'Now I will tell you stories of what happened long ago.
There was a world before this.
The things that I am going to tell about happened in that world.
Some of you will remember every word that I say,
some will remember a part of the words,
and some will forget them all –
I think this will be the way, but each must do the best he can.
Hereafter you must tell these stories to one another.
You must keep these stories as long as the world lasts;
tell them to your children and grandchildren
generation after generation...
When you visit one another, you must tell these things,
and keep them up always.'

– Henry Jacob, elder of the Seneca people, 1883

The Harvest Song
Painted in Taos Pueblo, New Mexico (Southwest)
by Eanger Irving Couse, c.1920

First published in the UK by Talking Stone 2018

Talking Stone
Swindonburn Cottage West, Sharperton
Morpeth, Northumberland, NE65 7AP

ISBN: 9780953745487

Cover illustration:
Haida Double Thunderbird, unknown artist, 1880

Patterns and motifs in chapter headings are based on
19th century Native American designs from each cultural region

NATIVE AMERICAN MYTHS

Collected 1636 – 1919

Rosalind Kerven

Dedicated to the wild creatures of North America,
without whom these stories would not have been told.

Kiowa tipi cover
Great Plains, 1904

The author owes a great debt to many men and women, long
dead: the Native American people who generously shared their
ancient stories with outsiders; and the ethnologists and other story
collectors who took the trouble to transcribe them and record them
for posterity. Where their names are known, these are given in the
notes after each story.

MAP OF NORTH AMERICA'S CULTURAL REGIONS

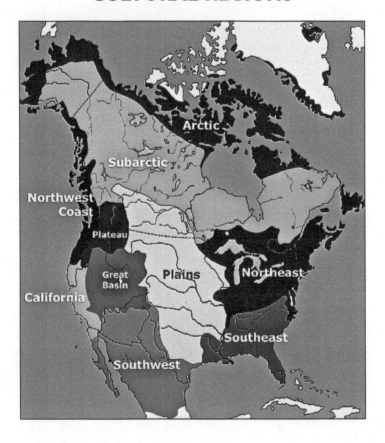

CONTENTS

MYTHS OF THE SOUTHWEST

MYTHS OF CALIFORNIA

MYTHS OF THE GREAT BASIN

MYTHS OF THE PLATEAU

MYTHS OF THE NORTHWEST COAST

MYTHS OF THE ARCTIC

MYTHS OF THE SUBARCTIC

MYTHS OF THE NORTHEAST

SOURCES AND BACKGROUND READING

TERMINOLOGY AND NAMES

There is no universally accepted term used to cover the numerous indigenous peoples of North America – those who inhabited the continent before the arrival of European settlers from the early 16th century. For most of the ensuing centuries, outsiders called the people 'Indians' – a term derived from the fact that the original European explorers of the Americas mistakenly believed they had arrived in India. Some now consider this term unacceptable. It has also become somewhat confusing, since people with roots in India itself also live in North America. Since the 1950s, 'Native American' has increasingly been used as a more accurate and respectful name, but this too is not universally accepted. In the United States 'Indian' is still widely used, with many groups using the term on their own websites, whilst others prefer to avoid the issue. Inhabitants of Alaska are often called 'Alaska Natives'. In Canada, the preferred terms are 'First Nations', 'Aboriginal Peoples' or 'Indigenous Peoples'.

Against that background, this book uses the term 'Native American', believing it to be accurate, all-embracing and generally inoffensive.

The use of the word 'tribe' is also controversial; some regard it as derogatory, yet many Native American peoples' own websites use it. Where applicable, this book uses the word 'people' instead.

When the stories in this book were collected, outsiders tended to call the various Native American peoples by names which they did not use for themselves. Since this is a historical collection, it uses the names recorded in the original texts; however, in the factual introduction to each cultural section, and under each story title, this is followed by the correct name in parentheses.

Where direct quotes from old sources are used, the original wording has been reproduced.

INTRODUCTION

This book presents some outstanding examples of historical Native American stories, collected in what is now the the United States and Canada between the early 17th and early 20th centuries.

By the latter date, most of North America's great indigenous civilisations had been either exterminated or severely damaged by white settlers, who imposed their lifestyle right across the continent. However, even 100 years ago, a good many Native American survivors still remembered their ancestral traditions. Fortunately, some were willing to share these with ethnologists. They in turn were eager to record them before they were lost for ever, and published their studies of Native American cultures over a number of years in books and academic journals. Preserved alongside them are less formal works written by explorers, travellers, geologists and missionaries. Within these archives – most of which can now be viewed in the original documents online – are thousands of sacred myths, oral histories, local legends and folk tales.

CHOOSING THE STORIES

Research for this book took over three years, and involved examination of nearly 2,000 stories from 130 different peoples. The oldest ones were collected by Jesuit missionaries in the 1630s (see p. 556). A cut-off date of 1920 was set, in order to present only material firmly rooted in the past, when the old cultures were more likely to be thriving. For example, a Cheyenne chief sharing his traditions with an ethnologist around 1907 said:

'My mother told me all these things. She is over a hundred
years old, and she learned these stories from her grandmother.'

Although myths are living entities, still being retold and developed today, more modern versions tend to have subtly different details and meanings.

The stories were selected for their 'world heritage' qualities – their expression of universal human concerns, their powerful allegory and imagery and their inspirational teachings; also for their strong plots, memorable characters and satisfying conclusions.

RETELLING THE STORIES

Rather than simply reproducing the oldest written texts, the stories have all been sensitively retold. This is because, although the sources appear to accurately record the narratives, some of the original transcriptions were themselves retellings, whilst others fail to convey the flavour and colour of the oral storytellers.

Many of the original texts comprised ethnologists' summaries or recounts as dry, factual records. Others, collected by sympathetic non-experts, were retold with somewhat less rigour than their more academic peers. Less common were stories recorded in the Native American narrators' actual words, formally and slowly dictated, often in the mother tongue, then translated into English, and transcribed sentence by sentence. The laboriousness of this method is described by J. William Lloyd in his collection of Pima (Akimel O'odham) stories, *Aw-Aw-Tam Indian Nights*, 1904:

'It was slow work. First he [Comalk-Hawk-Kih, an elderly Pima storyteller] would tell Ed [the bilingual Pima translator] a paragraph of tradition, and Ed would translate it to me. Then I would write it down, and then read it aloud to Ed again, getting his corrections. When all was straight, to his satisfaction, we would go on to another paragraph, and so on, till the old man said enough.'

There are also a fair number of stories written down by educated Native American people themselves; but close examination of even these reveals inconsistencies, repetitions and so on, which benefit from editing to reveal the original meanings and beauty.

Amongst many cultures there was never any definitive way to tell the stories, as they only existed in the oral sphere. In 1915, folklorist Paul Radin wrote:

'Anyone who has spent any time among Indians must have been impressed by the fact that only a few in any tribe have the reputation of being excellent raconteurs… If we are to judge from the Winnebago [Northeast cultures], where I made definite enquiries, one man was famous for the humorous touches which he imparted to every tale; another for the fluency with which he spoke and the choice of his language; a third for his dramatic delivery; a fourth for the radical way in which he handled time-worn themes; a fifth for his tremendous memory; a sixth for the accuracy with which he adhered to the "accepted" version; etc. As born raconteurs, with a different type of genius, they told the story for the sake of storytelling, as raconteurs have done in all ages. They used their specific gifts to attain the greatest effect.'

This book has been compiled in that spirit, with the intention of bringing these diverse recounts back to life as authentically as possible. All the plots and characters are entirely faithful to the originals. Stylistic guidance has been obtained from careful examination of sources which claim to reproduce the old informants' actual words and narrative structures; videos of modern Native American storytellers; and experience of contemporary oral storytelling performances from world cultures. Where appropriate, the original narrators' own imagery and turns of phrase have been reproduced.

CHARACTERISTICS OF THE MYTHS

Ethnologists and anthropologists typically divide Native North American cultures into ten distinct areas, and this book arranges the stories in the same way. Each region has its own very distinctive flavour and unique narratives. However, certain themes and motifs are common right across the continent, for example:

- **The fluid boundary between human beings and animals.** Many protagonists are named as specific animals and display that species' attributes; yet they also behave like humans. The most widespread animal character is the bear. Also frequently featured are the coyote, eagle, raven, snake and wolf, alongside many others. Sometimes they shapeshift between animal and human form, an ability which the old storytellers depicted quite matter-of-factly, as if it were normal and commonplace. People might marry a particular animal and give birth to hybrid offspring; or an animal might act as a kindly foster parent to an abandoned human child. This reflects a perspective in which human beings are an inextricable part of the wider natural world.

- **The concept that Earth is not the only world.** In many myths, there is also an 'above world' (or several layers of worlds) in the sky. Both people and animals might reach this Sky World by means of a rope, a chain of linked arrows, by climbing a tree which then grows right up to the heavens, or by darting quickly through the dangerous doorway which constantly opens and closes on the distant horizon. In some traditions, there are also further worlds under water or, less commonly, under the ground.

- **Significant numbers.** The most common 'significant' number is four, though in some regions it is three, five, seven or ten. Linked to this is the symbolic role of the four directions, sometimes complemented by three more: the sky above, the earth below and the spot where one is standing.

- **Creation and origin stories.** The most widespread of these open with darkness and water, and a primeval creator taking a variety of personas. The creator sends a series of animals to dive down into the deeps, searching for material from which to make the world. After several failures, at last one brings up a little mud, which the creator transforms into the Earth. Next, landscape features are shaped, plants made to grow and various forms of animal life created, culminating in humans. In some cultures, the first people live under the ground, from where they perform a ritual emergence.

- **The use of fantastical allegory to portray the human condition.** Some stories very subtly celebrate marital love, parental love, sibling love or platonic friendship. Others offer sympathetic insights into controversial issues such as inter-generational conflict, domestic violence, child abuse and mental illness. Some explore concepts such as wisdom and death. They tend to have a strong moral slant which would be recognised by all the great world religions.

There are also certain stereotyped characters who appear in numerous stories. For example:

- **Deities personifying the natural world.** Especially important are the sun, moon and stars; and the elements, particularly thunder and the winds.

- **The trickster.** He is always male, variously known as Old Man, Coyote, Raven and by many other names. His shockingly outrageous behaviour reinforces the need for correct social norms. However, he is often also a sacred character, playing a dual role and taking on a more sober persona for the purposes of creation or establishing customs.

- **The admirable young woman who refuses all offers of marriage.** This is portrayed as anti-social behaviour, which may lead to a variety of either good or bad adventures. Often she is a virgin who is mystically impregnated by a sunbeam, a drop of water or some other supernatural means; subsequently giving birth to a supernatural child who reaches maturity in a matter of days and achieves great deeds.

- **The orphan.** Usually (though not always) male, he begins life as a social outcast, either homeless or living with his elderly grandmother, but ends up as a revered hero. This transformation is often facilitated by divine intervention.

Each story is accompanied by short notes, giving details of the original narrator where known, and summarising related stories. No attempt has been made to explain or interpret them; for as ethnologist Natalie Curtis wrote in her collection of Native American songs and myths, *The Indians' Book*, in 1907:

'When questioned deeply as to the meaning of a myth, the Indian sometimes replies, "That is for each to think out for himself".'

Indeed, careful reading will reveal that most of the stories have various layers of depth and meaning, which often become more apparent on reflection.

Sioux Teepee
Painted by Karl Bodmer, 1833

MYTHS
OF THE
GREAT PLAINS

PEOPLE OF
THE GREAT PLAINS

Canada:
Southern regions of Alberta, Manitoba and Saskatchewan.

United States:
Kansas, North Dakota, Nebraska and South Dakota.
Parts of Arkansas, Colorado, Iowa, Montana, Minnesota,
Missouri, New Mexico, Oklahoma, Texas and Wyoming.

The Great Plains are dominated by vast open grasslands under huge skies, broken up by areas of semi-desert, wooded river valleys, cliffs, chasms and dramatic rock formations. Weather is an ever-present force, with strong winds, cloying summer heat, winter blizzards, droughts, floods and violent thunderstorms which sometimes leave wildfires in their wake.

Until the late 19th century, enormous herds of buffalo roamed the Plains. Men hunted them on horseback, using either thrusting lances or bows and arrows; they also pursued elk, deer and pronghorn antelope. Women butchered and processed the meat, and crafted the hides and body parts into housing, clothing and artefacts; supplementing the diet by gathering roots and berries.

The buffalo herds were constantly on the move, and Plains peoples typically followed a nomadic life in pursuit of them, moving home many times a year. To facilitate this, they lived in tipis, which could be very quickly erected or dismantled. These were weatherproof, conical tents, with frames of wooden poles covered by hides, often painted with symbolic images. Inside, bedding and storage were arranged around a central fire. Some peoples combined seasonal hunting with crop farming, using tipis when on the move but also living in permanent earth lodges near their fields.

When the men were not hunting, they often went 'on the warpath'. The aim was not destruction or conquest, but to attain prestige through bravery. A favourite tactic was 'counting coup' – humiliating an enemy from horseback with a blow from a ritual stick, then escaping without injuring themselves. White observers described them as peerless but cruel horsemen, and the richest bands reputedly owned thousands of horses. To replenish their herds they either caught feral horses, or raided enemy camps.

The women controlled the entire domestic sphere, making and owning all household goods, including the tipis. The dangers of hunting and warfare caused many men to die young. It was not unusual for two or more women – often sisters – to share the same husband. Where there was more than one wife, they often lived in separate tipis, with the first one usually asserting authority over the other(s). Amongst some tribes, it was the custom for male relatives to arrange a teenage girl's marriage, matching her to a much older man with proven status. She had the right to refuse, but this was unusual due to family pressure.

A typical household comprised a man, his wife or wives and their children, plus grandparents and unmarried siblings. Families lived together in bands of several hundred members, each with its own male chief. The bands often came together during the summer for tribal ceremonial gatherings. Independently of the bands, people also belonged to ritual societies which were organised for interests such as warfare, specific crafts and religion. Trade was an important activity, conducted between different tribes, and also with White settlers for their guns and metal utensils.

Great Plains religion held that all life was sacred, and that everything in the world was imbued with spiritual powers which needed to be kept in harmony. An individual with strong motivation and stamina would embark on a 'vision quest' which required a solitary four-day fast in the wilderness. Success was marked by a mystical dream that revealed a supernatural helper, often an animal, who offered power, advice and guidance through life. Professional 'medicine men' used their exceptional spiritual powers to treat the sick. An important sacred object was the personal 'medicine bundle', a leather container filled with remnants of birds, animals and plants, attached to clothing, carried or placed inside the lodge. Its contents were kept secret from outsiders and it was rarely or never opened. Some were family heirlooms, passed down through generations.

A major communal religious ritual was the four-day 'Sun Dance', held every summer to celebrate the renewal of life. It was sponsored by a man or woman in response to a vision, or to give thanks, and brought scattered tribal bands together. The male dancers often fastened themselves to a central pole by thongs and skewers pierced through their pectoral muscles, perceiving the 'ecstasy of pain' as a spiritual experience. Subsidiary ceremonies were held at the same time, for initiations and healing, and to glorify warrior deeds.

LIFE ON THE GREAT PLAINS
WHEN THESE STORIES WERE COLLECTED

The buffalo-centred culture described above reached its height in the mid-18th century, when horse ownership became widespread on the Great Plains, and hunting became more efficient with the acquisition of guns from White traders. Horses were originally introduced by Spanish settlers in the Southwest. Local peoples subsequently captured some of the huge herds, and sold them on to others in a chain that spread across the continent. This lifestyle lasted less than 150 years, ending abruptly in the late 19th century.

In the United States, after the American Civil War ended in 1865, rising numbers of gold prospectors and migrants began to cross the Plains peoples' hunting territories in wagon trains. This intrusion was exacerbated by the building of roads, forts, and the Transcontinental Railroad. The US government forced the Plains peoples into submission through hundreds of treaties, requiring them to cede huge tracts of land and allow safe passage for White travellers. In return they were promised concessions, including the right to live within designated reservations, grants of money and agricultural material, education and practical instruction. However, the government consistently reduced the size of the reservations, failed to provide the promised assistance to those whose livelihoods they were destroying, and deported many Native people to distant parts of the continent.

An increasing sense of betrayal caused a series of uprisings. These were brutally put down; but Plains warriors fought back bravely and sometimes victoriously. Their most famous triumph was the Battle of Little Bighorn in 1876, when thousands of Arapaho, Cheyenne and Sioux warriors succeeded in routing a major American battalion, which suffered multiple deaths and injuries. Government reprisals were ruthless and culminated in the infamous Massacre of Wounded Knee in 1890, when up to 300 unarmed Sioux men, women and children were slaughtered, with the survivors left to the ravages of winter storms.

Equally devastating was the settlers' destruction of the buffalo for the leather goods trade, and apparently also to starve the Plains peoples into submission. Estimates of the original size of the Plains buffalo herds vary widely, but all historians agree there were many millions. During the second half of the 19th century they were slaughtered by professional White hunters in unprecedented numbers, their hides shipped eastwards and their carcasses left to rot on the grass. It is said that by 1895 there were less than 1,000 buffalo left. Since the Plains peoples had totally depended on buffalo for subsistence and many material needs, it was now impossible to maintain their old way of life. Starvation was only avoided by accepting government rations on the reservations.

In Canada, the Plains buffalo hunt was transformed from a subsistence activity to a commercial enterprise run by the Hudson's Bay Company, which employed many Native American men as labourers and porters. The company virtually controlled the North American fur trade, supplying an insatiable market with pelts and pemmican. The company established trading posts in previously remote locations, which became centres where Plains peoples would congregate – and consume excessive amounts of alcohol, which exacerbated their many other problems. The Canadian Plains tribes too surrendered much of their land in a series of treaties which moved them onto reserves. Here they were allowed to continue hunting and fishing, and were given annuities, schools and equipment. However, they were directed to take up agriculture, their children were forcibly enrolled in schools, and traditional activities such as the Sun Dance were banned.

In both the US and Canada, periodic epidemics of infectious diseases, such as smallpox, quickly wiped out huge percentages of the Native American population.

Despite this widespread devastation, many Plains elders treasured their traditions, and continued to keep their ancient stories alive. In 1906 George Dorsey described what he had heard of the old Pawnee storytelling customs:

'Many years ago, in the winter…a person going through the village in the night would hear laughing and singing in nearly all of the lodges… The women had plenty of wood piled up… and the people felt that it was time to tell…stories and to make the children dance while they were singing.'

Robert Lowie reported similarly from the Crow people in 1918:

'Stories were told on winter nights when people were sitting by the fire or had stretched out before falling asleep. Old people with a reputation as raconteurs were invited for a feast and then expected to narrate their tales. The audience were required to answer 'e' (yes) after every sentence or two. When no one replied, it was a sign that all had fallen asleep and the storyteller broke off his narrative, possibly to resume it the following night… People were formerly afraid to tell stories in the summer because, one informant said…all the stars with names used to live in this world and only come out at night.'

There were conflicting reports as to whether there could be any variation in how particular narratives were told. George Bird Grinnell, who collected myths from the Blackfoot, Cheyenne and Pawnee, wrote in 1898:

'I have often been interested to see the pains taken to give each tale in its proper form – to tell the story exactly as it should be told. If in the course of his narration the speaker's memory proves at fault on any point, he will consult authorities, asking the opinions of old men who are best acquainted with the story, refreshing his memory by their assistance, fully discussing the doubtful point, and weighing each remark and suggestion with care before continuing his tale.'

In contrast, ten years later, Clark Wissler said of the Blackfoot:

'Each narrator has his own version, in the telling of which he is usually consistent. Myths are told by a few individuals, who take pride in their ability and knowledge, and usually impress their individuality upon the form of the narrative… Once, when discussing this matter with a Blood Indian, the venerable old man pulled up a common ragweed, saying, "the parts of the weed all branch off from the stem. They go different ways, but all come from the same root. So it is with the different versions of a myth.'"

THE PEOPLES BEHIND THE STORIES

Arapaho
The old Arapaho homelands included Alberta and Saskatchewan in Canada; and Colorado, Montana, South Dakota and Wyoming in the US. During the 19th century, the establishment of White trading posts and wagon trails through their hunting territories split the tribe into two groups. Today the Southern Arapaho live in Oklahoma, whilst the Northern Arapaho are based in Wyoming.

Blackfoot Confederacy (Niitsitapi)
It is said that Whites called them 'Blackfoot' because the soles of their leather moccasins were often dyed black. Originally one of the most populous and powerful Plains peoples, they comprised five different bands spread across Alberta and Saskatchewan in Canada, and Montana in the US, all sharing the same language and customs. Today the Northern Blackfoot (Siksika), the Blood (Kainah) and the Northern Piegan (Piikani) are based in Canada; whilst the South Piegan (Amskapi Piikani) are located in the US. The fifth band, the Small Robes (Inaxix) was destroyed by smallpox in the 1830s.

Crow (Apsaalooke)
'Apsaalooke' means 'children of the long-beaked bird', mistranslated by Whites as 'crow'. They were organised into three bands: the Mountain Crow, the River Crow and the Kick-in-the-Bellies. In the early 19th century they were reputed to be the richest nation in horses, with some individual men owning up to 100; to have less than twenty was to be poor. They are still based in their old homelands in Montana, where a majority speak the Crow language.

Gros Ventre (Atsina, Ah-ah-nee-nin)

'Gros Ventre' is French for 'big bellies', and is said to come from the Plains sign language which was once used for inter-tribal communication; the movement of hands over the stomach denoted hunger. They originally lived in the northern Plains. Following a 75 per cent population loss, due to smallpox during the 19th century, they allied themselves with the Blackfoot. Their modern reservation in Montana was established in 1888, and is shared with the Assiniboine (Nakoda) people.

Pawnee

In their old homeland of Nebraska, the Pawnee were divided into four main bands. Their culture differed from many neighbouring tribes for they were only part-time nomadic hunters, living for some of the year in permanent villages of conical earth lodges, where they grew corn, beans, pumpkins and squash. They ceded their territory to the US Government in 1800 and moved to their modern base, Pawnee County in Oklahoma, in 1875.

Sioux (Oceti Sakowin)

'Oceti Sakowin' means 'seven council fires', because the Sioux originally comprised seven closely related peoples, each subdivided into bands. The word 'Sioux' comes from an Algonquin word meaning 'little snakes' or 'little rattle', referring to the sound of a rattlesnake before it bites. The three main divisions – Lakota, Dakota and Nakota – are based on different dialects which developed along geographical lines. Today most Sioux people in the US live on nine reservations in South Dakota, with others based in North Dakota, Nebraska, Montana and Minnesota. In Canada, Sioux people are spread across Alberta, Manitoba and Saskatchewan.

Research for this section also covered stories from the following Great Plains peoples: Comanche, Kiowa, Omaha, Osage, Ponca and Wichita.

MORNING STAR
AND EVENING STAR

Pawnee

There is a power which rules over everything: Tirawa, the One Above, from whom all creation springs.

Before the Earth was formed, Tirawa made the Sky. Within the Sky, he made the first stars – one to the east where creation was planned; and one to the west where creation was fulfilled. Everything that these stars did was a prophecy, foretelling what would come to be on Earth.

The eastern star was the first man, Morning Star. The western star was the first woman, Evening Star. Between these two, Tirawa carved open a chasm, the sacred Pathway of Deserted Spirits. From either side of it, the two stars yearned for each other.

So Morning Star travelled westwards across the infinite reaches of the Sky. Evening Star saw him coming; her heart danced and she beckoned him towards her. Yet as he drew closer, her joy turned to unease. With whispered words and subtle gestures, she sought to delay him.

She made the ground split open before Morning Star's feet, and water gush from it, frothing and seething. A hideous, writhing, ravenous snake reared from the torrent and lunged towards him –

But Morning Star burst into song, drew a ball of fire from his pouch and hurled it. The flames overwhelmed the snake, the water dried and the ground closed up. Thus Morning Star passed on.

He strode closer and closer to the west. Evening Star saw him: again her heart leaped, then again she shrank from him. Once, twice, nine times more, she whispered and gestured, drawing on secret powers to delay her beloved. Nine times more she summoned obstacles to hinder his way: stinging cacti, savage animals, impenetrable forests, monsters and thickets of thorns. Nine times more, with his song and his fireball, Morning Star vanquished them all.

Finally, he reached the west. But still he could not go to her, for his way was blocked by her mighty guards:

Black Bear, Mountain Lion, Wildcat, Wolf,
Corn of four colours, Stars of four colours,
Spring, Summer, Fall and Winter,
Cottonwood, Elm, Box Elder, Willow,
Thunder, Lightning, Clouds and Wind.

Great was their power; but Morning Star's yearning was stronger. He conquered them all, forced his way past and entered Evening Star's dwelling.

'I have come for you,' he said.

Evening Star's voice trembled as she answered, 'You are welcome; but I will not yield to you yet. For first you must bring me a cradle-board for the child who will spring from our union. Fashion it from cottonwood, with a willow head-guard shaped like a rainbow. Bind it with bands of otter-skin in honour of rainstorms. Drape it with a wildcat hide, embroider it with stars.'

'I submit willingly to your desire,' said Morning Star, 'for then you will submit to mine.'

He turned away to the heavens. Before long, he returned with the cradle-board she had asked for.

'This is magnificent,' said Evening Star, 'but I cannot yield to you yet. For next you must bring me a mat for our child who is yet to be born.'

Morning Star willingly went back across the heavens, found a herd of buffalo, slaughtered one and butchered it. He fashioned a mat from its softest belly skin and took it to his love.

'This gift is wonderful,' said Evening Star, 'but still I will not yield to you. For finally you must bring me water, sweet enough to bathe the child who will soon be ours.'

This time, Morning Star crept secretly into Evening Star's own garden, waiting in the green shadows until an unknown old woman appeared.

'Why do you intrude on this private place?' she asked him.

'I am seeking sweet water,' he answered, 'for the child that Evening Star will bear me'.

'Come then, I am very glad to help you.'

The woman fetched a vessel made from the heart of a freshly killed buffalo, and called to her children to sing. As their voices rang out, she led him to a secret hollow, where aromatic flowers and grasses grew in rich profusion. Gently she pushed them aside, revealing a dark pool of rain and dew. She thrust a stick into it. Water gushed forth in a fragrant spring. She caught some in her vessel and offered it to Morning Star.

When he carried this sweet water to Evening Star, at last she drew him into her lodge. She lay with him, she let him overcome her. She gave him her power: the western power of storms. Into this he mingled his own powers of flint and lightening, of axes, knives and weapons. Thus everything each owned was given to the other, for the sake of the people who would come to walk upon the Earth.

Then Evening Star gave Morning Star a precious gift, a pebble. At her bidding, he dropped it from the heavens into the infinite waters beneath.

Aeons passed.

The four gods of the world quarters – the black, white, yellow and red stars – struck the pebble down with fisted hands. The pebble rose from the waters and transformed into the Earth.

Morning Star drew the fireball from his pouch and tossed it to the air, crying: 'Stay! Give light!' It transformed into the Sun, imbued with Morning Star's power.

Evening Star was swollen with their child. Soon she bore a beautiful daughter. When this girl was no longer helpless, Evening Star placed her on a cloud and gave her gifts: seeds of corn and all the plants in her garden.

The cloud drifted down. The girl tumbled from it, like rain.

On the Earth, the Sky girl wandered, planting her mother's seeds, listening and seeking. A boy came to her, born of the Moon and the Sun. They came together, just as Morning Star had joined with Evening Star.

Everyone in the world is sprung from their union.

Curtis: *The Indians' Book,* 1907
Curtis says that this myth was narrated by a man called Sakuruta ('Coming Sun'), one of only four priests who 'owned the right to tell this story'. He belonged to the Morning Star clan and was one of the heirs to

its medicine bundle (see p. 21). Curtis introduces his narrative with the following explanation of the Pawnee cosmic setting:

'Over all is the supreme, impersonal being, Tirawa, the infinite creator. After Tirawa, the Pawnee sees duality in all life. The very universe is divided into two great elements, male and female, finding their natural counterpart in day and night. Humanity is not the direct child of Tirawa, but the offspring of dual elements in the cosmic world.'

At the end of the story Sakuruta himself concludes:

'To the stars did Tirawa give power to watch over people. If the people were evil, the stars might send storms to embrace them. However, Tirawa himself is ever without anger. He is feared by none. Tirawa is changeless.'

There are many mysterious elements in this story, only a few of which are dealt with in Curtis' footnotes. She explains that the 'Pathway of Departed Spirits' is the Milky Way; Pawnee priests taught that, after death, the spirit passes along it to rest in the Southern Star. She says that the husband's gift of a cradle-board to his new wife was a Pawnee tradition; it was cut from a tree by his kinsmen and decorated with symbolic emblems. She mentions another story which describes how Morning Star won this cradle-board, but gives no details. The episode of the old woman fetching sweet water reflects a Pawnee custom of the midwife bathing a newborn child in a wooden bowl filled with water from a running stream.

Another version, from a man called Big Crow, appears in Dorsey's *The Pawnee Mythology* (1906). Here, Evening Star wants women to be higher than men, so she orders her daughter to kill all her suitors. Eventually, Morning Star himself approaches a poor mortal boy and urges him to win the girl. The boy uses Morning Star's own magic club and moccasins to overcome the girl's obstacles and challenges. When she finally agrees to accept him, Morning Star warns that her vagina is like a rattlesnake full of teeth (a theme which recurs in a number of other, light-hearted tales from the region) and gives him a stone to break them. After they have lain together, Morning Star gives him medicine bundles and sacred knowledge, then orders that girls from enemy tribes must be periodically sacrificed to him.

Both sources seem to be authentic and claim to have been obtained from men of high religious standing, so presumably the two versions co-existed. Writing an article summarising *Pawnee Mythology* in 1893, George Bird Grinnell remarks that such differences of belief are also true of Christianity. He says that the principle Pawnee deity, who he calls Atius Tirdwa ('Father Spirit'), is intangible, omnipotent and benevolent.

THE MAN
WHO MET THE SUN

Blackfoot (Niitsitapi)

There was a very beautiful girl from a good family. Many young men wanted to marry her, but no matter how rich, successful and splendid they were, she refused them all.

'Why are you behaving so arrogantly?' her father demanded. 'People are spreading rumours that you have a secret lover.'

The girl shook her head vehemently. 'Honestly, I long to get married,' she said. 'But it's forbidden.'

'Forbidden? What nonsense is this?' said her mother sceptically.

The girl blushed and drew a deep breath. At last she said, 'A couple of months ago, I was down at the river fetching water. No one else was around. Suddenly, I felt very strange, weak and frightened... Then I must have fainted. When I woke up, all I could see was dazzling light, all I could feel was heat. It was unbearable, I felt I was melting, like being in the heart of a fire. I knew at once that I had been overcome by that great Above Person – the Sun!

'I didn't know what to do, so I just lay on the ground, trying not to move, praying as hard as I could. I couldn't hear the river any more; everything had gone quiet. I was terrified the Sun would strike me dead. And then, like a loud drum slowly beating, I heard his voice:

'Girl, you are mine. I forbid you to marry. Obey!

'After that, the light gradually faded and the heat died down. I realised he had gone.' She began to weep. 'Oh Father, Mother, I dare not disobey the Sun. Imagine if I did: he'd scorch us with his anger, he'd send some dreadful disaster to all our people.'

The mother drew her daughter close, rocking her, soothing her tears. 'My poor child,' she whispered, 'you should have told us this before. If we had known, we would have stopped all those young men from pestering you.'

Her father nodded. 'The Sun dazzles us with his countless mysteries,' he said gravely. 'Yet everything he does has a purpose. What an honour that he's chosen you! You must indeed obey him; and we must all be patient and strong. In the long term, who knows what might happen?'

Now, in the same camp, there lived a youth who everyone called Scar Face, because his cheek was disfigured by a long, ugly scar. That wasn't his only burden, for both his parents had died at an early age, leaving him with no relations, no possessions and no home. He survived on scraps of food and kindness thrown to him by the elders. But the other young men constantly mocked him.

One day, they pushed Scar Face up against a cliff and started taunting him:

'Hey, great brave, why don't you have a go at that girl who refuses to marry anyone?'

'You're more handsome than the rest of us, *so* much richer, ha ha!'

'Pay her a visit, Scar Face!'

When they had finished kicking him and twisting his arms behind his back, they loped off to find a new distraction. Scar Face stood very still, deep in thought. After a while, he went down to the riverbank and hid in the brush.

Soon the Sun's Girl came down to the river with her bucket. As she held it in the water, Scar Face stepped from the bushes and called to her: 'May I speak with you?'

The girl saw that his expression was sincere. 'Come out into the open, where the Sun can look down on us,' she replied. 'What do you want?'

Scar Face stood before her. He said, 'I know I'm repulsive, and I've got nothing to offer you except my fearless heart. Even so, I long to win you as my wife. Tell me how I can do this.'

The girl gazed at the ground, scribbling in the dry soil with the point of her moccasin. Finally, she said, 'You seem decent, and you've been honest. So I'll be honest in return.' And she told him about her disturbing encounter with the Sun.

'So,' said Scar Face, 'is everything lost?'

'Only the Sun himself can answer that,' she said. 'If you could somehow travel to his lodge and persuade him to give me my freedom, then I would gladly marry you.'

'I'll go there at once,' he cried.

'But you must bring me a sign from the Sun, to prove you have won him over.'

'What kind of sign?'

The girl gave a hollow laugh. 'Isn't that obvious? You must get him to take away your horrible scar.' Then she picked up her full bucket and carried it up to her lodge.

Scar Face stared after her longingly, wretchedly, then wandered off in the opposite direction. What could he do? He didn't have a mother or a sister to equip him for such a journey. He had no father or uncle or older brother to offer advice.

As he walked on, he passed a lone tipi that stood on the edge of the camp, apart from the others. An old woman came hobbling out from it, then beckoned him over.

'It's Scar Face, isn't it?' she said. 'You've always been a courteous boy, so tell me what's the matter? You look as if you're in trouble.'

'I am, Grandmother. I need help to prepare for a long and dangerous journey.'

'Where are you going, and why?' she asked. When he didn't reply, she looked at him sharply, pursing her lips. 'Don't worry, I won't pry.'

She took him inside and rummaged through her storage bags. 'Now then. Have these seven pairs of moccasins, they're no use to me, and they'll make you fleet footed as a deer. And take this sack of pemmican: it's freshly made and will give you strength. I give you my blessing as well.'

Scar Face thanked her, then set out.

He walked for countless days. He trudged on and on for month after month. He crossed the prairie; he climbed steep hills; he tramped down lonely, echoing valleys. Summer faded into autumn, then froze into winter. He finished all his food. He wore out all his moccasins.

One frosty evening, he found himself on the edge of a dark, mysterious forest. He was utterly exhausted, so he sank down to rest for a while amongst the roots and leaves. As he dozed, a Wolf came padding up and stopped to sniff him.

'Greetings, my brother,' said Wolf. 'What are you doing so far from home?'

Scar Face sat up with a jolt. 'Oh, brother, I'm trying to find my way to the mighty Sun. Do you by any chance know the way to his lodge?'

Wolf pricked his ears but shook his head. 'Not me. I've never been anywhere near that Above Person's house. But don't despair, friend, for Bear is older and far more knowledgeable than me. If he hasn't already gone to sleep for the winter, he may be able to help.'

Scar Face thanked him. Taking Wolf's advice, he walked on towards a soft rumbling noise, and eventually came to the entrance of a cave. There he called: 'Brother Bear, if you're at home, I beg you to wake up!'

From deep inside, there came a rustle of dry grass. Very slowly, Bear came yawning out.

'What do you want of me, so late in the year, young brother?'

'I'm hoping you can guide me to the Sun's house.'

'Well I can't,' Bear said tetchily, 'I've never seen it. Go and ask that cunning old stripe-faced fellow – you know, Badger. His sett is just down that track, and he's more likely to know.'

Scar Face thanked him and crept on through the undergrowth to a large, neatly dug hole.

'Dear, generous animal,' he called down it, 'my brother Badger! I badly need to talk to you.'

Badger quickly poked his face out, his white stripes lighting up the gloom. 'What's your problem, brother?'

Scar Face told him.

'I'm sorry,' said Badger, 'I have no idea how to get there. However, let me think... Ah, yes! Go into that thicket over there and call for Wolverine. He's a great traveller, he's explored every inch of forest and mountains right to the world's edge. He's bound to know.'

Scar Face thanked him and ran onwards, calling: 'Wolverine my brother, I beg you to help me! Where are you? And where is the road that leads to the Sun?'

At first, he was answered only by silence. Then suddenly there came a soft crackling noise. He gazed around – and high above in the tangled branches, saw a gleam of eyes and teeth.

'I hear you, dear brother,' Wolverine called down softly, 'and I know the way. Just be patient until dawn, then I'll be glad to help.'

With great excitement, Scar Face sat down to wait. Sure enough, at first light, Wolverine came clambering out of the tree. He led Scar Face down a narrow, overgrown track, to the edge of a vast lake, then quietly slunk away.

In all his life, Scar Face had never seen such a barren, desolate place. The water was dark grey, restless with waves and currents, flecked with foam, and it was impossible to see the opposite shore. He stifled a sob, sat down and dropped his head between his knees.

'It's far too wide to swim across,' he thought, 'and even if I had enough strength left to build a canoe, it would never survive that treacherous water. This is the end: I'll never fulfil my quest.'

But at that moment, two big Swans swam up. '*Yuaah!*' they called. 'What are you doing here, brother?'

'Oh, my brothers, I'm sitting here in shame,' replied Scar Face. 'I've failed to achieve what I set out to do – I can't find the house of the Sun.'

'*Yuaah, yuaah!* You haven't failed – you're almost there! For beyond this very water lies the Sky where the Sun lives! We'll gladly carry you over.'

They told Scar Face to wade out to them and stretch himself across their two backs. In this way, they carried him over the dark, stormy water. He saw countless unearthly, unspeakable things writhing about just below the surface: vaporous shadows and grasping claws. But they reached the far side safely. The Swans dropped Scar Face onto a stony beach, and vanished.

Leading up from the beach he saw a broad, bright path, and set off to walk along it. However, he soon found his way blocked by a pile of treasures. There was a war-shirt, a shield, a bow and a quiver full of arrows, each one beautifully worked. He gazed at them longingly, but did not touch them.

Now he saw someone coming towards him, a handsome youth of his own age. His hair was extraordinarily long and glossy, he wore a robe of magnificent furs and his moccasins were embroidered with feathers of many colours.

'Did you see some weapons back there?' the youth said.

'I did.'

'Ah. And what did you do with them?'

'Nothing, for they are not mine.'

'Indeed,' said the youth, 'they are mine. It's good that you are honest. What's your name and where are you going?'

'They call me Scar Face. And I'm seeking the house of the Sun.'

'Well, you've struck lucky, Scar Face, because I am Morning Star – and the Sun is my father! Come home with me. As soon as night falls, you'll be able to meet him.'

He led Scar Face to a huge wooden lodge, painted all over with mysterious birds, animals and patterns. Inside, a pale, shining woman sat upon a shimmering blanket.

'This is my mother, the Moon,' said Morning Star. 'Mother, this is Scar Face, come to see Father.'

The Moon spoke to Scar Face very kindly and served him a tasty and generous meal. However, he scarcely had time to finish it before they heard heavy footsteps outside.

'Here comes my husband,' said the Moon. 'He's suspicious of strangers, so you'd better hide.'

She bundled Scar Face into a corner under a pile of sweet-smelling cedar branches. However, as soon as the Sun entered, he sniffed and growled: 'What's going on? I smell a person.'

'Father,' said Morning Star, 'it's my new friend. He's already proven himself to be honest.'

'Then come out, honest friend,' the Sun called.

Scar Face crept nervously from his hiding place, into a dazzling blaze of light. He flinched, fearing the Sun's heat would melt him; but the Sun took pity and put on a cloak of shadows that cooled the air around him.

'Sit down, sit down,' said the Sun. 'If you're a friend of Morning Star's, you're more than welcome. My boy has been very lonely since all his brothers died. Has he told you what happened to them?'

Scar Face shook his head.

'When you crossed the great water,' said the Sun, 'no doubt you noticed that it is full of monstrous birds. They have slaughtered all my other sons, torn them to pieces with their great, sharp beaks.'

In the corner, Moon began to weep quietly.

'So listen carefully to my warning,' the Sun went on. 'You may stay with us as long as you wish, and go out hunting every day with Morning Star. But don't ever go back to the great water – and don't let Morning Star go anywhere near it either. Obey me in this matter, young man, and everything will go well.'

And so he did. Scar Face moved into the Sun's lodge and stayed there for a long time. He and Morning Star became firm friends. The landscape of the Sky is very similar to our own world, and every day the two young men went out hunting together, always taking care to avoid the trails that led to danger.

However, one day their prey led them on a crazy chase, constantly changing tack and going round in circles, twisting and snaking here and there, until they lost all sense of direction. Thus at last they found themselves – totally unintentionally – standing on the great water's forbidden shores.

Scar Face dropped his weapons and seized his friend's arm, desperately trying to spin him round and pull him away. But like his ill-fated brothers before him, Morning Star was mesmerised by the water, spellbound by its shifting patterns and lights. He hurried towards it as if dragged by some invisible rope.

'Come back!' screamed Scar Face. But Morning Star paid no heed.

The next moment, the surface of the water broke in a shower of dark droplets and seven monstrous birds burst from it, thrashing their wings. They dived at Morning Star, circling around him, their needle-like claws and jagged beaks poised to kill. Morning Star froze…

But Scar Face sprang into action. He seized his spears and hurled them at the monsters. At each strike, one of the monsters fell – until all seven lay dead.

Morning Star's trance faded away like mist. He shook himself and hugged his friend. Together they cut off the monsters' heads and stored them in their packs. They were no longer disorientated and quickly found their way home.

There they rushed in and showed the monstrous heads to the Moon. She wept with joy to hear that the evil monsters were all destroyed. When the Sun came in, Morning Star proudly told him of his friend's great deed.

'My boy,' said the Sun to Scar Face, 'what can I do to thank you? What is your heart's desire?'

At once, Scar Face said, 'That girl that you once claimed – I wish to marry her. She longs to marry me too. Will you give us your permission?'

'Ah,' said the Sun, 'Her. Yes, I have watched and seen that she has always behaved wisely and never done anything wrong. She deserves a reward too. I give you two my blessing to marry. And I will allow you to live together to a very great age, as will all the children you shall have together.'

Scar Face bowed his head, wondering if he dared make the second part of his request; but as he tried to speak, the Sun interrupted him.

'Before you go home, I will give you some knowledge. Listen carefully.

'I am the only chief. Everything is mine. I made the Earth, the mountains, the prairies, the rivers, and the forests. I made the People and all the animals. I can never die. True, the winter weakens me – but every summer I grow young again.

'Which of all animals is cleverest? The Raven, for he always finds food, and is never hungry. Which animal has the most power? The Buffalo; of all animals, I like him best. I made him to provide the People with food and shelter. What part of his body is sacred? The tongue – that is mine. What else is sacred? Berries, they are mine too. Which is the best, the heart or the brain? The brain is; for though the heart often lies, the brain never does.

'Now come with me to look down upon the Earth.'

He took Scar Face to the edge of the Sky. Together they gazed down on the whole round, flat world below.

The Sun said, 'When any man is sick or in danger, his wife should pray to me and promise to build me a medicine lodge if he recovers. If she is pure and true, I will save the man. The lodge should be built like the world – round, with walls. A sweat-house must also be built, using a hundred sticks, shaped into a hemisphere, like the Sky. It must be painted half-red to honour me, and half-black to honour the night. Take these two Raven feathers and keep them safe. They are my sign: when any man in trouble recovers, he must wear them.

'Now I will give you your own sign, for the girl that you love.'

He rubbed a powerful medicine on the youth's face. At once, his scar disappeared.

Morning Star emerged from their lodge, carrying a set of exquisitely worked clothes. He pressed them into Scar Face's hands. Then the Moon came out and kissed Scar Face goodbye, weeping softly. 'You are my other son,' she said.

The Sun led Scar Face to the Wolf Road, a glistening, twinkling trail he had never seen before. Scar Face set off down it, and soon found himself back on Earth.

The weather had turned very hot. In the camp circle, all the lodge door skins were raised to let in the fresh air, and everyone was resting in the shade.

Scar Face skirted the edge of the camp, unnoticed, and walked on to a distant butte. He slipped behind it and dressed in the fine new clothes that Morning Star had given him. Then he draped his ragged old robe over them, pulling it around his head to hide his face. He sat down there and waited.

After a long time, he became aware of people's eyes on him. He didn't move. Footsteps approached and a shadow fell over him. Looking up, he saw two youths.

'Stranger,' said one. 'Our chief asks why you are sitting out here in the burning sun.'

Scar Face stood up and threw off his robe. The youths stared in amazement at his beautiful clothes, dripping with rich quillwork and beads. Then their gaze moved up to his face.

'It's you!' they cried in awe. 'Scar Face! But...but what has happened to you?'

Not waiting for his answer, they raced back to the camp, shouting, 'Scar Face is returned – but some strange medicine has changed him! His scar has vanished – and he's rich!'

Everyone rushed out to see. They showered him with questions, wanting to know where he had been and what had happened. Scar Face told them nothing, his gaze sweeping over the crowd... Until at last, he saw the girl he loved, the Sun's Girl.

He pushed through the others and went to her. He drew the two Raven feathers from his shirt and gently placed them in her hands.

'It was a long way,' said Scar Face, 'and more than once I nearly died. But, as I promised, my heart stayed strong – and I found the Sun. I did a good deed for him, and in return he has allowed me to claim you. See, he's taken away my scar. That, and these feathers, are his sign.'

'You were a long time,' whispered the girl, 'and more than once, I too thought I would die. I am so very happy that our test is over.'

And so they were married.

She made the first medicine lodge, as the Sun had ordered. The Sun blessed them with many children, good health and great age. And when the time came, he allowed their shadows to depart to the Sand Hills without ever knowing any further sorrow or pain.

Grinnell: *Blackfoot Lodge Tales*, 1892
Grinnell obtained this story from Cora M. Ross, a school teacher at the Blackfoot agency. Her phraseology is very similar to that of Grinnell's other stories, which he collected directly from Blackfoot informants. He says it was told to explain the origin of the Medicine Lodge Ceremony, also known as the Sun Dance (see p. 22). The Wolf Road, down which Scar Face returns to Earth, is the Milky Way.

There are two less-detailed versions of the same story in Wissler & Duval's *Mythology of the Blackfoot Indians*, from unnamed Piegan sources, containing a number of variations. Both claim that when the two youths bring the Moon the severed heads of the monsters, this is the origin of the Plains' warrior custom of scalping to prove the enemy is dead.

A Crow version says that the youth's scarred face is caused by burning and – incorporating a distinctly modern twist – the Sun cures it with the aid of a mirror. His journey to the Sun is made with the help of an eagle, in return for Scar Face killing the monster which ate its chicks. The eagle also takes him home again, and gives him the gift of special medicine. Here too, he wins his desired girl.

WHAT IS LIFE?

Blackfoot (Niitsitapi)

What is life?
It is the flash
of a firefly in the night.
It is the breath
of a buffalo in the wintertime.
It is the little shadow
which runs across the grass
and loses itself in the sunset.

– Chief Crowfoot (Isapo-Muxika) of the Blackfoot,
recorded in 1890
(Quoted in McLuhan: *Touch the Earth*)

THE WOMAN WHO MARRIED A STAR

>>>==o=K==<<

Blackfoot (Niitsitapi)

It was high summer. The Sun had scorched every corner of the Earth with his unrelenting heat. Even when night fell, the lodges were unbearably stuffy: it was impossible to sleep.

There were two young women who were good friends. One night they both took their beds outside, hoping it would be cooler there. But even in the open air under the wide Sky, they both lay restlessly tossing and turning.

'Oh, if only I could sleep!' said one.

'So you're awake too,' the other replied. 'Well, at least out here, we can enjoy looking up at the stars.'

'Yes, that's true. They're so beautiful, aren't they? Just look at that huge, bright one.'

'It must be almost dawn, because that's the Morning Star.'

'Hello, Morning Star,' said the first young woman. 'Ooh, I've never seen anyone so fine as you! I wish you were a *man*, so dazzling and splendid – I'd marry you at once!'

They went on talking and giggling in this idle manner until the Sun rose to herald another sweltering day. Then they got up, and went separately about their business.

A few days later, they met up again and went into the forest together to fetch firewood. It was much cooler under the trees. Both young women gathered big bundles of wood and tied them up ready to carry home. However, the one who had fantasised about the Morning Star had a problem: every time she tried to hoist the bundle onto her shoulders, the pack-straps snapped.

'You go ahead,' she said to her friend. 'Don't worry about me, I'll soon catch you up.'

So the friend went back to the camp by herself. Eventually, the first young woman got her bundle packed up securely, lifted it and turned to start walking back. But before she could take a single step, a young man appeared out of the bushes.

He was exceptionally handsome and very richly dressed. His robe was sewn from the finest beaver skins and he wore a single long eagle plume in his hair. He didn't say a word, but just grinned broadly, strode forward and stopped directly in front of her.

The young woman was flustered and embarrassed. 'Get out of my way,' she said sharply, and tried to skirt round him. But the young man immediately took a step to the side and blocked her path again. She tried to dodge round his other side – but he held out his arm, preventing her escape.

'Who are you, stranger?' she cried. 'Why are you tormenting me like this?'

At last the young man spoke. 'I'm not a stranger. Just the other night, you chose me to be your husband – so I've come to fetch you.'

'Don't tell lies. I've never seen you before in my whole life. Leave me alone!'

'Of course you've seen me – you said how splendid I was. I am Morning Star. I've come to grant your wish to marry me. Don't tremble like that, there's no need to be afraid. Come on, my parents are eager to meet you. Let's go to my home at once.'

Before she could argue, he drew out another eagle plume and gently placed it in her hair.

'Close your eyes.'

She didn't even try to disobey him; to tell the truth, she didn't want to. When he told her to open her eyes again, she saw to her wonder that she was no longer in the forest. Morning Star had worked some strange medicine and transported her to the Sky! They were standing in front of a magnificent lodge, painted with mysterious patterns. The door was wide open. Morning Star took her hand and led her inside, where a great chief and his wife were sitting, adorned in magnificent robes and feathers. The chief was the Sun himself, and the woman was the Moon.

'Mother, Father,' said Morning Star, 'Here is my new wife.'

The Moon smiled at the young woman. 'Welcome to the Sky. Sit down, my dear.'

The young woman took her seat beside her new mother-in-law. The Moon passed her a little dish, in which were four dark berries, and a small shell containing just a few drops of water.

'Eat and drink your fill, my dear,' she said.

The young woman looked at her sparse meal in dismay, for she was desperately hungry and thirsty.

However, the Moon said, 'Don't stint yourself, daughter-in-law. This dish contains all the food in the world, and the shell is filled with all the water in the ocean.'

The young woman soon found, indeed, that no matter how many berries she nibbled, and how much water she sipped, both the dish and the shell remained full.

Well! She soon settled in to her new life.

One day, the Moon gave her a long wooden stick fixed to a polished wooden handle.

'It's time for you to do your share of work,' she said. 'Take this digging stick out to where the purple turnip flowers are blooming on the prairie. Dig up the roots and bring home as many as you can gather. Then I'll teach you how to prepare and cook them.'

The young woman thanked her and turned to go outside.

'Not so fast,' the Moon called her back. 'I forgot to tell you something important. Not far from here you will see one purple flower that's much larger than all the others. I absolutely forbid you to dig up that one – don't even touch it.'

Naturally, the young woman wanted to know why.

'Because it's medicine,' said the Moon firmly. She refused to be drawn any further.

The young woman enjoyed being out in the beautiful Sky country, digging up roots, then taking them home to roast or to make into delicious soup. She flourished on the rich food and soon gave birth to a sturdy baby boy. She was so happy.

However, one thing marred her contentment – a niggling worry that she couldn't put out of her mind. Every day when she went out root digging, she would pass the outsized turnip that she was forbidden to touch. The more she saw it, the more she thought about it; and the more she thought about it, the more it disturbed her. At last, when her son had grown old enough to sit up on his own, she couldn't stand it any more.

She gazed furtively around. Neither the Sun, the Moon nor Morning Star were anywhere in sight. Gently, she placed the little boy on the ground, picked up her digging stick and poked it under the enormous turnip. It slid easily into the moist soil, right under the root. Her heart began to beat very fast. She put her weight on the handle and tried to ease the turnip out...

But it wouldn't budge.

The young woman began to panic that someone would see her. 'I'd best just pull the stick away,' she thought, 'and move on before anyone notices what I've done.' So she braced her feet on the ground and heaved with all her might.

But though she pulled and pulled – now the digging stick would not move.

What could she do? She was terrified that the Moon would punish her severely for her disobedience, and for losing the stick. Tears came to her eyes...

Woh, woh, woh! Two large white Cranes were soaring above her. They circled round for a few moments, then swooped down to land.

'You're in trouble!' whooped Crane Woman.

The young woman nodded and fell to her knees, holding out her hands in supplication.

'But you're also in luck,' said Crane Woman. 'For I have always been true to my husband here, and this has given me much power. You want to know why your stick is trapped under the medicine turnip, eh? It's because you don't know the songs needed to dig it out. Do as I say, and everything will be fine.'

Crane Woman began to sing. She took the young woman's hands in her own and placed them on the handle of the digging stick. Together, in this way, they easily pulled it out. Next, Crane Woman marched round in the direction of the Sun's daily journey, moving three times towards the turnip and back again. On the fourth movement, she pushed the digging-stick right underneath, dug the turnip out completely and gave it to the young woman. Then Crane Woman flapped her great white wings and flew away with her husband.

The turnip was very heavy, so the young woman put it down for a moment. She crept over to the hollow where it had been growing, knelt down and peered over its rim. She expected to see just the usual dark cavity filled with crumbling mud...

But there was a huge gaping hole there, awash with daylight, going down, down through the Sky, all the way to the Earth below. The young woman could see trees and rivers, the endless expanse of the Plains…and the lodges of her own camp. She couldn't stop gazing down at it. Her whole body ached with a desperate longing.

After some time, she picked up her child and walked back to the lodge, carrying the turnip. Her husband and his family were all waiting for her at the lodge door, their faces dark with sorrow.

It was Morning Star who spoke. 'You disobeyed my mother; you saw things that were best forgotten. Because of this, our marriage is over. Go back to your own people on Earth.'

'But what about our son?' asked the young woman, clutching the child close to her.

'You may take him with you,' said Morning Star. 'But listen carefully if you wish to keep him. Don't let him touch the ground – not even for a single moment – for twice times seven days. Otherwise he will be transformed…'

'Transformed?' she cried in horror.

'Yes indeed, transformed twice times over – and you will never see him on Earth again. Can you obey this?'

'Of course I can! I must!'

'How can I trust your word when you have already broken one prohibition?' said Morning Star. 'Hmm… Here's something to help you. When you get back to your own family's lodge, paint my symbol, the sign of the morning star, on the back of it, to help you remember what you must do.'

The Moon embraced her daughter-in-law sadly and bade her goodbye.

The Sun said, 'Wait. Someone is coming to help you descend.'

Very soon a man arrived, carrying a strong spider's web coiled over his arm like a rope. He told the young woman to clasp her child tightly, then wound one end of the web round them both. When they were well secured, he took the other end in his own hands and slowly let the two of them down on the spider's web, all the way back to Earth.

In the camp, a group of youths playing the wheel game looked up and saw the giant spider's web with the young woman dangling from it. They ran over in amazement as she untied herself and stepped onto solid ground, clutching her little son.

'It's the girl who vanished in the woods,' they cried. 'She's come down from the Sky!'

Everyone came rushing out of the lodges. When the young woman's mother saw her long-lost daughter carrying her grandchild, she was overcome with joy. She swept the pair into her arms, and took them home. The young woman told her parents everything that had happened, then repeated Morning Star's warning to her mother. 'Remember, Mama,' she said, 'he mustn't touch the ground, not even for an instant, for twice times seven days.'

'Of course I'll remember,' said her mother.

The young woman herself diligently obeyed the prohibition. However, unfortunately, she never explained to her mother what might happen if they forgot.

On the thirteenth day after her return home, the mother said to her daughter, 'Could you go down to the river to fetch some water this morning? I've woken up full of aches and pains, but you're young and strong.'

'I'm more than willing to work again,' the young woman answered. 'But just let me off for one more day, Mama, so I can keep my child safe until the period of danger has passed.'

'Don't you trust your own mother?' the older woman retorted.

The young woman argued a bit more, but she knew it was wrong to leave all the heavy work to her mother, so down to the river she went. 'Keep your eyes on him all the time while I'm gone,' she pleaded. 'Whatever you do, don't let him get off the bed.'

Her mother promised faithfully to take care of him. The young woman hurried away as fast as she could, her heart clouded with foreboding.

Sure enough, as soon as she had gone, the older woman turned her back on her grandson and picked up her sewing. The little boy sat on his bed, staring at her with his big black eyes. She didn't turn round. He cooed at her. Still she didn't move. Slowly, the little boy began to crawl. He reached the end of the bed and lowered one foot to the ground. His grandmother kept her back to him, her arm working up and down, up and down at her sewing. He lowered the other foot. Still she didn't notice. He tumbled to the floor with a loud crash.

At once the older woman jumped up. She saw her grandson squirming on the floor. Her head echoed with her daughter's voice: *Whatever you do, don't let him get off the bed*

She dashed over and scooped up the child. Thank goodness he wasn't hurt! She placed him back on the bed and scolded him sharply. He scowled and grizzled. She propped a big pile of hides, blankets and baskets around him, so he couldn't fall off again. The little boy kicked; the older woman scolded him again. The boy pulled his blanket over his head, then lay down. Gradually his breathing steadied and he fell into the stillness of sleep. The older woman relaxed.

Very soon, her daughter came hurrying home. She put down her water carrier and rushed over to the bed. 'Where's my little one?' she cried. 'You didn't take your eyes off him while I was out?'

'Of course not,' her mother lied. 'He covered himself up as you can see, and fell fast asleep.'

Breathlessly, with trembling hands, the young woman pulled back the robe – and gave a shriek of despair: 'Ach! I knew something dreadful would happen if I left him. Mama – he's vanished!'

'That's impossible,' said the older woman nervously.

'He's been transformed – just as my husband warned me – into *this.*'

She pointed at the bed. Where the little boy had lain, now there was only a deathly white blob of something soft and spongey – a large puffball fungus.

The young woman was heartbroken. She bent over the puffball and whispered to it urgently, she stroked it and sang to it. She went outside and called up desperate prayers to her father-in-law, the Sun. But nothing could wake the puffball, nothing could return it to the form of her beloved child.

In the end, she picked up the puffball and wrapped it in her shawl. Holding it close, she wandered away through the camp and out beyond to the empty prairie, constantly wailing and shrieking her prayers to the Sky: 'Above People, pity me! Give me back my child!'

She sat out on the grass as day cooled into evening. The wind dropped. Darkness fell. One by one the stars came out. She gazed up at them, searching as she did every night, for the hole in the Sky through which she and her lost little boy had descended on the spider's web rope.

But just like her child, tonight the hole had vanished. It was filled with a new star.

'Oh, my child,' she whispered, '*there* you are! Like he said, you've been transformed twice over!'

All night long she sat out there. The constellations travelled their slow trails across the Sky. But her child, the new star, was immobile, staying firmly in the same place.

That is how the Fixed Star, the one that always shines steady in the north, came to be.

Wissler & Duval: *Blackfoot Mythology*, 1908
The stories in the source book were collected amongst the various divisions of the Blackfoot Confederacy during 1903-7. Unfortunately, it does not name any of the original narrators, but says there were 21 in all, adding that:

> 'The method pursued with the most important myths was to discuss them with different individuals, so as to form an opinion as to the most common arrangement of incidents.'

At the end of the story the source book concludes:

> 'After this, the woman painted circles round the bottom of her lodge to represent the puffball, or the Fallen Star... She had already painted the Morning Star on the back of her lodge. This is why the people paint their lodges in the way that you see them... The doors of the lodges at that time faced the sun, and the sign of the Morning Star was made upon the back of the lodge, because he always travels on the other side from the sun.'

This was one of the most common Native American stories right across the continent, but especially in the Great Plains where it was also told by the Cheyenne, Dakota, Gros Ventre, Kiowa and Pawnee peoples. Most versions start with the same opening scene. Sometimes the ascent to the Sky is made by following a porcupine up a supernatural tree, which grows upwards as the young woman climbs it. Other variants include the little boy not turning into a star but maturing to become a heroic monster-slayer; and the woman making her own rope to return to Earth, but too short, so that she falls to her death, or is stoned to death by her celestial husband.

The myth explains the origin of the digging stick. The turnips that the young woman digs in the Sky are probably *psoralea esculenta,* a herbaceous perennial plant whose starchy, tuberous root was a staple food in the Plains, harvested between May and July. It was gathered by the women, then peeled and either eaten raw; or cooked by boiling, roasting in the embers, or crushing into powder for soup.

SPLINTER FOOT GIRL

Arapaho

It was late in the year, the grass had died and the prairie wind was sharp with frost, when seven young men eagerly set off northwards to prove themselves on the warpath.

After a few days, the seven came to a deep, rushing river. The only way across was by wading through the water barefoot, which the first six easily did. Unfortunately, as the youngest leaped out onto the opposite bank, he tripped against a fallen branch and a long splinter from it pierced his foot. Blood gushed from the wound and he crumpled to the ground, writhing with pain.

His friends ran over, extracted the splinter, bandaged the wound with strips from their tunics, then helped him up. He grabbed a stick to lean on and managed to hobble onwards. However, his foot was swelling alarmingly and he couldn't stop trembling, his face as grey as ash.

'You can't go any further in this state,' said the eldest. 'Don't worry friend, we won't abandon you. We'll set up camp here and stay put until you recover.'

The other six worked fast and soon knocked up a sturdy hut. The youngest collapsed inside it, groaning pitifully. The next morning, he was too weak even to rise from his bed. When the others went out hunting, he stayed behind, fitfully sleeping.

In this way, several days passed while the youngest man's condition got worse and worse. At last, as he lay feverishly alone in the hut, he leaned over and stabbed his bloated foot with one of his arrows. Pus oozed out in a new wave of pain that made him faint. When he came to, he found his whole foot had split right open, in a gaping gash from toe to heel. In the middle of the gash, there seemed to be something solid and alive...some kind of *creature*...

'This must be a dream,' he thought. 'I'm delirious with pain.'

He blinked, but his eyes had not deceived him: there really *was* something alive in there: a tiny, naked, perfectly formed little girl.

He reached down and gingerly brushed his fingertip against her. She was as solid as his own skin. Suddenly, with a squeal, she squirmed completely free. The next moment, the gash in his foot fused together, the swelling vanished and so did the pain. For the first time since his accident, he felt normal.

The tiny girl struggled to her feet, shivering. He reached for his knife, hacked a piece of cloth from his tunic and draped it carefully around her like a miniature blanket. The girl snuggled into it and smiled.

'Welcome, Splinter Foot Girl,' he whispered. 'I don't understand who you are, but I'm happy that you've come to me. I promise I won't hurt you. May I...? I would like to be your father.'

Splinter Foot Girl nodded solemnly.

'I'm afraid there aren't any women here to mother you, and no other children,' he went on. 'But I have six friends with me, all good men: they'll be your uncles and help me care for you.'

When the others came home, they were astonished and delighted to meet their mysterious new niece. They gave Splinter Foot Girl the tenderest pieces of meat to suck, treated her honourably, as uncles should, and helped the youngest man, her father, to look after her.

Under their care, she grew by the day – so extraordinarily fast that, within a single month, she was the size of a normal child. Before the last snow of winter had melted, she was as tall as a young deer. As the buds opened on the trees, she blossomed into a beautiful young woman.

Her father and six uncles were very proud of her. But they feared for her too – with good reason. For birds flying overhead saw their hut in the wilderness, and wheeled down for a closer look. They marvelled at the sight of Splinter Foot Girl moving gracefully around it, and carried news of her throughout the world. This reached the ears of an evil being called Bone Bull, an overbearing tyrant, with an insatiable appetite for young women. He wasn't a man – but a chief of the Buffalo.

As soon as he heard of Splinter Foot Girl's unearthly beauty, Bone Bull became mightily aroused. 'Ach, the thought of this girl is

51

like fire licking at my loins!' he bellowed. He snorted at a nearby Magpie. 'You! fly to Splinter Foot Girl's father and order him to send her to me at once!'

Magpie flew hastily to the seven young men's hut and there repeated Bone Bull's brutal marriage proposal. The girl's father and uncles were horrified.

'No,' they cried, 'she's much too young and precious!'

'You'll regret this,' Magpie chittered. But he carried their message as instructed.

When he heard it, Bone Bull summoned all the other birds, bellowing: 'Tell the seven men that unless they bring the girl to me, I shall tear down their lodge, gore them all to death, and seize her myself!'

The birds hastened to the seven young men to screech the Buffalo's warning.

'We'd better pretend we're willing,' said Splinter Foot Girl's father wretchedly, 'and present her to Bone Bull with all due ceremony. If we flatter him with gifts, maybe he'll treat her kindly for a while – which will give us time to work out how to rescue her.'

So they sent a message back saying that they would indeed give Splinter Foot Girl as a bride. She knew that her guardians loved her dearly and were acting in her best interests, so she accepted her fate calmly and didn't resist. The six uncles went to distant camps and bought magnificent gifts for her new husband: war-bonnets and quivers, blankets, moccasins, robes, pipes, knives, tobacco and fine medicine bags.

Finally, it was time to take her to Bone Bull. They found the Buffalo herd milling about in the middle of a barren plain. Bone Bull strode to meet them, poking out his long pink tongue lecherously. He snatched Splinter Foot Girl and quickly, brutally took his pleasure of her. When he was satiated, he pushed her to the ground, tossed her a magnificent painted robe and grunted his commands:

'Do everything I say, and do it at once. Never refuse me, never question me. Never wander away from the herd, never speak to anyone but me, your master; never even look at anyone but me. If you obey, you may be lucky and survive longer than the countless pathetic wives I've had before you.'

He lowered his head at her father and six uncles as if he were about to charge. 'Go!' he roared. 'Never come back – or I'll rip you to death with my horns!'

So the seven men were forced to leave their beloved girl in the evil Buffalo's charge. But they didn't forget her, not for a single day. Months passed. The year turned. Spring came again. The seven men sent messengers to seek news of Splinter Foot Girl: Magpie, Blackbird and Crow. They all reported that she was still alive, and as well as could be expected.

'Who will get her back for us?' the men begged them.

'I wouldn't dare,' said Magpie.

'I wouldn't have the strength,' said Blackbird.

'I don't know how to,' said Crow. 'And yet... I know two who do. Be patient. At nightfall I'll ask them to come.'

The sun sank and shadows spread their soft blankets over the prairie. All the birds fell silent. Soft footsteps came padding towards them, shapes scuttling over the ground: Badger and Mole.

'We've come to rescue your missing girl,' said Badger. 'But to succeed, we need arrows.'

The eldest man fetched a full quiver. Badger took it in his mouth. Mole pushed his head under a mat of grass, burrowed into the earth, and began digging. He squeezed into the hole and dug even further. Badger poked in his snout, widened the tunnel with his powerful claws, and slipped down after Mole, carrying the arrows before him.

Meanwhile, Splinter Foot Girl was sitting, hopeless and alone, in the wind-lashed patch of land where Bone Bull had left her. Her only comfort was the blanket she was sitting on.

Suddenly, the ground beneath this blanket began to vibrate and jiggle. As she leaped from it in alarm, the blanket jerked to one side, revealing a hole below. A fleshy nose and pale whiskers emerged, followed by a pair of claw-tipped hands and a small, dark body. Behind it, came a much larger head, striped with black and white.

Splinter Foot Girl screamed and backed away in terror. But Mole whispered, 'Have no fear, we've come to rescue you. Take these arrows from my friend, poke them into the ground to form a circle, remove your robe and drape it over them – never mind your modesty, we are two most honourable creatures. When your husband returns, his bad eyesight will make him believe that this effigy is you – giving us extra time to flee. Now, follow us!'

Mole scuttled back down the tunnel and Badger used his snout to nudge Splinter Foot Girl after him, coming up behind to protect her. At last, the passage turned upwards, and they emerged back at Splinter Foot Girl's home. She climbed out of the hole and fell into her father's arms, laughing and crying with relief.

But Mole ran back down the tunnel and returned, flapping his digger claws. 'We're in imminent danger!' he squealed. 'That effigy we left in your place didn't fool Bone Bull for long. He kept bellowing at it, and when it failed to submit to him, he flew into a rage and tried to mount it in full view of the herd. Of course, it collapsed under his weight – and all the other Buffalo saw his humiliation. Now he's seven times as angry as before – and leading his herd here in revenge!'

As soon as Splinter Foot Girl had dressed in a new robe, they all set off over the prairie, the men with weapons at the ready, running as fast as they could. They crossed rivers, waded swamps and squeezed through thickets, Splinter Foot Girl scarcely keeping pace. Finally, by an ancient Cottonwood tree standing alone in an ocean of grass, she threw back her head and cried,

'Oh, great Cottonwood, I can't run any more. I implore you to help!'

The Cottonwood rustled its leaves in reply: 'Of course! Run round me four times, then climb me, each man to a different branch. Splinter Foot Girl, you climb highest, to the fork. Crawl into the abandoned bird's nest there and hide.'

So it was done. Just as they were all settled in their places, they heard the thunder of approaching hooves. The seething dark mass of the Buffalo herd appeared on the horizon. As it drew closer, Splinter Foot Girl and her menfolk neither moved nor made a sound. The herd streamed straight under the Cottonwood, and ran on.

However, one small calf at the rear stopped for a few moments to rest in the shade of the tree. Splinter Foot Girl didn't notice him; thinking all the Buffalo had passed, she gave in to her fatigue and coughed, so that a drop of phlegm fell to the ground by the calf's feet. He sniffed it – and caught the scent of his chief's lost wife. At once, the calf rushed to catch up with the herd and pushed his way through to Bone Bull.

'Chief!' he grunted, 'I've found her – Splinter Foot Girl is hiding in that Cottonwood we passed!'

Bone Bull turned and squinted at the distant tree; he sniffed the air and listened.

'Herd,' he roared, 'turn and watch me! Admire how I shall punish the Cottonwood for sheltering my wife – who I shall then torture and gore to death!'

The herd spun round and thundered back to the tree. The seven men saw them coming and fitted arrows to their bows.

'Not yet,' the Cottonwood rustled. 'Let Bone Bull bring about his own ruin.'

The herd split into four and stampeded the Cottonwood from every side.

'Stand back!' Bone Bull bellowed. 'I am the mightiest creature on Earth!'

He positioned himself to the southeast, legs astride, lowered his head and charged at the Cottonwood. *Thunk!* His horns crashed against the tree, tearing a long cleft into the trunk.

The Cottonwood quivered but stood firm.

Bone Bull moved round and attacked from the southwest. His horns scraped noisily around inside the cleft, carving it wider.

Still the tree stood firm.

Bone Bull strode to the northwest and rushed at the Cottonwood from there, smashing into it with the force of a falling mountain boulder. However, this time, instead of causing further damage, the impact cracked the Buffalo chief's right horn and broke it clean in two.

The tree rustled its branches threateningly.

Bone Bull would not be cowed. He stomped to the northeast. There, using only his undamaged left horn, again he slammed against the tree, making the cleft twice as deep.

'One more blow and I shall destroy you completely!' he roared.

But the Cottonwood answered, 'Bone Bull, long before you were a mere speck in your father's seed, the Earth was nurturing me, giving me powers beyond your imagination. No matter how you try to hurt me, I shall always heal myself.'

These words stoked Bone Bull's fury as a hurricane inflames a fire. He pranced around, tossing his great head to roar his outrage, scraping up dust clouds with his hooves. Finally, angling his unbroken left horn, he charged at the Cottonwood's very core.

There was a loud crack. Bone Bull's single remaining horn was impaled in the heartwood! The mighty Buffalo bellowed furiously and tried to wrench himself free, twisting about, kicking the trunk with his massive hooves. But the struggle only dug his horn in deeper.

'Now is the time,' the Cottonwood rustled. 'Shoot him!'

The seven men let their arrows fly. Each found its mark in a soft part of Bone Bull's body: his neck, his flanks, the hanging folds of his belly. With each shot, the monstrous Buffalo's efforts grew weaker...until the last breath squeezed from him and he collapsed.

The herd was grunting in despair.

'You!' the Cottonwood called to them. 'You all supported your chief in his evil, and thus broke the sacred pact between living things. Our mother, the Earth, will punish you. She will cause your power to shrivel away. You'll fall to the mercy of the People. Your horns will shrink to half their former size and be useless against the hunters. Whenever you see People, you'll be overwhelmed by fear. No matter how far and fast you run from them, they'll always use their boundless cunning to outwit and kill you. They'll strip you of dignity, butcher your bodies and eat you; and cut up your skins to make blankets and robes. Now go!'

The herd fled in shame and vanished over the horizon.

The seven men and Splinter Foot Girl all clambered down from the Cottonwood tree. The corpse of Bone Bull was still firmly attached to the trunk by his horn, so they gave him a degrading burial under a pile of his own herd's dung, then left him to rot into the soil and feed the Cottonwood's roots.

Splinter Foot Girl walked away and smiled. She reached for her necklace, pulled off a small medicine ball of herbs and feathers, tossed it into the air, caught it, then kicked it. The ball soared up to the sky; and suddenly, her father began to rise too, light as a downy feather, drifting upwards in the wind. Splinter Foot Girl kicked the ball again and again; each time, one of her uncles rose up, until all seven men were floating towards the Sky. Finally, she herself began to rise; and high above the Earth, the clouds parted and let them all through to enter the Sky world.

And there Splinter Foot Girl, her father and her six uncles all made their home in a tipi covered with stars, and were never heard of on Earth again.

Buffalo were vital for subsistence in the Great Plains until their virtual extermination by Whites in the late 19th century. The spectacle of their herds was vividly described by George Catlin in the 1830s:

'They congregate into such masses in some places, as literally to black the prairies for miles together...several thousands in a mass, eddying and wheeling about under a cloud of dust, which is raised by the bulls as they are pawing in the dirt, or engaged in desperate combats... plunging and butting at each other in the most furious manner...the males are continually following the females, and the whole mass are in constant motion; and all bellowing...which, mingled altogether, appear, at the distance of a mile or two, like the sound of distant thunder.'

Once killed, the entire carcass was put to good use: the flesh and tongue for meat; the skin for tipi covers, clothing, cradles, shields, moccasins, musical instruments and horse equipment; the hair for headdresses, ornaments and ropes; the tail for fly-brushes; the horns for cups and spoons; the hooves for glue and rattles; the bladder for bags; the paunch to line basins and buckets; the bones for sledges, weapons and tools; the stomach for medicine and containers; the muscles for thread; the scrotum for rattles; the brain for dressing hides; and the skull for religious rituals.

The original text records four different versions of this myth, of varying length and detail, all collected amongst the Southern Arapaho of Oklahoma. Three of the narrators are not named, just identified by their initials; the other was a prolific storyteller called River Woman, who contributed eleven other narratives to the same collection, all featuring lively character development and dialogue. The longest version has an extra episode after the destruction of Bone Bull, with Splinter Foot Girl forced into a second violent marriage with a malevolent rock, and again saved by Mole and Badger. It also makes much of the wedding gifts presented to Bone Bull, listing them at length and linking each one to different parts of Bone Bull's body.

A Cheyenne story collected in 1900 follows a similar pattern, though here the heroine is not supernatural but just an ordinary girl with an exceptional talent for quillwork. She experiences a mystical calling to travel far to the north, where she joins a household of seven young men who accept her as their sister. She too is threatened with abduction by a malevolent buffalo chief; and here all seven escape in a 'growing tree' that takes them straight into the sky world, where they are all transformed into stars.

BLOOD CLOT BOY

Sioux (Oceti Sakowin)

Badger always hunted alone, yet always ended up with more buffalo than anyone else. That was because he had devised a very clever technique. He had built a special corral by his home, and disguised it in such a way that buffalo were constantly wandering into it. Every evening, he went down to the corral and shooed the buffalo out in a long line. Then he fitted his bow with an extraordinary arrow, the length of two trees laid end to end, and shot the leading buffalo. The long arrow always went straight through its heart, out again and into the buffalo behind, from there into the next buffalo, and so on. In this way, Badger achieved a mass kill with a single shot. So he always had a huge stock of meat for his family, who enjoyed a very comfortable life.

One day, Grey Bear called at Badger's lodge.

'Greetings, dear Brother,' Badger welcomed him.

Grey Bear looked at him mournfully. 'Huh! It's all very well calling me "brother",' he growled, 'but you don't treat me like one.'

'That's a terrible accusation,' said Badger with concern. 'Whatever do you mean?'

'You don't share things like a brother should,' complained Grey Bear. 'You have so much – yet I have almost nothing. Look how tall and plump your children are – then compare them with mine, who are stunted and skinny because I can't find them enough food.'

Grey Bear went on and on about his pathetic circumstances. Badger's eyes welled up with tears and he clasped his visitor's paws in sympathy.

'This is terrible, Grey Bear!' he cried. 'You must bring your family to live with us, and share our bounty. Go and fetch them here at once… Ah, but first let me give you something.' He nipped away, then returned with a large buffalo haunch, which he pressed eagerly into Grey Bear's paws. 'Take this back now, to keep your family from hunger until they arrive.'

The very next morning, Grey Bear came back, with his wife and children in tow.

Badger stood at the lodge door to give them a hearty welcome. 'Come in, come in!' he exclaimed. Our home is yours now too.'

Naturally, he expected his guests to reciprocate with similar courtesy. But instead, the Bears elbowed the Badgers roughly aside. They stomped around the lodge, poking their noses into everything and making insulting comments about the furnishings. Grey Bear's wife soon located the Badgers' meat store. She started poking her grimy claws into it and tossing enormous portions to her slavering family, who greedily gobbled them up.

'More, Mama, more!' the cubs squealed, over and over. When at last they were satiated, they wiped their paws and jaws on the Badgers' beautifully worked blankets, covering them with ugly smears of grease.

The Badgers hovered in the background, watching their guests in disbelief and shock.

'What are you gawping at?' snarled Grey Bear, signalling to his wife and cubs. They all pounced on the Badgers, dragged them unceremoniously outside and secured the door – the door to their own home! – firmly against them.

The Badgers stood outside under the frosty stars, lashed by the chill wind, overcome with dismay. For a long while they simply huddled there, shivering and whimpering.

'What a foolish mistake you made,' said Badger's wife. 'Fancy offering hospitality so freely to a heartless thug like him!'

Badger said nothing.

'Well, we'll just have to make the most of things,' sighed his wife. 'I'll get to work and build us a shelter; but I'm so cold and hungry, it won't be up to much. Husband, as soon as it's morning, take your long arrow and go hunting.'

'I can't,' said Badger miserably. 'All my weapons are still inside the lodge.'

That night the Badgers slept in a makeshift brush hut, their empty bellies rumbling. Early next morning they were woken by the *thud-thud* of heavy footsteps, followed by Grey Bear's booming voice:

'Oi! Get up, Stinky Ears! Yes, you, Badger. Your corral's overflowing with buffalo. Here's your bow and that special long arrow of yours – come out and shoot them.'

'Thank goodness for that,' mumbled Badger's wife. 'At least he's willing to work with you. Hurry up, husband. We'll all feel better once you've brought us some meat.'

So Badger ran to Grey Bear, collected his weapons and walked by his enemy's side to the corral. There Grey Bear watched as Badger skilfully herded the buffalo into line, killed four with a single shot and dragged the carcasses into the open.

'Right, Stinky Ears, you can go now,' growled Grey Bear.

Badger looked up at him nervously. 'Um...I'll just take my share.'

'*Your* share?' Grey Bear snarled, gnashing his yellow teeth. He seized Badger's scruff, lifted him off the ground and dangled him in the air. 'Don't think any of this is for *you*, Stinky Ears. You're my slave – which means you have to work for me and get nothing in return.' He snatched the bow and long arrow from Badger's paws. 'Now, get out before I kill you – and make sure you're on time for the hunt tomorrow.'

Badger slunk off to the makeshift hut – where he had to tell his starving family he'd brought them absolutely nothing.

Meanwhile, back at his lodge, the Bear family roared with laughter when Grey Bear described his dealings with Badger. They devoured all the fresh meat at a single sitting...

Ah, but not *quite* all of it. For the youngest Bear cub was different from the rest of his family. Badger's humiliation made him feel uncomfortable. Grey Bear had given this cub a big leg bone as his share, but he had only gnawed half the meat off it. He took the rest outside and played with it for a while, kicking the bone around like a ball. When he saw that his parents had both fallen into an overstuffed sleep, he crept across to the Badgers' hut and tossed the meaty bone inside for them to eat.

A month went by like this. Every morning Grey Bear forced Badger to hunt, then snatched away all the meat; and every evening the good Bear cub sneaked some leavings into the Badgers' hut. The Badgers just about managed to stay alive, but they grew steadily thinner and weaker.

One morning, after the kill, Badger begged: 'Please, please let me have some meat for my own family. We're all wasting away.'

'No!' Grey Bear growled.

'But if I die, who will hunt for you?'

'You're not indispensable, Stinky Ears. There's plenty more where you came from.' Grey Bear struck his massive paw against Badger's emaciated body, and pushed him hard, making him fall into a pool of buffalo blood.

As Badger sprawled there wretchedly, he noticed that some of the blood had congealed into a large clot. 'Hmm,' he thought, 'maybe that would provide some nourishment for my little ones.' He staggered to his feet, closing his paw around the clot. Clutching it carefully, he set off to shuffle home.

Next to his cold skin, the blood clot felt warm and solid. When Grey Bear was out of sight, Badger sat down and examined it. There was something...something rather strange about it. He sniffed it carefully for a long time, scratching his head. Then he tore up a clump of grass and wrapped the clot inside it.

When he reached his hut, Badger walked straight past it to a bare patch of ground. There he gathered twigs and fashioned them into a miniature sweat-house, with a bed of wild herbs in the middle. He unwrapped the blood clot and laid it gently on top of the herbs. Next to it, he lit a tiny fire surrounded by pebbles, and poured water on top. When the pebbles were sizzling, he shut the sweat-house door. Steam wafted out. He sat down and waited.

Suddenly he heard a voice coming from inside the sweat-house. It was singing. Badger jumped up and tipped more water through the twigs onto the stones. The singing stopped; but now he heard a soft breathing, and the voice called: 'Open up, let me out!'

With trembling paws, Badger wrenched away the sweat-house door. A figure squeezed out of it, shook itself, stood up on two feet and stretched to human size.

It was a young man. He was tall and splendidly built, with handsome features, dressed as a warrior chief. His fringed buckskin shirt was tanned almost as white as snow, and exquisitely embroidered with porcupine quills; his leggings and moccasins were lavishly decorated with beads; and his robe was sewn from countless otter skins. His hair fell to his waist, braided with strips of pure white weasel fur and crowned by a glossy eagle feather. He carried a bow and a quiver full of flint-headed arrows.

'Blood Clot Boy?' Badger whispered.

'I've been sent to help you,' said Blood Clot Boy.

'Thank you with all my heart,' said Badger. 'But I'm afraid I have nothing to offer you in return – except loyalty and honesty.'

'Such qualities are worth far more than a stash of treasures.'

'Will you allow me to adopt you as my son?' said Badger.

'I eagerly accept, Father,' said Blood Clot Boy.

'What an honour!' said Badger. 'This calls for a celebration feast. But unfortunately...' He shook his shrivelled old head in embarrassment, scattering dry moulted hairs into the breeze. 'Dear son, let me explain my tragic situation.' He told Blood Clot Boy all about the terrible things that Grey Bear had done.

'Father, that is why I have come to help you,' said Blood Clot Boy. 'Now, listen carefully. Early tomorrow morning, I shall hide. As always, Grey Bear will force you to go hunting. This time, after you kill the buffalo, ignore his jibes and start taking one of the carcasses for yourself. He'll try to punish you – but I will save you.'

The next morning, Grey Bear came out yelling as usual: 'Stinky Ears, get me some meat!' As usual, Badger scurried to obey, killing a set of buffalo with his long arrow. However, this time, instead of docilely cutting them up, Badger brazenly hoisted one of the carcasses onto his shoulder.

'Drop that!' Grey Bear roared. He punched Badger hard, making him spin round then reel away, quaking with shame. Grey Bear's wife and cubs were watching, dancing about and chortling with laughter. Grey Bear came at a run to strike Badger again...

But at that very moment, Blood Clot Boy strode from his hiding place. With firm steps he went to stand between Badger and his oppressor.

'Why do you treat my father like that?' he said coldly.

Grey Bear seemed to shrivel under Blood Clot Boy's uncanny gaze. 'Hmm...er...yes,' he stuttered. 'I do treat him very well, you know. I'm always urging him to take a good share home to his family, but he...'

'You're a liar as well as a brute,' said Blood Clot Boy.

Without further ado, he stepped back, fitted an arrow to his bow and shot it into Grey Bear's heart, slaughtering him on the spot. The other Bears squealed and tried to run away.

But Blood Clot Boy strode after them, shouting, 'I'll rid you of them all, Father!'

'Wait,' said Badger. 'There's one who doesn't deserve to die – a cub who's been secretly bringing scraps to my family and saving us from starvation. Let me show you...'

'I know how to recognise him,' said Blood Clot Boy.

He followed the Bears to the lodge that they had seized from the Badgers, kicked open the door and burst in. Grey Bear's Wife and her cubs were cowering against the back wall, heads bent in fear. Blood Clot Boy surveyed them and said, 'I hear one of you alone pitied Badger, my father, and took him food. Who was it?'

'Me,' rasped one of the cubs.

'No, no, it was me.'

'No, me.'

'They're all trying to win your favour,' said Grey Bear's wife snidely. 'Obviously it was really me.'

One cub alone squirmed behind the others, keeping his mouth shut tight.

'So,' said Blood Clot Boy, 'all you who claim to have pitied my father – what do you expect of me?'

'To spare us!' they cried with one voice.

In reply, Blood Clot Boy lifted his bow and shot each one dead. – except the silent one. By his modesty, that cub had revealed that it was he who had helped the Badgers.

Afterwards, Blood Clot Boy fetched his adopted family and took them back to their lodge. They were so happy to be home. Before long, Badger's wife had completely restored it and made it even more comfortable and splendid than before. The good Bear cub was allowed to live with them, for honourable deeds deserve reward.

After that, Blood Clot Boy went travelling and became widely acclaimed as a hero. However, Badger and his family stayed happily at home. They were safe, they were comfortable and their food never ran out again. Truly, they were rich.

Rigs: *Dakota Grammar, Texts and Ethnography*, 1893.
The source book reproduces this story as originally written out in the Dakota Sioux language by the Rev. David Grey Cloud, a pastor who belonged to the Santee (Eastern) Dakota Sioux people. Underneath it is a literal line-by-line translation, followed by a more easily understood summary. Grey Cloud says that, after the events retold here, Blood Clot Boy later becomes discontented and embarks on a journey. He ignores Badger's warning to avoid a particular old man, and ends up ensnared by the trickster Spider (Unktomi) – who humiliates him by turning him into a dog.

The same story, without the Unktomi incident, is recorded in two slightly later Dakota Sioux story collections. *Wigwam Evenings* (1909) was written by Charles A. Eastman, a renowned Santee Dakota Sioux doctor, writer, lecturer and campaigner, and his non-Indian wife. Its stories are retold in a somewhat sanitised style suitable for young children. *Myths and Legends of the Sioux* (1916) was written by Marie L. McLaughlin, whose grandmother was a Mdewakanton Dakota Sioux; McLaughlin was raised in a Dakota community and lived on Indian reservations for forty years, recording stories told to her by local elders. In her version, the victim of the Bear's selfishness is not Badger, but Rabbit and his family. The details of Blood Clot Boy's clothes, and of Grey Bear's death, are taken from her account.

The name Grey Bear is rather puzzling, since the bears of the Great Plains are either grizzlies or black bears, both of which range in colour from black, through shades of brown to blond; but not grey.

The story was also well known amongst other tribes; in Arapaho, Blackfoot and Gros Ventre versions the characters are not animals but human. The villain is a man polygamously married to two sisters, who forces his elderly father-in-law to hunt for him, but denies him any share of the kill. One of the wives surreptitiously gives her father just enough to stay alive, and Blood Clot Boy spares her when he arrives to take revenge. Typically in these stories, Blood Clot Boy later embarks on a series of monster-slaying adventures. The Arapaho have a story about a Blood Clot Girl.

A number of other supernatural-boy-hero stories circulated widely on the Plains, particularly amongst the Crow, Omaha and Wichita peoples. Many feature a set of twins, cut alive from their pregnant mother's womb by a male or female villain, who either throws both away or leaves one boy in the tipi but discards the other to fend for himself in the wild. The father raises the first child, who is later joined by the wild one. As they mature, the boys break a series of prohibitions on visiting certain places, bringing them face to face with various monsters which they successfully overcome. The Sioux and Gros Ventre told stories of Stone Boy, born to a woman from a stone. He embarks on a quest to discover the fate of his mother's four long-lost brothers, and eventually finds their lifeless bodies in the keeping of an evil witch. Stone Boy kills her, then restores his uncles to life in a sweat-house.

A sweat-house was typically made of bent and interlaced willow boughs. Inside, someone would sit and sweat in the steam produced when water was poured over hot stones, often accompanied by singing. It was used for both spiritual and healing purposes.

THE SEVEN BUFFALO FATHERS

Gros Ventre (Atsina)

There was a foolish young woman who was always preening herself and flirting. Before long, one of the young men persuaded her to slip away with him into the woods. Then the inevitable happened: she found herself pregnant.

'Which rascal got you into this condition?' her mother cried.

The girl's lover had already abandoned her for fresh prey and she was overcome by shame. 'I'm not saying.'

'Well, what's happened can't be undone,' the mother sighed. 'When the baby's born, I'll help you raise it.'

'I don't want you to,' the daughter said. 'I want to get rid of it.'

The mother had no time to argue, firstly because everyone else in their camp was packing up to move to a new location, and secondly because the young woman's labour pains had started. She sent her husband ahead, saying they'd catch up with him later, without giving any reason. Soon after everyone else had deserted the camp, she helped her daughter give birth to a baby boy.

The woman tried to put him into her daughter's arms, but the girl pushed him away and refused to suckle him.

'He'll sicken unless you feed him,' the woman chided.

'I don't care,' wept the daughter. 'Take him away!'

The older woman didn't know what to do. She was far too old to have any milk in her own breasts; and all the other nursing mothers in their band were far away by now. The last thing she wanted was to harm her grandson, but unless he could be fed quickly, he was bound to die.

'I suppose the kindest thing is to put the little mite out of his agony as fast as possible,' she thought wretchedly.

So she wrapped the newborn in a shawl and carried him to a nearby Buffalo wallow. There she dug a hole with her bare hands, and gently laid him in it, covering him with loose mud to drown his plaintive cries. Then, choking with tears, she ran back to her daughter, cleaned her up and led her to the new camp.

After they had gone, seven large Buffalo bulls appeared on the opposite horizon, walking towards the wallow. As they drew near, they heard strange, heart-rending noises coming from it. They stood very still, listening.

The eldest bull said, 'It sounds like some poor creature in distress down there. Come, friends, it's our duty to dig it out.'

So the seven Buffalo scooped the mud away with their horns. and were astonished to discover the abandoned newborn baby. Gently, they lifted him out and carried him to firmer ground. There they laid him on the earth and surrounded him solemnly.

'It's a young one of the People,' said a second bull.

'He needs caring for,' said a third.

'Why don't we adopt him?' said the eldest, 'and raise him as our son?'

This was a momentous proposal. The Buffalo bulls conferred for a long time, but at last they all nodded their agreement that this was the only honourable thing to do. They knelt before the abandoned baby and together licked away all the mud that covered him. As the child's body became clean, something remarkable happened. Before their eyes, he grew and strengthened. Within moments, he was no longer a helpless baby, but a strapping young boy.

He sat up, smiled at them and held out his hands pleadingly.

'It seems our tongues have worked some kind of medicine on him,' said a fourth bull in wonder.

The eldest said, 'There is a pact between the Buffalo and the People. That's surely the cause of this miracle.' He turned to the child and nudged him gently with his nose. 'Boy, have no fear. We are your seven adoptive fathers: we love you and will care for you. Tell us what you need, and we will bring it to you at once.'

'Oh my fathers,' said the boy, 'I'm very hungry – I need food.'

'There is food all around you, dear child,' said a fifth bull. 'The Plains are bursting with sweet grass and flowers.'

The boy did not move.

'People don't eat grass,' said a sixth bull. 'They eat...Buffalo.'

'I don't want to eat *you*!' cried the boy.

The bulls conferred again in low rumbles while the sun crossed the sky. Finally, the eldest said, 'My son, by the terms of our special relationship with the People, we must give you meat to live. We shall gladly bring it to you.'

The bulls ran across the Plains and found a young Buffalo cow, who had fallen behind the rest of her herd. They spoke to her quietly of the sacred duty that they wished her to perform. She bowed her head, then stood calmly to let the seven bulls charge her and gore her to death with their horns. Sharing the burden, they dragged her carcass back to the boy.

The boy said, 'I don't know how to eat it.'

After another discussion, the seventh bull ran off and soon returned, pushing a jagged rock before him. The others sliced shards from it with the tips of their horns, making a pile of rough stone knives. They explained to the boy how to use these to skin the carcass and slice off the flesh.

Once the boy had eaten his fill, he stretched, stood up and started gambolling and dancing before the seven bulls. They were enchanted by his antics and tried to mimic him until they were all quite breathless. Then they lay in a circle round the boy, licking him again, letting him clamber over their great, shaggy backs, tying feathers in their manes and grass to the ends of their tails.

The eldest bull said, 'I have long dreamed of this feeling. It is called happiness.'

The other six, and the boy himself, all grunted in agreement.

Days went by, months went by. Together, the seven bulls taught their human son how to make bows and arrows, and how to use them to hunt their sisters whenever he needed more meat. When it was time to move to new pastures, sometimes the boy ran with them, and sometimes he rode on their backs.

The boy became cleverer all the time, and also more mischievous. Sometimes, when the bulls were dozing, he would tie the legs of one of the bulls together, so that when the unsuspecting beast awoke and tried to stand, he tumbled over. But the boy was never scolded; the victims of his practical jokes always roared with laughter.

Years went by. The boy was no longer a child, but a lusty youth.

One day, the eldest bull said, 'My son, listen carefully, for I must give you a warning. Our trail today leads past an enemy herd. Its chief is a bull whose character is totally opposite to ours. He is domineering and violent. He has driven away all the other bulls, leaving only hundreds of cows to follow him. He guards them jealously and will not let any male creature near them. However, the cows all despise him, and are always on the lookout for a more biddable male, and approach anyone who they think might fulfil their needs. I urge you to walk straight past and ignore them.'

Unfortunately, the youth had inherited his unknown mother's tendency to recklessness. As they approached the enemy herd, he made a point of staring at the cows who mingled around their master; and when one approached, he foolishly stopped to speak with her.

'So,' said the cow. 'You must be the human youth we have heard of, the one who lives amongst our kind.'

'I am indeed,' grinned the youth.

'You're even more handsome than the rumours said,' the cow went on, rubbing her head against his shoulder. 'As for me, I badly need some male company, for the mighty bull who calls me his wife has ignored me ever since our miserable wedding day.' She put her soft nose to his ear. 'He's not looking: come, slip away with me!'

Before the youth could answer, a shadow fell over him. He spun round and saw a massive, heavy-maned bull. His long horns jutted forward in distorted, pointed spikes; his matted coat hung from him like a filthy, outsized blanket. He spat at the youth, giving off a foul, bog-like stink.

The seven Buffalo fathers stood at a distance, watching and trembling with dismay.

'You!' the massive bull roared. 'How dare you flirt with my youngest wife!'

'I was only greeting her as I passed by,' the youth stammered.

'You lie!' the bull roared. 'Your shoulder is wet with the grease of her caresses. You'll not get away with this. I will slaughter you – and your seven fathers too!'

At that moment, the seven Buffalo fathers came stampeding up. The evil bull charged at the eldest, his massive head lowered. There was an ear-splitting *crack!* as his misshapen horns broke his opponent's front legs. One after another, the other Buffalo fathers tried to attack, but all fell in the same way.

'You next!' the mighty bull bellowed at the youth.

Again he charged, his head angled to horn the youth, toss him high and smash him to the ground. But the youth quickly pulled a small white feather from his sleeve and held it up to the wind. The next moment, there was no one there – nothing but the feather, floating innocently in the breeze. Slowly, it drifted back to earth... and the youth stood there again, unharmed.

Many more times the evil bull charged at him. Just as many times the youth transformed into the feather and evaded him. The mighty bull began to tire and his attacks grew less forceful. The youth saw his chance. He drew out his bow and arrows, and shot the great brute dead.

'Aaahhh!' All the cows bellowed their happiness to the sky, then stampeded away to enjoy their freedom.

The seven fathers lay on the ground, panting in agony from their broken limbs. But the youth had found his power. He crept over to the eldest, took his bow, held it aloft and circled the bull four times, calling: 'Arise, my father – be healed!'

At once the bull staggered to his feet, shook himself – and was well and sound again. The youth repeated this with the other six. Soon all were back on their feet, as strong and healthy as if the battle had never taken place.

They stood in a circle around their adopted son. The eldest grunted softly and spoke: 'My dear child, no parent could have more affection for you that we seven. Nothing would make us happier than to live with you for ever. But we are old and will soon die, whilst you are young and have the best years of your life ahead. Moreover, we are Buffalo, we walk on four legs; we have no dwelling but the earth and the air; and all we need for nourishment is grass. But you are of the People; you use two of your legs for tools and weapons, and you cannot thrive without shelter to keep off the cold and rain, and meat to make you strong.'

'What are you saying, Father?' the youth asked fearfully.

'I am telling you that it is time for you to go home,' said the eldest bull. 'Time for you to find your birth family and return to the People from whom you came.'

The other bulls nodded sagely.

'But my home is with you,' the youth cried. 'I don't want to leave you. You've often told me how my human family didn't want me. And even if I could find them, I don't know the People's language, I won't understand a single word they say.'

'My child,' said the eldest bull, 'we share your sadness. But you must go back to your own kind. When you find your kin, you will know them. When you are with them, you will understand them. Listen carefully, do everything I tell you and all will come to pass as it should.'

The seven Buffalo led the youth to a human camp.

'This is where your family lives,' said the eldest bull. 'Do you see those women playing a ball game? Go and watch them until the ball rolls astray and comes to rest by your feet. Pick it up. One will ask you to return it. As you hand it over, say, "Here's your ball, my mother. I am your son." After that, follow your heart.'

The youth was bewildered and nervous; but he did as the old bull instructed. Eventually, the ball reached him. Using the words he had been told, he greeted the woman who came after it. She gasped, blushed furiously, turned her back and fled, tears welling from her eyes. Not knowing what else to do, he followed her, past the other women watching in surprise, all the way to her tipi. The woman dived through the door. The youth hesitated, then followed.

He had never been inside a tipi before and it took some time for his eyes to adjust to the gloom. He marvelled at all the furnishings and household equipment inside it, the like of which he had never imagined. The woman was crouching in a corner, head buried in her hands. Beside her sat another woman and a man, both much older, with grey hair and deeply lined faces.

'What's going on?' the old man cried, waving his arms at the youth. 'Who are you? Why is our daughter crying? How dare you burst in like this!'

The youth hesitated; then held out his hands and said, 'I am your long lost grandson.'

The old man stared at him in astonishment; for he knew nothing of his daughter's secret pregnancy, let alone the abandonment of her baby. But the old woman leaped excitedly to her feet.

'Is this really true?' she said. 'Are you really our daughter's lost child?'

The youth said, 'My seven adoptive fathers told me this. They are all Buffalo, Grandmother, and they speak only the truth. Long ago, they found me crying alone in a wallow and rescued me. They raised me and taught me everything, and now they have sent me home to you.'

The old woman turned to her daughter. 'I thought only you and I knew what happened on that dreadful day,' she said. 'If he knows of it too, he must surely be your son – and our grandson.'

The younger woman nodded and stood up. Slowly, she raised her eyes. 'My son,' she said hoarsely, stumbling on the words. 'I've always regretted what I made my mother do on that painful day when you were born. Is it possible for you to forgive me?'

'I forgive you,' said the youth.

He embraced his mother until all her tears were dry, went to his grandmother and embraced her too, then finally went to his grandfather.

'I knew nothing of this, nothing at all,' the old man said. 'But my grandson, I am glad to know you.'

'Sit,' cried his grandmother joyfully, 'eat.'

She stirred the pot simmering over the fire, ladled out a good helping of stewed meat and handed it to the youth. It was the first time he had ever tasted cooked food: its warmth and richness surged through his veins. As he ate, his body relaxed and his face softened. He talked to his family, on and on, telling them everything that had happened to him. They listened avidly, and when he had finished, they in turn told him everything he needed to know about their lives on the Plains.

Afterwards, he took his mother's hand, saying, 'You and I have an important task. Come.' He led her outside.

'Where are we going?' she asked.

'I want you to take me to my father.'

'I have nothing to do with him. He's not a man to be proud of.'

'Only yesterday, I was a wild boy who lived amongst the Buffalo,' the youth said. 'But today I am changed. Maybe my father can change too. Take me to him, Mother.'

She led him to the far side of the camp, to a tipi apart from the others. They went in and stood silently just inside the door. Before them, a group of dishevelled men were sitting in a circle, noisily playing a gambling game. There was a raucous cry: the guessing team had come up with the correct answer and the others tossed the playing pieces across to them. As one of the men leaned over to retrieve them, the youth's mother whispered, 'That's him!'

The youth stepped forward and cleared his throat. The gamblers all turned to stare at him.

'My father,' said the youth, looking at the man directly, 'many years ago you lay with a young woman in the woods and then abandoned her. She's here beside me now. I was the child she bore – *your* child too. Following your example, she then abandoned me. But I was saved by the Buffalo and they have sent me to claim you.'

The man turned pale. The playing pieces trickled from his fingers like sand. The others fell silent.

'Father,' said the youth, 'come home to your wife and child.'

His father bit his lip, then bowed his head and followed them outside. He walked through the camp with them and entered his one-time lover's tipi. He greeted her parents respectfully.

'Welcome!' cried the youth's grandmother. 'Two homecomings in a single day. Now we are truly a family.'

Kroeber: *Gros Ventre Myths & Tales,* 1907

Kroeber says that these stories were collected during the winter and spring of 1901, at Fort Belknap Reservation in Montana – which is still the modern cultural hub of the Gros Ventre people. He gives no details of the informant, who is simply identified by the initial 'P'.

Buffalo were intrinsic to Great Plains life, and there were numerous myths about them. Similar stories were told by the Blackfoot and Crow, who both also had a story about a young man who seduces a stranded buffalo cow. She has a baby boy who plays with the other children, but vanishes at night. Eventually, the cow transforms into a woman and they live together as a family. However, when the father breaks a taboo never to strike her, the woman and son both change back into buffalo and vanish; and the mourning father is killed by the herd. Another Blackfoot story tells how a woman playfully promises to marry a buffalo if his species allow themselves to be caught by hunters. After some buffalo are shot, she is seized by a huge bull and her father is trampled to death in revenge. However, a magpie helps the girl restore her father to life, and they return to the people with a special buffalo dance and song.

A Pawnee story tells how Moon Woman – whose appearance shifts from young to old to young again, like the phases of the moon – sends the first buffalo herd in response to prolonged prayer. According to the Cheyenne and Comanche, all buffalo were originally confined in a cave by an old woman, who eventually releases them. Another Cheyenne story describes a great race between the species, with the winners gaining the right to hunt the losers; the birds ensure that it is people who win and the buffalo who lose. In a Sioux tale, a mysterious woman appears out of nowhere, transforms into a buffalo and back again several times, then presents the people with the first peace pipe.

TWO SONGS

Sioux (Oceti Sakowin)

Far to the west,
Far by the Sky
Stands a blue Elk.
That Elk standing yonder
Watches over all the females
On the Earth.

– Chief Maza Blaska (Flat Iron),
Ogallalla Band, Dakota Sioux.

Friend,
whatever hardships threaten
If you call me,
I'll be your friend.
Ever enduring fearlessly,
I'll be your friend.

– Matoisto-Nakipin (Bear Claw Necklace),
White Horse Society, Dakota Sioux.

(Both quoted in Curtis: *The Indians' Book*, 1907)

THE ADVENTURES OF OLD MAN

>>=·=<<

Blackfoot (Niitsitapi)

OLD MAN AND FIRST WOMAN

Old Man created the Earth and all the plants and creatures in it, including the People. He was standing by the river admiring it all, when First Woman came along.

'I've been looking for you, Old Man,' she said. 'Don't go thinking the world is finished, because there are a number of matters we need to sort out together.'

'*Together?*' Old Man growled. 'I don't mind discussing a few things, but this creation is all my own hard work – so if there are decisions to make, I must have first say.'

'That's fine,' said First Woman. 'Because that means *I* get second say.'

Old Man sniffed. 'Go on then, what's bothering you?'

'For a start,' said First Woman, 'you haven't given us People proper faces; we need eyes, noses and mouths.'

'All right, I'll give you each two eyes, one on top of the other, a nose below and a mouth underneath – all in a neat straight line. There, I've done it. You can admire your reflection in the water.'

'That looks ridiculous!' First Woman complained. We need both eyes next to each other, like yours.'

'Oh, all right.'

'And another thing, Old Man. You've told the men to hunt buffalo, but you haven't told us women what work to do.'

'Just tan the hides,' said Old Man. 'It's very quick and easy.'

'How dare you undervalue women's work! Tanning is a lengthy and exhausting process…'

'If you say so,' said Old Man.

'… Anyway, we can't do it without hands to hold our tools.'

'I've already made plans for that,' said Old Man. 'I'll fix a hand at the end of each person's arm – each with ten fingers.'

'Ten fingers on *each hand*? That's far too many, they'll get in the way and we won't be able to grip our tools properly. Four fingers and one thumb on each hand is what we need.'

'All right, you win again,' said Old Man.

'Next,' said First Woman, 'you promised we could get together with men to bring more People into the world – but how?'

'That's one thing I've definitely thought of, First Woman!' cried Old Man, with a big wink. 'I've decided to make the whole business really pleasurable for everyone. That's why you all have special bits on your navels…ha ha!…let me show you how it will work…'

'Navels? That's no good. It'll make giving birth so simple that we women will think nothing of it, and won't bother looking after our children properly. You need to move the special bits down below – *there*,' she pointed.

'"Do this, do that" – that's all you say, First Woman!'

'That's because I'm always right. I know I'm only recently created, but I'm already much wiser than you. Now then, Old Man, here's the most important question of all. What shall we do about death?'

'Death?'

'Yes. Animals die, birds die, fish die, plants die. Even the moon and the seasons die. So what about People?' First Woman asked.

'Er…what about them?'

'Well, are we going to die for ever, like animals and birds? Or just for a short time, then come back to life again, like flowers and the Moon?'

'I don't know, First Woman. What do you think?'

'I don't know either. It's a really difficult problem, Old Man. There are good arguments either way.'

They both fell silent. At long last, Old Man sighed and said, 'I don't think either of us is clever enough to solve this. I tell you what, I'll throw this piece of buffalo dung into the water. If it floats, the People will only die for four days, then come to life again; but if it sinks, they'll die for ever. Right, here goes…'

'Stop, Old Man, not so fast! Smelly dung isn't at all suitable.'

'Yes it is. Look, First Woman, it's floating. That means…'

'No, no, we need to throw in a rock, and see whether *that* floats or sinks.'

First Woman heaved a boulder off the ground and tossed it into the water. It made a great splash and sank rapidly to the bottom.

'There,' said First Woman, 'that's decided. People will die for ever. That'll stop the world from being over-populated.'

Old Man said hoarsely, 'I'm sad about that.'

'Don't be silly, it's much better for death to be permanent. If the People didn't have to grieve, they'd never learn about sympathy. The fear of death will make everyone much nicer.'

Old Man shook his head. 'As you keep saying, First Woman, you know best. So it's pointless arguing.'

In this way, their great debate came to an end. Old Man and First Woman each went their separate ways and got on with other things. Time went by.

In due course, First Woman found that she was pregnant. Later, she gave birth to a beautiful, clever, affectionate daughter. First Woman adored her and was ecstatically happy.

But unfortunately, one day her beloved child fell seriously ill and died. First Woman's heart was broken.

Old Man expressed his sympathy.

'That's no use,' sobbed First Woman. 'What are you going to do about it?'

'I can't do anything,' said Old Man.

'Of course you can. You created everything.'

'But it's you who insisted that death should be forever.'

'But I had no idea how devastating it would be to lose a loved one!' First Woman cried. 'I admit now, I was totally wrong. Oh, I'm so upset! Please, please could we discuss this again? Look, I'm humbling myself before you. I realise now that your test would have been the best way to reach a decision. I beg you, let's reconsider it!'

'No,' said Old Man. 'We agreed that I have the first word on everything and you have the second. A third word doesn't come into it.'

Nothing would move him. That's why, once someone dies, it's impossible to bring them back.

OLD MAN AND THE ROCK

Phew! It was a sweltering day, with the sun blazing down like a ball of fire. Old Man was walking along, dragging his feet, dripping rivers of sweat.

'Maybe I'd feel better with less clothes on,' he thought.

So he yanked off his robe and draped it carefully over a rock that stood by the trail.

'Get off!' yelled the Rock. 'Why are you chucking your dirty old robe over me?'

'It's a gift,' said Old Man quickly, 'to thank you for all those times you've let me sit on you for a rest.'

'A gift, eh?' said the Rock. 'Hmm, I suppose it's not bad. Thanks, Old Man.'

'It's my pleasure.'

Now he was carrying less weight, Old Man strode forward with new zest. Soon he caught up with a young Fox who was travelling the same way.

'Can I walk alongside you, Old Man?' said the Fox.

'Of course you can, little brother.'

They went along side by side, with the Fox asking lots of questions and Old Man answering them, until suddenly the sun vanished behind a dark raincloud.

'Looks like there's a downpour on the way,' said Old Man. 'Little brother, I left my robe draped over that Rock back there. Go fetch it for me, will you, so I can keep dry when it starts to rain.'

The Fox ran off eagerly, but soon came back, bringing nothing and looking nervous.

'I'm sorry, Old Man,' he said, 'but the Rock won't give up your robe. He says he needs it to keep dry himself; besides, you gave it to him as a gift, so it's insulting to ask for it back.'

Old Man's face turned as dark as the sky. He elbowed the Fox aside, and marched back to the Rock, roaring, 'You selfish wretch, give me back my robe!'

The Rock didn't answer.

'You always managed perfectly well without it before,' Old Man raged, 'so don't pretend you need it now.'

The Rock didn't move.

'If you won't give it to me willingly,' said Old Man, 'I'll take it back by force.'

He seized the robe, put it on and strode back to the Fox, beckoning him to resume their walk. Very soon, it started to rain hard. The Fox's fur quickly became sodden, but Old Man stayed nice and dry, with the robe wrapped round him and pulled up over his head. Because it covered his ears, he didn't hear the rumbling noise that started up behind them. But the Fox heard. He turned round, and his amber eyes opened wide with horror.

'Old Man,' he yipped, 'look out! The Rock's rolling towards us!'

'Huh? I can't hear, what's the matter?'

'Get your ears out, Old Man! It's coming for us – run!'

The Fox darted down a hole and disappeared. Old Man shrugged sceptically, glanced behind him – and saw that the Fox's warning was true. He ran for his life, but the Rock moved even faster, rolling over and over, a blur of thunderous speed.

'My brothers,' cried Old Man to the whole of creation, 'help!'

A Rattlesnake stopped to shake his tail: *sh-sh-sh-sh!* He flicked out his forked tongue and reared up in the Rock's path... But the Rock rolled straight over him, crushing him flat.

'Help, help!' Old Man shouted.

Some Buffalo bulls heard and charged at the Rock; but it rolled on between them, scattering them to either side.

'Oh my brothers, I don't want to die!'

A Bear ambled up and stood before the Rock, holding up his great forepaws like a man spoiling for a fight. But the Rock rolled right into him, and left him sprawling, shaking up the ground, throwing up clouds of dust, coming closer and closer to Old Man...

'Help, help!'

A pair of Nighthawks came circling around overhead – then dived and broke wind over the Rock. *Fhhht!* The force of it cracked big fragments off the Rock. *Fhhht!* The next moment, a whole flock of them winged over to join in the fun. They flew round and over the rock, chipping away more and more pieces with their teasing: *fhhht, fhhht!!* Steadily, the swaggering Rock crumbled away until there was nothing left but a pathetic pile of shards and dust. The Nighthawks circled it one last time, then flew off.

But instead of being grateful, Old Man cursed: 'Darned Nighthawks, spoiling my fun!'

He crept into the forest and searched until he found a clutch of Nighthawk chicks, hidden in the moss. He reached into their nest, grabbed the chicks in his gnarled hands, flattened their heads, pinched off their beaks and stretched their mouths twice as wide as before. That's why nighthawks look all squashy-faced today. Then he sneaked away. When the adults returned to the nest, they were shocked and furious.

'Old Man won't get away with this!' shrilled the mother.

'Bad for good, is it, eh?' said the father. '*Prrr! Prrr! Prrr!* Come again my kin, help us!'

Hundreds of Nighthawks answered his call, circling high over the Plains, seeking out Old Man.

'There he is!'

'Get him!'

Splat! Thwack!

What were they doing this time? Excreting on him!

'*Prrt!* Nice robe you've got there, Old man! Pity we're going to spoil it…'

'Whoops, that one missed. Here, have another.'

Splat! Thwack!

'Ugh, get off you dirty creatures!'

'Tit for tat, Old Man. You spoiled our chicks, so we're spoiling you.'

Splat! Thwack!

Every time a piece of their filth landed on Old Man's precious robe, he tore off the soiled bit – until it was completely shredded to bits. Now the filth landed directly on his body. That really was too much for him. He plunged into the river with an almighty splash and swam away. When he finally dared climb out, he had to huddle up and hold his hands on his crotch for shame…

For his precious robe was gone for ever – leaving Old Man as naked as a newborn baby.

OLD MAN AND THE SUN'S LEGGINGS

Old Man fled. When he'd been running for some time, he came to a very grand lodge covered in extravagant decorations. It belonged to a person even more powerful than himself – the Sun.

The Sun heard someone loitering outside, and came out to see who was there.

'Oh, it's you,' said the Sun. 'Welcome! Step inside, make yourself at home.'

Old Man eagerly accepted the invitation. The Sun had a huge supply of meat, and he let Old Man eat as much as he wanted. But after a few days, the food ran out.

'We need to go hunting,' said the Sun, 'to get some more.'

He took down a large bag hanging on a hook near the back of the lodge, and pulled out a pair of fine calf-skin leggings, richly embroidered with bright porcupine quills and feathers.

'Oh my, what fine leggings!' Old Man cried.

'I always wear them when I go hunting,' said the Sun, 'because they're full of powerful medicine. They set the brush on fire and drive out the deer, making it easy to shoot them.'

The Sun put them on and they went out together. Sure enough, as soon as they reached a patch of brush, the leggings sent out a spark that quickly turned into spreading flames. The air filled with soft snorting noises as a mass of deer stampeded out in panic. Old Man helped the Sun shoot them. There was so much meat, they had to make several journeys to carry it all home.

'No doubt you're full of admiration for the leggings' power?' said the Sun.

'They're not bad,' said Old Man dismissively. However, in truth, he was so impressed that he desperately wanted them for himself. But of course, he knew the Sun would never give them away.

At bedtime, Old Man watched the Sun remove the leggings and put them back in the bag. As soon as he was sure his host was asleep, Old Man crept over, pulled out the leggings, tied them onto his back and fled. The Sun didn't even stir.

Old Man travelled a long way, avoiding camps, running through lonely grasslands. By the middle of the night, he was exhausted.

'I've put a long distance between us,' he thought smugly. 'By the time the Sun realises what's happened, it'll be far too late for him to catch me. I reckon it's safe to lie down now and get some sleep.'

He rolled up the leggings to form a nice plump pillow. As soon as his head touched it, he dozed off and slept like a baby until dawn...when he woke up with a start.

Someone was standing near him, talking. Whoever could it be out here, in the middle of nowhere? He opened his eyes, sat up... And was astonished to discover that the voice belonged to the Sun. Somehow, he was back in the Sun's lodge!

'Old Man,' the Sun was saying, 'how dare you lie on my precious medicine leggings?'

'Wh...what?' Old Man gabbled. 'How ever did they get here? I must have been sleepwalking and taken them without realising. Sorry.'

'All right, but don't do it again,' the Sun said gruffly.

'I wouldn't dream of it,' said Old Man.

However, the next night, as soon as the Sun was snoring, Old Man ran off with the leggings again. This time he went twice as far as before, and didn't stop until dawn. But almost as soon as he fell asleep, he was woken by the Sun berating him again: 'You liar! You thief!'

'No, no it's the leggings' fault, not mine. I told them: "You stay in that bag where the Sun's put you". But they jumped out by themselves and...'

'You can't fool me, Old Man. I see everything, I know everything that goes on. No matter where you hide, or what mischief you get up to, you can never escape my sight.'

What could Old Man say? 'I humbly apologise,' he muttered.

'All right, Old Man, I'll forgive you. And since you like my leggings so much, you might as well keep them.'

'Really?'

'Yes, go on, take them.'

'Thank you!' cried Old Man.

He put the leggings in his own bag, saying he thought it was time he went on his way. The Sun heartily agreed, and gave Old Man a good supply of pemmican for the journey.

Old Man went along again, eating at sundown and sleeping each night with the medicine leggings as his pillow. But of course, the pemmican eventually ran out and Old Man realised that he'd now have to hunt for himself.

'That's no problem, because I've got the Sun's leggings,' he thought.

He pulled them on with great excitement. Even though the Sun was much taller and fatter than Old Man, the leggings fitted him perfectly. He strutted around for a while, admiring the quillwork and decorative feathers, imagining he was showing off to a band of impressionable warriors and flirtatious young women. What a marvellous show he could put on for them! Then he heard the rustling of deer nearby. He ran over and stepped into the brush where they were hiding. At once a spark jumped from the leggings and the brush caught fire.

Old Man rubbed his hands together excitedly. Here came the deer, blowing and leaping, eyes wide with alarm. Old Man raised his bow, ready to shoot as they came out. But why was he getting so hot? What was that bright light almost blinding him? Oh-oh, it was the fire the leggings had started, creeping up... Any moment, the flames would leap out...and he would be burning too!

Old Man ran. Fire ran faster. It caught the leggings, turning them into a scorching mass of smoke, burning through them... Until his very legs were on fire!

Just in time, Old Man came to a river and plunged in. As the water quenched the fire, the remains of the leggings peeled from his blackened legs and floated away. There was nothing left of them.

That's how the Sun punished Old Man for being a thief.

OLD MAN PLAYS A GAME IN THE ASHES

Old Man went along further, until he heard the noise of excited squealing and singing. Soon he came to a band of Prairie Dogs, gathered around the remains of a large fire. They were taking turns to burrow into the smouldering ashes, while the others sang cheerfully. When the one in the ashes got too hot, he would spring out, laughing, and another would take his place.

'That looks good fun,' said Old Man.

'It is, it is!' the Prairie Dogs cried.

'Can I have a go?'

'Certainly not. This fire contains dangerous medicine that can harm anyone who doesn't understand it.'

'Aw, please,' said Old Man.

'No!'

'Please, please, please, please...'

'Oh, all right then, Old Man,' said the Prairie Dogs. 'But listen, only stay in the ashes for a very short time, otherwise you'll burn to death.'

Old Man assured them that he understood the rules. He lay down in the ashes while the Prairie Dogs covered him up. When he leaped out, it was his turn to cover them.

'Why not all lie down together?' he said. 'I can easily cover the whole lot of you at once. You'll be all snug in the ashes together; and when you get too hot, I'll quickly release you with a sweep of my hand.'

They agreed that would be even more fun and dived together into the ashes – except for one heavily pregnant female, who hastily scurried away.

Old Man scooped up great handfuls of ash and tossed it thickly over the Prairie Dogs. They all giggled and wriggled about in delight. After a while, they called: 'We're getting too hot now. Let us out quickly, like you promised.'

Old Man ignored them.

'Hurry up, we're starting to scorch!' they cried. 'Old Man, if you don't let us out, we'll all die!'

Old Man sniggered, turned his back and covered his ears.

'Help us, help us!'

Finally, the Prairie Dogs fell silent. Now, at last, Old Man dug them out.

'Good,' he chuckled, 'they're nicely roasted to death. Now I've got plenty of tasty meat.'

Only the pregnant one, who wisely fled, survived. She's the mother of all Prairie Dogs in the world today.

Old Man licked his lips, built a scaffold, butchered the Prairie Dogs and laid the meat on top of it, dripping with grease. He ate ravenously. Then he started to feel sleepy – and also worried.

'Supposing someone steals the rest while I'm dozing?' he thought. 'Hmm…I know, my nose doesn't go to sleep. Nose! You keep watch, and if anyone tries to steal my meat, make a noise to warn me.'

He shut his eyes and drifted off. Very soon, his nose started to snore: '*Chw-chw-chwghhh!*' Old Man sat up with a start. A Raven was hovering overhead. Old Man leaped up and waved his arms until it flapped away, then settled back to sleep.

The snoring started again: '*Chw-chw-chwghhh!*' This time, Old Man saw a Coyote circling the meat. He chased it off, then snuggled back down.

'*Chw-chw-chwghhh!*' Old Man was so exhausted that he didn't hear the next lot of snoring.

A big Bobcat crept out of the forest. It sniffed Old Man; but he didn't even twitch. '*Chw-chw-chwghhh!*' went his nose. Old Man turned over. The Bobcat leaped nimbly onto the scaffold and gobbled up all the remaining meat.

'*Chw-chw-chwghhh!*' At last Old Man woke up – just in time to see the Bobcat slinking away. When he realised the scaffold was empty, hah, he was angry! He sprinted after the Bobcat, seized him, pulled off the end of his tail, stretched him from end to end, and smashed his face on a rock to flatten it. That's why bobcats look as they do today.

When he was finished, he turned his anger onto his nose. 'Why didn't you wake me that time?'

Of course, the nose couldn't answer.

'Don't think you can get away with it by not speaking to me, Nose. I'll punish you for this!' Old Man broke off a twig, heated it in the ashes and pushed it up his nostril. 'There, that'll teach you!'

The next moment, he was screaming. 'Ow-ow, I've burned my nose! It's agony! I know, the wind will make it better.'

He ran up a nearby hill, tilting his nose towards the wind, which soon soothed it right down... But suddenly, the wind caught hold of Old Man and swept him up and away, higher and higher, right to the tops of the trees. He tried to grab branches as he passed, but none was strong enough to hold him...

Until at last a birch tree let Old Man cling to it, bouncing and bending up and down with the gusts, then finally letting Old Man tumble gently to the ground.

'You've saved my life,' he said to the birch. 'Let me reward you.'

He pulled out his knife and cut a series of delicate patterns into its bark. It's thanks to Old Man that birch trees look so pretty today.

OLD MAN AND THE FLYING EYES

Old Man kept going along, and some time later came to a small Bird standing underneath a tree. Every so often, the Bird's eyes would come loose from their sockets, fly up and hover in the branches. Then, with a quick cheep, he'd bring the eyes back and return them to their proper place on his face.

'However do you do that, little brother?' cried Old Man.

'I'm not telling,' said the Bird.

'Aw, go on.'

'No, it's my secret.'

'Please, please, please, please,' Old Man begged.

'Oh, all right,' said the Bird with a sigh, 'if it'll shut you up, Old Man. All you have to do is whisper, "I wish my eyes would fly out" – and they will. To bring them back, just wish the opposite.'

'That's easy,' said Old Man. 'I'll try it now…'

'Hold on, there's a rule you need to know,' said the Bird. 'It's very dangerous to do it more than three times in a single day.'

'Okay, I'll be sure to remember that. Here, watch me.'

Old Man stood by the tree and whispered, 'I wish my eyes would fly up there.' They did. 'Now I wish they would come back.' At once the eyes returned to their sockets. Old Man jumped up and down with excitement.

'Take care,' the Bird warned. 'Remember, only twice more today.' Then he flew off.

Old Man did it twice more. It was such fun!

'I don't care about that Bird and his stupid warning,' he thought. 'I'm going to have a fourth go. If it doesn't work, never mind. But if it does, I'll know for sure that he was just trying to spoil my fun. Here we go again: Eyes, fly to the tree!'

The eyes floated off to the uppermost branches.

'Heh, heh, heh,' Old Man chuckled. 'It's still working perfectly well. Hey, Eyes, come back now.'

Nothing happened.

'Didn't you hear me, Eyes? Come back at once! This isn't a wish, it's an *order*! Eyes, you lazy good-for-nothings, COME BACK!!!'

Just then, he heard footsteps.

'Bird, is that you?'

'No, it's Wolf,' said a voice. 'What's up?'

Old Man explained what had happened. The Wolf grinned and held his foot up to Old Man's nose. It had a festering wound on it. 'What do you think this is, eh?'

'It stinks like a buffalo corral,' said Old Man.

'Exactly,' said the Wolf. 'That means we're near a village. Ask there for help.' And he scampered away.

'Hmm,' thought Old Man, 'I'd better cover my eye sockets so I don't frighten the villagers.'

He tore a strip from his tunic and bound it over the top of his face, then stumbled off down the trail. Soon he met a young woman coming the opposite way. She had no idea who Old Man was, but saw that he was in trouble.

'What's the matter, Uncle?' she asked politely. 'Is there anything I can do to help?' Her voice sounded sweet and charming.

Old Man chuckled to himself, stood up straight, cleared his throat and said, 'Yes, there is, my dear. I've been hunting for so long, staring into the distance, that my eyes have become sore, so I had to bandage them. Would you be kind enough to lead me to the next village?'

'Ooh, you must be a mighty hunter to have hurt your eyes like that,' said the young woman admiringly. 'Here, take one end of this stick…' She thrust it into Old Man's hand '…and I'll hold the other end. Then we can go along nicely together.'

They walked like this for a while, with the young woman chattering away and singing. Old Man felt more and more attracted to her. He decided to avoid the village and take her for himself.

So he said, 'I'm too tired to go any further. Let's camp here for the night.'

The young woman went into the forest, cut some poles and quickly put up the framework of a makeshift lodge.

'Uncle, we need a hide to cover it,' she said.

'Help me kill a buffalo, then you can skin it,' Old Man replied.

A buffalo soon appeared. The young woman put her soft hand on Old Man's shoulder and helped him point his bow at it. Old Man enjoyed the feel of her so much, that he made sure he kept missing, constantly pulling her closer… So that, by the time they'd caught a buffalo, the young woman was getting suspicious. However, as night was already falling, she had no choice but to skin the buffalo and use its hide to cover the lodge poles. Then she made a fire and cooked some of the meat.

When they had finished their meal, Old Man strung the buffalo hooves together with a piece of sinew and shook them with a noisy rattle.

'Tie these to your dress,' he said. 'I've put medicine in them to keep you safe.'

The young woman guessed that Old Man really wanted her to wear the rattles so he would hear all her movements and thus stop her escaping; but she didn't dare disobey.

Night fell. Old Man lay down in the middle of the lodge; the young woman sat up, as far away from him as possible. When Old Man was snoring, she crept out, stood up and began to run. At once, the rattle started up: *clangle, clangle, clangle!* Old Man heard and jerked awake. Blindly, he fumbled outside, stood listening – and started after her.

The young woman veered towards the river, pulled the rattle from her dress, tossed it into the water and fled back to her village. Old Man hesitated, listened, then plunged after the rattle, head first into the river. He sank to the bottom then rose up again, blindly flailing his arms. Eventually, he managed to haul himself up onto the bank – where he collided with a Coyote.

'Look where you're going!' the Coyote growled.

'I can't,' said Old Man. 'I've lost my eyes, brother. Lend me yours, and in return I'll go to the nearest village and fetch some meat for us both.'

'All right,' said the Coyote. 'I'm getting old and it would be good to have a break from hunting. But only one eye, mind.'

He pulled one out and helped Old Man push it into his own empty eye socket. Old Man strode off happily and soon reached a big camp. He entered it boldly, turning his single eye from side to side, seeking out the chief. But when the villagers saw the gaping, bloody hole from his missing eye, they screamed, 'Help! A monster, hide, fasten the doors!'

Within moments, the camp was deserted. Old Man went on, but no matter how hard he looked, he couldn't find their stores of meat anywhere. He returned to the Coyote in a furious temper.

'I couldn't get any meat because you refused to give me *both* your eyes,' he raged. 'Well, it's never too late…'

He wrestled the poor Coyote to the ground, gouged out his remaining eye and placed it in his other eye socket. He was fine now, he could see very clearly.

And so he went blithely on with his travels.

OLD MAN SEEKS A WIFE

After a while, Old Man came to another village. In those days, men and women didn't live together, but in different camps, separated by a river. The men's lodges were lopsided and poorly built, with warped poles and hairy hides, full of fleas and lice, chucked untidily over them. The women's lodges, on the other hand, were beautifully made, with straight, polished poles and well tanned covers painted with beautiful designs.

Old Man went to the men's camp and asked for hospitality, which they readily gave him. As he was settling in, a messenger arrived from the women and announced to all the men: 'Greetings, friends. Our Chief has decided that we should all get married, and each of us must choose one of you as a husband.'

'What's "getting married"?' said Old Man.

'It's when a man and woman set up house together, cuddle up in private and get intimate,' said the messenger.

'Sounds good,' said Old Man. 'What's a "husband"?'

'A man who hunts and brings his wife lots of meat, protects her and gives her children.'

'Hmm, that sounds like hard work,' said Old Man.

'Oh no, it's a glorious way for a man to spend his time,' said the messenger. 'And giving his wife children is the most pleasurable thing you can imagine.'

'I see. And what's a "wife"?'

'A woman who keeps house for her husband. She builds the lodge, makes clothes and tools, gathers roots, does all the cooking and looks after their children.'

'Wa-hoah!' said Old Man. 'That sounds a really good deal. Can I join in?'

The messenger nodded. 'Anyone who hopes to become a husband must come to the women's camp tomorrow.'

That night, Old Man was too excited to sleep. The next morning, he bathed in the river, put on his best clothes, and sprinkled himself with sweet leaves. The other men all made similar efforts, but Old Man was by far the most magnificent. They all crossed the river to the women's camp. There the messenger told them to stand in a neat row while, one at a time, the women inspected them.

Old Man preened himself. 'I bet the Chief of the Women herself will make a beeline for me,' he thought. 'Ha! Once we're married, I shall usurp her and become chief over everyone myself. Then I'll have power over the whole world!'

Soon the first woman came out. She was hideous. Her hair was uncombed, her face filthy and her clothes in tatters. She walked clumsily along the line – and stopped by Old Man.

'Oh my, you're a good-looker,' she said. 'I can see you're a brave warrior and a successful hunter too. I choose you for my husband.'

Old Man wrinkled his nose at her stale breath and unwashed flesh. When she reached out to him, he slapped her hand away with a squeal, 'Ugh, no!'

The dirty woman raised an eyebrow. Then she called back to the other women waiting to come out: 'Keep away from this self-important old fool!'

Old Man grinned. 'No one will take any notice of *that* old hag,' he thought – and looked eagerly across to the other women, trying to work out who was their leader. But the next moment, he had a nasty surprise, as the other women answered the dirty one: 'Thanks for the advice, Chief!'

'Chief?' thought Old Man, 'surely not? Ach, it must have been a trick!'

One by one the other women came out and chose husbands from the line of hopefuls. They all ignored Old Man.

'Well, at least the Chief herself hasn't come back,' he thought. 'Despite my mistake, she obviously found me irresistible, so she's told the others to leave me for herself.'

As the number of solitary men dwindled, Old Man stood proudly, quivering with expectation. Suddenly, the Chief of the Women reappeared, this time moving gracefully, well groomed and splendidly dressed. Old Man almost swooned at the thought of lying with her. He stepped forward and waved frantically.

'Hey, Chief – here I am, over here. Come on, take me!'

The Chief of the Women strolled along the line of remaining men. Old Man was squirming with excitement. She glared at him coldly, walked straight past and, with a smile, selected another man further along.

'Hey!' Old Man shouted. 'He's the wrong one!' He started jumping up and down with rage, shouting and screaming.

The Chief of the Women turned to him. 'Old Man,' she said, 'your behaviour is abominable.'

Old Man stamped his foot. When he tried to lift it up again, he found it was stuck to the ground. He stamped the other foot. That one too was somehow rooted to the spot. He lifted his arms and punched the air with his fists; they remained suspended there. He shouted again – and the sound turned into the sigh of wind through branches. His skin darkened, then turned hard and rough. His clothes shrank away and were replaced by bristly, dark green needles.

And that was the end of Old Man. He'd turned into a pine tree. He's stayed that way ever since.

Grinnell: *Blackfoot Lodge Tales* (1892)
Maclean: *Blackfoot Mythology* (1893)
Wissler & Duval: *Mythology of the Blackfoot Indians* (1908)
Old Man – Na'pi, Napiw or Napioa – is the major divine trickster of the Great Plains. Like others of his kind, he is an enigmatic character with opposite and complimentary sacred and profane aspects. Another myth describes him creating the world in a similar way to the California story, COYOTE AND EARTH MAKER (p. 233). This suggests that originally he may have been a revered deity; indeed, cultural echoes of this can be found in short passages of the surviving texts. However, most 19th century Old Man tales portray him as malevolent, foolish, greedy and lewd; perhaps reflecting the Blackfoot people's conversion to Christianity, with its disparagement of indigenous spiritual beliefs. Wissler & Duval state:

'For several decades at least, the Blackfoot have considered the Old Man as an evil character, in most respects, trivial… Whenever the writer asked if the Old Man was ever prayed to, the absurdity of the question provoked merriment. The usual reply was, that no one had enough confidence in him to make such an appeal. In daily conversation his name is often used as a synonym for immorality.'

Numerous other Old Man tales feature similarly outrageous and comical charades, chases and deceits. Although usually imbued with vulgar and slapstick humour, they also explain characteristics of particular living creatures, landscape features and natural phenomena, and point to moral lessons. Parallel tricksters in other regions – sometimes with virtually identical stories – include Bluejay and Kweeti (Northwest); Coyote (California, Great Basin, Plateau and Southwest); Lox, Nanabozho, Wemicus and Wiskedjak (Northeast); Rabbit (Northeast and Southeast); and Raven (Northwest and Plateau).

THE THUNDERBIRDS

Crow (Apsaalooke)

There was a youth who constantly roamed over the prairie alone, searching for bigger, better game to impress his rivals.

One day, he noticed a strange white object in the middle of the grass. At first glance, it seemed to be a very large egg. However, when he looked more closely, he saw there was something uncanny about it. Its shell had a faint, luminous glow, and it was shifting about in the breeze as if it weighed no more than a feather. He knew he should be careful: it might be some kind of dangerous medicine. So he didn't touch it directly, but gingerly lowered the tip of his bow towards it, slowly, slowly…

Ssss! As the bow made contact, he was blinded by a dazzle of light. He reeled backwards. The sky spun, the ground rose into his stomach and he felt himself falling…

When he came to, he was no longer on the prairie – but on top of a mountain formed entirely of dark, barren rock. Only an icy wind broke the silence, slashing about his head like invisible whips. He had no idea how he had got there.

He got up and started to wander about nervously. Suddenly he found himself on the edge of a precipice, high above the glimmer of distant water. He was desperately thirsty; if only he could reach it! But it would be impossible to climb down there without falling to his death.

He cried out; but there was nobody to hear him.

He turned his back on the drop and walked on, feeling more energetic now, leaping from crag to crag, clambering up, then down again, clinging precariously to crumbling footholds. After a while, the wind dropped. In the new silence he became aware of a strange rustling noise coming from a hollow in the rocks close by. He leaned over and squinted into it.

He found himself gazing at an enormous nest with two huge, very ugly, young birds inside. They were the size of human babies, their dark bodies sprouting a smear of night-black feathers. Thunderbirds! They saw the youth peering in and stretched their open beaks towards him. Very warily, he put out his hand. The chicks flapped their half-formed wings with an urgent squawking:

'Brother, can't you hear? Our mother is on her way. Quickly, come inside with us to wait for her.'

The youth eased himself into the hollow and crouched awkwardly between the chicks. The sky darkened and thunder crackled. Huge clouds, edged with sickly yellow, rolled towards them, hurtled downwards and burst in a torrent of rain.

An enormous adult bird came soaring out of the deluge and over the peak. She landed above the nest and leaned over the youth, nudging him gently with her beak.

'So, you managed to find your way here, eh?' she rasped. 'Welcome! Now you may drink.'

The rain eased off as quickly as it had come, leaving all the rock crevices shining with newly formed pools. The youth stumbled across to the nearest one, cupped his hands and scooped water greedily into his mouth.

No sooner was he refreshed, than the chicks began squawking again: 'Now our father is coming!'

This time, the youth was ready for the hail and deafening cracks which signalled the approach of the male.

The two Thunderbirds perched side by side, looking sternly down on him. They were both black from beak to tail; and when they spread their wings, it seemed they could span the entire world.

Gradually, the air calmed and stilled. The youth drew on his courage and looked up at his hosts, expecting some dreadful punishment for intruding on their mountain fastness. But instead, the male said gently:

'My son, we have brought you here to carry out an important task. Every year we are plagued by a pair of evil Otters that crawl from the waters below to devour our children. We are very afraid that this year's chicks, your brothers here, will also be taken. Many animals have previously tried to save us from this curse, and all have failed. But you... Ah, we have watched the Earth for many days. We have seen that you are an unflinching hunter, and your aim is always true. We wish you to destroy these monsters.'

For the first time in his life, the youth bit his tongue to stop himself from bragging. He forced himself to follow the shrewd practices of the elders, taking time to consider his reply.

'I will do my best for you,' he said at last. 'But I need certain items to help me, and several days to prepare.'

'Four days and nights will pass before the monsters arrive to attack our young,' said the male Thunderbird. 'Whatever you need, we will fetch it for you.'

The youth requested elk meat to feed his strength. The Thunderbirds brought it. When he had eaten his fill, he asked for the carcass of a buffalo bull to work its body into tools. They brought that too. The youth skinned and butchered it, then fashioned its hide and paunch into two large buckets, which the Thunderbirds filled with hailstones. He used the skin of its forelimbs to make gauntlets, and the skin from its hind-limbs to make leggings.

Next, he asked the Thunderbirds to bring a well-seasoned dead pine tree, chop it into splinters, and place these in two piles. Then he requested two cherry trees, each with their branches trimmed away to form large forks. Everything he asked for, the Thunderbirds provided. In this way, the four days and nights passed quickly.

The following morning, the youth awoke to find the mountain top swathed in fog. It was so thick, he could scarcely breathe or see.

'This is the sign that the evil ones are approaching,' warned the female Thunderbird.

The youth quickly set to work. He set fire to each pile of pine-wood splinters and placed rocks on top of the blazing flames. He dressed himself in the buffalo-leg gauntlets and leggings. The sun rose and the fog lifted. He went to the precipice and looked down.

Far below, the distant water was seething. Suddenly, two enormous Otters emerged from it and began to climb the mountain with astonishing speed. Their long bodies were covered in evil slime, their mouths gaped ravenously. Their gigantic webbed feet scratched and scraped the rocks as they hauled themselves up.

The Thunderbird chicks cowered and squealed in terror.

The youth sang an arrow song and pulled four arrows from his quiver. One at a time, he fixed them into his bow and shot them all at the first monstrous Otter. It writhed in agony. The youth used a forked tree to pull hot rocks from the fire, and tossed them into the Otter's mouth. Finally, he poured down the melted hailstones from the buffalo paunch bucket. Steam exploded from the Otter. It stopped in its tracks, tumbled backwards, and hurtled down into the water below.

Now the other gigantic Otter came scrambling up with grasping feet and crashing jaws. Calmly, the youth attacked and killed it in exactly the same way. It fell to its death with a great splash that drained all the water from the lake below, leaving it completely dry.

The Youth strode triumphantly back to the nest, where the Thunderbirds were waiting to thank him. They sent a Raven across the sky to spread the news and invite all the birds to a victory feast. Soon the air was full of eagerly beating wings as a great swarm of birds landed, crowding over the mountain until there was scarcely room to move. A contest was held, from which a Blue Crane was chosen to carve up the monstrous Otter carcasses. Every bird, large and small, received a generous portion to eat.

At last, all that remained were the skeleton and the youth's four arrows protruding from it. The Blue Crane pulled the arrows free and passed them to the male Thunderbird.

'Come, stand before me,' said the Thunderbird to the youth. 'Do you wish to leave this mountain?'

'Yes, Father, I do.'

'Well, there is only one way down – and that is to fly like a bird. Because of this, you must change your shape. Which bird do you choose to be?'

'I would like to take the shape of an Eagle,' said the youth. 'Then I will be able to go everywhere and pick up everything.'

So the Thunderbird transformed him, giving him a yellow beak and a fierce eye. Only one aspect distinguished him from a real bird: in the feathers behind the Eagle-Youth's wing, the Thunderbird concealed two arrowheads. This was to ensure he did not forget that he was really human.

The Eagle-Youth flew away to the shore of a great lake. He spent the winter there, diving and feeding on the fish that lived within it. He remembered nothing about his old life, and was totally content.

However, when spring came, the Eagle-Youth was troubled by a niggling irritation – he had lice. He sat on a branch above a river and used his beak to root out the vermin and swallow them. As he poked about behind his wing, something long and sharp suddenly came loose and lodged in his nostril. He put up his claw to pull it away – and discovered one of the concealed arrowheads.

At once, his memory returned. Ah, he was not really a wild bird but a young man! His heart began to twist with longing: if only he could see his people again!

He flew up to the Thunderbirds' mountain. The chicks whose lives he had saved were thriving, but he soared straight past them and alighted at the feet of the old male.

'Father,' he said, 'I am ready to go home.'

'Then you shall,' said the old Thunderbird. 'I will accompany you some of the way, to make the last use of your powers, for there are still troublesome creatures to be destroyed.'

The Thunderbird and the Eagle-Youth set off, soaring in the skies above the Plains, seeking out enemies with their sharp eyes. Every so often they swooped down to the kill: a gigantic Beaver fell under their attack, as did another monstrous Otter, and a maverick Buffalo.

Then a great Elk bull appeared, his breath steaming like tobacco smoke in the spring air. Together they swooped down and tried to slaughter this one too. However, the Elk was blessed with unusual cunning. He dodged and escaped their attacks – then speared the Eagle-Youth on his antlers. He tossed the Eagle-Youth into the water, plunged in after him and dragged him down to the depths.

'Let me go!' the struggling Eagle-Youth cried.

'Not yet,' the Elk said quietly, 'And don't expect the one you call "father" to help you, for he has already flown back to his mountain. It is time for you to learn a fundamental lesson.'

'What can *you* possibly teach me?' the Eagle-Youth said scornfully.

'These things,' said the Elk. 'You are not of the Sky, but of the Earth. You are not invincible. You have killed too many of your fellow beings. It is time to change back to your true form and repent.'

He rose with the Eagle-Youth to the surface of the water. While they had been underneath, many river creatures had come together and prepared a sweat-house on the bank. The Elk pushed him inside. There, weighed down by a heat that even he could scarcely endure, the Youth shed his eagle feathers and turned back into a human being.

When, at last, the sweat-house door was flung open and he emerged, the Elk had vanished. The Thunderbirds' mountain was no longer visible, not even on the furthest horizon.

However, just across the prairie, the youth saw a familiar camp. He hesitated only briefly, then hurried eagerly back to his home.

Lowie: *Myths and Traditions of the Crow Indians,* 1918
The stories in this source book were enthusiastically recounted by the last generation of Crow warriors, who treasured vivid memories of life before they were moved onto a reservation some 50 years earlier. Lowie interviewed them in their homes. The stories were narrated in the indigenous language, and translated on the spot by a man called Jim Carpenter, a Piegan Blackfoot who had lived with the Crows since infancy. Lowie then immediately transcribed them into his notebooks.

He recorded two slightly different versions of *The Thunderbirds,* both narrated in 1914 by a man called Grandmother's Knife. Born around 1859 – when traditional Plains culture was still thriving – he was one of the most prolific storytellers on the reservation, providing over 30 myths for Lowie's collection. In his later years, he was also popular amongst his people for his knowledge of the old ritual songs, and for his prowess in the unique Crow sport of hurling feathered javelins.

The Thunderbird is described as follows by Charles Eastman, a renowned Dakota Sioux doctor, writer and reformer, in his book *Wigwam Evenings* (1909):

'The Great Bird of storm and tempest, who was appointed in the beginning of things to keep the earth and also the upper air pure and clean. Although there is sometimes death and destruction in his path, yet he is a servant of the Great Mystery and his work is good.'

Thunderbird stories were also told in the Arctic, Northeast, Northwest and Plateau regions. Other Plains myths feature thunder as a man or a god rather than a bird. In a Blackfoot story, Thunder is malevolent: he abducts a woman, whose husband rescues her with the help of a raven chief. A Cheyenne story features a more benign Thunder who obtains the first fire and teaches a supernatural hero how to use it. This describes Thunder's eternal struggle against Winter, whom he defeats every spring, to bring the life-enhancing rain. In a Sioux story, a youth is befriended by Thunder who gives him a white horse to ride through the sky, and a magic bow which protects against wounding and ensures victory in every battle.

ALL THINGS IN THE WORLD ARE TWO

Pawnee

All things in the world are two, man and woman...
Man himself is two in everything.
Two eyes, two ears, two nostrils, two hands, two feet...
Stand in the sunshine and behold how man is two –
substance and shadow, body and spirit...
In our minds we are two – good and evil.
With our eyes we see two things
– things that are fair and things that are ugly.
Through our nostrils we smell two things –
things that are good, things that are bad.
With our ears we hear two things:
things that fill us with joy, things that fill us with sorrow.
We have the right hand that strikes and makes for evil,
and the left hand full of kindness, near the heart.
One foot may lead us to an evil way,
the other foot may lead us to good.
So are all things two, all two.

– Letakots Lesa (Eagle Chief),
chief of the Pitahauerat Band, Pawnee,
(Quoted in Curtis: *The Indians Book,* 1907)

THE WOMAN WHOSE LOVER WAS A BEAR

Blackfoot (Niitsitapi)

There was a young woman of an age when she ought to be getting married. Several excellent warriors came to court her, but she turned them all away.

Her mother couldn't understand it. 'What kind of man is she waiting for?' she grumbled to her kin. 'She's lucky that some men are interested in her: although she's pretty, she's the most useless of all my nine children. She never does even half the tasks I ask her to, but goes sneaking off by herself, never says where she's been, then comes back with dirty clothes and bits of grass in her hair. I'm starting to get suspicious.'

The young woman's father was always busy hunting; and at that time her seven adult brothers were all away on the warpath. But she had a younger sister, who was still a child.

The mother said to this girl, 'Next time your elder sister goes off into the forest, I want you to follow her. Make sure you keep a good distance behind and go very softly, so she doesn't know you're there. Find out where she goes and what she does – and if you see anyone with her, take a good look so you can tell me who it is. Then creep away silently and run home before your sister guesses that you're spying on her.'

The girl nodded solemnly. Before long, she had her chance. She followed her elder sister very discretely, just as their mother had urged; then came scurrying home, wide eyed and trembling.

'Well, where did your sister get to?' the mother asked.

'Down to the river, into a big clump of trees,' the girl answered.

'Did she meet anyone there?'

'Um… yes.'

The mother cleared her throat and swallowed apprehensively. 'And what did they do together?'

'They lay down side by side in the grass,' said the girl. 'Then they started laughing and rolling around – they seemed to be playing a game. I only watched for a few moments, because I was scared they'd see me. So I quickly came back, like you said.'

'You've done very well to see so much and tell me everything,' said the mother grimly. 'Now, child, just one more question: how clearly did you see the man your sister was playing with? Could you recognise his face if you saw him again?'

'Yes, I saw, all right,' said the girl. 'But...oh Mama, it wasn't a man – it was a *bear*! A huge grizzly!'

The mother gasped. 'This is worse than I ever suspected!'

As soon as the father returned from the hunt, she shared the catastrophic news with him. He didn't waste any time, but ran round the camp to share it with the other men. Never mind the shame; he needed their help. They were all sympathetic, especially those with grown daughters of their own. As night fell, they gathered together with their weapons. The father ordered the younger sister to lead him back to the place where she had seen the Bear making love to the elder one. It didn't take long to find the offending beast lurking in the trees. Quickly, the men surrounded it and shot it dead.

When the father went home and told his elder daughter that he had killed her Bear lover, she was distraught. She screamed at him, wept and tore her hair, then ran out of the tipi, wailing.

'Oh dear, go after her,' the mother cried to the younger girl. 'See if you can soothe her.'

The girl found her elder sister just outside the camp, lying in the grass, ripping her dress to shreds and crying her heart out.

'Hush, hush,' she said, 'I've come to comfort you.'

Luckily, the young woman didn't realise that her own sister had betrayed her. She let the child stroke her hair for a long while, and gradually quietened down. Then she sat up and dried her eyes.

'You've got to do something for me,' she said. 'Take a knife, go back to the place where my beloved Bear lies dead, cut off one of his paws and bring it to me.'

The younger girl was always obedient, so she did as she was told.

Once the elder sister had possession of her Bear lover's paw, she wrapped it in a small medicine bag, which she sewed firmly onto her dress. She was constantly touching it and muttering prayers over it; but other than that, she gradually seemed to calm down.

The mother thought her elder daughter was reconciled to her loss and her hopes rose. She said to her kin, 'Oh well, lots of young women make foolish mistakes, but she seems to have put this disturbing incident right behind her.'

However, she spoke too soon, because the elder sister now returned to her old, bad ways. She didn't bother with her appearance and often even forgot to comb her hair. When she wasn't praying over her Bear paw, she did nothing but scowl. She still ignored her duty to help her mother, and totally neglected the practical skills needed to attract admirers.

Instead, she attached herself to her younger sister. Whenever the child joined her friends for a game, the elder sister was sure to be seen loitering around them. Soon the other children began to whisper about her, and poke fun:

'My mama says you'll never get married!'

'You play with bears, don't you?'

'Play bears with us, teach us what bears do.'

The elder sister almost seemed to enjoy their taunts. 'All right,' she said, 'I will.'

She ran into their midst, waving her arms and making noises like a bear roaring.

'Go on, shoot me!' she cried.

The boys mimed shooting her with bows and arrows. She pretended to fall down dead.

'Butcher me!' the elder sister cried.

The girls rushed forward and pretended to cut her up.

'Be careful,' the elder sister called. 'You mustn't touch my thighs.'

'Shut up, bear!' the children giggled. 'You're dead, you can't tell us what to do.'

And they began to tickle her in the very place that she'd forbidden. The elder sister gave another bear roar. The children shrieked and giggled, their small hands moving all over her. She roared again and again; each time, the roar sounded less like mimicry, and more like a real bear...

Suddenly, the children's laughter turned to screams:

'Aagh! What's happening to her?'

'Look at her skin – it's sprouting fur!'

'She's growing – she's enormous!'

The elder sister lumbered to her feet. They all cowered as she towered over them, a rearing colossus of muscle and fur – a Bear Woman!

A rasping sound broke from the back of her throat. She pounced – landed on top of the nearest small boy, seized him in her massive paws and tore him in two. She twisted round, jumped on another child, then another and another, squeezing, scratching, biting them all to death. There was no more laughter, not even any more screams; just the Bear Woman's sounds: panting, roaring and the crunching of teeth.

Within moments, all the children lay dead – all, that is, except the younger sister. She stood with her back pressed against a tree, cowering. The Bear Woman stared at her briefly, but didn't lay so much as a single claw on her. Instead, she dropped onto all four paws and moved away towards the camp, lumbering awkwardly at first – then breaking into a graceful run.

A woman emptying water outside her tipi saw her approach. She screamed a warning – but that didn't save anyone's life, least of all hers. Bear Woman charged at her, swiped her to death with a single blow of her massive paw, then turned to attack all the others who came out to investigate. Within moments, they were all dead.

The Bear Woman bit a big lump out of each victim and chewed it up. Just as she had finished the last one, the village men came back from their day's hunting. They saw what they thought was simply a large bear around the tipis, raised their bows and shot at it. But Bear Woman was more cunning than an ordinary bear. She dodged all the arrows then rushed at the approaching hunters one by one and easily killed them all.

After that, Bear Woman went back to the place where the children had been playing. There she found her little sister squatting on the ground, whimpering. Bear Woman seized the girl's hand, hauled her back to the camp and pulled her into their own family tipi. As soon as they were inside, Bear Woman turned back into her proper shape, of the elder sister.

'What's happened to you?' cried the younger girl. 'What have you done?'

'Never you mind,' said the elder sister. 'Just do as I say. You and I are the only two people left alive here, and you must be my servant. Obey all my orders, and I promise I won't kill you.'

She set the girl to cook and clear away, to gather firewood and fetch water – all the things that she herself had always been too lazy to do. And so they fell into a pattern of living, almost as if things were normal. The elder sister didn't turn back into a bear again, and she didn't harm the younger one.

One day, the younger sister was fetching water when she heard horses approaching. She looked up and saw her seven brothers riding towards her, returning festooned in glory after many months away on the warpath. She rushed towards them, fell into their arms with great sobs, and told them all the terrible things that had happened in their absence. They listened with mounting horror. She begged them to take her far away to a safe place; but the eldest brother thought for a moment and said,

'My dear little sister, first you must help us destroy this Bear Woman before she works any more evil. She's not our sister any more, she's a monster.'

'What can I do?' the girl wept. 'I've told you how she killed everyone else; it's impossible to destroy her.'

'It certainly won't be easy,' said the eldest brother. 'But we can do it with your help. Go back and talk to her. Without making her suspicious, find out in what way she is vulnerable.'

So the younger sister went back to the elder one, sat beside her and talked to her affectionately, as if everything were still normal. After a while, the elder sister began to confide in her.

'I hate what I have become,' she confessed. 'It makes me feel so lonely and frightened. Every night the horror of it comes crowding back and I find it impossible to sleep.'

'Why don't you go and lie down?' said the younger one. 'I'll sing to you and stroke your hair, like our mother used to – maybe that will make you sleepy.'

So the elder sister lay on her bed with the younger one sitting beside her, singing and smoothing her tangled hair. After a while, they began to chat.

'You of all people shouldn't be frightened,' said the younger one. 'I've seen with my own eyes that no one can hurt you.'

The elder sister sighed. 'Well, that's true enough, for my bear-paw medicine is so powerful that no one can shoot me or burn me or even drown me. But there's one possible fate that terrifies me.'

'If you speak this fear aloud,' said the younger one cunningly, 'it might help you overcome it.'

'That's good advice,' said the elder sister. 'I dread that when I'm in my bear shape with no moccasins, something will kill me through my paws.'

'Are you worried you might tread on a thorn?'

'Not a thorn,' said the elder sister. 'But even a bear's tough paws can't withstand the point of an awl.'

'Don't be silly,' said the younger one. 'All the women are dead now, so no one could possibly drop an awl in your path.'

'That's true…' The elder sister's eyelids drooped and at last she fell asleep.

As soon as she was snoring, the younger sister crept out. She ran around the whole camp, going into each deserted tipi and gathering awls from the dead women's work baskets. She took them back to her own tipi and stuck them all in the ground in front of the door flap, points facing upward. Then she ran down to the river where her brothers were waiting, and told them what she had learned and done.

'You've done really well,' said the eldest brother. 'Now, we seven will gather around the tipi with our weapons, ready to deal with her. But since she's half a bear now, her nose must be more sensitive than a human's, and there's a danger that she'll smell us. So take this jackrabbit to boil in the pot; the smell of it cooking will mask our own scent as we draw near.'

The girl carried the jackrabbit to the tipi. As she busied herself with the cooking pot, her elder sister awoke and asked what she was doing.

'I'm cooking a nice meal for you,' she said, stirring the richly steaming stew.

The elder sister sat up, scowling, scratched herself and stretched. Suddenly she was a bear again. 'I don't want to eat your stew,' she growled. 'I want to eat *you.*'

The girl screamed. Bear Woman came at her, rearing on her hind legs, her huge front claws grappling at the air. The girl dodged, darted out of the door-flap and pushed it back into place. She leaped nimbly over the awls, and made her escape.

Bear Woman dropped onto all-fours and lumbered after her, nosing blindly through the door-flap. She stepped outside – and trod straight onto the awls. First one front paw, then the other, then both back paws were impaled upon them. She bellowed with pain. She tried to wrench herself free, but each movement just worked the awls deeper into her flesh. She roared and roared…

The seven brothers leaped from their hiding place and shot her dead.

Then they gathered wood, lit a fire and heaved the bear carcass on top. Thick smoke rose into the air and consumed it. However, amongst the ash and sparks that scattered up from the pyre, there was a tiny piece of Bear Woman's finger. It fluttered down to the ground, and as it touched the earth – it turned back into Bear Woman – alive, full grown and angry!

Bear Woman's jaws chomped. She charged at her younger sister and her seven brothers. As they fled, the youngest brother pulled a small feather from his pouch and threw it up to the sky.

'I have powerful medicine too,' he cried. 'Let's fly!'

At once, the seven brothers and the younger sister left the evil Bear Woman behind, and went floating up to the dark sky. There they were all transformed into stars. The youngest brother became fixed up there as the bright North Star; whilst his little sister and their other six brothers became the seven stars of the Big Dipper.

Michelson: Piegan Tales (1911)
Wissler & Duval: Mythology of the Blackfoot Indians (1908)
This story is an amalgamation of the two sources, which have different details and endings. One has the bear stepping on prickly pear cacti instead of awls. The other says that instead of becoming a star, the younger sister is hidden under a rock by the trickster, Old Man (p. 74), who punishes the Bear Woman by shortening her ears and tail to make her look foolish.

Native American awls – pointed implements for piercing holes in hides being sewn into clothes or tipi covers – were typically made of bone.

Similar stories were collected from the Crow, Gros Ventre, Omaha and Ponca people, though some omit the 'bear lover' episode at the beginning and thus fail to explain why the elder sister undergoes the bear transformation. Some variants include a prolonged chase, with supernatural obstacles conjured up by the bear's siblings in an attempt to escape her. Related stories were also told in the Northeast and the Subarctic. It is interesting to compare their expressed antipathy to bears with stories from other regions which portray bears as enjoying complex but benign relationships with human beings; see THE BEAR STORY THAT BRINGS A WINDSTORM (p. 291), THE BEAR'S SONG (p. 406) and THE BOY WHO WAS RAISED BY A BEAR (p. 610).

The Big Dipper is the popular American name for the seven brightest stars in the iconic constellation Ursa Major (known in the UK as the Plough). The two brightest stars of the Big Dipper's bowl point to the North Star (Polaris), which is bright enough to be easily seen even by moonlight, and which always seems to be fixed in the northern sky.

THE ROLLING SKULL

Pawnee

Four young women went out together to gather firewood. When they had finished, one of them suddenly cried out in surprise, 'Oh, what a beautiful smell! Whatever is it?'

'It's like a scented root,' said another.

The other two joined in:

'I've never smelled one as sweet as that.'

'It seems to be coming from up there, to the north.'

'Let's go and find out what it is,' begged the first one.

So they all set off, but before long, two got tired and turned back.

The other pair went on a bit further, then one said, 'We've still got no idea where we're heading or even what we're looking for. It's so cold and it'll be dark soon. Let's go home.'

But the one who had first noticed the smell said stubbornly, 'It can't be far now. I'm not giving up until I reach it.'

'Don't be stupid!' said her friend. 'You know the night's full of dangers. There might be wolves or ghosts, monsters. You might freeze to death…'

'I'm not scared. The lovely scent is bound to keep bad things away. You go home if you want; but *I'm* going to keep searching.'

So she walked on alone into the twilight. The trail led uphill into a forest of towering cedar trees. At length she emerged to a clearing, where the path ended abruptly in front of a large lodge built entirely of rocks. The air around it was thick with the elusive scent.

She hesitated. Should she turn back, now that she'd found its source, or knock on the strange stone door? Before she could make up her mind, the door slid to one side – and out stepped an exceptionally handsome young man.

'Aha,' he cried, 'I thought I heard someone here. Welcome, come in.'

The young woman was dazzled by his good looks. Even so, she said cautiously, 'Um…I don't think I should… I'm just looking for the source of that wonderful smell.'

The youth smiled at her enticingly. 'You've come to exactly the right place; the source of the smell is in here. Come and see.'

Still the young woman hesitated, her friend's grave warnings echoing inside her head. However, the scent overwhelmed her common sense, and she followed him inside.

No sooner had she done so, than she heard a loud scraping noise behind her. She spun round, and saw that the stone door had closed by itself. In the glowing firelight she noticed a large medicine bundle hanging on the wall, with five gourd rattles dangling from it.

The youth sat down on a buffalo hide. The next moment, he transformed into a hideously ugly old man!

She gazed about fearfully, feeling dizzy from the scent. She couldn't see any way to open the door. The only other possible exit was the smoke hole in the roof, but it was too high and much too small to squeeze through. She trembled, and tears squeezed from her eyes.

'What's the matter?' the hideous old man sneered.

'You've tricked me,' she sobbed, 'you've trapped me!'

'Well, crying won't help you, so shut up and get busy.'

'How do you mean? What must I do?'

'Firstly, you've got to work for me; secondly, you've got to show me how happy you are.'

'Happy?' she cried, 'when I'm your prisoner – your slave?'

'Well, if you're not happy now, you never will be,' said the hideous man grimly. 'Want to know why? Ha ha ha! It's because in just a few days' time – I shall kill you!'

The night passed in a daze. The next morning, the hideous old man said to the young woman, 'I'm going out for the day. While I'm gone, cook me some meat from my store over there.'

He transformed back into the handsome youth and muttered some mysterious words. The stone door slid open, let him step through it, then at once sealed itself shut behind him. The young woman gazed hopelessly around the gloomy lodge and began to cry again.

'Woman!' called a strange croaking voice.

She jumped. 'Who's there?'

'*Caw!* Woman, if you want to be saved, do everything I tell you.'

She gazed fearfully around, down, up…and at last saw, perched above the smoke hole, a Raven.

'This brute that's captured you,' said the Raven, 'this shape-shifter – he's a monster. His true form is a skull.'

'Oh! A skull…?'

'Yes, a round, rattling, rolling skull. His name is Long Tongue, and he's a killer. *Caw!* Tomorrow, persuade him to let you out to relieve yourself. By the door, you'll see some hackberry trees. Pick some berries, hide them under your belt, then go back inside.'

'But once I'm outside, why can't I just run away?'

'Because he'll come after you.'

'Then how will I ever escape?'

'*Caw!* I'll tell you tomorrow.' The Raven flapped his wings and vanished.

She cooked the meat for Long Tongue. In due course, he returned and changed back into the hideous old man. They ate together, sitting on either side of the fire. Another night passed.

The next morning, Long Tongue grudgingly let her step briefly outside. She picked some berries, hid them and returned to the lodge. Then Long Tongue went out again, leaving her imprisoned.

Almost at once, she heard the Raven's croaks from the smoke hole: 'Woman, when Long Tongue returns, he'll place his head on your lap and tell you to pick the lice from his hair and chew them. But instead, chew the hackberries to make the right sort of noise. Once you've deloused him, Long Tongue will die – but only for a few moments. When this happens, go to the door and say, "Grandfather, move". The door will open. Step through it, throw all the lice away outside, then come back in saying, "Grandfather, close the lodge". Again it will obey you.'

'But why?'

'Never mind. But I'll tell you this much: some of my own skin is in his medicine bundle. Now, listen further. When the brute comes back to life, he'll announce that he's going on a long journey. Before he leaves, beg him to fetch you a dead buffalo; say you want to make tallow for him from its bones.'

Then the Raven was gone.

Some time later, Long Tongue returned and ordered her to delouse him. She did everything that the Raven had told her. Sure enough, when she had finished, he fell over and seemed to die. She ordered the door to open, and threw the lice outside. After a short while, Long Tongue revived, acting as if nothing strange had happened, and said he was going out again.

'Where to?' she asked him boldly.

'Upcountry,' he snarled. 'What's it to you?'

'I need to know when you'll be back, so I can prepare your food.'

'Not for several days.'

'I'll be bored,' she said. 'Can't I have something useful to do? Would you let me make tallow?'

'Mmm, I love tallow,' said Long Tongue.

'Then bring me a dead buffalo before you go, and I'll make some from its bones.'

Long Tongue went out and fetched the fresh carcass of a hefty bull, which he dumped before her.

'I'm off now,' he said. 'Make sure you have a good spread of tallow ready when I return. And be warned, if you try to flee, I'll quickly find out where you're going, I'll follow you and I'll kill you. Nothing in the world can save you.'

He stomped out, securing the door behind him. The young woman stoked the fire wretchedly, skinned and butchered the buffalo and started rendering the fat.

As she worked, the Raven came back. '*Caw!* Here's your chance. No, don't stop, finish the tallow while I make other preparations.'

He fluttered down, snatched Long Tongue's medicine bundle from its hook, opened it and pulled out some of its contents. First came a set of stones, the kind used to smooth arrows. Next, a clutch of flint arrow points, followed by a whole arrow; then a length of sinew and a feather; and finally a flint knife.

The young woman said that the tallow was ready.

'Shape some of it into a big ball,' said the Raven. 'Spread the rest over the floor and walls.'

When she had done everything, the Raven said, 'It's time to go. You're heading for a place four days' journey from here. Put the tallow ball and the treasures from the medicine bundle into this pack and tie it onto your back. You'll realise when it's time to use them: take them out and throw them behind you. Now then, wrap your arms around me.'

When she was ready, the Raven croaked four times: '*Caw, caw, caw, caw!*' then rose up through the air, carrying the young woman. They flew through the smoke hole, then soared above the cedar forest and out across the plains. On and on they flew. Finally, the Raven dipped down and alighted on the open grass.

'I've given you a head start,' he croaked, 'but I'm too tired to carry you further. Now you must run, while I fly overhead and guide you. Keep going eastward, and whatever you do, don't stop.'

'But what about when *I* feel tired?'

'You can't rest, woman, not for the next four days. Keep running. Any moment now, Long Tongue will return to his lodge, discover your escape – and then he'll be after you. Run, woman, run!'

Naturally, she did.

Meanwhile, Long Tongue came back to the stone lodge and quickly realised that the young woman had gone. Then he noticed that everything was covered with tallow, forgot his rage and started drooling. He fell to his knees and licked it up, his tongue growing longer and longer, waving about up and down, slurping tallow from the floor, twisting round to lick the walls, until he had devoured it all. He belched loudly and strode outside, bellowing, 'Woman, I'm coming to get you!'

Then he transformed into his true shape, the one that the Raven had spoken of, that of a skull. He had no body, no substance. His eyes were gaping hollows; his mouth a grinning nightmare of loose teeth that shook and rattled, gnashed and clattered every time he moved. And move he did! He rolled, he spun, he sped along like the wind; and all the time his teeth went *shucker-chucker, grittle-grattle.* The skull followed the young woman's trail, through the air then along the ground, faster and faster... Until he was almost upon her!

Just in time, the young woman remembered what the Raven had said. She pulled the stones from her pack and hurled them to the ground. Long Tongue saw them, turned into his old man shape again and paused briefly to snatch them up. Then he transformed back into the skull and rolled on after her.

And so it went on. Each time Long Tongue seemed to be closing in on her, the young woman pulled one of the other items from her bag to distract him: the ball, the flint arrow points, the whole arrow, the sinew, and the feather. Each one transformed into something Long Tongue desperately desired – a flood of tallow, a flight of arrows, a forest of perfectly straight trees, a herd of buffalo, a flock of turkeys. Each time, Long Tongue rolled into their midst, turned back to his hideous old man shape, gathered them up with his slavering tongue, then turned back to a skull and rolled on. One moment she seemed to be well ahead; the next moment the ground rumbled, the hills shook and the sky darkened, and there was the rolling, rattling skull again, almost upon her...

All the while, the Raven fluttered overhead, croaking: 'Run, woman, don't let him get you!'

Shucker-chucker, grittle-grattle... Long Tongue was about to overtake her! The young woman pulled the last item from her bag – the flint knife. She hurled it down behind her. At once a huge, deep ravine cracked open in the ground between them. The skull rolled on, toppled over the edge and plunged with a shriek right down to the bottom. It was trapped.

The Raven soared over the young woman, croaking, 'Well done! Just keep going a little further, *caw, caw,* you're almost there...'

He pointed with his wing. Her breath was coming in painful gasps, her legs were so tired they could hardly move. Ahead, she saw a huge mound and staggered towards it. As she drew near, she saw it was actually an earthen lodge. A man with an honest face was sitting outside it, busily making a bow. Somehow she managed to stumble up to him.

'Oh, please help me,' she groaned – then collapsed at his feet. 'I...I'm being chased by an evil monster... fleeing him for four days...can't escape. I can't go on...'

The man helped her up and led her inside to safety. Then he went back outside to await the monster. Very soon he heard the ground rumbling and the ghastly rattling noise: *shucker-chucker, grittle-grattle.* For somehow Long Tongue had managed to climb out of the ravine. Now the man saw a huge, hollow-eyed, dirty white, skull coming towards him, grinning as it rolled over and over in clouds of choking dust.

'Where's that woman?' the skull screeched. Its voice was like the chilling scrape of fingernails over horn. 'Give her to me, I know she's here, and I'm ready to kill her. Gimme, gimme...'

The man picked up a heavy stick and smashed it heavily on top of the skull – *crack!* – splitting it clean in two. But as soon as he removed the stick, the two halves joined back together.

'Gimme, gimme!' the skull snickered.

The man went round the side of his lodge, fetched his flint axe, hit the skull with that and split it again. But this time, he batted the two halves up to the sky – where one turned into the Moon and the other became the Sun.

Then he called through the open door of the lodge, 'My dear, the skull is vanquished. You are safe.'

'Thank you with all my heart!' said the young woman. 'But oh dear, I'm totally lost, for I wandered so far from home, I've no idea how to get back.'

The man smiled. 'Don't worry, you can make your home with us. I have many sons: the youngest is here with me to welcome you, and the other six will shortly return from the warpath.'

So the young woman moved in with the man and his youngest boy. When the other six brothers returned home, they were very pleased to meet her. They were all anxious to behave correctly towards the young woman and agreed to adopt her as their sister.

Now at last the young woman was at peace. She lived happily with her new family.

One day the young woman saw her adopted father fetch his medicine bundle. She watched intently as he opened it; and within its shadows, saw something that made her heart beat fast.

'Father,' she said, 'I believe I see an ear of corn in there.'

'You do.'

'Father, let me have it. Let me put it in the ground.'

'Why ever do you ask such a thing?'

'If I plant the corn,' she answered, 'soon it will grow into more corn, much more, and we can gather it to eat.'

'But this corn is sacred,' said the man, 'for it comes from our mother, Evening Star. I cannot take it out.'

The young woman sat in silence for a long while then said, 'Listen, my adopted father. I understand Evening Star's power, the power that lies within this corn to make it grow and increase. Again, I ask you: let me have it.'

Finally, the man consented and gave her the ear of corn. She planted it in the ground, and when it came up, she nurtured it. By the autumn, it had grown into a huge crop. She cooked some of it for her new family, and put the rest aside until the spring, when she planted it. Thus, from that time on, thanks to her, they always had plenty to eat.

The seasons turned. The next autumn there was even more corn to harvest. Yet the young woman's father was distracted, for he noticed disturbing signs about her.

'It's true,' she admitted. 'I am carrying a child.'

'How can this be?' the man chided her. 'You swore to live with my sons as a sister.'

'Of course I haven't lain with any of them. I've never been with any man. I don't know how this happened.'

She waited patiently until her child was born. Shortly afterwards, as she was nursing it, a strange man with shining eyes called at the lodge. When the old man challenged him, he said, 'Let me in to see the young woman, for I am the father of her child.'

But the young woman was mystified when she saw him. 'Who are you?' she cried.

'I am North Star.'

'You can't have fathered my child. I've never seen you before. Since I came to live here, I haven't seen any man except my adopted father and my seven adopted brothers.'

'But once,' said North Star, 'you admired a red bird singing on the bough of a tree. *I* was that bird. You were so entranced by my song, that I lay with you.'

And so the young woman understood that North Star was indeed her husband.

Some time after that, the young woman's father said, 'My daughter, it is time for us all to go to the Sky. Once we arrive there, our trails will part. You must go north with your husband and child, and when you arrive, you will stay there forever. Your brothers will go east, but not rest there, for every night they must make a journey westwards. Later, your birth sister and brother will join these seven stars, and so will my own blood daughter; thus people looking up from Earth will see seven stars first, and later ten. While I live on Earth, I shall live as a great warrior – a hawk; but when the world comes to an end, I too will join my sons.'

Dorsey: *The Pawnee Mythology,* 1906

The man who narrated this tale was called Little Chief. He was chief of one of the Pawnee's four bands, the Chaui; and also great-nephew of the head chief of all the Pawnee. Little Chief was keeper of a medicine bundle (see p. 21), and also of the 'buffalo pipe' which, when exposed, was said to cause windstorms.

The stars that the characters become at the end of the myth are the Pleiades, a small, misty constellation visible from almost every inhabited location on earth. Of its hundreds of stars, six or seven can normally be seen, though sometimes it is possible to see more. They are most visible in the northern hemisphere during the winter, usually rising in the eastern sky and setting in the west. It is interesting to compare the 'star' elements at the end of this myth with the other Pawnee story, MORNING STAR AND EVENING STAR (p. 27).

Corn was a staple food for the Pawnee, who were farmers as well as itinerant buffalo hunters.

There is another, much simpler, version of this story in the same source, with a few different details, narrated by a man called White Sun. He was apparently a famous storyteller, though his account lacks the richness and detail of Little Chief's narrative.

The monstrous rolling head or skull, which people escape by fleeing and conjuring up magic obstacles, is a popular motif in Plains mythology. Arapaho and Gros Ventre stories tell of starving people fleeing a skull which had been bringing them mysterious gifts of dead game; it is eventually smashed by falling into a canyon. In a Blackfoot tale, the rolling head is a woman's that had been cut off by her husband; one version says this is a punishment for her meeting a secret lover who is actually a rattlesnake; her body pursues the man, whilst the head chases their children. They succeed in drowning the head, but eventually the woman's body becomes the moon, still chasing the man, who becomes the sun. Similar 'animal lover' rolling head stories were told by the Cheyenne and Dakota Sioux.

Choctaw Village near the Chefuncte
painted by Francois Bernard, 1869

MYTHS OF THE SOUTHEAST

PEOPLE OF
THE SOUTHEAST

United States:
Alabama, Florida, Georgia, Louisiana,
Mississippi and South Carolina.
Parts of Arkansas, Kentucky, Maryland, North Carolina,
Oklahoma, Tennessee, Texas, Virginia and West Virginia.

The Southeast of the United States was once part of a dense forest that covered much of the eastern side of North America. Its landscape includes coastal and flood plains, low mountains, plateaus, winding rivers, lakes, swamps and wetlands. The climate ranges from warm to humid subtropical, with very hot summers and a tendency for hurricanes; winters vary from mild to very cold and snowy, depending on location. The soil is fertile, and the vegetation lush.

The Native American peoples of the Southeast were originally farmers who lived in semi-permanent villages. They grew corn, beans and squash – known as the 'three sisters' – supplemented by other crops such as sunflowers, gourds, melons and tobacco. The men did the heavy work of clearing the land, while the crops were generally planted and nurtured by women, often assisted by their children. They also hunted deer, turtles and other game, fished and gathered wild nuts and fruits.

Their villages were mainly built along river valleys. Houses could be rectangular or conical, typically constructed of wattle and daub. In the warmest areas during the summer, partially open-sided houses were often used for coolness. The focal point of each village was the central plaza, typically a square of beaten mud with a sacred communal fire in the the middle, surrounded by council and ceremonial buildings. Trails led between villages and far beyond, facilitating long-distance trade and warfare. Waterways were also commonly used for travel, in flat-bottomed dugout canoes propelled by poles or paddles.

Southeastern societies were typically matrilineal (i.e. descent was traced through the female line). They were divided into self-governing clans, each with its own chief. The clans were usually named after animals and birds, with membership inherited through the mother. Clan members co-operated in many ways, ranging from hospitality to shared vengeance. Marriage between members of the same clan was forbidden. Women owned the houses and were considered heads of their own households. Newly-weds normally lived near the wife's relations, and divorced women usually kept the children and marital property. The most important male elder in a person's life was not their father, but their mother's oldest brother. Polygamy was permitted for men wealthy enough to support more than one wife.

Society was organised around 'towns', which have been described as political units rather than places of residence. These were often divided into 'White' groups which were concerned with civic and religious affairs; and 'Red' groups, dealing with warfare and justice. Each town had its own council, comprising the chiefs of all its member clans.

Communal life was dominated by an annual cycle of religious ceremonies, based on the farming year. The most important was the Green Corn Dance, celebrated in the plaza at harvest time in late summer. It marked the first ripening of the corn, the end of the agricultural cycle and the beginning of the next one. It was also an opportunity for the community to purify and heal itself, to end quarrels and forgive misdemeanours. All fires were extinguished before a new one was ceremoniously lit and then distributed to every household. Old tools and clothes were replaced, and sexual abstinence was practised alongside fasting, feasting and dancing.

Another major communal activity was the playing of team ball games, known as 'the little brother of war' because of their role in releasing tensions and helping to keep the peace. For men, the favoured game was lacrosse using long-handled racquets. An observer of the Choctaw in the 1830s described up to 1,000 youths taking part in a day-long match, with an estimated 5,000 men, women and children spectating. The usual women's game comprised throwing the ball by hand. Other sports involved throwing sticks and rolling stones.

LIFE IN THE SOUTHEAST
WHEN THESE STORIES WERE COLLECTED

The Native American peoples of the Southeast were descendants of the highly developed Mississippian civilisation, which is believed to date from around AD 700 and to have lasted for some 900 years. Their ancestors built walled cities with great pyramids, and earthen mounds topped with temples and other important buildings. They made beautiful artefacts and had an extensive trade network. However, this civilisation was already in decline by the time the Spanish conquistadors arrived in the region in the 16th century, followed by missionaries, French fur traders and English colonists. During the 17th century, some Native peoples enjoyed flourishing trade links with these incomers; but others were enslaved en masse on White plantations. Such slavery caused multiple deaths, exacerbated by smallpox and other diseases imported from Europe.

By the late 18th century, many of the Southeast peoples had been completely exterminated. Moreover, the landscape was rapidly being transformed by White settlers: large swathes of forest were cut down, swamps drained, rivers dammed, wildlife destroyed and the soil degraded through unsustainable farming practices.

Against this background, the surviving Southeastern peoples faced a new catastrophe in 1830: the passing of the Indian Removal Act. This obliged them to give up their homelands, and move west of the Mississippi River to take up grants of land there. Some Native peoples managed to avoid this by taking up American citizenship; whilst others hid in remote areas where they attempted to preserve their ancestral traditions. For the rest, despite great opposition and resistance, and government promises of negotiation, the reality was brutal, forced removal under military supervision. Over the next two decades, tens of thousands of Cherokee, Chickasaw, Choctaw, Creek and Seminole people were forced onto the 1,000-mile trek westward – infamously known as the Trail of Tears – through the harshest conditions. Numerous people died en route, from starvation, disease, exposure and other traumas. The survivors were resettled in what was then known as Indian Territory – now the state of Oklahoma. There they united into a political organisation known as the 'Five Civilised Tribes', and sought to strengthen their position by embracing education, Christianity and other aspects of mainstream American life, including intermarriage. However, by the early 20th century, almost all the land they had formerly been granted was taken over by Whites.

STORYTELLING IN THE SOUTHEAST

Despite – or perhaps because of – the prolonged contact between the Southeastern Native peoples and Whites, there is a relative paucity of transcribed stories from local oral tradition. However, myths recorded around the turn of the 20th century amongst the Caddo and Cherokee peoples indicate that religious narratives once played a central role in the old Southeastern cultures, with a huge number presumably lost.

Writing in 1888, James Mooney tells how the so-called 'Eastern Band of Cherokees' managed to preserve their stories:

'Remaining in their native mountains, away from railroads and progressive white civilisation, they retain many customs and traditions which have been lost by those who removed to the west. They still keep up their old dances and ball-plays...their medicine-men, conjuring, songs, and legends. The Cherokee syllabary, invented by one of the tribe about sixty years ago, has enabled them to preserve in a written form much which in other tribes depends upon oral tradition, and soon disappears before the pressure of civilisation. The fact that many of these legends are connected with mountains, streams, and waterfalls with which they have been familiar from childhood also goes a long way towards keeping the stories fresh in memory.'

Most of the surviving Southeast traditional stories are not serious myths but light-hearted folk tales, and thus not included in the scope of this book. A good number tell of the trickster Rabbit, with storylines intriguingly similar to the popular *Brer Rabbit* tales collected from African-American slaves in the same region during the 19th century. There has long been academic debate about whether such stories are Native American or African in origin; or indeed, whether they represent a blending of the two narrative traditions during the era of slavery.

THE PEOPLES BEHIND THE STORIES

Caddo

The Caddo people originally came from Arkansas, Louisiana, Oklahoma and Texas. During the 19th century they were forcibly removed to Oklahoma, where they lost much of their reservation land. Since the 1930s they have been organised as the Caddo Nation of Oklahoma, and are active in preserving their culture.

Cherokee

Originally from Alabama, Georgia, North and South Carolina and Tennessee, the Cherokee are one of the largest and most powerful Southeastern tribes. They have a long tradition of adoption and intermarriage, both with other tribes, and with African Americans and Whites. In the early 19th century, a Cherokee man called Sequoyah invented a syllabary for writing in his people's language which is still used today. During the 1830s most Cherokee were removed to Oklahoma, but a small band managed to escape into the mountains, where they became known as the Eastern Band of Cherokees and managed to preserve some of their culture. Today there are three federally recognised Cherokee tribes in the USA. The Cherokee Nation, with headquarters in Oklahoma, is the largest Native American group in the United States. The Eastern Band of Cherokee Indians – descendants of those who managed to avoid removal – is based in the town of Cherokee, North Carolina. Members of the United Keetoowah Band of Cherokee Indians in Oklahoma are descendants of those who migrated to Arkansas and Oklahoma before the Indian Removal Act.

Hitchiti

The Hitchiti homeland was in Georgia. Even in the 18th century their population was very small. After enforced removal to Oklahoma, their identity gradually became submerged into other tribes of the Creek Confederacy or Muscogee, an alliance of diverse groups in Georgia, Alabama and Florida that came together during the 18th and 19th Centuries.

Research for this section also covered stories from the following Southeast peoples: Alabama, Biloxi, Caddo, Chickasaw, Choctaw, Creek, Natchez, Koasati, Seminole (Mikasuk) and Yuchi.

THE ORIGIN OF HUNTING AND FARMING

Cherokee

*When I was a boy, this is what
the old men told me they heard when they were boys.*

Long ages ago, when the world was still new, a young boy lived alone with his father, Lucky Hunter, and his mother, whose name was Corn. It's not told what this boy himself was called.

Every day, Lucky Hunter used to go off into the forest and return later with a large deer. Corn would cut it up and wash off the excess blood in the river, then cook it with a good helping of beans and corn. So the boy always ate well, though he had no idea how they got hold of all this food. His life was easy, but lonely.

One day, when the boy was playing by himself on the riverbank, he suddenly heard a voice calling him. He spun round – and was astonished to see another, slightly older, boy coming towards him.

'Who are you?' he cried. 'Where have you come from?'

'I'm your elder brother,' the stranger answered. 'I've come from the river.'

'The river? How ever did you get there?'

'My mother threw me in.'

'Whoah, that's cruel! Why?'

The strange boy didn't answer, but just said, 'Let's play.' Soon the two were immersed in a game.

The next day, the strange boy appeared again, and the day after that as well, and so on every day. It wasn't long before Lucky Hunter and Corn heard them talking and laughing, and asked what was going on. When the boy told them, his mother said, 'Ah,

121

the strange boy must be born from the deer blood that I put in the river. You'd better bring him home to live with us.'

'I don't think he'll want that,' said the boy, 'he's very independent.'

'Whether he wants it or not,' said his father, 'that's the best thing for him. If he won't come up to the house willingly, you'll have to help us catch him. When you're playing together tomorrow, challenge him to wrestle with you. As soon as you've got your arms tightly round him, shout loudly and we'll come and take over.'

So the boy did just that. His parents ran down and seized the strange boy. He struggled against them, crying and screaming: 'Let go, leave me be! You threw me away! I don't want to be with you!' But they dragged him home and forced him to stay. By and by, they managed to tame him…well, *half*-tame him, anyway. Despite their best efforts, he was still cunning and uncontrollable, and a bad influence on the other boy. Also, it turned out that he had magic powers. The parents called him Wild Boy.

One morning, the two boys saw Lucky Hunter go out with his bow and a pouch full of feathers. Wild Boy said to his younger brother, 'Look, there's our father, off to fetch the day's meat. It's time we found out why he calls himself 'Lucky' and where the meat comes from. Let's follow him.'

So they crept into the forest after Lucky Hunter, stealthy and silent, slipping behind trees whenever it seemed he might look back. Eventually they saw him emerge into a clearing, and stop at the edge of a swamp.

'Stay here,' Wild Boy whispered, 'watch what I do.'

Before the younger boy's eyes, he transformed into a wisp of bird down. The next moment, a wind blew up and carried the down onto Lucky Hunter's shoulder. Lucky Hunter didn't notice, but waded into the swamp, where he cut down a large bundle of reeds, then fitted a feather onto each to make arrows. When he had finished, he resumed his walk through the forest.

The wind blew the down back to where the younger brother was waiting. It turned back into Wild Boy, who told his brother what he had seen, and beckoned him to hurry on after their father.

They followed Lucky Hunter along a well-beaten forest trail that led up a mountain. Eventually, he stopped at another clearing, where a huge rock lay on the grassy slope. He stooped down and heaved it away, revealing a dark cave behind it. The next moment, out leaped a deer – a fat buck with a magnificent set of antlers. As it hesitated, blinking in the daylight, Lucky Hunter fitted an arrow to his bow and quickly shot it dead. He rolled the rock firmly back into place, lifted the carcass onto his shoulders and turned to carry it home.

The two boys nipped away into the trees and made a detour, racing back so fast that they arrived home long before their father. He had no idea that they had been following him.

A few days later, after Lucky Hunter had returned from his daily trip, they stole his bow and sneaked off along the trail. They stopped at the swamp to cut reeds and make arrows, then hurried up the mountain, where they hauled away the rock.

From the cave behind it, a deer leaped out. The boys cheered; they were so excited, they forgot all about shooting it. Moments later, out came another deer, then another and another...hundreds of them, thousands – a blur of thundering hooves, gleaming brown fur and towering antlers.

The two boys' mouths fell open, the bow and arrows dropped from their hands. Still more deer came out, more and more. In this way, the deer that Lucky Hunter had guarded so carefully in the cave since the beginning of time – their entire supply of meat – all vanished into the forest.

After them came other game animals: countless raccoons, rabbits and so on; then great flocks of birds – turkeys, pigeons, partridges – like storm clouds, the air rumbling with their beating wings.

Back home in the valley, the boys' parents heard the noise.

'That sounds like a thunderstorm,' said Corn.

'I don't think so,' said Lucky Hunter. 'To me, it sounds like Wild Boy leading his brother into mischief. I'd better go and investigate.'

He hurried out, soon found his sons' footprints on the trail and followed them up the mountain. When he reached the clearing at the top, there they were, loitering by the opening. Everything was still and silent. The boys watched him approach nervously, frozen to the spot. They didn't say a word, and nor did he.

Lucky Hunter stepped into the darkness of the cave and strode to a cranny in the far wall, where four large pottery jars stood. He kicked them, making the lids fall off. At once, a great mass of insects swarmed out of each jar. From one came gnats, from another fleas, from the third lice and from the last one bedbugs. In no time at all, they had all flown or crawled past Lucky Hunter, out of the cave to the two cowering boys. The insects landed on the boys' hands, hair and faces; they wormed their ways all over the boys' bodies. And with every tiny movement they made, came a vicious sting, an excruciating bite, a tortuous sucking of blood.

The boys screamed. They tried to slap the horrible creatures off, rolled on the ground, writhed in agony, wept and begged for mercy. Lucky Hunter watched until they were both close to dying from pain and exhaustion. Only then did he call the insects away.

When the boys' breathing came more evenly, when they had stopped twitching and crying, he spoke to them in quiet tones.

'You rascals! Do you realise what you've done? You've changed the world for ever, changed it for the worse. Before today, it was easy to get meat. There was no work involved, all I had to do was make the short trip up here and fetch it, always in the same place, an endless supply. But now you've let all the animals out, they've scattered everywhere, far away, all over the forest. From now on, I'll have to go all over the place looking for them; and even when I manage to track some down, I'll have to chase them even further and hope I can manage to kill them. And from now on all men, all over the world, will have to make the same effort to get meat.'

Wild Boy and his younger brother slunk home, nursing their wounds. By the time they arrived, they were as hungry as they were exhausted. Shame-faced, they went to their mother, Corn, and begged for something to eat. Corn knew the evil they had done, but took pity on them.

'As you know,' she said, 'there's no meat for you. But I can cook you something lighter.'

She picked up her basket and went out to the storehouse. It was built on high poles, to keep animals away, and the door was reached by a ladder. Although she went there every day, she had never once shown the boys inside.

Wild Boy whispered, 'Where does all that food she keeps inside the storehouse come from? Let's go and spy on her.'

No, he hadn't learned his lesson, and nor had his younger brother. When they heard the storehouse door close behind Corn, they sneaked round the back, clambered up the raised wall, scrabbled at the the log slats and made a chink to peer through.

An extraordinary sight met their eyes. Corn was standing in the middle of the room, leaning over her basket. She was rubbing her stomach round and round; and as her hand moved, a stream of corn grains came pouring out. When the basket was half full, she started to rub her armpits instead. From these there cascaded two streams of beans, one from each side, until the basket was full to the top.

The boys jumped down to the ground, gazing at each other in horror.

'That's revolting!' said Wild Boy.

'She must be a witch – our own mother!' said the younger brother.

'We'll have to kill her,' said Wild Boy.

When they got back into the house, Corn was already there.

'I know your thoughts,' Corn said quietly. 'You're planning to kill me.'

The boys didn't deny it.

'Well, that's how it must be,' said Corn. 'But listen carefully. Once I'm dead, there are certain things you must do to ensure plenty of food for the future. You must completely clear a large circle of ground in front of the house. Drag my body seven times round the edge of it, and seven times across the middle. If you do all this and stay up all night to watch over it, in the morning it will be overflowing with corn.'

Then she let her sons club her to death.

When this was done, they set to work clearing the ground, as she had told them. But instead of a complete circle, they only bothered to clear seven small patches. It's because of their laziness that corn only grows in a few places today, instead of all over the world.

They dragged the body round all the patches, spilling their mother's blood inside them. From each drop of blood, corn began to grow. But instead of dragging the body round seven times as she had told them, they only did it twice. It's because of their indolence that today we can only grow two crops a year.

Despite these failings, they guarded the plants diligently all night. By the morning, they were not only fully grown, but also ripe.

When Lucky Hunter came home and saw that they had killed their mother, he was outraged. He abandoned his sons and went to stay with the Wolf people, asking them to kill the boys in revenge. But Wild Boy again transformed into a wisp of down, spied on them and thus discovered the plan. He and his brother made a trap for the Wolves and killed almost all of them. Only a few survived, and from them are descended all the wolves in the world today.

After that, the boys settled down to enjoy their corn, baking it into delicious bread. News of this spread around the world, and people came from far away to beg a share of their wonderful food.

Wild Boy and his younger brother gave these people seven grains of corn, saying:

'On your way home, stop to plant these, then sit up all night to watch them. By morning, you will have seven ripe ears. Take these on your journey, and when you stop again the following night, plant them all and sit up to watch them again. By next morning each will have multiplied seven times more. Do this for seven days, and you will end up with enough corn for everyone.'

The visitors promised to do so. But their journey was long and the weather was hot. They found it ever more difficult to stay awake at night. On the seventh night, the last before they reached home, despite their best efforts, they succumbed to sleep. When they awoke in the morning, they were dismayed to find that the corn planted the previous evening had not even sprouted.

They gathered it up again, carried it home, planted it there and nurtured it carefully. It did grow in the end. But because of those people's sleepiness, ever since then crops have not grown instantly; instead, farmers must spend half the year tending them.

After a while, Wild Boy and his brother began to wonder what had happened to their father. To find him, Wild Boy rolled a wheel towards the Darkening Land in the west. It quickly returned, so they knew Lucky Hunter was not there. They tried rolling the wheel north and south, but each time it returned again. Finally, they rolled it eastward, towards the Sunrise Land – and this time it didn't come back. Thus they knew their father had gone that way, and set off to find him.

When they finally caught him up, the wheel had transformed into a little dog, trotting along beside Lucky Hunter. After all the trouble his sons had caused, he wasn't pleased to see them, but he let them walk behind him, on condition that they kept out of trouble. Along the way, they passed many dangers that Lucky Hunter expected them to succumb to – man-eating mountain lions, human cannibals and more – but through Wild Boy's cunning and magic, they survived them all.

By this time they had grown up into powerful men. They continued to follow Lucky Hunter's tracks, all the way to the end of the world – to the place where the Sky arch constantly rises and falls, allowing the Sun to emerge each day to shine on us all below. When the gap opened, they squeezed through it to the Sky, where Lucky Hunter and Corn had already arrived. They stayed with their parents for seven days, then travelled right across the Sky to the Darkening Land in the west.

They still live there now. They are known as the Little Men; and when they talk to each other, we hear low rolling thunder in the west.

Mooney: *Myths of the Cherokees*, 1888
Mooney: *Myths of the Cherokee*, 1902
Mooney says that he collected this story in the summer of 1887. It was
'one of the best known of the Cherokee myths of a sacred character, and in the old times anyone who heard it, with all the explanation, was obliged to 'go to water' after the recital; that is, to bathe in the running stream at daybreak, before eating, while the medicine man went through his mystic ceremonies on the bank. I heard the story in its entirety from two of the best storytellers, one of whom is a medicine man, and the other is supposed to be skilled in all their hunting secrets. Neither of them speak English. In addition, so many beliefs and customs turn upon this story...that I probably heard each of the principal incidents at least half a dozen times.'
The later version is almost identical except that this one identifies the boys as the Little Men – possibly the same who feature in SUN AND HER DAUGHTER (p. 128). It also adds a final paragraph in which some hunters, unable to find any game, send messengers for the two boys, now called Thunder Boys. They come to the town and sing seven songs which bring deer out of the wood for the hunters to kill. Before they depart, the boys teach the hunters the same songs for future use. The story concludes:
'It all happened so long ago that the songs are now forgotten – all but two, which the hunters still sing whenever they go after deer.'
Corn's role, particularly the dragging around of her body after she is killed by her own kin, bears a close resemblance to the Northeast story FIRST MOTHER (p. 546). The Creek and Natchez peoples had parallel myths. Caddo mythology says that Great Father gave the first seeds to Snake Woman, teaching her how to use them to grow and prepare food; and her two sons helped spread this knowledge around the world.
A number of other myths and folk tales from across North America tell of a supernatural brother (usually resulting from an abnormal birth, and sometimes a twin) who goads his younger sibling into forbidden adventure, though few are as meaningful as this story.

SUN AND HER DAUGHTER

Cherokee

The Sun is a woman. She lives on the far side of the Sky dome. You have seen her: every day at dawn, she rises and climbs up the the curving eastern side, walks right across the arc, then goes down again in the west to sleep through the night.

It's a long journey. But in the old times, she used to rest along the way, because she had a daughter whose house stood right in the middle of the Sky, directly above the Earth. Each day at noon, Sun would stop at her daughter's house and share a meal with her.

Sun loved her daughter more than anything.

But she hated all the People who lived below on Earth. Every evening at the end of her journey, she would pass her brother Moon going the opposite way, and she would grumble at him: 'Those People never look at me, but insult me by hiding their eyes behind their hands and grimacing. I can't stand them!'

Moon would try to soothe her, saying, 'No, sister, you're misinterpreting them. They only hide their eyes because your brightness dazzles them. *I* don't have any problem with the People, because my light's nice and soft; in fact, they often smile up at me and admire my beauty. Try thinking of them as your little brothers and sisters, as I do, and treat them more gently.'

This just made Sun jealous. She resolved to kill the People. So every day as she reached the zenith of the Sky, just before her daughter's house, she sent scorching hot rays down to Earth. They were so intense that the People could not bear to come out of their houses. Even indoors, it was insufferably hot. Many fell ill with a raging fever that no medicine could cure; and then, one after another, they began to die.

Every family lost several members. In the cool of the moonlit evening, the survivors held a council and discussed what to do.

'If we don't find a solution, there'll be no one left,' they said.

'We can't handle this ourselves. We need a stronger power.'

'You're right. Let's ask the Little Men to help.'

So a messenger was sent to the mountains, and very soon they heard the sound of drumming as the Little Men drew near. They themselves had not been harmed by Sun, for they lived safe in the gloom of their caves. However, they listened with great sympathy as the People spoke of their suffering. After they had debated the matter quietly amongst themselves they said, 'We can see only one way to resolve this. You must beat Sun at her own game: before she kills you, *you* must kill *her*.'

Nobody argued. Nobody thought through the consequences. The Little Men asked for volunteers, and two men stepped forward at once. The Little Men made some medicine, and in this way transformed one volunteer into Spreading Adder, and the other into Copperhead Snake. Then they used further medicine to send them up to the Sky, instructing them to wait near the door to Sun Daughter's house, concealed in the shadows, lying still and silent until Sun herself appeared. As soon as she reached Sun Daughter's door, they were to spring out and bite her.

At first, everything went well. The two snakes lay quietly, and when they heard Sun's footsteps approaching, Spreading Adder leaped forward ready to attack. But he was so dazzled by Sun, that instead of piercing her with his fangs, he just spat out a pathetic gob of yellow slime. Sun didn't even notice him as she hurried past into Sun Daughter's house. Spreading Adder slunk away in shame.

As for Copperhead Snake, he didn't even try to do anything, but retreated quickly after his companion.

So, back down on Earth, things stayed just as bad. In desperation, the People called the Little Men again. They asked for two more volunteers, urging no one to offer themselves unless they were confident of fulfilling the allotted task. After much hesitation, two more men stepped forward. The Little Men transformed one into Rattlesnake, and the other into the horned snake, Uktena.

'You are both better equipped than the last two,' the Little Men said, 'Don't let us down.'

They sent the new pair up to wait by Sun Daughter's door. Uktena was huge, broad as a tree trunk, with horns on his head, a blazing crest on his forehead and glittering scales. He was proud of his strength, and confident. He slid into a dark corner and settled patiently to wait for the right moment. However, Rattlesnake was so eager that he slithered excitedly past Uktena, right up to Sun Daughter's door, coiling up next to it on full alert.

He had only been there a short time, when the door opened. Rattlesnake tensed, ready for Sun to emerge. As soon as he saw a woman stepping out, he lunged forward and bit her.

But it wasn't Sun, after all; for she was still travelling across the Sky dome and hadn't arrived yet. Instead, it was Sun *Daughter*, popping out to see why her mother was late. As soon as Rattlesnake's poisonous fangs sank into her ankle, she swooned to the ground…and within moments, lay dead.

Rattlesnake was so excited, he couldn't think straight and had no idea that it was Sun Daughter he had killed, and that Sun herself was still alive. He raced back down to Earth, to boast of his great deed, and the People gathered round to congratulate him.

Uktena went back too; but in a terrible fury because Rattlesnake had got it all wrong. Down on Earth, his anger grew moment by moment, day by day…until he grew so dangerous that, in the end, the People had to banish him.

Meanwhile, up in the Sky, Sun arrived at her daughter's house – and found her lifeless body sprawled by the door. She fell on her knees beside it with a shriek of despair and tried desperately to revive her, caressing her, shaking her and chanting medicine songs, but nothing worked. Finally, she carried the body into the house, laid it down and sat next to it, weeping endlessly.

In this way, Sun stopped her daily journey and at last her rays stopped overheating the Earth. So the People saw an end to the heat-sickness and dying, which was a very good thing…

Except that, without the Sun, every day was dark and gloomy. The crops and wild fruits failed, the game animals wasted away and the People began to starve. They begged the Little Men for more advice.

'Ah,' said the Little Men, 'If you want Sun to shine again, you must send seven brave men to Ghost Country in the Darkening Land far to the west, to bring back Sun Daughter from the dead. Each must carry a rod made of sourwood, and between them, they must carry a box.'

At once, seven men offered to undertake this quest. The Little Men gave them careful instructions:

'When you reach your destination, you will see a great crowd of ghosts engaged in a dance. Stand just outside their dance circle, watching for Sun Daughter. When she steps past you, take turns to strike her with your sourwood rods until she falls; then seize her at once and put her in the box. Secure the lid tightly, then take her up to her house in the Sky, where Sun sits in mourning. But be warned: *do not open the box, not even a tiny crack, until you arrive there.*'

So the seven men set out on the prescribed journey, which took seven days to complete. As soon as they reached the Darkening Land, they heard the distant sound of music. Going further, they saw a mass of translucent figures swaying in time to the great dance of Ghost Country.

The seven men crept up and stood just outside the dance circle. When the limpid form of Sun Daughter came swaying towards them, one of the men reached out and struck her with his rod. She turned and gazed at him intently...then swung back to the circle and stepped on. The dance seemed to be endless. Again she passed them, and this time a second man tapped her; again she danced on. And so it went on, until six of the men had struck her and it was the seventh man's turn. This time, as soon as the rod touched her, Sun Daughter collapsed into a soft heap upon the ground. The box was open and ready. The men seized her, laid her carefully inside it, and shut the lid fast.

Nobody tried to stop them, nobody seemed to see. The other ghosts simply carried on dancing.

The men heaved the box up onto their shoulders and turned back to the east. They walked quickly, scarcely stopping to rest, conscious they must not open it. And so the first day of their return journey passed without incident. But on the second day, the box began to grow heavier. On the third day, they heard strange shifting noises inside it, as if Sun Daughter's ghost was beginning to return to life. On the fourth day, they heard her moaning...

On the fifth day, they heard her voice quite clearly. 'I'm hungry,' it called, 'oh, so hungry! Open up, give me something to eat. I beg you, please, please...'

Each time, the men remembered the warning and ignored her.

On the sixth day, the voice was even louder: 'At least, I beg you, give me a drink! You've returned me to life, so how can you now let me die again of thirst?'

Again they shuddered but still ignored her, striding on steadfastly.

On the seventh day, the voice cried: 'I'm smothering inside here! Even if you won't feed me or let me drink – surely you won't let me suffocate back to death? Open the lid, give me air, if you have even a grain of compassion!'

The men stopped.

'What shall we do?'

'No one can survive without air.'

'But the Little Men forbade us to open it until we get home.'

'We'll be there before the end of today. We don't want to arrive and find all our efforts wasted.'

They argued on and on. But in the end, they agreed to open the lid, just a tiny crack; for how could they not relieve the poor woman's suffering? At once, they heard a fluttering of wings, and a chirruping: *'Purdy-purdy, purdy...whoit, whoit, whoit, whoit!'* A beautiful Redbird flew out of the box and vanished into the bushes.

They slammed the lid shut again, shouldered the box and hurried on the last half-day's trek to the Sky. But when they arrived and opened the box properly, Sun Daughter's body was gone.

Ah, if only those fools had followed the Little Men's instructions properly! Then they would have brought Sun Daughter home safely – and *we* could have brought our own loved ones back from Ghost Country too. But because of their disobedience, the dead can never return.

Sun had seen the People's rescue party setting out to Ghost Land with soaring hopes. But when they returned with just an empty box, her grief welled up again.

'My daughter, my beloved daughter!' she shrieked. And her tears fell as torrents of rain, threatening to flood the Earth, so that now the People feared they would be drowned.

They held another council, and agreed to send a party of their most beautiful young men and women to the Sky, to try and cheer Sun up with their dancing and songs. The youngsters did their utmost to entertain her; but for a very long time Sun ignored them. Then the drummers set up a new tune, which happened to be Sun's favourite. When she heard it, despite her grief, she could not help but lift her face. The sight of all those beautiful youths and girls dancing pleased her so much, that she burst into a smile.

Mooney: *Myths of the Cherokee,* 1902

Mooney says that nearly three-quarters of the stories in this collection were provided by a man called Ayunini ('Swimmer'), who was born around 1835, just before the Cherokees' enforced removal.

'He was prominent in the local affairs of the band, and no…tribal function was ever considered complete without his presence and active assistance. A genuine aboriginal antiquarian and patriot, proud of his people and their ancient system, he took delight in recording in his native alphabet the songs and sacred formulas…and the names of medicinal plants…while his mind was a storehouse of Indian tradition. To a happy descriptive style he added a musical voice for the songs and a peculiar faculty for imitating the characteristic cry of bird or beast, so that to listen to one of his recitals was often a pleasure in itself, even to one who understood not a word of the language. He spoke no English, and to the day of his death clung to the moccasin and turban, together with the rattle, his badge of authority. He died in 1899, aged about 65, and was buried like a true Cherokee on the slope of a forest-clad mountain.'

Another important informant was Itagunahi, also known as John Ax, born around 1800 and thus about 100 years old when Mooney knew him:

'[He is] recognised…as an authority upon all relating to tribal custom, and an expert in the making of rattles, wands, and other ceremonial paraphernalia. Of a poetic and imaginative temperament, he cares most for the wonder stories…but he has also a keen appreciation of the humorous animal stories. He speaks no English and with his erect spare figure and piercing eye is a fine specimen of the old-time Indian.'

Other informants and advisors are named as: Ays'sta, 'one of the principle conservatives amongst the women'; Tsuskwanun'nawa'ta (James D. Wafford) who was of mixed race, spoke both languages and 'held many positions of trust and honour amongst his people'; Suyeta ('the Chosen One'), a Baptist minister; a doctor called Tagwadihi; Chief N. J. Smith; James and David Blythe ('younger men of mixed blood'); Salali and Tsesani.

It is not clear exactly who the Little Men are. On the one hand, they may be Wild Boy and his younger brother from the previous myth, THE ORIGIN OF HUNTING AND FARMING (p. 121). Alternatively, they may be the beings described in a different section as follows:

'The *Yunwi Tsunsdi,* or Little People live in rock caves on the mountainside… hardly reaching up to a man's knee, but well shaped and handsome, with long hair falling almost to the ground. They are great wonder workers and are very fond of music, spending half their time drumming and dancing. They are helpful and kind-hearted, and often when people have been lost in the mountains, especially children, [have] brought them back to their homes. Sometimes their drum is heard in lonely places in the mountains, but it is not safe to follow it, because the Little People do not like to be disturbed at home, and they throw a spell over the stranger so that he is bewildered and loses his way, and even if he does at last get back…he is like one dazed ever after. Sometimes, also, they come near a house at night and the people inside hear them talking…in the morning they find the corn gathered or the field cleared as if a whole force of men had been at work. If anyone should go out to watch, he would die. When a hunter finds anything in the woods, such as a knife or a trinket, he must say, 'Little People, I want to take this,' because…if he does not ask their permission they will throw stones at him as he goes home.'

Of the snake transformations in the story, the spreading adder – also known as eastern hog-nosed snake – is harmless. The copperhead snake is poisonous, though not normally deadly. There are numerous species of rattlesnake in the Americas. Bites from them are relatively common if provoked or threatened, but prompt treatment usually prevents death.

The original narrator concludes this episode by saying:

'Since then we pray to the rattlesnake and do not kill him, because he is kind and never tries to bite if we do not disturb him.'

The Uktena seems to be a mythical creature. Mooney describes it as:

'a great snake, as large around as a tree trunk, with horns on its head, and a bright, blazing crest like a diamond upon its forehead, and scales glittering like sparks of fire. It has rings or spots of colour along its whole length, and cannot be wounded except by shooting in the seventh spot from the head, because under this spot are its heart and its life… Whoever is seen by the Uktena is so dazed by the bright light that he runs towards the snake instead of trying to escape. Even to see the Uktena asleep is death.'

'Redbird' is a popular name for the northern cardinal, a common crested songbird which lives in much of the eastern side of North America. The male has vivid red feathers, though the female is duller.

Another Cherokee story tells of some youths who journey east, seeking Sun's home. One tries to squeeze through the shifting door between sky and earth, from which she emerges each day, but is crushed to death. The others flee, but are old men by the time they reach home. Another story tells of Sun tricked into an incestuous relationship by her brother; a similar story was well known in the Arctic.

Yuchi stories describe people as the offspring of the Sun's menstrual blood. In Choctaw myth, Sun is male. Two youths spend many years trying to discover where he dies, following him across the great waters to his house. His wife, Moon, scrubs them in a pot of boiling water before Sun sends them home on a buzzard's back, warning them not to speak for four days. However, their mothers pester them with so many questions that they break this prohibition and die. In an Alabama story, an old woman keeps the sun shut up in a pot; the trickster Rabbit manages to free it, and birds then take it to the sky.

ANIMAL POWERS

Caddo

In days of old
people knew the animals
and were on friendly terms with them.
All of the animals possessed wonderful powers
and they sometimes appeared to people
in dreams or visions
and gave them their power.
Often when men were out hunting
and were left alone in the forest
or on the plains at night,
the animals came to them and
spoke to them in dreams
and revealed their secrets to them.

– Wing, Caddo elder, Oklahoma
(Quoted in Dorsey: *Traditions of the Caddo,* 1905)

OLD DOG AND THE WOLVES

Hitchiti

As everyone knows, the Wolves and the Dogs are close relations. A long, long time ago, they used to be good friends and go around together.

However, that all changed when the People tamed the Dogs and took them to live in their houses. They gave the Dogs treacherous thoughts and taught them brutality; they made them catch any young wolves they found, and kill them.

Not surprisingly, the Wolves became very angry at this. They held a council to discuss the situation. Everyone there had a complaint about how their young pups had been killed by the Dogs. After they'd all had a hearing, the Wolf Chief stood up and said, 'I propose that we gather all the Dogs together and kill them.' This was unanimously agreed.

The Wolf pack trotted along to the houses where the Dogs lived with their People. They set up a loud howling, the Dogs howled back at them, and the Wolves howled in return.

'Come out, cousins,' the Wolves called. 'We want to tell you something.'

So the Dogs assembled eagerly in front of the houses.

The Wolves said, 'We're going to have a big feast in four days' time, at midday. We'd like you to come and join us.'

'What will there be to eat?' asked the Dogs.

'Chicken,' said the Wolves.

The Dogs all licked their lips. 'It's good of you to invite us. We'll be there.'

After they'd exchanged more pleasantries, the Wolves ran back to where they lived, and spent the next four days digging a big hole in the ground.

Soon the day of the feast arrived. Across in the house, the Dogs got busy smartening themselves up and getting ready to go. Amongst them was one who was extremely old and excessively slow. This Old Dog was getting ready too, but the others all chided him, saying:

'Don't bother, Grandpa. You know you're too decrepit to go visiting these days, you'll only cause problems for the rest of us. Stay at home where it's nice and comfy.'

'But I want to come,' said Old Dog in his soft, hoarse voice.

'Definitely not, there's no point: even if you manage to walk all the way there, you won't be able to join in the fun when you arrive,' said the others.

'I'll be able to eat,' said Old Dog.

But the others ignored him. And when they set off, they made sure to leave him behind.

They hadn't gone very far, when one of the Dogs happened to glance back. 'Oh no,' he groaned, 'Old Dog's following us. He's bound to ruin things. If only he'd stayed at home.'

But despite a lot of loud barking, they couldn't persuade him to turn back. So they all left him, bounded on ahead and quickly arrived.

'Welcome, welcome!' said the Wolf Chief. 'We've been really looking forward to you coming. Make yourselves at home.'

'Where should we go?' asked the Dogs. They looked around, expecting to see houses like the ones where they lived, but there was no sign of any.

'Into that hole,' said the Wolf Chief, pointing with his nose.

The Dogs were puzzled, but they all jumped down into the hole obediently. It was very roughly made, but they were too polite to complain.

'Everyone here?' the Wolf Chief called down.

Before any of the Dogs in the hole could reply, they heard a hoarse voice panting up behind them: 'Almost, not quite, just coming. Wait, please don't start without me.'

The Wolf Chief looked up and grinned mockingly. 'Ah, you too, Grandfather, eh? Come along, we don't want any of you Dogs to miss out on the fun, heh, heh, heh.' He stood back and waited while Old Dog slowly limped up, then showed him an easy way round the back, down into the hole.

Once he'd settled in, the Chief nodded at four other Wolves, who went and sat round the rim of the hole. After a few moments, one of them stood up. 'Ha!' he yapped, 'we easily got you trapped!'

He sat down and another Wolf stood up, growling: 'You've killed all our beautiful pups, you brutes.'

Then a third one spoke: 'We're going to take revenge.'

'Yes,' growled the fourth, leaping up as the previous one sat down, 'we're going to kill you all!'

Inside the hole, the Dogs were listening with pricked ears. When they heard their terrible fate, they began to whimper and cry, panting and huddling together fearfully...

Well, not *quite* all of them. For Old Dog staggered to his feet and pushed his way past the others. His usual doddering stance had suddenly changed: he leaned forward with curled lips and held his tail stiff and high, waving it slowly from side to side.

'Hold on,' he barked back at them. Now even his gruff voice had changed too; it was firm and clear. 'I have a confession to make. *I* am the only one who killed all your pups. *I* take all the blame. The other Dogs here are entirely innocent.'

His kennel mates glanced up at him in astonishment.

'So,' Old Dog went on, 'if there is to be death in revenge, let it be honourable. *I* am the only one you may justly kill.'

The four guard Wolves hesitated.

'Prove it,' the Chief Wolf snarled.

'Of course. I will show you one of my trophies.' Old Dog dug his teeth into the long, tangled underfur of his belly and pulled out from it a tail − a Wolf cub's tail. He held it in his mouth, raised his head and shook it at the Wolves. Then he sank to the ground, head lowered, trembling slightly, awaiting his violent fate.

For a moment the Wolves all hesitated, heads turned uncertainly to their Chief. He stared at Old Dog for a long moment. But the course he must take was clear: it would be cowardly and totally shameful to attack such an honest and venerable old animal. So he lowered his eyes respectfully and began to shuffle backwards... And when he had reached a respectable distance, he summoned his pack mates with an urgent yipping and led them away into the forest.

As soon as they were gone, the Dogs all leaped out of the hole and raced at top speed back to the house where they lived with the People. Well, not *quite* all of them...

For poor Old Dog was left behind to creep around, half-blindly sniffing, until he found the slope by which the Wolf Chief had led him down into the hole. At last he managed to clamber out and make his way slowly and painfully home after the others.

When he finally arrived, they all came to grovel around him.

'So,' said Old Dog, "Stay at home," you told me, and "You're too too decrepit to go visiting." Well, it's lucky I ignored you and came along anyway, so I could save you all from your own naivety.

'From this you have learned the importance of listening to your elders. Before long I shall pass away, but don't forget what you have witnessed today and take heed of it. In future, when you go about the world, if ever someone older than the rest offers you advice, trust him! Remember how this elder once saved all your lives.'

This is how it has always been told.

Swanton: *Myths of the Southeast Indians*, collected 1908-1914
Both dogs and wolves are popular characters in myths right across North America. A story such as this makes play of the fact that the two species are actually almost one and the same genetically, dogs being descended from wolves that have been tamed and selectively bred to live and work alongside humans for countless generations.

There are several Southeast versions of a story about a dog that informs its master that his wife is being unfaithful. In one, the secret lover is a snake that the man kills, chops up and serves his wife for dinner. In several others, the faithless wife neglects her sickly husband, spending all day with her lover. His dogs join together to carry him down to his boat and paddle him away, helped by various other animals, then return to kill the adulterous couple, finding a new wife for their master as they return home.

A Cherokee myth explains why they call the Milky Way 'Where the Dog Ran': it marks the route taken by a delinquent dog one night when he fled a whipping, having been caught stealing corn from a mill.

THE ORIGIN OF SICKNESS AND MEDICINE

Cherokee

In the old days all living creatures, from the biggest animal to the tiniest bug, lived side by side with the People in total peace and friendship.

However, as time went by, this changed. It was all the fault of the People. They had so many children, who in turn had countless children of their own, that their villages grew bigger and bigger and spread into every corner of the Earth – which didn't leave much space for the animals, birds, fish and insects.

And that wasn't all. For the People were very clever – *too* clever, in the view of the other animals – and always inventing things. Some of their inventions were simply useful, but others were exceedingly dangerous to the creatures that shared the Earth with them. Worst of all were their hunting weapons: bows and arrows, knives, blowguns, spears and hooks. With these, the People could easily kill and eat any creature that they wanted. Of course, they only targeted the bigger species; but that didn't mean that the smaller ones were safe from them. For even beings such as frogs, worms and flies met with horrible deaths – swatted, crushed or trampled – sometimes by accident, but more often out of sheer contempt.

After a while, all the non-human creatures realised they had to put a stop to this. There was no way they would let the People take over the whole world, no way they'd allow themselves to be wiped out completely. So each species called a council of its members and discussed how to control the People for their common safety.

The Bear Council was held in the Mulberry Place under the mountain, presided over by their Chief, old White Bear. He asked each of the others to state their complaints against the People. These came thick and fast:

'They've killed so many of my friends.'

'They butcher them, they eat them!'

'They cut off their beautiful fur and humiliate them by lying on it.'

After a while, Chief White Bear called for silence. 'There is no doubt,' he said, 'that the People must be controlled or even destroyed. I propose that we go to war against them at once. Does anyone disagree?'

Nobody did.

'Then that is decided,' said Chief White Bear. 'Now, how should we conduct this war? Who has a suggestion?'

At once a great chorus of voices shouted: 'Beat the People at their own game!'

'Yes! Attack them with the same weapons that they use against us!'

'But they have so many different weapons,' said Chief White Bear. 'It would take too long to learn how to make and use them all. Which type is best?'

A chorus of voices replied:

'Bows and arrows!'

'Yes, especially as they use our own innards, *Bear* guts, for the bow strings…'

'Which insults us as well as killing us.'

'Decision made,' said Chief White Bear. 'Now, who will gather locust wood and work it to fashion a bow?'

'I will,' cried a volunteer.

'And is there anyone here who will sacrifice himself, so that his guts may be turned into the bowstring?'

'Me,' called another. 'I sacrifice myself willingly for the common good.'

So the wood was fetched, the noble Bear was sacrificed and the bow was made and fitted with arrows. However, when one of the Bears tried to draw back the bow to let the first arrow fly, his long claws caught in the string and completely spoiled the shot.

'Trim his claws,' one of the spectators called.

This was done, and the next arrow flew straight out to land on its target. The other Bears all cheered and agreed to trim their own claws, so that they could join the fight with bows of their own. However, Chief White Bear held up his great forepaw and ordered them to stop.

'Are you all fools?' he roared. 'We need our long claws to climb trees. If we can't do that, we will be unable to find food and we'll all starve. We might just as well be killed quickly by the People rather than die slowly of hunger. We should trust in our own bodies, and accept that the People's weapons are not intended for us.'

All the Bears saw the wisdom of his words. Unfortunately, none of them could come up with a better plan. So, with many sighs of regret, the council broke up and all the Bears scattered away into the forest.

Meanwhile, the Deer were attending their own council, which had been convened by their Chief, Little Deer. They made more practical progress than the Bears, for they all agreed to punish the People's hunters by afflicting them with the aches and pains of rheumatism. However, this was not as effective as one might expect, for they were merciful enough to give the hunters a get-out. Not only did they send messengers to warn them about the punishment, but they also offered them the chance to avoid it – by only killing Deer when they were in desperate need, and always asking for forgiveness when they did.

In another spot, the Reptiles and Fish held a joint council, and came up with a cunning plan of their own. They resolved to haunt the People with dreams – as violent as the acts they committed against other living creatures. In some of these dreams, the snakes would appear, twining about them in slimy folds and blowing foul breath into their faces. In others, the victims were force-fed with rotten fish. Those People who suffered such dreams were condemned to lose their appetites so completely that they quickly starved to death.

However, it was the smallest creatures – birds, rodents, amphibians and bugs – that devised the most effective form of revenge. Their council was presided over by Chief Grubworm, who opened it by calling for an initial debate to confirm the People's guilt.

One after another, those present stood up to express their grievances against the People. They spoke of being kicked about for fun; of being snared then strung up on a spit over the fire and slowly roasted to death; and many more equally gruesome deeds. Only one spoke in defence of the enemy, and that was Ground Squirrel. 'I've never been attacked by any Person,' he said, 'so I have no wish to hurt them.' But his dissenting voice was angrily crushed by the others, who attacked Ground Squirrel so viciously that his back still bears stripes from their scratches.

Then a vote was held, which unanimously confirmed the People's guilt. They were condemned to suffer and die – just as they made all other beings suffer and die.

The council quickly got to work thinking up the most horrible diseases and ailments. All the illnesses and afflictions that affect people in the world today were invented and named at that time, by those worms and bugs, toads, rats, hummingbirds and other small creatures at their revenge council. With every new one, Chief Grubworm shouted, 'Thanks – excellent, wonderful! That'll kill even more of those evil People!' He couldn't stop quivering and dancing with joy. He grew so excited, that he ended up falling over backwards – and couldn't get on his feet again. So he was forced to move by wriggling along on his back, just as grubworms have done ever since.

Finally, the council ran out of ideas for more new diseases. And that's just as well, as otherwise no human beings would have survived to tell this story.

But that's not the only reason that plenty of us People are still around now. It's also thanks to all the plants. For at that time, they could think, speak and act too. And despite all the changes that had come about in the world, nothing had persuaded them to end their time-honoured friendship with the People.

When they heard about all the evil that the animals, birds, fish, reptiles and bugs had brought, they were shocked and disapproving. In fact, every growing thing – the trees, shrubs, herbs and flowers, even the grasses, mosses and lichens – all agreed that they wanted to save the People and defeat their non-human enemies. So each plant devised a cure for some of the diseases that the creatures had invented; and promised always to be there for the People in their time of need.

That's how medicine came into the world. Every plant has its health-giving use, though we don't yet know them all. Every plant has the potential to counteract the evil wrought by the vengeful animals, and to cure their victims. Even what we think of as weeds surely contain some good healing. One day we'll have discovered them all.

Mooney: *Myths of the Cherokee*, 1902
For information on the original narrator(s) of this myth, see p. 133.

The story includes several asides to explain how events in it affected Cherokee hunting practices. Of the Bears it says:

> 'Had the result of [their] council been otherwise, we should now be at war with the Bears, but as it is, the hunter does not even ask the Bear's pardon when he kills one.'

And of the Deer:

> 'Now, whenever the hunter shoots a Deer, the Little Deer, who is swift as the wind and cannot be wounded, runs quickly up to the spot and, bending over the bloodstains, asks the spirit of the Deer if it has heard the prayer of the hunter for pardon. If the reply be 'Yes,' all is well, and the Little Deer goes on his way; but if the reply be 'No,' he follows on the trail of the hunter, guided by the drops of blood on the ground, until he arrives at his cabin in the settlement... The Little Deer enters invisibly and strikes the hunter with rheumatism, so that he becomes at once a helpless cripple. No hunter who has regard for his health ever fails to ask pardon of the Deer for killing it, although some hunters who have not learned the prayer may try to turn aside the Little Deer from his pursuit by building a fire behind them in the trail.'

The Grubworm appears to be the larva of an unidentified beetle.

According to 19th century ethnologists, healing medicine played an important role in traditional Cherokee society. Of the medicinal potential of plants, the original narrator concludes:

> 'When the doctor does not know what medicine to use for a sick man, the spirit of the plant tells him.'

BEARS SINGING

Cherokee

A hunter in the woods one day heard singing in a cave. He came
near and peeped in, and it was a mother Bear singing to her cubs,
telling them what to do when the hunters came after them.

The mother Bear said to the cubs:

'When you hear the hunters coming down the creek, then –

Upstream, upstream, you must go,
Upstream, upstream, you must go.

But if you hear them coming up the creek, children, then –

Downstream, downstream you must go,
Downstream, downstream you must go.'

Another hunter out in the woods one day thought he heard a
woman singing to a baby. He followed the sound until he came to a
cave under the bushes. Inside was a mother Bear rocking her cub
in her paws and singing to it this song, which the people of the
Ani'tsa'guhi clan used to know before they were turned into Bears:

Let me carry you on my back,
Let me carry you on my back.
On the sunny side go to sleep, go to sleep,
On the sunny side go to sleep, go to sleep.

– Unnamed informant
(Quoted in Mooney: *Myths of the Cherokee*, 1902)

Moki Courtship
painted in Hopi Pueblo
by Henry F. Farny, before 1916

MYTHS OFTHE SOUTHWEST

PEOPLE OF
THE SOUTHWEST

United States:
Arizona and New Mexico.
Small parts of California, Colorado, Texas and Utah.
Extending into a large area of northern **Mexico**.

The area of the United States known as the Southwest is a land of huge, dramatic landscapes. Mountains, flat-topped mesas and strange, weather-carved rock formations rise above deserts and sweeping stretches of scrubland, crossed by two major rivers, the Colorado and Rio Grande. It is mostly very arid; a little rain falls mainly during a short period of the summer, and some higher areas have winter snow. Vegetation is sparse; depending on altitude and local climate, it varies from conifers to desert cacti, sagebrush and yucca. Wild animals include black bear, bobcat, coyote, various types of deer and rabbit, bighorn sheep, fox, mountain lion and wolf. There are numerous birds, snakes, lizards and other reptiles.

This terrain gave rise to various coexisting cultures which interacted through both trade and aggressive encounters. They had different patterns of settlement, housing and social organisation; yet all sourced food in similar ways.

One dominant culture was that of the pueblos – small towns comprising rows of permanent, multi-storey housing blocks. A favoured location was on a mesa top, which made the town difficult for enemies and other outsiders to access. They were constructed of adobe or stone, with ceilings and roofs formed from beams covered with poles, brush and mud. The different levels were connected by ladders. Each comprised a number of separate apartments, typically built around a central courtyard. Pueblos such as Acoma, Hopi, Isleta and Zuni were originally built hundreds of years before the first White settlers arrived and are still occupied today.

Other peoples, including the Apache, Navajo, Papago and Pima, lived along rivers in the desert lowlands. They used temporary housing, the structure and location of which varied according to the season. Apache wickiups were dome-shaped huts built of wood and covered in brush, overlaid with hides in winter for weatherproofing. Navajo hogans also had a wooden framework; during the summer they were covered in brush and were partly open to the elements for coolness; but in winter they were commonly clad in mud for warmth. In areas bordering on the Great Plains, some peoples used tipis. Seating and bedding comprised brush and grass spread with blankets.

Farming was practised by most Southwestern cultures, though some spent more time on it than others. The main crops were variously beans, corn, melons, squash, sunflowers, tobacco, sugar cane and cotton. In many areas there were sophisticated systems of irrigation canals, first constructed in ancient times. Some peoples, particularly the pueblo dwellers, had well-tended and irrigated permanent fields. Others were semi-nomadic and practised shifting agriculture, often by rivers, moving around from season to season. Raising turkeys, which are indigenous to North America, was a long-established tradition in some pueblos. Since European livestock was introduced by Spanish settlers in the 16th century, the herding of cattle, sheep, goats, horses and donkeys had become widespread. This was supplemented by the hunting of antelope, deer, rabbit and many other kinds of large and small game, in some areas including buffalo. Many types of wild plants were also gathered, including fruits, nuts, seeds, roots, leaves, berries, cacti, and agave crowns and shoots.

Women held a prominent role in many Southwest societies. It was common, though not universal, for descent and inheritance to pass down through the female line, for a husband to live with his wife's extended family, and for the children to belong to their mother's clan. In such circumstances, a woman and her birth family owned the house, livestock and rights to their grazing areas. Women had both political and leadership roles amongst some peoples.

In the pueblos, social life was egalitarian and non-individualistic, based on the extended family and group consensus. Town residents worked together and shared their produce. Each town was autonomous, with its own chief or chiefs; in some cases the office was split between those who presided over community activities, and those in charge of war. Non-pueblo peoples lived in small bands of extended family groups, each with its own male leader. Trade was an important activity, linking individual pueblos and other regional peoples over wide networks.

Religion was important to Southwest life. The land itself was considered sacred; colours and the cardinal directions held particular spiritual significance.

In the pueblos, the community leader was also the religious leader. Ceremonies were held to maintain harmony with nature, and to induce good weather conditions, particularly rain. They took place in underground chambers called kivas; most towns had several. In ritual, 'kachinas' – spirits of the natural world and revered ancestors – were represented by elaborately masked and costumed male dancers. They were often complemented by 'sacred clowns' who used humour and mockery to remind the audience of correct ethical behaviour.

Outside the pueblos, the Navajo used religious rites particularly to repel evil and heal illness. Sand or 'dry' paintings depicting the myths were created as temporary altars, and corn pollen was used as an offering. Sacred chants and prayers were recited during long ceremonies, which might last up to nine days.

High quality craftwork was created by both women and men, for example fine pottery and baskets decorated with exquisite geometric designs; and woven fabrics in both wool and cotton. Turquoise work was an ancient regional specialism; from the late 19th century this was combined with silversmithing, a skill imported from Mexico.

LIFE IN THE SOUTHWEST
WHEN THESE STORIES WERE COLLECTED

Contact with White culture had begun in the 16th century with the arrival of Spanish colonists, who introduced horses and other domestic livestock. There was mass conversion to Roman Catholicism, but with mixed success, since some peoples also maintained their ancestral religious traditions. During the 19th century, the states of Arizona and New Mexico were both transferred from the governance of Mexico to the United States. Reservations were established to isolate the Native Americans within areas of their traditional homelands. At the same time, attempts were made – with limited success – to destroy traditional methods of subsistence and compel assimilation with the settlers, for example by forcibly sending Native children to distant schools. Epidemics of diseases such as smallpox and influenza decimated certain tribes. In the 1880s the building of railroads ended the cultural isolation of the pueblos and brought large numbers of new settlers; in the same decade the last Apache rebel guerrillas were defeated. Native American farmers adapted to White agricultural technology, whilst some people became waged workers for White employers. The craft goods that they had previously made for their own use – woven textiles and baskets, pottery, painting and jewellery – now also sold amongst the settlers, bringing new sources of income.

STORYTELLING IN THE SOUTHWEST

In the late 19th century, traditional storytelling was still very much alive amongst some Southwest peoples, and ethnologists were able to collect a large number of sacred myths, and also more mundane folk tales.

Writing in 1897, Washington Matthews gives the following interesting information about the Navajo men who revealed their ancient stories to him:

'[They] were…popular shamans or medicine-men, who had numerous engagements to conduct ceremonies during the winter months, and it was [also] only during the winter months that they permitted themselves to tell the tales. It was usually with difficulty that arrangements were made with one of these shamans to devote a period of two or three weeks to the service of the author. Then, too, they had farms and stock which demanded their care.'

Of the stories themselves, he explained that there were no set formats:

'The legends of the Navajos have many variants. No two men will tell the same tale exactly alike, and each storyteller will probably maintain that his own version is the only reliable one... Notwithstanding these varieties, the tale tellers agree substantially in the more important matters... The narrators sometimes acknowledged that they had forgotten episodes which others had remembered and detailed... The tales were told in fluent Navajo, easy of comprehension, and of such literary perfection as to hold the hearer's attention... The original was often embellished with pantomime and vocal modulation which expressed more than the mere words.'

In contrast, other peoples of the region had already been persuaded to downgrade their narrative heritage to mere relics of a bygone, inferior age. In 1907, the *Journal of American Folk-Lore* published a collection of short recounts of ancient tales written by Pima and Papago children attending the Industrial School at Tucson, Arizona. Many of these were also recorded in other, more formal collections made by ethnologists. The children's versions, which were printed without any editing, seem to be fairly accurate, though greatly abridged. However, the comments by some of the youngsters themselves show how the US education system had devalued their heritage. For example, a seventh grade (adolescent) boy called Johnson Azul wrote:

'These legends are no longer believed, as the Indians are coming out of their superstition into a better knowledge.'

This was echoed in the comments of J. William Lloyd, who published a long collection of Pima myths at around the same time. He wrote in his introduction:

'As these Indians are all Christianised now, and mostly zealous in the faith, I could get no traditions on Sunday. And indeed, when part way through, this zeal came near balking me altogether. A movement started to stop the recovery of these old heathen tales; the sub-chief had a word with [his informant], who became suddenly too busy to go on with his narrations.'

It was only financial offerings and the intervention of the Indian Agent that enabled him to complete his compilation.

THE PEOPLES BEHIND THE STORIES

Acoma Pueblo (Haak'u)
Situated near Albuquerque in New Mexico, and originally established around AD 1200, this is said to be the oldest continuously inhabited community in North America. It stands on top of a 122-metre high (400-foot) mesa. Today it is known as 'Sky City' and still contains over 250 traditional-style dwellings. Many Acoma people regularly return to their ancestral homes there for special cultural occasions.

Apache
The traditional homelands of the various Apache peoples are spread across the mountains and deserts of Arizona, southern Colorado, New Mexico and western Texas, down into northern Mexico. They were mainly semi-nomadic hunters and gatherers, and obtained further food and goods by raiding White settlers and other Southwest peoples on horseback. To avoid retaliation, they retreated to small communities in the mountains and canyons, but suffered their final defeat in 1880. Today the Jicarilla Apache reservation is in New Mexico. Most White Mountain Apache people live on their reservation in Arizona.

Hopi Pueblo
Twelve Hopi villages dating from ancient times stand on three mesas in northeastern Arizona. Their name is a short form of Hopituh Shi-nu-mu ('The Peaceful People' or 'Peaceful Little Ones'), and traditional ethics emphasise the importance of behaving in a peaceable and civilised way. Traditional Hopi culture, language and religion continue to thrive today.

Isleta Pueblo (Tuel)
Situated in the Rio Grande Valley near Albuquerque in New Mexico and established in the 1300s, this was a centre for Tiwa-speaking peoples of the area. Its name comes from the Spanish for 'Little Island'. In the 19th century it was a prosperous farming community at the centre of a wide trading network.

Navajo (Dine)

The Navajo are a sub-group of the Apache tribes. Traditionally they were semi-nomadic herders, farmers, raiders and weavers. During World War II, Navajo 'Code Talkers' used their mother tongue to develop a secret code that helped the US to defeat its Japanese enemy. Today they are the second largest Native American group in the United States, both in terms of population and the size of their reservation, which extends across Arizona, New Mexico and Utah. The Navajo language is still widely spoken.

Pima (Akimel O'odham – 'River People')

The Pima homeland is in Arizona, where they have long lived on the banks of the Gila and Salt Rivers. Today many live in the Gila River Indian Community, still using their ancient irrigation systems. Traditionally they were farmers, hunters, gatherers and traders, and also expert textile and basket weavers. They are closely connected to the Papago (Tohono O'odham – 'Desert People').

Zuni Pueblo (Shewena)

Archaeologists believe that Zuni ancestors may have begun farming in their current location, in western New Mexico, at least 3,000 years ago; and that in the 14th century there were twelve Zuni pueblos, some containing up to 1,400 apartments. Their home was traditionally called 'the Middle Anthill of the World'. Today they occupy just a single Pueblo.

Also researched for this section were stories from the following Southwest peoples: Cochiti Pueblo, Laguna Pueblo, Papago, Tewa, Yuma (Quechan) and Zia Pueblo.

EMERGENCE: THE FOUR WORLDS

Navajo

*I know the White men say the world is round, and that it floats in the air.
My tale says the world is flat, and that there are five worlds, one above another.
You will not believe my tale, then, and perhaps you do not want to hear it...
I shall tell you all that I heard from the old men who taught me,
as well as I can now remember. Why should I lie to you?...
I always tell the truth. I hold my word tight to my breast.*

They say that down in the First World there lived twelve kinds of winged people. They were Dark Ants, Red Ants, Dragonflies, Yellow Beetles, Hard Beetles, Stone Carrier Beetles, Black Beetles, Dung Beetles, Bats, White-Faced Beetles, Locusts and White Locusts. The houses of these winged people all stood along the banks of three great rivers, which flowed from a central spring. By day, when white light dawned in the east and blue light shone in the south, these winged people moved around busily. But when yellow light in the west signalled the coming of evening, they became slower; and as soon as blackness came from the north, they lay down and slept.

Unfortunately, the winged people didn't behave well; they were always quarrelling. Also, they were wildly promiscuous, with husbands and wives constantly unfaithful to each other. Sometimes they tried to mend their ways, but they couldn't control themselves.

The First World was surrounded by four oceans, each of which was ruled by a sacred chief. These chiefs summoned the winged people to a council and told them: 'We are outraged by your disgusting behaviour. You are all banished from this world. Get out, go away!'

The winged people ignored them. They continued to sleep around wantonly, and their arguments grew louder and even more violent.

The chiefs repeated their banishment order every four nights, four times over, but it didn't have any effect. Finally, the Chief of the Eastern Ocean said, 'If you continue to disobey us, we will make it impossible for you to stay in this world any longer; we will *force* you to leave.'

Four mornings later, the winged people awoke to see water coming at them from all directions. The oceans were rising fast, swallowing up all the land. If they wanted to avoid death by drowning, they had no choice but to flee.

In this way, the winged people became the Exiles.

They all spread their wings, spiralled round, then flew up to the sky. Looking down, they saw that, far below, the First World was now completely flooded; there was nothing but water wherever they looked. And above them, the sky seemed to be impenetrable. How could they possibly escape?

As they fluttered up there in despair, they suddenly saw a stranger thrusting his blue head from the sky. 'Here,' he called, 'come to the east. There's a hole there that you can easily squeeze through.'

They followed his directions, and thus passed up to the Second World.

The First World had been red; but this place, the Second World, was entirely blue. It was arid and barren, scattered with rough, lumpy houses. These were the homes of the blue-headed Swallow people. The Swallows crowded round and stared at the Exiles, but didn't say a word.

The Exiles were desperate to find somewhere good to settle, and to meet other people like themselves. So they despatched a Locust and a White Locust to explore. First they flew east, then they flew south, then west, then north. When they finally returned, they brought the following gloomy tidings: 'We have flown in every direction, as far as it was possible to go. But each time we found only bare, flat, dry ground, surrounded by great cliffs above a bottomless abyss.'

Shortly afterwards, the Swallows came to visit them again. 'Where have you been flying and why?' they asked.

'To view the land and seek out people like us,' the Locust and the White Locust answered.

'And what did you find?'

'No living plant and no living creature in any direction,' they answered.

'Ah,' said the Swallows, 'you should have asked us: we could have told you that and saved you the trouble. We are the only beings who live here.'

The Exiles consulted each other. Then one spoke up as follows: 'You speak the same language as we do. Like us, you have bodies, legs, feet, heads and wings. Let us become friends.'

'Let us indeed,' agreed the Swallows.

So the Exiles and the Swallow People mingled together and treated each other like kin. They addressed each other in the warmest terms, as 'my sister', 'my father' and so on. In this way, they lived very pleasantly and in great happiness for twenty-three days. However, on the twenty-fourth night, everything changed. For one of the Exile men went back to his old sins: he lured one of the Swallow Chiefs' wives aside and tried to seduce her. Her husband was outraged.

'How could you do this?' he cried. 'We gave you a wonderful welcome – but with this insult you've just flung it back in our faces. When you arrived and sought sanctuary with us, we did not pry into your affairs or ask why you were banished from the First World below. Now we can guess the reason: it was surely a punishment for your immorality down there. Well, now we realise the truth, we too banish you. Go from here, get out!'

The Exiles flew up to the sky in shame, as high and fast as they could. This sky too was smooth, hard and tightly sealed; but again a stranger came to their aid. This time it was the White Wind who poked his face through at them, calling, 'Fly to the south. Look up there for the slit in the sky and pass through.'

They did as he suggested, and in this way entered the Third World.

Everything here was yellow. Just as last time, the Exiles sent out a Locust and a White Locust to explore each of the four directions. Just as last time, they returned to report that, no matter which way they travelled, there was nothing but barren wasteland. The only inhabitants they had spotted, far in the distance, were the Grasshopper People, who lived in holes in the banks of a great river.

The Grasshoppers had seen them too. Now they came and spoke with the Exiles very amicably. Here too, the two groups befriended each other, mingling and embracing, treating each other as kin. But it was no use. Just as last time, on the twenty-fourth day of their stay there, one of the Exile men tried to molest the wife of one of the Grasshopper chiefs.

'What a way to treat us, after our hospitality,' the chief raged. 'No doubt you behaved in a similarly depraved way in each of the two worlds below, and that is why you came up to us. Well, we shall expel you just as the chiefs below must already have done. Do not dare to drink our water or breathe our air any more – begone!'

So once more the Exiles had to fly up to yet another impenetrable sky, which they circled beneath in despair – until suddenly the voice of the Red Wind called to them: 'If you wish to pass through here, fly west.' They did, and found the passage that the Red Wind had made, twisting around like the tendrils of a vine. They circled up through it and thus made their way to the Fourth World.

Four of the Grasshopper People came with them, a white, a blue, a yellow and a black one. That's why there are grasshoppers of these colours today.

The Fourth World had no colour; it contained only the pure black of night and the pure white of day. The Exiles could not see any sign of life. The only visible features were four great, snow-capped mountains on the horizons in each direction.

Again, they sent out a Locust and a White Locust to explore. When they flew east, south and west they found nothing. However, this time they returned from the north with exciting news:

'Dear friends, this world, the Fourth World, is the largest of all, and also the best. We have met strange people here, marvellous people – human beings! They live in houses in the ground. Also in the ground, they grow plants for food. When we came upon them, they were busy gathering in their harvest. They called us over straight away and treated us most agreeably. They even shared their food with us.'

These were the Pueblo People. The next day, they came to visit the Exiles, with gifts of corn and pumpkins. 'We would like to be your friends,' they said.

The Exiles were so happy to meet them, that they all agreed amongst themselves to permanently mend their ways. Thus they settled down beside the Pueblo People in the Fourth World.

Time went by. The seasons turned.

Late in the autumn, a voice was heard in the distance, calling very softly, four times. It drew closer, growing louder. Then, out of nothing, four mysterious beings – four gods – appeared. Each was a different colour: White Body, Blue Body, Yellow Body, and Black Body. They tried to speak to the Exiles; but instead of using words, they gestured in signs. They seemed to be giving instructions, but the Exiles could not understand them at all. Then the four gods vanished, leaving the Exiles to puzzle over what they had meant.

The same thing happened on a second and a third day. On the fourth day, after the gods had made their mysterious signs, only three of them vanished, leaving Black Body behind. This time he spoke, in the Exiles' own language.

'My friends,' he said, 'I see you do not understand our sacred signs, so I shall tell you what they mean. We wish you to make people in the same form as us – in human form. Your bodies are similar to ours, but your teeth, your feet and your claws are not human; they belong to animals and insects. We wish the new creatures to resemble us gods in every way.'

The Exiles nodded.

Black Body went on, 'Do not think you can accomplish this in your present state. For you are dirty and foul-smelling. We will return in twelve days; make sure you have cleansed yourselves thoroughly by then.'

With that, he vanished.

Time passed. On the morning of the twelfth day, the Exiles washed themselves well. The women dried themselves with yellow cornmeal, and the men with white cornmeal. No sooner had they finished, than they heard shouting in the distance, four times over; and after the final call, the gods again appeared. Blue Body and Black Body were each carrying a buckskin. White Body was carrying two fine ears of corn, one yellow and one white.

The gods laid one of the buckskins on the ground. They placed both ears of corn on it; and under each one an eagle feather in the same colour. They covered all this with the other buckskin, so that the tips of the feathers could just be seen.

'Stand at a distance!' cried the gods. 'Let the winds come in!'

At once two winds blew up: the White Wind from the east and the Yellow Wind from the west. At the same time, eight Mirage People appeared and circled the buckskins four times. The feather-tips began to twitch. When the Mirage People had finished their walk, the gods carefully lifted the upper buckskin.

Underneath it, the white ear of corn had turned into a male human being – First Man. The yellow ear of corn had turned into a female human being – First Woman.

It was wind that gave life to them. Today too, it is wind that comes from our mouths and gives *us* life. When it ceases to blow, we die. In the skin at the tips of our fingers we can still see the wind's trail, showing where it blew so long ago, when the First People were created.

The gods turned to the Exiles and ordered them to build a hut of brushwood. When it was finished, they said to First Man and First Woman: 'Arise! Enter your new home. Live together as husband and wife.'

This they did, and four days later, First Woman gave birth to twins, the first children. She birthed another set of twins every four days, until five sets had been born in total. The first set were both hermaphrodites and barren. The other four sets each comprised a girl and a boy. Within four days, they had grown into adults, and each sister married her brother.

Four days after the last birth, the gods took First Man and First Woman away to the eastern mountains, where they instructed them in secret for four days. After that, they instructed their children in the same way.

When they returned from the mountains, the four sisters ended their marriages to their four brothers, and each took a husband or wife from the Mirage People. Many more children were born to these couples. They spent only four days in the womb, grew to maturity within another four days, married and had further children of their own, all on the four-day cycle.

They built great farms, irrigated by dams and ditches. The hermaphrodite twins watched over them, and invented wicker water bottles and pottery.

Eventually, some of First Man and First Woman's great-grandchildren married Pueblo People. Others married amongst the Exiles who had emerged from the worlds below into the Fourth World – our world – where we, their descendants, still live today.

Matthews: *Navaho Legends*, 1897
The original narrator of this myth was an elderly priest called Torlino, who introduced it to Matthews with the words quoted at the beginning, then proceeded to recite it with 'literary perfection' in the Navajo language, which was then translated. Torlino knew a little of White culture from his son, whom he had sent away to school.

This story forms part of a longer origin myth which, Matthews says, is the property of the whole tribe:

'Several versions…complete or partial, were recorded. The one here published was selected as being the most complete, extensive, and consistent of all. Other versions often supplement it. The narrators sometimes acknowledged that they had forgotten episodes which others had remembered and detailed.'

Although Torlino mentions five worlds in his introduction, only four appear in the actual story; perhaps the fifth world refers to the sky. In the source book, the myth continues at some length. Key episodes describe the temporary separation of men and women; a great flood caused by the divine trickster, Coyote, who also introduces the phenomenon of death; the making of the sun and moon; and the origin of monsters.

It is not clear which two species the Locust and White Locust characters refer to: there is only one recorded variety of American locust, which became extinct in the late 19th century. The source gives no further information about the 'Mirage People', who are also briefly mentioned in the Apache myth, THE SUN'S HORSES (p. 182).

Parallel myths of emergence from an underworld were recorded from Acoma Pueblo, the Jicarilla Apache, the Mohave Apache and the Hopi.

THE THREE GODDESSES CREATE PEOPLE

Hopi Pueblo

Aliksai!

Long, long ago, the whole world was nothing but water, a boundless ocean. At that time there were four divine beings: three goddesses and the Sun.

Two of the goddesses were Hard Treasure Women – guardians of shells, corals, turquoise and beads. Their underground kivas were at either end of the ocean, one at the east and the other at the west. The other goddess was Spider Woman, who lived in the southwest.

As for the Sun, he was always on the move. Every morning he rose from Eastern Hard Treasure Woman's kiva, dressed in a grey fox skin that hung from her ladder, and displayed the white light of early dawn. Later, he changed into a yellow fox skin, brightened things up with the yellow dawn, and began his journey across the sky. At the day's end, he reached Western Hard Treasure Woman's kiva, and shook the rattle on her ladder to announce his arrival. Then he went down into her house, passed through it to a doorway in the far end, and continued his course underwater. By next morning, he was ready to rise again in the east.

One morning the two Hard Treasure Women got together and set to work, making a great stretch of dry land appear in the middle of the boundless water. This was the Earth.

The next day, as the Sun travelled across the Sky, he gazed down and saw the Earth. When he arrived at the kiva of Western Hard Treasure Woman that evening he said, 'I really like this Earth you've made, it's beautiful. But it's a shame that nothing lives on it.'

Western Hard Treasure Woman agreed and asked the Sun to take a message to her sister, inviting her to come and discuss this matter. As soon as she received it, Eastern Hard Treasure Woman made a rainbow and hurried over it to the western side of the ocean.

'Sister,' she said, 'I'm here! What kind of creatures should we make to live on Earth?'

Eastern Hard Treasure Woman had already given it some thought and said, 'Let's start with a little bird.'

She reached all the way down to the land far, far below and scooped up a handful of clay. She shaped this into a Wren and covered it with a piece of cloth.

'How shall we bring it alive?'

'With a song.'

The two goddesses sang sweetly. After a while, the cloth twitched and Eastern Hard Treasure Woman gently lifted it. Out hopped Wren, fully alive.

'What do you want of me?' Wren asked.

Eastern Hard Treasure Woman said, 'We wish you to fly in every direction, all over the Earth below, and see if you can spot any other living beings.'

'Surely if such beings existed,' said Wren, 'the Sun would already know. He travels over the Earth every day.'

'That's true,' said Western Hard Treasure Woman, 'but he only ever passes directly from east to west, over the middle of the land. If there are any beings in the north or the south, he wouldn't see them.'

So Wren flew all over the Earth, in this direction and that, north, east, south and west, looking around carefully wherever he went. When at last he returned, he said, 'I couldn't see anyone anywhere.'

He hadn't noticed Spider Woman's kiva in the southwest, for its entrance was very carefully concealed.

Western Hard Treasure Woman thanked Wren. Then she set to work making more clay birds, of many different sizes, shapes and colours. She placed them all under the cloth, and again, the two goddesses sang until the cloth began to move, then pulled it away. This time, it revealed countless living birds of every species.

'What do you want of us?' they all cried.

'We wish you to inhabit the Earth,' the Hard Treasure Women said. 'Go and fill it with song.'

'But we don't know how to sing,' the birds protested.

'Don't worry,' the goddesses replied. 'We'll teach you.'

The two goddesses spent a long time teaching each kind of bird its own unique tunes. When at last they had all mastered them, the birds scattered across the world.

Western Hard Treasure Woman set to work again, this time shaping the clay into all different kinds of animal, which she brought to life in exactly the same way. Between them, the goddesses taught each species how to speak with its own noises, and how to behave. Then they sent the animals out to live in their own parts of the world.

'Hmm,' said Western Hard Treasure Woman. 'What shall we do now?'

'I think it's time to create People,' Eastern Hard Treasure Woman replied.

'What are they?' her sister asked.

'Let me show you.' Eastern Hard Treasure Woman took some more clay. She shaped some into a woman and the rest into a man, then brought both to life in the same manner as the other creatures before them.

'What do you want of us?' these People asked.

This time, after the goddesses had given their usual answer – 'We wish you to inhabit the Earth' – they added: 'We wish you to have great understanding too.'

'How?' the People asked.

Eastern Hard Treasure Woman took some more clay. This time she shaped it into two tablets, took a wooden stick and used it to paint patterns of lines on them. The newly created woman and man gazed at them in bewilderment.

'Why are you showing us these meaningless squiggles?' they asked.

Eastern Hard Treasure Woman seized the woman's hands and rubbed the palms with her own. She did the same thing with the man's hands.

'Now look at the tablets again.'

This time, the People's eyes lit up with interest. They saw that the lines represented spoken words; and even better, they understood exactly what they meant. They were the first White People, and it was the Hard Treasure Women who taught them to read and write.

The Goddesses sent these White People down to Earth to make a home for themselves. They travelled around for a while until they found a place they liked, then built themselves a house there.

Meanwhile, over in the southwest, Spider Woman saw what the other two goddesses had been up to. She decided to create some People too.

So she made a clay man and a clay woman, brought them to life with song, and taught them to read and write, just as the Hard Treasure Women had done. They were another kind of White People, the first Spaniards. Spider Woman made donkeys for them, and sent them away to settle down. They were very clever and quickly learned to make themselves metal tools and guns.

After this, there was no stopping Spider Woman. She created more and more human beings, giving a different language to each pair. She worked so hard at this, for such a long time, that she got into a muddle. She made a man but forgot to create a woman to go with him; and a while later, she made a woman, but forgot to make an accompanying man.

She said to this single woman. 'Go down to Earth and find the single man I made earlier. See if he'll accept you, so you can settle down together.'

So the single woman went searching around the world, and it wasn't long before she found the single man. They got together, and the man built a house for them to live in. But after a while, they began to argue.

'Oh, go away!' the woman shouted. 'I'd far rather live by myself!'

'But who'll get wood for you?' the man protested. 'Who'll work the fields? You need me. It's much better to stay as a couple.'

So they made up, but only for a bit; before long they argued again. They separated for a while, came together again, separated again, and so on. From this stupid pair, other couples learned to quarrel too; that's why there are so many squabbles today between husbands and wives – it was Spider Woman's fault.

The Hard Treasure Women didn't approve of Spider Woman's creations. So they made some more People of their own, better People – always married couples.

Unfortunately, there was often conflict between these two groups of people. The Hard Treasure Women were so offended by this that they both retreated to their secret kivas, vowing never to return to Earth.

The Spaniards sent two of their men to hunt the two goddesses down, using their great skill and cunning. After a long journey the two men finally arrived at the kiva of Eastern Hard Treasure Woman, brandishing their guns.

She guessed at once why they had come; but she was not afraid. She came calmly out of her kiva and said, 'Welcome! I know you've come to kill me; but first let me show you something marvellous.'

They were struck with awe standing before her. Eastern Hard Treasure Woman brought a glowing white stone from her kiva, and laid it before their feet.

'What's that?' the Spaniards asked.

'Lay down your weapons, then lift this up,' she answered. 'You'll soon understand.'

One of the men put down his gun, reached forward, placed his hands underneath the stone and tried to heave it from the ground. But it was far too heavy; he could not make it budge at all. Cursing, he tried to pull his hands away…and discovered they were stuck fast to the stone.

'Help me!' he growled at his companion.

The other man put down his own gun and tried to assist. But his hands also stuck fast to the strange white stone. So now neither man could move; they were Eastern Hard Treasure Woman's prisoners.

She smiled and picked up their guns. 'Look,' she said, 'these are worthless.' She rubbed them between her hands – and at once the guns crumbled away to dust.

'Now,' she said, 'listen to me. You People who Spider Woman made believe that you alone know everything. But the People that my sister and I made also know many things. Some of this knowledge is shared between you all; but each group also knows many things that the others don't know. It's pointless fighting over it; you should share your knowledge instead, and learn from each other. If your People possess or know something good, exchange it with the others for some of their own unique good things. Learn to live in peace with everyone else. If you wish me to release you, promise to do as I say.'

The two Spaniards were humbled.

'We swear to follow your teachings,' said one.

'And we won't ever again try to kill you, Goddess,' said the other.

Eastern Hard Treasure Woman went back into her kiva and worked her power on the white stone. At once, the two men were released. They left her quickly and quietly.

She did not fully trust them. However, after that the Spaniards always left the Hard Treasure Women in peace.

Voth: *Traditions of the Hopi*, 1905

Little information is given about the narrator of this myth, except the name, Qoyawaima. He or she lived in the Hopi village of Oraibi (Orayvi) in Arizona and was clearly a prolific storyteller, having also given 23 other narratives to Voth's collection, including THE COYOTE GIRL (p. 205). Oraibi was first built some time before the year AD 1100, and had around 900 inhabitants in 1890. An introductory note says that the stories 'were collected in the vernacular and without an interpreter' in the two years leading up to publication; apparently Voth was fluent in the Hopi language. The exclamation at the beginning of the story seems to have been the Hopi storytellers' standard opening word.

In the Hopi text, both creator-goddesses are given the same name, 'Huruing Wuhti', and are distinguished only by the different locations of their homes. Voth says in a footnote:

'The nearest literal translation that can be given of this name, which appears so frequently in Hopi mythology and ceremonies, is Hard Being Woman, i.e. woman of that which is hard, and the Hopi say she is the owner of such hard objects as shells, corals, turquoise, beads, etc.'

They have similarities with two important Navajo deities, Woman Who Changes and her younger sister White Shell Woman, who are also strongly linked with the Sun.

Spider Woman is a popular character in Southwest stories, although she does not normally play a creative role. Usually she is a supernatural helper who appears when the main protagonist of the story is facing some kind of difficulty. Typically, she invites him or her into her underground home to give advice and practical help, often making use of her ability to spin threads. See THE SUN'S HORSES (p. 182) and THE COYOTE GIRL (p. 205).

An interesting aspect of this myth is its blending of comparatively recent history (the arrival of Europeans in the Southwest from the 16th century) into what is probably a much older sacred narrative. Some passages of the account given by Qoyawaima are rather confusing, perhaps due to the way the Hopi text was translated, and it is not clear why a distinction is made between the Spaniards and other White people.

TOBACCO AND CORN

Pima (Akimel O'odham)

These are stories which I used to hear my father tell,
handed down from father to son.
When I was little I did not pay much attention,
but when I grew older I determined to learn them,
and asked my father to teach me, which he did, and now I know them all.

A powerful shaman had a daughter called Tobacco, who was of the age when most women are already married. However, no man wanted her. This made her very unhappy, so she begged her father to bury her alive, saying: 'All those men who rejected me will soon regret it!'

Reluctantly, her father carried out her request. A tobacco plant grew from the top of her grave. Her father plucked some leaves from it and smoked them. They gave off a pungent scent which drifted around the village.

Shortly after this, Tobacco came back to life. She stepped out of her grave and walked calmly across to her old home.

News of her astonishing revival spread rapidly, far and wide. It reached the ears of a man called Corn, who travelled to her village urgently to court her. However, their meeting did not go well. They talked for a while, then sat down to play a gambling game. Corn was by far the better player, and beat her every time – until he had won everything that Tobacco owned. But she was only willing to hand him a few meagre possessions, things that she didn't really want anyway, and refused to give him any more.

'That's not enough,' said Corn.

'Well, that's all you're getting,' said Tobacco.

'No wonder you're still unmarried,' Corn scorned her. 'You selfish little cheat – you're no use to anyone!'

'No use?' she screamed at him. 'Nobody realises it yet, but it's impossible to live without me!'

'Don't be stupid,' sneered Corn. '*I'm* the one everyone needs, because they eat me, they can't ever get enough of me. Everyone loves corn. But no one wants tobacco, apart from a few crusty old men who don't mind stinking of smoke.'

'You're wrong,' said Tobacco. 'The shamans need me to make rain; and without rain, *you* can't grow, Corn.'

And so the quarrel went on, with neither giving way to the other, until Corn walked out on her.

Tobacco knew she was right; but she also knew that the rest of the villagers didn't appreciate her worth. They were always whispering maliciously about her, laughing behind her back. She became more and more miserable, just as she had been before.

This time, she took matters into her own hands. She made herself sink through the floor of her house, deep, deep down into the ground. She did not emerge until a long time later, and by then she was in a totally different place, far to the west. She walked even further westward, on and on, calling up a strong wind to blow away her tracks, leaving no trace. Eventually, she reached a towering mountain and climbed its sheer cliff to a secret opening. There she made her hideout.

Corn remained in the village, strutting around and enjoying everyone's admiration. However, at planting time, things changed. There had been no rain all summer, so the ground was much too dry and hard to plant any corn seeds.

People began to mutter, and then to complain quite openly:

'The drought only started after Corn drove Tobacco away.'

'Yes, she must have remarkable power, that woman – there was always plenty of rain when she was around.'

'Well, we all know who's fault it is, then.'

They summoned Corn to a council and told him:

'You foolish, wicked man! If you hadn't upset poor Tobacco, she'd still be here and our crops would already be coming up.'

'Get out of here, you troublemaker!'

'But you can't get rid of me,' protested Corn. 'You can't live without me.'

'And now we realise that we can't live without Tobacco either,' they said. 'Go and find where she's hiding. Beg her to come back and bring us rain.'

'Very well,' said Corn, 'if that's what you want, I'll go too. But you'll soon be sorry. Without me around, things will be even harder for you – you'll all starve. And to make sure you do, I'm taking my friend Pumpkin with me. We'll go and find a place where there's plenty of moisture in the land, a place where we can thrive; and we won't give another thought to you lot wilting away here.'

Corn refused any further discussion. He stalked off, called Pumpkin, and soon the two young men were striding away, singing raucously at the tops of their voices.

Back in the village, there was no rain for a whole year. There were no crops, and there was barely enough wild food to keep the people alive. What little water they could find had to be severely rationed.

There was another powerful shaman who lived there, called Geeheesop. He vowed to try and save the situation. He took his Stone of Light and his Square Stone, a clutch of down and some feathers from the tail of an eagle; and with these managed to divine and reach the secret place where Tobacco was now living.

'Tobacco!' he called up to her. 'All your people are suffering for lack of water. Now we realise what an important woman you are – for only you have power to make rain.'

Tobacco didn't answer. Geeheesop went on:

'The ground around our village is full of buried seeds, but they're all being burned up by the endless sun. Tobacco, every seed in the ground is begging for water. Every tree that has not yet died from the long drought is suffering terribly too. Please come back!'

At last Tobacco spoke. But all she said was, 'What about Corn? He's still with you, isn't he?'

'No,' said Geeheesop. 'We sent him away.'

'Well, why don't you bring *him* back?' said Tobacco. 'As he told me himself, everyone loves him and they can't get enough of him. But nobody wants *me*.'

'We all want you!' Geeheesop said. 'We need you desperately. Please, Tobacco, come back at once. Please, please.'

He went on and on, begging and pleading. Tobacco still refused to come with him. But she did yield a little. She came down and put four balls into his hands.

'What are these?' he asked.

'They are pressed together from the seeds of the plant that bears my name.'

'Thank you, Tobacco. And what should I do with them?'

'Take them home. Find some tobacco-worm droppings, and smoke them in a cane tube. That will soon bring the rain that you all long for. After it has moistened the ground, plant these seeds. They will start to grow within four days. When the leaves are ready, pick them, smoke them, and call on the winds. Then many clouds will come, bringing all the rain you need.'

Geeheesop took the seeds and went back to the village, where he did everything Tobacco had advised him. When he smoked the tobacco-worm droppings, a little rain fell, and then he planted the seeds in a secret location. Sure enough, within four days they began to grow. But then they wilted, looking as if they would completely wither away. Hastily, the shaman picked some of the new leaves and smoked them. Almost at once, the wind blew again with another rain shower, this time much heavier, and the plants revived. He repeated this over and over, until the plants had grown lush and tall. Then he picked a big bunch of leaves, put them in his cane-tube pipe, and took it to the place where all the villagers gathered in the evening.

As he approached, he lit his pipe and began to smoke it, blowing out huge puffs. The villagers all came over to see what he was up to. Geeheesop passed the pipe around and they all sampled it. When each had taken a turn, the shaman let it go out, then stuck the pipe in the ground.

The next day Geeheesop came to the same place with a new pipe. As he lit it, the other shaman, Tobacco's father, said, 'Yesterday after I had a smoke, I didn't feel well.'

Some agreed with him, others did not.

At last another man spoke up, saying: 'My friend, I believe it was not the act of smoking tobacco that made you feel bad. I believe it was because of the way we passed the pipe around between us. We did not share it properly as relatives should. As we handed it to the next person, we should have greeted him by name. We should have said, "here you are cousin", "here you are brother", and so on.'

'I believe you are right,' said Tobacco's father. 'In future, that's what we must always do whenever we smoke.'

The next day, Geeheesop showed them where the plants were growing. They gathered the seeds, saved and replanted them. That is why tobacco grows all over the place today.

As for Corn and his friend Pumpkin, they had gone in the opposite direction to Tobacco, far to the east, where they settled down to live for many years. During all that time, despite the new rains, the people were unable to grow either corn or pumpkins. However, eventually Corn and Pumpkin decided to return to the village. They didn't hurry on their journey, but stopped here and there at many of the places they passed through on the way.

One day, they made camp on the slopes of a mountain. While they were resting there, they saw a woman and her brother, a young boy, wandering around the bottom, gathering wild cacti. When they had a good pile of them, the pair built a fire and started to roast the cacti. Corn went down to them.

The boy saw him and called his sister, 'Hey! I'm sure that's Uncle Corn coming towards us!'

'Don't be ridiculous,' the young woman retorted. 'Corn's gone far, far away. That's why we're so hungry all the time and reduced to eating cactus.'

However, she soon realised that the boy was right – for Corn came ambling right up to them and, without a word, sat down near the fire. He stayed there all the time that the cacti were cooking, watching them intently. Every so often, he took an arrow from his quiver, fitted it to his bow and shot it upwards. Each time, the arrow whirled around and fell straight onto the roast. After he had done this many times he said, 'Don't you think it's time you uncovered the corn, to see whether it's cooked yet?'

The woman looked at him in wonder. 'That's not corn,' she said. 'It's just wild cacti.'

'Is it?' said Corn. 'Uncover it anyway.'

So she did – and gasped. For the cacti had been transformed into a neatly baked cake of pumpkin and corn.

'Eat it,' said Corn. 'Enjoy it.'

Ah, how good it tasted after all those years of famine! When they had finished, the young woman turned to Corn and said, 'Uncle, how can we ever thank you?'

'By answering this simple question,' said he. 'Is Tobacco married yet?'

'No,' said the young woman. 'She's come back to the village, but she still lives alone.'

Corn turned to the boy and said, 'I want you to run an errand. Go to Tobacco's father and ask if he and Tobacco would like me to come to them. If the answer is no, I'll keep away. But if they want me, I'll come at once.'

The boy dashed to the village and passed on the message. Tobacco's father said, 'Tell Corn I have nothing against him and that he should certainly come.'

The boy ran back and repeated the answer to Corn.

Corn said, 'Good. Now go back to her father and tell him to build a small roundhouse as quickly as he can. Tell him to take Tobacco into it and wait for me to arrive. Then go right round the village and tell everyone to sweep their houses clean, inside and out, ready to receive me. I'm coming back openly, no more secrets.'

The boy conveyed the new message, and everything was done as Corn had ordered. Soon the whole village was looking spick and span, and Tobacco was installed in a newly built roundhouse. Then Corn came down from the mountains to greet Tobacco – his bride.

The sun was just beginning to sink when he arrived. A black cloud gathered above the roundhouse. It began to rain – not water, but corn, every so often mixed with little pumpkins. This continued right through the night, while Corn and Tobacco celebrated their marriage.

In the morning, the people went out and gathered up all the corn and pumpkins that had fallen, until their storage jars and baskets were full to the brim with food.

Lloyd: *Aw-Aw-Tam Indian Nights*, stories collected 1903
The myth as originally narrated continues rather mysteriously with Tobacco giving birth to a baby – a deformed pumpkin. This is accidentally killed by the village children and eventually transforms into a giant cactus.

Lloyd gives an interesting account of how he obtained this and the other stories in his collection, thanks to a chance encounter with an educated young Pima man called Edward Hubert Wood ('Ed'), who was selling Indian blankets and baskets at the Pan-American Fair in Buffalo in

1901. The two got talking and became friends, later entering into correspondence:

'And so I came to know that one of my Indian friend's dreams was that he should be the means of the preservation of the ancient tales of his people. He had a grand-uncle, Comalk-Hawk-Kih, or Thin Buckskin, who was a…professional traditionalist, who knew all the ancient stories, but who had no successor, and with whose death the stories would disappear.'

Eventually it was arranged for Lloyd to visit the Pima Gila River Reservation in Arizona. There he met up again with Ed, who introduced him to Comalk-Hawk-Kih. Lloyd describes him thus:

'The strong, friendly grasp he gave my hand was all that could be desired. Tall, lean, dignified, with a harsh yet musical voice; keen, intelligent black eyes, and an impressive manner, he was plainly a gentleman and a scholar, even if he could neither read nor write, nor speak a sentence of English.'

Lloyd stayed on the reservation for two months, living exactly as his hosts did. He describes one evening of storytelling:

'Ed sitting on the ground, against the wall, nodding when I wrote and waking up to interpret; the old man bent forward, both hands out, palms upward, or waving in strange eloquent gestures; his lean, wrinkled features drawn and black eyes gleaming; telling the strange tales in a strange tongue… My interpreter was eager and willing, and well-posted in the meaning of English, and was a man of unusual intelligence and poetry of feeling…as far as possible I have kept his words and the Indian idiom and simplicity of style. Sometimes he would give me a sentence so forceful and poetic, and otherwise faultless, that I have joyfully written it down exactly as received… All was grave and serious, as befitted the scriptures of an ancient people.'

Lloyd goes on to say that sometimes another Pima man, Miguel, came in with his flute, which he occasionally played as Lloyd transcribed the stories.

The arid climate of the Southwest stimulated the development of a number of other drought and famine myths. A parallel story from the Pimas' close relatives, the Papago people, blames a prolonged drought on Whirlwind being banished from the neighbourhood, in punishment for blowing up an arrogant young woman's skirt, exposing her to her rejected suitors. Whirlwind takes his close friend Rain with him, and thus no rain falls for four years; finally a bird persuades them to return once the people have called him four times. It concludes that Arizona's dry climate is due to modern people's failure to call Rain very often.

Related stories were also told in some of the Pueblos.

FIVE SACRED THINGS

Zuni Pueblo (Shewena)

Five things alone are necessary for sustenance and comfort:
The Sun who is the father of all,
the Earth who is the mother of People,
the Water who is the grandfather,
the Fire who is the grandmother,
our brothers and sisters…the Seeds of growing things.

Who could live without the Sun father?
For his light brings day,
warms and gladdens the Earth mother with rain,
which flows forth in the Water we drink
and that causes the flesh of the Earth mother
to yield abundant Seeds;
while these – are they not cooked
by the brand of Fire which warms us in winter?'

– Unnamed priest
(Quoted in Cushing: *Zuni Breadstuff*, 1884)

THE BATTLE OF WINTER AND SUMMER

Acoma Pueblo (Haak'u) & Isleta Pueblo (Tuel)

There was a very beautiful young woman called Kochin-ne-nako, daughter of the Chief of Acoma. Many men tried to win her hand, but none of them succeeded.

One day Kochin-ne-nako was filling her water jar at the spring, when she heard footsteps climbing the nearby cliff ladder, then crunching boldly over the sand towards her. She turned and saw a tall, confident young man, very handsome but with a stern expression. His clothes were covered in tiny white crystals that glistened exotically in the sunlight.

'Lady,' he said, 'my name is Winter. I have come to marry you.'

He was so different from all the other men, that this time she did not refuse. Her father, the chief, gave permission and very soon they were living together as husband and wife.

Almost as soon as Winter settled in the town, there was a great change in the weather. The sun all but disappeared and it grew very cold. Sleet and snow fell daily, often in blinding blizzards whipped up by strong winds. The water regularly froze.

The townspeople sat it out, waiting for the weather to turn with the seasons. But it never did. The storms cleared just enough for them to plant their crops, but the corn only grew to half its usual height and failed to ripen. So they were forced to abandon farming and go out into the desert to gather wild cactus fruits and pads. That was the only food they could find, and it was barely enough to survive.

Kochin-ne-nako greatly regretted her marriage. Her husband's manner was as chilly as the temperatures around him. Her only solace was that he went out each morning to the far north and never returned until early evening. She took advantage of his daily absences by going out to forage alone.

One morning she had to wander an exceptionally long distance before she could find any cacti worth gathering. She picked a big pile of the fleshy pads, lit a fire and carefully singed off all the spines. As she rested for a while, nibbling her harvest hungrily, she suddenly noticed a movement from the corner of her eye. She looked up and saw a man of similar age to her husband striding eagerly towards her.

However, whereas Winter always looked grim and wore heavy grey clothes, this young man had a broad smile and was dressed in the colours of the cornfield. His shirt was woven from yellow corn silk. His leggings were bright green, like the moss that grows round a watering place. His hat and belt were both fashioned from broad green leaf-blades, decorated with corn tassels. His moccasins were beautifully ornamented with butterflies and flowers.

'Good morning,' he greeted her. 'Why is such a fine lady reduced to eating wild cactus?'

'That's all the food we have where I come from,' she answered sadly. 'We've been plagued by endless bad weather for the past year, and our crops just wither away in the fields.'

The man reached into his shirt and pulled out a fat, ripe ear of corn, which he thrust into her hands.

'Here,' he said, 'treat yourself to this. And wait – I'll go and fetch some more.'

Before she could ask any questions, he was sprinting away towards the south, and within moments had melted into the horizon. Was he real – or merely a vision brought on by hunger? She chewed on the corn in bewilderment, relishing the sweet juices...

Before she had even half finished it, the man came running back, his arms weighed down by a whole bundle of ripe corn. He dropped it at her feet, then turned to go.

'Wait!' she called. 'Tell me who you are.'

'My name is Summer.'

'Where did you find this corn, Summer, when the fields round here are all so barren?'

'I brought it from my home, Kochin-ne-nako, which lies far to the south.'

'How do you know my name?' she said.

Summer grinned broadly, making her glow with a warmth she had long forgotten. 'I know many things about you, Kochin-ne-nako. I know that your father is the chief of your town, and that your husband, Winter, has a heart as cold as his name.'

'Well, Summer,' she said, 'I wish I could see your home, where the corn grows so richly. Will you take me there?'

'And *I* wish I could,' he answered. 'But I mustn't make your husband angry.'

'What do I care if you do?' said Kochin-ne-nako. 'I regret the day I married Winter. He's brought me nothing but misery and hunger.'

Summer looked at her searchingly for a long moment. Finally he said, 'Kochin-ne-nako, you can't come with me. But I promise I'll return here tomorrow and bring you more corn.' With those words, he turned his back on her, walked away and vanished again.

Kochin-ne-nako bent down and picked up the corn. Each ear was very fat, wrapped in glossy green leaves. It took her a long time and much effort to stumble home without dropping any. When she was only halfway there, she heard voices calling her name – and was relieved to see her sisters.

'Where have you been?' they cried. 'What's that you've got? You were out so long, Mother sent us to search for you.'

She told her sisters everything truthfully. They helped her carry the corn. When they reached home, their parents asked exactly the same questions, and received the same explanation.

'So,' said her father, the chief, 'you've met Summer have you? You should bring him here as our guest, so we can all benefit from his kindness and warmth.'

'Winter won't like it if I do,' she said nervously.

'Ach, he's always out in the north all day,' the chief reminded her. 'Let Summer come while he's away.' He turned to his wife. 'My dear, get this corn roasting at once. As soon as it's ready, we'll share it out with everyone, before Winter comes home to cause trouble.'

This was done. By the time Winter returned in the evening, everything seemed just as gloomy as normal.

Early next morning, as soon as her icy husband had departed, Kochin-ne-nako hurried back to the place in the desert where she had met Summer. He was there already, waiting for her with his usual smile and a heap of corn at his feet. He had brought even more than the previous day, far too much for Kochin-ne-nako to carry. But that did not matter, for this time Summer accompanied her all the way to town. There she took him to her family house, where the chief gave him a hearty welcome. Summer sat down with his hosts, shared their meal and awaited the coming of his rival.

As the sun set and the sky darkened, they heard heavy footsteps. The air grew chill and damp; a bitter wind blew up. Winter came stomping into town, growling loudly and spitting out sleet. As he approached the chief's house, he stopped and sniffed the air.

'Who's there?' he bellowed. 'Father-in-law, what brute have you accepted as your guest? Ach, you don't need to tell me – I'd know the stink of my arch-enemy anywhere. Summer, it's you, isn't it? Get your hands off my wife!'

Summer leaped from his seat, threw Kochin-ne-nako a quick smile, climbed hastily up the ladder to the apartment roof, and jumped down to the street. Winter was advancing towards him, surrounded by a blizzard. Summer strode to meet him, breathing out a mild breeze. As they drew close, the icicles and rime that always covered Winter began turning to water and melting away.

All the townspeople crept out of their houses to watch. For the first time, they saw Winter as he truly was: not a shimmering frost-warrior, but a thin, snivelling thug, shivering in a ragged undergarment of wind-bleached rushes.

'I'm ready to fight you, Winter,' Summer greeted him. 'If you win, you can keep your wife. But if I beat you, Kochin-ne-nako will be mine.'

'All right,' growled Winter. 'I can't refuse you. But I need time to prepare – and so, I guess, do you.'

'Of course,' said Summer. 'Meet me here again in four days' time.'

And so it was agreed. The two men parted and went their separate ways: Summer to the warm, lush green meadows of the south; Winter to the icy blasts of the north.

In the south, desperate to win Kochin-ne-nako and save her people, Summer got busy. He begged help from all the animals and birds of the summer lands – even the insects. He appointed Bat to be his advance guard, for his skin was tough enough to withstand his enemy's storms. He sent an Eagle messenger westwards, summoning his old friend, Hot Shale Rock, to build an enormous fire. When it was blazing, they piled thin black stones in it to heat and billow out choking clouds of smoke.

By the fourth day, everything was ready. Summer rode out on Hot Shale Rock's smoke-cloud, flanked by all the southern animals. The cloud covered them in soot – which is why, today, these animals are all either brown or black. Winter came to meet him in a tempest of darkness and snow, with all the white-frosted animals of the north in his wake. The two parties met in the centre of town with a flash of lightening.

Winter blew up a great gale and hurled freezing rain and snow at his opponent, smothering all the houses in thick drifts. Summer, from his smoke-cloud, gusted back with a whirlwind of heat, melting the snow into warm rain. Winter stirred up his tempest again into a hissing, blinding sheet of hail. Summer's fire-powered breath quickly thawed it, softened it, bathed it in mildness and warmth.

Both were strong; neither could totally vanquish the other.

In the end, it was Winter who called a truce. 'No more!' he roared. 'We are equals and so it must always be. Let us split the year between us, half the months to you and the other half to me.'

'Agreed,' said Summer quietly. 'But there is still one more thing to settle. Which of us should get the woman?'

'Ach,' snarled Winter, 'she and her family are too soft for me. You have her.'

And so it was that Kochin-ne-nako divorced Winter and married Summer instead, with whom she found great happiness. And so it was too that the seasons came into the world.

Lummis: *The Man Who Married the Moon*, 1894
Pradt: *Shakok and Miochin*, 1902
Gunn: *Shat-Chen Traditions and Narratives of the Queres Indians*, 1917
Judging by the number of different outsiders who collected this myth, it seems to have been well known in the pueblos.

Although the story is based in Acoma Pueblo, the only collector who gives any information on his original source is Lummis – who actually heard it in Isleta Pueblo. Lummis lived amongst the Pueblo people of New Mexico for some years. He paints a vivid picture of a storytelling session he witnessed in the late 19th century:

'The room is long and low, and overhead are dark, round rafters... The walls are white as snow... built of cut sods, plastered over and whitewashed. The floor is of adobe clay, packed almost as hard as a rock, and upon it are bright-hued blankets, woven in strange figures. Along the walls are benches, with wool mattresses rolled up and laid upon them. By and by these will be spread upon the floor for beds, but just now they serve as cushioned seats. Over in a corner are earthen jars of water, with little gourd dippers floating, and here and there upon the wall hang bows and arrows in sheaths of the tawny hide of the mountain lion; woven belts of red and green, and heavy necklaces of silver and coral, with charms of turquoise... There is a fireplace, too, and we are gathered all about it, a dozen or more... A hearth of clay rises a few inches from the floor; a yard above it hangs the chimney, like a big white hood; and a little wall, four feet high, runs from it out into the room, that the wind from the outer door may not blow the ashes... Three or four gnarled cedar sticks, standing on one end, crackle loudly.

'Some of us are seated on benches, and upon the floor. His back against the wall, squats my host...a withered, wrinkled old man... He must be a century old. His children, grandchildren, great-grandchildren, and great-great-grandchildren are all represented here tonight. His black eyes are like a hawk's, under their heavy brows, and his voice is musical and deep. I have never heard a more eloquent storyteller... I can tell you the words, but not the impressive tones, the animation of eye and accent, the eloquent gestures of this venerable Indian... His father and his father's father, and so on back for countless centuries, have handed down these stories by telling, from generation to generation, just as Tata Lorenso is telling his great-great-grandsons tonight...

'Lorenso is ready with his story. He pauses only to make a cigarette ... pats the head of the chubby boy at his knee, and begins...'

This seems to be the only major story of the seasons in the Southwest. It is interesting to compare it with the Northeast myth, SUMMER AND HER GRANDMOTHER RAIN (p. 586).

THE SUN'S HORSES

White Mountain Apache

Old Man Water's daughter lived by herself. One day, she was sitting in her open doorway watching the rising Sun. Its blood-red rays came streaming straight towards her so strongly, that it was impossible to dodge them. Before she knew what was happening, they had entered her. In this way, she became pregnant.

When her son was born, it was obvious that he was no ordinary child. He looked very strange; to tell the truth, he was grotesque. His hands and feet were webbed like a duck's. He had no hair on his head at all. Strangest of all, he had neither ears nor a nose.

The grotesque boy grew up very quickly, unnaturally fast. He seemed to be a deep thinker, for he was always asking awkward questions. One day he said to his mother, 'Why haven't I ever met my father? Who is he?'

'I'm afraid you'll never be able to meet him,' his mother answered, 'because your father is the Sun.'

'Why should that stop me?' said the boy. 'If he's too busy to come to me, I'll pay him a visit. Where does he live?'

'In the Sky, at the sunrise place,' said his mother.

'I'll go there at once,' said the grotesque boy.

'Don't be stupid,' said his mother. 'It's further away than you can imagine, and the trail there is blocked by insurmountable obstacles. My son, you'd never manage to cross it.'

But the grotesque boy said stubbornly, 'Nothing can stop me visiting my own father.' And he set out on his quest at once.

He walked a long, long, long way. Eventually, he found his path blocked by a vast row of cliffs that stretched as far as the eye could see on either side. Every so often there came a sharp creaking noise, as the cliffs rose briefly off the ground, exposing a low gap at the bottom, then quickly crashed down again. 'Ach!' the boy groaned, 'I'll never be able to dart under that gap without being crushed. I might as well give up.' However, as he stood there in despair, a storm broke in the distance, and a great bolt of lightning came streaking towards him. Before the grotesque boy knew what was happening, the lightning had shot him like an arrow, straight through the gap.

Once he had recovered from this shock, he continued to walk on, until he met a new obstacle: a towering thicket of cacti, stretching to the horizon on either side. 'Ach, how can I get past *this*?' he cried. As if in answer, a whirlwind arose, swept him up and twisted him right through it.

On the far side, he went on – only to be overwhelmed by a humming swarm of mosquitoes. 'This is the worst thing yet,' he wept. 'How can I escape?' The next moment, heavy rain began to fall. It soaked the mosquitoes' wings until they all collapsed into a silent, motionless heap.

He easily waded through them, and walked still further, to a wide range of mountains. They kept splitting apart to reveal a valley in their midst, before quickly closing in again. Each time the valley appeared, the boy tried to dart through it, but always without success. He sat down and buried his head in his hands. At that moment, a small, dark, stripy creature came wriggling towards him. It was the caterpillar, Black Loopworm. 'Hey, friend, climb on my back,' he called. So the boy did, and Black Loopworm carried him safely through…

Right into the Sky World!

Here the going was much easier. A house gleamed brightly ahead in the distance. 'That must be where my father lives!' the boy thought excitedly. And as he drew closer, beyond the house, at last he caught a glimpse of the Sun himself in all his dazzling glory, riding high in the sky. The grotesque boy stopped to stare in awe.

When he tried to continue on his way, he tripped heavily and fell. He jumped back to his feet and took another step, but tripped again. Examining the ground, he soon discovered the cause: a spider's thread, almost invisible, was stretched right across his path.

'Grandson,' called a friendly, voice, 'where are you going?'

At first the boy couldn't see who the voice belonged too. Then he noticed a tiny, dark-grey head projecting out of an equally tiny hole in the ground. Spider Woman!

'Oh, Grandmother,' he answered politely, 'I'm on my way to visit the house of my father, the Sun.'

'Poor child,' said Spider Woman. 'You'd do better to come into *my* house instead.'

'How can I, Grandmother?' said the grotesque boy. 'I'm far too big to squeeze through your little door.'

'Try it,' said Spider Woman.

The boy did. To his surprise, he managed to slip down into her house very easily. Inside, he found that she already had company: a big crowd of Spider Girls was gathered around the fire. They were lying on the floor in a circle, end to end – and they were all completely naked.

'Stop staring at them,' Spider Woman scolded. 'Take off your shirt and give it to me.'

He did as she told him. Spider Woman took the shirt and pulled it apart, until its threads were all unravelled. All through the night, she wove them back together, and sewed the new cloth into beautiful tunics and skirts for each of her girls. She shook them awake, and as the Spider Girls dressed, rays of morning light came seeping in; the Sun was beginning to rise.

The grotesque boy stood up, eager to go. But Spider Woman said, 'It's too early to visit your father. You must wait through the day until he starts to sink towards the horizon.'

At last it was time. Spider Woman led the boy to the Sun's house, and left him there. But how could he get in? The house had twelve doors, but each was tightly shut. He was about to try opening one of them – when he realised he was already inside! A big, bright woman was standing before him, looking at him curiously.

'You!' she said to the boy. 'What kind of person are you? Why are you here?'

'I'm the Sun's son,' he answered boldly. 'I've come to see my father.'

'Hmm,' said the woman. 'Let me tell you, the Sun is my husband, and he doesn't allow anyone apart from me to enter his house. How did you find your way in here?'

'I don't know.'

'Well, since you've arrived, I'd better hide you.'

She fetched a blanket woven from soft filaments of cloud, beckoned the grotesque boy to lie down on it, rolled the blanket around him and tied it securely with a cord of lightning. Then she hid him in a narrow place by the head of the bed.

Soon after that, it got dark. There was a great commotion of stamping and cursing – and then the Sun himself strode in.

'Wife,' he roared, 'what's going on? As I was setting this evening, I saw a youth making his way here. Where is he? You're keeping something from me. You're hiding him, aren't you?'

Sun's wife looked at him grimly. 'Husband,' she said, 'you're a liar. You've been lying to me for a long time. All the years we've been together, you've sworn that you've never been unfaithful, never had an affair with anyone. Now I know the truth about what you really get up to during your daily journey. That youth you spotted, he arrived here this morning – claiming to be your son!'

The Sun flushed deeply. He didn't deny it. All he said was, 'Hmmph. You'd better show him to me.'

So Sun's wife went to the bed, untied the lightning cords and helped the grotesque boy out of the cloud blanket. 'Well, husband,' she snapped, 'what do you say?'

'I admit the truth,' said the Sun. 'It was just a brief encounter, but I think I probably did indeed father this young man. Hmm. Just to be sure, I'd better test him.' He turned to the grotesque boy. 'Come over here.'

The boy went to him.

'Do you like to smoke?'

The boy had never tried, but naturally, he nodded. The Sun showed him his twelve pipes, then filled each one with tobacco. This was not ordinary tobacco, but the deadly poisonous kind. He gave one of the pipes to the boy and ordered him to smoke it.

The boy took a single draw on it. At once, all the tobacco vanished. The Sun nodded and gave him a second pipe. This time the boy drew on it twice. Again he wasn't harmed, but all the tobacco burned out. The Sun filled a third pipe, a bigger one. The boy had to draw on this one three times, after which all the tobacco was consumed. The Sun gave him a fourth pipe, even bigger than the others, crammed to the top with the noxious leaves. The boy didn't flinch, but calmly drew on it four times. Again, the tobacco was entirely finished, and the poison had no effect on him at all.

'Don't think that's all you need do to prove yourself,' growled the Sun. He seized the boy and hurled him with great force eastwards – into a blazing, black fire. The grotesque boy did not burn up, but transformed into a downy feather. He floated up with the smoke, spiralled back to his father, and resumed his human shape.

'So you think you're as strong as me, do you?' the Sun yelled.

He grabbed the boy again and this time flung him southwards, into a fire that was blazing blue. Again, the boy turned into a feather and returned to the Sun's feet. So the Sun threw him westwards into a yellow fire, and finally northwards into a fire made entirely from white lightning. The boy survived these tests too.

The Sun made no comment, but called to his wife: 'Prepare a sweat-bath for my son.'

Sun's wife carefully spread out four cloud blankets: black, blue, yellow and white, one in each direction. That was the sweat-bath. The Sun led the way into it, and the grotesque boy followed him.

'Now,' said the Sun, 'it's time to meet your brothers.' He gave a loud shout – and the next moment, eleven other boys came crowding in with them.

While the grotesque boy was in the sweat-bath, wonderful things happened to him. The webbed skin between all his fingers and toes fell off. A nose grew in the centre of his face, and ears appeared, one on each side of his head. His hair, eyebrows and eyelashes all grew, as did nails on the ends of his fingers and toes.

When they emerged, the Sun made all the youngsters stand in a straight line.

'Wife,' he said, 'which is my new son, the one who just arrived?'

'I swear I don't know,' she said. 'Now he's been in the sweat-bath he doesn't look strange any more, he's just like all the others.'

The Sun was satisfied. He took his new son aside, and showed him a shelf containing two very different weapons: a metal gun, and a bow and arrows.

'Which one do you want?' he asked. 'You may take whichever you choose to shoot this target.'

The boy examined the gun and shuddered. Then he examined the bow and quiver and smiled. He picked them up and shot two arrows. Both hit the target, right in the centre.

Then the Sun called the other boys to bring their own weapons and shoot at each other in fun. The others all had guns. They easily beat the boy with his arrows, and drove him off.

The boy didn't care. He wandered away and soon found himself in a valley between two mountains. In the side of each was a great cave. The slopes of one mountain were brown and arid. The boy peered into its cave, and saw that it was full of White men's things: metal tools and guns, with herds of cattle, goats, sheep, pigs, mules, donkeys and horses wandering around them. The slopes of the other mountain were very beautiful, smothered in yellow flowers. When the boy peered into *that* cave, he saw sunflowers, cactus, agave, yucca, pinyon, oaks and juniper. There were also many kinds of wild roots and leaves, all ripe and ready to pick.

The Sun had come out after him. Now he asked, 'Which mountain do you prefer, my son?'

'The yellow one,' the boy answered at once. 'It's full of good things to feed my people.'

'Then all the plants growing in it will continue to belong to your people in the future,' said the Sun. 'The guns and livestock in the brown mountain will be for the Whites.'

The Sun went into the brown mountain and waved his arms to drive out all the animals. The boy watched listlessly...until suddenly, right at the end, the horses emerged. Their bodies flowed like music; their manes and tails drifted in the wind. The boy's eyes opened wide and he cried, 'Father, I wish I could have some of those!'

'I gave you a choice,' said the Sun. 'It's too late to change your mind.'

He snapped his fingers. A crowd of Mirage People came running from the east. The boy blinked...and they vanished. So did the horses, leaving only a cloud of red dust behind.

'I want some horses,' the boy repeated.

'The horses have gone,' said the Sun.

'Even so, I beg you to give me some.'

'Why didn't you choose the horse mountain while you had the chance?' snarled the Sun.

'Please, please,' begged the boy for a fourth time, 'let me have some horses.'

This time, the Sun took up a rope and strode away. A few moments later he returned, leading a magnificent chestnut stallion. He called the boy over and helped him onto its back. At once the boy knew how to handle the horse, how to ride. He thanked his father, then rode the stallion at a gallop, all the way back to his mother's house, completing the long journey in a single day. Once he arrived, he set the stallion to graze; but it refused, nickering and pawing the earth. So he rode it straight back to the Sun's house and set it free.

'What are you doing back here after such a short time?' the Sun demanded.

'That horse you gave me was no good. I need a better one.'

The Sun stared at him. 'Not one, but two, no doubt.' He strode off and returned with another stallion, and also a mare.

'I suppose I should have given you these two in the first place.,' he said. 'Here, you'll need this equipment as well.' He handed the boy a rope, a halter, a saddle blanket and a saddle.

The boy offered his thanks again. He led the two horses away to the place that marks the very centre of the Earth. There he laid the rope, halter, saddle blanket and saddle under four different cottonwood trees, one in each direction, then sent the two horses away to graze. However, when he checked on them, they were not feeding; instead they were gambolling and playing. After four days, he drove them up a valley; and after another four days, he went back to see how they were getting on. At first, he couldn't see them anywhere; but the ground was marked with many sets of small hoof-prints, the size that is made by young foals.

They led back to the centre of the Earth. And there the boy saw a magnificent herd of the Sun's own beautiful horses, walking with their young beside them.

They were the first horses that came into the world.

Goddard: *Myths and Tales from the White Mountain Apache*, 1919
This was one of eleven stories narrated in 1910 by a sixty-year-old man, who 'was still a growing youth when he left the White River country'. His name is not given, but he is identified as 'the father of Frank Crocket', who translated the texts from White Mountain Apache dialect to English. The same source gives another, slightly different and more complex version of the same myth from a different informant.

The first horses arrived in the Southwest with the Spaniards in the early 16th century, transforming local peoples' lives with dramatically increased mobility for hunting, trading and raiding. As with THE THREE GODDESSES CREATE PEOPLE (p. 162), this relatively recent history has been blended into what seems to be a much more ancient story. Elsewhere, in a Hopi creation myth, horses are said to be a transformation of scales falling from the body of a woman who is bathing. There are also a few minor horse myths from other regions, particularly the Great Plains, where horses were intrinsic to the culture of buffalo hunting and warfare.

The obstacles and challenges that the boy has to overcome are typical of numerous Native American myths and folk tales right across the continent.

SONG OF THE HORSE

Navajo (Dine)

How joyous his neigh!
La, the Turquoise Horse of the Sun.

How joyous his neigh!
There on precious hides outspread he stands.

How joyous his neigh!
There on tips of fair fresh flowers he feeds.

How joyous his neigh!
There of mingled holy waters he drinks.

How joyous his neigh!
There he spurns dust of glittering grains.

How joyous his neigh!
There he is hidden in sacred pollen mist.

How joyous his neigh!
There his many offspring grow and thrive for ever.

How joyous his neigh!

– Unnamed singer, Arizona
(Quoted in Curtis: *The Indians Book*, 1907)

DOCTOR MOUSE

Isleta Pueblo (Tuel)

In the first days, after the People had broken through the crust of the Earth; after they had emerged from the Underworld and crossed the great Black Lake of Tears to reach our own land... At that time, the animals were created by the Trues, the invisible spirits who rule everything.

When they had finished, they called Coyote and ordered him to carry a mysterious heavy bag to the Peak of White Clouds. 'Come what may,' they commanded him, '*do not open this bag until you arrive.*'

But Coyote disobeyed them. Long before he reached his destination, he untied the cords that held the bag shut, and peered inside. At once, a mass of dazzling stars exploded in his face! They spun round and round, then flew up to the Sky, scattering in all directions.

The Trues punished Coyote by afflicting him with excruciating toothache. No matter what he did, he couldn't get rid of it. That's what set Coyote off howling: '*Owowow-wooooh!*' That's what caused him to embark on a life of restless wandering.

The other animals sympathised. But when they tried to help, not only did they fail, but the malady spread into all *their* mouths too. Soon almost every animal in the world was suffering with a swollen face and unbearable pain.

However, there was one who did not suffer, for he kept apart from the rest. This was Mouse. He lived alone in a secret nest, well hidden beneath a thick, spreading chaparral bush; and he always kept to his own private underground tunnels.

As he travelled along them, Mouse often found interesting roots, which he took back to his nest, building up a huge collection. He liked to experiment by grinding them up, mixing them together and adding other ingredients. In this way, he developed extraordinary knowledge and skills, inspired by the sacred powers of the Trues.

After the terrible toothache epidemic had raged for some time, Mountain Lion, chief of all the four-footed animals, called a council to discuss it. All those who were well enough staggered along to it. Even Coyote attended. He was afflicted worse than anyone, but he forced himself to come out of guilt and duty; for in his heart he knew that his disobedience to the Trues was ultimately to blame for the sickness.

Mountain Lion asked all the animals, one by one, if they could suggest a cure for the terrible suffering. No one could... Until it came to Prairie Dog's turn.

He pointed at Mouse, who was crouching diffidently in an ill-lit corner close to the door. 'Ask *him*,' said Prairie Dog. 'Don't be misled by his apparent insignificance. He has secret powers.'

All eyes at once turned to Mouse.

'What kind of powers?' said Mountain Lion.

Prairie Dog said excitedly, 'I'd heard that Mouse keeps certain roots with healing properties, so when my toothache got so bad that my mouth seemed to be on fire, I burrowed down to consult him. I persuaded him to try one of his potions on me – and I got better straight away!'

'Mouse,' Mountain Lion called. 'Step out and show us what you can do.'

Mouse scurried forward, carrying his little pouch. He opened it, took out some flat leaves and laid them neatly on the ground. On top of them he poured a small heap of thick ointment.

'What's this?' asked Mountain Lion.

'A mixture of pulverised sweet root and fat,' said Mouse. 'This is what cured Prairie Dog.'

'Then demonstrate what it can do on another sufferer here, Mouse. Who will volunteer?'

'*Owowow-wooooh!*' howled Coyote.

Mouse beckoned him to step forward. He staggered across weakly, panting and jittering with pain. Mouse told him to lie down, then carefully and gently pressed a leaf of root-paste against Coyote's cheek. As the others watched, Coyote gradually seemed to relax. Then he let out a long sigh and jumped to his feet with a joyful yip: 'It's stopped hurting!'

Everyone clapped. Mountain Lion held up his great paw for silence.

'Extraordinary!' he roared. 'We have all just seen that Mouse is the father of a marvellous new power, the power of medicine. Because of this, he is surely sacred. We must call him 'Doctor', and make a new law to protect him. From this time and for ever, it is forbidden for anyone to kill him, or even harm him. And no one may touch any of Doctor Mouse's kin either, be they alive or dead.'

All the four-footed animals agreed.

However, there were no birds or snakes at that council. That is why, to this very day, they do not respect mice but often kill and eat them.

'Now, Doctor Mouse,' said Mountain Lion, 'it would benefit us all if you would share your knowledge and skills with as many other animals as possible.'

'Of course,' said Mouse.

So an elder of each species went to stay with Mouse for a while, learning how to use his medicinal roots to heal illness, injury and pain. Once their training was complete, they all returned to their own kind, and used their new skills on anyone who needed them. However, in the case of really serious illness, they always deferred to Doctor Mouse, bringing him gifts of cornmeal and requesting his help. His cures were always successful.

Despite this, one of the animals that Doctor Mouse had trained was sceptical. Although Badger had sat beside all the others, listening to Doctor Mouse's lessons and watching his demonstrations, he did not really believe that Mouse was as wise as everyone thought.

After the training was finished, Badger went home and said to his wife, 'I reckon that Mouse is a fraud.'

'He cured Coyote, didn't he?' said Badger Woman. 'You saw with your own eyes.'

'Hmm. But that Coyote's such a trickster, he might have faked the whole thing. I'm going to test Mouse, play a trick on him myself. I'll only believe in him if he sees through it.'

So Badger went on a long fast. He didn't eat a single morsel for four whole days; and he didn't drink either, not one drop. Of course, this made him very ill: too weak to stand up, scarcely able to speak. On the fifth day, he groaned hoarsely to his wife, 'Go and fetch this so-called "Doctor" Mouse and tell him I'm dying. He'll pretend to cure me, and I'll pretend that he can't. That will easily expose him.'

Badger Woman prepared a gift of cornmeal, hurried over to Mouse and pleaded with him to visit her sick husband. Mouse came immediately, carrying his pouch of roots. However, once he had looked carefully at Badger, he didn't even bother opening the pouch. Instead, he sang the following song:

'*Old Man Badger,*
Silly old fool!
Trying to deny
That Mouse has power,
Four days starved himself.
Needs no medicine –
Just a good meal!'

Then he said, 'Get up, Badger, go and eat something. Don't ever dare waste my time like this again.'

As soon as he had left, Badger did indeed get up. 'Well, well,' he said grudgingly, 'he really is a clever fellow.'

His wife cooked him a huge meal, and by the time he had finished it, Badger was bursting with his usual energy. He invited all the other animals round to hear about his experience. As a result, they all respected Doctor Mouse even more.

Many years later, some People caught Doctor Mouse, imprisoned him and took him before their elders.

'We've heard rumours about you, small one,' they said. 'Is it true you can cure the sick?'

'It is,' said Mouse.

'Then teach us your power.'

'Why should I?'

'If you do, we'll set you free; but if you refuse, we'll kill you.'

Mouse had no choice but to agree. They brought him to their town and treated him as an honoured guest. He went into their kiva with the elders and stayed there with them for twelve days and nights. By the time they emerged, the elders had acquired Mouse's knowledge of all the healing plants, and perfected the skills to use them.

After that, they called up a strong guard to take Doctor Mouse back to his own house under the chaparral bush. Just as the animals had made a law to protect Mouse, now the People did too. They gave him full liberty to enjoy their fields and everything that grew in them.

To this day, all True Believers honour Doctor Mouse and sing of him in sacred places. For he was the father of medicine, and taught us how to cure the sick.

Lummis: *Pueblo Indian Folk-Stories,* 1910

For information about the original narrator, see notes to THE BATTLE OF WINTER AND SUMMER, p. 176.

The chaparral bush where Mouse has his home is probably *Larrea tridentata*, an aromatic desert shrub found throughout the Southwest, growing up to six metres high. In ancient times, Native peoples used it to treat various illnesses; and modern herbalists still claim it can heal swelling and infections in a variety of conditions.

A footnote to Lummis's text says that the cure that Mouse uses on Coyote's toothache,

> 'is still practised... The sovereign remedy for toothache, however, is to go to the kiva after dark, carrying food in the left hand, march round inside the big circular room three times, leave the food under the secret recess in the wall where the scalps taken in old wars are kept, and then come out. The toothache is always left behind.'

Another Isleta story says that people almost won their ongoing war against mice – until the mice secretly crept in and disarmed some sleeping human warriors by gnawing their weapons. Since then, it has been impossible to rid local homes of mice.

THE YOUTH AND HIS EAGLE

Zuni Pueblo (Shewena)

In the days of the ancients, there lived a youth who had a pet female Eagle. He kept her in a cage on the roof of the lower terrace of his family house.

The youth loved his Eagle dearly and could not bear to be separated from her. He spent all his time caring for her: winter and summer, morning, noon and night, he was constantly feeding and petting her. Because of this, he neglected all his duties in the cornfield and melon garden.

Naturally, his brothers and other male kin despised his idleness, and constantly criticised him for not earning his keep. Every evening, as they returned home wearily after a long day of labour in the fields, they would pass the Eagle cage. Eventually, one of the uncles said: 'I'm fed up with scolding this useless, work-shy boy. How can we force him to stop wasting all his time?'

'Let's kill the wretched bird,' said another. '*That* will cure his infatuation.'

All agreed this was an excellent plan. They resolved to carry out the killing in the next few days, then passed on into the house.

It had not occurred to any of them that the Eagle would understand what they were saying; but she did. She brooded on it long and hard. When the youth next brought her food, she turned her back and lowered her head on her breast in gloomy silence.

'Are you ill?' the youth cried in alarm.

To his astonishment, the Eagle answered him in human speech, saying, 'I'm not ill, just too upset to eat.'

'What's the matter? Have I neglected you?'

195

'Of course not,' said the Eagle. 'It's just that today I heard your kinsmen plotting to kill me.'

The youth looked at her in horror. 'My beloved Eagle,' he cried, 'I swear I won't let them. I'll guard you every moment of the day and night, I'll…'

'Don't worry,' said the Eagle, 'I can protect myself very easily. If those villains dare open my cage, I'll simply fly away and escape to my other home in the Sky. But I'll have to leave you behind – and I can't bear the thought of never seeing you again.'

The youth began to weep. 'I can't bear it either,' he cried. 'Let me join you!'

'My beloved friend,' said the Eagle, 'how can you? You can't fly. You don't know the long trail through the high skies and into the world above.'

'Please, please,' begged the youth, falling to his knees. 'There must be a way to overcome those obstacles. I can't live without you!'

'Ah,' said the Eagle, 'I wish with all my heart that you could come with me. But even if you managed the journey, things would not go well after we arrived. For you could not stomach our food: unlike you People, who ripen everything with fire to make it edible, we live on raw meat alone.'

'But if you leave me behind, I won't be able to eat anyway,' the youth said. 'I'd rather starve by your side, than stay here and waste away with a broken heart.'

The Eagle shook her head. Again the youth begged her. Again the Eagle refused him. However, when the youth implored her a fourth time, she finally gave in.

'Very well,' she sighed, 'so be it, we will try. Go home for the last time and prepare a large pack of food. It will need to last you a long time if I succeed in taking you up to the Sky. If we arrive safely and your food eventually runs out, we'll have to find another solution. I'll be waiting for you tomorrow morning.'

The youth bid his friend goodnight, and slunk into his house. Before his family returned from their day's work, he secretly prepared and hid a large bag of food, then went to bed.

The next morning, as soon as his family had all gone to the fields, he jumped out of bed, ate a quick breakfast, slung the food pack over his shoulders and ran to the Eagle's cage. She was ready for him. He opened the wicket. She stepped out of the cage, crouched on the ground and spread her wings.

'Climb on my back,' she said. 'Grasp the base of my wings, and rest your feet above my thighs. Are you ready? Then let us begin our journey.'

Saying this, the Eagle slowly rose above the town, whistling:

'Huli-i-i Huli-i-i
Pa shish lakwa-a-a
U-u-u-u
U-u-u-u-a!'

The family working below heard her call and cried, 'Look! That Eagle is carrying away our lazy boy!'

The news quickly spread, until the whole town was gazing up at the youth, riding the Eagle high in the sky. There was nothing anyone could do to bring him back; in truth, maybe nobody really wanted to. Gradually, the song died away in the distance and the Eagle grew smaller, soaring upwards until she was a mere speck that finally vanished.

She flew on with the youth. At last, at the zenith of the Sky, they reached an opening. The Eagle rose easily through it and emerged, on the far side, into the Sky World. Here she flew still further, to a wondrous place where everything glowed bright blue.

'Huhua!' said the Eagle wearily. 'At last we can rest for a while. Welcome to my world.'

The youth got down and went to stand by her side, looking around in awe.

'This is the Turquoise Mountain,' she said. 'When your People look up from the Earth below, it's what makes the sky appear blue.'

She raised her wings until the tips touched above her, lowered her head, caught hold of her crown, shook it from side to side and pulled at it. As the youth watched in wonder, her suit of feathers fell away – to reveal a beautiful young woman, with eyes so dark, deep and unearthly that he blushed before their gaze.

'You have always loved me so well,' she smiled, reaching out her hand. 'Come, let me take you to meet my people.'

They walked slowly down the mountain together. Soon they saw ahead a dazzling city of gleaming white walls, tainted by neither ladders nor smoke. Eagle Woman donned her feather-suit again, told the youth to mount her and carried him to the city. They hovered above it for a few moments, so he could appreciate its full glory. Then she swooped down, swept grandly through one of its wide roof-doorways and came to rest on the floor.

At once, a great crowd of other Eagle people stepped forward to welcome them. 'Sit,' they cried, 'rest.'

The Youth took a seat beside Eagle Woman and looked around. The great room into which they had descended was high, broad and long, lit by many windows, all beautifully clean and finished. Around the walls were hooks, from which hung many feather-suits belonging to the Eagle people who lived there. As he gazed around in wonder, a stately old man came up to them and said, 'May you two always be happy, for you are fated to be wife and husband. What do you say?'

The youth and Eagle Woman exchanged glances and said together, 'Yes!'

And so they were married.

A few days later, the youth was presented with a fine feather-suit of his own with broad, strong wings and beautiful plumage. Once he was comfortable wearing it, they gave him lessons as if he were a chick, teaching him to spread the great wings, leap into the air and finally to fly. Whenever he faltered as he tried to soar over the valleys and plains around the city, Eagle Woman was by his side to help and encourage him. Soon he became as agile in the air as she was.

One day, as they were flying together, he said, 'I want to ask you something. Why do we never go south?'

'Oh, my husband!' she cried. 'Promise me never to fly in that direction. For that way lies a truly fearful land, which no living being should ever enter.'

She refused to tell him any more. Nevertheless, he agreed to follow her advice.

Although the youth often joined the Eagles when they went hunting, he could not share their catch since, as his wife had warned him at the outset, no cooking was done in the Eagles' city and their raw meat made him ill. Eventually, the supply of human food he had brought with him was all used up.

Seeing this, his wife told him to fly out to the east, saying, 'There you will find people who cook their food, as you are used to.'

'Are they human beings like me?' he asked.

'No, they are your grandparents, the Storks. I know you are growing hungry, so go to them, my husband. They will feed you all you need, and allow you to bring more of their food back here.'

She showed him the way to go, warning him again in the strongest terms never to fly south. Soon he reached the house of the Storks. They were delighted to welcome him, and at once called him inside to eat, setting before him bean-bread, bean-stews, bean-bakes and bean-and-meat-mushes, all even tastier than the human food he was used to. He ate his fill and, with many thanks, took the surplus back to the house of the Eagles.

Thus they continued to live very happily, with the youth now often flying between the Eagles and the Storks. The Storks became very fond of him, and regularly warned him – as his wife still did – to beware the dreadful region that lay to the south. But the warnings came so often that he began to resent them. 'Why shouldn't I see this place for myself, and make up my own mind?' he thought. 'No one can harm me now I'm an Eagle; with my strong wings I can easily escape any danger.'

So one day, in secret, he went the forbidden way, gliding over a low range of mountains. Rising from the plains beyond, he saw another magnificent city. Its walls were built of stone, like the mysterious ruins of our long-dead ancestors. Smoke rose from the rooftops in extraordinary spirals. The whole place was teeming with life. He flew closer, hovering over it for some time, observing and admiring it, then turned and flew back to the Eagles.

As soon as he arrived, his wife came out to greet him, with tears in her eyes. 'Husband,' she cried, 'you've ignored all my warnings, and disobeyed your Stork grandparents too! How could you?'

'What do you mean?' said the youth.

'You have been to the forbidden city in the south – and though you did not realise it, the evil people who live there saw you. As a result, they immediately sent messengers, who travelled here far faster than you could. They've invited us all to a great dance festival, which will put us all in mortal danger. It is impossible to refuse their invitation. And you must come with us.'

The Youth bowed his head in shame.

Eagle Woman went on: 'I have always loved and trusted you. I thought that you loved me too – yet you defied me. Still, I accept that perhaps you did not understand what you were doing, so I will explain. The city we are forced to fly to tonight is cursed – perilous

beyond imagination. You will see truly marvellous things there…
But oh, my husband, do not ignore my next warning!'

'What do you ask of me now?'

Eagle Woman said, 'Listen carefully. This city is full of temptations. Do not give in to any of them. Above all, do not laugh. Do not even smile. Not even once, not even a little, not at all.'

'That is easy.'

'You will discover, once you are there, that it is not. I will support you as much as I can, I will stay by your side and help you concentrate all your thoughts on what I have told you. Once again, I tell you, *do not even smile*. If you truly love me and wish to stay with me for ever, I implore you to do as I say.'

The youth promised over and over.

Night fell and he flew again to the forbidden city of the south, this time with his wife and all the other Eagle people beside him. They alighted in the central courtyard, and he saw it was even more splendid than it had seemed from the air. Its smoking chimneys were festooned with gleaming sparks, and red firelight shimmered from countless windows. As they made their way through the streets, hoards of laughing people carrying brilliant torches went scurrying past them. Soon they found themselves ushered into a great dance hall, where an excited audience was already assembled.

The next moment, they heard music. The atmosphere seethed with expectation. The fires blazed up, lighting the room almost as bright as day. A troop of women came dancing down the ladders to the floor, clad in rich garments, their faces gleaming with merriment and pleasure. They made their way past the youth's seat, to the middle of the room – jostling, playing grotesque pranks, assuming ridiculous poses, pointing at one another and at the audience, calling out in shrill voices:

Dead!
Dead this!
This, this!'

All through the long dance, the youth could not take his eyes off them. He was tickled with amusement by their strange antics and jokes. Yet, remembering his beloved Eagle Woman's warning, he made sure never to smile, his face never even twitched.

The dancing women whirled out, and were at once replaced by some more, even merrier than the first ones. Amongst them was one dancer of surpassing beauty, flanked by two attendants. She kept glancing towards the youth flirtatiously, fluttering her eyes and directing all her high spirits to him alone.

The youth could not help himself: she mesmerised him and everything else left his mind. He leaned forward, totally absorbed in this brazen woman, dazzled by her. Eagle Woman clutched his arm and whispered in his ear, 'Be strong!' But he did not even hear her. The dancing woman ran towards him and grasped his hands, stroking and teasing them.

The youth's lips quivered...and slowly cracked into a smile.

She gestured at him obscenely. All at once, he began to giggle, helplessly and lewdly. She hauled him to his feet, and he allowed her to drag him into the dance.

Eagle Woman gave a shriek, ran from the dance hall, donned her feather-cloak, flapped her wings and soared away. All her people rose to follow in a single dark, keening mass.

But the youth did not even notice, for he was totally besotted. Up and down the great lighted hall he stepped, hanging on to the one who had taken him into her power, copying her crude gestures, roaring with laughter.

By and by, the fire burned low. The woman began to purr and murmur into his ear, saying, 'Why go back to your home? We can give you a much better time than your prudish wife – not just me, but my two attendants as well, all three of us. Stay, pass the night with us here!'

Then the chant started up again:

'Dead!
Dead this!
This, this!'

Still laughing and jostling, they led the Youth away; and in truth, he was very willing. They escorted him to a distant, private room, exquisitely furnished. There he lay down on the softest of blankets while the women gathered around him. The one who had chosen him pillowed his head on her lap and gently caressed him. The others, smiling, lay down close on either side. In this way, the night passed until he was satiated with pleasure. And then he fell asleep...

The youth opened his eyes with a start, blinking at the brilliant daylight. He looked around – and was overwhelmed by horror and self-loathing. What had he done, what had become of him?

The splendid room of the night before had transformed into a barren ruin. Wind shrieked through great cracks in the walls and broken windows. The rotting roof had fallen in; sand and filthy grit were blowing around him.

He could still feel the weight of the dancing woman, half lying on top of him. But when he pushed her off, his hands felt only a dry tangle of bones. Two more skeletons lay on either side.

He sat up and shuddered violently. It was like being in a ransacked cemetery, strewn with broken bones and skulls. Here and there, a hideous face with peeling skin, half-buried in the sand, seemed to glare at him with cold, sunken eyes. Disembodied fingers and feet were everywhere.

He stumbled up and trod gingerly amongst the litter, making no noise. But when he tripped against a bone, it let out an eerie shriek; and the other bones took up the cry, howling like creaking forest branches, groaning and whistling. At the sound, many skeleton fragments arose and came towards him. He sprang from the building in terror and raced away for his life.

On and on he ran, while his macabre pursuers drew ever nearer. They caught him up, surrounded him, pressed against him…

But just then, the youth heard someone calling: 'Grandson! We've come to save you!'

Somehow, he found strength to turn his head. He saw a group of Badgers rushing towards him. They caught him up and one seized his trembling hand in its paw and pulled him away, yelling, 'Stay strong, Grandson – down here.' The next moment, he found himself drawn down into the warmth of a dark tunnel. They went along it and eventually reached the innermost chamber of an underground house. Here all the Badgers bustled round, urging each other: 'Hurry, heat water!' When a pot was boiling, they scattered foul-smelling herbs and roots into it, stirred it, then ordered the youth to drink four draughts.

'Now,' said the Badger Chief, 'how do you feel?'

'Better than before,' he answered shakily.

'Then you are ready for your scolding,' the Badger Chief said. 'You fool, you faithless lout! How could you fall in love with Death? Ach, don't try the excuse that she was irresistibly beautiful. You are lucky that we found you, and used our power save to you. But your luck won't hold. Your wife can't still love you after your obscene unfaithfulness. Dancing with Death, lying with her – and with all her cronies too!'

The youth began to weep.

The Badger Chief went on more gently. 'Go. Not to your marital home, of course that is out of the question, they won't have you there. Nor can you return to your own people on Earth below, for you've forfeited your feathers, and you can't fly without wings. But your grandparents, the Storks, will take you in: go there.'

So the youth did, with dragging feet and a heavy heart. The Storks greeted him sorrowfully and reproached him over and over: 'Your beloved wife will never forgive you!'

'I will go and plead with her,' said the youth. 'She must realise my ignorance, she must understand I had no idea what was going on.'

'She told you never to go south, as we did, but you ignored and disobeyed us all,' said the Storks. 'Even then, you might have survived with your wife's support; but instead, you chose to ignore her and succumb to temptation. Why were you not strong?'

The youth had no answer to that.

The next day, he crept out and journeyed on foot to the house of the Eagles. When he arrived, he was too ashamed to enter, so he lingered outside its high walls, moping and softly moaning. The Eagles saw him as they came and went, but none offered any greeting.

At last Eagle Woman herself appeared on the housetop and called down: 'You disgust me. Don't dare call yourself my husband ever again. Go back to your grandparents, for they still have some love for you. But not me. You have lost my love for ever.'

So, with great sadness, the Youth went to live with the Storks. Every so often, despite his wife's ban, he returned to the house of the Eagles; but each time with no success.

However, one day an elder went to Eagle Woman, saying, 'You have punished your husband enough. We have discussed this case, and agree it is time to forgive him and take him back.'

'How can I touch him again, after he has lain side by side with Death?' she wept.

Many other elders now came to speak with her. Some counselled her with time-sharpened wisdom, others simply appealed to her heart. They wore down her resolve until at last she seemed to give in.

When the youth made his next visit, Eagle Woman came down to meet him. She handed him an old, thin, tattered feather-suit and told him to put it on, then follow her.

In these rags, he flew after her to the summit of the Turquoise Mountain. There she allowed him to rest briefly, then led him to the Sky-hole, and straight down through it.

As they descended together, she seized a corner of his feather-suit in her talons, drew the whole garment off him and bade him a cold farewell. Then she soared up, back through the Sky-hole and vanished.

The youth gasped and shrieked, tumbled over – and fell fast as an arrow to the very centre of the town where once he had lived with his beloved pet Eagle. In this way he perished.

Thus it was in the time of the ancients; and thus ends my story.

Cushing: *Zuni Folk Tales*, 1901
Cushing himself translated the stories in his collection, which were narrated to him in the Zuni language. He says his chief informant was a man called Waihusiwa, who told him over 50 tales of varying length. When pressed for even more, Waihusiwa colourfully excused himself saying, 'my word-pouch is as empty as the food-pack of a lost hunter'.

In a Hopi variant of this story, the young hero is abandoned by his pet eagle as soon as it has carried him up to the Sky, but he is rescued by Spider Woman (see THE THREE GODDESSES CREATE PEOPLE (p.162), THE SUN'S HORSES (p. 182) and THE COYOTE GIRL (p. 205). A related Navajo myth tells of two Pueblo men who trick a Navajo beggar to be lowered in a basket down a cliff, and capture eagle chicks for their use. The Pueblo men abandon him, but the beggar eventually finds his way up to the sky world, where he is welcomed by Eagle people in feather-suits as in the story here. He achieves some noble feats, also with Spider Woman's help, and receives eight chief's daughters as wives. After learning the eagles' sacred songs and rituals, he temporarily returns to earth, then lives permanently in the sky with the gods.

Two different species of eagle live in the Southwest: the bald eagle and the golden eagle. Eagle feathers were traditionally used in the sacred ceremonies of a number of Native American peoples.

THE COYOTE GIRL

Hopi Pueblo

Aliksai!

A long time ago, there lived two girls who were very close friends. Their names were Blue Corn Maiden and Yellow Corn Maiden. They spent most of their time together, chatting away all day as they worked at grinding corn.

As the pair grew up, their conversation turned increasingly to the subject of marriage. But unfortunately, they both happened to fall in love with the same young man. This led to constant quarrels over which of them should have him, with neither girl willing to yield to the other. So far as Blue Corn Maiden could see, there was no way to resolve this.

However, unbeknown to her, Yellow Corn Maiden possessed secret supernatural power, and she decided to use this to get her own way. Early one morning, she called at her friend's house saying, 'It's stupid to argue, let's make up. Come for a walk with me outside the town; let's go to the spring and fetch water.'

Blue Corn Maiden was so relieved to be friends again, that she eagerly agreed.

When they had both filled their water jars and were carrying them home, Yellow Corn Maiden suddenly said, 'Oof, this is heavy! Let's sit down for a rest on top of that sandhill.'

So they did.

After a while, Yellow Corn Maiden said, 'There's no hurry to get home. Let's play a game first.' She reached into the folds of her dress and drew out a small hoop. It was very pretty, glimmering with rainbow colours. 'Go down there,' she said. 'I'll throw this hoop, then you catch it and throw it back.'

Blue Corn Maiden ran down and stood at the bottom of the slope, hands at the ready. But the rainbow hoop was much heavier than she'd anticipated, and her friend threw it with unexpected force. When Blue Corn Maiden tried to catch it, the hoop knocked her right down...

And when she struggled back to her feet, she discovered something truly dreadful: the hoop was filled with evil medicine which had transformed her into a wild animal! She had four legs, thick fur, pricked ears and a tail – a coyote! She let out a great howl of horror and dismay.

Yellow Corn Maiden laughed callously and shouted down to her, 'What's the matter? You've only got what you deserved for trying to steal my lover.'

The coyote girl found her balance and started to creep back up the hill.

But Yellow Corn Maiden shrieked, 'Ugh, go away you horrible, dirty animal, get lost!' She picked up her water jar, turned round and marched back to the village.

The poor coyote girl didn't know what to do. She stumbled awkwardly on her four legs, and managed to make her way back to the spring. There she tried to pick up her jar – then quickly realised that she couldn't. 'I'll have to go home without it,' she thought. 'Oh no, I can't. No one in the village except Yellow Corn Maiden will have any idea who I am, and she certainly won't confess her wicked trick to anyone.'

She lay down, buried her new black nose (how strange it felt to her!) in her new scruffy tail (even stranger!) and whimpered herself to sleep.

The coyote girl woke up as the sun was setting. She stood up, looked down at her front legs and paws, turned her head to examine her long back with its mottled fur – and felt totally wretched.

She was hungry. When it got completely dark, she went back to the town, using the stars to guide her. But on the outskirts, the dogs smelled her and all rushed out to drive her away, having no idea that she was really one of their people. She slunk off, skirted the town in a wide circle, then tried to enter it from the other side; but there too the dogs repelled her.

She lay down and whimpered some more. Fortunately, she could still think like a human being. It was autumn, and she remembered that some of the townspeople had set up temporary huts by the fields to watch over their crops. 'If there's no one in them tonight,' she thought, 'maybe I can steal some food from there.' So she ran over, using her new coyote sense of smell, and soon discovered some roasted corn ears on a roof. She leaped up, grabbed them in her mouth and gobbled them up. Then she made a final effort to get into the town, but was again driven away.

She sat down, ears cocked, nose twitching. 'I'll go westwards,' she thought, 'maybe I'll find more food there.'

She ran through the night, on and on. Just as dawn was coming up, she found another hut, this one built by hunters. They had gone out very early in search of game, leaving the door ajar. The coyote girl peered cautiously through it, then crept in – and was at once overwhelmed by the delicious smell of roasted rabbit meat. In no time at all, she found where it was stored, and devoured it greedily. When her stomach was so swollen that she couldn't swallow any more, she lay down and fell into an exhausted sleep.

She slept right through until evening, when the two hunters returned. As they came through the doorway, the first thing they saw was a coyote curled up by the embers of their fire, and a mess of gnawed bones strewn around. One pulled out his bow and fitted an arrow to it. But as he took aim the other touched his arm and said, 'Stop, don't shoot! There's something not right about that animal. Look.'

As he pointed, the first hunter's mouth dropped open in amazement. For the coyote girl had sprung awake at their voices and struggled to her feet... And *tears* were trickling from her eyes, with a noise more like a human sob than a coyote howl.

'What kind of coyote cries like a human?' said the second hunter. 'We ought to try and capture it alive, then take it to Spider Woman to ask her advice.'

The first hunter readily agreed. They went in and spoke in soft voices, coaxing the trembling creature not to be afraid. They offered it more meat, which the coyote girl could only nibble, since she was still satiated from her stolen meal. They ate heartily themselves, then packed the remaining meat and skins, and bound up the coyote girl's four feet. One carried her over his shoulder, the other carried everything else, and they started out. After a long, long trek, they reached Spider Woman's house.

There they stopped and called, 'Grandmother, please come out, we need your help! We've brought you some meat. We've also brought you an animal: there's something wrong with it that we don't understand.'

There was a scuffling noise as Spider Woman emerged from the top of the house ladder, beckoning them inside. They clambered down after her, removed the burdens from their backs and gave them to her.

She thanked them for their gift of meat. Then she scurried over to the coyote girl and examined her carefully, running her fingers lightly all over the animal's body.

'Oh, the poor thing!' she cried. 'This isn't a real coyote, you know. Thank goodness you didn't kill it. Wherever did you find it?'

The men told her and she listened carefully. Then she sent each of them on an errand to fetch what she needed: one to find devil's claw pods from the town, and the other for juniper branches from the forest. While they were gone, she boiled up a big pot of water. When the man returned with the pods, Spider Woman removed hooks from two of them, sticking one into the coyote girl's neck and the other into her back. Then she poured the hot water into a wide jar, dropped the coyote girl deep into it and covered the jar with a piece of cloth. Reaching under it, she seized the two hooks and started twisting and turning them... Until suddenly, with a great splash, she pulled the loosened coyote skin right out of the water. She tossed it away, then finally pulled away the cloth. There was Blue Corn Maiden back in her true form, fully dressed, with her hair tied splendidly in whorls!

'You poor child,' cried Spider Woman. 'How ever did this happen?'

Weeping and trembling, the girl told her.

'What an evil betrayal,' said Spider Woman. 'To do such a terrible thing, and to her own friend! But take comfort, dear child: you will have revenge.'

When the other hunter returned with the juniper branches, Spider Woman used them to scent some fresh hot water, then led Blue Corn Maiden into another room, where she helped her to bathe. She looked after Blue Corn Maiden very well.

Some days later, Spider Woman said, 'My dear, it's time for you to go home. Your mother is missing you badly and grieving for you.'

'I don't know the way,' said Blue Corn Maiden.

'Don't worry,' said Spider Woman. She climbed up to the top of her house and called out: 'Where are my neighbours? I need your help.'

A few moments later, many people appeared, running towards her – not ordinary people but Kachinas, spirit people. They went down into her house and listened while Spider Woman told the sad story of Blue Corn Maiden's suffering. The Kachinas were all very sympathetic.

Spider Woman now called the girl and dressed her up in a fine new ceremonial robe.

'The Kachinas will see you home safely,' she said. 'When you arrive, tell your father to reward them with these ceremonial sticks and feather ornaments, as prayer offerings. And now listen carefully, for I shall tell you how to take revenge on Yellow Corn Maiden for her wickedness.'

Spider Woman whispered instructions, repeating them over and over, testing the girl to be sure she understood exactly what to do.

The Kachinas formed a long line, and danced all the way to the girl's home town, with Blue Corn Maiden in her fine clothes running behind them. They arrived at dawn. The Kachinas told the girl to stand aside while they continued to sing and dance. The commotion immediately caught the attention of some early risers, who ran over to find out what was going on. They watched in awe for a while, then scattered to spread the news that Kachinas were dancing in the plaza – with the missing girl, Blue Corn Maiden herself! Naturally, the first people they told were her grieving parents. Initially, they refused to believe it; but after four separate messengers insisted it was true, they went out to see for themselves. When the mother saw her lost child, she rushed forward and burst into tears of joy.

'Come home, my child, come home!' she cried and began to lead her away.

But Blue Corn Maiden followed Spider Woman's instructions and urged her mother to wait while her father presented the Kachinas with the prayer offerings, to thank them for leading her home. Once this was done, she went happily with her parents. The Kachinas returned to their own village and were not seen again.

Blue Corn Maiden rested at home for a day. Next morning, following Spider Woman's instructions, she went outside to grind corn, singing loudly. Yellow Corn Maiden heard her, and hurried shamelessly over to greet her.

'I've missed you,' she said. 'I'm really glad to see you safe at home.'

Blue Corn Maiden received her politely, for Spider Woman had warned her to bide her time. She let Yellow Corn Maiden sit next to her, and the two girls spent the whole day grinding corn together, just like old times.

As the sun sank, they put their work aside. Blue Corn Maiden said, 'I'm going to the spring to fetch water for my mother. Would you like to you come?'

The other girl nodded.

As they crouched at the spring, side by side, Yellow Corn Maiden noticed that her friend was scooping up the water with a very curious dipping cup, which made it sparkle with extraordinary colours.

'What a pretty cup,' she said. 'Where did you get it?'

'Oh,' said Blue Corn Maiden carelessly, 'when I was out on my adventures, Spider Woman gave it to me.'

'You met Spider Woman?' cried Yellow Corn Maiden excitedly. 'You lucky thing! Can I see it?'

'Of course,' said Blue Corn Maiden. 'Take a drink. The cup doesn't just make the water sparkle, it makes it taste sweeter too.' She passed it over.

Yellow Corn Maiden examined the cup carefully, admiring the exquisite, gossamer-fine patterns painted on it. Then she dipped it into the spring, filled it and took a long sip.

At once she fell down – transformed into a bull snake!

Blue Corn Maiden shuddered, but quickly recovered herself. She gazed down at the snake and said coldly, 'There! This is in return for what you did to me. Spider Woman said you don't deserve to ever change back, you'll have to stay in this shape for ever.'

She picked up her water jug with trembling hands, and carried it slowly back to the village.

There was nothing the bull snake could do except wriggle away. Eventually she found her way back to her own house. When her parents saw her there, they did not realise the snake was their daughter, and so they killed her.

Voth: *Traditions of the Hopi*, 1905
This story was narrated by Qoyawaima, the same person who also gave Voth the myth THE THREE GODDESSES CREATE PEOPLE (p. 162).

After Yellow Corn Maiden is transformed into a bull snake – a non-venomous species – the original narrator comments:

'The bull snake left the place and wandered about. It often gets hungry, but as it cannot run very fast it has difficulty in getting its prey, hence it captures its prey by charming and drawing it towards it by its powerful inhalations, which is still frequently observed by the Hopi. It lives on little rabbits, mice, birds, squirrels, etc., which it charms by its inhalations and then kills them.'

Following the killing of her in snake-form by her parents he says:

'Hereupon the maiden, or rather her soul, was liberated and could then go to the Skeleton House [the dwelling of dead souls]. Ever since, some of the sorcerers will occasionally leave their graves in the form of bull snakes. Bull snakes are often seen coming out of certain graves still wound in the yucca leaves with which the corpse was tied up when laid away. If such a bull snake in which a sorcerer is supposed to have entered happens to be killed, the soul of the sorcerer living in it is set free and then goes to the Skeleton House.'

Several other versions of this cautionary tale were told in different pueblos, though none feature Spider Woman. In one from Acoma Pueblo, the unfortunate girl is rescued from her coyote transformation with the help of her lover. In Isleta Pueblo there are two variants; in both, the victim of the enchantment is a young man.

'Devil's claws' are a group of plants which have seed pods with two hooks. For information on kachinas see p.150.

There are a number of other Southwest stories about coyotes. Most feature Coyote as a sacred trickster, either taking part in creation, sometimes mischievously; or playing the familiar role of the archetypal trickster. These are related to the California stories, p. 233 ff.; also, the Great Basin story on p.277 and two Plateau stories, p. 329 and 338.

For further Spider Woman stories, see THE THREE GODDESSES CREATE PEOPLE (p. 162) and THE SUN'S HORSES (p. 182).

MOUNTAIN CHANT

Navajo (Dine)

The voice that beautifies the land!
The voice above,
The voice of the thunder,
Among the dark clouds
Again and again it sounds,
The voice that beautifies the land.

The voice that beautifies the land!
The voice below,
The voice of the grasshopper,
Among the flowers and grasses
Again and again it sounds,
The voice that beautifies the land.

– From one of the great nine-day ceremonies of the shamans,
told by unnamed informant.
(Quoted in Matthews: *Navaho Legends*, 1897)

THE SERPENT
OF THE WATERS

Zuni Pueblo (Shewena)

In the time of our forefathers, under Thunder Mountain there stood a town called Home of the Eagles. The priest-chief there had several daughters who were all very attractive. However, one was blighted by a strange habit: she was obsessed with cleanliness, and could not bear the slightest speck of dust or dirt on herself or her clothes. Because of this, she spent almost all her time bathing and washing her possessions. The place where she did this was a spring below the town, which was sacred to Kolowissi, the Serpent of the Waters.

To use a sacred spring for such mundane purposes, to fill its waters with dirt, was total sacrilege. Kolowissi was outraged.

So one day the Serpent transformed into a pretty little boy-child, a toddler, and in that shape sat down on the edge of the pool below the spring. Soon the young woman came down there for her next washing session; but before she could even begin, she saw the child sitting there, playing in the sparkling water, splashing and cooing. She was so charmed, that her desire to wash went straight out of her mind. She looked around in all directions, but could see no sign of anyone who might be looking after the child.

'His mother must have abandoned him here,' she thought. 'Oh, what an evil woman! He could have fallen into the water and perished, poor thing! I must take him home and look after him.'

Still forgetting herself, she spoke softly to the child. He gurgled back at her. Soon she felt confident enough to scoop him gently into her arms. She hurried up the hill to her house with him, climbed the ladder to the top apartment and carried him into her bedroom. This was completely separate from the rest of the family, because she could not bear to sleep near anyone else, due to her fear of dirt. She sat on the floor and played with him, laughing at his antics and smiling into his face. He answered her with coos and smiles of his own, making her heart swell with love. She was so happy, that she totally forgot the passing of time.

Meanwhile, her younger sisters had prepared the evening meal, and were awaiting her return, saying, 'Where can she be?'

'Down at the spring, no doubt,' said their father, 'bathing and washing her clothes as usual. Run and call her.'

The youngest girl went down there, but found no trace of her. So she climbed the ladder to her elder sister's private room, peeped in – and was astonished to find her playing with a baby. The elder girl was so absorbed, that she didn't even notice she was being watched. The younger one hurried back and told the rest of the family the extraordinary scene she had just witnessed. The other girls and their mother were all very excited, and jumped up at once to go and see the baby for themselves.

But the father yelled at them: 'No, no, stop, you fools! Have you forgotten? That spring where your sister spends all her time is sacred. There's something unnatural going on.'

He sent the youngest daughter back up the ladder to order her sister to come down. But again she returned, shaking her head. 'She refuses,' the younger girl said. 'She won't bring the baby down here, and she won't leave him on his own either.'

So they ate their meal without her.

Meanwhile, in the top room, the little boy at last seemed to grow sleepy. The young woman laid him gently on her bed, then stretched out by his side and soon fell into a deep, contented sleep.

However, as she slumbered innocently, something extraordinary happened. The infant began to change shape and grow. Gradually, steadily, his body elongated and became scaly and gleaming. Kolowissi was transforming back to his Serpent shape. When the metamorphosis was complete, he coiled himself tightly around the young woman, his head by hers, his tail in his mouth.

In this way, the night passed.

In the morning, when the eldest girl did not appear for breakfast, the youngest sister was sent back to her room. There was no answer when she called, so she tried to open the door – but could not, because the Serpent's enormous coils were firmly pressed against it. She pushed with all her might, but failed to budge it.

214

Fearfully, she asked the rest of the family to help. All the womenfolk rushed up. Side by side, the mother and her daughters all pushed against the door, and managed to open it a tiny crack – enough to glimpse the scales and great loops of the Serpent. They let the door bang shut and all rushed screaming downstairs.

There the old father said quietly, 'I expected this would happen.'

He walked out of the house and round the plaza, pondering the matter. Then he climbed the ladder to his eldest daughter's room and banged on the door shouting:

'Oh, great Kolowissi, Serpent of the Waters, it is your own priest who prays to you. Let my child go free just for now, I beg you, let her see her mother one last time before you punish her mistakes.'

He repeated his entreaty over and over. When he fell silent, he heard a rasping sound inside the room. The great Serpent was loosening his coils, scales scraping the walls like the sound of flints under the feet of a runner. The whole building shook.

Now the young woman herself woke up. She quickly realised that she was the Serpent's prisoner. As she began to weep and scream, the coils were loosening around her. Cautiously, quivering with fear from head to toe, she managed to stand up. At this, the Serpent bent some of his coils to form an arch by the doorway and hissed at her, 'Pass through.'

She did; then ran from the room like a frightened deer, hurried down the ladder and almost fell into the room below, where she hurled herself onto her mother's breast.

Her father, the priest-chief, stayed at the top, continuing his prayer. Finally, he said, 'I will keep my promise; you shall have her.'

Then he backed away, hurried outside and sent messengers to summon the other town priests in council. He told them all that had happened. After much discussion, they agreed to perform sacred ceremonies for four days. In the course of this, they prepared plumes, prayer-wands and other offerings of treasure.

When everything was ready, on the fourth morning, the old priest went back home and sent for his wayward daughter. His face was dark but his words were firm.

'It is time for you to do penance for your disrespectful behaviour to mighty Kolowissi,' he told her. 'We have consecrated these treasures for him. You must offer them to the Serpent; and also offer yourself.'

She thought back to the dreadful morning when she had woken smothered in the serpent's heavy coils, and began to tremble.

'What's the matter?' said her father coldly. 'Isn't this what you always wanted? Why else did you constantly go to his sacred waters and show your body there? The consequences of that are inevitable. Come now, daughter: give up all thoughts of your family and home, and prepare yourself for him.'

He allowed her only enough time to cling briefly to her weeping mother and sisters; then dragged her outside to the plaza, shivering with terror. By now, all the townspeople knew what was happening, and had gathered there to show sympathy for her terrible plight. They watched as her family dressed her in ceremonial robes of elaborately embroidered cotton; adorned her with earrings, bracelets, beads and other precious jewellery; and painted her cheeks with red spots as if for a dance. Then they laid out a road of sacred cornmeal leading from the western side of the plaza to the spring of the Serpent of the Waters.

When it was ready, the old priest – who all this time never shed a single tear – instructed his daughter as follows: 'Go and stand on the sacred road that has been made for you. Call to the Serpent that you are ready for him.'

She went and stood there, crying in a quivering voice, 'Kolowissi, you may come for me.'

At once, a door was heard opening on the top floor of her father's house, and the great Serpent appeared in its frame. He began to descend, not using the ladders, but letting his head and breast down to the ground in great undulations. When the front of his body had reached the plaza, he lifted his head and placed it on the young woman's shoulder, hissing, 'It is time for us to go.'

Very, very slowly, she started to take faltering steps towards the west, cowering beneath her burden. The Serpent was far longer than anyone could imagine; for even as they set out together, part of his body was still in the plaza and his tail still lingered in her bedroom. Gradually his coils moved after her. Every so often she stumbled with fear and weariness and seemed to lose her way; each time, the Serpent gently straightened her course and urged her onwards. In this way, they eventually left the town behind them and continued out into the empty lands beyond. He steered her towards the river, then over the Mountain of Red Paint. Even by then, the tail-end of the Serpent was still emerging from the top room of her father's house; not until they were well past the mountain did his last section come out.

Out in the wild lands, something else extraordinary happened. The Serpent began to contract, as if his front was swallowing the rear, over and over. At the same time, his shape changed. The young woman, plodding on under her burden, staring at the ground in despair, was not aware of any of this... Until he startled her by suddenly lifting his weight from her shoulder.

'Look at me!' he hissed.

She answered with a quiver of fear and a gasp. Ignoring the change in her burden, she plodded on with eyes cast down.

He followed her a short way behind saying, 'It is time to talk.'

Still she gave no pause, no answer. A third time he spoke to her in a similar vein, his voice gradually growing less hoarse, more smooth and pleasant – like the voice of a man who seeks to impress a woman that he desires. Finally, she dared to turn and look at him. She blinked in astonishment, her mouth dropped open and she came to an abrupt halt. For the Serpent had vanished. A handsome young man was standing in his place, dressed, like her, in ceremonial robes.

'Why won't you speak with me, why won't you let me walk by your side?' he said.

'Because I am terrified, and filled with shame,' she answered.

'What do you fear? What are you ashamed of, and why?'

'Because I was forced to leave my home in the company of a repulsive, monstrous creature,' she said. 'He made me carry the weight of his head on my shoulder...and even now I feel his presence there.' Gingerly, she lifted her hand to the place where the Serpent's head had rested, and shuddered.

'Really?' said he. 'But I have walked all the way just behind you, and I saw no such creature as you describe.'

She stared at him. 'You came all the way too? Then the monster must be your friend. Wherever he is hiding, I beg you to take him away, and ask him to leave me in peace and go home.'

'He will not allow that, because he thinks very highly of you.'

'What do you mean? Where is he?'

'He is here,' said the young man, laying his hand on his own heart. 'I am the one whose head was your burden throughout the journey.'

'*You?*' cried the girl. 'How can this be? I don't believe you.'

'Yes, my dear, I am the Serpent of the Waters,' said the young man. From under his flowing mantle he drew out a long, shrivelled snakeskin. 'There, this is proof of my word.'

The girl was overwhelmed. He was so fine, so gracious. She looked at him long and hard, and he steadily returned her gaze.

'Then you and he are the same?'

'Yes. I am the snake and the young child, and now I am as you see me. And I wish to declare my love for you. Will you come and live with me? Will you allow me to love you properly, for ever? Will you learn to love me?'

'Where will you take me; where do you live?'

'All the waters of the world are my home,' he answered.

And so she agreed. As they journeyed on, the girl completely forgot all her previous worries and sadness, and she also forgot her old home. She followed Kolowissi gladly, and descended with him into the Doorway of the Serpent of the Waters. There she dwelt with him in great happiness ever after.

Because of these momentous events of old, the ancients avoided using springs for anything except drinking water. To this day, flowing springs are considered the most precious things on earth, never to be used for anything profane.

Thus ends my story.

Cushing: *Zuni Folk Tales*, 1901

As with the other Zuni stories presented here, this was told to Cushing by a man called Waihusiwa (see p. 204). Cushing says he introduced this myth as follows:

"'Son ah tehi," he exclaimed, which may be interpreted:"Let us abide with the ancients to-night."

'The listeners reply "E-so," or "Tea-tu" ("certainly" or "be it well")'.

Cushing translates the snake's name as 'Serpent of the Sea'. However, as Zuni pueblo is some 450 miles (750 km) from the nearest coast, it seems more accurate to use the term 'Serpent of the Waters'.

Another Zuni myth tells of a young man who, after a series of adventures, marries a rattlesnake woman. Their hybrid children are bullied by other children in the man's town, so his wife takes them to her own home, first teaching her husband the antidote to rattlesnake bites. A Hopi story also features a man who marries a shapeshifting snake woman, bringing about the origin of the Hopi Snake Clan.

Snake stories were common in many other regions of North America. In particular, 'snake marriage' stories related to this one were also told in California, the Great Plains and the Northeast.

THE WAR TWINS
AND THE UNBORN

Zuni Pueblo (Shewena)

Our grandfathers say that the Underworld was once inhabited by very strange beings. They lived in towns like those of living people, yet in form they resembled the dead; they were like ghosts. However, they were less complete than ghosts, for they had never lived in the daylight. These beings were the *unborn*.

The dead are like the wind, and take shape by their own will. But the unborn Underworld People were more like smoke. They could not control their bodies, which were soft and pliable like swollen seeds which have not yet started to grow.

At that time the Twin Gods of War, Ahaiyuta and Matsailema, lived on Earth. They were also rather strange. They used to go wandering around looking for trouble; and delighted in things that normal people found disturbing and abhorrent. For example, if they heard someone crying and groaning, they would get really excited, as if these distress calls were really an invitation to a dance.

One day, when the world was quiet, the War Twins were sitting by the side of a deep pool, listening to curious noises rising up like bubbles through the water.

'Wha-hoa!' cried the elder Twin. 'What a lovely sound, just like people weeping.'

The younger one put his ear to the water to hear it better. 'You're right, it sounds like funeral mourners. There must be some kind of dire trouble in the Underworld. Let's go down there and join in the fun.'

Without wasting any time, they covered their heads with their upside-down shields, shut their eyes, plunged into the pool and sank down through the water. Somehow, in all that wetness, they managed to stay completely dry – just as light moving through dark places always maintains its glow.

When they reached the Underworld, Matsailema exclaimed, 'Pshaw, what a stink! The poor wretches here must be dead already, and that's the smell of them rotting.'

'Then it's been a waste of time coming,' said Ahaiyuta.

'Not necessarily,' said Matsailema. 'Even if they *are* dead, it will be interesting to see their town and find out how they once lived.'

Ahaiyuta agreed, and they strode on eagerly. Although the Underworld was completely dark, they soon saw the town quite plainly. How was that? Well, here in the Upper World, when we shut our eyes, it seems as if we're in the dark. Likewise, down in the Underworld, when the War Twins opened their eyes, it made the darkness seem light. That was their way, that was their power.

'Just look at all those people milling around,' said Matsailema as they drew closer. 'They stink like corpses, yet they're still alive.'

'Yes,' said Ahaiyuta. 'That's because the smell isn't of dead people after all – it's coming from that heap of rotting food over there. I wonder why they haven't eaten it.'

'We can only find out by watching,' replied his brother. 'Come on, let's hide and spy on them.'

So they crept right into the town, pressed themselves against a wall, and peered through a window into a house. The people in there were about to have a meal. They took a steaming cooking pot off the fire, carefully served the contents into dishes, then gathered around. However, they did not touch the food at all; indeed they seemed terrified of doing so. Instead, they just cautiously held their faces over the steam and let the vapours flow over them.

'Look,' whispered Matsailema, 'they can't eat properly because they haven't got mouths!'

'Ssh,' hissed his brother. 'They must be feeding just on the *smell* of food. That means they can probably hear our whispers louder than if we were talking normally. We'll have to think how best to deal with such peculiar folk…'

But it was too late, for the Underworld People had already discovered their presence. Naturally, they were angry, for no one likes strangers spying on their meals. They came swarming out to shoo away the culprits, like ants in a rain shower. The War Twins were already on the run from them, racing for the nearest hillock; but the Underworld People saw them. At once they set off in hot pursuit, with a deafening war cry:

'Flush them both out!
Strike them!
Death, death, death!'

The War Twins broke into raucous laughter and quickly loosed a volley of arrows with a loud *p'it-tsok!* However, the arrows were completely ineffective; they failed to strike a single Underworld Person dead.

'What's the matter, why won't they work?' growled Ahaiyuta.

'Never mind why, let's club them instead,' said Matsailema. He drew out his war club, sprang to meet the leading Underworld Person, and pummelled him hard over the head and shoulders. However, the man was so soft that this caused him no harm at all.

Just then another Underworld Person came rushing at them from the other side. As he did so, he brushed against one of the feathers on the edge of Ahaiyuta's shield...then crumpled to the ground like smoke subdued by a hawk's wing.

'Brother, that's the way to get them!' cried Ahaiyuta. He snatched up a bunch of dry plume-grass, leaped forward and swept it, *swish, swish!* this way and that, against the faces and breasts of their pursuers. And it worked. To the right and the left, one by one, the enemy fell. The survivors screeched in despair, begging for mercy. Now the War Twins only had to hold the grass up threateningly to make them cower.

'Don't worry, we won't fight you any more,' Matsailema called to them. 'It's your own fault if you're scared.'

'We came in friendship,' said Ahaiyuta. 'We were simply looking around, as strangers always do in strange places.'

'Anyway, now we're hungry. Please give us something to eat.'

Thus peace was made. The Underworld People led the War Twins to the town plaza, told them to be seated and brought out some food. It was steaming hot, far too hot to eat, so the Twins blew on it to make it cool. At this, the Underworld People cried out in dismay: 'Stop, you shameless brutes. How dare you blow all the steam away and waste precious food!'

'Don't be stupid,' said the War Twins, 'it's impossible to "waste" steam: it's just empty air. It's this solid stuff that *we* eat.'

They began scooping up huge helpings of food, cramming it into their mouths, and wolfing it down. The Underworld People were horrified. They broke out into pungent sweats, insistently shouting and scolding: 'No, stop, stop! Ach, it's too late! Touching food will make you fall ill and die!'

'Die?' the War Twins retorted, eating more greedily than ever. 'Nonsense. Proper food is what you soft, pathetic creatures all need. That'd soon toughen you…'

Before they could finish, the Underworld People set up a new commotion, screaming and flapping around in panic. They turned their backs on the War Twins and all rushed to the shelter of their houses, shouting to their guests to follow.

The War Twins looked around but could not see anything amiss.

'Terrible danger!' the Underworld People screamed from their shelters. 'The gods are angry with us today, they're blowing arrows at us. If you don't come in, they'll kill you both! Hurry!'

There was actually nothing happening at all except for a strong wind blowing over the town, scattering slivers and straws before it.

'Brother,' said the elder War Twin, 'these people need hardening up. The best way to do that is by teaching them to eat properly.'

'Exactly,' replied the younger one. 'Let's take a quick nap, then sort them out.'

They propped themselves up against a wall, set their shields in front of them, and dozed off. However, they had only slept for a few moments, when they were suddenly jerked awake by the Underworld People setting up another great wailing: 'Help, war, murder! Look, listen!'

This time, a big flock of jays was flying above the town.

'If one of those birds lands on someone, he'll die at once,' the Underworld People cried.

Even as they spoke, they were fleeing. But one or two stragglers could not go fast enough. Some jays swooped on them – and sure enough, they dropped dead at once – as if struck by lightning.

'It's pathetic,' scoffed the elder War Twin. 'Dropping dead at the touch of a mere bird.'

'We can soon deal with that,' said the younger one. 'Watch and copy me.'

He pulled some hairs from his scalp-lock, twisted them into nooses and held them up. His brother did likewise. When the next bunch of jays flew in to attack, the nooses quickly snared and entangled them. As each one was trapped, the War Twins struck it dead. Then they took the dead birds to the nearest fire, roasted them, and settled down to enjoy a hearty meal.

The Underworld People came crowding around in amazement. 'Look,' they cried 'those strangers are putting the enemy inside their own bodies!'

Now they treated the War Twins with great respect and awe, and gave them a fine apartment to stay in.

The very next day there was yet another alarm. The Twins ran out to investigate – and this time were greatly amused to see some Underworld People fleeing through the streets from a cooking pot! It was decorated with rings made of eye-wateringly strong onions and boiling furiously, belching out hot steam, spluttering mush in every direction. Every time a splash hit an Underworld Person, he keeled over and died.

The War Twins burst out laughing: 'That's ridiculous, it's all the wrong way round – people being chased by food!'

They rushed out, quickly caught up with the pot, tipped it upside-down and gobbled up all the mush. Finally, they kicked the pot with all their might, completely smashing it to pieces.

The Underworld People gathered round them again.

'You're such heroes!' they cried.

'Amazing: to vanquish your enemies by eating them!'

'Teach us how, we beg you!'

'We will help you gladly,' the Twins answered. 'But first we must understand you more.'

So the town council was summoned to explain the situation to the War Twins. They learned that, long ago, when the Underworld People were first created, they were left half-finished. Because of that, they could not eat solid food, and lived in constant fear.

So the War Twins called forward all those who were brave enough to change, and cut slits in their faces – in other words, mouths. They also gave them the gift of digestive organs, filling the cavities inside their bellies which, until then, had been totally empty. As a result, these people were now able to eat solid food, especially meat. And so they soon became hard, strong and brave. Now they were ready to ascend to our world of daylight, ready to take up their proper places as children, born to our people up here.

From this, you may now understand two things. Firstly: why does a newborn child only eat air until his cord of invisible sustenance has been severed; and then, only sucks milk, and with much distress? Secondly: why do the very old resemble newborns – toothless and unable to digest anything except soft food and broth?

Both questions have the same answer. It is because babies come from the Underworld, the land of insubstantial mist; and the aged are on their way to return there.

Thus ends my story.

Cushing: *Zuni Folk Tales*, 1901
This was originally narrated by Waihusiwa (see p. 204).

The Twin Gods of War are ambiguous characters. Waihusiwa portrays them in various stories as heroic and helpful, but also often as comical and endearing, sometimes with a malicious streak. In some of the tales, they live with their long-suffering grandmother who scolds their bad behaviour, with no effect. In one such story, they persuade Centipede to help them steal thunder and lightning from the Land of Eternal Summer, causing a terrible storm with floods, in which their grandmother drowns. A mysterious plant grows on her grave: the first pepper, which was widely cultivated on Zuni farms. In another, they save two girls by killing a cannibal monster. They skin and stuff its body, then play with it to terrorise their grandmother. She is so disgusted by their teasing that she abandons them, and they transform to the morning star and evening star.

However, in Cushing's earlier collection, *Outlines of Zuni Creation Myths*, an unnamed informant presents the Twin War Gods more reverently as significant deities born of the Sun and Earth Mother. They take part in creation and give important instruction to the first people. Later, following various cataclysms, they became dwarfed and hideous, heartless and evil, specialising in terror and magic. Effigies of the War Gods were apparently prayed to for protection and victory in battle.

There are parallel 'twin brother hero' characters in Navajo mythology. Here too their father is the Sun; but they are actually half-brothers, whose respective mothers are the goddesses She Who Changes and White Shell Woman. They too were prayed to for success in war.

A footnote to the myth explains the Underworld People further:
'The universe is supposed to have been generated from haze produced by light...out of darkness. The...analogy of this in nature is the appearance of haze (both heat and steam) preceding growth in springtime; the appearance of...growing and living things through mist seemingly rising out of the darkness each morning. In harmony with this conception of the universe...[the soul of] every being passes through many successive states...always beginning as a haze, and passing through the raw or soft, the formative, variable, fixed...and finished or dead states.

SONG OF BLESSING FOR A NEW HOUSE

Navajo (Dine)

May it be delightful, my house.
From my head may it be delightful,
To my feet may it be delightful.
Where I lie may it be delightful.
All around me may it be delightful.

Man flinging a little meal into the fire:
May it be delightful and well, my fire.

Man tossing a handful or two of meal up and through the smoke hole:
For this gift may it be delightful, Sun, my mother's ancestor,
May it be delightful as I walk around my house.

Man sprinkling two or three handfuls out of the doorway:
May it be delightful, this road of light, my mother's ancestor.

Woman making a meal offering to the fire:
May it be delightful, my fire.
May it be delightful for my children; may all be well.
May it be delightful with my food and theirs; may all be well.
All my possessions, may they be well made.
All my flocks may they be made well

– Recorded amongst unnamed people,
(Quoted in James: *Indian Blankets and their Makers*, 1914)

Detail from *Mariposa Indian Encampment, Yosemite Valley, California*
(Miwok people)
painted by Albert Bierstadt, 1872

MYTHS
OF
CALIFORNIA

PEOPLE OF CALIFORNIA

United States:
Most of the modern state of California,
extending into small areas of Arizona, Nevada and Oregon;
and south into the Baja California region of **Mexico**.

The cultural region of California is a land of contrasting scenery, climate, flora and fauna. Part of the north, east and centre comprises high mountains. Below these lies a flat and fertile valley, bounded on the west by lower slopes, with the Pacific beyond. Much of the south is desert. There are several lakes and major rivers. The region is volcanic and susceptible to earthquakes and tsunamis. Much of California enjoys dry summers and mild, damp winters; however, in parts the weather is alpine, subarctic, temperate or subtropical.

Even today, almost half its total area is forested, containing some of the world's oldest and tallest trees: the ancient giant sequoias and redwoods. On slopes above the tree-line, the terrain resembles tundra, whilst the deserts support a variety of cacti. Wildlife includes antelope, black bear, bighorn sheep, bobcat, condor, deer, elk, hummingbird, jackrabbit, mountain lion, opossum, roadrunner, tortoise and many snakes. Most important to traditional Native American storytelling is the ubiquitous coyote.

Some historians believe that, before European settlement, this was one of the most densely populated regions of North America. Its abundant foodstuffs supported a simple but sustainable lifestyle.

An important staple food was acorns. Harvested from over twenty different species of oak tree, they were made edible by pulverising and straining through sand or baskets, or by immersing in mud or water; then processed into soup, bread or porridge. Surplus acorns were stored in big baskets on poles to protect them from animals. Some groups actively managed their local oak trees. Where oaks were scarce, supplies were obtained through trade.

Hunters caught a variety of small game, whilst fishermen concentrated on suckerfish or salmon. Fish were preserved by sun drying, light roasting or smoking, then stored in bark-covered baskets. Many other foods were gathered: shellfish, caterpillars, grasshoppers, worms, grubs, locusts, gnats and maggots; berries, roots, mushrooms, clover, seeds, peanuts and pine nuts.

Houses varied according to local climate and community styles. They were usually constructed from brush, grass, reeds, bark, mud or a bulrush mat, on pole frameworks. Most were cone-shaped; some were sunk into the ground, with dome-shaped walls and roof. In hot areas during the summer, open shelters were used. In the north, some peoples constructed plank houses as on the Northwest Coast (see p. 364). Each house normally accommodated just a single family, but most villages also contained a larger ceremonial/community building, and sometimes a special hut for women's seclusion during menstruation.

There was no central political organisation. It has been estimated that there were about 150 distinct tribal groups, many speaking different languages or dialects. Life centred on thousands of small villages, each containing between 50 and 500 people, usually a group of related families. Often a central village was linked to neighbouring smaller villages, sharing a single headman with limited powers, who either inherited his authority, or was chosen for his religious status or wealth. Some villages moved location with the seasons, others were permanently settled. Trade was important, extending as far as the Great Plains and the Southwest, using shell beads for currency.

Marriage was informal, usually involving payment by the groom to the bride's parents, presumably with her consent. Wealthier men might have two or more wives, sometimes sisters. There was no universal system of inheritance: some peoples were patrilineal, others matrilineal. Shared entertainments such as athletics and ball games brought all ages and both sexes together.

Many Californian peoples were – and indeed still are – famed for their exceptional skill in making baskets. These were fashioned from a variety of materials: willow and hazel twigs, pine and fern roots, grass, bark, twigs and yucca leaves, with the different colours and textures finely woven into geometric patterns. They were put to multiple uses: for beating and winnowing; for fish traps, weirs and nets; for carrying seeds or heavier burdens; and for storage. Some, being watertight and fireproof, were used for heating liquids over a fire; others were fashioned into hats or cradles. Bulrushes and logs were used to make boats, rafts and dugout canoes; bone and horn were fashioned into hooks and spear points.

Religion was expressed by rituals such as puberty ceremonies for both boys and girls, mourning, ceremonial dances, healing, reverence for sacred locations and intervention with the spirit world. The Maidu, Pomo and Wintun people all followed a cult known as 'Kuksu', named after a supernatural being associated with healing. It involved elaborate rites conducted in secret exclusively by men, in underground dance houses. Some peoples had shamans who could cure people from spirit 'pains', inflicted on them by other, hostile shamans; and used fetishes such as bundles of feathers, quartz crystals and giant moth cocoons.

LIFE IN CALIFORNIA
WHEN THESE STORIES WERE COLLECTED

By the late 19th century, life for many Native Californians had been irrevocably transformed by two phenomena.

The first was the influence of over twenty Christian missions, originally established in the coastal area by the Franciscans during the late 18th century. Native peoples were forcibly relocated to them, with many suffering appalling conditions and devastating exposure to European diseases. These so-called 'Mission Indians' were baptised into the Catholic faith, their traditional cultural practices were banned and they were forced to adopt Spanish names. Their ancient gathering, hunting and fishing lifestyle was replaced by unskilled employment on White farms and in workshops. California was originally politically part of Mexico, which became independent in 1834 and was ceded to the United States in 1848. After that, the missions were gradually secularised and transferred to new owners; the Native people living on them found themselves working for new masters as indentured labourers.

The other transformational phenomenon was the Gold Rush. From 1848, this brought vast numbers of White prospectors into California to set up mining camps. They destroyed countless Native American villages, with the occupants driven away, terrorised by mass rape and other violence, or killed. Those who survived saw their waterways tainted by mining activities and lost access to ancestral food supplies and sacred sites. Further dramatic changes came with the arrival of the stagecoach in the latter half of the 19th century. Some communities sought solace and hope in the Ghost Dance movement, which spread from the Great Basin into California from the 1870s (see p. 270).

It is estimated that the Native American population of California fell by over 90 per cent, to 10,000 people in 1900. Meanwhile, Indian reservations or 'rancherias' were established around existing Native American settlements in California. Some were later broken up by official allotment programmes, which assigned property to individual households, in an attempt to force assimilation.

STORYTELLING IN CALIFORNIA

Despite all this displacement and hardship, some of the old culture survived into the early 20th century. Surviving photos from that period show Native Californians wearing European dress but still practising traditional activities such as processing acorns and basket making. Moreover, a rich catalogue of stories continued to be passed down, and seems to have been willingly shared with the ethnologists who came to record them. An account of traditional storytelling amongst the Miwok people during 1913-14 states:

'These stories were formerly related at night in the circular assembly houses of the Miwok. Certain men versed in the myths often travelled from village to village, telling the tales in the assembly house of each village. Such a raconteur was known as an "utentbe"... Each utentbe was paid for his services, his audience presenting him with baskets, beads, furs, and food. Thomas Williams, who was formerly an utentbe, said that the telling of a myth often took all night. Not infrequently the myth was chanted. Each myth, whether chanted or told in ordinary prose, was accompanied by the songs of the various characters.'

Many of the surviving stories are lighthearted folktales. However, a good number seem to be based on ancient beliefs. Most notably, and in contrast to other regions, the iconic trickster, Coyote, had not been downgraded to a fool, but survived in his original form as a sacred character of great complexity and inspiration.

THE PEOPLES BEHIND THE STORIES

Achomawi
Originally from northeastern California, their name means 'river dwelling'. Today many still live in their ancient homelands, as one of eleven autonomous bands of the modern Pit River Tribe.

Maidu
Based in northeastern California, they were once split into three groups, the Southern, the Northeastern and the Konkow. Today many live on seven rancherias, and work to preserve their culture.

Miwok
Originally from north California. Today there are eleven federally recognised Miwok tribes and seven unofficial groups. Attempts are being made to revive their old language, dances and songs.

Pomo
Originally from the north California coast and hinterlands, some still speak the old language and practise traditional rites. Pomo basket making has an international reputation.

Shasta
Originally from north California and southern Oregon, mainly along rivers. Today most live on two reservations. Few speak the old language; but they maintain a vibrant tribal website.

Yokuts
There were once 60 Yokuts groups in a sizeable central area. Today many are enrolled in the federally recognised Yokuts tribe.

Yuki
Based on the northern coast of California, many still live on a reservation there, alongside a number of other peoples with whom they are closely integrated as the Round Valley Indian Tribes.

Research for this section also covered stories from the following Californian peoples: Atsugewi, Dieguenos, Gallinomero, Hupa, Juaneno, Karok, Luiseno, Maidu, Rumsen, Serrano, Shastika, Sinkyone, Tolowa, Wappo, Wintu, Yana and Yoruk.

COYOTE AND EARTH MAKER

Maidu

SONGS OF THE BEGINNING

In the beginning, there was no land: just water, water everywhere. On top of it, Earth Maker floated. As he floated, he talked to himself, saying, 'Soon the world must come into existence. But where? And how?'

At once, out of the void, someone answered him: 'Earth Maker!'

'Who's there?'

'It's me, Coyote.'

'Coyote? What do you want?'

'Earth Maker, I'm impressed by your power to speak of such momentous things.'

Earth Maker sighed. 'I'm just trying to work it out. Hmm... I reckon the world will begin...over there.'

'Where? How do you know?'

'Come with me, Coyote. You'll see. Let's float in that direction.'

So they did. But nothing happened, nothing changed.

After a long while, Earth Maker began to sing, over and over:

'Where are you, little world?

Where are you, mountains,

My great world mountains?'

Coyote listened, then took up the song, adding his own words:

'Where are you, world?

Where are you, foggy mountains

Mountains for us to walk on?'

Still nothing happened, nothing changed. They went on singing together until they both grew tired.

Coyote said. 'I don't believe you, Earth Maker. There's never been a world; and there won't ever be one either.'

'You're wrong,' said Earth Maker. 'I just have to find something to start it off. Once I do, I'll make it really good.'

All this while, they were still floating along. Suddenly, the surface of the water looked different. Something was drifting towards them – a lump of mud, the size of a bird's nest.

'Is *that* what you've been waiting for?' said Coyote.

'Hmm,' said Earth Maker, 'maybe.'

'That's much too small to make into the world,' said Coyote.

'No it isn't. I can stretch it.'

Earth Maker drew out five ropes and fixed them around the edge of the lump of mud. He spaced them out evenly, one to the east, one to the south, one to the west, one to the northwest and one to the north. When they were all secured, he began to stretch them. Sure enough, the mud grew bigger: wider and longer.

'You see, Coyote, it's working,' he said. Then he called out into the emptiness: 'Who sent this mud to me? Who found the fragments and stuck them together? Who found the stuff from which the world will be made? Whoever you are, sing! And show yourself. For in the time to come, people must know who you are.'

Earth Maker and Coyote listened. Suddenly, through the stillness, they heard a sound. It was a bird singing – the voice of Robin, the first created being in the world. He was singing his world-making song – the sweetest song that has ever been, or ever will be. He sang as Earth Maker hauled the ropes and stretched the lump of mud to make the Earth. He continued singing after the stretching was finished. Then finally he stopped.

'Coyote,' said Earth Maker, 'it's your turn again.'

So Coyote sang:

My world, where people will travel
By the valley edges!
My world of many foggy mountains,
My world where people will go zigzagging
here and there, through range after range!
I sing of the country I shall travel in.
In such a world I shall wander.'

Then Earth Maker also sang about the world he had just begun to create. Eventually he stopped and said, 'This world would be even better if it was even bigger. Let's stretch it some more.'

'As well as bigger, it needs to be more beautiful,' said Coyote. 'We ought to paint it with something. Don't you agree, Robin?'

'I have no idea,' said Robin. 'You two are both much cleverer than me. You thought about the world, you talked about it – and then you made it. You have the power to change evil to good.'

'So,' said Coyote, 'I shall paint the world with blood. There will be blood everywhere: people will be born with blood and so will animals; all creatures without exception shall have blood. And there will be red rocks too. Blood will make the world beautiful.'

'I believe your words are wise,' said Robin. And he flew away.

When he had gone, Earth Maker said, 'Coyote, lie on the ground, face down.'

Coyote scowled, but obeyed. While he was lying thus, Earth Maker continued to stretch the world, this time with his foot, east, south, west, northwest and north. When he was finished he said, 'All right, Coyote, you can look.'

Coyote stood up and gazed at the Earth. 'Is that the best you can do?' he snorted. 'I could run round that tiny world in no time.'

Earth Maker thought for a long moment. Then he said, 'Lie down again, flat on your belly. Whatever you do, don't look up.'

Coyote obeyed again. Earth Maker stretched the earth with his foot even more – this time until it was impossible to stretch it any further. 'All right,' he said at last.

Coyote stood up and gazed at it again. Now he couldn't help but be impressed. He nodded, then set out to walk eastwards.

Earth Maker stood still, watching him for a while. Then he set out too; first south, then west, northwest, north, east – and back to the spot he had started from.

There he began to make People. He started off with two White People, then made other pairs in slightly different shades. As he worked, he counted them. He kept making more and more, each pair a different colour. Then he counted out an equal number of countries, giving each pair its own home.

'You are a country of this name, and you shall have these People,' he said. 'They will grow through many dawns and winters. They will have children, girls and boys; and when these children grow up, they will have children in their turn. Thus, after many winters have passed, there will be countless people.'

He went travelling through the world, making more and more People, giving each pair their own country, some big and some small. He promised that no country or People should ever lack anything they needed to flourish. He gave them all instructions on how to live.

When he had finished, he said, 'One day, a long time in the future, this world will become bad. Although it is spread out flat, it is not stable. When it turns bad, all I need do is pull this rope a little, to make it shake. Afterwards I will make it over again, and the People will be reborn.'

Then Earth Maker's mood changed. 'But for now,' he said, 'let there be plenty of songs!' He began to sing, many different songs, one after another. 'These songs are for the People,' he said. As he sang, he walked along, on and on, until he reached the very centre of the world. There he built a house to live in, and stayed there.

THE BATTLE OF STRENGTH

Over there, just across from where the Sun goes down, long ago in the olden time, Earth Maker met Coyote going along.

'What are you up to?' said Earth Maker.

'I'm travelling through the world,' said Coyote. 'I'm going to spoil it.'

'How dare you! What will you do?'

Coyote spoke of things that made Earth Maker seethe with fury. 'If you talk like that,' he said, 'I shall have to destroy you.'

Coyote shrugged and went on his way.

Earth Maker called all the People, from all the countries he had made, to a feast. When they were all assembled, he said:

'Listen. I have grave things to tell you. When I made this world, I told Coyote that I wished it to be perfect. Inevitably, events happen and sometimes People must die. But I intended that, if the dead were laid full length in the water, they would come to life again the following day. Coyote opposed this. He said, "No, all beings must be mortal and only live for a certain time. Once they die, they must stay dead for ever." He is evil. I tried my best, but although I am the great chief, I could not override him. So now Death is permanent – and it is Coyote's fault. You will all share my anger with him – an anger that knows no bounds.

'That is why I have called you together here. I want you to hunt for Coyote everywhere; if necessary, right to the water on the furthest edge of the world. If you find Coyote, kill him at once. Yes, kill him, my People! Also, seek out every place where he has scent-marked, left his dung or scratched up the earth; every corner that he has fouled. Any trace of him that you find must be destroyed.

'However, beware. After you think you have killed him, you must wait four days; if you hear him howling during that time, you will know you have failed and he is still around. Only after four silent days have passed, can you be sure that we are rid of him for ever.'

The people listened to him carefully and answered, 'Yes.'

Meanwhile, Coyote had gone far away towards the west. He had no worries for he believed he was inviolable. He scent-marked bushes, scratched up earth and left huge piles of droppings for everyone to see. Even the rivers weren't safe from his excrement: wherever there was a raised patch of pebbles or grass, he swam out to it and ostentatiously relieved himself, then went away. He desecrated all the most beautiful places that he passed through.

However, Coyote did not realise that his time was nearly up, his freedom had a limit. For now the People were after him. Everywhere they went, they stumbled over his filth and damage that soiled the clean earth. They followed his traces, on and on… Until at last they caught him up.

They snared Coyote in a rope and led him along to the edge of the great water. They waded through it, dragging Coyote shamefully behind them, out to a tiny, barren island far, far from the shore. There they bound him tightly on top of a rock.

'You'll never escape,' they said. 'You'll die here. Despite all your arrogant boasting, you'll starve to death.'

Coyote grinned but said nothing.

The People went back to Earth Maker and told him what they had done.

Earth Maker said, 'This sounds excellent. But as I warned you, it might not be the end of Coyote yet. Go home and listen carefully. Only if you hear nothing of Coyote for four days, can you be certain that he is completely dead.'

So they went off. A night passed. In the morning, all over the world, they listened. Good, no noise. The next morning they listened again, and again all was silent…

Meanwhile, Coyote was still bound to the rock. He stayed calm and, after some effort, he managed to pass some dung. He looked down to examine it – and at once Gopher popped out.

'Ah,' said Coyote, 'so it's you. Help me!'

'Don't ask me,' Gopher said, 'I can't do anything.'

Coyote strained again. This time, a matted bunch of Grass popped out.

'Help me!' said Coyote again. 'Tell me how to save my life.'

The Grass answered him at once: 'It's easy. Make yourself like mist.'

'What good is that?'

'Wait in that form until dawn,' said the Grass. 'When the mist outside lifts and floats up, mix yourself with it. In that way you'll be able to free yourself, drift along, and get back to land.'

'You've spoken well,' said Coyote. '*Ts-ts-ts!*' He restored the Grass to where it had come from, and added Gopher as a plug. Then he transformed himself into mist and waited.

Just before dawn, as the first streaks of light appeared in the sky, the real mist outside began to rise. Coyote mingled with it and rose too. In this way, effortlessly, he floated across to the shore.

As soon as he was standing there, he howled. At once, many other howls – from his scent marks, droppings and scratchings – took up the chorus. The People heard them and were dismayed.

'Oh no! We tried our best to kill him properly, but we failed.'

'Go after him again,' said Earth Maker. 'This time, make sure you do not lose him.'

So they caught Coyote once more, and imprisoned him inside a hollow tree. They forced him to stand up on his hind legs, like a human being, leaving no space to put his front paws down, which caused him great pain. Then they blocked up the opening of the hollow with layers of thick wood. Thus he was completely enclosed on all sides, above his head and below his feet.

'Stay here and suffocate to death,' they said. 'This will certainly be the end of you, Coyote. You'll never get out of here, never bring trouble to the world again.' Then they all went home.

A short while after they had gone, Woodpecker flew to the hollow tree, looking for insects to eat. *Tap, tap, tap!* His beak worked hungrily across the bark, over and over, and found plenty. When night fell, he went away; but first thing the next morning, he returned to resume his meal. *Tap, tap, tap!* He worked on and on and, by the end of the second day, had made a sizeable opening into the hollow.

'My cousin!' Coyote called. 'Help! I'm imprisoned inside this tree. I beg you to make your hole bigger and let me out.'

'Who's there?' said Woodpecker suspiciously. 'Who's calling?'

Coyote didn't answer. So Woodpecker put his eye to the hole and peered inside. When he saw it was Coyote, he gave a squawk of disgust and flew straight off.

Now, for the first time, Coyote felt regret. 'I've been a fool,' he said. 'I shouldn't have argued with Earth Maker.'

He began to grunt and strain, over and over. Despite the cramped space, at last he managed to squeeze out Gopher.

'Help me,' Coyote begged, 'tell me what to do.'

'There's nothing you can do, except wait here to die.'

'Why can't you say something nice to me?' Coyote whined.

He grunted and strained some more until Grass came out.

'Help me!' Coyote cried.

'Why do you ask again?' said Grass. 'What I told you last time will work this time too. Make yourself like the mist.'

So Coyote transformed himself again, shaking off both form and shape. In this way, with the dawn mist, he easily drifted up, and out of the hole that Woodpecker had made.

The People were all listening out for him. A day passed: no sound. A second day passed: nothing. Then the third day: still silence. They grew more confident, daring to hope that this time they really wouldn't hear Coyote ever again. The fourth day dawned. It was almost wholly daylight. The People got careless, hardly even bothering to listen.

Suddenly: '*Owowow-woooo! Owowow-woooo!*'

'That's Coyote howling!' they screamed. 'He's escaped. It's truly impossible to get rid of him!'

Earth Maker heard their anguish and called them all back.

'Listen,' he said. '*I* will take responsibility for dealing with Coyote once and for all. I will send a deluge of rain, followed by heavy snow. The snow will melt and mix with the rainwater; together they will flood the whole world. The water will rise so high that even the tallest mountain peaks will vanish beneath it. Coyote will have no chance: he will drown in it and be destroyed once and for all.'

'But what about us?' the People cried.

'Together you must make an enormous canoe with enough room for you all. That way you will be saved and survive.'

The People set to work at once, building this canoe. It took them many months – two whole winters – to make it big enough to hold them all. When it was half finished, Earth Maker came to see how they were getting on. He admired their handiwork, then told them to stop for a few moments and listen carefully.

'I want to give you a warning,' he said. 'Be on your guard. Coyote may well play a trick to spoil our plan, he might even find a way to sneak amongst you in a desperate attempt to save himself.'

All the People nodded.

'Don't worry, Earth Maker,' one of the men called out. 'I'll make it my special duty to watch out for him.'

'You speak well,' said Earth Maker. Then he went on his way.

He hadn't realised that the man who had promised to be the lookout was actually Coyote himself! Yes, Coyote had cleverly disguised himself to look exactly like one of the men. They had unwittingly welcomed his offer to work on the canoe with them. The disguise was so effective that no one had the slightest suspicion.

At last the canoe was ready. Straight away, Earth Maker sent the rain. The water rose fast and flooded the People's houses. Then it snowed, and the snow melted into the flood. Day by day, it swallowed up the land and mountains. But inside the enormous canoe, rising on the surface of the flood, the People were safe.

'How is it?' called Earth Maker.

'We're fine,' Coyote answered for them all. 'And we're all overjoyed to think of that villain Coyote drowning!'

The mountains vanished. The whole world was water, just like at the beginning of time. The canoe kept drifting about…

Then one day, very slowly, the flood began to subside. A strip of flat land appeared on the side of a mountain. The canoe came to rest there and all the People climbed out. They were so happy to be safe and on dry land again.

However, as soon as they were all ashore – Coyote threw off his disguise.

When they saw him and realised he had outwitted them yet again, a great commotion broke out. In the midst of it, Earth Maker came. He stared at Coyote in thunderous silence.

'What's the matter?' said Coyote. 'Go on, speak out.'

'Coyote,' Earth Maker said at last, 'for a long time I have been trying to kill you, but you have always defeated me. I have to accept that your power is equal to mine. Because of this, I shall hunt you no more.'

Then Earth Maker and Coyote parted. And all the people went their separate ways, back to their own countries.

Dixon: *Maidu Texts*, stories collected 1902–03
Coyotes are wild dogs unique to North America, slightly smaller than wolves. Prolonged attempts have been made to eradicate them from the United States as troublesome predators. However, whereas numerous other species tragically succumbed to White persecution, coyotes have not only continued to thrive but have also expanded their range in recent years; suggesting that the cunning survivalist character of Coyote portrayed in the second part of this myth is based on observed fact.

Dixon says the story was translated line by line, from the northeastern Maidu language. He collected it, alongside other myths:

'from Tom Young, a half Maidu, half Atsugewi man who, although only about 30 years of age, possessed an extensive knowledge of the myths of the Maidu of this region... The Creation Myth [was] obtained in two parts in successive years.'

In the source, the myth continues with an episode about the killing of a being called Salt Man, resulting in the establishment of a place for gathering salt. Earth Maker and Coyote then resume their dispute, arguing about death, marriage and childbirth, taking turns to give way to each other. Next, Earth Maker goes around the world, destroying monsters; and finally the pair work together to shape the landscape.

Coyote also plays an important role in creation myths of the Achomawi, Atsugewi, and Yokuts. In Karok and Miwok myths there is a particular twist: Coyote makes all the animals then calls a council to discuss creating human beings. Each animal wants humans to have qualities similar to their own, but Coyote's trickery ensures they are created with *his* wit and cunning.

Many humorous Californian tales depict Coyote as a trickster who is not only exceptionally lewd, but also malevolent. A Maidu story begins comically, with him disguising himself as an old woman, carrying his penis like a 'baby'; however, he then uses it maliciously to carry out mass rapes. In another, Coyote plays a trick to marry his own daughter. A Karok tale describes Coyote wanting to dance with the stars – and ending up permanently dangling from one by a single paw.

For further Coyote myths see the following pages, the Great Basin story on p. 277 and the Plateau stories on p. 329 and 338. He was also an important character in the Southeast and Southwest.

COYOTE DANCES
FOR THE SUN

Pomo

There was a time when something went badly wrong with the Sun. Previously, it would rise right up into the Sky and travel across it each day. But now it just came a short way above the horizon, then quickly sank down again. Because of this, the world was constantly bathed in shadows.

In those days, the Sun was in the care of the Sun People. They lived in the east and were very powerful.

Their chief was called Sun Prophet. He had visions that showed him everything that happened in the world. If there was ever a problem down there, he was the one who dealt with it.

Second to him was Sun Man. He was responsible for carrying the Sun across the Sky each day. Sometimes he carried it in his hand; at other times, he wore it round his neck on a rope made of softened grapevine. As he travelled with it, he kept a sharp watch on the People who lived on the Earth below.

There were also four Sun Messengers, who went out with Sun Man each day. If Sun Man noticed someone on Earth doing evil, he sent the Messengers to shoot the wrongdoer with invisible arrows. Then they would drag the spirit from his body and carry it beyond the southern edge of the world to the Land of the Dead. There Sun Prophet – the chief – decided whether the wrongdoer should die permanently, or be restored to life.

So the Sun People had a lot of important work; carrying the Sun across the Sky was only part of it. Maybe that's why they forgot to raise the Sun high enough at this time.

Now, amongst the People on Earth, it was Coyote who had the most power, for he had created them. He had also appointed their chiefs and given each type of person their particular jobs as hunters, fishermen, fire tenders and so on. So when the People began to suffer from the lack of sunshine, they all asked Coyote if he could help.

'Yes I can,' he said. 'A group of us need to go to the Sun People's country and seize the Sun from them. Once we've got hold of it, we can fix it permanently in its proper place, high in the Sky. I shall choose the best men to come with me, and then I shall lead the way.'

The men he chose were all excellent dancers, and also strong enough to bear the great weight of the Sun disc.

Before they left, Coyote dressed in his ceremonial clothes and told the others to do the same. While he was waiting for them, he took a large hunting sack and packed a bunch of medicine feathers inside it. Then he ordered four Mice to run into the sack.

When everything was ready, the whole party set off towards the east in a long line, dancing and singing as they went. At last, just before dusk on the fourth day, they arrived at the Sun People's village, and went straight to the dance house.

They danced around it four times in each direction. Next, without waiting to be invited, they entered the house itself. Here they danced round the fire, round the centre pole, and then round the fire and pole together. Finally, they all sat down.

Sun Man had seen them arrive and sent a Messenger to greet them.

'Welcome,' he said. 'Why do you honour us with this visit?'

'We wish to dance with you tonight,' said Coyote.

'Excellent!' said the Messenger. 'My chief will be happy to hear this. Rest here while everything is made ready.'

Coyote and his party waited quietly. In due course, they heard footsteps and the other Sun People came in, led by Sun Man himself. He was wearing the Sun disc round his neck. It was so brilliant, that even a mere glance at it was almost blinding. He carefully removed the disc, stretched up his arms and attached its grapevine rope to one of the rafters of the dance house. There it hung, swinging gently, its glimmering golden surface flashing.

Sun Man turned to Coyote and his followers and greeted them warmly, repeating his Messenger's welcome. Wood was brought, the fire was lit and other preparations were made for a great dance.

Then Sun Man said, 'My honoured guest, you shall choose the first dance.'

'I request the Fire Dance,' said Coyote. 'And I would like everyone present to join in.'

'A good choice,' said Sun Man. And he signalled for the dance to begin.

As everyone stepped around the flames, Coyote quietly slipped out of the circle into the gloom beyond. He fetched his sack, let out the four Mice hidden inside, and spoke to them in a whisper: 'Friends, run up the central pole and along the rafters to where the grapevine rope is fixed, with the Sun disc dangling from it. Gnaw through the rope as fast as you can.'

The Mice nodded and scampered off. Coyote returned to the dance, which was getting faster and faster.

Suddenly there was a soft thud, and a shower of sparks flashed out of the fire. One of the Mice had lost his footing and fallen into it. He wasn't harmed, scarcely even scorched, and at once sprang out and dashed away. But one of the Messengers saw him and snatched him up before he could escape.

'So, little intruder, what are you doing here?' he cried. He held up the Mouse by the tail for Sun Man to see.

'Hurl the wretch into the fire,' Sun Man ordered. 'Let him have a quick death by burning.'

But before the Messenger could do so, Coyote strode forward and snatched the Mouse from his hand. 'Don't waste good food,' he said. 'Mouse is my favourite meal.'

Sun Man roared with laughter. 'Each to their own taste, Coyote. Go on then, eat him if you will.'

Coyote put the Mouse to his mouth. But instead of devouring him, he whispered, 'We can easily trick these people. Run down my arm and out of the dance circle into the dark. From there, sneak back up the pole and continue gnawing.'

As he spoke, he made a great show of waving his hand about and thrusting it into his mouth. The Mouse scurried away, while Coyote pretended to munch and swallow him. He even made a loud noise as if he were crunching bones, for he had secretly crammed a piece of charcoal into his mouth for that very purpose.

'A tasty titbit, eh?' laughed Sun Man. He was too busy joking with Coyote to notice the Mouse shinnying back up the pole.

Shortly after this, a second Mouse fell into the flames in a cascade of sparks. Again a Messenger rushed forward to kill him, again Coyote snatched him to safety and pretended to eat him, while the Mouse fled back up to continue gnawing. The same near-catastrophe happened with the other two Mice as well.

When the fire dance was over, everyone went off for their usual plunge into the sweat-house followed by a short swim. Then they performed two other very long dances, continuing well into the night. By this time, all the Sun People were exhausted. One by one they sat down, gleaming with sweat and yawning.

However, Coyote was still bursting with energy. 'One more dance, to round it up to four,' he cried.

'I'm afraid you'll have to do this one alone, if you really have strength left for it, Coyote,' said Sun Man.

'I certainly have,' said Coyote. 'And I have some extra decorations to wear for it too.' He went to his hunting sack, pulled out the bunch of medicine feathers he had brought and fixed them carefully to an ornamental stick. As he danced, he waved the feather-stick gracefully about; and as he waved it, the medicine seeped out and scattered through the air. It was sleep medicine. Its effect was immediate: very soon, all the Sun People were snoring.

However, the medicine did not afflict Coyote's followers. Those on the dance floor stood at the ready for the Mice – who did not let them down. As the last Sun People dozed off, the Mice finished gnawing through the grapevine rope – and thus freed the Sun disc, which went tumbling towards the floor. However, before it could smash there, all Coyote's men rushed forward with hands outstretched and caught it.

'Dance backwards!' Coyote yelled. 'Then flee!'

So they resumed their dancing in reverse order, round the fire and the central pole, round the pole alone, round the fire alone and out through the door. They circled the entire dance-house one way and then the other; and finally turned westwards, towards home.

They were all very weary and it was a vast distance. However, Coyote helped them by crying, 'Earth, shrink to speed my People on their way!' The Earth obeyed, so that in no time at all their journey was almost over.

Back in their village, Red-Headed Woodpecker saw the dazzling light of the Sun disc signalling their approach. It grew clearer and even brighter as they drew near. Red-Headed Woodpecker called out all the other villagers to see it, and they waited in an excited throng to greet the adventurers.

When they arrived, Coyote laid the Sun disc carefully on the ground in the centre of the village for all to admire.

'What shall we do with it?' everyone wanted to know.

'We must hang it up in the Sky, as high as possible,' said Coyote. 'Who will volunteer?'

There was a great clamour as all the birds fought to be chosen. Chief Hawk called for silence.

'All shall have a chance to try,' he said. 'Two of each kind of bird, two at a time.'

Two Hummingbirds went first. They failed. Next, two Loons tried, then two Eagles, then many other types. They all failed too. For the Sun disc was extraordinarily heavy, and none could fly very far up with it before the weight dragged them back down. The air filled with squawks of frustration and dismay.

'We haven't tried yet,' said the Crows.

'You?' the others mocked them. 'How can *you* possibly succeed when the most capable among us have already failed?'

The two Crows did not bother to answer. They strutted forward to the Sun disc, which still lay uselessly on the ground. One Crow grasped its edge, just as all the other birds had done; but the other wormed his way right underneath the disc, taking its weight on his back. Then they rose together, crying, '*A-a-a-a!*'. Their method was a clever one: their ascent was slow but much steadier than any of the others. Every so often, they swapped positions so that neither had to bear the greater burden for too long. In this way, they reached such a height that they could scarcely be seen.

'They're almost near the correct spot where the Sun should hang!' cried Red-Headed Woodpecker. 'Ach, now they've slowed down, they must be tiring, they've stopped to take a rest.'

Everyone waited with bated breath.

'They're flying again...' said Red-Headed Woodpecker, '...only a very short distance from the top... Yes! They've reached it! There, they have hung it up. The Sun is in its rightful place in the Sky! Now they are coming back down.'

Free of their burden, the Crows shot down to Earth in an eye-blink. Everyone crowded round to congratulate them, bathed in the glowing light and warmth of the Sun.

Then everyone went into their houses and brought out gifts of beads and blankets, baskets and food, which they piled at the feet of Coyote, his followers and the Crows.

After that, there was only one thing left to do: they had a celebration dance.

Barrett: *A Composite Myth of the Pomo Indians*, 1906
This story is noticeably similar to widespread fire myths – see THE THEFT OF FIRE, p. 277. Barrett says that it was collected in 1904 from an unnamed informant, who in term had learned it from some older people. It was part of six linked narratives about Coyote's exploits; but apparently this episode was often told as a stand-alone myth.

The five linked Coyote myths open with him as a lecherous, vengeful and destructive deceiver, who destroys the world by fire. He is taken up up to the Sky world by Spider on a rope of feathers, where his elder brother Mamumda – the chief deity – scolds him and orders him to mend his ways. Coyote returns to Earth, where his great fire has left no water anywhere except in the sea. There Coyote drinks his fill, but becomes ill and collapses. A shaman jumps on his belly, causing the water to gush out of him and thus replenish all the rivers and lakes. He builds a village and plants feathers inside each house; these transform into animal-people. He invites them all to a dance where he designates Eagle and Grey Squirrel to be joint chiefs. Wood Duck – who in the first story had suffered from his lechery – is made the woman chief, and she appoints Hawk as the supreme chief. Coyote now announces his retirement. Next comes the story presented here. Finally, Coyote turns the animal-people into the actual animals and birds that live in the world today, and gives them their typical characteristics.

A number of other sun myths were collected in California. In some the sun is an object, in others a person. One Achomawi myth briefly tells how the sun fell down from the sky, and was caught and held by Mole until some people came along and pushed it back. Another features some Buzzard brothers who accompany Woodworm to Sun's house, trying to discover why Woodworm's brothers had all been killed. Woodworm marries Sun's daughter, and after some dramatic adventures, restores his brothers to life. A third Achomawi story describes Sun leaving his daughter at home in winter, and carrying her around in his basket during the summer. She is stolen by Fish Hawk in revenge for Sun's disparagement of poor people. Sun is grief-stricken, and so relieved when the shaman Kingfisher finds her, that he does not punish her abductor.

A Maidu story portrays Sun as kidnapping children. When he snatches Frog's grandson, she pursues Sun and swallows him. Inside her belly, Sun swells up until he kills her, transforming her into a real frog.

In a Miwok myth, Sun is a beautiful woman, covered in dazzling abalone shells. When she vanishes, Coyote sends a gang of men to bind her in ropes and drag her back.

THE TEN MOONS

Shasta

In the old times, there wasn't just one Moon; there were ten of them. These Moons lived far away in the east. They controlled the weather, in a bad way. One of them sprayed blizzards everywhere, another spat rain, a third filled the air with icy balls of hail, a fourth blew out strong gales with every breath, and so on. Together they had inviolable power; and they used it ruthlessly to ensure that the world was either battered by storms or blighted by perpetual winter.

Because of this, the People's lives were a misery of shivering and struggles. Every day they discussed what they could possibly do to change things for the better, saying:

'The only way would be to kill those heartless Moons.'

'But that's not so easy. They go wandering about all over the place every day; and they cover such vast distances here and there, that we'd never be able to catch them.'

'Even if we could, we wouldn't be able to kill them, because their house is guarded by the great bird Toruk.'

'Yes, and the Moons have cut out the bones from both his legs to stop him escaping. He's in such pain and so frustrated, it's turned him completely savage; we'd never get past him.'

Thus they all worried and grumbled over and over.

However, one day Coyote said: 'I know how to do it. I can overcome the bird Toruk with my tricks – and I can kill the ten Moons too.'

'Whoah, Coyote! Can you really?' they all cried.

'I can,' said Coyote, 'and I will. I'll go at once.'

He set out on the long journey to the east. When he finally arrived at the Moons' house, it was the middle of the day, and all ten Moons were out. Only Toruk was at home, perched uncomfortably on his boneless legs just inside the door, moaning quietly to himself. When he saw Coyote approaching, he flapped his wings threateningly, stabbed his beak at the air and screeched a warning cry.

Coyote didn't cower or flinch. Instead, he said soothingly: 'Hush, Uncle, it's only your friend – me, Coyote.'

'Coyote? What do you want?' Toruk squawked suspiciously.

'To make you better, Uncle. Look, I've brought you some tasty food. And when you've eaten it all, I'll mend your poor broken legs.'

He passed the bird a big dish of meat. Toruk didn't hesitate, but started gobbling it up at once. As he did, Coyote spoke to him in a kindly voice: 'If I help you, Toruk, would you help me in return?'

'Maybe. Hmm…I must admit, that meat was good, better than the dry roots those brutes the Moons feed me on. If you can really mend my legs, Coyote, then you can ask whatever you want of me.'

Coyote had brought two branches freshly cut from a young oak tree. He quickly shaped them into bird legs, then fastened them to Toruk's body.

'These are good, Coyote, very good,' said Toruk. 'Yes, in return I'll do what I can for you.'

'Firstly, Uncle,' said Coyote, 'I need you to tell me everything you can about your masters, the ten Moons.'

'Well,' said Toruk, 'there's not much to tell. They go out every day…'

'So I've heard,' said Coyote. 'What for?'

'Gathering roots,' said Toruk.

'Ah. And do they share these with you, or leave you to starve?'

'As I've told you,' said Toruk, 'I get dry roots to eat. They wouldn't starve me, because they need me to guard their house from intruders like you. We have an arrangement that, when I get hungry, I call them. Then one of the Moons comes back to feed me right away until I'm satisfied.'

'Call them now, will you, Uncle,' said Coyote. 'Get them to come to the door.'

'Don't be stupid!' Toruk cried. 'If any of the Moons find you, they'll slaughter you at once.'

'Uncle, don't worry, just call.'

So Toruk gave a sharp cry: '*To-o-oo!*'

They waited for a short time. Then suddenly the Sky burst open in a torrent of rain.

'Quickly,' whispered Toruk, 'hide, Coyote – in here behind me!'

Coyote sidled inside the Moons' house and waited on the far side of the door, peering surreptitiously around it. Very soon he saw the rainstorm Moon rolling towards them, in a halo of shimmering water. As the Moon approached the house, he yelled, 'What's the matter, slave? Are you hungry?'

'Yes, master,' said Toruk humbly.

'Here,' said the Moon, 'I'll scatter some roots for you. Come and fetch them.'

'I can't, master, I'm too weak from lack of food, and anyway, you've hobbled my legs. I beg you, bring them inside.'

The Moon spat with impatience; but he went right up to the door and poked his head in, peering around for the bird.

At once, Coyote pounced. He seized the Moon's hair, sliced off his head, then dashed out and tossed both head and body behind the house.

By the time this was done, he was quivering with damp and cold. He squatted down and warmed himself by the fire.

'Well done!' said Toruk.

'Yes, that's one out of the way,' said Coyote. 'Now, I'll hide again while you call the next Moon, Toruk.'

So the great bird repeated his squawk: '*To-o-oo!*'

Very soon, a violent wind blew up and came whistling across the plain towards them. The second Moon came spinning along in its wake.

'What is it, slave?' he hissed. 'Didn't my brother feed you enough?'

'No master. You've no idea what hard work it is keeping your house safe from prowlers,' Toruk simpered. 'No matter how much I eat, I'm soon famished again. Would you be so kind as to drop some more roots just inside the door for me?'

The Moon huffed and puffed irritably, but he did as he was asked. Once again, Coyote leaped out at him, chopped off his head and tossed the Moon's remains out of the way.

'That's two of them gone, Coyote, just like that!'

'Yes, this is going well. Summon another.'

'*To-o-oo!*'

This time, the earth under their feet began to harden with frost. Huge snowflakes came drifting down, whirling around and settling on top of them.

'Snow and ice,' said Toruk. 'That means the biggest Moon is on his way.'

The next moment, they heard this Moon booming through his blizzard, 'Slave, why do you keep bothering us? Surely you've had enough to eat by now?'

'No, master,' the bird called back. 'My stomach is like a bottomless pit, it's such hard work being on guard here, driving all your enemies away.'

'Very well then. I'll toss you some roots,' said the Moon.

'No, master,' Toruk wailed. 'You know I'm a cripple and I can't reach them outside. Please bring them right up to me. Without enough food, I can't do my work properly, master. Then one of your enemies could break through and cause you no end of trouble.'

The Moon hesitated for a moment, then came right up to the house and made ready to toss some roots in through the open door.

'Master, come closer,' Toruk urged him.

So he did. And Coyote beheaded him, just like the rest.

In this way they went on, one Moon after another falling into Toruk's trap, to be decapitated by Coyote. But he didn't get off unscathed. For each Moon brought a new wave of wild or freezing weather with him; and even when each was dead, his cold lingered on. Coyote grew more and more chilled. He became numb; he could scarcely move his limbs, and his insides were like a glacier. As he tried to thaw by the fire, suddenly he heard Toruk calling him urgently: 'Coyote, we've got to flee!'

'Why, Uncle? Have we killed all the Moons now?' Coyote asked.

'Not all of them. There's still one left. But when you tossed the last Moon's head out of the way, his hair fell into the edge of the fire. Can't you smell it burning?'

'Ah, so that's the cause of the awful stink! Even though my nostrils are blocked up by ice, I can certainly smell it.'

'It's so strong, Coyote, and it's drifting across the world so fast, that the Moon who's still left alive will soon smell it and realise something has happened to his brothers. He's the fiercest one of all. We've got to get out of here before he comes to take revenge!'

And so they left at once, Toruk running beside Coyote on his fine new legs. They got home safely, and with only one Moon left, the weather soon settled down and grew warmer.

It's a great thing that Coyote did this. Otherwise, there would still be ten moons in the world – and life would be really uncomfortable for everyone.

Dixon: *Shasta Myths*, 1910
This was one of a number of myths collected at Shasta reservations in California and Oregon. The halting style and inconsistencies of the original suggest that it was in the unnamed narrator's actual words, perhaps recounted randomly from memory. In a parallel Shastika myth, Coyote not only destroys nine surplus moon brothers who have been freezing the world, but also nine out of ten sun brothers who were threatening to burn everything up.

A number of other moon myths were told in California. Another Shasta tale features an old woman transformed into the moon by a hero who had escaped her attempts to destroy him; whilst a Luiseno story says the moon was the reincarnation of a great wise man, killed by Frog Woman in revenge for him spying on her when she was bathing. In a Dieguenos story, the People hold races to stop the moon waning. A Maidu story is centred on an argument between Coyote and the Moon, the latter wanting the dead to rise again as he does, but Coyote overriding him. In an unfinished Yana tale, Fox, Mountain Lion and Wolf visit Moon's house to court his daughter, but are overcome by his fire and pipe smoke. A Yokuts myth tells of Coyote asking the Moon not to rise any more. His wish is granted, as are similar requests made to Thunder and the Sun; he then persuades Night to stay all the time, but eventually everything returns to normal. A Tolowa story, recorded in 1860 from 'a daughter of the oldest woman then living' in the tribe, says that the only fire that survived a great flood was kept on the moon; it was brought back to Earth by the Spider people, who climbed to the moon by a gossamer rope and floating ball.

RATTLESNAKE SONG

Yokuts

The kingsnake said to the rattlesnake:
'Do not touch me!
You can do nothing with me,
Lying with your belly full.
Rattlesnake of the rock pile,
Do not touch me!

There is nothing you can do,
You rattlesnake with your belly full,
Lying where the ground-squirrel holes are thick.
Do not touch me!

What can you do to me?
Rattlesnake in the tree clump,
Stretched in the shade,
You can do nothing.

Do not touch me Rattlesnake of the plains,
You whose white eye
The Sun shines on,
Do not touch me!'

– Performed by an unnamed shaman at a Rattlesnake Ceremony
(Quoted in Kroeber: *Handbook of the Indians of California,* 1919)

THE SINGING TREE

Miwok & Yokuts

It was the beginning of time – before People came into the world.

Condor lived on top of a high mountain. From its peak, he could see everything in all directions, even as far as the ocean. Every morning he flew out hunting. Every evening he returned to roost on his favourite rock, on the eastern side of his mountain.

One morning when he woke up, the rock looked somehow different, somehow *weird*. He felt sure something was wrong with it.

Now, on a small creek nearby, there lived two wise bird doctors: the Snipe brothers. Condor flew down to consult them.

'I believe that my rock has fallen sick,' he said. 'Doctors, I beg you to heal it. Come with me, let me show you.'

The Snipe brothers followed him up the mountain. When they reached his rock, they walked round it several times and poked it gently with their long beaks. At last they said, 'What is your relationship with this rock, Condor?'

'I am very fond of it,' he answered. 'I roost on it every night.'

'Ah, that is just what we suspected. This is no ordinary rock, Condor – it is your wife.'

'My *wife*? But...but... Is there something wrong with her?'

'Nothing is wrong. She is about to give birth to your child.'

'My child! But how?'

The Snipe brothers strutted around, gathering logs and branches, piling them up and setting light to them. Once these were ablaze, they went to the rock, prised it loose and rolled it into the middle of the fire. The rock heated up and began to glow... then suddenly burst open with a deafening clap like thunder. From its midst a shadowy figure shot out with a loud '*Wek!*'

'My son!' Condor gasped. 'Falcon!'

The Snipe brothers withdrew, leaving Condor to gaze in amazement at his son. Falcon was already fully grown. He did not greet his father, but rose hastily into the air and flew away. North he flew, then west, then south, not once diving down to explore the Earth stretched out below. But when he turned east and flew to that distant, sacred place where the Sun rises... Ah, there was a sight and a sound which made him sink to the ground in awe.

It was an elderberry tree. Its branches and leaves were heavy with luscious bunches of berries. At that time, in the beginning time, it was the only elderberry tree in the whole world. It grew on top of a round hill, surrounded by a den of writhing rattlesnakes. The tree was constantly shaken by the wind, and the swaying of its branches made wonderful music, an everlasting song of sweetness. As soon as Falcon saw it, the moment he heard its music, he thought, 'I must have this tree for myself!'

He hovered over it for a long time, wondering how he might manage to obtain it. Then he noticed a movement close to the tree and swooped lower to investigate. Two chiefs of the Star Women were hard at work with their digging sticks close by. They were Morning Star and Pleiades, and both were dazzlingly beautiful. He alighted on the ground and walked up to them.

They exchanged greetings, then Morning Star said, 'Why have you come to us? What do you want?'

'Oh, sisters, I long to know everything about this wondrous tree.'

'Ah,' said Pleiades gently. 'We make the tree sing without cease, to keep us awake all day and night, and thus continue our work.'

'But why is it surrounded by rattlesnakes?' Falcon asked.

'To protect the berries from all the birds who wish to steal them.'

At these words, Falcon − a bird himself, of course − flew guiltily away. Swiftly he went, and soon arrived back at Condor's house.

There he said, 'Father, I have flown far and even further, to the sunrise place in the east. There I saw a marvellous tree, that plays on the wind all day and all night, making the sweetest, most exquisite music. I long to snatch this tree away and bring it back here so that we can enjoy it too. Can you tell me how to do this?'

'I am not wise enough to help you fulfil your wish,' said Condor. 'But ask your grandfather, for he knows everything.'

'My grandfather? Who is he? Where can I find him?'

'He lives in the ocean,' Condor replied.

'Father, I flew over the ocean when I was exploring the world to the west. And I flew back over it again, when I turned and made my way east to the sunrise place and the singing elderberry tree. But I did not see anyone who might have been my grandfather.'

'He is not a bird like us, my son. Fly back to the ocean now and look for a stump of wood bobbing in the waves, making soft noises as it rises and falls. Your grandfather lies within it. Do not try to seize the whole stump. Instead break off a fragment of the wood, small enough to carry in your beak.'

So Falcon hurried back to the ocean and flew low over the waves until he found the bobbing stump of wood his father had spoken of. He darted at it with his sharp beak, tore a long splinter from it and carried it home to the mountain top.

When he woke the next morning, the splinter had vanished. In its place, a strange new house had suddenly appeared.

Falcon went up and called through the door, 'Who lives here?'

'My dear grandson, I do,' a voice answered him; and the next moment – he saw none other than Coyote!

Falcon was astonished and hurried back to Condor. 'Father, is Coyote really my grandfather?'

'So you've met him at last,' said Condor. 'Ask him about the singing tree, my son, for he knows everything and will surely be able to give you the advice you need.'

Falcon went back to Coyote and said humbly, 'Grandfather, I have been to the sunrise place in the east. There I have seen the Star Women's marvellous tree, playing the sweetest music in the world. I long to bring the tree here. How can I do so?'

'Ah,' said Coyote. 'So you've found it already, have you? Well, let me warn you that bringing it here will be very difficult. Unless you follow my instructions, it might even cause your death.'

'I'm not afraid of dying, Grandfather. I want it. I *must* have it.'

'Well, in that case, I give you my permission to buy it.'

'Buy it? But how can I pay for it?'

'You must gather shells, my grandson, as many as you can carry. But wait! Before you go, listen further and be sure to heed my advice. You already know that the Star Women chiefs are irresistibly beautiful and charming. They will be expecting your return, and this time, they will do all they can to delay you. They will lure you with smiles and friendly, tender words; they will invite you to linger and play with them. Do not give in to temptation unless you wish to die.'

'Thank you, Grandfather; I will remember and obey you.'

Falcon flew back to the ocean. He gathered up countless shells and threaded them on a string so long that one end was out of sight of the other. Then he flew back eastwards to the sunrise place, with the shells streaming out behind him.

The Star Women were waiting for him.

'What have you brought us?' Morning Star asked.

'Money,' said Falcon. 'I will give you all these shells, in return for the singing tree.'

'That's fair payment,' said Pleiades. 'We happily accept.'

She held out her hand and took the shells. Then Morning Star held out *her* hand, and led Falcon to the round hill. As they approached, the snakes all rose and hissed and shook their rattles. But the Star Women scolded them and shooed them away down their holes, until the ground was completely clear.

'Now,' said Morning Star, 'Use this digging stick to break off a small piece of the tree to take home.'

'I want more than a small piece,' said Falcon boldly. 'In return for all the shells I paid you, I want it all.'

'Do what we say,' said Pleiades. 'You won't be disappointed.'

Falcon remembered how the splinter of wood from the stump bobbing in the ocean had transformed into Coyote. Perhaps a piece of this tree would produce a similar result? He took the digging stick and did as Morning Star had told him, breaking a large piece of the tree away. But before he could fly off with it, the Star Women began to dance round him, flashing enticing smiles and stroking his feathers.

'Don't go yet,' they urged him. 'We like you. Stay and play some games with us. Let us love you. Oh, Falcon, you can't imagine the fun we shall have together if only you will stay!'

'No!' said Falcon, remembering Coyote's warning.

'Has someone spread ill rumours about us? Ignore them, Falcon. Stay with us and be happy.'

'No!' he cried again. Then he rose into the air and sped back to the mountain top where Coyote was awaiting him.

'Grandfather,' he cried, 'I've brought the singing tree!'

He held out the piece he had carefully carried back with him. 'Shall I plant it here, so we can enjoy its music at once?'

'No, not here but everywhere,' said Coyote. 'We must plant pieces of it all over the Earth. Everywhere it grows, it will make not just music, but also food and medicine for the People.'

'But Grandfather, there *aren't* any People.'

'There will be soon,' said Coyote, 'for the Earth will burn and then cool again; and after that, you and I shall make People out of feathers. For now, come round the world with me to prepare it.'

So Falcon and Coyote travelled together, north, west, south and east. At each place they came to, they planted a piece of the singing tree; and each one they planted sprouted and grew – ready for the People's creation.

Merriam: *The Dawn of the World*, 1910

Merriam attributes this story to the Hool Poom Ne people who 'are now extinct'. He includes it in his collection of Miwok tales, but a modern online commentary claims that both the story and the people who told it were really of the Yokuts tribe, who mixed and intermarried with the Miwoks as a result of the troubled events of the 19th century.

The episode here is part of a longer myth. The next section tells of Falcon gambling against a giant, resulting in Falcon's death. The grieving Coyote plays a return game against the giant, and kills him. As fire spreads across the world, Coyote restores Falcon's life and sends him into the sea. Once the fire has cooled, Falcon returns home with Coyote and they use three different types of bird feather to create human beings, which turn into a male chief, a female chief and ordinary people. Coyote and Falcon now transform into their animal and bird forms. The only fire still left in the world is guarded by the Star Women, in the original elderberry tree in the east; Hummingbird is sent to fetch it, and places it in other trees so that the newly created people can easily obtain it.

The California or blue elderberry tree grows up to six metres (20 feet) high, particularly near rivers and streams. Traditionally, its berries were eaten either fresh, dried or cooked; and were also used as dyes for basketry. Its dried flowers were brewed into tea, used to treat childhood fevers, and its crushed leaves were used on sprains and swellings. Its hollowed stems were made into whistles or flutes, whilst other parts of the tree were fashioned into musical instruments.

The California condor is actually a vulture, the largest land bird native to North America, a scavenger of carrion. It became extinct in the wild in the 1980s, but has since been reintroduced to its previous range. Condor is a character in several other Yokuts stories.

Two species of falcon live in California, the peregrine and the prairie falcon; both feed on small birds and mammals. The former is one of the fastest birds in the world. Snipes are water birds with long beaks.

It is interesting to note that, in contrast to the myths of the Great Plains, the Star people here are women.

THE END OF DARKNESS

Achomawi

In the beginning, when the world was still new, only the animals went out and about. The People had been created, but they stayed shut up inside their houses, fast asleep. For it was always night time and the whole world was dominated by Darkness.

Darkness was a woman. She lived in the east with her two daughters.

Darkness wanted to find a husband for these daughters of hers. She'd heard much talk of a chief called Chickenhawk, and reckoned he would be a fine match for them. Unfortunately, Chickenhawk was already married. But Darkness didn't let that put her off. One night, she took her daughters on a long journey. Eventually, they reached Chickenhawk's house and Darkness knocked on the door. It was opened by Chickenhawk's wife, Wildcat Woman.

'What are you lot doing here, Darkness?' said Wildcat. She wasn't pleased to see them.

'We've come to gamble with you,' said Darkness.

'It's not convenient. We're all just about to eat our evening meal.'

'Aren't you going to invite us to share it with you?'

'There's not enough food for three extras, and the house is already crowded,' said Wildcat. 'My husband has lots of followers.'

'That's all right,' said Darkness. 'We won't eat much. It's the games we've come for.'

Of course, Wildcat couldn't refuse to give hospitality, so she had to let Darkness and her two girls come inside. Sure enough, all sorts of animals were already gathered there to eat, including Coyote.

As soon as the food was finished, Darkness stood up and called out, 'Wildcat, are you ready? It's time for our game. Get the playing pieces ready.' She sat down on one side of the fire, shooing everyone else out of the way.

Wildcat spoke quietly to her husband: 'Hmm, I'm not sure it's wise to do this.'

'What else can you do?' said Chickenhawk. 'Darkness has great power and she'll take revenge if you turn her down.'

So Wildcat laid out her gambling sticks, then sat down on the far side of the fire, opposite Darkness. 'Right,' she said, 'what stakes shall we start with?'

'If I lose, you can have both my girls,' said Darkness at once. Everyone gasped.

But then she added, 'Don't make the mistake of thinking I'm wildly generous – because I'm betting them against your husband, Wildcat. If you lose, I win Chickenhawk. You'll have to hand him over, to marry my daughters.'

'No!' said Wildcat.

'Are you arguing with me?' snarled Darkness.

There was a long silence. Coyote crept forward and whispered into Wildcat's ear, 'Go along with what she wants. This is how it has to be. I'll help you with the singing.'

Wildcat guessed that, if she won Darkness's daughters, she'd have to give them to Coyote. But she knew Coyote's advice was always worth listening to. So she said, 'All right, Darkness, I agree.'

The two players started singing, and the game began. Everyone joined in the song, with Coyote loudly encouraging Wildcat to play well. And it worked. Wildcat guessed correctly over and over again.

Then suddenly, just as Wildcat had won almost all the sticks, her luck turned. Darkness won the next round, and the next – and the next one too. Wildcat's winnings vanished. Darkness's pile of sticks grew bigger and bigger...

'So!' Darkness cried, 'I've won them all! Chickenhawk, you are mine. Release him to me, Wildcat.'

'No.'

'Trying to keep your mangy claws in him are you?' sneered Darkness. 'Hey Chief Chickenhawk, you'll be glad to exchange that mean old wife of yours for my two beautiful girls won't you, eh? As for you, Coyote, I heard you cheating with your song, trying to guide Wildcat into guessing right. Well, you know what you deserve? This!'

She seized hold of Coyote, snapped him into two – *wump!* just like that – and hurled the pieces outside. Everyone else in the house wailed in dismay.

'Be quiet, all of you!' screeched Darkness. 'Chief Chickenhawk, come to me. From now on, you are my son-in-law. But the game isn't finished yet. I want to gamble some more. Wildcat, I'll stake my girls again if I lose. And you lot gathered here – are you cowards? Or will you dare to offer yourselves as stakes in return?'

Few wanted to be accused of cowardice, so almost everyone in the house agreed that they should be paid to Darkness if she won the next game. Only three refused to do so. They were Caterpillar, Lizard and Rabbit.

Wildcat Woman played the next game as hard as she could. But without Coyote to guide her, she quickly lost.

'People,' cried Darkness, 'I've won you all! You're mine, mine! Don't expect me to be merciful.'

Wildcat gave a hiss of despair. 'I'm so sorry. I've failed you all.'

'Let *me* take over,' said a soft voice. Caterpillar slithered forward. 'Darkness, I wager myself against your daughters.'

Darkness laughed scornfully. 'You? You're so small, I'm surprised you can even speak. But I'm enjoying myself, so why not?'

'These gaming sticks of yours are getting hot from overuse,' said Caterpillar. 'Let's use these nice fresh ones of mine.' He brought out a set of sticks that were cool and slippery to the touch, like ice.

They began to play. The slippery sticks unnerved Darkness and distracted her. She kept making foolish mistakes, so that Caterpillar won round after round. Soon Darkness only had one stick left.

'Stop wriggling and twitching,' Caterpillar ordered her. 'Be still.'

'How dare you tell me what to do!' screeched Darkness.

'If I can't tell you, I'll have to show you,' said Caterpillar. He slithered across to her, seized the last stick and shoved it at her – deep into the shadowy mass of her body. At once, with a deafening crash, Darkness burst! Bits of her scattered all over the house.

'Be gone!' cried Caterpillar. And he kicked her remains outside.

All this time, Darkness's two daughters had sat very still, not saying a single word. But as soon as their mother was destroyed, the eldest leaped to her feet.

'You'll not get away with this, Caterpillar,' she screamed. 'Don't think the game is over. Now you must play against me, and be warned, I can play even better than my mother. Come, set out the sticks for a new game.'

'No, *you* be warned,' said Caterpillar. 'As you've already seen, to play against me is to beckon death.'

'You'll not frighten me so easily, you pathetic creature.'

They began to gamble. True to her boasting, the girl played strongly, and in no time at all was almost victorious. But at the last possible moment, Caterpillar suddenly turned things around and quickly won all the sticks back from her. 'You see,' he cried, 'I am the winner!' To prove his point, he slid another of his icy gaming sticks straight at her. It entered her body and she too exploded, exactly like her mother.

Now the younger of Darkness's daughters was left alone in this house of hostile strangers. She sat there shaking with violent sobs.

'What are you crying for?' sneered Caterpillar.

'How can you ask? Thanks to you, I've lost my mother and my sister – I've lost everything.'

'You've got nothing to complain about. I've lost far more than you – my chief and all my people. I shan't let you get away with this. I shall win them back. Now it's *your* turn to play against me.'

The girl protested, but Caterpillar insisted. It was a long game, very long. First he let her almost win. Then he suddenly bounced back against her – retrieved all the winnings – then reversed it again, letting her think luck was on her side – until finally he swept everything to himself.

'I have beaten you, girl. I claim back all your mother's winnings – all my people. As for you – go the same way as the rest of your abominable family!' With those words, he slid his icy stick one more time and slaughtered her too.

Caterpillar turned to Chief Chickenhawk and his people, who had all been huddled in the back of the house, awaiting their sorry fate.

'So, my friends, you are saved, you are free! Pass these words down to your children. Teach them to say, "It was Caterpillar, that callow youth, who won everyone back from Darkness!"'

So it was. Yet despite the end of Darkness and her daughters, their shadow had not left the world. Still nothing could be seen, nothing could grow.

None of the animals had any power left, except Caterpillar and two who had refused to be gambled, Lizard and Rabbit. Caterpillar had already completed his work. Now Lizard stepped forward. He went to the fire, snatched a burning log from it and held it up. A small circle of light glowed around it. He carried the log outside and made his way through the gloom until he reached Big Lizard's house. Rabbit went with him.

Big Lizard came out to greet them saying, 'I've heard such noise and commotion! Whatever is going on?'

Lizard told him. 'Now Rabbit and I have come for your help, to chase the last dregs of dark from the world, and flood it with light.'

Big Lizard nodded and went back into his house. He returned with a great mask made from the head of a grizzly bear. 'Put this on, Lizard, then dance. And you, Rabbit – you must sing.'

Lizard donned the hat. Rabbit burst into song:

'Daylight is coming,
Daylight is coming,
Daylight is coming…'

As he sang, Lizard danced. By and by, very slowly, a hint of light appeared in the Sky. Then Lizard's grandmother came out and joined in, singing:

'Daylight is coming,
My lover is coming,
My lover is coming…'

'Stop!' cried Lizard angrily. 'You mustn't sing such profane words, Grandmother. All you ever think about is men!'

'Sorry, sorry,' the old woman cackled. 'The words came out wrong because my teeth are all gone…'

Lizard turned his back on her in disgust. 'Rabbit,' he said, 'go and see if the light is coming.'

Rabbit paused in his song. He walked towards the north. Nothing. He walked towards the west. Nothing. He walked towards the south. Nothing. Finally, he walked towards the east…and saw dawn just starting to come up, streaking the Sky with soft shimmers of light. But the light was so dim, he wondered if he were dreaming it. So he went back and told Lizard, 'It's not coming yet.'

Lizard danced some more while Rabbit continued to sing. Then Lizard sent Rabbit out again. This time he returned and said, 'Brother, daylight *is* coming! Look!'

Lizard turned and saw it. Together they stood and watched as the light seeped across the Sky, just as a flood spreads over the ground. As they watched, the world emerged from the shroud of gloom that had held it in suspense. Birds began to sing. Trees and mountains revealed their shapes. Grass and flowers unbent and thrust their way up towards it. It was the first spring.

All the People woke up and rose from the beds where they had been waiting since the beginning for this dawn of time.

Lizard ceased his dancing. 'People,' he called. 'Now you are properly born. Open your doors and greet the morning. Go out and live!'

Dixon: *Achomawi and Atsugewi Tales*, 1908 / 1909
This was one of a number of myths collected during the summers of 1900 and 1903. Dixon says that some were given as text, but nearly half were obtained only in brief form in English; and that his chief informants were men called Charley Green, Charley Snook and 'Old Wool'.

Although the source names Darkness' gambling opponent as Wildcat, that is not a specific North American species; coming from California she is most likely a bobcat or a mountain lion. 'Chickenhawk' is the popular American word for three species of hawk, supposedly derived from their favourite prey, although this is just one of many birds – usually wild ones – that they attack.

The gambling game in this story was probably a form of the stick guessing game played by many tribes in North America, described as follows in 1907 by Culin in *Games of the North American Indians*:

'The number of sticks or disks varies from ten to more than a hundred, there being no constant number. The first operation in the game, that of dividing the sticks…into two bundles, is invariably the same. The object is to guess the location of an odd or a particularly marked stick. On the Pacific coast the sticks… are usually hidden in a mass of shredded cedar bark. The count is commonly kept with the sticks or disks themselves, the players continuing until one or the other has won all.'

He adds that most gambling games were accompanied by singing. In an Achomawi version of the game:

'Four rods – two bound…and two plain…are juggled behind a large, flexible basket plaque…and the relative position of the rods guessed at. The game is counted with ten counters.'

Stories about gambling were widespread across North America; see the Subarctic myth, THE BOY WHO GAMBLED HIS FAMILY AWAY, p. 507.

The original source says that the three animals who refused to be used as gambling odds were Caterpillar, Rabbit and Weasel; however, there is no further mention of Weasel. For consistency, the retelling here has substituted Lizard for Weasel, since later in the source Lizard is named as an important survivor. Lizard appears in a number of other Californian stories, sometimes playing a role in creation, or the acquisition of fire. A few stories depict him as malevolent; however, more frequently he is a neutral or helpful character.

CHILDREN'S INITIATION SONG

Yuki

This rock did not come here by itself.
This tree does not stand here of itself.
There is one who made all this,
Who shows us everything.

– Sung by unnamed shamans.
(Quoted in Kroeber: *Handbook of the Indians of California*, 1919

Bannock hunting party fording the Snake River southwest of the Tetons,
illustration by Frederic Remington, 1895

MYTHS OF THE GREAT BASIN

PEOPLE OF
THE GREAT BASIN

United States:
Nevada and Utah.
Parts of Arizona, California, Colorado,
Idaho, Oregon and Wyoming.

The landscape of the Great Basin is is characterised by parallel rows of canyons and mountain ranges, with areas of desert, and encircled by peaks and plateaus. It is predominantly arid, with warm summers and cold winters; rainfall is generally low but there can be considerable snow in winter. Its rivers and streams all either drain into saline lakes, including the Great Salt Lake, or are absorbed by underground inland 'sinks'. Vegetation is sparse and typically comprises grass, sagebrush and open forest, in which important trees are pinyon (small pines with edible seeds) and juniper. Animal life includes coyotes, deer, mountain lions, pronghorn antelopes, rabbits, lizards, snakes and golden eagles.

Traditional Great Basin society was organised into small bands of around five households. They lived nomadically, moving with the changing seasons to harvest wild plants as they ripened, and to follow game animal migrations. Tribal identity and ritual were less developed than in other regions. However, when the need arose to make major decisions affecting the wider community, councils were convened; and big social gatherings were held to mark natural events, such as the pine nut harvest and fish spawning. These assemblies provided opportunities for trade, and for organising joint action against shared enemies. They were also a time for arranging marriages, which simply involved setting up new joint households without formal ceremony. Amongst the Ute, a major social event was the Bear Dance to celebrate nature's spring awakening; this was followed by the summer Sun Dance, adopted from the Great Plains (see p. 22).

Great Basin life was dominated by the seasons. Spring and early summer was the time to gather roots, seeds and berries; and to socialise with other bands. In late summer, root digging became busier, and small game hunting began. Autumn activities were fishing, harvesting pinyon nuts, hunting large game and drying meat for winter use. Winter was the time for making clothes, and repairing tools and weapons.

The main means of subsistence was gathering wild seeds, nuts and berries, and unearthing roots with digging sticks. It is said that the Paiute knew 96 different species of edible plants. Pinyon nuts were especially important and nutritious; they were roasted in pits or ground into meal for gruel or cakes. Other useful foods were prickly pear cactus flowers and fruit, and the inner bark of trees. Plants were also collected for medicinal purposes. Grasshoppers were caught and processed into paste, roasted or cooked in soup. Hunting concentrated on small game such as rabbits, rodents, snakes, lizards and birds; and, less commonly, larger animals such as deer, mountain sheep, elk and pronghorn antelope. Groups of men often travelled to the Great Plains to hunt buffalo. Salmon and other fish were caught in long-handled dip nets or trapped in weirs. Some Paiute bands were small-scale farmers, growing corn, squash, melon, gourds and sunflowers.

A common form of summer house was the wickiup – a small, conical building constructed from a pole frame covered with brush and reed mats. Tipis covered in buffalo hides were also widely used. Winter housing often comprised clusters of mounds with underground chambers. Land travel was conducted on horseback. Water travel used rafts made of reeds.

Great Basin craftwork included utensils made from mountain sheep horn, bags made from salmon skins, quillwork, beadwork and watertight coiled baskets covered with pitch. The yucca plant provided raw materials for rope, baskets, shoes and sleeping mats. The Ute fashioned ceremonial pipes from alabaster and rare black pipestone. Their rattles filled with quartz crystals flashed when shaken in the dark, and were believed to have strong powers to summon spirits.

LIFE IN THE GREAT BASIN
WHEN THESE STORIES WERE COLLECTED

By the late 19th century White settlers, dominated by members of the Mormon Church, were rapidly encroaching on the Great Basin. This caused inevitable conflict over land and natural resources, and also brought in devastating diseases. Some Native peoples reacted by raiding Mormon farms; however, many eventually converted to Mormonism.

One of the iconic movements of 19th century Native American history, the Ghost Dance, originated in the Great Basin. In 1870, a Paiute healer called Wodziwob was greatly disturbed by the large numbers of his people dying from European diseases, and dreamed that he had power to restore the dead to life. He organised his followers to paint themselves and perform a circle dance, during which he claimed to visit the dead and receive their promise of return. The Ghost Dance rapidly spread around the region and also into California and the Plateau; but two years later Wodziwob brought it to an end. However, in 1889, with Native American communities continuing to suffer widespread devastation, it was revived by another Paiute holy man called Wovoka, who worked on a Mormon ranch and was training to be a traditional 'weather doctor'. He claimed that he had visited Heaven in a vision and had come back to preach virtue, the adoption of some 'White ways', industry and peace. He also promised that the five-day Ghost Dance would enable people to be reunited with their lost loved ones. Special Dance shirts were made, that supposedly protected wearers against bullets and evil spirits. The movement quickly spread into the Great Plains, where officialdom regarded it as seditious; its presence there helped provoke punitive US Government policies and the tragic Wounded Knee Massacre (see p. 23).

STORYTELLING IN THE GREAT BASIN

Traditionally in the Great Basin, winter was the time for sharing news and stories with visitors around the fireside. However, the stories collected by ethnologists in this region before 1920 are fewer in number and less rich in content than those from other regions in

North America. It is not clear why this should be; perhaps many older narratives were lost as part of White suppression and assimilation into a culture dominated by the Mormon ethos.

In the surviving Great Basin stories, as in California, the divine trickster Coyote is often an important protagonist.

THE PEOPLE BEHIND THE STORIES

Paiute

The first Paiute Reservation was established in 1891 with others following. Today many people belong to the officially recognised Paiute Indian Tribe of Utah, which is divided into five bands, based on ancient community identities. Other Paiute live on the Warm Springs Reservation in Oregon alongside Sahaptin and Wasco and people from the Plateau.

Shoshone

Their name comes from a word meaning 'high growing grasses'. Some neighbouring tribes and early European explorers referred to them as 'Snakes'. They are related to the Comanche people of the Great Plains, who broke away from them in around 1700. Today most Shoshone live in the community of Shoshone-Bannock Tribes on the Fort Hall Reservation in Idaho, established in 1868. The Northwest Shoshone are an independent group within the larger tribe, with their own farmlands in Utah.

Ute

The Ute were one of the first Native American tribes to obtain horses. Historically, they had a reputation for being fierce raiders and warriors, with women and even children fighting to defend their camps. Today over half their enrolled members live on the Uintah and Ouray Reservation in Utah; and there is a separate Southern Ute reservation in Colorado.

Research for this section also covered stories from the Chemehuevi people.

WOLF AND IRON MAN
SMOKE TOGETHER

Shoshone

Wolf was the father of the Indians. He lived under the ground. Iron Man was the father of the White people. He lived on the great water.

One day Wolf called his younger brother, Coyote, and said, 'I want you to take a message to Iron Man. Travel across the water to his house, then call out that I send him my greetings.'

Coyote scowled, but did what his elder brother told him. Iron Man heard him approaching, and came out to shake Coyote's hand. He listened to Wolf's message then said, 'Send my own greetings back to your elder brother. More than that, tell him to pay me a visit. Does he like competitive games?'

'He loves them,' said Coyote.

'Excellent. We've obviously got more in common than either of us realised. When he comes here I'll set up a couple of contests, a bit of fun to test which of us is stronger. I'm looking forward to it.'

Coyote hurried home and gave his brother the message. Wolf grinned and got ready to go. He set out the very next morning, running eagerly over the ground, then paddling across the great water. Coyote followed him, silent as a shadow. When Wolf reached Iron Man's house, the door was wide open. He slipped straight through it and found Iron Man awaiting him inside.

'Welcome, Wolf!' he cried. 'Come in, make yourself at home.'

So Wolf did, putting down his bow and quiver and settling himself by the fire. Iron Man went to fetch his pipe. It was so big and heavy, he had to drag it along the floor. Its bowl was as wide as his own wrist, and its stem was longer than his arm. He set it before Wolf.

'I hear you like competitions,' he said. 'So let's try this one: see which of us can smoke the longest.'

Wolf licked his lips and nodded.

Iron Man brought out a fat wad of tobacco, cut it up and crammed it into the pipe. 'You go first,' he said.

Wolf picked up the enormous pipe as if it weighed nothing and lit it from the fire. When it was burning steadily, he put the end of the stem to his lips and breathed in deeply, then blew out a cloud of smoke three times. Next, he pointed the stem to the east, drew on it and exhaled three more times. He turned it to the south, the west, the north, then up towards the Sky and finally down to the ground, each time doing exactly the same. Then he continued to puff away at the pipe very calmly – until all the tobacco was gone.

'I'm impressed by your stamina,' said Iron Man admiringly. 'But I'm certain you'll find that I am more than your equal.'

'Indeed,' said Wolf. 'Now, my friend, since I had the honour of smoking your pipe, I would like to honour you in the same way, by offering you mine.'

He went to his quiver and drew from it a pipe that was already full to the top of its bowl with tobacco. It was just as splendid as Iron Man's pipe, but less than half the size.

'You make it far too easy for me,' Iron Man protested. 'I'll have finished that tiny morsel of tobacco in no time at all.'

'Try it,' said Wolf, 'and see.'

He lit the pipe, sending out a billow of sweet-smelling smoke, then passed it to Iron Man, who took it and began puffing away. Wolf sat very still, watching in silence.

Iron Man smoked on and on. After a while, he took the stem from his mouth and peered into the bowl. It was just as full of tobacco as when he had started smoking it. He drew on it some more. The smoke drifted round and round his house, growing thicker with every puff. Wolf still said nothing, still watched him. Gradually, Iron Man's breathing grew shallower, and the smoke he exhaled grew thinner. Through the fug, Wolf saw him swaying in his seat with glazed eyes. Suddenly, Iron Man vomited violently; then he fainted.

Wolf went over to him and gently released the pipe from Iron Man's hand. Then he blew out gently, and his breath dispelled the smoke into nothing.

After a while, Iron Man came round from his stupor. The two of them sat in easy companionship, watching the fire.

Eventually, Iron Man stretched and said to Wolf, 'You certainly beat me at that contest, my friend. Ah well, I'm ready for another.'

'So am I,' said Wolf.

'This time it should be on *my* terms,' said Iron Man, 'with materials which my people have used for as long as yours have used tobacco.'

'That's only fair,' said Wolf.

Iron Man went to a basket and drew out two enormous, dark balls of iron. He gave one to Wolf and kept the other for himself.

'Let's make these into guns,' he said.

Wolf readily agreed.

So the two of them set to work, melting the iron balls over the fire and breaking them into pieces. They beat, bent and rolled each piece into the shape of a gun. Iron Man worked feverishly and soon had a towering pile of fine finished weapons. But when he looked up, he saw that Wolf had made even more.

'Well?' said Wolf.

'You've beaten me again,' said Iron Man.

'So – which of us has greater power?' said Wolf.

'It seems that you do,' said Iron Man reluctantly. 'And yet...I find it hard to believe, for the White people who *I* made have grown far more powerful than your Indians. Maybe you have been cheating.'

Now, all this time, Coyote had been hiding silently outside Iron Man's house, spying. As soon as Iron Man spoke those slanderous words, Coyote slunk in through the door and revealed himself, staring at Iron Man with his amber eyes.

'Iron Man,' he snarled, 'you speak lies about my elder brother. Even I can prove that our power is far superior to yours.'

'*You?*' said Iron Man with a roar of scornful laughter. 'All right then, prove it by taking down the Sun from the Sky!'

'You don't mean that?' Wolf said quietly.

'Yes I do,' said Iron Man, 'and I know that it's impossible.'

'It's not impossible,' said Wolf. 'But it's an immensely dangerous thing to ask of us. My friend, take back those words.'

Iron Man hesitated.

But Coyote didn't hesitate at all. He dashed outside, threw back his head and howled at the Sky. His cries echoed on and on. And at last – the Sun itself came tumbling down, just like that! The instant it touched the Earth – all the light in the world, and all the warmth, were both completely extinguished.

The next moment, Iron Man began to shiver violently as his blood seized up and froze. In the darkness, he staggered to his feet – but immediately smashed his head against the wall. Trembling with cold, blindness and rage, he spun round and tried to stumble towards the door...but instead, crashed against another wall.

'What's going on?' he shouted. 'I can't see! Wolf, where are you...? Ach, my head... Get that detestable midget brother of yours to put the Sun back. All right, I admit it, your power is far greater than mine.'

At those words, Wolf himself ran to the place where Coyote had dumped the fallen Sun, seized it and tossed it back up to the Sky.

In this way, the world at once returned to normal.

Lowie: *The Northern Shoshone*, 1909
This was one of a number of stories that Lowie collected from unnamed narrators in 1906 at the Lemhi Agency in Idaho, just before the Shoshone people who lived there were forcibly removed to Fort Hall Reservation in the same state. He says:

'The majority of the myths were told by old informants and taken down from the translation of my interpreters. Several stories were told in the Shoshone-English jargon of a middle-aged Indian sufficiently conversant with English to make himself understood.'

He gives two versions of this myth, both similar and very sparsely told, with some different details; they are combined in the retelling here. Wolf and Coyote appear together, often as brothers, in other Shoshone stories.

The description of Wolf's pipe-smoking ritual comes from the journal of White explorer Meriwether Lewis, who experienced it amongst the Northern Shoshone in 1805. He says that the pipe they used was made of a dense, highly polished, semi-transparent green stone.

The myth is an example of how Native American storytellers wove the tensions caused by White settlement into their narratives. An Ute folk tale in a similar vein, from 1909, describes Coyote outwitting two White men by transforming a tree and a rabbit into two horses, which easily win a race. The Whites are so impressed that they insist on buying the prize animals; but the following morning, find they have vanished into thin air.

A Paiute myth cites Wolf as a major deity, saying, 'The Sun and Wolf created everything'. It opens with an unnamed creator and his wife burning all the earth to ashes, then vanishing. Wolf and the Sun make a flood, and after it subsides, they create people, plants and animals. When the people start fighting, Wolf kicks them out, to form the various tribes.

SUMMER DANCE SONG

Paiute

Already the summer moon is rising,
Coming to clothe everything [with leaves].
It will clothe the chokecherry,
It will clothe the serviceberry,
It is coming to clothe everything.

Now the summer moon is half risen,
The first big moon.
Such it was taught by the forefathers,
Thus we are going along singing.
Such is the song of the big moon that we have,
This is the dance song.

— Patotzi, leader of the Wadatika Band of Northern Paiute
(Collected before 1913. Quoted in
Kroeber & Marsden: *Notes on Northern Paiute Ethnography*)

THE THEFT OF FIRE

Ute

Back at the beginning of time, the People had a very strange way of cooking and keeping warm. Every day, they used to collect a load of big, flat rocks and heap them together in a great pile. As the day went on, the rocks in the centre would heat up, and then the People would take them out to use, throwing water onto some to make steam. It wasn't easy, and it wasn't very effective either.

In those days, wise Coyote was the chief. He was very dissatisfied with this system, and sure there must be a better way.

One day, out of the blue, it came to him. He was lying on his bed, gazing aimlessly out of his tipi, when he noticed a mysterious object drifting down through the air and landing by his doorway. He hurried out to investigate, and found a small fragment of a plant. It was a piece of reed, yet unlike any he had ever seen before. It was almost black, and so dry and brittle that it almost crumbled away at his touch. He placed it carefully in a shallow basket, then shouted for his headmen.

As they came hurrying in, Coyote excitedly showed it to them, saying, 'Look at this, so dark and brittle. I believe it has been burned on a fire.'

'What is "fire"?' they asked.

Coyote answered, 'Fire is wood and flames, smoke and heat, power and light. It transforms everything it touches. If we could only get hold of this fire, we could use it to cook our food and warm our houses. I believe this mysterious fragment originated in the centre of a fire in a distant land; that it rose up on a column of smoke and was carried here by the wind. My friends, let us find the place where this marvellous fire burns. Let us seize its power and bring it back here to improve our lives!'

The headmen all nodded solemnly.

'You winged ones,' Coyote cried, pointing to them, 'Crow, Eagle, Grouse and Owl, Hummingbird, Hawk Moth and all you others – bring your best men to help. And send runners to the tribes that live further out, summon them all to do the same.'

When they had departed, Coyote sent another headman to fetch a large bundle of fresh tree bark. Once he had brought it, Coyote sent everyone home, telling them to prepare to set out early next morning. Alone, he started work, beating the bark with a stick, so that, by sunset, it was entirely crushed into shreds. He dropped these into a bucket of dark paint, left it to soak and went to bed. At sunrise, he fetched the bark from the bucket; it had now turned deep black. He pulled it out, shook it dry and placed it on his head. It looked exactly like a long-haired wig, hanging to the ground. He took it off and wrapped it up carefully in a carrying thong.

Shortly after that all the strongest and most able men from near and far arrived, ready to begin the quest. Coyote showed them the mysterious fragment, and explained that it was a piece of fire, saying, 'It arrived here on the wind. The strongest wind blows from the west, so that is where it must have come from. Let us go!'

He hoisted the carrying thong onto his back, and led the way.

They walked for several days, camping briefly at night. On the third night, they slept below a mountain; and next morning they climbed it. From its peak, they could see the whole world spread out far and wide before them.

Coyote said, 'Do you see that big grey object in the distance like a cloud, constantly billowing about and changing shape? I believe that is smoke, coming from the fire. That is our destination.'

When they descended to the flatlands and made camp, they could no longer see it, so Coyote sent flying scouts to check its location.

First, he sent Red-Tailed Hawk, who returned and said sadly, 'I saw nothing, Coyote. Perhaps I did not go quite high enough, but I had no strength to fly any further.'

Then he sent Eagle, who soared up so far that they all lost sight of him. When he finally returned, Eagle said, 'Chief, I went as high as it was possible to go, and far beyond many mountains, waters and great plains, I again glimpsed the billowing smoke.'

'Who can find out more?' said Coyote.

'Send Hummingbird!' the others cried with one voice. 'Though he is small, his wings beat faster than anyone's.'

Coyote called Hummingbird and asked if he would undertake this task. For a long while, Hummingbird just hovered there, not saying yes nor no. Then, with a sudden short chirrup, he flew off. He was gone much longer than the other two birds – so long that they began to fear he had fallen from the Sky and was lying dead. At last, when they had given up hope of ever seeing him again, he reappeared. After another long silence, he said, 'I flew further than it is possible to imagine – to the place where the edge of the earth meets the edge of the Sky! And from there I made out, even further away, a strange, jagged mass of light – yellow and orange on a base of darkness, bending with the wind.'

Coyote gave a cry of joy. 'My friend, what you say warms my heart! This is the very thing we are seeking!'

The next morning he led them on as before, over endless mountains, valleys and plains. Every so often, Coyote sent out his winged scouts to see how they were progressing.

At last Hummingbird announced, 'that jagged light is much closer now – just beyond the three great ranges ahead.'

So Coyote led them across those mountains and the canyons that lay between. When they stood on the last peak he said, 'Dear loyal and courageous friends, we will stop here to prepare. We must wash the long journey from our bodies, dress in clean clothes and decorate ourselves.'

This they did, and soon everyone was finely attired. But none could match Coyote's splendour when he draped the shredded bark wig over his head. It flowed like real hair over his shoulders to his feet, richly woven with gleaming ornaments.

Now Coyote divided the People into groups, saying, 'When we arrive in the Fire People's village, each group must seek hospitality in a different tipi. I myself will stay with the Fire Chief and use my cunning to work out a way to steal their fire. Guard this secret with your lives! When the time comes, I will give a signal, so be alert. It will take the form of two loud whoops. When you hear it, prepare to carry the fire to our home.'

They all nodded eagerly. Coyote went on, 'Be warned: the Fire People will put up a strong fight to try and stop us. They'll chase us, attack us, try to kill us. Some of you will certainly die in the process. Is anyone too afraid to take part?'

No one spoke against Coyote. Each man promised his support.

Coyote led the way down into the village. They received a very warm welcome. As planned, Coyote spent the first night in the Fire

Chief's own tipi, whilst the rest of his men lodged with the other villagers, who all gave generous hospitality.

The next day, the Fire Chief said, 'Friend Coyote, you have travelled so far to honour us with your presence. What is the reason for your journey?'

Coyote replied, 'We have heard that your People are outstanding dancers. We travelled here to witness one of their performances. For my People are keen dancers too, and eager to learn from yours.'

'I am truly delighted,' said the Fire Chief. 'Dancing is indeed our greatest pleasure. I will arrange a performance this very night, as soon as the Sun sets, and your People must join in. Tell me, is there any way we can make the experience especially enjoyable for you and your companions?'

'Since you are kind enough to ask,' said Coyote, 'I do have one special request. Where we come from, there is no such thing as fire. I myself have no fear of the smoke and flames, but my companions tell me that the fires in the tipis they slept in last night caused them all much alarm and distress. Is it possible to extinguish all those fires before the dance begins?'

'Of course,' said the Fire Chief. 'I will arrange for water to be poured over to quench them all. But we do need to keep our great central fire burning; and we will be dancing around it. I hope your People can accept that?'

'Oh, they won't mind a single fire burning outside,' said Coyote quickly. 'It's the numerous fires indoors which unnerve them.'

Thus it was agreed. That afternoon, the Fire Chief went about ordering each household to put out its fire and soak the embers in water. By the time this was completed, it was growing dark. The Fire People all gathered round the bright flames of the central fire alongside Coyote's People, all dressed in their best clothes and ornaments. When Chief Coyote emerged in his richly bedecked bark-shred wig, everyone gasped in awe.

The dance began. Both hosts and guests swayed and spun vigorously and joyfully, on and on. Every so often, some would sink to the ground to rest before leaping to their feet again.

But Coyote danced ceaselessly all night long. Only when the first light of the new dawn began to streak the Sky, did he pause. And then he let out a loud whoop: *'OOOH-YIPP!'*

At the sound, every other dancer stopped. The Fire Chief hurried over. 'Whatever is the matter, friend?' he cried. 'Are you hurt or ill?'

'There's nothing wrong,' Coyote assured him. I whooped to express my delight at the wonderful night I'm spending here. We never have such good dances in our own country.'

The Fire Chief nodded and retreated. But Coyote's People were now on full alert. They watched him resume his dance, saw him move closer and closer to the great fire.

'OOOH-YIPP!'

At the second whoop, Coyote's People moved away from their hosts and tensed up, ready to spring into action. Suddenly Coyote pulled off his wig and flung it into the fire. The fine shredded bark was perfect tinder: it quickly burst into flames.

At once, Coyote ran, dragging the flaming bark hair in his wake, carrying every single last spark. The flames rippled behind him like a snake of shimmering light, leaving nothing behind. Where, only moments before, the central fire had burned brightly, now there were just cold ashes.

Since all the other village fires were already extinguished, the only fire left in the whole world was now in Coyote's hands.

He raced off with it. Behind him ran his People, guarding his back, thundering over the ground. The Fire People were dismayed at Coyote's cruel deceit and followed their own chief in hot pursuit. But by the time they set out, Coyote and his followers were already well over the first mountain ridge, racing faster than a horse caught up on the wind.

But after a while, as Coyote pounded along, even he began to tire. He shouted to Eagle: 'My friend, you can fly much faster than I can run. Take this from me and flee!'

Eagle seized the flaming wig in his talons, soared into the air and carried it thus for a long distance. When he too tired, he passed it to Hummingbird, who took it willingly, flapping his small wings in a blur.

By now, Coyote had fallen right back, he was at the very rear. He called after the others, 'Listen, friends! The Fire People are now our sworn enemies. If they catch any of us, they will kill us. Those of you who are exhausted may hide to save your lives − and thus live on for the future.'

Some heeded his words and dived into holes and caves, lying low until the danger was over. Meanwhile, Hummingbird handed the fire to Hawk Moth, who in due time passed it to Chicken Hawk, and so on. Coyote took it back for a while, then passed it again to the flying People... Until gradually, one by one, they ran out of strength, dropped out and went into hiding.

The only one left was Coyote.

The pursuers closed in on him, eager for the kill. Coyote ran over a hilltop, dived into a hole and pulled a stone over the opening to seal it. From outside, his hiding place was invisible. He crouched within, clinging tightly to the remnant of fire, which was now reduced to a dull, tiny spark.

After a while he emerged, changed direction, leaped into a ravine – and was spotted again. But this time, the Fire Chief said, 'Ach, let the wretch tire himself out. I will make a storm of rain and snow to drown and freeze him to death. It will also extinguish the fire he stole. For since we cannot enjoy it any more – neither shall *his* People.'

The next moment, rain began to bucket down, flooding the valleys knee-deep. Coyote waded on through the seething flood and hauled himself up onto a small hillock, sparsely covered with cedars. On top of it, Black-Tailed Rabbit was sitting nonchalantly in a puddle.

'Help, friend!' yelled Coyote. 'I have just fetched fire from a distant country – and my enemies are trying to steal it.'

'Fire?' Rabbit cried. 'That's a treasure indeed!'

'It is,' said Coyote, 'but I fear it will cause my death, for the enemy I snatched it from has made this great flood. I beg you to save me from it – and thus save fire for everyone in the world!'

'I could hold the fire for a while, if that's any help,' offered Rabbit.

So Coyote gave him the meagre piece of smouldering shredded bark. Rabbit, thinking to protect it, promptly sat on top of it.

'Fool!' Coyote shrieked. 'You've put it in the water – get it out before the flame dies for ever!'

Rabbit thrust it back angrily. 'Huh! Look after it yourself, Coyote, and don't ever ask for *my* help again.'

'I apologise,' said Coyote humbly.

Rabbit grunted. 'Oh, all right then, I'll tell you this: there's a cave in the rocks over there that you could hide in.'

Coyote thanked him, hurried to the cave and crawled inside. The flood had not penetrated; it was completely dry. Near the back, he found a big pile of dry sagebrush and cedar twigs. He spoke to the twigs in a trembling voice: 'You are here to be used. I shall make you into a fire and teach you how to burn.' He placed the smouldering fragment of bark under the pile and blew on it.

At once, the flame flared up and spread. The sagebrush and cedar caught light. In no time, an excellent fire was blazing.

Meanwhile, outside, the Fire Chief transformed the rain into a snowstorm and the floods into thick ice. But, safe inside the cave, Coyote warmed himself by the fire. He fell into a long sleep, dreaming that the weather had cleared. Sure enough, when he awoke and peered out, the south wind was starting to blow. In no time, all the snow and ice had melted.

Coyote picked up a thick stem of sagebrush, bored a hole into it, filled this with glowing embers and sealed it up. He emerged from the cave, put the stem of fire under his belt and hurried away with it. Refreshed now, he travelled without resting once until he finally reached home.

There, Coyote called all those who had stayed behind in the village and showed them the sagebrush. He used an arrow to bore a small hole into it, then told two men to hold it firmly on the ground. He put a small heap of dry grass next to it and blew.

At once the grass caught light. Fire had survived!

Coyote said, 'Take this into every tipi. From now on there will be fire in every house.'

Thus spoke the chief of old. And thus it was that fire came into the world.

Kroeber: *Ute Tales,* 1901
The bringing of fire to the people, stolen from outsiders or supernatural powers who had been keeping it exclusively for their own use, is very common in Native American mythology. It is interesting to compare this to the California story, COYOTE DANCES FOR THE SUN (p. 242).

Kroeber does not give any information about the person who narrated it to him, saying only that all the Ute stories in this source book:

> 'were collected in the summer of 1900 from the Uintah Utes, now in northeastern Utah. They were [almost] all obtained in English... They are given as nearly in the form in which they were heard as was thought possible.'

This story portrays Coyote in his sacred, creative role. However, in most Great Basin stories, Coyote is portrayed simply as a trickster, often with plots similar to the Great Plains story, THE ADVENTURES OF OLD MAN (see p. 74).

Kutenai Woman
Photographed by Edward S. Curtis, 1910

MYTHS OF THE PLATEAU

PEOPLE OF THE PLATEAU

Canada:
Part of British Columbia.

United States:
Parts of California, Idaho, Oregon, Montana and Washington.

The ancestral homelands of the Plateau peoples cover some 200,000 square miles of inland western North America, where the great Columbia and Fraser Rivers and their numerous tributaries flow through deep valleys and canyons towards the Pacific Ocean. Some parts are thickly forested; in others little grows apart from sagebrush and grass. It is often windy, but much of the region has little rain.

Plateau life was based on seasonal migration in search of food and medicinal plants. It was common to travel over wide areas, enabling different families to regularly meet up for harvesting foods, and also for social occasions such as feasts, ceremonial dances, sporting activities and gambling.

The men were primarily drawn to the great rivers to harvest the salmon runs, and also to their hunting grounds. Salmon was the most widely consumed fish, but other important species included trout, whitefish, suckerfish and sturgeon. Fishermen used a range of technologies: spearing, netting, hooking or trapping in weirs. Game was less abundant than in other regions; but hunters caught antelope, bear, beavers, deer, elk, jackrabbit, mountain sheep and otters. Some travelled to the Great Plains to shoot buffalo. The women gathered wild fruits and roots, particularly berries, camas, bitterroot, wild carrot and wild onion.

In the autumn the people congregated at permanent riverside villages, which had facilities for preserving and storing food, and from where the men continued to hunt. Among most Plateau peoples, a number of extended families lived in each village, and the villages were linked in to larger communities. The prevailing ethos was of individual autonomy, egalitarianism, co-operation and responsibility to the group. Chiefs, at both village and regional level, were usually advised by councils. Some chiefs were hereditary; others were elected by kin or council on the basis of past achievements. They were usually male, but there were also women chiefs who might deal with issues such as serious misdemeanours or emergencies.

Trade was an important and long-established aspect of life. It was conducted between different local bands, and also between different peoples – sometimes extending as far as the Pacific coast and the Great Plains. There was also much trade with White settlers, who bartered manufactured utensils in return for local pemmican, hemp rope and spoons made of mountain sheep horn. Some Plateau peoples supplied the Hudson's Bay Company, which controlled much of the North American fur trade (see p. 23)

The traditional mode of travel was along rivers by canoe. Horses, which arrived in the Plateau in the early 18th century, were widely used for long distance journeys overland. Some peoples became rich in horses, particularly the Nez Perce. Horses were also used for warfare; old photographs show them as ostentatiously decorated with paint and ornaments as their riders.

Some Plateau houses were built for seasonal use only, others were permanently occupied. There were three main types. Large, circular 'pit houses' were sunk into the ground with poles across the top, covered with wood, bark and earth; entry was usually down a ladder from the roof. There were also conical, tipi-style structures, covered with mats of woven plant fibre. Finally, there were communal longhouses, each housing many families, often related by kinship, who cooked on fires ranged side-by-side along the centre. Some villages had a sweat-house (see p. 64), and a special pit-house where pubescent girls were temporarily confined to mark their first menstruation.

Traditional religion was based on respect for the natural environment, particularly animals and plants. It emphasised living in harmony with one's fellows, working together and sharing both wealth and hardships. A major spiritual event for boys and girls, was the 'dream vigil'. This involved spending several days in a solitary place, fasting, to be rewarded with a vision of the animal which was to become their lifetime guardian spirit. An insight into traditional Plateau education was given by a Klamath writer called Lucy Thompson (Che-na-wah Weitch-ah-wah) in 1916. She describes how:

> 'My father…took me at a very early age and began training me in all of the mysteries and laws of my people. It took me years to learn and the ordeal was a hard one. I was…given the true name of God, the Creator of all things, and taught the meaning of every article that is used in our festivals, together with all the laws governing our people.'

LIFE ON THE PLATEAU
WHEN THESE STORIES WERE COLLECTED

The Plateau people had little contact with Whites until the early 19th century, when they began visiting the newly established trading forts to barter their furs and other hunting products. A gold rush on the Fraser River brought the first smallpox epidemic in the 1860s. This decade also saw the first roads being built across ancestral homelands, bringing in White settlers to establish farms and ranches. Some Plateau people set up their own small enterprises, whilst still spending much of their time on the old subsistence activities. Later, large areas of land were seized from the indigenous population, amidst broken promises made by both the Canadian and US governments. In many cases, the Plateau peoples adapted to their new conditions, working for the settlers as wage labourers, changing their clothing and even their names to match White convention, and actively seeking a formal education.

However, the loss of their territories was both irredeemable and devastating – not just in terms of livelihood but also because it impinged on their sacred relationship with the landscape.

STORYTELLING ON THE PLATEAU

During the late 19th century, ethnologists made some truly excellent and comprehensive collections of certain Plateau peoples' stories, whilst those of many others were recorded more briefly. It seems that, in this region, the old myths continued to be greatly valued and frequently told. The stories themselves, the topography described in them and the animals which shared the land, were still all widely regarded as sacred. Writing of the Modoc people in 1912, Jeremiah Curtin stated that their holy places:

'are before [their] eyes in [their] own birthplace, where every river, hill and mountain has a story connected with it, an account of its origin.'

This outlook has survived to the present day; for example the Lillooet people on an official website state that their history is 'written upon the land'.

THE PEOPLES BEHIND THE STORIES

Lillooet (St'at'imc)
They are based in British Columbia, occupying only a tiny fraction of their original territory. Today most live on reservations, where there is much community action to restore ancient rights. They continue traditional harvesting of wild foods, and make intricate basketry and hand drums, both for community use and for sale.

Modoc
Originally from northeastern California and southern Oregon, in 1864 they were forced onto a reservation alongside their former enemies, the Klamath. The resistance of some resulted in the 1872-3 Modoc War. Survivors were relocated to Indian Territory in Oklahoma, where a few still live; a larger number are still based alongside the Klamath Tribes of Oregon. It is said there are no longer any full-blooded Modoc people.

Nespelem
They originally lived along the banks of a river in Washington that bears the same name. They are now one of the Confederated Tribes of the Colville Indian Reservation.

Nez Perce (Nimi'ipuu)

Their original homeland was spread across Idaho, Oregon and Washington. In 1877, they split into two. One group accepted enforced relocation to a reservation; the other fled on an epic 1,170 mile trek, but finally surrendered. Long famed for their hardy, fast horses, they now operate a major horse-breeding programme.

Sanpoil (Nesilextcl'n)

Their original villages stood along two tributaries of the Columbia River in Washington. In 1872 they were moved alongside eleven other peoples to become part of the Confederated Tribes of the Colville Indian Reservation, where they continue to be based.

Thompson River People (Nlaka'pamux)

Since the mid-19th century their ancient homeland has been split between British Columbia and Washington. In 1900, their 70 villages each contained up to 100 inhabitants. Today they actively promote traditional values such as peaceful conflict resolution, modesty and respect.

Wasco and Wishram

These two peoples were closely related. The homelands of both were along the Columbia River near the Dalles in Oregon, which had been a regional trading centre for thousands of years before the arrival of White settlers. Today Wasco people are one of the Confederated Tribes of Warm Springs Reservation in Oregon; whilst Wishram people are part of the Confederated Tribes and Bands of the Yakama Nation in Washington.

Research for this section also covered stories from the following Plateau peoples: Chilcotin (Tsilhqot'in), Coeur D'Alene (Skitswish), Flathead (Salish), Fraser River People (Sto:lo), Ivlickitat, Klamath, Okanogan (Syilx), Pend d'Oreilles (Kalispel), Sahaptin and Yakama.

THE BEAR STORY THAT BRINGS A WINDSTORM

Modoc

There was a chief's son who was absolutely useless at hunting. One day, when he came home dragging his feet and empty-handed as usual, his father completely lost patience with him.

'Where's the game you caught?' he demanded.

The young man flushed and lowered his eyes. 'Sorry…er, I didn't manage to catch anything today, Father.'

'You lazy, good-for-nothing!' the chief yelled at him. 'You're no son of mine: get out of my sight!'

The young man flinched and slunk away in shame. He slipped outside and started to walk towards the lonely lava flats. His mind was swirling like a river in full spate; his eyes were fixed on a distant, snow-capped mountain.

As he walked on, a violent wind suddenly blew up from the frozen mountaintop, bringing blinding flurries of snow. He sheltered under a cedar tree until the storm blew over, then resumed his trudge across the hard ground, not once looking back. He reached the lower slopes of the mountain and started to climb steadily, leaping over rocks, slithering on stretches of scree. Every so often, he stopped to gaze up at the icy heights, where he had spotted an upright pole with something hanging from it – a sign that people must be living up there. 'Perhaps they'll let me stay with them for a while,' he thought, 'give me a fresh chance.'

At last he reached the snow line, and saw the pole just a short way ahead. The object hanging from it was a deer hide. He waded through the snow right up to it. There was no one around, but next to the pole, smoke was rising from a hole in a low mound.

Beside it, a ladder led down into a house. He hesitated, then cautiously climbed down – into a fine dwelling, richly furnished with splendid furs. At first, he thought it was unoccupied; but then he became aware of a woman sitting in the shadows, watching him. In the soft firelight, she was exceptionally beautiful. Her long, thick hair hung loose; her eyes were uncannily bright.

'I wondered how long you would take to get here,' she said. 'Welcome!'

'How did you know I was coming?' he whispered.

'I lured you here myself, by hanging up the deer hide outside.'

'But…why?'

'Because I felt sorry for you. I've often watched you down there, listened to you grumbling, heard you upbraiding yourself silently for your failure and your lack of friends. I want to help you.'

The young man shivered. If she'd been able to watch him from so far away, heard his moans, even knew his secret thoughts – she must have astonishing power.

'Who are you?' he whispered.

'My name is Bear Woman. Now, take a seat and I'll give you something to eat.'

She got up and fetched him a plate of woven straw, with a small heap of fine powder in the centre.

'What's this?'

'Yelalwek – sweet seeds. I am the only person in the world who knows where they grow. Taste them.'

Gingerly, the young man took a pinch of the tiny seeds between his fingers and dropped it onto his tongue. At once, his whole mouth was overwhelmed by the most delicious sensation.

'This is the best thing I've ever tasted!' he cried.

'Eat up, go on, enjoy it.'

So he took a little more, then more. No matter how much he ate, he was never satisfied; yet strangely, after every mouthful, there was always exactly the same amount left on the straw plate.

After a while, Bear Woman took the yelalwek away and brought him a dish of pounded deer meat. There was no sign of any man who might have supplied this.

Bear Woman laughed softly as he ate it. 'You don't need to speak your mind, my friend, I can hear all your puzzled thoughts. I'll explain things to you tomorrow.'

He was afraid to be in the house with such a powerful woman, yet no one had ever treated him so kindly.

After the meal, they sat quietly around the fire for a while, until the young man couldn't keep his eyes open any longer. He dozed off, then suddenly jerked awake to find her standing over him.

'Come,' she said, 'sleep in the bed I've made up for you.'

It was impossible to argue with her, so he went over and huddled under her thick blankets. Then she sang soft medicine songs over him, sending him quickly back to sleep.

However, the medicine was not quite strong enough: halfway through the night, he woke up. He sat up, blinking at the glowing embers of the fire, and spied his hostess's bed across the room. The next moment, he stifled a cry. For it wasn't the woman sleeping there – but a huge black bear! It was lying on its back with its mouth wide open, revealing long yellow fangs.

The young man shrank back against the wall. The movement disturbed the bear, which woke up and sat up too, gazing back at him – with eyes that were the eyes of Bear Woman. When it spoke, its voice was hers too: 'So: you were bound to discover my secret, sooner or later. Yes, I'm this kind: a woman in the daytime – and a Bear at night.'

'I don't understand.'

'You will. I belong to the Mountain: that is my father. The Earth is my mother. It is they who give me food, and keep me alive.'

Later, as dawn started to show through the smoke hole, she transformed back into a beautiful woman. Then she rose and gave him water to wash his face, stirring it into foam with her finger. Just as the previous night, she conjured up food for him from nowhere.

Bear Woman insisted that the young man stay with her. He soon got used to her strange ways. After a while, he asked if he could try his hand at hunting, hoping he might be better at it now his situation was so changed.

'Of course,' she said, 'but don't stray far from the house.'

As soon as he went outside, he saw a big deer standing there. It didn't flee when it saw him, but stood motionless as if waiting to be shot. He couldn't believe it was so easy. He dragged the carcass back to the house, butchered it and gave Bear Woman the meat.

'Now I live here, I've become successful!' he cried. 'I can hunt for you every day, I can be a proper husband and make you proud.'

They lived together in this way for a long time.

Then one day, Bear Woman said, 'I've seen men from your village scouting over the lava beds and climbing the Mountain. They're looking for you.'

The young man grimaced and didn't reply.

'Also,' she said, 'I can hear people crying and wailing down in your village. It's your mother and sisters mourning for you. Maybe you should go back to them?'

'No,' he said. 'My father treated me really badly, and my mother just stood by. I want to stay here with you for ever.'

Bear Woman smiled and said, 'Then I must tell you some important things. Wherever you go up here, you are walking on my mother. Don't harm anything that grows on her – not a single tree or bush, not even a leaf, nothing. When you track a deer, concentrate completely. Ignore any small animals that try to distract you, or you'll lose your mind and get lost.'

The young man always followed her advice. He became a brilliant hunter and filled Bear Woman's stores with excellent meat.

One day he heard a loud commotion of blood-chilling whoops, then saw a deer perched on a high rock. He shot at it, but the deer stretched out its head, causing the arrow to strike one of its horns, then bounce back to his bow. The young man spun on his heels, sprinted home and told Bear Woman what had happened.

'Ah,' she said, 'that great noise was my father, the Mountain, warning you not to kill deer in that place. If you'd tried to shoot it a second time, you'd have been in trouble. Don't go there again.'

The young man began to tremble. It seemed to him now that, despite conquering his past faults, life was still full of difficulties. Nothing Bear Woman said or did could comfort him.

'Let me stay inside with you, away from danger,' he begged. 'You've often told me that your mother and father always bring enough food, so there's no point in me hunting.'

Bear Woman agreed with this new arrangement. They stayed in the underground house together for a whole year. At the end of it, Bear Woman gave birth to a baby boy. After he was born, she rubbed him all over with red paint three times every day: at sunrise, noon and sundown. Because of this, the boy grew fast.

One night the child started crying and thrashing about. Nothing would persuade him to stop.

'He's getting too big for that cradleboard,' said the young man. 'Let's take him out; he can sleep on the mat with us.'

'No,' said Bear Woman quickly. 'One of us might roll over on top of him by accident and smother him.'

'I won't let that happen,' said the young man. 'Let him sleep by me; I promise to be really careful.'

Gently, he lifted his son from under the tight covers, and laid him down beside him on the sleeping mat. He loved that boy of his. He brought the child's face up next to his own, so that he'd hear at once if the little one got distressed. The boy was happy too, now he was free of restriction, and they both quickly drifted off to sleep.

When the young man woke up, in the middle of the night, he could feel his child's warmth beside him and opened his eyes to admire the boy by the light of the embers. But his little son had turned into a Bear cub, covered in fluffy, dark fur.

'So that's why she didn't want him next to me at night,' he thought. 'Our child's a shape-shifter, like she is.' He gazed at the cub, who twitched his nose and paws as he slept, just as he did in his human form. The young man didn't love him any less, yet he was apprehensive. 'Bears aren't like humans,' he thought. 'It's possible that one day my wife and child could kill me.'

In the morning, when both Bear Woman and the boy had turned back into humans, she asked if they'd slept well together.

'The little one turned into a Bear,' the young man answered.

'And?'

'I thought how nice he looked; he reminded me of you.'

And so they went on together, the child growing very fast. In no time at all, he was running around.

'You really ought to take our son to meet his grandparents,' said Bear Woman. 'He's old enough to behave now.'

The young man knew this was the right thing to do. But he was very nervous, with bad memories of his father; and he was terrified of what would happen if they saw the boy transformed into a cub.

'He'll miss you – come with me,' he begged his wife.

'No, I'm too busy doing my beadwork,' she answered. 'Once you're on the way, our boy will be so excited, he'll forget he's left me behind. Everything will be fine, so long as you keep to these rules: when evening comes, don't let him play with the other children. He usually only turns into a Bear in his sleep; but it might also happen if he's up too late.'

'Is that all?'

'Also make sure you keep him well away from a fellow called Skunk,' said Bear Woman. 'He's a spiteful joker, and if he teases our boy, that could hasten his transformation too.'

'If my family sees him as a Bear, they'll kill him!'

'Yes, but if you're on your guard, they won't.'

Bear Woman wrapped a handful of yelalwek seeds in a bundle of deerskin, and said, 'When you reach your parents' home, lay five white deerskins on the ground; then put five pinches of these on each skin. They'll grow into enough food to feed your family and all the villagers. But don't let anyone steal them – because that would spoil the medicine, and we'd never be able to use it again.'

The young man carried the little boy on his back all the way to the village. When they reached his parents' house, his youngest sister came along. She let out a shriek of joy, burst into tears and called out: 'My brother's come home!' She was *so* glad to see him.

The young man carefully laid the bundle of seeds on the roof, then carried his son down the ladder into the house. All the women of the family were gathered inside. Sitting in their midst, the young man saw a handsome, sly-eyed stranger wearing a hat of thick, white and black fur. It was Skunk. The young man showed them all his child. Everyone admired him greatly except for Skunk, who sniggered and said, 'Heh, heh, he's as bad as one would expect.'

'Leave him be!' cried the little one's grandmother. 'He's a lovely lad, we must make him feel at home.'

All the other women murmured their agreement and shouted, 'Shut up, you loud-mouthed fool!' Then they crowded round Skunk and slapped him until he promised to be quiet.

'I've brought you a wonderful gift,' said the young man.

He sent his sister up to fetch the bundle of seeds. Then he asked his mother to find five white deerskins. When she had laid them out, he placed five pinches of yelalwek seed in the centre of each one. As everyone watched, the seeds quickly multiplied and spread across the skins, growing constantly before their eyes.

'Ooh!' they all gasped.

'Hmm, that looks tasty,' smirked Skunk. He grabbed a big handful of yelalwek and crammed it into his mouth. The next moment, he started to jerk about and writhe in pain – for inside his body the seeds were continuing to increase. They came pouring out of his nose, his ears and his eyes; while those he had already swallowed made his stomach swell so alarmingly that it seemed about to burst. He rushed outside, choking and screaming.

When he was gone, everyone looked pleased.

'It seems you've done well for yourself after all,' said his mother.

At sundown, the men came home. All the children went outside for their last game before bedtime. 'Can we take our new cousin out to play?' they begged.

The young man, busy talking to the menfolk, enjoying his unexpected welcome, completely forgot his wife's warning. Luckily, his son was more careful, and shook his head silently at the others.

'Oh come on,' they begged. 'You're so sweet. We won't hurt you, we promise.'

The little boy became very upset. It so happened that a wise man called Eagle was going up the ladder out of the house at that moment, and he heard what was going on. He peered at the little boy shrewdly, then told the other children, 'Don't pester him.'

So the boy stayed indoors, sitting quietly against the wall. After a while, his aunt – the young man's sister – came down and spotted him there. She scooped him up in her arms and started cooing at him. He wriggled and groused, begging to be put down; but she couldn't resist him and wouldn't let him go.

'Don't be shy,' she said. 'Let's go and watch the others.'

She carried him up the ladder, set him down on the ground outside, then took his hand and led him over to where the other children were playing.

'Come and join in!' they called.

His aunt ran with him into the game. It was such fun that the little one quickly forgot himself. He copied the other boys and girls, running around with them...

Until suddenly one of the boys cried, 'Whatever are you doing?'

For the little one had fallen onto all-fours and started lolloping about in a very strange way. He ran up to the boy who had called out, lifted his hand and cuffed him.

'Stop it!' the others shouted.

But he started hitting them too, one after another. Still on all fours, he chased them here and there, shoving them all to the ground, climbing on top and pummelling them.

'Ugh!' they screamed, 'he's like a wild animal!'

'That hurt! How can someone as small as him be so strong?'

'The way he's running – that's how a *Bear* moves!'

'Oh, look at him! he's turning all dark – he's got fur!'

The child didn't mean to be vicious; he'd simply found his courage. He honestly thought he was playing normally – because that's how Bear cubs play. He wanted to make the others join in his play-fighting, and couldn't understand why they were all running away.

Lurking in the bush, Skunk heard the children screaming.

'Oho,' he muttered, 'everyone ignored me, but this has turned out just as I thought.' Then he raised his voice, calling: 'People, there's a Bear eating your children! Don't worry, I'll deal with it.'

He ran over, raised his bow and skilfully shot an arrow right under the bear cub's arm. The cub squealed, fell to the ground... and in that instant, turned back into a boy.

Down in the underground house, talking with the others, the young man heard the commotion, Skunk's shout and the cub's squeal. It was like an arrow to his own heart. Yelling frantically, he almost flew up the ladder, and raced across the grass to intervene.

But it was too late: his beloved child was already dead.

On the mountaintop, Bear Woman had been feeling restless. The more she thought about the journey she'd encouraged her husband and child to take, the more agitated she became. She rushed outside and stood in the snow, listening. She heard the children's screams, and guessed at once what was happening.

Bear Woman let out a terrible roar. It echoed around the mountains and down across the lava beds like thunder. She shook herself, making the Earth tremble. She pulled up trees. She tore great rocks from the ground and hurled them around as if they were mere pebbles. She ran down the mountain. As she neared the village, the thudding of her footsteps made the roofs fall off many houses. Then she called up a wind – a whirlwind, a storm of dirt, darkness and spiralling air.

Back in the village, everyone heard her approach. They hastily held a council; but were all too terrified to work out what to do.

However, one of the village girls was an orphan; she was small for her age but cunning and feisty. To protect herself from bullies and wild beasts, she always carried a long stick, sharpened at both ends. When her grandmother came back from the council, weeping with despair, this girl said, 'Grandmother, paint my stick red. Then paint red lines across my forehead, my chest, my stomach and my arms.'

It was done. The girl walked boldly through the windstorm, out to the trail that led to the mountains, and sat down in the middle of it. Very soon, the ground began to shudder under her. Through the darkness of the whirlwind, an even darker shape suddenly loomed ahead, moving rapidly towards her. It was Bear Woman, running in her Bear form. The orphan girl jumped up and plunged her pointed stick into the heart of the whirlwind.

The wind dropped. There was a loud thud. The ground steadied and the air cleared.

Before the orphan girl's feet, there lay a beautiful woman, wearing a dress richly embroidered with beads and porcupine quills, totally motionless – dead.

The villagers ran up to see what had happened. The young man pushed through them and knelt beside his dead wife, tears streaming down his face.

'If only I had remembered your instructions,' he wept, 'then you and our child would both still be alive.' He turned to the villagers. 'Please, I beg you… Is there anyone here who can help?'

The shaman, Crow, stepped forward. 'Take my medicine basket,' he rasped, 'lay it on your child then step over him.'

The young man went back to his dead son, worked the medicine – and at once the little boy sprang back to life.

'Now try it with your wife,' said Crow.

The young man did. But no matter how many times he tried – five, ten, twenty times – no matter how carefully, still the beautiful woman in her rich dress lay there deathly still.

The young man curled up on the ground beside her, weeping uncontrollably. Everyone felt very sorry for him.

Someone said, 'There's an old medicine woman who lives on her own among the rocks on the far shore of the lake. It's said that she's in direct contact with a spirit. Maybe she can help.'

So the medicine woman was sent for. She came at once, hobbling as fast as she could. For a long moment, she stood over the dead woman's body, cocking her ear, screwing up her eyes into the distance. Finally she said:

'This person's spirit has already travelled almost to the place at the end of the world where the Sun goes down. But it has not quite passed over yet, and it may still be possible to call her back. Who is willing to scream for her?'

A man stepped forward. At once, he was possessed by the medicine woman's spirit guide. '*Aaaiieeee!*' His scream spun right across the lava beds to the far horizon.

The medicine woman stood very still, listening. At last she said, 'Her spirit has turned, it's coming back!' And then: 'It's here, returning into her body!'

Right away Bear Woman stood up – beautiful and bright as ever. She gazed around, and when she saw the orphan girl, she said with a smile, 'Who ever would have thought you were so strong?'

Bear Woman stayed in the village with her family for three days.

Then the young man said to his mother and sister, 'We're going back up the Mountain for ever. I can't risk coming back here.'

Bear Woman made sure she took all her yelalwek seeds with her – which is why no one since then has ever tasted them. After they left, they were never seen again. Sometimes, the young man's family and friends went out searching, but they never caught even a glimpse of them in the distance.

But to this very day, sometimes it is still possible to hear the voices of Bear Woman and her family, drifting down from the snowy peaks on top of their Mountain. And to this day too, telling this story is sure to bring a windstorm.

Curtin: *Myths of the Modocs,* collected 1884, published 1912
Curtin obtained his stories from two different informants. He does not state who told which tale, and since they are all beautifully narrated it is difficult to distinguish between them. He met one of them living in exile far from home in Indian Territory, Oklahoma, and described her as:

'Ko-a-lak'-ak-a, a woman who was then old and feeble... She was remarkable for her intelligence and her wonderful memory. In childhood her grandfather had instructed her in the religion of her people, in other words, taught her all the myths of the Modocs, and to old age her tenacious memory retained many of them.'

The other was one of those still living in his ancestral homeland, though in wretched conditions. This was a man called Sconchen:

'the oldest Indian there... Though old and infirm, his mind was still clear and active. For years, in the prime of his life, he was chief of his people, and in his old age they revered him.'

The story's setting is explained by the source book's introduction, which says that some of the original Modoc lands, straddling Oregon and California, were of volcanic formation with areas of lava beds and surrounded by mountains, some topped with snow for much of the year.

There were numerous other bear myths told on the Plateau, often bleak and gruesome, but occasionally humorous. Many also feature either a man or a woman marrying a bear, with a variety of outcomes.

THE EARTH IS OUR MOTHER

Nespelem

Old One, or Chief, made the Earth out of a woman,
and said she would be the mother of all the people.
Thus the Earth was once a human being, and she is alive yet;
but she has been transformed,
and we cannot see her in the same way we can see a person.
Nevertheless she has legs, arms, head,
heart, flesh, bones and blood.
The soil is her flesh, the trees and vegetation are her hair,
the rocks her bones, and the wind is her breath.
She lies spread out, and we live on her.
She shivers and contracts when cold,
and expands and perspires when hot.
When she moves, we have an earthquake.

– Red-Arm (KwElkwElta'xEn), Nespelem elder
(Quoted in Boas: *Folk-Tales of Salishan and Sahaptin Tribes,* 1917)

THE DEER PEOPLE

Thompson River People
(Nlaka'pamux)

A man was totally obsessed with Deer. He spent virtually all his time hunting them, and was always outstandingly successful in the kill. He constantly talked about Deer or thought about them; when he was asleep, they regularly filled his dreams.

He had two wives, one of whom had a son. But the family always came second to his Deer hunting. The two women and the child accepted that, for the Deer were his guardian spirits.

One day, this hunter discovered a set of fresh Deer tracks. He could tell they'd been made by a doe and a fawn. He followed them until they stopped abruptly at the bottom of a grassy mound. There he scouted around carefully, but it was as if the animals had suddenly sunk into the earth at that spot.

He stood there at a loss – and suddenly felt someone's eyes upon him. He looked up. An attractive woman was sitting on top of the mound, watching him with a half-smile on her face. A young boy was squatting next to her, about the same age as his own son.

He greeted them, asking, 'Did a couple of Deer pass this way?'

'No,' the woman answered. Her smile grew wider.

'Then...excuse me,' he said. He went on a little further, thinking that the Deer must have sprung so lightly around the mound that their hooves had left no mark, and that he would surely be able to pick up their trail again on the far side. But still he had no luck. He'd never been caught out like this before.

He went back to the woman. 'Look,' he said, pointing, 'these tracks were only made a very short time ago and they stop right here, just below where you're sitting. You *must* have seen them?'

The woman and the boy both burst out laughing. At last, she quietened and grew serious. 'Stop troubling yourself,' she said. 'The tracks are of no consequence. There's something much more important you need to think about.'

'Well?' he said impatiently.

The woman answered, 'I love you.'

'*What?*' the hunter snapped. 'Don't be ridiculous, leave me be. I already have two wives and a child. My duty's to look after them.'

The woman stood up and came down the hillock to stand close to him. 'I've often seen you and secretly longed for you,' she said. 'It's time for you to come home with me.'

The hunter turned his back on her. He heard the boy come down behind her, then their footsteps crunching over the ground as they walked off together. The hunter couldn't stop himself turning round to gaze after them...just as the woman paused and looked back at him. Their eyes met. Something strange happened in the hunter's heart. Despite his good intentions, he found himself turning to follow them. They waited for him to catch up, and the three continued their journey together, walking silently side by side.

The hunter's mind was like a whirlpool. Over and over he kept thinking, 'This is wrong. My wives and my little boy are at home waiting for me. They depend on me, they'll starve if I don't bring them some meat tonight.'

He didn't utter a word of this aloud; yet a few moments later the woman said, 'I know what you're thinking. Please don't worry. You're *my* husband now, and I promise you'll never regret it. In the long run, you'll do more for your family this way; you'll do more for all your people.'

The hunter realised that something uncanny was happening to him, and managed to still his doubts. He walked on beside his new wife and her child, matching his stride to theirs, wondering where they were going and what would become of him.

At length, the landscape changed from barren flatlands to a region of high hills, one beyond the other, rolling away to the horizon. The woman led the way to the base of a steep slope which opened into a cave. She plunged into it and he followed after the boy. In the darkness at the far end, the cave narrowed to a passage just high and wide enough to walk through, leading gently downwards into the Earth itself. They went along this for some time... And suddenly emerged into a blaze of firelight and noise.

'Welcome to my home,' the woman cried.

They were standing inside a very big house, full of men, women and children milling around, in a glow of chatter and laughter. They were all very well dressed, in clothes made of exquisitely worked Deerskin. Suddenly one of them noticed the woman and her two companions, and a shout went up: 'Our daughter's back – and she's brought her husband at last!'

The rest of the day was a blur of confusion. The woman's people seemed very pleased to meet him, especially two young men who introduced themselves as his brothers-in-law. He was fed generously and made to feel very comfortable. However, at last people started to bid him goodnight, and go off in family groups or couples. The hunter stood there uncertainly, until the woman came up to him and led him away by the hand.

'So,' he said, 'are we really married now? Do we share a bed?'

Again she laughed. 'Of course, husband. But be careful, don't get carried away. You may embrace me but we can't fully consummate our love just yet. You have to wait until the rutting season begins.'

'The rutting season? Why?'

'You understand all the ways of the Deer, husband; well, they are our ways too. You know the rut only takes place once a year. When that month comes, you'll realise it was well worth the wait – there'll be no holding back then! You'll be able to make love as much as you want, not just to me – but also to my sisters and cousins.'

So that night the hunter lay chastely beside her, trying to make sense of what she had told him. His confusion only grew worse after they rose the following day. For people kept coming up to him saying, 'Son-in-law, we hear you're an unsurpassable hunter. We've completely run out of meat here, and we're worried we'll all go hungry. Could you get some for us?'

The hunter wasn't sure how to answer. So he went to their chief and asked if he was permitted to do this.

'Of course,' the chief said. Then he repeated his new wife's words: 'But be careful.'

'Careful in what way?' the hunter said. 'I'm constantly mindful of danger, and I always kill cleanly.'

'Indeed,' said the chief, 'but here you must take care in another way. We have a special law that must always be followed: once you have killed an animal, never throw away any part of it.'

The hunter promised to remember this. He took up his bow and arrows, and a youth showed him the way out into the open air.

There he scouted about for some time, and eventually saw two young Deer standing a short distance ahead, seemingly heedless of his approach. He quickly shot them both, then set about skinning and butchering them. When this was done, he carried them back to the house in the hill, leaving nothing behind but their dung.

That night, the household feasted on the meat he had provided. Everyone joined in; well *nearly* everyone, for the hunter couldn't help noticing that two of his new brothers-in-law, the ones who had made a point of befriending him last night, were missing. All the others praised him lavishly for his hunting success.

In his old home, when a meal was finished, they used to simply throw the bones aside; but here one of the men stepped forward and bundled up the bones neatly, then carefully carried them out.

'Where's he taking those?' the hunter asked his wife.

'He's throwing them into the river,' she answered. 'That's what we always do with the Deer bones after we've eaten the meat.'

'Why?'

'You'll see, husband. Then you'll understand some of the things that are still mysterious to you. Just wait.'

Towards the end of the evening, the man who had taken the bones away came back. Behind him came the two missing brothers-in-law. They ran straight up to the hunter and flung their arms around him in greeting.

'Where have you been all day?' the hunter asked, bewildered.

'We were with you much of the time,' they answered. 'We ran ahead of you, you shot us, then you butchered us and brought us back for the feast. Afterwards, our friend here took us down to the water to bring us back to life. That's what we all take turns to do here. That's the way we Deer People live.'

After a while, the hunter got used to this way of life. He lived happily but chastely alongside his new wife, and always volunteered to go hunting whenever needed. He never came back empty-handed, for there were always youngsters eager to be temporarily killed for the benefit of their people.

So time went by until the rutting season began.

The Deer Chief called the hunter. 'Now you will truly become one of us,' he said. And he transformed the hunter into the shape of an old buck.

In this form, the hunter went back to his wife, who now had the body of an agile doe, and finally made love to her. He was ecstatic; but his joy did not last long. For as soon as they went outside together, they were surrounded by several other bucks, all much younger than him. They charged at the old buck, the hunter, and soon routed him. Then they took possession of the doe, his wife, who happily allowed them all to have their pleasure with her. The old buck slunk away feeling miserable and outraged.

That night everyone assumed their human forms and there was much merrymaking and gossip. They all kept shooting glances at the hunter, who sat alone in a corner, looking very downcast.

'What's the matter with our son-in-law?' the older people wondered. 'Why isn't he joining in the fun?'

'He's sulking because the young bucks took his wife from him.'

'But that's all part of it.'

'He's got to learn the rules of the game.'

The chief listened to their banter for a while, then called the hunter over. 'Son-in-law, cheer up, I've decided to take pity on you. Tomorrow I'll decorate you and make you strong. Then you'll be able to keep your wife to yourself.'

The next morning, he transformed the hunter, giving him the body of a buck in its prime. His coat shone with health, rippling with toned muscles, and a magnificent set of antlers crowned his head. He strode out eagerly to meet his rivals, and soon beat them all off, wounding many in the process. His Deer mind felt no remorse; instead he took back his wife, and when they had satisfied their need for each other, he sought out and won for himself many other does: all her sisters and female cousins. When he was finally tired of mating, he looked around to see how the wounded were faring, and was happy to see a group of shamans busy healing them and restoring their strength for their next battles.

And so it went on for a whole month, until the antics of the bucks quietened down and the does went off to quiet places, nursing their pregnancies. The rut had come to an end.

Some time later, his Deer Wife gave birth to a son. As he grew up, the youngster shifted easily between his human and animal forms. The hunter was very proud of him.

Years passed. The Deer Wife said to the hunter, 'I've been thinking: it's not fair that you should live with my people all the time. We ought to visit your old home, so that our son can meet the other side of his family.'

The hunter eagerly agreed.

The wife got busy, making ready for the journey. She prepared a large quantity of Deer fat, then used her powers to reduce it to a handful. She did exactly the same thing with sizeable quantities of dried venison, raw and dressed skins. As soon as this was all packed, the hunter, his wife and his son set out together.

At first they travelled in their human forms. But the Deer Wife complained that this was too slow, so they all transformed into Deer and in that way made much faster progress. Even in their Deer shapes, they still needed to eat plenty of meat and fat to fortify them. But they didn't touch any of the provisions the wife had prepared. Instead, one of her brothers constantly ran alongside them, and whenever they needed food he would let the hunter briefly become human and shoot him. After they'd eaten, they put his bones into water and thus he would revive, ready to be shot again another day

Eventually they arrived at the hunter's old village. What a long time it was since he had last seen it! They all changed back into humans, and he was eager to press forward at once; but his Deer Wife put a warning hand on his shoulder and drew him back.

'Wait,' she said. 'Don't approach your people straight away – unless you're ready to die.'

'Then what must I do?'

'You must spend eight days preparing yourself first, by bathing in a herbal decoction that I'll make for you.'

Just at that moment, the hunter noticed a young woman outside one of the lodges. It was his own sister! His heart began to pound, and despite his wife's warning, he waved and called out to her: 'Sister! It's me, I've come back!'

She stared at him in astonishment, then let out a squeal of joy. 'Oh, my beloved lost brother! We all thought you were dead.'

She started to run towards him; but the Deer Wife shook her head urgently, calling, 'No, listen to my warning: go back!'

'I'm sorry,' the hunter called, 'but it's not safe to come near me for eight days. After that, I'll tell you everything.'

'Meanwhile,' his Deer Wife called to the sister, 'you must all clean your houses. Get ride of everything old, and any bad smells.'

The sister recognised that the Deer Wife spoke with authority, and ran off to share this extraordinary news with her neighbours.

The Deer Wife gathered herbs, boiled them in water, then began the eight-day cleansing process of her husband. Once this was over, it was safe for them all to visit his family.

They were thrilled beyond words to see the hunter again after such a long time. Long mats were already laid out, in anticipation of a feast to celebrate his return. His first wife, the one who'd borne him a son before he vanished, had remained faithful to him. However, his second wife, the childless one, had given up all hope of his return, and thus married again. The hunter greeted both women warmly.

His Deer Wife pulled out the small bundle of fat from under her robe and tossed it onto one of the feasting mats, where it spread out like a solid puddle, until it had resumed its original great size. Everyone gasped and cheered. She did the same with the venison. Then she asked to be shown into a separate lodge, where she laid out the raw deerskins that she'd brought. They multiplied at once into such a quantity, that the lodge was filled almost to the ceiling. And so, thanks to the Deer Wife, the whole village enjoyed a truly magnificent feast and everyone was happy. The dressed skins, however, she kept to one side.

The hunter and his family stayed there for a long time. His second son, the Deer Boy, was well grown now, and the hunter taught him to shoot Deer himself. His shots were always true. The wild Deer that lived in the area recognised him as their own kin and let him catch them, especially as he always threw their bones into the water to restore their lives. The hunter's elder son – the one by his first wife – went out with the Deer Boy; they became firm friends and the elder son eagerly copied the Deer Boy's ways.

One day the Deer Wife said, 'It's time we returned to my own people now. But I don't want to leave you all, after the kindness you've shown to me and my son. I invite you to come with us.'

This threw the hunter's people into a fluster. At last one of the elders spoke up: 'It's not possible for us to make this long journey because we don't have enough moccasins to wear.'

The Deer Wife smiled and drew out the small bundle of dressed buckskins from their hiding place. She threw them onto the floor, and at once they multiplied into a huge pile, perfect for fashioning into moccasins. The village women set to work, sewing and decorating them, and soon there was more than enough footwear to keep everyone comfortable during their travels.

So they set out, the hunter's people walking alongside the Deer Wife and the Deer Boy. When they reached the Deer People's country and entered their house inside the hill, they were given a hearty welcome.

The hunter's people stayed there for a long time, but at last decided to return home to their own country. The hunter himself stayed behind and became one of the Deer People. But his son, the Deer Boy, had grown very fond of his half-brother, so he went back with him to their father's people.

There the Deer Boy grew up to be an even mightier hunter than his father. Although he was now an ordinary man, he had brought with him the wisdom of his mother's people, a wisdom that still has resonance today:

> When you kill Deer,
> always see to it that the bones are not lost.
> Throw them into the water. Then the Deer will come to life.
> A hunter who does this pleases the Deer.
> They have affection for him, are not afraid of him,
> and do not keep out of his way,
> for they know that they will return to life
> whenever they give themselves into his power.
> The Deer will always remain plentiful,
> because they are not really killed.
> If it is impossible to throw the bones into water,
> then burn them. Then the Deer will really die,
> but they will not find fault with you.
> If a man throws Deer bones about and takes no care of them,
> if he lets the dogs eat them, and people step on them,
> then the deer will be offended and will help him no more.
> They will withhold themselves,
> and the hunter will have no luck in hunting.
> He will become poor and starve.

Boas: *Folk-Tales of Salishan and Sahaptin Tribes*, 1917
No information is given about the original informants of this tale; though footnotes in the source book indicate that there were at least three versions of it. The teaching given at the end of the story reproduces the exact wording of the original text.

The deer most commonly hunted on the Plateau were white-tailed and mule deer. Although they were not the most important food source for the Plateau peoples, their significance is reflected in several other myths. In a Lillooet story, it is impossible to hunt deer successfully, because they can jump between mountain peaks in a single bound. The other animals lure the deer to a feast and give them so many gifts to carry home that the weight prevents them from leaping in their former way.

THE HUNTER AND THE ELK SPIRIT

Wasco

There was a youth who was an excellent shot; his arrows never once missed their target. However, the only animals he ever killed were birds and squirrels. Because of this, his father was constantly criticising him.

'You pathetic namby-pamby! Still shooting birds like a little boy who's only just left his mama's breast! I'm ashamed to call you my son. You ought to be bringing home good solid elk-meat by now. *I* was, long before I reached your age.'

The youth hung his head.

'You coward,' his father taunted him, 'you're scared of being attacked by one, eh? But you'll never be a real man unless you face up to something like that. Look at this scar on my forehead, boy. I won it when I was even younger than you are now, when a huge bull elk gouged its antlers across my face – moments before I shot it dead. I'm proud to bear it as a sign of my conquest over a great beast. But *you'll* never have anything to show that you're a man.'

The youth didn't argue. Instead, he went out alone into the mountains and stayed there for many days, fasting and praying. Eventually he was rewarded – with a visit from the spirit of an elk.

'I am your master and your guardian,' said the Elk Spirit. 'Serve me and always heed what I say. Do not be arrogant. Never kill more than enough to fulfil your own present needs. So long as you obey, I will always help you.'

'I will serve you, I will heed you,' the youth whispered.

After that, the youth went home. To his father's relief, he ceased chasing after trivial small game, and soon became a great hunter.

He shot elk, deer and even bear. He always knew exactly where to find them, tracked them down quickly and shot them with great skill. He brought home plenty of meat to feed his own family, but never any surplus.

That didn't satisfy his father. 'I used to kill double that amount – treble! – when I was your age,' he sneered.

The youth ignored him. Every day through summer, autumn and winter, he brought back just enough food to share with his family. And every day, summer, autumn and winter, his father continued to mock him.

These constant jibes made the youth's heart swell with a new yearning. He became obsessed with the desire to prove that he was as good as, or even better than, his father.

The Elk Spirit watched the youth's secret struggle. One morning, he tested him by calling up a great herd of elk, and making them run directly across his path. The temptation was too much; the youth raised his bow and shot them all, one after another, until the whole herd lay dead. Just as he ran forward to begin butchering them, he heard the drumming of hooves over the hill. He spun round and saw another herd coming over the crest. 'It'll really put my father in his place if I slaughter this lot too,' he thought. 'He won't know what to say when I overload him with so much meat.' No sooner had he killed all of these, than a third herd appeared from the opposite side, then a fourth herd, and finally a fifth. The youth raced here and there, up and down, along river banks and lake shores. His supply of arrows seemed to be inexhaustible, imbued with fail-proof medicine. Long before the sun had moved right across the sky, all the elk from all five herds lay dead.

He was breathless with exhilaration. He set to work, hauling the fallen animals into piles, until there was only one left, lying in the shallows of the lake. He waded out to fetch it. However, when he touched it, he was surprised to feel the warmth of its life-blood still surging through its veins. How had this one survived his arrows, when all the others had perished at a single shot?

The truth is that this was no ordinary animal. It was the youth's own Elk Spirit.

The Elk Spirit dragged him down into the water. Far into its depths they sank, mysteriously joined together, until darkness overwhelmed him. At last he came to, as if he were emerging from a deep sleep. He found himself in the underwater world; yet strangely, he could breathe as if it were the open air. All around, he saw large, dark shapes drifting like clouds, floating in and out of the shadows. One moment, they all seemed to be people; the next, some re-shaped themselves into elk, others into deer, and others still into bears. Before his eyes, they morphed back into human form, then out of it again, until he was dizzy from trying to make them out. The elk-shaped ones kept fixing him with their wretched eyes, groaning at him piteously.

As he stared at them in remorse, he became aware of a voice calling: 'Draw him in.' A few heartbeats passed, then it was repeated: 'Draw him in, draw him in.' He made no effort of his own; yet somehow, slowly, he found himself moving towards the largest shape of all. As he drew close, he saw it was his guardian, the Elk Spirit. The youth lay prostrate on the ground before him.

'Look around you,' the Elk Spirit said. 'All the people in this underwater place are the spirits of those you killed. Countless numbers of my brothers and sisters are still groaning in pain from their wounds – the ones that you needlessly inflicted today. Why did you ignore what I commanded?'

'It was my father,' the youth protested. 'His scorn broke me. I was desperate to be his equal, desperate to be *better* than him.'

'You fool. Your father goaded you to achieve far more than he ever did.'

'No, no, *he* began killing elk when he was still a young boy. He showed me the scar where one of your people once gored him. I was determined…'

'Your father lied to you,' said the Elk Spirit. 'He received that scar long after he had grown up, and it was not caused by one of my people's antlers, but by a mere piece of wood that fell on him and scratched his skin. You believed his lies and chose to follow his false example rather than my advice. You wounded and slaughtered countless elk without good reason. Because of this, I am no longer your guardian.'

The youth had no chance to argue or protest. For the next moment, he heard the same disembodied voice calling five times: *'Cast him out, cast him out, cast him out, cast him out, cast him out!'*

He sank into the darkness again, felt the sensation of rising through water. Then he found himself lying on the lakeshore, his clothes and hair completely sodden. There was no sign of the elk carcasses he had worked so tirelessly to pile up. He dragged himself to his feet and made his way, shakily, shamefully, home.

His father was sitting in the house, talking loudly. The youth strode past him without a word and went to bed. He lay in it silently for five nights and days. After that, he washed himself, asked for five elk-hides to be laid beside his bed, and called for his friends.

'I'm a fool,' the youth told them. 'Instead of following the wisdom of my guardian Elk Spirit, who had given me so much help, I listened to the deceits and taunts of my father and obeyed him. I killed more than was needed and wronged my guardian spirit – so now he has abandoned me.'

And with those words, he died.

Sapir: *Wishram Texts,* 1909
The source gives no information about the person who supplied this story, which was collected at Warm Spring Reservation, Oregon, in 1885.
A footnote to it says:
'The fact that the young man divulges his guardian spirit is itself indicative of approaching death, for only upon the death-bed was it customary to communicate…the greatest secret of one's life.'
The North American elk is a very large deer – one of the largest of its kind in the world (not to be confused with the European 'elk', known as a 'moose' in North America).
A superficially very similar story was collected amongst the Wasco some 70 years later in 1953. By then it had evolved in various ways. The youth, who is anonymous in the original, is given the name Plain Feather and is elevated to the status of a young warrior. The mockery comes not from his father but from his peer group, who criticise him for not hunting for enjoyment as well as necessity. Instead of his father, an evil old man called Smart Crow, persuades him to disobey his guardian spirit, on the pretext of a vision predicting a long, hard winter for which large stores of meat will be necessary. These apparently minor changes, which seem to 'explain' the events more clearly, actually alter the whole dynamic of the story. They remove the subtle but profound mystical point of the original that a spirit guide's instruction should override that of a father.
The story is set near the Dog River, a tributary of the Columbia in Oregon. The 1953 account adds that the lake under that mountain had become known as the Lake of Lost Spirits because of this myth.

FOX AND THE DAUGHTER OF DARKNESS

Modoc

Ah, Fox! The women were always talking about him, constantly warning their daughters to be careful:

'They say he's a really handsome fellow, always half smiling.'

'His eyes are the colour of dry leaves in the autumn sunshine, and he gazes at you intently.'

'He uses all the tricks of sweet-talking love – but he's a liar and a philanderer.'

However, to one young woman, Twilight, this wasn't a warning – it was an enticement. The more they tried to protect her from Fox, the more she found herself thinking about him. When she was on her own, she even sang songs about him:

'Oh, Fox if only I could see you,
If only I could go with you,
And make endless love with you…'

Fox heard her songs and, straight away, his passion was aroused. But it wasn't so easy for him to have her, because Twilight's father was Old Man Darkness – a domineering, suspicious man who repelled intruders by shrouding his house in thick gloom.

This didn't put Fox off. 'If I can't call on Twilight at her father's house,' he thought, 'I'll bring her to me instead.'

Whatever Fox wished for, it always came to be. He wished for fire, and at once fire ran across the ground, burning away all the scrub. He wished for 'ges' roots; and at once, the whole area was full of ges, growing thickly, almost ready to harvest.

A few days later, Twilight's three brothers returned from hunting and told her they had seen a rich patch of ges growing on the far mountainside. Twilight went off to find it with her digging-stick. It took her most of the day just to walk there, and the sun was low in the sky by the time she got started digging out the roots.

Fox hid in the trees, watching her and grinning to himself, licking his lips. Then he transformed into an old woman and came out hobbling towards her, smiling kindly.

'Greetings, my dear,' he called.

'Oh, good evening, Grandmother,' Twilight replied politely.

'You're hard at work, I see. You've dug up a fine pile of roots.'

'Yes indeed, Grandmother. But now I'm so tired, and I live too far away to carry them straight home. I'll have to camp overnight, all by myself.'

'Oh dear, poor girl. Shall I stay with you, keep you company?'

'That's really kind of you, Grandmother. I'd like it very much.'

So Twilight went with the old woman, little suspecting she was really Fox. Even so, she had a feeling that something wasn't quite right – because the sun set extraordinarily fast, like a ball tumbling through the air, and it grew completely dark within moments.

'Oh dear,' said Twilight, 'I can hardly see to make my camp.'

'Don't worry,' said the old woman, 'I'll help you. But first, have a little rest. Lie down here and I'll sing some songs to soothe you.'

Twilight did, and within moments, she sank into a deep slumber. Fox threw off his disguise, leaped up and rushed around, gathering brushwood and fashioning it into a splendid house. Twilight slept soundly until dawn – when Fox wished her awake.

She sat up sleepily, then gazed around in utter astonishment. 'Oh! Wherever am I? How did I get into this beautiful place? I've never seen such bright walls or such colours in the decorations... And I wonder what's happened to that kind old woman...?'

At that moment, Fox strode forward in the form of a breathtakingly handsome man, with clothes fashioned from the softest skins, and exquisite beads.

'Who are you?' cried Twilight, shrinking back against the wall.

'I'm the one you've been singing about and longing for, day after day after day,' he answered. He fixed her with his beautiful, yellow-brown eyes. 'I am Fox.'

Thus Fox made her his wife.

The very next day, Twilight gave birth to their baby, a beautiful little boy, perfect in every way – except that his ears stood up on the sides of his head, and were covered with soft fur. When Twilight saw them, she burst into tears.

'What's the matter?' Fox asked her. 'After all those songs about me, surely you're happy we're married and have a child together?'

'Of course I'm happy to be with you, Fox! But I'm so scared of what will happen when my family sees that our baby has animal ears. They'll kill him!'

'I'll easily stop them,' said Fox. 'I have power to do anything.'

Later, she dropped back to sleep, and Fox wished their son's ears to human shape. When Twilight woke up and saw this, she was greatly relieved. She asked if she could take their baby to show her parents, saying, 'They'll be so excited to have a grandchild.'

Fox said he was happy for her to go. He swaddled the baby for her, and tied him to a cradleboard. He was an extraordinarily beautiful little boy, as bright as a rainbow. Twilight strapped him onto her back. Then she set out, alone, for her family home.

Now, Old Man Darkness and his wife had been very worried when their daughter had vanished. They'd sent their three sons out to search for her, without any luck. So you might expect them to be ecstatic when she arrived home safely, with a beautiful baby on her back. But Old Man Darkness soon wiped away Twilight's smiles.

'Where have you been? Staying out for all those days and nights!' he growled at her. 'Gallivanting off with some man, were you? Who is he, eh? Bring the child over here, let's have a look at it.'

She stepped closer, holding out the cradleboard.

Old Man Darkness took a quick look. Without pushing back the covers, he pushed her away, wrinkling his nose: 'Ugh! There's something uncanny about it. It smells disgusting. Confess to me, girl: what filthy, good-for-nothing wretch have you been with?'

'Father, I haven't "been with" anyone. I'm a married woman now. My husband's the man I always longed for.'

Her mother said, timidly, 'Those songs you used to sing... Surely it isn't...?'

'Fox!' yelled Old Man Darkness. 'Get out, girl! Never come back to this house.'

'But Father, I love him. Please let me show you your grandson.'

Gently, she pulled back the cradleboard covers – and screamed. For the little one no longer looked like a human baby. Instead, he was covered all over in thick fur, with whiskers, a black nose and pricked ears.

Old Man Darkness took one look at the creature – the Fox Cub – then snatched him from his daughter's arms, carried him to the door and hurled him onto the ground outside. Twilight wept.

From far away, back in the bright house he had made, Fox was spying. He had transformed the baby into a cub to torment Old Man Darkness for his hostility. Now, to punish the old man even further, he transformed Twilight too.

The bloom of youth drained out of her, like water leaking from a punctured kettle. Her skin folded into wrinkles, her hair turned grey, she groaned and clutched her back. She had become a decrepit old woman. Her family stared at her in disbelief.

Meanwhile, outside, the Fox Cub lay where his grandfather had thrown him, wailing with pain and hunger.

'The baby!' old Twilight gasped hoarsely. 'He needs feeding.'

She turned feebly to the door, but she was too bent and helpless to get outside. Luckily, her youngest brother took pity: he leaped to his feet, rushed out and fetched the hapless Fox Cub. He helped Twilight lie down under a blanket and put the Cub into her arms.

'I don't care whether you're young or old,' he told her. 'You're my sister just the same.'

He lay down to sleep beside Twilight and the Fox Cub. By morning, Fox had undone his mischief: Twilight had regained her youth, and the cub had turned back into a human baby.

Twilight spoke to her brother in whispers, telling him everything about Fox. As the mist rose from the grass, they sneaked out together, and Twilight led the way to the bright house. Fox greeted his wife and baby affectionately, and made his brother-in-law very welcome. Then he said he wanted to pay his respects to his father-in-law, Old Man Darkness himself.

Old Man Darkness was not pleased to hear they were on the way. He snorted with scorn. 'I don't want to meet Fox, the promiscuous lecher! He's totally shameless, he goes around pissing on other people's roots and seeds. He's...'

'Tsk, tsk!' his wife scolded. She elbowed Old Man Darkness out of the way, and spread mats and blankets splendidly across the floor. She managed to make everything look nice just in time before Fox and Twilight arrived together and sat down.

For a while, nobody spoke. Then Fox said, 'Father-in-law, I shall catch some game as a gift for you. Wait here.'

He hurried outside. Old Man Darkness glowered at the door, watching. Fox ran some distance, then suddenly fell onto all fours

317

and changed into his animal form. He sniffed the air with his long nose, he cocked his head, he twitched. Then he went bounding off, his thick tail waving proudly; he leaped, he pounced. Soon he came back, turned into a man again and handed a bulging sack to his mother-in-law.

'Here, Mother, take these outside to roast.'

Before she could even thank him, let alone move, Old Man Darkness snatched the sack from her and tore it open.

'*Mice!*' he roared. 'How dare you give such rubbish to my wife! They stink even more than you do. Chuck them away!'

His wife ignored his outburst and took back the sack. She roasted the mice and served them to her sons – who all ate them with relish. But Old Man Darkness refused even to taste them. He stood nearby, belly rumbling with hunger, muttering under his breath.

'What's the matter?' Fox said. 'Why are you so angry?'

Old Man Darkness turned his back on him.

'Make peace with me,' said Fox.

Old Man Darkness spun round to face him. 'Never! You've stolen my daughter…'

'I didn't steal her,' said Fox. 'She was desperate to marry me.'

'You smell of evil. I despise you. Get out of here!'

Fox stood watching him for a long moment. Then he said quietly, 'In which direction can you see furthest?'

'I can see far off in any direction I choose,' snarled Old Man Darkness.

'Well then…what do you see when you look straight east?'

Despite himself, Old Man Darkness couldn't help turning towards the east. At that moment, Fox caused a great wind to rise in the west and made it blow straight at the old man's back. The wind made his body melt, turning it to murky slush. The liquid steamed, rose into the air and formed a black cloud. The wind hurtled against the cloud, and blew it away towards the east.

Fox grinned and called after him: 'From now on, old man, you will have no sense. You are no longer a person: you are darkness itself. Whenever you come, wherever you go, people will fall asleep. But I, Fox, shall never sleep in your presence. I shall sleep in the daytime, and travel in the darkness to oppose you. People will use your name, Darkness, to do evil: they will steal, and commit murder. For you yourself are unyieldingly evil, and your presence will give people evil thoughts.'

Curtin: *Myths of the Modocs*, collected 1884, published 1912
For information about the Modoc informants, see p. 300.

The Modoc word for Fox is 'Wus'. He is an iconic character who appears in many other Modoc stories. Curtin comments that he 'was the greatest trickster in the world; he delighted in deceiving people'.

In the source book, the myth develops into a new story with a more melancholy tone. Fox takes his wife and family away and gives them the 'water of life' to drink, filling them with good feelings. Twilight has another baby. However, their household becomes troubled. The two children are fostered by Fox's grandmother, and one accidentally dies. This causes Fox to lose his mind, which is restored after a period of prayer and austerity on the mountaintop. Fox now permanently abandons his family to go on a journey. He overcomes an ogre who had devoured an entire village and marries the only survivor. She is a mature medicine woman with only one leg and a magic cane that enables her to cover vast distances with a single hop. They have countless children, but they begin to fight – bringing the phenomenon of conflict into the world. Fox now divides his children into tribes, each speaking a different language, then travels to the end of the world with his wife and five youngest children. On the way they discover a river full of small fish, which Fox turns into the first salmon. Later he quarrels with his wife, and they are both transformed into birds.

There is a second Modoc story in which Fox courts Twilight. Here Fox is warned against her by his companion, Grey Fox:

"'What could you do with Twilight?" asked Grey Fox. "You can see
her only a little while just before dark. No one can see her in the
night or in the daytime. That is why she doesn't get a man."'

Nevertheless, Fox is determined to win her, so he goes to her father's house and turns himself invisible. However, as soon as he touches her, she recognises him and screams, forcing him to flee.

Fox's womanising features in a number of other stories. Usually, his lust is regarded as both unwelcome and dangerous. In one episode, Fox tries to court a Butterfly girl; on being rejected because he is too old, he transforms the girl and her friends into the first butterflies. In another, Old Snowbird's two daughters ignore her warning and get caught by Fox, who transforms them into ugly old hags. Fortunately everything comes right in the end and they are able to marry their husbands of choice.

In a more serious myth, Fox organises the stealing of fire from two sets of brothers on the edges of the world (similar to the Great Basin story on p. 277). This also precipitates the origin of Summer and Winter, and the end of the primeval age, when 'all the people turned to common animals, for real people were coming'.

Elsewhere he appears as a typical trickster. In this guise, he also appears in Flathead and Nez Perce stories, often as the sidekick of Coyote.

RITUAL MORNING SPEECH

Nez Perce (Nimi'ipuu)

I wonder if everyone is up.
It is morning.
We are alive, so thanks be!
Rise up! Look about!
Go see the horses, lest a wolf has killed one!
Thanks be that the children are alive –
and you older men, and you older women;
also that your friends are perhaps alive in other camps.
But elsewhere there are probably those who are ill this morning,
and therefore the children are sad,
and therefore their friends are sad.

– Unnamed herald on horseback,
giving the day's orders for the village or camp
(Quoted in Teit: *Folk-Tales of Salishan and Sahaptin Tribes*, 1917)

MOUNTAIN GLACIER AND THE DAUGHTER OF CHINOOK WIND

Lillooet (St'at'imc)

Mountain Glacier is exceptionally cold, slow and unyielding. Even so, he has the same needs as any other man.

That's why, long ago, he decided to find a wife to comfort and take care of him. The women who lived near him up in the mountains all feared his harshness and refused him. But instead of despairing, Mountain Glacier went looking further afield.

South he went, through the valleys, down the river, into lakes and out of them, then further still. How many human lifetimes did his journey take him? Many, for the distance covered by a man in a single step took Mountain Glacier a whole day. But he was in no hurry, he was determined; and at long last, he reached the ocean.

There he ambled along the shore to a village and entered the wooden house of Chinook Wind. He was given a hearty welcome, with a feast and magnificent gifts; then his host asked why he had come.

'I wish to marry your daughter,' said Mountain Glacier.

'Ah,' said Chinook Wind. 'I see that you are a mighty man. I give her to you gladly.'

So Mountain Glacier took Chinook Wind's Daughter away. After another impossibly slow journey back to his distant home, they were husband and wife. But right from the beginning, she wasn't happy up there in the mountains.

'What's the matter?' Mountain Glacier growled.

'I can't stand the cold,' she said.

Mountain Glacier answered cruelly, 'That's how life is up here.'

His wife was dismayed. Realising that she would have to look after herself, she went down to the forest on the slopes far below their house, and gathered wood there. She brought it home and lit a fire, then sat by the flames and warmed herself.

But when her husband came home and felt the heat...ach! Mountain Glacier began to melt! In a frenzy, he threw ice on the fire to extinguish it. Then he seized the unused firewood and hurled it away.

'Husband,' said Chinook Wind's Daughter softly, 'you may be mighty but you're also a fool. It's impossible for me to live in this cold. Let me have a fire, I beg you! Otherwise you will lose me.'

Mountain Glacier didn't want to lose the wife he had travelled so far to fetch. But he didn't want to melt either. So he said, 'Very well, I understand your needs. But it's undignified for my own wife to forage for firewood. I shall order our servant, Water Ouzel, to undertake this task for you.'

This promise gave his wife hope. She did not hear the heartless instructions that Mountain Glacier gave to the small grey bird. 'When you bring my wife firewood each day,' he said, 'make sure it is always wet.'

Water Ouzel obeyed. He hopped into the water, found fallen branches and logs drifting down the river, hauled them out and dragged them, still dripping, up to his master's house.

There Chinook Wind's Daughter tried to light a fire with them.

'Now surely you must be happy?' Mountain Glacier chided her.

Chinook Wind's Daughter shook her head. 'No, husband, I'm not. For a fire of wet wood gives out no heat; and it smokes so much I can scarcely even see my own hands.'

Mountain Glacier shrugged and sighed irritably: 'Huh! Maybe I was better without a wife, after all, for this one is never satisfied.'

In this sorry way their lives together went on. Eventually she gave birth to a child; but that did not relieve her misery. So, constantly shivering with cold, she sent another bird to take a message to her family, describing the horrors of her marriage.

Her brother was devastated to hear of his sister's suffering and called all his friends to help. A large band of these bold young men set out in a canoe, up the river, through the mountains and along the lake to rescue her. The further they went, the chillier they got. Their breath froze and their skin grew sore with cold-burns.

'No wonder my sister is in such despair,' said the brother.

Ahead of them loomed a bleak and frozen place, shadowed by barren slopes: Mountain Glacier's abode. They paddled on to the top of the lake, where the water merged into a solid expanse of ice.

There all the young men transformed themselves into snowflakes. They were light as air, laughing silently. They rose, drifted over Mountain Glacier's house and danced around it.

Inside, Chinook Wind's Daughter suddenly felt a draught of warm air. She jumped up, ran to the door and saw the snowstorm. 'Snow only falls when the weather turns milder,' she thought. 'That must mean my brother has come!'

But her joy was short-lived. For at once, her husband came to challenge them, raising his hands to the sky. The air chilled, every rock became smothered in frost; every remaining drop of water froze.

The snowflakes flurried back to their canoe, which was now marooned in ice. But the young men did not give up. They transformed this time into sleet. In this guise, they returned to Mountain Glacier's house to taunt him again with their dancing. Again, he drove them back with cold fury. They withdrew just long enough to renew their strength, then made their final attack – this time as torrential rain.

The rain pelted down on Mountain Glacier's house. Piece by piece, it melted. Mountain Glacier tried one last time to retaliate; but could manage only a light spattering of hail. The young men laughed out loud at this feeble show, and easily blew it away with a strong, warm wind.

Mountain Glacier was lost, for this wind born of the ocean was far stronger than his own primeval powers. Nothing could be done to stop it. He abandoned his house. He abandoned his wife. He began to retreat, slowly, heavily, into the depths of the mountains.

Chinook Wind's Daughter ran to greet her brother, laughing with relief. He helped her into the canoe, and the young men at once started paddling back towards the south. Halfway along the lake, they put ashore, built a fire and gathered around it to eat. There, the brother noticed that his sister's hip was disfigured by a big lump.

'Oh, my poor sister, what is wrong with you?' he cried. 'Did your cruel husband wound you? Are you stricken by a dreadful disease?'

Chinook Wind's Daughter blushed as if he had discovered some shameful secret. 'No,' she answered lightly, 'that is my baby son.'

'Let me see him,' said her brother.

'Don't touch him!' she cried. 'He's the only good thing I got from my marriage. Don't make me leave him behind!'

But her brother insisted. He wrenched the lump from her side and unwrapped it from its blanket.

'Look, sister,' he said gently. 'You were nursing no child. It's merely a lump of ice, as cold as its father's heart. In this way too he deceived you.'

Then the young woman wept: 'The place where I carried him is still cold with grief, my brother.'

But he had strong words to comfort her. 'From this time on,' he said, 'in this land, cold and ice will have mastery for only a few months each year. For we shall make the chinook wind blow each spring and drive them away, just as we have done today.'

With those words, he paddled his sister all the way home.

Since then, the deadly blasts of winter on the Plateau have always been overcome each year by the warm wet winds of spring.

And since then too, in memory of the ice baby that Chinook Wind's Daughter once carried on her hip, women have always been more stricken by winter chills than their husbands.

Teit: *Traditions of the Lillooet Indians*, 1912

The story is set in the Coast Mountains of southwestern British Columbia. No information is given in the source book about the original narrator.

The chinook wind blows warming, wet gusts from the northwest coast, over the mountains and inland, rapidly increasing winter temperatures in the interior, melting and evaporating stands of snow. Its name comes from the Chinook people of the Northwest.

Stories such as this illustrate the old Plateau belief that the landscape was alive and imbued with spiritual presence. Another example appears in the source book's introduction:

'There are two springs, one hot and one cold...in the Lower Lillooet district. They were a married couple whom the Transformer changed into springs at their own request. They said, "Let us be two springs, one hot and one cold, side by side. People who bathe in us and drink our water will become well".'

The battle between cold and warm weather is a recurrent theme in the region – see the next story.

NORTHERN LIGHTS, EXTREME COLD AND THE SOUTH WIND

Sanpoil

Northern Lights was the proud mother of five sons. The eldest of these was called Cold. After him came Colder, then Coldest, next Extreme Cold and finally the youngest of all, Most Extreme Cold. They all lived together in the far north, in a lodge made entirely of ice. They were unable to endure heat of any kind.

Every night, the youngest son, Most Extreme Cold, went out spreading frost over all the leaves and grass that he passed, causing them to wither and die. After a while he would run back home saying, 'I've done what I can, Mama. There are many living plants still to destroy, but I'm not brave enough to travel any further.' Then his eldest brother, Cold, would sigh disparagingly and go out to finish the deadly work. The other three sons all stayed at home in the ice lodge with their parents.

Northern Lights loved them all, but she had special affection for her second youngest son, Extreme Cold. She was very protective – some might say *over*-protective – and always fussing around him. Not surprisingly, Extreme Cold found this annoying. As time went by, he grew restless to leave both the ice lodge and his mother, for he was eager to see the world beyond.

So he said, 'Mama, I've decided to go on a journey.'

'Oh! Where to, my favourite boy?'

'I haven't decided yet,' he said. 'No special place, just here and there. I'll travel south and see where my feet take me.'

'Don't go!' she begged him. 'I worry you'll get into trouble.'

'You know I'm strong, Mama. I can look after myself.'

'But I'm worried that you'll bring trouble back here to us.'

'Of course I won't. You mustn't stop me.'

Northern Lights began to weep. 'My son, at least promise that you won't speak to any human being that you meet along the way. More than that…promise that you'll *kill* every one of them!'

Extreme Cold didn't say no to that, and he didn't say yes. But Northern Lights could not hold back her son. So she helped him prepare for his journey and watched with trepidation as he set out.

Thus Extreme Cold went into the world, travelling far to the strange lands that lay to the south. As he went, his breath froze all the plants, which perished as he passed them. He laid waste the spring, destroyed the summer and eliminated any hope of the fruits of autumn. Thus every land he passed through lost its seasons; the animals died and the people began to starve.

In one of the countries that he blighted like this, a chief called his people to a council, hoping to find a solution.

'This calamity has surely come from the Cold People of the far north,' he said. 'But I have never met anyone who knows where their ice lodge lies, let alone how to find it. If any of you can suggest how we might reach that place and persuade these cruel people to stop our suffering, let him speak up now.'

Everyone assembled there shook their heads gloomily. Then suddenly the door of the lodge blew open and a tall, shrewd-looking stranger strode in.

'Who are you?' the chief cried.

'My name is South Wind,' said he. 'I am a shaman. I have studied the trouble which currently afflicts us. It is caused by one of the Cold People who has dared to enter our land. I offer my services to find and confront this being.'

'You seem to have knowledge that none of us can even dream of,' the chief answered. 'If you are brave enough to attempt this on behalf of us all, I give my blessing.'

So South Wind went to seek his enemy, blowing this way and that until he located Extreme Cold walking ahead of him. He saw how Extreme Cold spread ice and death on every side, turning the whole landscape grey and brittle.

South Wind drew closer then called out, 'Wait there!'

Extreme Cold spun round, his face twisted with malicious glee. 'Who are you who dares slow my journey?' he snarled. 'Well, whatever you hope for from me, the only thing I offer you is this!'

He brandished his thin hands in a rush of glacial air, sending out a shower of ice. At once South Wind blew it back at him; then smiled and held out his own hand in friendship.

'Nephew, that's no way to greet your uncle,' he said softly. 'Besides, it's pointless to try and abuse me – because, as you see, my strength is far greater than yours.'

'Nephew?' said Extreme Cold uncertainly. 'Uncle?'

'Yes indeed,' said South Wind. 'Have you not heard of me? I am the brother of your mother, that good woman Northern Lights.'

Extreme Cold hung his head in shame. 'Accept my apologies, Uncle. How can I make amends for dishonouring you?'

'Take me to see your mother, my sister,' said South Wind. 'It's too long since we were last together, and the world has changed so much that I cannot find the way without a guide.'

'In that case, I will end my journey at once and take you to our home,' said Extreme Cold humbly.

He turned round and led South Wind back through the bleak landscape, blighted by his deadly touch. South Wind did not comment as they made the way north; but he blew out his warm breath behind him and to every side. Thus the hard earth began to thaw at last, and under the surface living roots and seeds stirred.

The warmth that South Wind exuded had an effect on Extreme Cold too, as if he were melting inside. By the time the pair reached the ice lodge, his whole body was steaming.

Extreme Cold plunged into the ice lodge with relief, taking deep breaths of the frozen air within. South Wind came in softly behind him.

'My dearest son! Welcome back!' cried Northern Lights. 'But who is this you've brought?'

South Wind stepped forward and embraced the freezing woman. 'My dear sister! Don't you recognise your own lost brother? It's been so long... But surely you remember me?'

Northern Lights stepped back and stared at him with frost-glittering eyes. 'My brother...?' she said uncertainly.

Her husband leaped to his feet, crying, 'This is no brother of yours, Northern Lights. He's trying to fool you. How many times have we both bemoaned the fact that neither of us have any siblings?' He lowered his voice and took Northern Lights to one side, turning his back on South Wind. 'This must be some malicious deceit. Whatever this stranger is up to, we must meet his mischief with cunning of our own and destroy him.'

'Wise words, husband,' Northern Lights replied. 'Most likely he has come to harm our beloved sons. But this is easily dealt with: I'll offer him hospitality for tonight, then while he sleeps we can freeze him to death.'

South Wind was waiting uncertainly by the foot of the ladder. 'Brother,' said Northern Lights, smiling broadly, 'you are most welcome. Come, let me make a bed for you, and in the morning we can talk about old times.'

So Northern Lights, her husband and their sons all went to bed alongside South Wind. Northern Lights and her husband both lay wide awake, listening for South Wind to succumb to slumber. On the far side of the lodge, South Wind lay awake too.

Who would give way first?

The long winter's night went on. Finally, Northern Lights and her husband stopped whispering and both began to snore. Beside them, their five sons were already lost in the land of dreams.

South Wind lay in his bed a short time longer. Then he rose and quietly climbed the ladder that led out of the house. In the moonlight outside, he spotted a heap of fallen fir trees, their trunks split open by frost. Quickly, he drifted over to them. The cold had rotted them away to their cores, revealing a mass of sticky pitchwood. He dug this out, carried it back to the ice lodge and threw it down the entrance hole, blowing the breath of fire after it.

At once, the pitchwood exploded into flames. The roof of the ice lodge thawed and caved in. Beneath it, Northern Lights, her husband and their five sons were overcome by heat and the greedily spreading fire, in which they perished.

So it was that the South Wind overcame the Cold People, and thus regulated the seasons to be as they are today.

Teit et al: *Folk-Tales of Salishan & Sahaptin Tribes*, 1917
The source gives no information about the original narrator.

Many other Plateau stories reflect the weather extremes that dominate the region. In a Coeur d'Alene myth, Heat and Cold are two brothers who alternate the seasons. An Okanagan story tells of Coyote destroying the Ice People who killed their enemies with cold; but their daughter survives, thus freezing weather still exists in the world. In a Wasco story, an endless hard winter is punishment for a girl who struck a bird; the villagers must float her away downriver on an ice-floe to melt the snow.

COYOTE AND HIS SON

Thompson River People
(Nlaka'pamux)

Long ago, a great flood covered the whole world. The surging waters submerged everything except for a few mountain peaks. Almost everyone drowned in it...

But Coyote didn't. He turned himself into a piece of wood and floated on top of the water. It tossed him around, here and there, but he never sank into the depths. At last the flood subsided, leaving the piece of wood high and dry. Then Coyote changed back into his true shape.

He was full of vigour, full of lust, but there were no other beings in the world to share it. However, the flood had enriched the land and made it full of growing things. So Coyote took trees to be his wives; and from them were born the ancestors of all people.

Time passed until there were again numerous people in the world. Yet despite this, Coyote was very lonely. He was filled with longing to have a proper child – a son – of his own.

So he took a lump of clay and kneaded it into the shape of a boy. The boy drew breath and came alive.

'My dear son!' cried Coyote joyfully. 'Make me proud. Work hard and train yourself to be strong and wise.'

The clay boy ran off eagerly.

'Take care,' Coyote called after him. 'Keep away from water!'

The clay boy tried diligently to obey his father. But soon the sun came out and made him too hot to concentrate on his training. He went down to the river and gazed longingly at the cool water.

Despite his father's warning, he gave way to temptation, stripped off his clothes and jumped in. Within moments, he had dissolved. Nothing was left of him.

Later, Coyote found the clay boy's clothes on the riverbank and realised what had happened. 'My son was disobedient,' he said sadly. 'But I must share the blame, for I didn't create him well enough.'

Coyote went into the woods, collected some gum from the trees, shaped this into another boy and brought him alive.

'Welcome, my son,' said Coyote. 'May you live long and work hard. Learn to be strong and wise... But always stay in the shade.'

The gum boy also set off eagerly and diligently. But the shade made him gloomy, and beyond the trees he saw sunshine. So he crept out there to a large, flat rock, lay down on it and fell asleep. Within a short time, he had completely melted away.

Later, Coyote found a patch of sticky gum in the middle of the rock, and realised what had happened. 'My second son was also disobedient,' he said sadly. 'But I must share the blame, for I didn't create him well enough.'

Coyote found a big piece of stone. He dipped it into the river, and when he pulled it out again, the stone was still intact. He laid it in the sun for a whole day, and the stone was unharmed at the end of it. He hurled it hard against the rocks several times over; but the stone didn't break or even chip. So he fashioned it into a third boy.

'Welcome, my third son,' said Coyote. 'May you live long and well. Work hard, train yourself to be strong and wise. Go to the water often to cleanse yourself; lie in the sun to absorb its power.'

The boy did all these things, and no harm came to him. He completed his training and grew up fast into a fine young man, skilled in all the masculine arts. News of him spread, and many people came to admire him. When the time was right, he took the daughters of Mallard Duck and Loon to be his wives. One was dark and the other was fair; both were beautiful and hard working.

Well and good. But Coyote was jealous of his son's good fortune, and filled with longing to have a proper wife of his own.

'What a good time I could have with a couple of ripe young women like that!' he thought. And he devised a plan to steal them.

He went off alone, defecated on a bare patch of ground and transformed his dung into an eagle's nest with a clutch of chicks inside. He caused a tree to grow under the nest, lifting it high into the crown of branches. Then he hurried to his son's house, calling,

'Beloved son, I've found an eagle's nest on top of a lonely tree. It's a great place to gather some of their precious feathers.'

'Show me where it is, Father,' said the young man eagerly.

Coyote took him there and pointed up to the nest.'Let me give you some advice,' he said slyly. 'Climbing a tree fully dressed is an encumbrance. You'll reach the top more quickly if you strip off.'

The son agreed, left his clothes by the roots, then began shinning up the tree. As he went, Coyote kept lifting up his eyelids with his fingers; and each time he did this, the tree grew taller.

After a long while, his son called, 'Father, this tree's higher than I realised. I still can't reach the nest, so I'm coming down.'

'Nonsense,' Coyote called back. 'Don't give up, keep going!'

So Coyote's Son continued to climb with renewed effort. Finally, he came level with the eagle's nest. He reached into it, hoping to pull out some loose plumes. However, as soon as he touched it, the entire thing turned back into dung. Even worse, the tree below his feet had somehow vanished; it was impossible to go back down.

'Ach, how could my own father trick me like this!' he cried.

He stepped off the branch where he was balanced – and thus entered the Above World, the Sky. It was very similar to the Earth, with a vast, flat, treeless, grassy plateau stretching as far as he could see. Wind gusted harshly across it, chilling his naked body to the bone. He had no idea where to go, but started running fast, to save himself from freezing to death.

The plateau was dotted with wild potatoes, so he stopped to pull one up. Maybe he could eat it? However, at once, a different kind of wind blew up from the hole where it had been. He peered into it and saw the Earth far, far below. For these 'potatoes' were really stars. Hastily, he dropped it back into place and hurried on.

Soon he came to a door in the roof of an underground house, and went down its ladder. Inside, it was snug and cosy, but there was no sign of anyone at home. A row of baskets was lined up along the wall. Since there was no one to stop him, he decided to take one. However, as soon as he stooped to pick it up, all the other baskets came to life, springing up to attack him, crashing into his face and hurling themselves at his body.

'Stop, stop!' he yelled, and dropped the basket he was holding. At once, the others resumed their places like normal, lifeless objects.

He beat a hasty retreat, but halfway up the ladder, he turned back to curse them: 'Baskets, you'll suffer for this! From now on, you'll have no life of your own: you'll be people's slaves for ever!'

He walked on, still naked and directionless. As he went, he entered three further houses, and in each had a similar weird adventure. One was occupied only by a set of awls, another by some sharp-toothed combs, and the last by a clutch of birch-bark containers. Each time, he tried to take one of the objects – only to be attacked by the others, causing him to escape at full speed. He cursed all these too, and thus they became the eternal slaves of human beings.

'What a bizarre country this is,' he thought. 'I wonder if there are any normal inhabitants.'

By now he had reached the edge of the plateau, and made his way down a slope dotted with trees. At the bottom, he came to an encampment where he did indeed catch sight of some real people.

There were only two of them, both very old women, both blind. They were huddled over a fire, fiddling sightlessly with their pile of logs. They kept losing hold of the logs and clutching at thin air, arguing fiercely. Coyote's Son decided it was safest to just hurry past them. However, as he did, one of their flailing hands inadvertently grabbed his naked manhood and the old woman gave a shriek of disgust. This sent Coyote's Son into a rage; he seized both women and hurled them into the trees, where they were at once transformed into grouse. Then he strode on.

In time, he reached yet another underground house, and descended its ladder with trepidation. But, to his immense relief, he discovered that this was the home of old Spider and his wife.

'Welcome, young man, welcome!' Spider greeted him.

'Welcome indeed,' said Spider's Wife. 'But whatever's the matter with you? Where are your clothes? You look blue with cold. And your stomach looks hollow, as if you're starving to death.'

'You're right,' said Coyote's Son. 'I beg you to help me.'

'Of course we will. Sit down, make yourself comfortable. Here, put on these warm clothes. That's right. And help yourself to as much food as you can manage from our pot.'

After Coyote's Son had fed and warmed himself, Spider's Wife said, 'Stay here for as long as you like. We'll be your grandparents and take care of you. I'll feed you up on deer-fat and lots of other treats. You'll soon get your strength back, you'll see.'

So Coyote's Son settled down with them. His adopted grandfather, Spider, eagerly taught him everything he needed to become full of sacred power. When this training was complete,

Coyote's Son went out hunting and filled the Spiders' house with piles of meat, fat and skins. They were delighted.

Time went by very pleasantly in the Above World. But Coyote's Son couldn't help feeling homesick. He went to Spider saying, 'Grandfather, I miss my own country and my wives.'

'That's only to be expected,' said Spider kindly. 'We'll be sorry to lose you, but even so, it's right that you return to your real home.'

'How will I get there, Grandfather?'

'I'll let you down in a basket,' said Spider. 'But beware the four obstacles you'll meet on the way: clouds, mist, tree tops and grasses waving in the wind. As you pass each one, keep your eyes tightly closed; otherwise you'll rise back here again. But when you hear the cry of meadowlarks, open your eyes and climb out.'

Spider brought a splendid basket and fixed it to a rope. He lifted up the fire-stone in his house, revealing a hole. Far, far below, Coyote's Son saw crowds of people looking no bigger than flies. He entered the basket, closed his eyes, and sat still while Spider lowered it through the hole. Every so often, the basket bumped against one of the obstacles and, despite himself, he opened his eyes, making it rise again; but once he closed them, it resumed its descent. Eventually, it came to rest amidst a loud chorus of meadowlarks. He opened his eyes for good, climbed out, tugged on the rope, and watched as the basket was hauled back to the Sky.

Here on Earth, the flowers were in bloom – the season when his people travelled to the summer hunting grounds on the lakeshore. He set out that way, and saw a crowd of his people walking ahead. He soon caught up with the slowest stragglers: Ant, Beetle and Caterpillar. They were overjoyed to see him.

'Wherever have you been, friend?' Ant asked.

Coyote's Son told them about his father's malicious trick and his curious adventures in the Above World. They listened with great interest, and then it was his turn for questions: 'What's my devious father been up to since I left? How are my wives?'

'Ah, there's an equally interesting story,' said Beetle, 'and you won't be pleased to hear it. Just after you vanished, Coyote turned up, dressed in your clothes, pretending he was you. In this disguise, he presented himself to your wives. Your dark wife wasn't taken in at all, but your fair wife believed his deceit. This suited Coyote fine, because he only lusted after her anyway. He moved in with her, and didn't object at all when your dark wife moved out.'

'What's become of her?' asked Coyote's Son.

Caterpillar took up the tale: 'She cut her hair to show she was in mourning for you, and set up home on her own. She's been well supported by the charity of the rest of us. For we all guessed that Coyote had done something terrible to you. She's very well, I'm pleased to say. And here's some special news for you, friend – some time ago, she gave birth to a little boy.'

'My own son!' cried Coyote's Son excitedly. 'On the very last day I saw her, she told me she was carrying our child.'

'You must be impatient to see him as soon as possible,' said Ant.

'I am.'

'Well, listen,' said Beetle. 'Your dark wife and child are travelling more slowly than the others, in between us and the main body of people. If you walk quickly, you'll catch them up.'

'Thank you, friends. Please don't tell anyone you've seen me.'

'Your secret is safe with us,' Caterpillar assured him.

Coyote's Son walked on and soon recognised the familiar form of his dark wife ahead, carrying a child in her arms. A moment later, he heard the little one's voice carried back on the wind: 'Mama, my father's walking behind us.'

'Don't be silly,' the dark wife scolded. 'Your father died before you were born and you've never met him.'

But when the good woman glanced over her shoulder and saw Coyote's Son coming up, she stopped and shrieked with joy. She put the child down and raced to meet him, throwing herself into his arms.

After they had embraced, and told each other all that had happened, Coyote's Son told her to camp at a distance from the others. There he visited her every night, bringing good quantities of deer meat and fat.

'Wherever did you find such food husband?' she asked fondly. 'I keep hearing the other men complain that all the deer have vanished; everyone's just been living on roots.'

'Ah,' he smiled, 'I've driven the deer to a secret place to be sure that our family never goes hungry again. Don't tell anyone else.'

Because they were camping alone, at first no one realised their good fortune. However, Raven's eyes are sharp and his brain even sharper. He noticed that the dark wife had stopped wailing in grief and singing mourning songs. So he went to her lonely tent, listened outside and caught the sound of happy voices. Then he burst in – and saw the dark wife and her little boy enjoying a rich meal of fat.

'Can you spare a few pickings for my own hungry children, Sister?' Raven begged.

The dark wife hesitated, then gave him a generous portion.

'Thank you, thank you,' Raven cringed. 'Where did you get this good food, if I may ask?'

'From my hus…' she started to say; then clapped her hand over her mouth.

'Your husband? Coyote's Son? No! Surely he hasn't returned?'

'I beg you to keep this secret!' she cried in remorse. 'Listen, Raven, if you do, I'll give you more meat every evening.'

'You can trust me, Sister,' said Raven. 'I won't tell a soul.'

And he didn't. He carried the meat to his own home, cunningly wrapped up in moss – which was all his family had been living on until then. But when he took it out, his children immediately fell to quarrelling and fighting for a larger share. This commotion brought the neighbours round to find out what was going on.

'It's just that my poor little ones are complaining about only having moss for supper yet again,' said Raven.

However, the neighbours grew more suspicious and one went to spy on them. When the young ones' noise started up, this man rushed in, seized one of the children and forced him to disgorge his food. The man snatched it and took it to show the others.

'That's deer fat!' they cried. 'Where did Raven get it?'

They hauled Raven up before a council. 'No one's managed to kill any deer for ages,' the chief said. 'Tell us where you found this meat, Raven – or we'll kill you.'

'I swore not to tell,' said Raven. 'Hmm, but I suppose I must, to save my life. I got it from Coyote's Son.'

'*What?!*'

'Yes, he's come back! And his lodge is filled with meat.'

He led them to Coyote's Son's tent.

'Welcome back!' they cried. 'We're so very glad to see you!'

Coyote's Son came out to greet them. 'And it's good to see all of you too, my friends. Help yourselves, there's plenty of meat.'

The next day, he threw a celebration feast. Almost everyone came; but his father, Coyote, pointedly stayed away.

Coyote's Son plotted revenge on his father. He fashioned some deer entrails into a net, beautifully crafted and finely decorated, then snipped it with notches to weaken it. He used the net to hang up some meat in a tree, then visited his father's tent.

'Father, haven't you heard? I've returned safely!'

'Why have you taken so long to visit me?' said Coyote snidely. 'Fancy leaving your own father to depend on rumours to discover you're back.'

'I've been busy preparing a gift for you,' Coyote's Son said. 'I've hung some meat in a tree on the far side of the creek. No one else knows about it – I put it there secretly, especially for you.'

'Good,' snarled Coyote. And he hurried across the creek to get it.

His eyes lit up when he saw the net full of meat. He cut it down with greedy fingers, and hastened back to the creek. This was very deep, but easily crossed on a log. Coyote had just carried the net to the log's half-way point, when the notches gave way. The meat tumbled out of it into the water, making Coyote lose his balance – so that he tumbled into the water too.

At once, it seethed into a violent torrent. It carried Coyote swiftly downstream, into the wide, rushing Great River beyond…

As he was carried away, Coyote transformed into a piece of wood, just as he had done during the Flood. In this form, he drifted downriver with the current, passing through countless unknown regions, on and on…until at last his journey came to an abrupt end, as the water dashed him hard against a fish-dam.

This dam was the property of two elderly sisters who used it to catch salmon. At that time, salmon only lived in the lower reaches of the river, for the dam stopped them all swimming upstream.

The next morning the sisters came down to fetch their night's catch – and found the piece of wood tangled up amongst the fish.

'That could be useful,' said the first sister. 'I'll take it home.'

There she fashioned the wood into a bowl, then served up a fish on it. But before either woman could taste it, the fish vanished! They both shook their heads in bewilderment, and put another fish into the bowl. Exactly the same thing happened again.

'I'm not having this nonsense,' said the one who'd made it. And she hurled the bowl into the fire.

As it started to burn, they heard a strange noise, '*Wah, wah!*' coming from the heart of the flames.

'That sounds like a baby in there!' cried the second sister. Hastily, she poked around in the fire – and, very soon indeed, pulled out a baby boy. 'Oh, you know how I've always longed for a child!' she cried. 'It must have been sent to me.'

From that day, she nursed him tenderly. He quickly grew into a strong lad. Together the sisters did their best to care for him; however despite all their efforts, he was wayward and difficult, impossible to control.

In a dark corner of the sisters' house, there stood four large wooden boxes. 'Whatever you do, naughty boy,' they told him, 'don't you dare take the lids off any of those.'

'Why?' the boy wanted to know. 'Why, why, why?'

They refused to tell. So one day, when they were about to go out, the boy pretended to be sick and took to his bed. The sisters made him comfortable then went off. As soon as he was alone, the boy turned back into his true form. Yes, of course – it was Coyote! He sneaked into the corner and wrenched the lids off the four boxes.

A great cloud of smoke rushed from the first one – the first smoke in the world. Swarming masses of many different kinds of insects rushed from the others – the first insects in the world.

Then Coyote ran down to the fish-dam and forced it open. At once, all the salmon waiting below rushed through it and swam upstream, into the Great River and all its tributaries.

That's how the annual autumn salmon run began. It was all due to Coyote's mischief.

Teit: *Traditions of the Thompson River Indians*, 1898
A number of unnamed informants must have supplied this story, since Teit's footnotes mention different variants, using phrases such as 'it is also said'. Similar myths were widely recorded amongst other Plateau peoples.

This story has no precise beginning or end. After the final episode here, the source book spins on, with Coyote running ahead of the salmon run, bringing fish into other rivers and their tributaries. As he travels, he encounters various young women; he sexually abuses some and propositions others. Wherever his victims manage to evade him, he sets rock barriers across the water, ensuring that such places never receive any salmon. The myth continues with Coyote's many other marvellous feats and malicious tricks. Each episode is explicitly linked to a particular location or river. This was an important aspect of narratives in the region. The humorous fantasy motif of the trickster turning faeces into a useful object was also widely used in Plateau stories.

Although Coyote does not dominate myths here as much as in California and the Great Basin, he plays an important role in a large number of them. Some tell of ordinary humans outwitting and even killing the sagacious trickster, albeit only temporarily.

COYOTE AND THE SECRETS

Wishram

Coyote went to visit the Sun, thinking he could take over her work.
When he arrived, he said to her, 'Well, this is good:
I shall become your slave and follow you about.
Because you are chieftainess, I'll work for you for nothing,'
The Sun agreed.

Early next morning the Sun rose;
and wherever she went, Coyote followed her there.
He looked down and saw the various things that people got up to:
women being abducted, people being killed,
goods being stolen and other bad things. Oh dear.
'People,' he yelled, 'I can see what you're all up to,
I can see what you're all doing!'
Because of this, the Sun didn't want him.
'I've taken you with me long enough,' she said.
'You're too mean. It's no good.
If you keep telling on people, there'll soon be trouble.'

Thus Coyote's attempt to become the Sun
was all in vain, he had to give it up.
And because of this, we can't find everything out.
But if Coyote had become the sun,
everybody today would be betrayed in their secrets.

– Pete McGuff, half-Wishram elder.
(Quoted in Sapir & Curtin, *Wishram Texts*, 1909)

HOW SICKNESS CAME INTO THE WORLD

Modoc

The three Gletcowas brothers stood out from other men because they were all very small – they'd never grown any bigger than children. Despite this, they were all brilliant at catching deer. They crafted snares from knotted ropes of twisted grass and suspended them from trees; then every morning they went out and drove their prey into them. When they'd caught enough, they carried the carcasses home to skin and butcher.

Two other brothers lived nearby. They were of normal height but both somewhat strange. The elder one, Keis, was lazy and hot-tempered. He sat at home all day making bows and arrows; but though he had piles and piles of them, he never used them. The younger one, Snoutiss, spent his time digging roots, like a woman. So these two had to make do with no meat to eat.

That's not to say they didn't wish they had some. Whenever they heard the Gletcowas brothers removing the catch from their snares, Keis and Snoutiss would grouse and grumble:

'Those three always have far more meat than they need.'

'They ought to share it with us.'

'Well, since they don't,' said Keis, 'let's help ourselves, take some from their snares. We'll just cut off a joint or two, they won't notice.'

'Yes they will,' said Snoutiss, 'because they always carry all the deer home whole. Go to their house, brother, ask for some.'

'I'm not lowering myself by *begging*,' said Keis.

As soon as Snoutiss had gone out root digging, Keis sloped off to the Gletcowas' favourite patch of woodland. It didn't take him long to find a nice, fat dead deer dangling from a branch in one of

339

their snares. He couldn't manage to untie the knot round its neck because it was too tight, so he tried biting it. Unfortunately, the knot still didn't loosen, and all he managed to do was break his teeth. Blood started pouring from his mouth – just as the two elder Gletcowas brothers came along to fetch their day's catch. They saw Keis standing guiltily next to the snare.

'What are you doing here?' they asked.

Keis didn't bother to answer. He just watched with greedy eyes as they untied the deer. Then he sprang on it, hissing, '*Mine!*'

'No, it's ours,' said the eldest brother calmly. 'But I tell you what, come home with us and we'll cut you off a good portion.'

'I want it *now*,' said Keis.

'Sorry, friend, but it's taboo to butcher deer out here in the woods. If we broke this rule, we'd never be able to catch any more. It's not far to our house. Come there with us, we've got plenty of meat and we're happy to share it.'

Keis snarled at them, turned his back and slouched off home. Blood was pouring down his chin from his broken teeth and he was in terrible pain, which aggravated his habitual smouldering rage. By the time he reached home, this rage had grown so huge that he couldn't think of anything beyond it.

'Everyone's against me, they all hate me,' he muttered. 'Well, I'll show them who's the strong one; they won't know what's hit them.'

He started to mix up medicine – bad medicine, poison. Black vomit, he made, shivery chills, high sweaty fever, really terrible stuff, a huge batch of it. Then Snoutiss came home.

'Hey, brother, what are you up to? Pshaw! What's that stink?'

'Poison,' Keis said shortly.

'*What?* You can't make that! It might escape from here, spread all over the place. All sorts of people might catch it. They'll get ill and die.'

'I'll do what I want,' said Keis. 'It's my revenge against those mean Gletcowas brothers. Look at my ruined teeth! It's their fault, for knotting their snares so tightly.'

Snoutiss tried to reason with him. Keis pretended to be deaf and just carried on with what he was doing. The foul smell grew stronger; the heaps of poison grew steadily higher. This was serious. Snoutiss rushed over to the Gletcowas house to try and smooth things over.

The three brothers welcomed him in. They were really concerned to hear that their brief encounter in the woods had tipped Keis over the edge. They pressed a whole deer haunch on Snoutiss. 'See if that calms him down,' they said.

But when Snoutiss reached home with it, he didn't even dare climb down the ladder; for peering down the smoke hole, he could see Keis still hard at his evil work. The entire inside of the house was dripping with sores; aches and pains of all kinds were floating about in the air and there was a terrible stench of sickness.

'Keis!' he yelled.

His brother didn't even look up.

'You've gone crazy,' Snoutiss called down. 'There was no reason to lose your temper – the Gletcowas brothers have given us a load of venison as a gift. It's out of all proportion to behave like this.'

'I'll do what I want,' Keis growled.

'But don't you realise, you'll never get rid of this evil stuff you've made. It'll be in the world for ever.'

'Good.'

Snoutiss went away in despair, and hurried to the house of his wise Uncle Wewenkee to ask for advice. Wewenkee listened intently as Snoutiss explained what had happened. The old man thought for a long while. Then he said, 'I own a painted wildcat-skin blanket; I'm much stronger than your crazy brother. Wait here while I go to your house and try to talk some sense into him.'

So Wewenkee went off, but soon came back looking very grim.

'It's even worse than you told me,' he said. 'I painted red stripes across my forehead and around my wrists, to stop Keis realising I was there. Then I made myself small and crawled in through a crack in the wall. He had blankets of sickness doubled around his body, one over another, and he's covered all over in sores himself now. He's unleashed something dreadful into the world! I managed to get away before the poison got hold of me. We've got to stop him before it spreads any further. I'm going back there right now to deal with it. Are you coming?'

Snoutiss shook his head. So his uncle went back alone.

After he'd gone, Wewenkee's wife said, 'Fancy not going along to help, you coward! What are you afraid of? Wewenkee is far more powerful than your brother: he can even raise a whirlwind.'

Snoutiss felt ashamed and went slinking after his uncle.

Ahead of him, Wewenkee reached the house and ran down the ladder, shouting at Keis: 'You fool! All this bad stuff will sink into the earth…we'll never get rid of it…it'll cause so much trouble!'

He pulled a big strip of soft bark from his clothes and moulded it into a ball, which he started rolling all over the walls. As it rolled, it soaked up the sores and sickness that were clinging to them. He did the same thing over the floor. Then he turned to Keis and rolled the bark ball over his body.

After that, he held up the bark ball to squeeze out all the muck it had gathered. Then he rolled it over some more sickness, concentrating on the bits he'd missed the first time. 'I'm catching as much as I can,' Wewenkee said, 'but loads of it has already escaped. It's too late to stop that soaking into the ground all over the place. You'll see: when the weather turns hot, it'll rise up and make people ill; and do the same in the chill of winter too. You fool! Why ever didn't you just ask the Gletcowas brothers for some meat instead of losing your temper for no reason? Why did you choose to do this evil?'

Keis said nothing – because there was nothing he could say.

'What happened to your teeth?' Wewenkee asked him.

'I broke them trying to get some meat. That's partly why I'm so furious.'

'Are they all gone?'

'All except two.'

'Would you lend them to me?' Wewenkee asked slyly.

But Keis snarled, 'No, I won't. You thought you'd seized *all* the poison from me, Uncle, didn't you, eh? But I managed to keep some back, hidden in the ends of my remaining teeth. No doubt people will try to attack me in revenge for what I've done – but they won't achieve anything, because my poison bite will kill them! Don't look so disapproving, I'm not the only evil one in the world.'

Wewenkee sighed. 'Can't I stop you choosing the wrong path, nephew? Can't you live in peace like I do?'

'So if people pelt you with dirt,' said Keis, 'you just meekly accept it, do you?

'I'm above all that,' said Wewenkee. 'I'm one of those pious people who go up the mountains at night to swim in lonely pools.'

'They'll get you,' sneered Keis. 'They'll skin you alive!'

'Ah well, let them. The Earth will soon give me another skin.'

'I've no desire to be like you, Uncle. I'll get angry when it suits me; I'll poison people to death whenever I want.'

Wewenkee begged for Keis to change his ways: 'You should do as I say. I'm your uncle, and I'm a chief, too.'

'So what?'

'So together we could put all this sickness back inside our two bodies. The world's changing, Keis, strange things will happen soon. A new kind of people is coming. You don't have any quarrel with them, but you're acting as if you *want* them to hate you.'

Wewenkee talked on and on. At last Keis pulled out all the different illnesses he was still hoarding, tied them up in a bundle and put it in his quiver. 'All right,' he said, 'here's a compromise: I'll only get these out when people actually abuse me.'

All this time, Snoutiss had been crouching on the roof, listening to what was happening inside. He thought they didn't know he was there. But suddenly Keis yelled up at him, 'Oi! We know you're up there, little brother. Stop eavesdropping and come in.'

Snoutiss climbed down the ladder.

Wewenkee greeted him warmly. 'I'm glad you're here, young nephew. You no doubt heard everything I said, but there's more to tell and you're more likely to remember it than Keis. Firstly, those Gletcowas brothers...'

'Those pathetic midgets,' said Keis disparagingly. 'I'll easily deal with them.'

'Don't underestimate them,' said Wewenkee. 'They can transform into all sorts of things to stop you getting hold of them – fish or bugs, the wind, dangerous animals, a molehill to trip you up. Now then, Keis, stand up.'

Keis did so, scowling. Wewenkee paced slowly round him, examining him from every side.

'I don't like what I can see, nephew, and no doubt your hidden thoughts are even worse than your body. Lie down, cover yourself right up and sleep for a whole day. Maybe that will heal your thoughts so you don't fly into a rage so easily. Do you understand? Can you do this? Good. And remember, *don't touch the bundle of sickness that you've put away in your quiver.*'

Keis went into his bed, covered himself up and closed his eyes. Wewenkee beckoned Snoutiss to one side.

'Watch your brother,' he whispered. 'If you see him move anywhere near the bundle, come and fetch me straight away.'

'Can't we just destroy all the sickness once and for all?' Snoutiss asked nervously.

'Unfortunately, it's too late. Keis has blighted the world for ever,' said Wewenkee

Keis slept peacefully all night. The next morning, as soon as he woke up, he sent Snoutiss out to fetch water.

343

'But there's some in a jar here, brother,' said Snoutiss.

'It's stale,' said Keis. 'I need fresh water.'

Snoutiss was suspicious, but he didn't want to provoke Keis into a new fit of temper, so he went down to the river. While he was out, Keis pulled out the poison bundle; but he didn't have time to untie it before he heard Snoutiss returning. He hastily put it away again and pulled the blanket back over him. Keis, peering down the smoke hole, saw all this. Instead of bringing in the water, he dashed straight over to their uncle's house to tell him.

Wewenkee was outraged. 'I must stop him!' he cried.

He stretched himself out full length and went out to search for all the places where Keis might try to conceal himself: hollow trees, holes in the ground and so on. Each time he found one, he encircled it and squeezed it hard. Suddenly he saw Keis, slipping into a narrow crack in the middle of some rocks! Wewenkee went straight after him; but though he squeezed them with all his might, it wasn't enough to crush Keis.

'I see you wish to be master of your own destiny,' said Wewenkee at last. 'Well, I leave you to it.' And he slipped away.

Inside his hiding place, deep in the hole, Keis began to sing, a medicine song, a shaman song. The three Gletcowas brothers heard him, and went to investigate. Wewenkee heard him too, and sent Snoutiss to find out what he was up to. When they reached the rocks, they all smelled tobacco, for Keis was smoking as well as singing. The Gletcowas brothers went off to discuss how to kill him once and for all, while Snoutiss reported to his uncle.

Keis continued to sing. The Gletcowas brothers grew more and more impatient, waiting for him to emerge. The youngest started running backwards and forwards in front of the rocks where he was hiding, and suddenly tripped over. The noise of his fall finally brought Keis out. His mouth was wide open, exposing his venomous teeth. His body began to stretch, higher and higher towards the Sky.

The Gletcowas brothers darted behind some rocks, prepared their bows, then stood up to shoot. Keis lunged towards the youngest to strike him with poison – but at that moment, all three released their arrows and shot him.

Keis collapsed, but his medicine song continued. The eldest brother grabbed a tree stump, wrenched it out of the ground and started pounding it on top of Keis's head, over and over – until finally Keis fell still. He was dead.

344

The brothers butchered him into small pieces and tossed them about disdainfully. 'You're finished!' they cried. 'Your power's gone. Even old women can kill you now.'

But Keis wasn't really destroyed; for every scattered piece of him turned into a vicious, venomous rattlesnake.

Wewenkee and Snoutiss saw it happen. 'Ach,' said Wewenkee, 'This is the end of us all. Only our memory will live on.'

'Why, what's happening, Uncle?' Snoutiss cried in alarm.

Wewenkee gave a bitter laugh – then turned himself into a whipsnake and went slithering away. The next moment, Snoutiss became a common little blowsnake. As for the three Gletcowas brothers, they all transformed into birds and flew across the Shasta River to the north.

But the sickness stayed right where it was, scattered all over the earth.

Curtin: *Myths of the Modocs*, 1912
For information on the original narrator, see p. 300. Curtin notes:
    'It is not known who the Glatcowas brothers were. When asked, the Modocs said: "Glatcowas is just a name".'

The story is set around the Shasta River that runs through Northern California, west and north of the iconic Mount Shasta, a volcanic mountain whose snow-capped peak rises starkly above the surrounding landscape. In the 19th century, a number of other Native peoples lived alongside the Modoc in this area.

Rattlesnakes are poisonous. They are characterised by the 'rattle' at the end of the tail – a set of interlocking scales, which click together through muscle contractions to warn off predators. The most common species in the old Modoc territory are the northern Pacific rattlesnake, which grows up to 60 inches (150 cm) long; and the great basin rattlesnake, up to 40 inches (100 cm) long. Their normal diet is small mammals, which they strike from a coiled position with their venomous fangs, normally eating only once every two weeks. They inhabit a variety of terrains, living for up to 25 years. Whipsnakes are non-poisonous, but fast moving and can strike if threatened; they grow up to 45 inches (120 cm) long, eating insects, reptiles, birds and small mammals and inhabiting a variety of terrains, from open desert to woodland. Blowsnakes, sometimes known as western hognose snakes, are also non-poisonous and usually docile. They look superficially like rattlesnakes but are much smaller at only 20 inches (51 cm) long. They prefer sandy and gravelly areas and feed mainly on amphibians.

THE CHIEF WITH A HUNDRED WIVES

Wasco

Over the mountains, by the ocean, there was a village that once had a giant for its chief. He was known as Big Foot, because his feet were three times as long as an ordinary man's. The rest of his body was just as outsized too, every single limb and organ.

Big Foot's power was equal to his size. Everyone was in awe of him. His longhouse was enormous, ostentatiously carved all the way round with images of animals and fish. Then there was his sexual prowess, which no other man could hope to match: he kept no less than 100 wives, and imposed himself on each and every one of them every single night. The only consolation for these unfortunate women was that he got his business over exceptionally fast: by midnight he'd already satisfied himself with half of them, and well before sunrise he had finished.

By the side of his house there stood another building, housing 100 slaves. Their job was to ensure that no one else could possibly sneak into the longhouse to meddle with Big Foot's wives. They started work at sundown, tramping to the seashore to fill colossal baskets to the brim with sand, which they carried back and scattered ankle-deep around the chief's house to 50 paces from the walls. They smoothed it so perfectly that even a mouse couldn't sneak across without leaving clear footprints to show its guilt.

For Big Foot was constantly on his guard. He despised and distrusted all other free men; he didn't fraternise with any of his male kin or villagers. His only company was his wives and their numerous children – all of whom, without exception, were girls. For every time a wife bore him a boy child, he immediately murdered it. He was terrified that if any son of his were allowed to live, he would grow up even mightier than Big Foot himself, and usurp him.

But he couldn't get enough of women. Even forcing himself on 100 wives every night didn't calm his insatiable lust. So when he heard that a Wasco chief's beautiful daughter had just become ready to marry, he immediately vowed to add her to his collection.

Whatever Big Foot wanted, he always got. He filled 50 canoes with 50 male and female slaves and ordered more slaves to transport him up the Great River to Wasco Village. On arrival, he dragged up the 50 slaves as payment for the young woman – such a generous offer that the Wasco chief could not refuse it. Of course, the young woman herself didn't have a say in the matter. Big Foot tossed her into his own canoe without ceremony and spent the whole journey back to his longhouse lecherously tormenting her.

The young woman's name was Nadaiet. All the other wives did their best to make her feel welcome, given the nightmare of their shared situation. Five of these women took a particular liking to her: they let her play with their daughters and warned what would happen if she were unlucky enough to give birth to a son.

Which, a year later, is exactly what she did.

'I don't want that monster of a husband to kill my baby!' Nadaiet wept.

'We won't let him,' the five soothed her.

'But you told me it's inevitable, that nothing can change his mind, that you've all lost sons to his rage.'

'That's true. But we've been discussing this, Nadaiet, and we've decided not to put up with it any longer. We've come up with a plan. We'll disguise your little one as a girl, and in that way keep him safe from Big Foot until we can smuggle him away to safety.'

No sooner had this been agreed, than Big Foot himself came striding into their corner. 'I hear you gave birth last night, Nadaiet,' he growled. 'Let me see the baby.'

'She's only just fallen asleep,' the young woman whispered. 'Please don't wake her, husband.'

'Girl, is it?'

'Yes.'

'Are you sure? Let me see.'

'Of course I'm sure. Please husband, she's been so fretful all morning, it would be cruel to disturb her now.'

'How dare you hide her from me! Unwrap her.'

At that moment one of the five older women gave a loud shriek: 'Ugh! Pshaw! Big Foot, can you smell that awful stink? She must have soiled herself again.'

The other women held their noses. Sure enough, a mass of soft, foul-smelling goo came seeping from the baby's swaddling clothes.

'Clean her up,' snarled Big Foot. 'Make sure you show her to me later on.'

But the five managed to help Nadaiet avoid that fateful moment with a string of lies. They told Big Foot that the child had picked up a stomach illness during the birth so that her private parts were constantly dirty. By the time they had to admit that the ailment had passed, Big Foot had totally forgotten that he'd never had a chance to check on the child. So Nadaiet was able to raise her little boy in peace, craftily dressed in girl's clothes.

The boy thrived in the women's care. They all loved him: not only was he their beacon of hope, but he also began to display noble qualities that his evil father totally lacked. The only problem was that he grew and developed almost too fast. Before long he was starting to look like a boy, and behaving like a boy too.

'Any time now, the brute will realise what the child really is,' said Nadaiet. 'Then he'll snatch my precious son and slaughter him!'

'No he won't,' said her five friends. 'We've thought of a way you can smuggle him away from here while there's still time.'

So that night, when Big Foot threw himself on top of Nadaiet to ravish her, she gave way to her bottled up feelings and began to shake with sobs.

'Keep still, you little bitch,' Big Foot snapped. 'What's the matter? You'd better not be complaining about my love making.'

'Of course not, dear husband, it's wonderful,' sobbed Nadaiet. 'It's just that I'm terribly homesick. I wish so much that I could show our beautiful daughter to my parents. I want them to admire the result of your famous virility.'

'Well,' said Big Foot, standing up with an extra swagger at this flattery. 'I suppose you could take her on a short trip to your family home. You can go upriver with a few of the other women...only for a few days, mind. I don't want the pair of you getting too settled there.'

Nadaiet was delighted. So were her five friends. They helped her prepare for the journey, secretly making and stowing away various items the boy would need once he was in a safe place. They helped Nadaiet and her child into the canoe and paddled as fast as they could upriver from Big Foot's house. As soon as they were a safe distance away, they pulled into the shore.

'Get out, young one,' they said to the child.

He did. They helped him take off his girl's dress and necklaces, and handed him a fine beaded and fringed war-shirt and trousers that they'd secretly made for him. He pulled them on eagerly; and as soon as he was wearing them, he seemed to grow in stature and maturity. He grinned in bewilderment and wonder.

'What's going on?' he asked his mother.

'You can be your true self at last,' Nadaiet told him. 'You are a *boy*, a young one moulded from Big Foot, your father.'

'I don't want to be like Big Foot, Mother,' he said. 'He's a brute.'

'Yes, my son, and he's also a coward. If he'd discovered who you really are, he'd have been so terrified that you'd become his rival, that he'd have killed you on the spot. He's already killed countless numbers of your half-brothers, the ones that his other wives – your aunts – brought briefly into this world.'

The boy gasped in horror. For a moment, tears welled up in his eyes. Then he blinked them away and drew himself up straight. 'I'm not afraid,' he said staunchly. 'I despise my father. Now I know the truth, I vow to kill *him* in revenge for all these past murders.'

'That's just what we all hoped to hear,' said Nadaiet proudly; and her companions cheered.

The five friends paddled the boy and his mother up to Wasco village. After they'd refreshed themselves there, and bestowed many words of encouragement on the boy, they returned home, sworn to continued secrecy. Nadaiet introduced the boy to her parents, who were naturally besotted to meet their valiant grandson – especially when she revealed how he had survived such terrible odds. Nadaiet settled back happily in her old home for a few days. But the boy was restless and angry.

'I shouldn't be wasting time, Mother,' he said. 'What must I do to overcome my evil father?'

'You had better go into the mountains, my son, and seek guardian spirits to help you.'

So the boy walked off alone, relishing his new-found strength and endurance. He ran across the plateau, scrambled up the foothills, then climbed right up into the snowy peaks. He stayed away for four nights; and at sunset on the fifth day he returned.

'Well, my son, did you find the help you sought?' his mother asked him.

'Yes, Mother. I met five Thunders and five Spirits of the Lightening. They all promised to give me strength.'

'You've made a good start,' she said, 'but I believe it's nowhere near enough. Go back and seek some more.'

The boy took her advice without arguing. She waited for him patiently; and on the fifth evening he returned again, his smart new trousers all in tatters.

'How have you got on this time, my son?'

'Mother, I met five bands of fierce Grizzly Bears. They've shared their strength with me and given their solemn word to support me.'

'That's still not what you need, my son. Go back and seek more.'

Again he took her advice. Again he stayed away for five days. This time he returned with scratches on his cheek saying, 'Mother, now five massive bands of Elk with enormous antlers have all given me a share of their strength.'

'Dear boy, you are trying hard and anyone would admire your great endeavour. But still that's not enough.'

'Mother, please tell me what else I must do and why I have failed to get what I need so far.'

'Perhaps it is *my* failing, for not telling you enough about the supernatural ways of your father. The fact is that, despite his prodigious weight, he has power to walk over the surface of any stretch of water. That means that even the boldest warriors always fail if they try to attack him by canoe, for he simply walks out, plucks the vessel from the water and destroys them. If you are to have any chance of overcoming him, my dear son, you must find a way to match this. So I suggest that this time, you seek help from the water itself.'

The boy nodded eagerly and hurried to the river at the place where the banks were furthest apart and the water deepest. He was gone for another five days – so long that his mother feared he had drowned. But on the fifth evening he came running in once more, squeezing water from his sodden sleeves.

'Mother, guess what! The Spirits of five seething Whirlpools have now joined my side.'

'That may prove very useful, my brave son, but I believe it is still not enough. Go back and seek something else, something with the ultimate power to overcome the venom of your father.'

So the boy set off once more. On the fifth evening of his fifth expedition he came home dishevelled and tattered, but with eyes shining so bright that his mother knew he had succeeded at last.

'Have you found more help, my son?'

'Yes, Mother. I made contact with five long-legged Water Spiders and told them of my plight. They gave me a wonderful gift: the ability to run – not walk, but *run*, Mother – over the water exactly as they do. And after that, five Yellow Flies came swarming around me and pledged to help me practise this skill.'

Nadaiet hurried him back out to a quiet spot on the riverbank and asked him to demonstrate what he had learned. So the boy stepped out onto the rushing water and moved lightly over it, walking, dancing, running back and forth. When he had finished, she called him back onto dry land and folded him into her arms.

'My son,' she wept, 'now I really believe you have found everything you need. How tall you have grown during this quest and how strong!'

Nadaiet's father helped his grandson to gather a band of men, weapons and canoes. The boy led them downriver to make war against his evil father, Big Foot.

They did not attack at once, for the boy's long spirit quest had also brought him the wisdom to proceed with subtlety and cunning. They camped on the opposite riverbank, some way from Big Foot's village. When night came, the boy used his new skill and ran silently across the water to his father's house, skimming so lightly over the barrier of sand that he left no sign of his passing. He slipped inside, where Big Foot had just finished defiling one of his unhappy wives and was making his way to the next one. The boy followed him through the night. Big Foot was oblivious to his stalker, but the women saw him in the shadows – and when dawn came up and their husband had gone, they nudged each other and whispered, 'Our young chief has finally come!'

The boy repeated this trick on the following night; but this time he left tracks in the sand; and in the morning, Big Foot found them. He was outraged – especially when he realised that the footprints were even longer and broader than his own.

'There can be only one cause of this,' he snarled. 'No man could equal my size unless he were born of my own seed. My youngest wife – the devious bitch! – must have given birth to a son and deceived me. I must destroy him at once!'

So he called up a force of armed warriors from his village. They came quickly in 50 huge canoes, driven by the Chinook Wind, and immediately attacked the boy's encampment on the far shore.

But the boy was ready for them, with the East Wind for *his* ally. His canoes sallied out; and when they met Big Foot's canoes mid-river, they collided so violently that the crash echoed far and wide across the ocean.

Big Foot's canoes shattered into jagged splinters of driftwood, causing many men to drown. Thus the evil chief was forced to fight against his son, hand to hand. They fought on top of the water, charging and counter-charging, leaping and slithering over the liquid surface. Each had his own awesome wind – the Chinook and the Easterly – at his back to bolster him. This went on for four days, and the boy showed no sign at all of tiring.

But by the fifth morning, Big Foot's strength was almost spent; his medicine power was waning. Now the water refused to hold his weight any longer and began to draw him in. However, the boy, fortified by the Water Spiders and the Yellow Flies, was as full of vigour as ever. As he saw his hated father start to sink, he rushed at him and dealt his death blow.

In this manner, Big Foot was vanquished and his 100 abused wives finally won their freedom. The boy, now a fully fledged man, became the new chief of the village. He realised his youthful promise and was soon famed far and wide for ruling his people well. All his vanquished father's wives regarded him as a hero, and ten of them willingly agreed to set up household with the young chief as their new husband.

As for Nadaiet, she returned to Wasco village. The happiness of her life there was enhanced 50 times over, whenever her noble son paid her a visit.

Sapir: *Wishram Texts*, 1909
There is no information about the person who supplied this story, which was collected at Warm Spring Reservation, Oregon, in 1885.

The village where Nadaiet hailed from shared its name with the people who lived there: 'Wasco' (Wa'sqlo) means 'small bowl' after a nearby bowl-shaped rock containing a bubbling spring. It was located near a site called The Dalles, on the Columbia River in Oregon. This was a major fishing, trading and socialising centre for thousands of years, stimulating interaction between distant peoples – as reflected in this story. From the early 19th century, it was also a place of rendezvous for white fur traders, Hudson's Bay Company boatmen, trappers, explorers and military expeditions.

THE DRESSES, THE SPIRIT
HOUSE AND THE BONES

Modoc

Kumush is the Father. At the beginning of time, he lived by Tula Lake. Mysterious things happened there: creations and killings, burnings, rebirths and deceits.

Afterwards, Kumush went wandering all over the Earth to the very edge of the world for many years. When he finally returned, he had his daughter with him. No one knows who her mother was, for there were no other living people then; they were entirely alone.

Kumush's daughter was only a few days away from her entry into womanhood, that most significant of times. Kumush worked hard to prepare for it. His most important task was to make her ten special dresses.

The first dress was to wear in her last days of childhood.

The second dress was for her maturity dance.

The third dress was for the day the dance ended, to wear when she emerged from the sweat-house.

The fourth dress was to wear on the following day.

The fifth dress was just an everyday dress.

The sixth dress was for beginning the work of a mature woman, by fetching wood.

The seventh dress was for the other kind of women's work, gathering roots.

The eighth dress was to wear on a journey.

The ninth dress was to play the ball-game.

And what of the tenth dress, the most splendid of all, the one fashioned from finest buckskin, exquisitely covered with close sewn, moon-bright shells? Ah, that last dress was the terrible one, her burial dress. She must keep that one safely. It was not to be worn until she died.

When the day of her maturity dance came, Kumush told his daughter: 'Beloved one, soon you will hear a song. Dance to it for five days and nights; and afterwards, bathe in the sweat-house.'

'Father, I will do it.'

'But take care, my daughter: beware of sleep and especially of dreams. For if you doze off during your dancing, or while you are bathing in the sweat-house, you may dream of death. And if you do – oh daughter, there is no way I can save you.'

What can a young girl do, but try her best? Kumush's daughter listened and soon heard a sound like an old woman singing – though as no other people lived at that time, it was the voice of Kumush himself. She danced to it and after the allotted time, went to cleanse herself in the sweat-house, while Kumush waited outside. When she emerged, she had painted her face, her hands and her body with red root.

As she stood by the fire to dry the paint, she turned to her father and told him, 'Despite your warning, I fell asleep. In my sleep I dreamed; and in my dream…oh Father, I saw someone die!'

When Kumush heard this, he was filled with dread. 'That means your own death,' he said. 'You dreamed of yourself.

'Give me the burial dress,' said his daughter. 'I am ready to meet my fate.'

'It's too soon for that,' Kumush protested. 'For you haven't yet worn the dress to celebrate your emergence from the sweat-house.'

'Father,' she said, 'there's no need for any other dresses now. I'll never wear those you made me for fetching wood or gathering roots; nor for travelling or playing the ball game.'

'Ah,' said Kumush slyly, 'but you haven't rejected *this* one, daughter.' And he tried to press upon her the dress that she'd worn during the last days of childhood.

She shook her head and pushed it away. 'Father, I'm a grown woman now, I can't wear that. You made everything in the world and destined how things should be. You fated me to dream of death. That's why you prepared the burial dress. Give it to me.'

Kumush could not argue because she spoke the truth. Weeping, he gave her the burial dress. However, as she began to put it on, he tried to cling to it and hinder her.

'Father,' she chided him, 'my spirit is eager to leave my body and begin its journey.'

'I can't abandon you, beloved daughter,' Kumush said hoarsely. 'I'll come with you. I'll leave my own body behind here and travel to the spirit world beside you.'

'That's impossible, Father,' she answered. 'For as you yourself have taught me, my spirit will travel without touching the ground. You could never keep up with it.'

'You are wrong,' said Kumush. 'Remember, I know everything. Whatever is needed above, below, and in the world of spirits, I know how to do it.'

He let her put on the burial dress; and in that instant, she died.

Although Kumush was not dead himself, he managed to make his own spirit leave his body, just as his daughter's spirit had left hers. He took her hand, and thus they started on the long journey together, both leaving their bodies behind.

Death had endowed the daughter with wisdom. So she told her father, 'Keep your eyes closed, otherwise you won't be able to follow me, you'll have to go back.'

They found themselves travelling along a road that led westwards, towards the place where the sun sets.

'What can you see?' Kumush asked her.

'Oh Father, we are passing such tempting foods: goose eggs, wild cherries and crawfish.'

'Don't taste them,' Kumush cautioned, 'don't even touch them. For if you eat the cherries you'll be sent back to the world we've just left as a homeless spirit without a body; while the goose eggs and the crawfish will cause you to wander for ever, carrying them in a broken basket which you must constantly labour to mend.'

'I heed your warning, Father,' she answered. And she floated straight past these temptations, not looking at them, moving fast.

They went on. After a while, Kumush said, 'I wonder how far we've already gone and how much of our journey still lies ahead.'

'I believe we are almost at our destination, Father, for I see beautiful wild roses growing in the distance.'

'Ah,' he said, 'only the spirits of those who lived good lives can see those. You may pluck one if you wish.'

Some time later, the road ahead changed into a very steep slope, leading downwards. Beside it, a rope was dangling from the branch of a willow tree. The daughter pulled it gently. The next moment, they heard music, and voices calling. They squatted at the top of the slope and slid down it to the bottom. When they landed, they were in the lower world. At first sight, it seemed to be a vast and beautiful plain. However, in truth, it was not open country, but an enormous house surrounded by high walls on every side.

As they stood there, spirits came floating towards them. 'Welcome!' they cried to the daughter. But to Kumush they said, '*You* shouldn't be here, Father: you're too raw, you're not ripe at all. Ah, pity on you, pity on you for being alive!'

But they didn't send him away. So Kumush and his daughter explored the spirit house together. They found that it stretched in each direction twice as far as they could see. Only one road led down into it, and another led up out of it. No one could enter by the way leading up, and no one could exit by the way leading down. Countless spirits dwelt there: more than every star in the Sky, more than all the hairs on the heads of every living person.

At first, even Kumush's daughter couldn't see them; they both just heard the spirits' voices. However, after sunset, when darkness shrouded the world above, it grew light in the spirit house. The daughter looked around curiously, but Kumush still kept his eyes closed fast, for if he were to see things forbidden to the living, he would be compelled to leave her and return to the world above.

He shrank himself to a tiny speck, then told his daughter to hide him in a cranny high on a wall, and to call up a mist to shield him. No sooner was this done, than the keeper of the spirit house appeared. His name was Wus-Kumush.

When it became dark again, Wus-Kumush said, 'I want fire!' At once, a big, round, bright fire sprang up in the centre of the house, spreading its light all around. Crowds of spirits came towards it and made a great circle round Kumush's daughter. Then they danced a dance not of our world, and sang a song not of our world. Kumush watched them, hidden high in his corner.

This ceremony went on for five nights in a row. All the spirits sang, but only those in the circle danced. Each time a new day dawned, they went away to their own places, lay down – and turned into piles of dry, loose bones.

Wus-Kumush called Kumush's daughter. 'You must be very hungry,' he said. 'It's time for you to eat.' He offered her goose eggs and crawfish. 'Don't worry, they won't affect you now in the way that your father warned of.'

So Kumush's daughter ate them innocently. But though Wus-Kumush's assurance was correct, he did not tell her the true consequence. For as soon as she finished her meal, she too turned into a set of bones. That was what happened sooner or later to most of the newly dead. Only the few who managed to resist food for five whole years escaped this fate; they lived in shining settlements set in a circle outside the spirit house.

The spirit of the daughter's bones went to her father in his hideout; and on the sixth night, she moved him to a new place, on the eastern side of the house.

There Kumush told her, 'I've had enough of this place, I'm going back soon. I'll take some spirits with me, to fill the upper world with people. Once they've settled in, I'm going to travel some more and find a good place to build a house.'

Unbeknown to them, Wus-Kumush was spying. Now he revealed himself and said, 'My friend, that sounds a fine idea – but the spirits will refuse to go with you. In fact, they're all so angry that you managed to enter our house while you're still alive, that they're planning to kill you.'

Kumush laughed. 'How naive you all are, how ignorant! I am the Father of everything. All the spirits are born of my own power. If they try to kill me, I'll immediately come back to life.'

At that hour, the spirits were all in the form of bones, but they still heard him. They creaked with anger at Kumush's arrogant words.'Rise, rise!' they hissed. 'Let's crush that old man's heart!'

As soon as Wus-Kumush was out of the way, the bones jumped up and threw themselves at Kumush, striking him like sharp elbows, trying to beat him to death. However, he easily dodged them; their blows all fell on empty air. When morning came, the bones had to lie down and become disconnected. Then Kumush's daughter moved him to a different cranny. But the next night the bones rose again in the form of people. They danced and sang, hunting him out, and when they found him, they attacked him. And so it went on, night after night.

Kumush put up with these constant attacks until he was ready to leave. When that day dawned, he scooped up his daughter's bones and put them into a great basket. Then he squatted down and began sifting through the countless other bones lying around. He was very specific about what he wanted: only shin bones and wrist bones, no other kind. As he worked he kept muttering to himself: 'Hmm, this is of good quality but that one's not so good; never mind there'll be room in the upper world for them all.'

Soon the basket was full to the top, almost overflowing. Kumush fixed it round his head with a strap, hoisted the weight onto his back, then strode to the road at the eastern end of the spirit house, the one that led upwards. It was just as steep as the road he had previously slid down with his daughter, and very slippery too. Even Kumush found it difficult to climb; he kept slithering about and stumbling. But he didn't give up, he kept on as well as he could.

When he was halfway up, the bones started to move about in the basket, then rose up and rained blows on his back and neck, trying to kill him. He shrugged them off and continued on his way. But just as the top was almost within reach, the commotion made the strap slip from his forehead. The basket fell right off, and at once, the bones transformed into whooping, shouting spirits. They rolled all the way back to the Spirit House, where they became bones again, dragging Kumush after them.

Kumush put the bones back in the basket and started up a second time. Half-way up he cried: 'Pathetic things! You can't stop me carrying you to the upper world!'

At once, his strap broke again and he tumbled down after the basket, with the spirits whooping and shouting all the way.

Kumush filled the basket a third time. He was so angry that he flung the bones in really hard.

'You think you want to stay down here,' said he, 'but that's only because you can't remember the other world where you lived before you died – my place up there, where the sun shines. Once you see it again, you'll want to stay there always and never come back to this gloomy house.'

This time, the bones stayed silent. Perhaps they'd decided to heed him after all, perhaps he'd roused their interest and they wanted to know what he would say next.

Kumush went on, 'When I was up there recently, when there were no people left except me and my daughter, I felt lonesome. That's why I'm taking you up there – and this time, I'll succeed.'

He was about to lift the basket onto his back for the third time, when he realised that the strap was broken beyond repair. 'I wish I had a new strap,' he cried, 'a better, stronger one than before.'

Right away he had it.

Then he said, 'I wish I could get right to the top with this basketful of bones.'

The second wish didn't work straight away. By the time he reached the mid-point of the slope, the bones started up their battering again. Kumush struggled against them with all his might, tugging at his precious basket. At last, he reached the top of the slope. He pulled the basket round, released it from the strap and, with a single great heave, threw it up to the level ground above.

He leaped up beside it, opened it and threw the bones in different directions. 'Live!' he cried. As each set of bones flew through the air, he named all the nations they would become and said what kind of people each would be.

The last bones he threw, he named for the Modoc people. 'You will eat what I eat,' he said. 'You will keep my place when I am gone, you will be bravest of all. Even if you are only few in number and numerous enemies attack you, you will overcome them.' As he threw each handful of bones, he went on, 'If you meet trouble, you must find the power to save yourselves. Send men to go and ask the mountains for help; they must request wisdom, courage and medicine power; then they must swim in the water and dream.'

Kumush named the different kinds of food that should be eaten: catfish, salmon, deer, rabbit and so on. He named more than 200 different things; and as he thought of each one and named it, suddenly it appeared in the rivers or the forests or the plateaus. Then he decreed how the people should live: 'Women shall dig roots, fetch wood and water, and cook. Men shall hunt and fish and fight. It shall be this way for ever.'

He decreed how people should be punished for behaving badly: 'If a shaman tries to kill someone; or if he refuses to put medicine in the path of a dangerous spirit to repel it – if you are sure he has done this then you should kill him. But if an innocent shaman is killed, you should kill the man who killed him, unless he pays for the death. This is everything I have to tell you.'

Finally, Kumush finished his great work. He took his daughter's hand and led her on their final journey, towards the eastern edge of the world. They waited until dawn; and when the Sun came out, they followed him on his road to the very middle of the Sky. There they stopped and Kumush built a house.

He lives there still today.

Curtin: *Myths of the Modoc*, 1912
For the Modoc informants, see p. 300.
    The original story in the source book was told both comprehensively and evocatively, and this retelling closely follows its style. Curtin says:
        'Many of the Modoc firmly believe that their tribe originated as described in this myth. They call Kumush father, and live by the rules he laid down for them. They believe that he gave...all gifts that

support existence, that it is through him that the Indians live and prosper... When old men are asked what their ideas are regarding life hereafter they tell of Kumush's visit to the great house in the underground world; of what he saw there, and of the terrible effort he made to bring spirits to the upper world, and create Indians. The underground house of the Modoc dead is in the west.'

In the source, the story opens with Kumush leaving Tula Lake then, after many wanderings, returning to a place called Nihlaksi. The latter seems to be a mythical place; but Tula Lake, California, was old Modoc territory.

Kumush is powerful and ambiguous, operating outside ethical restraints. In an earlier myth, he restores life to a supernatural youth who had been killed by his lover's jealous brothers. However, Kumush himself becomes jealous of the youth, kills him and his lover, then steals their baby son. Once the child grows up, Kumush tries but fails to get rid of him by using a trick similar to that described in COYOTE AND HIS SON (see p. 329). Other Modoc myths about him concern the origin of cremation; and the transformation of Kumush's brother into the mysterious Wus-Kumush of this story. ('Wus' in the Modoc language means 'fox' – see p. 319.)

The strap that Kumush uses to carry his basket of bones up from the spirit house is a tumpline, traditionally used for moving loads. A strap, attached to the load at both ends, is placed over the top of the head, just behind the hairline and in line with the spine. The bearer leans forward, so that the back as well as the head supports the weight.

When Kumush throws the bones out to become different tribes at the end, the myth reveals Modoc feelings about some of their allies and enemies. The source says:

'When he named the Shastas he said: "You will be good fighters." To the Pitt River and the Warm Spring Indians he said: "You will be brave warriors, too." But to the Klamath Indians he said: "You will be like women, easy to frighten."'

The Klamath people were longstanding enemies of the Modoc. Despite this, the Klamath had a parallel creation myth about Kumush, which similarly featured his daughter and the scattering of spirit bones – here gathered in 'the Place of Darkness' – to form the first people.

Several other Plateau stories tell of failed attempts to rescue the prematurely dead. A Klickitat story is set on a real island in the Columbia River which was formerly used by local people for death rites, and considered to be the repository of dead spirits. A young woman travels there, seeking her departed lover. She finds him and spends an ecstatic night with him; but in the morning he and all his companions have turned into skeletons. She flees home, but her parents send her back to the island, fearing she will bring bad luck. On the island she gives birth to a baby, half-human and half-spirit. Her lover's old mother comes to see it, but breaks a taboo not to look at the baby for ten days, causing it to die. Compare with THE KEEPER OF THE BRAINS OF THE DEAD (see p. 551).

AN OLD WOMAN'S PRAYERS

Modoc

The old woman took roots and talked to the mountains.
She said: 'You must give us wood that won't burn us.'
To the springs she said:
'Old grandmother,
you always have water under your care;
give us plenty of good water.'
To the house she said:
'You know us, our house that we built.'
She talked to each part of the house.
If people didn't talk to the posts of the house they would fall.
To the posts she said:
'Hold up this house; be good to us.'

– Unnamed storyteller
(Quoted in *Myths of the Modoc*, 1912)

Chief Highest Peak in Mountain Range
in front of House Where People Always Want to Go
Photographed in the village of Haina by Richard Maynard, 1888

MYTHS OF THE NORTHWEST COAST

PEOPLE OF THE NORTHWEST COAST

Canada:
Coastal British Columbia.

United States:
Parts of coastal Alaska, Oregon and Washington.

The Northwest Coast cultural area is a long, narrow strip of land on the Pacific seaboard of North America. It extends from the Alaska panhandle down to the northern tip of California, with numerous rivers, inlets, fjords, channels and islands. Its eastern edge is bounded by a string of mountains, isolating it from the interior. Much of the original temperate rainforest still remains: mainly cedar, fir, hemlock, spruce and yew, with an undercover of moss and ferns. The climate is mild and wet: wind, rain, fog and storms are common, but there are few extremes of temperature.

These benign conditions gave the Northwest Coast peoples a reliable and abundant supply of food. Most important was fish from both sea and river, particularly salmon and eulachon, but also cod, flounder, halibut, herring, perch, sturgeon and trout. Porpoise, seal, sea lion, sea otter and whale were hunted at sea; whilst inland game included bear, deer, elk and mountain goat. Other important foods were forest roots and berries, shellfish and seaweed.

This diet supported a relatively dense population, living in numerous small 'towns', usually facing either a river or the sea. Each comprised a collection of 'big houses' spread out along a beach, built of cedar planks with plank roofs, sometimes painted and brightly ornamented. A single big house was occupied by a number of different families, related by blood or clan. Each had its own separate living area, marked out by internal screens and posts. Food was stored in the rafters.

The beach below the town was used to store canoes – the only form of transport – paddled by both sexes for fishing, hunting, visiting, raiding, trading and ceremonies. During the summer months many families left their town to live in brush-shelter camps, where fish were caught and preserved by drying and smoking.

Women's work comprised gathering food and weaving materials from forest and beach, processing food, tanning hides, cooking and making clothes and baskets. The men did most of the hunting and fishing, made canoes and hunting equipment, prepared timber, built houses and produced carvings and painted artefacts. Leisure activities enjoyed by all included music, storytelling, races, gambling games, ice hockey and laughing competitions.

Northwest culture was rich and complex, organised around the town, the extended family, the lineage and the clan. Power mainly lay with local chieftains, whose status was based on heredity and wealth. Below them, came nobles, commoners and slaves. In some towns, slaves formed up to one third of the total population; some were captured in raids, others enslaved for unpaid debts, and the rest born into slavery. Amongst the free, lineage defined social status, clan membership, rights to local resources and ceremonial privileges. Northern cultures such as the Haida, Tlingit and Tsimshian were matrilineal; there a male hereditary leader would be replaced by his sister's son rather than his own. Further south, amongst the Bella Coola, Kwakiutl and Nootka, children inherited status and goods from both parents.

Wealth was reckoned by ownership of material goods which could include 'money' such as abalone, clam and dentalium shells alongside blankets, carvings, coppers, furs, hides and ritual masks. Warfare was fairly rare; conflict usually took the form of raids for slaves or plunder, or to settle feuds ignited by an insult.

A typical household contained around 50 people, members of a single clan. They all claimed shared descent from ancestors who had once interacted with a particular supernatural being, as recorded in their unique clan myth. Clan membership sometimes crossed tribal divisions.

Links between families and other groups were important, and facilitated by marriage. It was commonly forbidden to take a spouse from one's own lineage or clan. Ordinary people usually married for love, but marriages between nobles were often made for political alliances. Noblemen could take several brides, with each proposal accompanied by gifts and a feast. Amongst the Tlingit, high status women could have several husbands. Divorce was easily arranged though not admired; amongst some peoples, a divorced wife kept both children and wedding gifts.

One of the most important social customs was the 'potlatch'. This was a ceremonial feast at which a rich and powerful host gave away a large quantity of personal treasures to his guests – a ritual display of wealth and social status. Many men accumulated surplus goods specifically for this purpose. Those who had insufficient possessions to give away, had to borrow from others when it was their turn to hold a potlatch, eventually repaying this loan with interest. As well as goods, the host also distributed 'titles' to use specific hunting, fishing and berry-gathering grounds, and rights to hold particular roles during ceremonies.

The Northwest peoples were, and still are, renowned for their striking art with its heavily stylised mythical images and patterns. The cover of this book is a good example. Women used bark, roots and woven plant and animal fibres to fashion baskets, blankets, capes and hats. Men used antler, bone, stone and wood to make storage chests and boxes, tools, dishes and canoes. Even everyday objects were often richly decorated with black, red and turquoise paint, intricate carvings and glistening abalone and dentalium shells. Towering wooden totem poles, up to 164 feet (50 metres) high, were erected both inside and outside houses. Some were structural, forming a decorative entrance or internal supporting post; others stood independently to welcome visitors at the town beach. They also marked graves and were used in funerals, with the deceased person's remains placed at the top. Their elaborate, brightly painted carvings represented family crests.

LIFE ON THE NORTHWEST COAST
WHEN THESE STORIES WERE COLLECTED

There was a long tradition of bartering goods between different groups on the Northwest Coast. From the 18th century, this was expanded to trade with British, Spanish and Russian merchant ships, which were fulfilling demand from the insatiable European market for furs. The Native peoples supplied these in abundance, particularly sea otter which was hunted to the brink of extinction. In return, they eagerly bought European iron tools and guns.

Contact expanded rapidly from the early 19th century, as Europeans found an overland route to the Northwest through the Rocky Mountains, and the Hudson's Bay Company (see p. 23) established trading posts in the region. By the end of the century, the Native population had dropped dramatically, due to the introduction of alcohol and deadly European diseases. Despite this, some survivors initially flourished, for the fur trade brought them wealth on an unprecedented scale. This had a knock-on effect, with potlatches becoming bigger and more frequent, and rich men vying to outdo each other in the display of wealth.

From the mid-19th century onwards, Christian missionaries of various denominations arrived, opening churches and schools. The European incomers began to establish their own settlements, designating the Native American towns as 'reserves', though without any formal treaties. Local traditions and ceremonies were denounced or outlawed; potlatches were officially banned in Canada and died out in Alaska due to fear of the authorities. Children were forcibly removed from their parents and sent to live for years in residential schools where they were forbidden to use their own language and culture; many eventually returned home with no sense of belonging anywhere.

More recently, the situation has improved. The region's Native American population is rising again, and renewed pride in their culture is enhanced by outsiders' admiration for their art which is in great demand by collectors. Many have taken up employment in the fishing and canning industries, and are active in the conservation of local forests and wildlife.

STORYTELLING ON THE NORTHWEST COAST

It was believed that shamans could move between the human and spiritual (mythical) dimensions, the latter being the world of myths. Writing about the Nootka in 1919, Edward Sapir noted that they had two different types of narratives:

'One of these consists of numerous stories of the pre-human mythological epoch, in which animals [with] more or less human form, and mythological beings...form the chief characters... Such myths...are the common property of the whole tribe, and are told without reserve.

'The second type of legend is much more elaborate in form, and more clearly reflects [their] ritualistic and social idea... [Each belongs] to some specific family, whose legendary history is recounted in them, and members of which alone have the right to tell them. [These] are believed...to possess in a much higher degree the element of historical truth than the general body of myths... Beginning with the origin of a particular family or sub-tribe, they [relate] the traditional history of the ancestors and later generations... They tell of how various chiefs in the past gained supernatural powers from mythological beings, such as the Thunderbird, the Lightning Serpent Belt, the Whales, Mountain Fairies, and other beings. These powers, together with associated songs, which they are taught by these various beings, and names referring to the legendary incidents, are supposed to have been handed down from the remote beginning of things through successive generations to the present representatives of the family... They constitute the historical guarantee, as it were, for the various privileges claimed by a particular family of today.'

Myths were also preserved and kept alive by ceremonial dancing and singing, totem poles, carvings and painted decorations.

THE PEOPLES BEHIND THE STORIES

Bella Coola (Nuxalk)

Decimated by disease in the 19th century, the modern Nuxalk have a thriving community. They have never ceded, sold or surrendered any land, and today work to maintain traditions and their mother tongue. They are based around the village of Bella Coola in British Columbia, where fishing for salmon and eulachon is still central to the local economy.

Haida

The Haida still live in their ancestral homes, the islands of Haida Gwaii (formerly the Queen Charlotte Islands) in British Columbia, with a smaller community on the southern half of neighbouring Prince of Wales Island, Alaska. They have two matrilineal clans, the Eagles and the Ravens. Today many work in commercial fishing, forestry and eco-tourism, and co-operate with Parks Canada to preserve and study the archaeology of their ancestral towns. A number of modern Haida artists are held in high renown in Canada.

Tlingit

The Tlingit – 'People of the Tides' – are the most northerly Northwest Coast culture, based on the mainland and islands of the Alaskan panhandle. Their three matrilineal bands are Eagle, Raven and Wolf, each divided into many clans. They have long interacted with the neighbouring Haida and Tsimshian, sometimes trading peacefully but also conducting raids and battles for slaves and treasures. In the late 19th century many converted to Russian Orthodox Christianity, mingling it with traditional beliefs.

Tsimshian

Their name means 'inside the Skeena River'. Today, most still live around that waterway in British Columbia, with another community on Annette Island, southern Alaska; their four dialects are still widely spoken. Their lineages are: Eagle, Killer Whale (or Fireweed), Raven (or Frog) and Wolf. Fishing is a major livelihood. They have both male and female ceremonial chiefs and still hold community feasts to celebrate weddings and other major events.

Research for this section also covered stories from the following Northwest Coast peoples: Alsea, Coos, Cowichan, Hupacasath, Kwakiutl, Makah, Nootka, Quileute, Quinault, Siwash, Tillamook and Tseshaht.

THE COSMOS

>>> <<<

Bella Coola (Nuxalk)

The Earth – the Land Below, our beautiful world – is an island floating in the boundless ocean between two Sky Worlds and two Lower Worlds.

A giant holds the Earth in place with two strong ropes attached to a great stone bar. Sometimes it becomes too heavy for him and he has to shift his hands, causing an earthquake. If he moves it westwards, it brings sickness; but that is easily cured when he turns it to the east. The surrounding ocean contains a being who swallows the salt water twice every day and then disgorges it, making the tides.

There are two Sky Worlds over the Earth, one above the other.

The highest is a vast, treeless prairie plagued by ceaseless winds. These blow everything far, far eastwards to a house that stands in complete solitude and calm.

In front of this house is a stretch of black, blue and white pebbles; behind it is a saltwater lake. A huge winged monster stands before the house, its mouth forming the door. This is the home of Our Woman, who is also called Afraid of Nothing. She is supreme, above everything and everyone, a formidable warrior. At the beginning of time, when the gigantic mountains made the Earth uninhabitable, Our Woman went to war against them, conquered and diminished them. It is said that she still sometimes visits the Earth, but she brings with her only sickness and death.

A river – or, some say, simply an opening – leads from the higher Sky World down to the lower one. Right in the centre of this country stands the House of Myths, which is also called The

House Where People Were Created. Its front post is painted with birds and a white crane sits on top.

The master of this house is the Sun, Our Father, the Sacred One, who works alongside another spirit called Alk'unta'm. Together they created the People, and together they now often try to destroy us. It is the Sun himself who makes children, and the young of animals too, but he does not do it alone. For a female spirit gives each one its individual features, and another rocks them all in a cradle, before sending them down to Earth to be born.

Many other spirits, both male and female, live in the House of Myths. Amongst them is one who orders the deaths of both People and animals; but two others offer protection from sickness, and wake the People from sleep. Another guards the Moon, cleaning her face each month, restoring her to her full size. The Mother of Flowers also lives there, giving birth to all plants each spring; she is helped by a shaman and two old women. Four brothers live in a high room at the back, carving and painting, giving the People on Earth inspiration for their own designs.

Below the Sky Worlds, and below the Earth, is the first Lower World. This is the Country of Ghosts. There, the spirit houses stand along the sandy banks of a great river, under a hill whose base is covered with enormous boulders. The ghosts all walk on their heads. The seasons there are opposite to our world; so that during winter in our world, it is summer in the Country of Ghosts.

When the newly dead arrive in that country, some choose to climb a rope ladder that leads up, directly to the lower Sky World. From there, eventually they return to Earth, reborn as babies into their old families. However, others prefer to stay in the Country of Ghosts permanently. They enter the town dance house, die a second death there, then sink to the Lowest World from which none may ever return.

Boas: *Mythology of the Bella Coola Indians*, 1898
This very simplified version gives a flavour of the extremely complex mystical information that Boas obtained in 1890, alongside many actual stories, when he 'fell in with a number of Bella Coola who were fishing for salmon in the Fraser River.'

Other Northwest Coast peoples also believed that the Sun was the most important deity, but they did not offer ethnologists any evidence that they had a systematic mythology. Boas says:

'The Bella Coola, on the other hand, have developed a peculiar mythology in which a number of supernatural beings have been co-ordinated. A system has been evolved which justifies our terming the supernatural beings "deities".'

His account mentions numerous other deities and their roles, which were often related to an ancient sacred winter ceremony. His description of the Country of Ghosts was:

'...principally obtained from shamans who believe they have visited that country during a trance. According to the statement of an old woman, who believed that as a little girl she had visited the country of the ghosts during a trance, the entrance...is through a hole situated in each house, between the doorway and the fireplace.'

Boas gives a number of examples of prayers to the Sun, both supplications and thanksgivings, which he translates as follows:

'Look on us where we are going, Father!
Father, take care of our road, take care of us!'

After a long spell of rain:

'Wipe your face, Father, that it may be fair weather!'

A successful hunter, or a woman gathering berries prays:

'Father, you make me happy, you give me what I desire.
Thus I find what I wished for.'

He also describes offerings to the Sun, with hunters seeking success by throwing slices of seal meat or mountain goat tallow into the fire, and the sick requesting cures by burning pieces of clothing decorated with red cedar bark.

RAVEN STEALS DAYLIGHT

Tlingit

In the beginning, the Creator lived in a house at the head of Nass River. Though he wasn't married, he had a daughter. No one knows the daughter's name, or who her mother was. She was cared for by two wise old men. Every day, they would carefully check the water before she drank it, to ensure it was perfectly clean.

The Creator also had a sister. She had given birth to many children, but every single one had died almost as soon as it was born. Not surprisingly, the poor woman was constantly weeping.

One day, a very tall being called Heron came to her. 'What's the matter?' he asked.

'Every time I have a baby, it dies,' she answered.

'That's because your brother knows you are destined to raise a son,' Heron told her. 'He fears that when your son grows up, he will become a rival, and therefore he ensures that no child of yours can ever reach maturity. But I know how to overcome this. Go down to the beach at low tide, and find a small, smooth stone. Bring it back and drop it into the fire. When it's red hot, swallow it. Don't be afraid.'

The woman did this. As a result, some time later, she gave birth to Raven. Since he had been fathered by a stone, he was so tough that even the Creator could not kill him. He grew up clever and strong. The Creator was so impressed that he stopped worrying about him, and instead made Raven headman of all the world.

Some time after that, the Creator decided to make the first human beings, the People. He started by trying to forge them out of rock, but they wouldn't come alive. After many attempts, he managed to create People who could breathe and move by fashioning them from leaves. That's a shame, because rock People would have lived for ever; whereas we leaf People eventually wither, rot away and die.

The first People found the world very difficult to live in, because it was completely dark and they couldn't see a thing. The Creator had already made the stars, moon and daylight, but he kept them all locked away in his house.

Raven pitied the People and wanted to bring light into the world for them. So he carefully studied the habits of everyone in the Creator's household, and soon came up with a cunning plan.

He had noticed that the Creator's daughter came out every day to fetch water from a nearby spring. Raven flew to this spring, and transformed into a hemlock-tree needle. He floated about in the water, drifting idly from side to side, waiting. Soon the daughter came out with her bucket. She dipped it into the water and filled it almost to the brim – with the hemlock needle floating on top.

Of course, she wasn't supposed to drink any of it until the two wise old men had checked it. But Raven sent an unbearable, raging thirst into her throat, a longing to take a drink at once. She looked around and saw that neither her carers nor her father were there to stop her. So she lifted the bucket to her lips and took a long draught. She was so relieved to swallow the sweet water, that she didn't notice the hemlock needle sliding smoothly down her throat.

Soon after that, she *did* notice something unusual: she was pregnant. Her father noticed it too. Fortunately, he wasn't angry, but very excited. He had a special shelter built for her confinement, and lined it with luxurious furs. However, her labour went on and on, and still the child did not come forth. So the Creator replaced the furs with soft moss, and in no time at all, his daughter gave birth to a beautiful baby boy with bright, quick eyes.

It was the Creator's nephew, reborn as his grandson. Yes, Raven!

Raven Child grew very fast. He was soon crawling everywhere, all over the house. The Creator was immensely fond of him. He let the little boy do whatever he wanted, and play with everything that he asked for… Well *almost* everything.

Because even the indulgent grandfather refused to let him have the three big, round, sacred bundles that hung from the walls.

At first, the little boy didn't notice them. But when he did – oh, how he wanted them – more than anything else! He crawled round and round, pointing up at the forbidden bundles, constantly whimpering. His whimpers turned into cries, and his cries turned into the furious screams of a tantrum. The Creator tried to ignore him, but each scream stabbed at his heart like a knife. In the end, he couldn't bear it any longer. Carefully, he unhooked the smallest bundle and gave it to the little boy.

Raven Child gurgled with happiness, grabbed the bundle and started rolling it all over the floor. Then suddenly, with unexpected strength, he tossed it straight upwards, above the firepit. The bundle got caught in the heat of the fire, which pushed it straight up, making it fly out of the smoke hole. As soon as it reached the open air, it burst open. Myriads of glittering stars came flying out! They scattered across the Sky and fixed themselves into constellations. Raven Child burst out laughing.

But he soon started grizzling and wailing again, pointing at another of the bundles. Again, his grandfather refused at first, but eventually gave in and let the boy have it. Again, this calmed him for a short while, as he rolled the bundle around the floor. And again – he suddenly tossed it upwards, sending it flying up above the fire, and out through the smoke hole.

When this bundle burst, it let out the beautiful pale, glimmering Moon. It shot up into the Sky and hung there.

Now there was only one bundle left, the biggest one. Raven Child crawled to a spot directly underneath and pointed up at it. His grandfather ignored him, and ordered the rest of the household to do the same. The little boy began to sob.

'No,' said the Creator.

'Wah!' sobbed Raven Child. 'WAAAAAGH!' His screams grew so loud that it was painful to hear them. His face turned red. His chest heaved, tears streamed from his eyes and he gasped for breath.

The two wise old men who cared for his mother watched the boy dubiously for a long time. At last they approached the Creator.

'Master,' said one, 'your little grandson is making himself ill. We're worried he'll cry himself to death.'

'Look at his eyes,' said the other old man. 'See how they spin round and round, constantly changing colour. He is no ordinary child…'

'No, indeed,' said the Creator. 'He is Raven. And if *he* wishes for the last bundle, how can I refuse? Bring him to me.'

They lifted the screaming boy and put him in the Creator's arms.

'Be calm, my grandson,' said the Creator. 'For I am going to give you the most precious thing in all the world.'

He took the bundle down and put it into Raven Child's arms. The boy took it. He quietened...

Then, suddenly, he transformed. He grew bigger. He sprouted a cloak of glossy black feathers; his nose and mouth became a beak. He gave a cry: *'Gaaa!'* He flew up and out through the smoke hole.

Raven soared through the air, carrying the bundle in his strong beak. He flew from his grandfather's house at the head of the Nass River, all the way to the estuary. There was a crowd of men and women gathered there, enjoying the new, soft light of the stars and moon. They were all fishing for eulachon, shouting and yelling loudly as they worked.

Raven hovered above them. *'Gaaa!'* he croaked. 'Be quiet.'

The People couldn't see him, but they recognised his voice. 'Go away, Raven,' they called back. 'You can't tell us what to do.'

'Gaaa! Shut up! If you don't, I warn you, I'll break this bag of daylight over you!'

'Daylight? You? Only the Creator himself has daylight,' they scoffed. 'And you're certainly not the Creator, you're just a scruffy old bird.' They shouted even louder than before, just to annoy him.

Raven lifted a claw to the bundle dangling from his beak, and made a small hole in it. Shards of lightening shot out, scattering across the Sky.

'You disobedient fools!' Raven squawked. *'Gaaa! Gaaa! Gaaa!'*

He wrenched the bundle right open, so that the rest of its contents came spilling out, spreading daylight everywhere.

The People were dazzled and terrified. Some jumped into the water and transformed into seals. Others fled into the forest, where they became martens and bears.

Since then, the stars and moon have always lit the night Sky; and every day is filled with light.

Swanton: *Tlingit Myths and Texts,* 1909
Raven is the dominant sacred trickster of the Northwest Coast and numerous stories about him were collected around the turn of the 20th century. This is one of the most widespread.

This retelling combines two complementary versions from Swanton's collection, with a few extra details added from Haida and Tsimshian versions, which are also set on the Nass River.

Swanton says he heard one account at Wrangell, an island in southern Alaska, in 1904. It was narrated by a chief called Katishan, whose mother also provided a number of stories. Katishan was

'...a church member [who] shows a moralising tendency...he [is] considered the best speaker at feasts in past times, and is supposed to have a better knowledge of the myths than anyone else in Wrangell.'

Katishan begins with the following statement:

'In olden times, only high-caste people knew the story of Raven properly, because only they had time to learn it.'

He then describes the sacred beings who lived with the creator, Raven at the Head of Nass:

'At the beginning of things there was no daylight and the world lay in blackness. Then there lived in a house at the head of Nass River a being called Raven At The Head Of Nass, the principal deity to whom the Tlingit formerly prayed, but whom no one had seen; and in his house were all kinds of things including sun, moon, stars, and daylight. He was addressed in prayers as My Creator, and Invisible Rich Man. With him were two old men called Old Man Who Foresees All Troubles In The World, and He Who Knows Everything That Happens. Next to Raven At The Head Of Nass [the people] prayed to the latter of these. Under the Earth was a third old person, Old Woman Underneath, placed under the world by Raven At The Head Of Nass.

'Raven At The Head Of Nass was unmarried and lived alone with these two old men, and yet he had a daughter, a thing no one is able to explain. Nor do people know what this daughter was. The two old persons took care of her like servants, and especially they always looked into the water before she drank to see that it was perfectly clean.'

Swanton collected the other version from an unnamed storyteller at Sitka, also in Alaska. According to him:

'No one knows just how the story of Raven really begins, so each starts from the point where he does know it.'

The Nass River flows through British Columbia for 240 miles (380 km) from the Coast Mountains, reaching the Pacific Ocean just below the bottom of the Alaskan Panhandle. Its name comes from the Tlingit word, *Naas*, said to mean 'belly' because of the large supply of fish in it.

There are numerous other Raven myths from many Northwest Coast peoples, covering matters such as the origin of death, fire, fresh water, people, salmon and other fish, shells, the tides and general ethics. There are also 'Raven' versions of the outrageous trickster tales popular throughout the continent.

RAVEN AND THE MASTER OF THE SOUTH WIND

▶▶▶ ◀◀◀

Tsimshian

At one time, Raven was married. His wife was called Bright Cloud Woman. Like him, she was a supernatural being; it was she who made the streams overflow with salmon. For a while, she loved Raven deeply, making him glow with happiness. But then the fool falsely accused her of being unfaithful. Bright Cloud Woman was so upset that she abandoned him, transformed into a cloud and took all the salmon away.

As for Raven, he went back to being dark and ugly. He built himself a small hut on a lonely part of the beach, and spent much of his time there by himself, grumbling and weeping.

To make matters worse, he couldn't find any food. This was nothing to do with his despair – it was because there was constant bad weather, blown in by a strong south wind. The wind caused problems for all his neighbours too; they were also running out of supplies. On top of all that, inside their houses, the wind kept blowing the smoke back down the smoke holes, turning their homes smoggy and murky. So as well as being hungry, everyone was constantly coughing and their eyes were very sore.

Raven knew it was *his* responsibility to deal with the problem. So he summoned all the fish to his house for a council.

'My father's tribe,' he said to them, 'if these appalling conditions continue much longer, we'll all either starve or choke to death. We must urgently discuss how to overcome the wind.'

Octopus rose at once. 'Chief,' said he, 'Let me speak my mind. I propose that we all go and make war against the Master of the South Wind. That's the only way to calm the weather.'

Halibut was the next to leap up, saying, 'I totally agree. Let's go to war at once, to save our children from dying.'

Thus it was decided.

Octopus spoke again. 'I propose that we ask our brother, the Killer Whale, to lend us his canoe, for it's more than strong enough to withstand a gale.'

Again, everyone agreed, and Red Cod was sent to fetch the canoe from Killer Whale, who was glad to help.

As soon as Red Cod brought it back, Raven told the council: 'Brave brothers, prepare yourselves! Be ready to set out first thing tomorrow.'

Early the next morning, they launched the canoe with all the warriors aboard. Octopus and Halibut sat in the stern alongside Raven. Red Cod sat in the bows, watching out for danger.

As they skimmed through the water, the little shellfish Cockle suddenly hopped forward, and made a great display of taking up a seat in the bows beside Red Cod. 'Watch me, everyone!' he cried in his shrill, thin voice. 'I know you all mock me for being small and hiding inside my shell, but I'll show you! I have a grand plan: I'll kick that evil Master of the South Wind all the way down the beach and drown him in the sea!'

The others all stared at the little fellow in great surprise. But since he seemed so sure of himself, no one contradicted him.

Killer Whale's canoe sped on southwards, a long, long way. All the time, Cockle kept bragging: 'You watch, I'm the one you need to vanquish that villain!'

Raven was impressed. When, at long last, they reached the Master of the South Wind's town, he gave orders to the three warriors he believed to be boldest, Octopus, Halibut – and Cockle:

'When we arrive, you three go ashore. The rest of us will wait in the canoe. When you reach the Master of the South Wind's house, Halibut, you lie down in front of the door. Octopus, hide to the side of the door, and as soon the Master starts to emerge, suck him right out. He won't be able to stop himself from stepping onto Halibut, which will make him slip; and then bold Cockle here can kick him down the beach into the sea, as promised.'

The canoe drew up in front of the Master of the South Wind's house. Halibut hurried up the beach and lay down before the Master's door, his most slippery side facing upwards. Octopus made to follow him... But just then, little Cockle nudged him aside and jumped out eagerly onto the sand. He opened his shell and pushed out his long, fleshy foot. Then he wriggled, jumped and rolled up to the Master's house. The door was open. He slipped past Halibut and peeped in.

He saw the Master of the South Wind at once. He was lying down, with his back towards the door, squirming about, apparently in great discomfort. Within a few moments, Cockle understood two things: firstly, what was wrong with the Master, and secondly, why he was causing the rest of the world such trouble. For the Master was suffering from terrible flatulence. He couldn't stop breaking wind – and he couldn't help doing so with unspeakable violence! *That* was the root cause of all their problems, that was why the south wind constantly blew so hard.

Brazenly, Cockle rolled inside, right up to the Master. As soon as he reached him, he stuck out his little foot, waved it around and kicked the Master with all his might. But of course, Cockle was so ridiculously small and feeble, that the Master didn't feel his kick at all, not even as a tickle.

Cockle kicked him again and again, battling hopelessly. Then he heard Raven's voice calling: '*Gaaa!* Cockle, come back here at once!'

And so he did, feeling thoroughly ashamed.

When he arrived, Raven didn't give him any chance to make excuses – but seized him and broke his shell wide open. 'You little braggart,' he hissed. 'Your words were big, but your actions were less than useless.' He picked Cockle up in his long beak and, without any ceremony, swallowed him.

Now Red Cod volunteered his services. He jumped straight from the canoe, and hurried all the way into the Master of the South Wind's house. He didn't waste time assessing the Master's disgusting, flatulent habits. Nor did he attempt to attack him personally. Instead, he seized the fire-drill and began working it until flames sparked out. He dragged some red cedar bark from under the master's blanket and flung it onto the flames. In this way, the house began to fill with thick, acrid smoke.

Red Cod rushed out to safety while he had time.

The Master of the South Wind began to cough and wheeze. He fumbled about and managed to stand up; then stumbled backwards blindly, sneezing and coughing, all the way to the door. Without knowing what he was doing, he stepped backwards, straight onto damp, slippery Halibut, who was still patiently lying in wait. The master's feet slithered apart on a streak of slime – and thus he slid all the way down the beach, to Killer Whale's canoe.

Octopus raced after him, seized the master in his arms and squeezed him.

'Squeeze harder, tighter!' Raven cried. 'Bite him, suck him if you need to. The rest of you – hurl stones at him, club him, kill him!'

But the Master of the South Wind struggled valiantly against Octopus, and began to plead for his life: 'Oh, Chief Raven, no, no! I never meant any harm, I'm innocent. Why are you doing this to me?'

Raven answered, 'We are punishing you for your foul and selfish behaviour, which constantly devastates us with gales and terrible weather.'

'Forgive me, I beg you, give me at least a chance!' the master cried. 'Listen, let's reach a compromise. I'll control myself, I promise. How about this? I'll make it so that, in future, after every bad weather day, there'll always be a fine day.'

'What use is that? It won't help us, if every other day the bad weather resumes,' Raven sneered at him. 'Brothers, continue with your work, kill him!'

'No, no,' the master begged. 'How about this? I'll control myself so well that there will always be *two* good days in succession, one after another each time, after just a single windy day.'

'That's not much better,' said Raven. 'Go on, brothers, kill the brute!'

'Wait, listen!' the master pleaded. 'If you spare my life, I...I promise I'll cause no more trouble at all. I'll make sure that the air is always still, that it's always balmy summer.'

'Ah,' said Raven softly, 'now you're talking. But your latest proposal is too much. It will be enough to have four days of fine weather at a time.'

'I'll do that, I promise!' the master cried.

Raven said, 'That is good. But don't you dare lie. If you agree to this bargain, you must keep it. Otherwise, we shall come to your house again, and if that has to happen we will kill you without mercy.'

The Master of the South Wind swore to be true to his word. So Octopus released him. The master walked slowly back up the beach and retreated into his house.

Then Raven and his bold warriors all boarded the canoe and paddled home. When they arrived, each went back to his own house. Later, they all went out into the newly still, clear air, and each found plenty of his own food.

It's good that Raven and his fish brothers fought that battle. That's why nowadays we often have good weather.

Boas: *Tsimshian Mythology*, 1916
This story was one of a large collection that Boas says:
    '...was recorded during the last twelve years by Mr Henry W. Tate, of Port Simpson, British Columbia, in Tsimshian, his native language. Mr Tate died in April, 1914. The translation of the tales as here presented was made by me, based on a free interlinear rendering by Mr. Tate... At the time when I received these tales I called his attention at once to the necessity of keeping strictly to the form in which the traditions are told by the Tsimshian; and by far the greater part of the tales bear internal evidence of being a faithful record of the form in which the traditions are transmitted among the people.'
However, despite this, he says that it seems:
    '...that Mr Tate felt it incumbent upon himself to omit some of those traits of the myths of his people that seem inappropriate to us, and there is no doubt that in this respect the tales do not quite express the old type of Tsimshian traditions... I have had the personal experience that informants were reluctant to express themselves freely in the traditional form, being impressed by the restrictions of what we call proper and improper.'
According to the Tsimshian, Raven was originally a supernatural youth, first given the name 'Giant' by his father, a chief. When he steals daylight, in a similar way to the previous Tlingit story (see p. 373), he dons a raven skin to carry it from the Sky, down to Earth; thus the people re-name him 'Raven'. Boas recorded a large number of Raven stories amongst the Tsimshian, including both serious myths and light-hearted trickster tales.

Belief in Raven was very much alive at the turn of the 20th century. Tate's cousin met a man who, wandering in the mountains 'not many years ago', stumbled on a lonely hut where he came upon a gigantic man who told him he was Raven. Tate adds, 'Many young people have gone trying to find Raven, but they cannot do it, because he hides in the mountains.'

Old Northwest Coast texts usually refer to octopuses as 'devilfish' – presumably a term which came into use when Christian missionaries brought the concept of 'the devil' to the region. A passage from a later story in this source book clearly identifies it, saying:
    'The devilfish's mouth is in the middle of its arms, and it draws its prey into it. In the middle of very many suckers is a skin which can be pulled back; and when this is drawn back, the sawlike edge of the mouth is pressed against the victim.'

SONG TO
CALM THE WIND

Haida

Ocean spirit,
calm the waves for me.
Get close to me,
my power.
My heart is tired.
Make the sea very calm for me,
ye ho ye ho lo!

– Isaac of the Ei'elanqe'awai family, 1900
(Quoted in Swanton: *Haida Texts and Myths*)

A JOURNEY TO SALMON COUNTRY

Bella Coola (Nuxalk)

A chief's wife was hard at work on the riverbank, busily cutting up some freshly caught salmon. When she sliced open the last one, she got a huge surprise. In the place where its guts should have been, she found a tiny baby boy! He was perfectly formed, but no larger than her hand.

Once she got over her shock, she carefully scooped him out, carried him down to the water and washed him. Then she laid him on the grass by her house, and hurried inside to call to the other women: 'You'll never guess what I just found inside a salmon!'

'A spear head?' they asked. 'A necklace?'

'No, no,' said the chief's wife, 'something far more wonderful. Quickly, come and see!'

They all hurried out. When they saw the miniature baby they all gasped:

'Oh, isn't he sweet!'

'So tiny, yet so beautiful!'

The chief's wife said, 'What do you all think I should do with him?'

'Bring him indoors, definitely,' said one. 'This is no ordinary child.'

'You need to take extra special care of him, coming from where he does,' said another.

The chief's wife already had a baby son of her own, so she laid the foundling in the cradle next to him. At once, her own baby boy opened his eyes, gazed at the Salmon Boy and gave a broad smile, as if in welcome. Salmon Boy grinned back at him and gurgled. All the women cooed in delight.

Then her own baby, the chief's son, began to cry with hunger, and Salmon Boy joined in. The chief's wife lifted them both out and put one to each breast as if they were twins. They suckled with equal relish. But all the time that Salmon Boy was feeding, his eyes were darting around, as if he were listening intently to the women's conversation, and considering everything they said.

They all slept soundly that night. When they woke the following morning, the chief's wife was astonished to see how much Salmon Boy had grown. Another day went by, and then another; very soon Salmon Boy had grown as big as his foster-brother. After that, *both* babies grew extraordinarily fast, quickly mastering the skills of walking and talking. Within a few days, they were not babies any more, but mature boys, big enough to go outside and play by themselves on the riverbank.

One morning, Salmon Boy suggested they build a hut together. The chief's son agreed. When it was finished, they both made arrows to shoot birds.

Then Salmon Boy said, 'I'm going into the hut. You go home for a while. Come back later, when the Sun's high in the Sky. But brother, listen carefully, this is really important. Before you come into the hut, you must always shout first to let me know that you're on the way.'

'Why?'

'If you don't, I'll die!' said Salmon Boy. 'Please, please make sure you do it every single time, don't forget.'

'I'll try my hardest not to,' said the chief's son. 'But just supposing one day I *do* forget...brother, I don't want you to die! Is there anything I could do to bring you back?'

'I'm not sure... Maybe you should carry me down to the water and place me on some sticks.'

'Then what?'

'I don't know,' said Salmon Boy. 'You'll have to watch and see.'

Then Salmon Boy went inside the hut, and the chief's son went home. At midday he returned, shouting at the top of his voice, 'I'm here!' and Salmon Boy beckoned him in. The chief's son found the hut full of freshly shot birds. Together they piled them into his canoe, which the chief's son paddled home to his father's house. Salmon Boy spent the night very happily in the hut on his own.

The chief was delighted to receive such an excellent catch. He got his people to stew the birds, and that night everyone in the town ate well. After that, every other day the chief's son found Salmon Boy in his hut, surrounded by plump, newly shot birds, which he took home. This went on for some time.

However, one day the chief's son forgot to shout his usual warning. He just ran up the bank from his canoe, his bare feet padding silently over the sand, and burst through the door. Only then did he remember to call out, 'Brother, here I am.' But it was too late.

In the gloom, at first he thought the hut was completely empty. Then he noticed a movement on the floor. He squatted down – and saw a half-dead salmon lying there. It was quivering violently, vomiting up what looked like shards of shimmering quartz. The boy recoiled, spun round, raced back to the canoe and paddled home as fast as he could.

'Mother!' he yelled. 'Come quickly, I've done something terrible! I forgot my promise to my foster-brother – I opened the door of his hut too soon – and he's died!'

The chief's wife stopped only briefly to scold him, then called all the townspeople to get into their canoes and paddle as fast as they could to Salmon Boy's hut. There the chief's wife took the half-dead salmon in her arms.

'Carry him to the water,' wept the chief's son.

She did so, and the chief's son got the men to lay out some sticks on the surface. Tenderly, the chief's wife placed the salmon on top.

No sooner had she done so, than they heard paddles swashing and saw a canoe full of people coming rapidly upstream towards them. When the canoe reached the place where the dead salmon lay on the sticks, one of the men stood up and shouted, 'Salmon Boy, we've come for you!'

Every eye turned to the salmon. It twitched. It murmured, '*Hmm.*'

'Come aboard, come on,' the man called.

'*Hmm. Hmm.*' The salmon twitched some more. Then suddenly it jumped and landed in the strangers' canoe – which at once began to pull away.

'Wait!' shouted the chief's son. 'Don't leave me behind, let me come with you!'

'All right,' the man called back. 'We'll keep close to the bank until you catch us up.'

The boy raced alongside the canoe, until he managed to jump aboard. Then the paddlers deftly turned the canoe round, carrying the chief's son and the twitching, half-dead salmon back down the river.

'My son!' his mother shouted after him. 'Come back!'

But it was too late. The canoe, with her two beloved sons inside, was already completely out of sight.

The canoe sped on and on. As it went, the half-dead salmon continued to thrash around, making desperate noises. Gradually, before the eyes of the chief's son, it began to transform... Until, at last, it was no longer a fish, but back in the living, laughing shape of Salmon Boy. He hugged his foster-brother gladly. Then they sat side by side in the canoe, watching the changing countryside.

'Whoah, look at that weird place ahead,' the chief's son said. 'And yuck! What's that horrible stink coming from it?'

'We've reached Smelt Country,' said Salmon Boy. 'Quickly, brother, hold your breath and cover your nose with your hands before we reach it.'

The chief's son did as he was told – just as the stench became overpowering. But they soon passed safely through it.

Salmon Boy nudged his brother. 'It's all right, you can breathe freely again. Are you ready for the next place? It's just ahead – Herring Country. A load of stuff like bits of dirty snow will fall on us there, but don't worry it's completely harmless. Here we go...'

Sure enough, masses of grey flakes were beginning to drift lightly down around them. 'What is it?' asked the chief's son.

'Herring scales,' said Salmon Boy.

'Ugh!'

'Shake yourself,' said Salmon Boy, 'and they'll fall off you. There, we're through it already. Next place coming up!'

Now they sailed past a town where all the buildings were gleaming with sticky grease.

'Another strange place!' said the chief's son. 'Why's everything so greasy here?'

'Because it's Eulachon Country and, as you know, they're very oily fish. Phew, we've passed all the nasty places now. Not long till we reach the best place in all the world!'

The canoe passed through an opening into a broad inlet, and towards a large, beautifully constructed town that stood just ahead.

As they drew closer, they saw crowds of children playing around the houses, and rows of ornate canoes drawn up on the beach.

'We're home at last!' Salmon Boy cried. 'My dear brother, welcome to Salmon Country!'

The canoe drew to a halt and the two boys leaped ashore.

'Let me show you around,' said Salmon Boy excitedly. 'You see that house there? That's where the Spring Salmon people live. Next door is the Sockeye Salmon people's home, and that one's for the Humpback Salmon. There's the Calico Salmon house, that's for the Dog Salmon and that's where the Coho Salmon live.'

They walked on together. As they passed the children, one of them suddenly stopped in the middle of their game and said, 'Hello Salmon Boy. Why do you smell so peculiar today?'

The others gathered round.

'Yes, you smell of something strange,' said another. 'Something that doesn't belong here.'

'*I* know what it is,' said a third. 'It's like the smell of that country where we have to go every spring.'

None of them could see the young human being, the chief's son, with him.

Salmon Boy led him on, peering through the open doors of each house. Inside one, right in the centre of the town, they saw a young woman with very pale skin, eyes as big and clear as rock crystal, and copper-coloured hair that reached down to the floor.

'Whoah, she's a beauty,' said the chief's son.

'We'll go inside here,' said Salmon Boy. 'Watch me, brother, and copy everything I do. We need to be very careful because the door of this house tries to bite everyone who enters.'

At that moment, the door snapped shut. As soon as it re-opened, Salmon Boy leaped through it – just in time before it snapped shut again. When it opened once more, the chief's son managed to jump inside too. A lot of friendly looking people gathered round to greet them, crying, 'Welcome, make yourselves at home!'

So the two boys sat down. Slaves appeared, offering them dishes of food. But although the chief's son was starving after the long journey, he couldn't bring himself to taste the food; it looked so revolting.

'Go on, brother; try it,' Salmon Boy whispered, licking his lips. 'It's delicious algae, the very best stuff that grows on fallen logs lying underwater.'

But the chief's son shook his head.

One of the men was watching them. 'Don't worry, young friend,' he said. 'Maybe you'd rather eat a couple of our children, eh?'

'Oh no!' the chief's son cried.

But the man went on, 'Don't worry, it's fine. Choose two children that you like the look of, take them to the river, then toss them in.'

The chief's son looked at Salmon Boy uncertainly.

'It's okay,' said Salmon Boy. 'That's what human beings are supposed to do. Go on, try it.'

So the chief's son slipped outside and approached the children playing in the sunshine. They still couldn't see him. He picked up one little girl and one little boy. They both weighed hardly anything. He carried them to the bank and forced himself to throw them in. As they went under and sank to the bottom, he turned away with a shudder. After a short while, he forced himself to peep at the water – just as they came floating up again. They were not children any more, but two plump salmon, one male and one female. They drifted to the shore, where the boy caught them easily with his bare hands, then carried them up to the house.

The same man was waiting for him. 'Well done,' he said. 'Put them on the fire until they're nicely roasted, then eat and enjoy them! But make sure you put the bones and innards carefully to one side.'

The chief's son did. When he had eaten his fill, the man told him to take the remains and throw them into the river, then turn quickly away, and run straight back to the house without looking. On the way back, just as he reached the door, he heard footsteps behind him. He spun round – and saw the same girl and boy that he had originally thrown into the river, both come back to life!

But the girl was covering one of her eyes with her hand, and the boy was limping.

'Whoops,' said the man, 'it looks as if you've been careless.' He turned to the other people. 'Everyone have a good look around, please! See if you can find one lost eye and one lost leg bone!'

The two items were quickly found. The man sent the boy to throw them back into the water, alongside the two injured children. In no time, both children reappeared, completely whole and well.

Shortly after that, the chief's son married the beautiful young woman he had seen earlier. She was the daughter of Spring

Salmon, and her own name was Salmonberry Bird. She soon gave birth to a son and a daughter.

Some time later, Spring Salmon launched his canoe, with his daughter and family seated behind him. All the townspeople followed him upriver in their own canoes. They paddled a long way, landing just below the town where the chief's son had come from. There, Spring Salmon sent messengers ahead. They reported back that the townspeople had just built a new salmon weir.

Spring Salmon sent his daughter and the chief's son up to the town, laden with gifts. However, neither were in human form; the man who was watching the weir just saw two splendid salmon swimming into his trap, followed by a lot of other fish. When the trap was full, he took them all out.

The chief's son was very nervous. He thought, 'If only he would treat Salmonberry Bird and me gently!' – and his wish was granted. Although the watchman broke the heads of all the other salmon, he left the chief's son and his wife intact. He carried all the fish up to his own house, and hung them from a pole.

During the night, the chief's son and Salmonberry Bird both transformed back into humans. As soon as morning dawned, the chief's son hurried to his father's house, calling, 'Father, Mother! It's me, your long lost son! I'm back!'

The old couple stared at him in astonishment.

'But we thought you'd gone to the Salmon Country.'

'I did. I've lived there for some time, got married and we have two children. But now the Salmon have brought me back. They're staying a little way downriver at the moment. It pleases them greatly to see the People eating fish.'

'We're very glad to hear that, my dear son,' the chief's wife said.

'Yes, Mother. But listen carefully, for I have something very important to teach you. From now on, when you cut up salmon, you must always be very careful. Don't break any of their bones, and don't throw them away. Instead, you must put them all back into the water. Now please, come down to the fish trap. I want to show you something there.'

His mother and father followed him down to the weir.

'Look,' he said, 'do you see those two small salmon? Those are your grandchildren!'

He scooped his little son and daughter out of the trap and passed them to the chief's wife. Then he placed some leaves on the ground, covered with layers of cedar bark and eagle down and said, 'Mother, lay your grandchildren here.'

The chief's wife did so. At once, hordes of salmon came swarming up the river, over the weir and into the traps. The People pulled them out and prepared them, following the instructions of the chief's son. When all was done, they threw the bones back into the water. At once, the salmon all returned to life and swam back to their own country, leaving their meat behind.

So it has been with salmon, from that long distant day to this.

Boas: *Mythology of the Bella Coola Indians*, 1898
For information about the source, see p. 371.

> In a footnote to the final episode in his collection of stories, Boas says:
> 'This custom prevails up to this day [late 19th century]. When the first salmon are caught, a stick wound with red cedar bark is stuck into the ground at the bank of a river... A line is attached to it, and the salmon, after they have been caught, are strung on this line, which lies in the water. Then the Indians spread leaves of skunk cabbage on the ground, which are covered with a large coarse mat made of cedar bark. On this mat, red and white cedar bark is placed as a pillow for the salmon. The people...take small strips of cedar bark and offer this to the salmon... Next, they strew eagle down over the salmon, which is placed with its head on the cedar bark. All the salmon that have been caught are laid side by side on the cedar bark. Then they are carried up to the house and roasted.'

The story is actually part of a longer myth. It continues with the chief's son transforming into a feather and floating up into the Sky world, where he turns back into human form. Here an old woman gives him a bag of cold wind to protect him from fire. He enters the House of Myths (see p. 370), where the Sun tries to heat him to death many times, but on each occasion the bag of winds cools and saves him. Finally, after a series of challenges, his conflict with the Sun ends and he returns home.

Salmon are still considered very important today: the Nuxalk people's website says that 'when the first spring salmon return to the Bella Coola River, the Nuxalk gather to give thanks,' pointing out that 'fishing is the heart of our people.'

'Salmonberry bird' is a common Northwest Coast name for the bird known to scientists as Swainson's Thrush. It arrives in the area in May, just when salmonberries (a type of bramble) are ripening in the forests.

It is interesting to compare this story with the Subarctic myth MOULDY SALMON GIRL (p. 489), and similar tales told by the Haida and Tlingit. The conservation of the salmon's remains is parallel to Plateau people's care for deer bones (see p. 309).

THE COUNTRY UNDER THE SEA

Tsimshian

There was a chief called Dragging Along Shore who went to sea with three companions. They were hunting sea otters, sea lions, and seals, but they had terrible luck; although they were gone for days and days, they caught nothing. Eventually Dragging Along Shore said, 'I've had enough. Let's go home.' The others agreed.

They turned their canoes and started paddling back along the narrows, but by then the sun was sinking and they were all yawning, so they decided to stop for the night. The steersman cast his anchor-stone down into the waves. Then he lay down in the stern, with the chief in the bows, and the other two in the middle. In no time at all, they were all fast asleep.

Round about midnight, Dragging Along Shore suddenly jerked awake. *Swish, swish...* Something was swimming close, *too* close, to the canoe. He peered over the side. In the moonlight he saw a beautiful silvery fish, Cod Woman, gliding through the water.

'Shut up, you're disturbing our sleep!' he yelled.

Cod Woman ignored him and continued noisily circling the canoe: *swish, swish*. He leaned over and grabbed her. Desperately, she gasped and tried to squirm free. He dangled her above the waves for a long moment, twisting and tugging at her fins, until two of them tore. Cod Woman screamed, bleeding heavily. Dragging Along Shore tossed her callously back into the sea, wrapped his blanket over his head, and was soon snoring loudly again.

As he and his companions slept, monstrous fins and hands came slithering out of the darkness and seized their canoe. They dragged it down, down through the deep, dark water, all the way to the bottom of the sea.

Some time later, the steersman woke up, disturbed by the sensation of something gripping his face. He opened his eyes, brushed it off – and was astonished to find a sea anemone. How ever had *that* got into the canoe? He sat up gingerly and looked around, blinking as the air shimmered around him like sun-dappled water. The canoe was no longer floating. Somehow, it had run aground, balanced on top of a high platform, at the rear of a very large and magnificent house. On the floor below, many people – all strangers, and all very strange looking too – were gathered around the central fire, facing a splendid chief.

The steersman crept quietly over to each of his companions, shook them and whispered urgently: 'Quickly, wake up. We're in terrible danger!'

One by one, the others came to and sat up carefully, poised to defend themselves. For a long while, nothing happened. Then the strangers' chief turned and bellowed, 'Guests, come to the fire!'

Chief Dragging Along Shore stood up and led the way. When they reached the hearth, the strangers' chief told them to sit.

As they did so, Dragging Along Shore felt a light touch on his ankle. He squinted down into the gloom and found himself staring into a pair of tiny, bright eyes – Mouse Woman.

'*Psst!*' she squeaked. 'Don't be afraid, my dear.' Her voice was softer than a whisper. 'Take my advice and all will be well. But first, throw your ear ornaments into the fire.'

Surreptitiously, while his host was distracted, Dragging Along Shore removed his precious woollen ear ornaments and tossed them carelessly into the flames like mere splinters of wood. At once, Mouse Woman darted into the embers and retrieved them.

'You look bewildered,' she hissed. 'Do you know where you are?'

'No.'

'You're in the Country Under the Sea. This is the house of Chief Naguna'ks. He got his slaves to drag you down here.'

'Why?'

'It's your steersman's fault. When he cast the anchor-stone last night, it crashed down onto the roof of Naguna'ks' house. He was furious! As you saw, he sent his slave, Cod Woman, to find out what was going on...'

'I thought that cod was just any old fish.'

'Foolish man! When you met her, you should have apologised for your steersman's error and offered reparations.'

'I had no idea...'

'No idea, indeed! Instead you made matters a hundred times worse by attacking the poor woman and breaking her fins. She returned in such distress and pain, that Chief Naguna'ks sent his male slaves to drag all four of you and your canoe down here.'

'This is disastrous,' whispered Dragging Along Shore. 'I assure you, the damage to his roof was an accident. And my encounter with that fish – I mean, Cod Woman – was a complete misunderstanding. What do you advise me to do?'

'That's obvious,' said Mouse Woman. 'Offer him everything you have in your canoe. With any luck, that may save you.' Then she scurried away into the shadows.

When Chief Dragging Along Shore looked up, he saw Chief Naguna'ks watching him intently. Dragging Along Shore asked if he could go back to his canoe for a moment. Permission was granted. In the canoe, he rooted around amongst the remains of their supplies and quickly filled several boxes with the last of their mountain goat grease, crab apples, dried cranberries and tobacco. He also took out a large copper and two caskets, one filled with eagle down and the other with red ochre. He carried everything over to the fire and presented it all ceremoniously to Naguna'ks – who accepted it graciously and thanked him with equal ceremony.

Then Chief Naguna'ks ordered his slaves to prepare food for his guests. They filled four huge vessels with water, heated them with red-hot stones, then dropped a whole seal into each one. The seals were neither skinned nor butchered before cooking. When they were ready, a slave pulled one out with a hook fixed to the end of a long pole and brought it over to Dragging Along Shore. 'Here you are, sir,' he said with a big smile, 'eat up and enjoy it!'

Dragging Along Shore hesitated, aghast. But Mouse Woman nudged his foot: 'Don't worry, it's not poisoned, it's quite safe.'

'But how am I supposed to eat it?' he whispered. 'Surely they don't expect me to swallow that huge thing whole?'

'What crest do you belong to?' asked Mouse Woman.

'The Killer Whale,' he answered.

'Perfect,' said Mouse Woman. 'It'll slide down nice and easy.'

So Dragging Along Shore opened his mouth as wide as it would go. The servant held the seal by the tail and dropped it straight in, head first. Sure enough, he swallowed it with no discomfort at all – and, in fact, with a great deal of pleasure. The second hunter copied him, and so did the third; they too belonged to the Killer Whale crest.

However, the steersman belonged to the crest of the Eagle. When he tried to copy the others and gulp down a whole seal, he choked, spluttered and retched. They all glanced nervously at Chief Naguna'ks, fearing he would take offence. But he just ordered his slaves to cut the last seal into small pieces, and in that form the steersman ate it with relish.

From that moment, things went well for the four hunters. They worked hard to adapt to the ways of their hosts in the Country Under the Sea – which pleased Naguna'ks very much. He quickly forgot his anger with them; in fact, he grew so fond of them, that the four hunters ended up staying there for a very long time.

Word of their presence spread amongst the other spirit beings who lived in the Country Under the Sea. They sent messages to Chief Naguna'ks, asking to meet them. So Naguna'ks invited his neighbours to emerge from the rocks where they lived, and attend a grand feast in honour of the hunters.

When it was time for the feast to begin, he commanded his slaves to open the door of his house. At once, water rushed in, filling it almost to the top. The hunters hastily jumped into their canoe to save themselves from drowning. Then the waters subsided almost as fast as they had risen, until the floor of Naguna'ks' house was completely dry again.

Many guests arrived on the flood. To the hunters' unaccustomed eyes, some looked weird, grotesque or even horrific, but their manners were all very civilised. As for Chief Naguna'ks himself, he had dressed for the occasion in a Killer Whale robe, ornamented all over with horns.

He made a formal speech as follows: 'Friends, fellow spirits, welcome to my feast. I wish you to meet my new brother, Dragging Along Shore, his two nephews, and his brother-in-law. They arrived at my house in unfortunate circumstances, having committed a great crime against my property. However, they quickly made amends with courteous behaviour, and by presenting me with all their remaining provisions, and also several treasures. I have given them hospitality for a whole year, and now it is time to send them back to their own home. Thus I have called you all here today, to pass on to you what these human beings once gave to me.'

Thus he re-distributed the hunters' gifts. The spirit chiefs of the rocks were all delighted with them.

Naguna'ks went on, 'Dear friends, please do not do anything to frighten these four hunters, for they are now my brothers. When you see them hunting, help them, for they greatly need good luck.'

The spirit beings of the rocks all readily agreed. After that, they all departed.

The following day, Chief Naguna'ks' re-opened the door of his house, bringing the water rushing back in, so that the hunters again had to take refuge in their floating canoe. This time, when the water subsided, two extraordinary new rooms were revealed, one on each side of the house. One was adorned with carvings of two Killer Whales, their noses joined together. The other was decorated with green seaweed, surrounding a copper canoe with copper paddles, stern-board and bailer.

Naguna'ks said to Dragging Along Shore, 'I give all this to you. I also give you my own garment covered with my crest. Tomorrow you shall return home. In future, whenever you go hunting, make sure you first come to the waters above my house here and make me an offering. Then I will help you and give you the luck to find everything you need. But always heed this warning: *do not hurt any fish*. If you disobey, you will be in great danger.'

Then he turned to the steersman and presented him with his own hat, a large sea-apple shell, carved in the centre with the likeness of a man. He also gave him a box inlaid with abalone.

Finally he said, 'Board your canoe and sleep there tonight.'

Early the next morning, they awoke to find they were no longer in their own canoe, but in the copper one that Naguna'ks had gifted them. And somehow they had been transported onto the sea, surrounded by foaming waves as high as mountains.

Gradually, the waves subsided and the foam transformed into fog, so thick they could scarcely see each other. They all fell silent, paralysed with foreboding. There came a noise like rolling thunder... Then suddenly, the fog gave way to bright sunshine... And they found they were back in the very spot in the narrows where their adventure had begun, exactly a year before. The copper canoe was filled with living sea treasures of all kinds, overflowing into their clothes. They began to row away; but it was hard going, since the heavy copper paddles were entangled with seaweed. Whenever they touched the side of the canoe, there was a great clanging noise. Even so, they were soon skimming through the sea as fast as a bird flies through the air. By midnight they had reached the waters of their home town. They cast the anchor-stone and settled down to sleep.

Dragging Along Shore had an elder sister who had never got over the loss of her brother. Early every morning, she would go down to the beach and gaze out over the waves, desperately watching and longing for him, but with ever-diminishing hope.

That morning when she went out, she could hardly believe her eyes. It seemed to her that a large monster was floating on the waves in front of the town. Its skin gleamed dark orange in the rising sun and every so often it made a clanging call. In great alarm, she fetched her husband. He came out and called boldly, 'What are you, who's there?'

To their surprise, it was a familiar voice that answered: 'It's us – your chief who was lost last winter and his three companions. We've come back safely, with marvellous treasures!'

The whole town gathered in excitement. As the lost hunters waded ashore, the townspeople were struck by their curious clothes and hats, exquisitely ornamented in seaweed and sea anemones. As for the copper canoe decorated with glistening shells, no one had ever seen such a thing before.

Some youths rushed forward, eager to help by carrying up the canoe; but it was so heavy, even the strongest could not lift it. Two of them did manage to stagger up with the copper paddles, and others joined forces to carry the treasures that the hunters had brought back from the Country Under the Sea. Finally, the four hunters themselves heaved the copper canoe onto their shoulders, two men at either end.

As soon as they had settled back in, Chief Dragging Along Shore told everyone about their wondrous adventures. Afterwards, he invited the neighbouring tribes to a great feast, requesting every chief to wear his own crest-hat and decorated garment. When they were assembled, the steersman opened his most precious gift, the abalone-inlaid box. The next moment, Dragging Along Shore's house was engulfed by thick fog. When the box was closed again, it vanished, revealing an extraordinary transformation...

The house was now decorated with hanging sea anemones and every imaginable type of seaweed. The copper canoe had somehow moved onto the top of the main platform. Even curiouser, two new rooms had miraculously appeared on either side, exactly like in Naguna'ks' house: one adorned with carvings of two Killer Whales, the other draped in green seaweed. Even the guests themselves looked different, for they too were now richly clothed in ornaments from the sea.

From that time on, Dragging Along Shore prospered. He was always lucky in his hunting and brought home huge quantities of game, because of Chief Naguna'ks' blessing. He was so successful, that he could afford to hold potlatch feasts almost every year. His fame spread right across the world.

A long time after this, Chief Dragging Along Shore took three youths to hunt with him. Before they set out, he made a point of warning them not to hurt any fish.

They caught plenty of animals, then went ashore to camp. The youths wandered off to explore, and one of them spotted a bizarre-looking fish swimming about in the shallows.

'Yuck, look at that ugly brute!' he guffawed. He grabbed a stick and made to club it.

'Stop, don't do that!' cried another. 'Don't forget the chief ordered us to leave all fish unharmed.'

'All right,' said the first, 'I won't kill it. But it won't hurt to take a good look at it, eh?'

The third chuckled. 'That's the weirdest fish I ever saw. Look at its big mouth.'

'Hey, ugly mug,' grinned the first. He scooped it out of the water, put his hands into its mouth and yanked them to both sides to stretch it. He and the third youth fell about laughing. But the second youth felt uneasy. He sidled off to tell Dragging Along Shore what was going on.

As soon as he heard about this mischief, the chief leaped up and rushed over to the youths tormenting the fish. 'You idiots! Why ever did you ignore my warning?' he shouted. 'You've brought us all into terrible danger! We must leave at once.'

He turned to the second youth: 'Run up the hill and watch the sea. If anything happens to us, it's your responsibility to go back and explain to my people.'

He ordered the others back into the canoe with him. They paddled away as fast as they could. The youth on the hilltop saw them make it round the headland. But then, to his horror, a great whirlpool suddenly appeared out of nowhere, making the canoe spin round. Faster and faster it went…and then the sea swallowed it right up.

He raced away and made his way home overland. That's how the townspeople found out that their master and the two others had perished…

But some say that Dragging Along Shore himself did *not* perish. They say that he was saved by Chief Naguna'ks; and that he still lives with him as an honoured guest, far away from his own people, in the Country Under the Sea.

Boas: *Tsimshian Mythology,* 1916
For information about the original narrator, see p. 382. According to the source book, the myth originally had the purpose of explaining the provenance of a local name, for Dragging Along Shore changes his family name to Git-naguna'ks, which is clearly derived from Naguna'ks.

A parallel Quileute story tells of some seal hunters who find a way down to the seals' underwater house, enabling them to greatly increase their catch. Resentful rivals kill the man steering the successful canoe, and cut the rope linking it to the surface. Thus his companion is stranded below with the seals, who befriend him. They lend him a sealskin which he uses to tow the murderers out to sea and drown them. Afterwards he promises his benefactors that he will never hunt them again.

There is evidence that copper was used by Northwest Coast peoples for at least 3,000 years, originally worked with stone and wooden tools. It was probably both locally sourced and imported from distant rivers in the Arctic and Subarctic; later it was also obtained by trade from Europeans. Regarded as precious, it was often beaten into the shape of a shield, decorated with family crests and other designs. Such artefacts were known as 'coppers', and were commonly given away at potlatch feasts (see p. 366), or used as marriage gifts, often increasing in value as they changed hands. See also the Subarctic story, COPPER MOUNTAIN (p. 514).

Mouse Woman is a common character in Tsimshian, Haida and Tlingit tales. She helps both male and female protagonists with information and advice, in return for them throwing their ear ornaments into the fire, presumably for her own use. None of the sources give any further details of her background.

MOSQUITO TOWN

Tsimshian

One winter, ten brothers and their ten wives all went out hunting together in the mountains. They trekked up and down slopes and valleys, crossing frozen rivers, travelling a long, long way. Each night they made camp out in the wilds.

After many days of living like this, they reached the top of a high mountain. In the remote valley below, they saw columns of smoke rising from a town. They couldn't resist the opportunity of a good night's sleep in a warm house, so they made their way to it, sliding down the mountainside in their snowshoes. They arrived just as the wintry sun was setting. A big crowd of townsfolk came out to greet them, buzzing with friendliness.

'Welcome!' cried the chief. 'We don't get many travellers passing here, so it's a real treat to meet you. How many of you are there?'

'We're ten couples,' they replied. 'And one of the women just gave birth to a little one while we've been travelling.'

'There's plenty of room for you all,' said the chief. 'Each couple can sleep in a different house. And the new family with the baby must honour me by being my own guests.'

The travellers were very happy to find such kindness. Each went off to stay with a different family. The couple with the newborn baby were the youngest ones, and they were overwhelmed to be hosted by the chief himself.

He took them into his house, which was quite magnificent, gave them the best seats by the fire, and had his slaves serve them generous quantities of delicious meat. But just then, the baby started to cry, *'Wah, wah, wah!'* On and on he went, screwing up his little eyes and bawling inconsolably. The mother nursed him, rubbed his back and jigged him up and down playfully, but nothing would comfort the poor thing. Then the father tried, but he had no success either. It was embarrassing and distressing; the inexperienced young parents didn't know what to do.

At length, an elderly lady on the other side of the fire stood up and came over to them.

'I'm so sorry!' the young mother cried. 'I can't calm him down.'

'Don't apologise my dear,' said the old lady, 'I'll be very glad to help. Heh, heh, yes I know *exactly* what to do. Let me take the little one for a while.'

The young mother was reluctant to pass her baby to a complete stranger, but she was hungry, and she'd hardly managed to eat anything yet because of the child's tantrum. So she let the old woman carry the baby over to her seat immediately opposite, on the far side of the fire.

As the little one screamed and cried, the old woman put her mouth very close to his ear, and started to chant a strange song over and over:

'A-a-a-ye-hmmmm!
A-a-a-ye-hmmmm!'

Gradually he quietened, his sobs became slower…and finally he stopped.

'He's fallen asleep,' the father said.

'I'll go and get him,' said the mother. She swallowed her last mouthful, then hurried round the fire to the old woman. As she got closer, her heart missed a beat. She could see that the baby had gone very limp; he was lying in the old woman's arms like a piece of cloth. She reached out for him, the old woman handed him over – and she realised that her tiny son was dead.

His ear, the place where the old woman had put her mouth very close to sing to him, was covered in blood.

The old woman had nodded off to sleep with her hands folded over her belly, which looked curiously swollen. The young mother shuddered, gasped and began to weep silently. Fearfully, she carried the baby back round the fire and showed him to her husband, who turned white with shock. The young mother bit her lip and whispered, 'I don't think these are real people. They're…they must be…some kind of supernatural beings. We've got to get out of here as fast as we can – and warn the others.'

She sat down by the fire, rocking the corpse of her dead son. Her husband got up and slipped out, telling his hosts he needed to relieve himself. He dashed round the other houses, slipped inside and, in hasty whispers, told his kin what had happened.

When he got back to his wife, their hosts were preparing for bed. They were shown where to sleep and did likewise.

'Whatever you do, stay awake!' hissed the husband.

'I'll never sleep in this nightmare house,' the wife replied.

The pair lay side by side, sharing their grief. After a long while, they heard someone quietly getting out of bed. It was the chief. He padded towards them softly. The young couple clutched each other fearfully. The husband coughed. The chief stopped in his tracks. The husband coughed again, over and over. The chief retreated.

They lay still, listening. After a while, another man rose, and approached them. At once, the wife had a coughing fit. The man retreated. Then a woman came, and they repelled her by the same method. So it went on, with the terrified couple taking turns to thwart their attackers.

Exactly the same thing was happening to the other brothers and sisters-in-law in all the other houses.

At dawn, the young couple realised that at last all their hosts were asleep. They crept out of bed and slipped through the door. From the other nine houses, the other nine couples also emerged. They met up at the edge of the town, and all hastily ran out to the wilderness, up the mountain from where they had arrived.

Halfway up, they stopped for a rest, and looked back at the weird town from which they had made such a lucky escape. But it turned out they hadn't escaped at all – for a great crowd of townspeople was following them, climbing the mountain in their tracks.

'They're going to attack us!' one cried.

'What can we do?' said another.

'Fight back with our hunting equipment?'

'That'll be useless – they've got supernatural powers.'

Hastily, they pooled ideas. Then, using their climbing staffs, they dug out a huge bank of snow. As their pursuers came closer, they pushed it over the cliff, making a great avalanche. It seemed they had managed to kill all the malignant townspeople in one blow... But then they spotted another huge crowd swarming up behind. The ten men and ten women all groaned. But the youngest couple, the ones who'd lost their beloved baby, were aflame with fury and courage, and urged the others on. Together they made another avalanche, then another and another, until at last all the townspeople were dead...

...All except the chief. In the brightening day, they saw him properly for the first time.

He was a short man, with a huge belly that seemed to glow red as he moved, as if bloated and engorged by blood. Behind his arms was a pair of transparent, grey-veined wings. His nose was very long and thin, sharp as a needle. He skimmed up the mountain so fast, that they had no time to try and stop him.

'So my friends,' he shouted, 'let me introduce myself properly. I am Chief Baboudina, and the place you have just left is Mosquito Town. That baby you brought us provided a fine meal for my grandmother when she bit him and sucked his tender young blood completely dry. But now you have dared to swat my people to death, I come in revenge. I warn you, there is no escape from my proboscis, for it is not flesh but crystal.'

He rushed up and killed the man nearest him in a single blow with his proboscis. The other men seized their wives and made to flee. But Chief Baboudina rose into the air and flew after them. He was here and then he was there, darting around so fast, his aim so true, it was impossible to evade him.

But the woman who had lost her baby was younger and braver than the rest, and her hatred for Chief Baboudina knew no bounds. Somehow, she managed to shake him off, then ran as fast as she could. Glancing over her shoulder, she saw him flying in hot pursuit, his crystal proboscis viciously prodding the air.

She reached a lake. Beside it stood a huge old tree, with a great branch hanging over the water. She waded out, grabbed the branch, hauled herself up onto it and climbed high into the tree.

When Chief Baboudina arrived at the lake shore, he was mystified at the sudden disappearance of her tracks. Then he saw her reflection in the water, and thought it was the young woman herself. So he plunged in and attacked it, stabbing with his proboscis many times over, but with no result. For when he withdrew, after the mud he'd stirred up had settled – the woman's reflection was still there.

He attacked again and again, growing ever angrier. The woman, watching him safely from high above, couldn't help laughing at his pathetic efforts. Chief Baboudina saw her reflection laughing, and it stirred his murderous attack even more. Over and over, he plunged in and stabbed it. The short day ended and grew dark; stars lit the frosty sky. The north wind blew up, with flurries of snow. Chief Baboudina crawled out of the lake one last time, shivering from head to toe. He lay down weakly on the freezing ground, letting his wings merge with the spreading ice. Slowly, the monstrous mosquito froze to death.

The woman was too afraid to believe she was safe. She tossed some branches at him; he didn't even twitch. So she shinned down, slowly approached and boldly kicked him. Still nothing moved.

He was well and truly dead.

She took the shell knife she wore round her neck, sliced open the body of Chief Baboudina and cut out his heart. She put it carefully into her pouch and ran back the way she had come.

She found the bodies of her husband and nine brothers-in-law, lying alongside her nine sisters-in-law. She went to her husband's corpse, held the freakish heart gingerly by one corner, and swung it over him once, twice, three times...

On the fourth swing, her husband sighed. He stretched. He yawned. Then he stood up – alive!

They embraced each other joyfully. The courageous woman turned to their kin and repeated the same trick over each of them. Soon they were all returned to life.

Afterwards, she led them back to the body of Chief Baboudina. They examined it carefully and exclaimed with wonder over its curious anatomy. Then they built a big pyre, placed the body on it with the severed heart on top, and set it on fire.

In no time at all, it was all turned to ashes.

Just then, a soft wind blew up, bringing the first warmth of the coming spring. It caught the ashes in its breath, and blew them about. At once the ashes flew up and transformed into mosquitoes, with exactly the same form as Chief Baboudina and his evil kind, only much smaller – just like the ones that still plague us today.

Boas: *Tsimshian Mythology,* 1916
For information about the original narrator, see p. 382.

Mosquito myths were told in most regions of the continent. Boas gives two other Tsimshian versions of the one here, in which the ancestor of the mosquitoes kills victims by sucking out their brains through their ears. The Haida have a similar story. A lengthy Bella Coola tale tells how mosquitoes originated from the ashes of the burnt body of an evil witch.

The motif of bringing the dead back to life by a simple ritual is particularly common in Northwest Coast stories, and also appears in a number of stories from the Northeast and, to a lesser extent from the Arctic, Plateau and Southwest.

LIFE IN THE OLDEN DAYS

Tsimshian

In olden times there was a very happy people
who lived in a very pretty town of three rows.
They built their houses on top of the hill, the second row
under the first, and the third row under the second one.
The town was on the bank of a very good river, near a large lake.
They went there often in the summer for picking berries,
which grew along the sides of the lake,
which was their hunting ground.
Sometimes the people would live there in summer
for drying berries for winter use,
and in winter the hunters would live there.

In those days the people were in the habit of going for one or two
days to catch salmon to be given to the chief, to use in winter;
and in the winter the people would often go to the chief's house,
and the chieftainess would feed them.
So the men caught salmon for their chief, and
the women worked for their chieftainess, picking berries for her.
The chief and his wife did not work for themselves.
The chief also had many slaves, male and female, and many wives;
some chiefs had as many as twenty, some ten, and others four.
These slaves and wives would work for the people,
but the head wife did not work like the others.

– Henry W. Tate, Tsimshian Elder
(Quoted in Boas: *Tsimshian Mythology*, 1916)

THE BEAR'S SONG

Haida

You ask me to tell you something of bygone days. I will tell you a tale, as I have heard it told round the lodge fires by the old people, on winter evenings.

Not long ago, as our old people tell us, the Bears were a race of beings quite similar to humans. They used to talk, walk upright, and use their paws like hands. When they wanted wives, they used to steal the daughters of our People.

There was a young woman called Kindawuss and a youth called Quissankweedass. She was the town chief's daughter, while he was the son of common people. They were both the same age, and had been playmates since they were children. They were so fond of each other that people would say, 'If you want Kindawuss, just look for Quissankweedass'. When they grew up, this ripened into a love so strong, that each seemed to live only for the other.

However, they knew they could never become husband and wife, not just because they were of different social rank, but also because they both belonged to the Raven crest. The ancient laws decree that a person from the Ravens is only allowed to marry into the Bear, Beaver, Eagle or Frog crests; it is forbidden to marry one of their own. Despite this, the two young people continued to spend all their time together, oblivious to the laws and to gossip... Until, one day, they were both rudely awakened from their dream.

Over at Kindawuss's house, her mother sat her down in a quiet corner and had a serious talk with her: 'It's time for you to choose a husband, my girl,' she said. 'And don't you dare say that you've already chosen Quissankweedass, because you know full well that you can't marry a Raven man.'

'I want to marry Quissankweedass,' the girl answered stubbornly.

Meanwhile, in Quissankweedass's house, his father had taken him aside for a similar talk, man to man: 'Son, it's high time you took a wife. And don't you dare say that you've already chosen Kindawuss, because you know full well that that you can't marry a Raven woman.'

'I only want to marry Kindawuss,' the youth retorted.

The two sets of parents scolded and nagged their children to change their minds, but it was no use. Every evening, Quissankweedass and Kindawuss continued to meet up. So their parents tried to separate them by confining them at home.

However, the pair had already anticipated this might happen and made a plan to overcome it. At an agreed time, they both got permission to go out to relieve themselves – then seized the chance to flee into the forest together. They hurried deep through the trees and undergrowth, to an area where no human had ever trodden before. Here the forest was so dense that only the smallest animals ever scurried through it. In a clearing, they excitedly built a simple but cosy hut. By night they laughed and loved there together, in illicit bliss. By day they went out together, he hunting, she gathering the berries that were ripening in abundance. They took utmost care to keep away from any beaten tracks, and to avoid areas where their kin might look for them. And they succeeded.

Kindawuss, being a chief's daughter, was used to living in luxury; but she far preferred her new, simple life with her strong, attentive lover. They lived like this for several months until the nights drew in, and the soft summer rains gave way to heavy autumn storms.

Then Quissankweedass said, 'My love, before winter, should we visit home briefly, to reassure our families that we're safe and well?'

'Definitely not!' said Kindawuss. 'I know exactly what would happen: my father would accuse me of shaming him, punish me and lock me away. Then our happiness would end for ever!'

'I don't believe my own father will act so harshly,' said Quissankweedass. 'To be honest, I miss my parents and want to do the right thing by them. I understand your fears, but I still feel it's right that *I* at least should go. My only worry is how you'll cope alone here in the middle of the forest. Will you be afraid?'

'Afraid?' she retorted. 'No! This is our home, Quissankweedass. Every time I sit in it, I'll imagine you're sitting opposite me. The only thing I do fear is that you won't come back. Promise you won't stay away for more than four days.'

'I promise, my love,' he said.

Early next morning, Kindawuss walked with Quissankweedass through the towering trees, until the thought of drawing any closer to their town made her shudder. They embraced, each promising to think of the other constantly. Then they said goodbye.

As he went on alone, Quissankweedass began to feel misgivings; but he hurried on, and in no time at all reached his parents' home. They were overjoyed to see him, and at first, Quissankweedass thought they would forgive him. So he lowered his guard and told them everything. However, when his parents realised he and Kindawuss really were living together, against all the norms and sacred laws, they were furious.

'Son, I beg you,' his mother cried, 'never go back to her!'

'But you know I've always loved her,' he protested. 'I can't live without her!'

'Of course you can,' his father snorted. '*Love* has nothing to do with it. It is absolutely forbidden to marry within your own crest, and that's the end of it. Even worse, you've led our chief's beloved daughter astray. Think of the implications for us, especially as mere commoners, if we condone your disgraceful behaviour. Since you refuse to listen to the wisdom of your elders, we'll have to force you to behave by keeping you prisoner. No doubt, in a short time, that foolish girl will come creeping back to look for you. Her father will know how to punish her, in a way that suits her high status.'

So Quissankweedass was kept indoors, racked with worry and guilt, imagining Kindawuss's dismay when he failed to return after four days. Eventually, however, his father dropped his guard a little, enabling the youth to sneak out. He made his way back to their secret home in the forest, heart pounding. He could not wait to hold his beloved in his arms again; but he was terrified that she might have come to harm, or that she would not forgive his long absence.

At last, he arrived at the spot where they had parted. Her small footprints still showed in the soft mud, leading back to their secret hut. He took a deep breath and stooped in. Everything was quiet and the fire was cold. He could tell at once that Kindawuss too had been away for a long time. Where could she be?

Desperately, he searched the hut for some clue; there was none. He went outside, pacing up and down the stream, pushing through trees and thickets, constantly calling her. But the only reply was his own voice, echoing back from the mountains.

He searched for days, without success. At last he returned to the town, his heart totally broken. He went around confessing everything to everyone, and begging for help. Once they realised the chief's daughter was in mortal danger, many people put aside their disapproval and joined the search for her. Among them were her father, the chief himself, who was racked with anguish and fear; and Quissankweedass's father, who was full of regret for detaining his son and thus perhaps causing the young woman's death. They searched for ten whole days, but found nothing.

Months went by, then years. Gradually, the chief and his people stopped even mentioning Kindawuss's name. Yet Quissankweedass believed with all his might that, somewhere, she was still alive. Finally, he consulted a shaman.

'I know why you've come,' the shaman said. 'You're still seeking your lost lover, eh? What have you brought to help me find her?'

Quissankweedass gave him a fragment from a cedar-bark cape she had once worn. The shaman held it in his palm, and after a while, he said: 'I see a young woman lying on the ground. Yes indeed, it is her. She seems to be asleep. There is something among the bushes. It comes towards her: a large, dark shape…'

Quissankweedass gasped.

The shaman raised his other hand to silence him, then went on: 'I see a lake, and a large cedar tree. Now I see your lover there…'

'Where is the lake? Where is the tree?' Quissankweedass cried.

'I can take you there,' the shaman answered.

Now, let us go back to Kindawuss.

After she said goodbye to Quissankweedass, she stared after him wretchedly for a long while. Then she retraced her steps towards their hut; but through her streaming tears, she could scarcely see the way. So she lay down in a shady place amongst the ferns, and sobbed uncontrollably until she fell asleep.

As she lay there, a hulking, dark figure emerged from the trees and came padding towards her on all fours –

A male Bear.

He came close and sniffed her. Through her troubled dreams, Kindawuss felt his warm breath on her face. She sprang awake – and screamed.

'Hush, sweet girl,' the Bear said in a deep, rasping voice.

'Aaargh, go away!' she cried.

'No,' the Bear answered, 'unlike your human lover, I will not abandon you. Do not waste your life hiding and waiting for him. I have come to free you from this trouble, by making you my wife.'

Kindawuss backed away, trembling violently. She stared at the Bear, aghast. 'How can you ask such a thing? Never, never!'

The Bear went on, 'You have nothing to fear. I promise to treat you well. I'm much better than Quissankweedass, for I am a chief, like your father – the Chief of the Bears. Will you come and marry me willingly?'

'No, go away!'

The Bear Chief sighed deeply. He reached out his great paw and pressed it on her, gently yet so firmly that she was trapped. He scooped her up, very carefully, in his huge jaws, and carried her into the trees.

'Stop,' she screamed, 'I beg you, put me down!'

The Bear did stop, dropping her softly and restraining her again with his paw. 'Will you come of your own free will?' he asked again.

'I see I have no choice,' she said hopelessly.

So she followed the Bear Chief down a secret forest trail. Once or twice she tried to slip away, but each time he quickly brought her back. Eventually, they came to a lonely clearing where a silver lake shimmered in the sunshine. The Bear led her to an ancient cedar tree, towering almost to the Sky. Its gnarled, indented trunk was as broad as the lovers' secret hut.

'There is my house,' he said, pointing up into the leaves. 'It is comfortable and cosy for you, my dear Kindawuss. Follow me up, and you will see.'

'But I can't climb a tree,' she whispered.

'Ah,' said the Bear Chief sagely, 'you humans have such different ways and abilities from us! Wait, I'll make you a ladder.'

He scratched long strips of bark off the trunk, twisted them deftly into two ropes, lashed footholds between them, climbed the tree with the contraption and dangled it down. Kindawuss clambered up it into the foliage, and thus entered the Bear Chief's home.

Its interior was only just big enough for a single family, but otherwise it was as splendid as her father's house. The Bear Chief showed her to a bed, thickly lined with moss. She lay on it and was surprised to find it very soft and comfortable.

That night, she wept constantly. The Bear Chief kept away and let her grieve. In the morning he said, 'Please don't cry any more. I will do everything in my power to make you happy, Kindawuss. Listen, I have composed a special song to cheer you up.'

He began to sing in a voice as beautiful as it was deep:

'I have taken a fair lady
from her Haida friends
to be my wife.
I hope her kin won't come,
and take her away!
I will be kind to her.
I will give her berries from the hill
and roots from the ground.
I will do all I can to please her.
For her I made this song,
and for her alone I sing it.'

The song touched her heart deeply. She decided to try and make herself at home in this strange place with her strange new husband; and as time went by, it grew easier. The noble Bear cared for her tenderly, and she began to return his love.

Eventually she gave birth to their children: twin sons. Then she stopped even thinking about Quissankweedass, realising that her new life was truly happy.

After Quissankweedass consulted the shaman, he ran home and gathered some other other young men into a new search party. The shaman used his powers to lead them to the Bear Chief's house, high in the great cedar tree on the shores of the lonely lake.

There he said, 'Make your plans carefully. You have only one chance to rescue her.'

The men conferred together. When they were all ready, Quissankweedass called, 'Kindawuss, are you there?'

At first there was only silence. Then they heard a rustling in the branches and saw the face of a woman gazing down.

'Who are you?' a familiar voice called back. 'What do you want?'

'It's me,' he shouted back, 'your own faithful Quissankweedass. I've been searching for you, Kindawuss, for endless years. I beg you, come down and come home!'

'Ah,' she said, 'you are much too late. I am married to the Bear Chief now, and we have two children. I can't leave them.'

Her words stabbed at Quissankweedass's heart. 'Well then…will you at least come down and let me see you properly, even if only for a moment?'

He kept begging and cajoling her, until she took pity and climbed slowly down the ladder to face him.

At once, Quissankweedass's companions seized her. Ah, how fiercely she resisted them! However, the men easily overpowered her and carried her off to their town.

Naturally, her parents were overjoyed to have their lost child safely back. They gave her a wonderful welcome; they did not scold her at all. Quissankweedass was overjoyed too. Just as before, Kindawuss saw that she had no choice. She tried to settle down with him this time; yet she could not stop weeping.

'You've forced me to leave my two small sons behind,' she said, 'my own flesh and blood, who I love more than you, more than the Bear Chief. How can you expect me to live without them? Let me go back!'

'No, my love,' Quissankweedass replied. 'I'm not losing you again. I shall go with my friends and fetch your children here.'

'The Bear Chief will never allow it,' she said.

However, Quissankweedass nagged her, day and night, until finally she said, 'My Bear husband has the kindest of hearts and it may be possible to persuade him. I will teach you the special song he made for me. Go to the tree, sing it, then beg him to send our children here. He will believe you speak on my behalf and grant your request.'

She taught him the words and tune until he had it perfectly, though it sounded poor and hollow in his thin human voice. He led his companions back to the tree by the lonely lake, and sang it.

The Bear Chief had been broken-hearted since he lost Kindawuss. When he heard their special song, his heart leaped with hope that she had come back, and he hastened down. Only when he found himself surrounded by men did he realise the trick. He growled fiercely at them, but they were well armed and threatened to take the children by force. Eventually, fearing for the little ones' lives, the Bear Chief gave in and let them go.

Thus Kindawuss got her children back. Now at last, her father, the chief, agreed to let her break the prohibitions and live with Quissankweedass as husband and wife. He helped her raise her half-Bear sons.

These two grew up with quite different dispositions. One stayed with his mother's People, married a local girl and raised a family there. However the other went back to his father, and lived peacefully amongst the Bears until he died.

Deans: *The Story of the Bear and his Indian Wife*, 1889 (collected 1873)
Deans & Triggs: *Tales from Totems of the Hidery*, 1899
Both sources reproduce the story almost identically, though with different dates and spellings of names. Deans describes its provenance as follows:
'Looking over my papers a few evenings ago I found the following tale, bearing the date of May 1870, the time when it was recorded. My informant was a very intelligent Haida, by the name of Yak Quahu, whose memory was stored with legends like the following, which he used to repeat of an evening, seated by the camp-fire.'
The first two paragraphs of this retelling almost exactly reproduce the original, which presumably recorded Yak Quahu's own words, though the rest of his narrative is rather sparse and lacking in detail. Deans adds:
'I have heard it told often by others since then, and at each time of telling a great deal of the original was lost or forgotten, showing, I fear, that after a few more years, these fine old legends would have been lost beyond recovery, had I not collected them when I did.'
He says that Yak Quahu said of the characters' names:
'In all old tales I have never found the name of the hero of the tale, and when a name has been given, it appears to be one given by the storytellers, rather than the original name of the hero ... So I have given names of...a youth and maiden in my native village.'
Of the Bear Chief's song he says,
'To this day [it] is known among the children of the Haidas by the name of the Song of the Bears. I have heard it sung many a time... This is the song of the bears, and whoever can sing it has their lasting friendship.'
Human marriage with a bear is an important theme on the Northwest Coast. A common story amongst the Nuxalk, Tlingit and Tsimshian opens with a girl slipping in a pile of bear dung, causing her to drop and spill the basket of berries she has been picking. In her fury she shouts out insults to the bears for fouling her path. She is then abducted by a young man, who turns out to be a shapeshifting bear, and forced to marry him. There are various versions, each with a different outcome.

413

MOON WOMAN AND THE ARROW CHAIN BOY

Tlingit

The young son of a town chief was close friends with another boy also of noble ranking. They were always visiting each other's houses, where they spent their time making great quantities of arrows, then practising shooting.

One fine spring evening, the Moon was shining bright enough to see by, so the two boys took their bows and arrows, and set out for a hill behind their town to shoot them. The second boy ran ahead, pointing at the Sky, laughing and shouting, 'Whoah, look how funny the Moon is tonight. It's exactly the same shape as that stupid old wooden ornament my mother wears in her lip! Hee hee! And it's the same size too, it's tiny!'

'Sshh!' the chief's son scolded him. 'You mustn't insult the Moon like that, it's danger –'

Before he could finish, the Moon suddenly vanished, and so did all the stars. The night turned pitch dark; it was impossible to see. The chief's son stood rooted to the spot, hardly daring to breathe. After a while, the darkness was broken by a shimmering ring of rainbow light, circling the spot where his friend was standing.

'Look at that,' he whispered.

The other boy did not reply but gave a bloodcurdling shriek. Slowly, the rainbow light faded. The stars winked back into the Sky, and the Moon drifted out from the clouds, lighting the whole hillside. The chief's son could not see his friend anywhere.

'Where have you gone?' he yelled. 'Stop hiding, come out!' But only silence answered him.

'He must have been scared of that weird light, and run right up the hill to escape it,' the chief's son thought. So he went up there himself and searched everywhere, but still didn't find his friend.

He sat down and thought about what had happened. Whichever way he looked at it, he couldn't escape a frightening conclusion. 'It must be because he said those rude things about the Moon,' he thought. 'He must have been snatched away as a punishment!'

The chief's son sat very still, thinking what to do. He didn't dare seek help in the village, for fear of getting into trouble. 'I'll have to find a way to climb up to the Sky myself and try to rescue him,' he thought. 'But how?'

Soon he had an idea. He fitted an arrow to his bow and shot it up, aiming for the Moon. It flew through the air, *phat!* and met its mark. He shot another arrow, which joined on to the bottom of the first one. He shot another and another and another, on and on – until the linked arrows hung all the way down from the Sky in a long chain, with the last one dangling just above him. He put his ear to the bottom of the arrow chain….and far, far away, heard his friend's voice crying, moaning and groaning.

The chief's son wanted to rush up there at once to help his friend, but he was exhausted from all the shooting. So he lay down by the bottom of the arrow chain and fell straight asleep. When he awoke, dawn had broken. He jumped up and turned to the arrow chain. It had transformed to a long ladder.

'Excellent,' he thought. 'I'll climb it at once… Hmm, no, first I'd better get some food for my journey.'

So he ran around the hilltop. Every time he came to a fruit bush, he broke off a branch and stuck it into his hair. Then he started climbing the arrow-chain ladder. He went as fast as he could, up and up, climbing all day; but by nightfall, he was still a long way from the Sky, and he was exhausted again. So he settled himself as comfortably as he could on the ladder, and camped there overnight, dozing fitfully.

He woke early the next morning feeling very strange, as if his head were pressed down by a great weight. He reached up, tugged one of the branches from his hair – and found it was now smothered in big, juicy salmonberries. He gobbled them up, then felt much better and stronger.

He set off climbing again. Again, at around midday, he felt both hungry and weighed down by something on his head. This time he took a branch from the other side, and found it loaded with huckleberries. For although it had been spring when he'd started his climb, up there in the Sky it was already summer and all the berries were fully ripe.

Thus he went up and up, dozing whenever he grew tired, eating endless berries from the branches in his hair. Eventually, in this way, he reached the top of the arrow chain. He stepped off into the Sky World and looked around.

The first thing he saw was a large lake. He gathered great armfuls of moss by the shore, spread it out and lay down on it. Ah, it was so comfortable after all those nights of balancing on the arrow chain! He fell at once into a wonderfully deep sleep...

But he could not rest for long, because suddenly someone was shaking him awake and shouting in his ear: 'Get up!'

He opened his eyes and looked around. A girl was standing beside him, in neat clothes beautifully ornamented with porcupine quills. 'My grandmother wants you to come,' she said.

The chief's son followed her down a dark trail. At its end she led him into a very small house, where an old woman was waiting.

'Welcome, grandson,' she said. 'What brings you to the Sky?'

The boy answered, 'I'm looking for my friend. He was snatched away, and I think he was carried up here, because I heard him crying. I'm worried he's in terrible trouble. Grandmother, if you've seen him, if you know where he is, I beg you to tell me!'

'Indeed, I do know,' answered the old woman. 'He is held captive in Moon Woman's house, just a short distance away. I've heard him crying too. He is suffering terribly because Moon Woman tortures him.'

'Oh no! How can I rescue him?'

'Grandson, I can see you are very hungry, so before we talk further, let me give you some food.'

The old woman put her hand up to her mouth. At once, a fat salmon appeared. She put it in a dish and offered it to him. He ate it ravenously. In the same way, she produced berries, then a large hunk of meat, and waited while he ate them all.

When he had finished, she said, 'Moon Woman has tied your friend to a high platform in her house, just below the smoke hole, and abuses him cruelly. However, sometimes she leaves him alone there for a while to nurse his pain. That's when you should be able to rescue him. Let me give you some useful things to help you.'

She fetched some items from a dark corner and passed them to him: a spruce cone, a piece of devil's club shrub, a spray of wild roses, and a small piece of stone. 'Take these. When the time comes, throw them and see their great power. Afterwards, bring your friend here, and I'll help you both return home.'

The chief's son wrapped the objects carefully in his blanket. The old woman took him outside and pointed out Moon Woman's house. As he set off towards it, he heard his friend's moans and screams even louder. How he pitied his poor friend! When he reached the house, he clambered onto the roof, crawled along to the smoke hole and peered down it. The other boy was just below, bound by thick ropes.

'Hey, it's me,' the chief's son hissed, 'I've come to rescue you.'

The other boy gave a gasp of joy. 'Oh, it's so good to see you!'

'Where's Moon Woman?' said the chief's son.

'She's gone off somewhere,' the other boy whispered up at him. 'I'm alone right now.'

'Then stretch both your hands up towards the hole.'

The other boy did so. The chief's son reached down and tugged him with all his might until the ropes snapped. His friend broke free and clambered out. They were so glad to see each other! But the chief's son didn't let emotion overcome him. Instead, he felt inside his blanket, pulled out the spruce cone and tossed it down to the platform below. To their astonishment, at once the cone began moan and wail, sounding just like a boy.

The friends jumped to the ground together and started to run. However, before they had gone very far, the cone rolled off the platform and the cries stopped. At once Moon Woman realised her captive had got away. She rushed up and began to pursue the boys.

Here she came, feet pounding behind them! The one who had escaped glanced back and almost fainted. 'Help!' he cried. 'She's going to snatch me away again…she'll get us both…!'

But the chief's son pulled out the devil's club and hurled it to the ground behind them. At once it grew into a mass of dense, spiny shrubs, rooted between Moon Woman and the boys. But Moon Woman was strong, Moon Woman was angry. She fought and struggled through…and quickly emerged to gain on them again.

So the chief's son tossed back the spray of roses – which at once transformed into an enormous thicket of tangled, sweet-smelling thorns. But Moon Woman could take any pain, Moon Woman would not be beaten. She plunged through the prickles… And now she was almost treading on their heels!

Finally, the chief's son pulled out the fragment of stone and hurled it back. It landed right by Moon Woman's feet. The next moment it had become a towering cliff with sides as smooth and slippery as ice. Moon Woman gave a cackle of fury and tried to climb up it. But since she was shaped like a round, white ball, she just kept rolling off it, down and back, down and back...

At last, the boys reached the house of the kind old woman. She made them very welcome and gave them another good meal to celebrate their escape. When they had finished eating, she said to the chief's son, 'Go back to the place where you first entered the Sky. Lie down there together and think of nothing but your home. Keep thinking of it until you arrive.'

So they went to the lake shore and lay down side by side. Each boy tried to empty his mind of all thoughts except home. Gradually they floated down, like feathers on a breeze. However, every so often, one of them remembered their strange adventure; then they both immediately bounced back up, and had to start over again. But, at last, they managed to concentrate all the way – and found themselves back on the hilltop just outside their town.

They ran home at once. Their parents were overjoyed! The chief had been in the middle of organising a big funeral feast for the boys, as everyone had assumed they were dead. As soon as he saw them alive and well, he turned it into a thanksgiving celebration.

Swanton: *Tlingit Myths and Texts*, 1909
This story was narrated by an elderly lady who Swanton does not name, but identifies as the mother of a man called Katishan, a chief at Wrangell, Alaska. He says that although she had lived amongst white people for a long time, this did not seem to have influenced her storytelling.

After the incident in which the insurmountable cliff stops Moon Woman from chasing the boys, the storyteller comments:
'It is on account of this cliff that people can say things about the moon nowadays with impunity.'
The woman's lip ornament, that one of the boys insultingly compares to the moon, was a 'labret', once a very common decoration of Tlingit women. Writing in 1786, a European traveller called La Perouse said:
'All [the women] without exception have the lower lip slit close to the gum the whole width of the mouth, and wear in it a kind of wooden bowl without handles, which rests against the gum, and which the slit lip serves as a collar to confine, so that the lower part of the mouth projects two or three inches.'
The motif of an arrow chain to the sky appears in several other stories from the Northwest, and also in myths from California, the Great Plains and the Plateau. The use of 'magic objects' to save a hero or heroine from a malevolent pursuer is a common motif in myths throughout North America – see THE ROLLING SKULL (p. 105).

THE WISDOM
OF PORCUPINE

Tsimshian

A long time ago, Grizzly Bear summoned his fellow large animals to a council. Black Bear came, as did Caribou, Elk, Mountain Lion, Wolf and Wolverine. When they were all assembled, Grizzly rose to his feet and addressed them with these words:

'I bring you here today because, as you all know too well, we are facing an increasingly difficult situation with regard to the People. Until recently, we were happy to allow them to hunt some of us, because they only took as many as they needed for meat and clothing. Besides, they only went hunting in good weather, so in winter we were at peace to breed and replenish our numbers.

'However, of late they have been developing both their skills and their weapons to such an extent that they have taken to hunting all the year round. Because of this, they are killing our fellows in ever-increasing numbers. To be frank, unless we do something about this, we are in serious danger of being totally wiped out!'

All the others nodded in melancholy agreement.

'So,' Grizzly went on, 'this is what I propose. We should approach He Who Made Us, and request that, in future, he makes the winters so cold that the People themselves are forced to stay in their houses all the time. In that way, they will not be able to come out to kill us. Then we shall be able to raise our children free from worry, and thus grow both numerous and strong again. May I have your support to do this?'

The other animals all carefully considered it. One by one, Black Bear, Caribou, Elk, Mountain Lion and Wolverine raised their paws or hooves, and nodded their approval.

However, there was one dissenter, and that was Wolf. He stood up and said, 'One aspect of your proposal worries me, Grizzly Bear. Those of us assembled here do not represent all the animals on Earth – for you have only summoned us large ones. We have many other brothers and sisters who are much smaller than us, and their opinions are equally valid. I am thinking of those such as Beaver, Marten, Mink, Porcupine and Raccoon; and, indeed, also those who might be classified as *extremely* small – not just the Mouse nations, but also the various Insects. If He Who Made Us did indeed make the winter more severe, these extremely small ones may well protest. That would cause friction between us when we should be friends, and our plan will become totally worthless.'

'That is indeed true, Wolf, my brother,' said Grizzly. 'So let us hold another council tomorrow – and this time, we will invite *all* creatures, of all sizes, to attend.'

'Except for the People, of course,' a Caribou called out.

'Naturally, except for the People.'

So the following day, representatives of every living creature on Earth, except the People, met together. To make sure there was enough room for everyone to fit in, and every voice to be heard, they assembled out in the open on a wide prairie. The large animals sat on one side of it, and the small ones, including the various Insects, faced them on the other side.

This time, Grizzly opened the council by explaining to his small friends what the large animals had agreed the previous day. 'And so,' he concluded, 'if any of you have any objections, this is your chance to voice them. Please consider the situation carefully. We very much hope we can count on your unanimous support when we approach He Who Made Us with a request to turn winter colder and more severe.'

When he sat down, there was a very long silence. Then some of the small creatures started whispering amongst themselves. For a long while, none spoke up. Then, at last, Porcupine rose to his feet.

'*Quaah!*' he said. 'I would like to express an opinion and I hope you will listen to it carefully. The plan you have suggested certainly seems very clever and effective... But not for all of us. It will only help you big animals, for you are all covered in thick fur, which grows even thicker in the winter. But look for a moment, I beg you, at the very smallest of our friends sitting with us on this side of the prairie. I refer, of course, to the Insects. Do you see any fur to clothe their little bodies and protect them from ice and snow? Of course you do not. If future winters become as cold as you would like them to, they will all most certainly freeze to death. Are their lives not as valuable as yours?'

No sooner had Porcupine stopped speaking and sat down, than Grizzly leaped back to his feet. This time, he addressed his remarks solely to the large animals who surrounded him.

'Brothers,' he said, 'I ask you this: having already agreed a plan of action, one that will certainly be in all *our* interests, should we dismiss it now, just to please a minority?'

A chorus of voices from the large animals answered:

'No, certainly not!'

'We've already made our decision.'

'It's impossible to please everyone.'

'Porcupine's just causing unnecessary problems.'

Porcupine jumped up again. *'Quaah!'* he cried. 'Listen once more! I want to make a point that you probably haven't thought of. You big ones are always wandering about in the mountains, looking for tasty roots, grasses and berries to eat. Don't deny it, I've often seen you. Caribou and Elk eat nothing else, and the rest of you all need plants as much as meat to keep you healthy. Well then, consider what will happen if the weather turns as cold as you wish. It will make all your food plants wither away and crumble to nothing. They'll never be able to regrow, even when summer returns.'

None of the large animals could think of an answer.

'I know what you're thinking,' Porcupine went on. 'You believe I'm making up excuses to get my own way over you. But the fact is, it wouldn't worry us small ones if there weren't any berries or roots or grasses. We equally enjoy eating the bark of trees – but none of you lot have the right teeth for that. And such a scarcity wouldn't affect the Insects at all, because they can find all the food they need in the soil.'

Still the others stayed silent. Porcupine shook his head angrily. Then he put his hand to his mouth, bit off his own thumb and spat it out. (That's why all porcupines today have four fingers but no thumb on their front paws.) *'Quaah!* Why won't you listen to me, you great fools!'

But this time he was wrong. The big animals *had* been listening to him, very carefully. Grizzly lumbered to his feet. He looked slowly around at all the creatures assembled on the prairie, turning last of all to Porcupine; and then he hung his head.

'Porcupine, my brother,' he rasped, 'I am ashamed. Your wisdom is far, far greater than mine. Indeed, it has struck us all quite speechless. What you say is absolutely correct. I would now like to propose that you should be appointed chief, over all of us.'

'Yes, yes!' all the other creatures cried. And then: 'Wise Chief Porcupine, speak again!'

'Thank you, my brothers,' said Porcupine. 'Now listen carefully to what *I* propose to benefit us *all*, both great and small:

'In spring there will be showers of rain, to make the plants grow.

'In summer it will turn warm and the salmon will swim up river.

'In autumn the leaves will fall, rain will make the rivers overflow. and those animals that like the long sleep will go to their dens.

'And in winter the level of cold, the amount of ice and snow, shall stay exactly as it is now.'

Thus it was agreed. And that is exactly how things have been in the world ever since.

That is the end.

Boas: *Tsimshian Mythology*, 1916
For information about the source of this story, see p. 382.

The source gives a twist to the story at the end. It describes some of the larger animals continuing to oppose Porcupine. In the end, he gets so angry with them, that he strikes them dead with his long, sharp tail quills, concluding: 'Therefore all the animals are afraid of Porcupine to this day.'

Another Tsimshian myth about the seasons begins with the origin of the sun and moon, again with Porcupine overcoming the other animals' views, this time to agree the length of the lunar months. The animals then name the twelve months of the year, which Boas translates as follows:

October to November, 'Falling Leaf Month'
November to December, 'Taboo Month'
December to January, 'The Intervening Month'
January to February, 'Spring Salmon Month'
February to March, 'Month when Eulachon is Eaten'
March to April, 'When Eulachon Is Cooked."
April to May, *[no translation given]*
May to June, 'Egg Month'
June to July, 'Salmon Month'
July to August, 'Humpback Salmon Month'
August to September, *[no translation given]*
September to October, 'Spinning Top Month'.

PROVERBS

Tsimshian

A deer, although toothless, may accomplish something.
(Don't judge someone by their outward appearance.)

You are not the only one to whom Raven gave intelligence.

He wants to die with all his teeth in his head.
(He acts so foolishly that he will not live to be a toothless old man.)

What will you eat when the snow is on the north side of the tree?
(A reproach to the wasteful, referring to the end of winter, when food is scarce.)

You mistake the corner of the house for the door.
(Signifying a gross mistake.)

Go where your ears will be full of grubs!
(Said to someone who goes foolhardily to their own destruction.)

It is not good to have too much one's own way.

– Collected by Mrs. O. Morison in British Columbia in 1889.
(Quoted in *Tsimshian Proverbs*.)

Oopungnewing, an Inuit village near Frobisher Bay on Baffin Island
Drawn by unknown artist based on sketches by C.F. Hall, 1865

MYTHS OF THE ARCTIC

PEOPLE OF THE ARCTIC

Canada:
Most of Nunavut.
Northern regions of Newfoundland and Labrador,
Northwest Territories, Quebec and Yukon.

United States:
Coastal Alaska, including the Aleutian Islands.

Also **Greenland** and northeastern **Russia**.

The Arctic cultural region extends right across the far north of North America and beyond to the coasts of Greenland and northeastern Siberia in Russia. Throughout this region, the indigenous way of life and outlook was very similar, moulded by harsh terrain and cold climate.

The landscape is mainly vast, open tundra, bounded by rocky coastlines. The sea freezes in winter and carries drifting icebergs in summer. The soil is permanently frozen, limiting plant life to low growing mosses, lichens, grasses, sedges and creeping shrubs. Winters are long, dark and very cold, averaging minus 28°C, with the entire landscape covered in snow; summers are cool. Snowmelt and poor drainage contribute to numerous lakes, ponds, marshes and areas of soggy ground. Fog is common, as are gales, which cause blizzards and snowdrifts in winter. This environment supports a variety of land and sea mammals, which are joined by teeming bird life during the summer.

Much of the region is the homeland of the Inuit (singular Inuk). Formerly they were known by outsiders as Eskimos, a name still used in Alaska, but now considered derogatory in other regions. The Inuit were originally semi-nomadic. In winter they lived in permanent villages; but during the short summer they travelled in search of food, living in skin-covered tents, each housing up to twenty people. Separate but related peoples are the Alutiit of the Kodiak Islands and neighbouring parts of Alaska, and the Aleuts (Unangan) of the Aleutian islands.

There were various styles of winter houses. In some locations, they were built of stones and turf over a wooden frame; in others of bones and stones; and elsewhere of blocks of snow, known as 'igloos'. Whatever the construction, entry was always through a long, narrow passage that dipped in the middle to keep out cold air. Inside, the single main chamber was divided by low screens into a separate room for each of the two or more families who shared the house, each room with benches for sitting and sleeping,

A dome-shaped igloo, three-and-a-half metres (twelve feet) high, could be built by two men within two hours. Inside, beds comprised a solid snow foundation covered with wood, then a thick layer of shrubs and finally a number of heavy deerskins; clothes removed for the night formed pillows, and the whole family slept under a single cover of deerskins sewn together. Lamps were made of soapstone filled with blubber. Over the fireplace was a pole framework, from which hung cooking pots and drying clothes. There were small side rooms for storage and cooking.

The Alutiit and Aleuts lived in semi-underground houses, built over a square pit. The upper walls and roof had a driftwood frame covered with grass thatch and earth. Inside was a central fire, and benches along the walls. Some were occupied by several families, usually related, who each had their own separate apartment within the structure. Entry was through the roof hole, descending by a notched-log ladder.

The most important Arctic food was seal. During the winter, men worked in pairs around seal breathing holes in the ice to harpoon or shoot them; in summer whole villages of men, women and children went sealing. Other important game animals were bear, caribou, deer, musk ox, otter, narwhal, sea lion, walrus and whale; and to a lesser extent Arctic foxes, Arctic hares and wolves. In the summer, huge amounts of salmon were caught, alongside various ducks and other waterfowl. Hunting weapons included harpoons, bows and arrows, spears and guns traded from Europeans; traps were also used. The women gathered roots, berries, shellfish, crabs and seaweed. Surplus food was preserved by drying, smoking or roasting. Favourite delicacies included a concoction of berries, fat and fish; and boiled whale blubber and skin. During the height of winter when the weather was at its worst, people lived on their stores of preserved meat, fish and berries.

Tools, clothes, boats, sledges and weapons were mostly made from animal and fish bones, skins, intestines and sinews; and ivory from walrus tusks and narwhal horn. Driftwood, which was rare and thus valuable, was also widely used, as were flint, slate and soapstone. Boats and kayaks were made with driftwood frames covered in sealskin. Sledges were constructed from driftwood, whalebone, ivory and deer antlers, and pulled by teams of dogs with sealskin or deerskin harnesses. Dogs also played an important role in hunting, tracking land game and sniffing out seals.

Traditional Inuit society was egalitarian, based on kinship and links between families. Status came from success in hunting, or special expertise in skills such as needlework. Property belonged to the community, apart from personal items. Decisions were made through community consensus, and good behaviour was maintained by fear of public shaming and retaliatory blood feuds.

Monogamous marriage was the norm, but some men took a second wife with the intention of having more children. Divorce and remarriage were easily arranged; in such cases children normally stayed with their mother. Orphans, widows, disabled people and unmarried men and women were cared for by their relations. Children were raised with much affection by the elders.

Most communities were self-sufficient. However, there was some trade through barter, particularly of soapstone, whalebone, narwhal, walrus ivory, skins and craftwork. Despite the extremes of weather, Arctic people were by no means isolated. During the long, dark winter, it was common to travel by dog-sledge to socialise in distant villages. In spring and summer, people would travel up to 200 miles (320 km) by boat to stay with friends. Communal festivities at different times of year included feasting, singing, drumming and dancing, gambling, satirical songs, ball games, wrestling and kayak races.

Traditional Inuit religion was based on the belief that everything in the world, both living and inanimate, has a spirit; and that everything is controlled by supernatural powers. This belief permeated every aspect of life. It was important not to offend any of the spirits by inappropriate behaviour, to ensure good hunting and general wellbeing, and to keep the cosmos in balance.

Shamans had the ability to communicate and mediate with the spirits by entering a trance, which was often achieved through a dramatic masked dance.

LIFE IN THE ARCTIC
WHEN THESE STORIES WERE COLLECTED

In the late 19th century, most of the high Arctic belonged to Canada. Alaska was a Russian colony until 1867, when it passed to the United States. Greenland was a colony of Denmark.

In more accessible coastal areas, the Arctic peoples had long been accustomed to whaling ships from both western Europe and Russia, and were familiar with European food and trade goods such as iron knives, kettles and guns, and nets. Many had found paid work in the whaling industry. Others supplied the European marine fur trade, particularly with sea otters – which were in such demand that they were hunted almost to extinction – or worked in the new Alaskan industries such as commercial fishing, canning and copper mining. European diseases took a severe toll; in the Aleutian Islands they decimated the local population by over 80 per cent. Inevitably, traditional ways of life were severely disrupted. By the early 1920s, virtually all peoples in this part of the Arctic were in contact with traders, missionaries and government agents, and had been converted to Christianity.

In the more remote regions, the only European visitors were explorers and ethnologists, who found many local people still living in the time-honoured way. The harsh climate kept most settlers away from these parts until the late 20th century.

STORYTELLING IN THE ARCTIC

Around the turn of the 20th century, ethnographers transcribed numerous Arctic myths and folk tales, and also recorded much information about storytelling practices.

Boas, writing about Baffin Island, said that storytelling was particularly popular during the long winter nights:

'Old traditions are always related in a highly ceremonious manner. The narrator takes off his outer jacket, pulls the hood over his head, and sits down in the rear part of the hut, turning his face towards the wall, and then tells the story slowly and solemnly. All the stories are related in a very abridged form, the substance being supposed to be known. The form is always the same, and should the narrator say one word otherwise than is customary, he will be corrected by the listeners.'

On the other side of the continent, by the Bering Strait which separates Alaska from Russia, Nelson noted similar formalities:

'[In some areas] important tales are given by two men, who sit cross-legged...facing each other; one is the narrator and the other holds a bundle of small sticks in one hand... At certain points one of these sticks is placed on the floor between them, forming a sort of chapter mark. If the narrator is at fault he is prompted by his companion. Some of the tales are long, occupying several successive evenings in their recital. The narrators are very careful to repeat them in a certain set phraseology... The voice is intoned to imitate the different characters in a more or less dramatic manner, and with the gestures makes a very effective recital. The listeners are quiet and attentive, and at certain incidents express by a word or two their feelings of surprise or satisfaction. These tales are heard with pleasure over and over again.'

In Greenland, Rasmussen found the storytellers were more relaxed:

'The aim of the Eskimo storyteller is to pass the time during the long hours of darkness; if he can send his hearers to sleep, he achieves a triumph. Not infrequently a storyteller will introduce his chef-d'œuvre with the proud declaration that 'no one has ever heard this story to the end'. The telling of the story thus becomes a kind of contest between his power of sustained invention and detailed embroidery on the one hand and his hearers' power of endurance on the other.'

In the Hudson Bay area, Turner noted a similar ambience:

'Sitting in the hut, engaged in their evening work, the old men tell what they have seen and heard. The old women relate the history of the people of former days, depending entirely on memory, often interspersed with recitations apparently foreign to the thread of the legend. The younger members sit with staring eyes and countenances which show their wondering interest in the narration. Far into the night the droning tone of her voice continues reciting the events of the past until one by one the listeners drowsily drop to sleep.'

THE PEOPLES BEHIND THE STORIES

Alaskan Eskimo

This name embraces two main groups. The **Inupiat** are based in northern and northwestern Alaska. Since the 1970s, the oil industry has become an important source of revenue to them, but it also threatens their traditional way of life. The **Yup'ik** live in western and southwestern Alaska. Their mother tongue is widely spoken, promoted by bilingual education. Today, both peoples combine subsistence hunting, fishing and gathering with a modern lifestyle.

Canadian Inuit

They still occupy their ancestral lands, spread across 53 high Arctic communities. This region, known as Inuit Nunangat, covers some 35 per cent of Canada's landmass and 50 per cent of its coastline. More than half still speak the Inuktut language, and maintain traditional hunting practices.

Greenlanders (Kalaallit)

Today almost 90 per cent of the population of Greenland are Kalaallit. Most are bilingual, speaking Danish alongside one of three local dialects. Many work in commercial fishing and tourism. However, traditional sustainable hunting is still practised, particularly in the north and east of the country. Their own name for their country is Kalaallit Nunaat, 'The Land of the People'.

Also researched for this section were stories from the following Arctic peoples: Aleut and Alutiit.

OUR FOREFATHERS HAVE TOLD US MUCH

Greenland (Kalaallit Nunaat)

Our forefathers have told us much
of the coming of Earth, and of People,
and it was a long, long while ago.
Those who lived long before our day,
they did not know how to store their words
in little black marks, as you do;
they could only tell stories.
And they told of many things,
and therefore we are not without knowledge of these things,
which we have heard told many and many a time,
since we were little children.
Old women do not waste their words idly,
and we believe what they say.
Old age does not lie.

– Unnamed Greenlandic storyteller in
Smith Sound, northwest Greenland, early 20th century
(Quoted in Rasmussen: *Eskimo Folk-Tales*)

THE WOODEN BOY AND THE WINDS

Alaskan Eskimo (Yup'ik)

A woman and her husband had been married for many years, but they had no children.

One day, the woman said to her husband, 'When I was out on the tundra some time ago, I noticed a lone tree growing in the middle of nowhere. I wish you would go out and find it, then fetch back a piece of wood from its trunk.'

'What for?' the husband asked.

'So you can carve it into a model of a child,' said the woman, 'to cheer us up in our loneliness.'

The husband agreed and went outside into the deep winter night. His wife hadn't been able to remember exactly where this tree was, but a long beam of moonlight was shining on the snow like a path, so he decided to follow that. He trudged down it, on and on. Eventually he saw something upright sparkling in the light, standing out clearly from the flat, featureless land. It was surely the tree his wife had spoken of. He took out his hunting knife, cut a chunk of wood from the trunk and carried it home.

There he sat down and began carving it into a lifelike model of a small boy.

His wife was delighted and called it 'Wooden Boy'. When the carving was finished, she cut up some furs and sewed them into miniature clothing, then carefully dressed the model boy in them. She got her husband to shape the offcuts of wood into a set of tiny dishes. 'These are for you, Wooden Boy,' she said.

By then the man was getting tired of it all. 'What's the point of all this?' he grumbled. 'What do we want with a silly toy? It's ridiculous, it won't make us any happier.'

'It's not doing any harm,' said the wife. 'And it'll give us something new to talk about, instead of just going over the same old problem and disappointment all the time.'

The husband rolled his eyes and shook his head.

The wife ignored him. She carried the model to the place of honour on the bench opposite the entrance and propped it up there. She filled the tiny wooden dishes with food and water and placed them next to the model. Then they went to bed.

In the middle of the night, they both woke up suddenly and opened their eyes. The fire had died down completely; the room was in total darkness.

'Sshh,' the woman whispered. 'What's that?'

Now the man heard it too: a soft, clear whistling.

'Maybe it's Wooden Boy,' said the woman. She rolled out of bed, lit a lamp and padded over to the bench where they had left the model. 'Oh, it is!' she cried. 'Come here, quickly!'

The husband got up, rubbing his eyes and went across to her. The first thing he noticed was that all the food and water in the miniature dishes had gone. The model was still propped up just where the woman had left it – but, somehow, its eyes seemed to be moving. Could it *see* them...? Surely not... Yet its eyes definitely seemed to have shifted to look at them directly.

'He's coming to life!' the woman cried in delight.

She snatched the model off the bench and held it in her arms, cradling it like a baby, rocking it up and down, talking to it, singing childish songs. Her husband just watched her speechlessly. Eventually, she grew tired of this play and replaced the model on the bench. Then she and her husband went back to bed and both fell into a deep sleep.

When they woke up in the morning, the model had vanished.

They searched all over the house, but there was no sign of it anywhere. They went outside – and at once saw a set of fresh, child-sized footprints in the snow. These led away from their own door towards the snowbound expanse of the open tundra.

Hastily, they pulled on their outdoor parkas and boots, and followed the small footprints. At first they led along the banks of a small creek. Then they turned onto the tundra – all the way to the lonely tree from which, under the moonbeam two nights

434

previously, the man had cut wood to make the model. And there the footprints abruptly stopped.

'Something strange is going on,' said the man. 'I think we ought to turn back.'

His wife agreed. Sad and puzzled, they went home and got on with their everyday lives.

Meanwhile, Wooden Boy kept on walking along the path that the bright moon showed him. He walked right to the edge of the day, to the place where the Sky walls slope down and meet the Earth, thus keeping the daylight in place.

Wooden Boy stopped and looked around. He quickly spotted something rather strange just close to where he was standing in the east. It was a gut-skin cover, fastened over a hole in the Sky wall. As he stared at it, the gut-skin kept moving, bulging in and out, as if some very strong force on the far side was pushing it.

Wooden Boy said: 'Hmm, the Earth is very quiet and boring today. I reckon that's a wind behind there. If I let it out, perhaps it will make the world more lively.'

So he took the wooden knife from his belt and carefully eased it round the rim of the cover, pulling it away. At once, the strong East Wind came blowing through it. Every so often, its force tossed out a live caribou, its hooves scarcely skimming the ground.

Wooden Boy went close to the hole and peered through it. On the far side he saw another world, very similar to our own world here on Earth. 'Don't blow too hard all the time, East Wind my friend,' he shouted. 'Sometimes you should blow more lightly. And sometimes it would be better not to blow at all.' Then he fixed the cover back on the hole and walked on.

He followed the curving line of the Sky wall, and soon reached the southeast. Here too there was a hole in the wall with a gut-skin cover billowing towards him from behind. Now he cut this one open. It released a violent gale, scattering a great debris of caribou, bushes and trees before it. Hastily, he pressed the cover back into place, calling again: 'Don't blow too hard all the time, Southeast Wind, my friend. Sometimes you should blow more lightly. And sometimes it would be better not to blow at all.'

On he walked, along the wall. In the south, he reached another hole. He cut this open as before, and at once was bathed in a warm wind that brought with it the fresh scent of rain, and salt-spray from the distant ocean. Wooden Boy breathed the smells in deeply before he closed it, saying: 'Don't blow too hard all the time, South Wind my friend. Sometimes you should blow more lightly. And sometimes it would be better not to blow at all.'

On he walked, on and on, to the western part of the Sky wall. As soon as he opened the hole there, he was deluged by a violent rainstorm, laced with sleet and rougher salt smells from the sea. Hurriedly, he rammed it shut, shouting out the usual instructions against the tempest's din.

He went on and reached the northwest. When he pulled off the cover there, a squall of cold wind came blasting through, full of snow and ice, chilling him right through to his dry, wooden bones. Breathlessly, he repeated his orders, then forced the cover quickly back into place.

Now Wooden Boy was on the last lap, heading along the curving Sky to the north. As he walked, it grew colder and colder. Every so often, he kept stopping and retracing his steps a short way, then circling back on himself and creeping on, delaying his arrival at the final destination. When he finally came face to face with the last hole in the Sky wall, it was covered in frost. Even with the cover on, his wooden fingers turned numb and could scarcely perform their work. However, eventually, he managed to cut the gut-skin cover away. He was greeted by a hurricane, thick with huge lumps of snow and ice.

'Not too hard!' Wooden Boy bellowed, struggling to make his voice heard. 'I beg you, North Wind my friend, sometimes at least, blow more lightly – and sometimes please don't blow at all!' Then he slammed the last cover shut.

Wooden Boy turned and travelled back the way he had come, away from the Sky wall into the open, walking steadily until he reached the very centre of the Earth. This is the place where it is possible to clearly see all the Sky arches overhead. They are supported by long, slender poles likes those of a conical house, but made of some strange material unknown to human beings.

After that, he went back to the village where he had started from – the place where his own life had begun, thanks to the wishes of the childless woman and the handiwork of the childless man. He walked round it in a wide circle. Then he started going into all the houses, one by one, introducing himself to the people who lived in them, making sure they became his friends. Once this was done,

Wooden Boy went back to the woman and her husband, his foster-parents, and settled down.

He stayed in the village for a long, long time. When his foster-parents died, his friends in the village willingly took care of him. He lived there through countless generations, far longer than anyone else has ever lived. But in the end, he too finally died.

It was Wooden Boy who taught the people how to make masks, and how to use them. And it was his life that inspired the custom for parents to make wooden dolls for their children to play with, just like the one that he was once was, so very long ago.

Nelson: *The Eskimo About Bering Strait,* 1899
Nelson gives no information about the informant, saying only that this story comes from the lower Yukon.

In another part of his book, Nelson gives some interesting information about wooden dolls and masks in the region:

'The girls play with dolls made of ivory or other material, and also have small models of dishes and other women's household utensils, with which they amuse themselves...playing at housekeeping and women's work of various kinds... [They] frequently have a number of dolls varying in size, the smaller ones being made so that they will stand upright... In connection with these toys, girls have also a complete outfit of toy bedding made from the skins of mice or lemmings, small grass mats, toy boots, mittens and clothing, all patterned after those used by the people of the locality.'

About wooden masks he says:

'Shamans are believed to have the power of seeing through the animal mask to the manlike features behind... Masks may also represent totemic animals, and the wearers during the festivals are believed actually to become the creature represented or at least to be endowed with its spiritual essence... Many of the masks from this region are very complicated, having numerous appendages of feathers and carved wood; these either represent limbs or are symbolic. The masks are also painted to represent features or ideas connected with the mythology of the being. Mask festivals are usually held as a species of thanksgiving to the shades and powers of earth, air and water for giving the hunters success.'

The tundra is often afflicted by strong winds.

GRANDMOTHER, TELL A STORY

Canadian Inuit

'Grandmother, tell a story!'

'I don't know any stories; go to sleep.'

'Grandmother, tell a story!'

'Before I can think of a story,
a little lemming without hair
will come out of the corner of the house.
It will crawl under your armpit, *totuto'q*,
and will crawl out again, *totutoto'q*.'

– Unnamed informant, Baffin Island, 1883
(Quoted in Boas: *Eskimo Tales and Songs*, 1897)

438

THE MAN IN THE MOON

Greenland (Kalaallit Nunaat)

There was once a very obstinate man. No one in the world was as obstinate as him. He always had to have his own way in everything. The only person who dared to oppose him was his wife. But although she tried hard to argue against him, it was really quite pointless, because he always got his way over her in the end.

Things came to a head between them at a very sad time – when their baby died. His wife went into mourning according to the time-honoured laws, which meant that she stayed at home and did absolutely nothing except grieve.

But the obstinate man himself just carried on as normal, going out fishing in his kayak as he always did. It infuriated him to see his wife sitting around idly, staring into the fire, weeping and neglecting all her work. At last he couldn't stand it any longer, so he went in to her and said, 'Oi, you lazy woman! Get up and do something useful. My kayak's leaking. Go and re-sew the skins.'

'But it's forbidden to work while I'm in mourning,' she protested.

'Forbidden?' he snorted. 'I'll tell you what's forbidden in *this* house – wasting time. Go down to the shore and mend my kayak, like I told you.'

'No.'

'Go and do it, go and do it, go and do it, go and do it, go and do it – or else! You'll be sorry, I tell you, unless you do it. Go and…'

He went on and on, nagging and threatening, over and over. In the end, the poor woman gave in and went down to the beach to obey her husband, just to shut him up. But she was really scared that the spirits would punish her for breaking the ancient laws.

Sure enough, after she had been working on the kayak for just a short time, something very strange happened. The sinew she was sewing with started to twitch in her hand as if it had a life of its own, making strange noises like someone hissing and muttering. The next moment, she heard a great splash. She looked up from her sewing, heart pounding – and saw an enormous, monstrous dog rise from the deeps and dance on top of the waves.

'Grrr!' he growled at her. 'Woman, why are you sewing? You know it's forbidden to work while you're mourning.'

'Oh dear, I'm so sorry, forgive me,' she called back. 'I *told* my husband I mustn't work, but does he listen to me? – of course not. He never does. He's the most obstinate man who ever lived in all the world!'

The monstrous dog gave a yelp, sprang out of the water onto the beach and raced up to their house. The obstinate man was waiting outside for his wife to finish her task so he could go out sealing. The dog threw threw himself at the man, and started biting him with sharp teeth, tearing claws through the man's thick clothes and into his flesh...

Ho! But the obstinate man wasn't having *that*. He wasn't going to let any creature, or even a spirit, get the better of him. He fought back fiercely, refusing to give up... And although he didn't have vicious teeth or claws of his own, his determination and endurance ensured that the dog eventually dropped dead of exhaustion. The obstinate man stepped back, folded his arms smugly and gazed down at the lifeless body, feeling mighty pleased with himself. As usual, he'd got his own way; he'd won.

However, just then, he heard someone urgently calling his name. He spun round – and was astonished to see a rotund, glowing figure standing there, glaring at him. It was the Moon Man!

'I've come to take revenge on you,' the Moon Man said. 'That dog you just killed was mine. How are you going to make amends?'

'The dog got what he deserved for attacking me,' the obstinate man retorted. 'I'm not making amends.'

'You'd better,' said the Moon Man.

'No,' said the obstinate man.

'In that case,' said the Moon Man, 'I'll have to kill *you* in return.'

He leaped at the obstinate man and started beating him. But, of course, the obstinate man wasn't going to just stand there and take it. For the second time, he fought back fiercely. He caught the

Moon Man by the throat and squeezed him – almost strangling the Moon Man to death!

'Stop!' the Moon Man gasped. 'Don't you realise? If you kill me, the tide won't be able to come in or go out any more, so your wife won't get any pickings off the beach.'

'So what?' the obstinate man retorted. 'I don't care.' And he gripped the Moon Man's throat even tighter.

'Stop, I tell you!' wheezed the Moon Man. 'If you kill me, the seals will stop breeding and you'll run out of meat to eat.'

'So what?' the obstinate man retorted. 'I don't care.' And he gripped the Moon Man's throat tighter still.

By now the Moon Man could barely even squeak: 'If you kill me, there...*argghh*...there'll never be another dawn. So you'll nev... *argghh!*...never see day...daylight again.'

And at last... Well, would you believe it? For the first time in his whole life, the obstinate man actually hesitated. He imagined how awful it would be to live in darkness for ever and ever. So he gave in, and let the Moon Man go.

The Moon Man turned his back and shouted at the corpse of his monstrous dog. At once the dog sprang up, alive again.

'Time to go home,' said the Moon Man. He whistled and many more dogs appeared out of nowhere, running towards him. As each one reached him, the Moon Man tossed it up into the air – until a whole team of sledge dogs was hovering above them.

'Right,' said the Moon Man, 'I'll be on my way.'

'No you won't,' cried the obstinate man, 'not until you've told me how *I* can travel up to the Moon myself. I want to follow you up there and pay you a visit.'

The Moon Man sighed and said, 'Oh, all right, if you must. All you have to do is make your dogs fly like mine, and they'll easily find the way. But let me warn you to take great care. On the journey, you'll have to pass an enormous rock that blocks your path. Make sure you drive your sledge the long, winding way right round it, the *dark* way.'

'Why?'

'Because anyone who drives past the rock on the straight, sunny side gets his heart ripped out,' said the Moon Man. And with those words he got on his sledge, cracked his whip and drove up to the Sky.

The obstinate man stared after him for a moment, then hurried home to prepare for his journey to the Moon. His wife asked what he was doing and where he was planning to go, and he told her.

'You'll never manage to get up to the Moon!' she sniffed.

'Of course I will,' he said. 'I can do anything I want.'

He called out his dogs and started tossing them up in the air, one by one. Straight away, they all crashed heavily back down to Earth.

'I told you it's impossible,' said his wife.

'No it isn't,' said the obstinate man. 'It's because they've been lying around inside doing nothing for so long, just like you; their dirty coats are weighing them down. I'll soon deal with that.'

He drove the dogs to the sea and forced them all into the icy water.

'Poor things, they'll freeze to death!' squealed his wife.

'No they won't.'

Every time the dogs came out shivering, he pushed them back in until, finally, they were all gleaming clean. Then he tried tossing them up in the air again, and this time, they were light enough to stay up there.

'See?' he said. 'I told you I could do it. Now, even while I'm away, make sure you do as I say, and get on with your work.'

'I keep telling you, I mustn't,' said his wife.

'Huh!' said the obstinate man. 'If I don't find you busy when I come back, there'll be trouble.'

He called the dogs down, harnessed them to his sledge and jumped into it. With a crack of his whip, the dogs strained – and the next moment they began to pull the sledge, with the obstinate man inside it, up off the ground, towards the Sky. His wife watched him go, shaking her head in frustration and disbelief.

The dogs pulled the sledge on and on, up and up. After a long while, the obstinate man saw an enormous rock looming ahead. He realised it was the one the Moon Man had told him about, with that warning to avoid the easy trail that passed on the sunny side. He could see an alternative trail leading through shadows into the pitch darkness. It looked winding and forbidding, most uninviting.

'I'm not going that horrible way,' the obstinate man said to himself. 'I don't have to do what *he* said.'

So he drove the sledge straight towards the sunlight. As he drew closer, he heard someone singing drum songs, and saw an old woman. She was hard at work sharpening her knife and scraping it rhythmically so that it hummed in time with her song.

'Halt!' she shouted when she saw him. 'You can't pass here.'

'Oh yes I can,' said the obstinate man. 'You can't stop me.' He jumped off his sledge and tried to knock her over. But the old woman raised her knife at him and, the next moment, he fainted.

When he returned to his senses, he'd come over all weak, and his chest felt hollow and painful − for there was a gaping hole in it. Yes, that old woman had ripped out his heart, just as the Moon Man had warned. For the second time, the man found himself wondering whether being stubborn was always a good thing.

He had no choice now but to continue his journey the long, dark, winding way. He was surprised to find that, actually, this got him to the Moon in no time. As soon as he arrived, he saw the Moon Man himself, waiting to greet him.

'You were a long time,' said the Moon Man.

'I know,' said the obstinate man. 'It's because I thought I knew better than you, so I ignored your advice and took the trail that you explicitly warned me against. And just like you said, I've lost my heart, and I feel awful.'

'Come inside,' said the Moon Man. 'I'll sort you out.' He led the obstinate man into his house. A pure black sealskin was spread out on the floor. 'Lie down on this.'

The obstinate man was about to refuse on principle, but then he realised that would be stupid. So he lay on the sealskin as he'd been told. The Moon Man nodded and went out. When he came back in, he was carrying the obstinate man's heart, which he had retrieved from the old woman. He stuffed it back into the obstinate man's chest, and sewed it up neatly.

The obstinate man quickly felt completely better and started to sit up.

'Not yet,' said the Moon Man. 'Stay there, roll over onto your belly, so I can show you something.'

He pulled up one of the stones from the floor nearby, revealing a big hole in the Sky underneath. 'Look,' he pointed down through it. 'There's your home on Earth down there. What can you see?'

The obstinate man peered down. 'Oh, there's my wife. Good, she's obeying the orders I gave before I left.' She was indeed: sitting on the bench, busily plaiting sinews to make sewing thread.

'What else can you see?' said the Moon Man.

'Smoke.'

'From the fire?'

'Hmm…no,' said the obstinate man, 'the fire's only smouldering. It's very strange: the smoke seems to be rising from my wife's body.'

'Why do you think that is?' said the Moon Man.

The obstinate man shook his head.

'It's evil rising from her,' said the Moon Man, 'because she's disobeyed the sacred laws by working while she's still in mourning.'

'That's disgraceful!' said the obstinate man. 'She shouldn't be doing that.'

'She knows she shouldn't,' said the Moon Man. 'She's only doing it because *you* forced her to.'

The obstinate man realised that the Moon Man knew everything, and felt very ashamed.

The obstinate man stayed on the Moon for quite some time. On another day, the Moon Man lifted up a stone under the passageway into his house, and let his guest look down it. The obstinate man saw a very strange country below, overflowing with big walruses – so many that some were sitting on the others' backs.

'It's a great joy to catch such animals,' said the Moon Man. He demonstrated by tossing a harpoon at one of the walruses, which died instantly, and then hauling it up by a rope. He told the obstinate man that he could take the carcass with him; and then showed his guest the way home, down to Earth.

And the good news is this: after the obstinate man arrived safely home, he was totally changed. He stopped being obstinate, never asked his wife to break laws or go against custom again, and let her do whatever she wanted.

Rasmussen: *Eskimo Folk-Tales*, 1921

Rasmussen was born and raised by a Danish missionary family in western Greenland; his mother was half-Greenlandic and he spoke the language fluently, enabling him to collect myths and folk tales verbatim directly from local storytellers during several expeditions around the country in the early 20th century. He gives the location of this one as southeastern Greenland, an area that he first visited in 1904.

The moon is a very common theme in Arctic stories. A widespread myth tells of its origin as follows: a girl is seduced by a secret lover, under cover of darkness. Desperate to find out who he is, she smears his back with soot while they are embracing – and discovers to her horror when the lamps are lit that it is her own brother. In her disgust, she cuts off her breasts and orders him to eat them, since he cannot control his desire for her. This arouses the brother's incestuous passion even more, and he pursues her. As she flees, she rises to the sky and is transformed into the sun; her brother, chasing her, becomes the moon.

Another myth also tells of a visit to the Moon Man's house, this time by a shaman, making a 'spirit journey' whilst in a trance. There he is forced to watch a comical dance performed by the Moon Man's wife, and warned to resist laughing at her, for if he does, she will cut out his intestines. He rises to the challenge, and is rewarded with a gift of a deer and a seal to send down ahead of his return to earth. One version mentions that the Moon Man's dog, called Tirie´tiang, is 'dappled white and red'.

In a note to material collected from western Alaska, Edward Nelson wrote in 1899:

'A shaman…told me that a great chief lives in the moon who is visited now and then by shamans, who always go to him two at a time, as one man is ashamed to go alone. In the moon live all kinds of animals that are on the earth, and when any animal becomes scarce here the shamans go up to the chief in the moon and, if he is pleased with the offerings that have been made to him, he gives them one of the animals that they wish for, and they bring it down to the earth and turn it loose, after which its kind becomes numerous again.

'[This] shaman…had never been to the moon himself, but he knew [one] who had been there. He had been up only as high as the sky… by flying like a bird and found that the sky was a land like the earth, only that the grass grew hanging downwards and was filled with snow. When the wind blows up there it rustles the grass stems, loosening particles of snow which fall down to the earth as a snowstorm. When he was up near the sky he saw a great many small, round lakes in the grass, and these shine at night to make the stars.'

A Baffin Island story tells of an abused orphan boy who desperately prays for help. The Moon Man comes down and beats him severely; not as a punishment, but to imbue him with supernatural strength, enabling him to overcome his oppressors.

The Alutiit of Alaska have a moon myth which resembles the 'star husband' stories common in other parts of the continent (see THE WOMAN WHO MARRIED A STAR, p. 42). Two girls fantasise about marrying the Moon. He comes down to fetch one and makes her his wife. Although he allows her free run of the Sky, he warns her never to look under a set of curtains. Inevitably, she disobeys, and under each curtain finds a different moon in a different phase. She sticks the full moon on the side of her face, but is unable to pull it off. The Moon is not angry with her, but allows her to continue wearing it and help him in his work.

SONG OF A MAN WAITING FOR A SEAL TO RISE

Canadian Inuit

I heard it diving
suddenly into the water.
It is difficult to catch.

Now it is at the beach,
where the other man is,
who wants very much to see it rise.

I thought so!
It has been tired of coming up,
and after I am gone it will show itself.

– Unnamed informant, Baffin Island, 1883
(Quoted in Boas: *Eskimo Tales and Songs*, 1897)

THE GIANT

Alaskan Eskimo (Yup'ik)

There was a woman whose husband was constantly beating her. He abused her so brutally, that at last she decided her only option was to flee him. So one winter's night, while he was out with the other men, she dressed in her warmest clothes, packed a small bundle of food and walked off.

There was no moon and there were no stars; it was very dark. She hurried through the village to the tundra as fast as she could, keeping away from all the houses, for she was terrified that her husband would chase her. She headed towards the north, trudging slowly on through the thick snow. After many days out in the wilderness, she had no food left, so she survived by eating snow. It grew colder and colder. The constant wind lashed against her, like her husband's cruel blows.

As she walked on through the dim wintry gloom, she suddenly saw a curious-looking hill looming ahead, with five rounded peaks on its crest. She climbed to the top and stood looking around, trembling with hunger and weariness.

'What a strange place,' she said aloud. 'Those five small peaks over there look to me just like toes, as if I'm standing on the main part of a foot. I must be getting delirious from the cold.'

She trudged over to a hollow between two of the peaks. It was quite sheltered from the wind there. She knelt down, scraped away all the snow, curled up on the soft grass underneath it, and quickly fell asleep.

In the morning she woke up feeling refreshed, so she walked on to the next hill, way ahead in the distance. She reached it just as the darkness thickened, and clambered down to a big cave

447

underneath, where she laid her makeshift bed. As she went to sleep, she thought drowsily, 'I must stop imagining things. This cave reminds me of the hollow under an enormous bent knee.'

Again, she slept then walked on. The next night she stopped under another hill, and couldn't help thinking that the shape was very similar to an outsized thigh. The following evening, she camped in a deep pit – and was struck by its uncanny resemblance to an outsized navel. She spent the night after that in a snug spot between two breast-shaped hillocks. She was sleeping much better now, and was able to walk quite a long way the next day, bedding down for that night in a hollow that was both spongy and mysteriously warm.

When she woke up the next morning, she was greeted by an alarming, very loud noise: *b...b...boo-boom-boom!* It seemed to be coming from underneath her feet. She jumped up in shock, anticipating an earthquake. But when she heard it again, she realised it was actually a very deep, loud man's voice. Straining her ears, she managed to make out its words: 'Who are you? Human beings are normally too afraid to come near me. What has driven you here?'

At first the woman couldn't speak. But then she remembered she had nothing in the world to lose, so she found courage and told the disembodied stranger all about the cruelties of her husband. 'I couldn't stand the way he treated me any more,' she finished, 'so I ran away. I've been wandering in the snow for days; I've lost count of how many. I've completely run out of food.'

The voice boomed again: 'I pity you. You are welcome to stay here with me as long as you wish. But let me warn you, don't sleep near my mouth again.'

'Your *mouth*?' the woman cried.

'Yes indeed,' said the voice. 'That is where you are standing. I've had to breathe very gently all the time that you were lying there, for fear of blowing you away.'

Then at last the woman understood. For the last five days, she had been travelling not on the tundra, but on the body of the great giant, Kin'ak!

'You are hungry,' said the giant. 'I'll get you something to eat.'

The next moment, the daylight was obscured by what seemed to be a great black cloud. As it came closer, she realised it was actually the giant's hand moving about. It spread open, and dropped a freshly killed caribou by her feet.

'Here you are. Eat this.'

There was some brushwood lying close by. The woman gathered a big bundle of it, lit a fire and roasted the caribou on top. In no time at all it was cooked – the most delicious meal she had ever tasted. When she could eat no more, the giant said:

'You must be wondering which is the best place for you to rest on my body. I suggest you go into my beard, the part where it grows most thickly. Hurry up and move there straight away. For I have a load of hoar-frost caught in my lungs and it's making me very uncomfortable: I need to cough to clear it.'

The woman barely had time to reach the giant's beard before everything jerked. There was a great roaring noise, and a furious wind came rushing over her head, accompanied by a blinding blizzard. It spread out across the tundra below, then cleared in an instant.

The next day, Kin'ak said, 'If you wish, you may use some of my hairs to build yourself a house.'

'Where shall I build it?' she asked.

'Oh, anywhere on my face, so long as it's not near my mouth.'

By now she knew her way around the giant's head, and understood how the various slopes and bumps she walked over made up his facial features. She chose a spot on the left side of his nose. Then she plucked some hairs from his moustache and, taking care not to hurt him, used them to build herself a very cosy little hut, close to one of his nostrils.

The giant was very kind and said she could stay on him as long as she wanted. Whenever he saw that she was hungry, he would reach out his great hand and catch her a caribou, deer or seal – whatever she fancied. He also caught wolves, wolverines and other fur-bearing animals, so that she could use their skins to make herself new clothes. When she was cold, he told her to pluck hairs from the side of his face for kindling.

One day, after the woman had lived on Kin'ak for quite some time, he said to her, 'My dear, I have grown stiff and uncomfortable from lying so still for so long in one place. I need to turn over. But I can't while you're living on me, because it would crush you. So I must ask you to get off me for a while. Have you ever thought of returning home?'

449

'I would dearly like to,' she said. 'Only I am so afraid that my husband will start to beat me again. I might not manage to escape him next time.'

'Is there no one in the village to protect you?'

'No.'

'Then *I* will protect you,' said the giant. 'Now listen. You know those animal skins you've been collecting? Go and cut off all the ear tips, and put them in your basket.'

'Why?' the woman asked.

'You will find out when the time comes. For now, I have one more thing to tell you: if ever you are in danger, just call my name and I will come to help you. Right, is your basket full? Good. Stand in front of my mouth.'

The woman did so. At once, a great storm of wind and fine snow blew up. She found herself driven helplessly before it, until she fell into an exhausted sleep…

When she woke up and opened her eyes, she was astonished to find herself lying on the ground just outside her own village. How familiar it looked! Was she really there? Yes indeed, there was the sound of the dogs howling.

Hastily, she crept away and hid until darkness fell. Then she slipped into her old storehouse, put the basket of ear tips inside it, closed the door, and went into her house. Her husband was sitting in there all alone. When he saw her walk in, he gave a yelp of astonishment and delight: 'Wife! I thought you were dead!'

'I could have been,' she answered. 'You beat me so hard, you almost killed me, you brute!' Then she told him how she had fled and wandered in the wilderness until she met the kindly giant who had helped her.

'I'm very glad to see you back safely,' said her husband.

'And…?' she asked.

'And I swear I'll always treat you kindly from now on,' he promised.

So the woman moved back in with him.

That night while they slept, each of the ear tips she had brought from the giant was transformed into a complete animal skin. The next morning, they found the storehouse overflowing with valuable furs. Her husband traded these and became very rich. This new-found wealth brought him popularity and respect, so that he became one of the village headmen.

In due course the woman gave birth to a son. She called him Kin'ak, in honour of the giant. He grew rapidly, and was soon stronger and more agile than all the other boys.

So for a while, everything went really well. But as time went by, the husband returned to his old ways. He became just as bad-tempered and aggressive as he used to be; no, even worse.

One day, he fell into a fury, cornered his wife, grabbed a huge stick and started to beat her with it mercilessly. She dodged past him, raced down the entrance tunnel and out of the house. But as she stepped outside, she slipped on the ice and fell heavily. Her husband rushed after her, cursing and swinging back the stick to strike her again...

Just in time, she remembered the giant's promise.

'Kin'ak!' she screamed, 'Kin'ak, help me!'

Within moments, a blinding blast of wind blew up, swirling around the house, sweeping away everything before it. When it finally cleared, she found herself alone.

For the giant's windstorm had blown that brutal man right to the end of the Earth, never to be seen again.

Nelson: *The Eskimo About Bering Strait,* 1899
In the source, the story continues with another, rather sad episode. The son grows up to be as ill-tempered and violent as his father. After killing several men in the village, his mother persuades him to leave. Like her, he walks out into the wilderness, and he too finds his way to the giant's body. He lives there quietly until he breaks the rule not to go near the giant's mouth; the angry giant blasts him out to meet the same fate as his father.

Several other stories about domestic violence were collected in the Arctic, suggesting that it may have been a fairly common problem, but also frowned upon. Another Alaskan story tells of a woman fleeing her cruel husband and ending up on an island alongside a man who has fled his abusive wife; they survive when a jellyfish mysteriously brings them food. From Greenland comes a story of a woman who walks into the sea to escape her violent husband. She lives on the sea bottom and gives birth to their son, who grows up to take revenge on his father's people. See also THE MAN IN THE MOON (p. 439).

A FESTIVAL SONG

Canadian Inuit

The whale!
The white whale!
The hooded seal!
The salmon!
The caribou!
The ground seal!
The seal!
The walrus!
The polar bear!
The fox!
The bird!
The wolf!
The bone!

– Sung as a chorus, by people assembled at a religious festival
in a village 'singing house' on Baffin Island in 1883
(Quoted in Boas: *Eskimo Tales and Songs*, 1894)

SEDNA'S FINGERS

Canadian Inuit

A very beautiful young woman called Sedna lived alone with her widowed father. Many men wanted to marry her, and her father urged her to choose the best of them. However, she was so proud and particular that she turned every one of them down.

One spring, when the ice was breaking up, a Fulmar came to woo her. He flew over the melting sea, fixed her with his intense gaze and squawked: 'Come with me, my love. Let me take you to live in the wondrous Country of Birds.'

'What can you offer me if I do?' asked Sedna haughtily.

'Perfection,' was Fulmar's answer. 'In Bird Country there is no such thing as cold or hunger. If you marry me, your pot will always overflow with meat. Your home will be in a tent thickly covered with the warmest skins. Your bed will be piled with the softest white bear furs. My friends will pluck out their lightest down feathers with their own beaks, and weave them into tunics for you to wear. Your lamp will always burn brightly, full of oil. You shall have everything your heart desires!'

'He's lying,' whispered her father. 'Ignore him, resist him.'

But Sedna could not help herself; she was enchanted by his smooth white head and neatly folded wings. No man had ever courted her with such shining promises before. For the first time ever, her heart melted.

'Very well,' she said, 'I will come with you.'

So she said farewell to her father and flew with Fulmar over vast, lonely stretches of sea. So far, so difficult! But at last she arrived in Bird Country – only to discover she had been cruelly deceived.

For her new home turned out to be on a narrow ledge of rock, balanced precariously high above the waves. All day and all night her ears were battered by the deafening cries of countless birds, swooping and screeching around her. Instead of the promised warm hides, her tent was covered with tattered fish skins, constantly billowing in and out with the ravaging wind. Instead of soft fur, her bed was made of stiff walrus skins that scratched her into an agony of sores. Worst of all, she was offered not a single scrap of meat – only meagre leftovers of stringy, rotten fish. How she suffered!

In despair, Sedna made a song about her sorrows. Every day, she sang it, begging the wind to carry it over the water to her father:

'Aya!
Oh dear Father, hear me!
The birds despise me,
treat me cruelly,
feed me food that's foul and putrid,
batter me with ice and wind.
Surely you will come to save me?
Take me, Father, how I beg you,
in your boat across the water!
Aya, fetch me safely home!'

Months passed. Her father did not come. A whole year passed.

At last, when spring warmed the tundra and the sea, her father heard her calling. He sighed deeply and shook his head. How could he ignore his own flesh and blood? So he left the comforts of his own home and paddled far across the sea to Fulmar's distant land. There he climbed the steep cliff to Sedna's flimsy tent.

'I am so relieved to see you, Father!' she cried. 'I bitterly regret my past arrogance. Have you come to rescue me?'

'I have,' the old man answered. 'For I see with my own eyes how your husband has abused you. Though you have brought this on yourself through your own foolishness, I will take revenge.'

He lay in wait for Fulmar's return. As soon as the great bird landed, the father struck him dead. Then he helped Sedna down the cliff to his boat, and sped away with her across the waves.

Shortly afterwards, the other birds found Fulmar's lifeless body and saw that Sedna had fled. They cried out their grief, over and over, just as all seabirds still cry and mourn today. Then they set off in pursuit of Sedna and her father. Soon they saw them, paddling frantically to escape.

'Revenge stokes revenge!' the birds cried. 'Storm, arise and help us!'

At once, the sea stirred into monstrous waves.

'They're trying to destroy us!' screamed Sedna.

Now her father looked at his wayward daughter with new eyes, thinking of the trouble she had caused. He remembered how she had spurned all the excellent young men who had courted her, how she had ignored his wise advice and thrown in her lot with a stranger. In the darkness of his fear, he thought, 'I shall offer her to the sea. Then maybe it will spare my own life in return.'

So he seized Sedna and flung her overboard.

She sank at once, then quickly rose again, swam urgently to the boat and clung to the gunwale, her fingers stiff and blue with cold.

'No!' she screamed. 'Don't let me die! Help me, Father, save me!'

The father was overwhelmed by panic and fury. Grimly, he showed his answer – by pulling out his knife and slicing off the top joints of Sedna's fingers. The bloody tips dropped into the sea…

There, the water bloated them. Each one grew bigger and bigger, long and fat and grey. Each one sprouted small eyes, a huge mouth and a pair of flippers. They skimmed off through the waves, jumping and diving.

The first whales.

Sedna was still bobbing in the water close by her father's boat, screaming and crying. She clung to the frame with the broken remains of her hands, begging again, 'Help me, Father, save me!'

But still the father had no pity. This time, he sliced off the second joints; and when she clung on with her finger stumps, he cut those off too. The fragments of her pale, bleeding flesh tumbled into the seething waves. These too grew and transformed into living creatures. Short, sleek fur spread across them, mottled like shadows on white sand. The ends inflated into round faces, fringed with whiskers. For a long moment their big, liquid eyes stared at Sedna darkly; then they slipped under the surface and sped away.

The first seals.

The birds, soaring overhead, looked down, saw the father's callous work and thought that Sedna was drowned. So they called off the storm and flew back to Bird Country.

At last, the father took pity on Sedna. He allowed her to climb back into the boat, and took her home.

Thus Sedna lived again with her father. But hatred for what he had done to her grew in her heart.

455

One night, while the old man slept, she set her dogs on him. When he awoke, he found she had caused them to gnaw his hands and feet right off. He roared a string of curses at both Sedna and the dogs. As his words rang out, the Earth split open and swallowed up Sedna, her father and the dogs.

They all went down to Adlivun, the country under the sea where people's souls go after they die; and Sedna became its mistress.

Boas: *The Central Eskimo,* 1888
Boas says that this myth, from Baffin Island, also appears in an old song, with slightly different details. He says that since she descended to Adlivun:

'...she has been the mistress of the country... She has a large house, in which no deerskins are found. There she lives with her father, each occupying one side of it. The father, who is unable to move, lies on the ledge and is covered with old skins. In the entrance across the threshold lies Sedna's dog, watching her house. Like her, the father has only one eye, and he never moves from his place while in the house. The dead, who are seized by Sedna's father, Anguta, are carried to this dwelling. The dog moves aside only a little, just enough to allow the souls to pass. They have to stay in this dismal abode during a whole year, lying by the side of Anguta, who pinches them.'

Boas quotes an earlier study which says that her father, Anguta, is apparently the supreme being, who created the Earth, sea and heavenly bodies. In that source, his daughter, Sedna:

'...is supposed to have created all things having life, animal and vegetable. She is regarded also as the protecting divinity of the Inuit people. To her their supplications are addressed; to her their offerings are made; while most of their religious rites and superstitious observances have reference to her.'

A number of similar Arctic stories feature a different 'animal husband', most commonly a dog. A widely reported one tells of a woman who has ten children with her canine husband; half are human children and the rest puppies. Because the children are all very greedy, their grandfather forces them to live on an island, but allows the dog to carry food across to them in boots slung around its neck. One day the grandfather fills these boots with stones, so that the dog drowns. In one version particularly reminiscent of the Sedna myth, the grandfather throws the mother overboard and, as she tries to cling on, cuts off her fingers, which are transformed to seals and whales.

TRULY THE WORLD IS GREAT

Greenland (Kalaallit Nunaat)

Once there were two men who desired to travel round the world,
that they might tell others what was the manner of it.
This was in the days when there were people in all the lands.
Now we grow fewer and fewer. Evil and sickness have come upon
us. See how I drag my life along, unable to stand upon my feet.

The two men made themselves cups of musk ox horn,
each making a cup for himself from the same beast's head.
And they set out, each going away from the other,
that they might go by different ways and meet again some day.
They travelled with sledges,
and chose land to stay and live upon each summer.
It took them a long time to get round the world.
They had children, and they grew old,
and then their children also grew old, until the parents
were so old that they could not walk, but the children led them.

And at last one day, they met.
Of their drinking horns there was but the handle left,
so many times had they drunk water by the way,
scraping the horn against the ground as they filled them.
They had been young at their starting,
and now they were old men, led by their children.
'Truly, the world is great indeed,' they said when they met.

– Qilerneq, 'the oldest man in the tribe', northwest Greenland
(Quoted in Rasmussen: *The People of the Polar North*, 1908)

GHOST COUNTRY

Alaskan Eskimo (Yup'ik)

There was a girl who became seriously ill. She got worse and worse
– so ill that she hardly knew what was going on around her. At last
she fell into the blissful oblivion of sleep...

But suddenly, she was woken up by someone shaking her, and a
familiar voice saying urgently, 'Get up, get up! You don't need to
sleep any more, you're dead!'

She opened her eyes and saw she was lying in a grave box.
Standing beside it was her grandfather – her *dead* grandfather. He
held out his hand and said, 'Here, let me help you out of the box.'

She climbed out and found she felt perfectly well – in fact, much
better than she had felt for a long time. But where was she?

Her grandfather said, 'Don't worry, everyone's confused when
they first arrive here in Ghost Country. But look around my dear,
and tell me if you see anything familiar.'

She gazed about in all directions. They were standing on the
edge of a village, but it looked quite different from any place she
had ever seen before; and much bigger too, extending right up to
the horizon. Then she noticed some men and women wandering
around the houses, and gave a squeal of surprise.

'Oh, yes! I recognise some of those people over there. They're all
from our village, people who've died.'

'Exactly,' said the old man. 'Now, come with me and take a look
around.'

They entered the strange village and wandered about for a bit.
Then her grandfather said, 'I want to show you something. You see
that house over there? Go into it, go on.'

She did. Inside, sat an old woman whose face was twisted with anger. Instead of greeting the girl, she spat at her and screeched: 'What do you want, what are you after, sneaking in here, you dirty little cur? Get out – before I *beat* you out!' The old one seized a wooden club and raised it as if she were about to strike the girl... who screamed, cowered, then turned and ran out in terror as fast as she could.

She burst into tears and went back to her grandfather. 'Who was that nasty old hag?' she wept. 'Why did you send me in to her?'

'So that you could learn,' the old man answered. 'In this village there are many dog ghosts. They take revenge on people who have been cruel to living dogs. Those who experience their anger are being punished for the suffering of dogs beaten by people in the other world. Now come along, I have more to show you.'

They walked together out onto the tundra and soon came to another village, with a large community house in the centre. As they drew close, the girl saw a very curious sight. A man was lying on his side, with grass growing up through all his joints. He could wave his hands and feet about, but it was impossible for him to get up.

'Who is he?' the girl whispered. 'Why is he suffering like that?'

'Ah,' said her grandfather, 'when he was alive on Earth, he used to constantly pull up grass stems and chew them; this is his punishment.'

She shook her head and stared at the grass man in pity for some time, then turned back to her grandfather. But he had disappeared.

What should she do? The path she was standing on stretched onwards to more houses in the distance, so she decided to continue along it. However, she did not get very far before she found the way completely barred by a deep, rushing river. She looked up it and she looked down it, but could not see anywhere to cross in either direction. She was so frustrated, that she started to cry again. Her tears fell into the river, where they mingled with the tears of people on Earth, who were weeping for their dead loved ones.

When at last she dried her eyes, she saw something floating on the river towards her. It was a great mass of straw and rubbish, bobbing up and down on the surface. It came level and drifted in to wedge itself between the banks on either side. Cautiously, she tested it with one foot. It held her weight, so she walked right onto it and used it like a bridge to cross to the opposite side. Once she was on dry land again, the mass of straw disintegrated and vanished.

She walked towards the next village. As she drew near, she found herself surrounded by many ghosts. They came crowding around her, whispering and hissing:

'*Ssss, Ssss*. We smelled you coming.'

'*Hhhhh.* Who are you?'

'*Ssss, Ssss*. Where did you spring from?'

Their shadowy fingers reached out touching her clothing, pulling it towards them, examining it closely.

'*Aahh.* We see your totem marks.'

'Now we know, *hhhhh,* we know who you are.'

She stood frozen to the spot; and at that very moment heard her grandfather's voice again, calling: 'Is she there? Where is she? Ah, I see her.' The comforting shape of his ghost came drifting rapidly towards her. He seized her hand again and led her into another house.

And – oh joy! – inside that one, she found her own dead grandmother.

'Come in my dear,' this ghost called, 'come and sit by me. Now then, you must be thirsty, eh? Would you like a drink?'

The girl nodded. There were many tubs of water standing by one of the walls, mostly of a very weird design. However, one was identical to the water tubs in her own village. Her grandmother pointed towards it and said, 'Only drink from that one, my dear, for it contains water from our own Yukon River back home.'

'But there's not much left in it,' said the girl.

'No matter. Don't even think of drinking from any of the other tubs, for they are all filled with ghost water.'

'How did you manage to bring the Yukon water here, Grandmother?'

'It was given to me by my son, your father, at one of the Festivals for the Dead. He also gave me all this lovely deer fat. My dear, you look hungry. Have a piece of it to eat.'

After she had refreshed herself, the girl felt much better. 'May I ask you a question please, Grandmother?' she asked.

The old woman nodded.

'How did Grandfather know I was coming here? Why was he waiting for me when I opened my eyes?'

'That's because, as you were dying, you thought about him,' her grandmother answered. 'Your thought was heard by everyone here in Ghost Country. As soon as your grandfather knew you were on your way he went to wait for you, so he could welcome you and show you around.'

Back on Earth, in the country of the living, it was time for the Festival of the Dead. As usual, the girls' home village sent two messengers to invite the neighbouring villagers to the festival. It was a long journey, and the messengers didn't arrive until nightfall. There was a drum dance going on inside the community house. The messengers went in and delivered their invitation.

They didn't realise – nobody realised – that the ghost of the dead girl was sitting on a bench amongst the people at the drum dance, in-between the ghosts of her two dead grandparents. All three were invisible, which is why nobody could see them. When the messengers returned to their own village the following day, the three invisible ghosts followed them.

The Festival of the Dead began. The three ghosts stood watching almost right the way through. However, towards the end, they got up to go outside the community house, to await the ceremony of dressing the dead people's namesakes. On the way, the ghost-girl slipped and fell over. When she got up, her ghostly grandparents had vanished. She stood in the corner of the entrance passage under a lamp, expecting them to return any moment; but they did not. Meanwhile, the living people began to troop out from the festival, all dressed up in splendid new clothes.

When most of them had gone, an old man, one of the living, came out, tottering along with a walking stick. As he passed through the entrance, he looked up – and saw the ghost-girl in the shadows, hovering a full handspan above the ground.

'Whoah!' he cried. 'Is it *you*? Surely not! Everyone knows you died.'

She did not reply.

The old man hurried back into the community house, where many of the other men were still gathered, and shouted excitedly: 'Come quickly! There's the strangest creature in the passageway. She looks exactly like that girl who died recently – and she's floating.'

The other men came crowding out to gawp at her, carrying lamps. 'It must be her ghost,' they cried.

'Her parents will be so glad to see her.'

461

'Come on, let's try and get her along to show them.'

They all waved their hands, shooing the ghost across the village towards the house where the girl's parents lived. Somehow, they managed to drive her down the entrance passage and right inside. But as her startled parents gazed at the spectre, all the colour faded from the ghost girl's face, and her body began to shrink and shrivel away. They pressed her to sit down; but by the time she had managed to do so, there was nothing left of her but a heap of transparent skin and bones.

However, that was not the end of it. For at the festival another girl from the same village had been given the dead one's name. Early the next morning, she too died. Then *her* spirit went away to Ghost Country, to take the place of the first girl, the one who had died before.

After that, the ghost of the first dead girl came back to life. With each day that passed, she became stronger and stronger. In the end she became like any normal human being; and she went on to live healthily and happily for many years.

Nelson: *The Eskimo About Bering Strait,* 1899
Nelson says that this story:
'is known all along the lower Yukon, and was related by an old shaman who said that it occurred several generations ago. It is believed by the Eskimo to have been an actual occurrence, and it gives a fair idea of their belief of the condition of the shade after death.'

He gives some interesting information about a Festival of the Dead that he observed at a village he calls St Michael, as follows:

'Every year the [Festival of the Dead] is held during the latter part of November or early in December. It is repeated two days after the Bladder Feast of autumn and just before the beginning of the salmon fishing in spring. It is given for the sole purpose of making offerings of food, water and clothing to the shades of those recently deceased, and of offerings to the dead who have not yet been honoured by one of the great festivals. The makers of this feast are the nearest relatives of those who have died during the preceding year.'

Describing a communal festival he says:

'Those making the festival plant...stakes of invitation bearing... symbols before the graves of those to be honoured, and by these graves are sung songs of invitation to the shades, informing them of the approaching festival. It is said that…the shades are in their graves and come thence to the 'kashim' [community house], where they assemble in the fire pit, under the floor. At the proper time they ascend…entering and possessing the bodies of their namesakes in the kashim, and thus obtaining for themselves the offerings of food, drink, or clothing which are made to these namesakes for the benefit of the deceased. It is by means of such offerings that the shade is believed to obtain the supplies necessary for its wants in the land of the dead. When the offerings have been made and the songs concluded, the shades are sent back to their abiding place by stamping upon the floor… All are supposed to take part in this festival whose nearest relatives have died, and in proportion to the care and generosity exercised on these occasions the shade is made happy and comfortable.

'These Eskimo fear to die unless they have someone to make offerings to their memory, and childless persons generally adopt a child so that their shade may not be forgotten at the festivals, as people who have no one to make offerings for them are supposed to suffer great destitution in the other world. For this reason it is regarded as the severest punishment possible for a shade to have these rites neglected by its relatives. When a person has been very much disliked, his shade is sometimes purposely ignored.'

He explains the role of a deceased person's namesake as follows:

'When a child is born it is given the name of the last person who died in the village, or the name of a deceased relative who may have lived in another place. The child thus becomes the namesake and representative of the dead person at the feast to the dead.'

Interior of a Cree Indian Tent
Aquatint print by Edward Francis Finden, 1820

MYTHS OF THE SUBARCTIC

PEOPLE OF THE SUBARCTIC

Canada:
Much of Alberta, British Columbia, Manitoba,
Newfoundland & Labrador, Northwest Territories,
Ontario, Quebec, Saskatchewan and Yukon.
Southern part of Nunavat.

United States:
Interior of Alaska

The Subarctic is North America's largest cultural region, extending across the whole continent from west to east. Much of it is forested – mainly pine, spruce, fir, aspen, willow and birch – giving way to open tundra in the north. There is water everywhere: lakes of all sizes, ponds, streams, swamps, bogs and mighty rivers. Vast areas are flat or undulating, but there are also mountains and plateaus, particularly in the west. Winter in the Subarctic is long and severe; summer is short and plagued by insects. At the turn of the 20th century, the population density was low and widely scattered.

The Subarctic peoples were traditionally nomadic hunters, fishers and gatherers. Depending on where they lived, they hunted or trapped bear, beaver, buffalo, caribou, deer, hare, marmot, moose, muskrat, otter, rabbit, squirrel, wild sheep, wild goat and wildfowl such as ducks and geese. Game was brought down with bows and arrows or spears, or by driving the animals into corrals. Fish were caught with weirs, traps, fish hooks, nets and spears; in winter, fishing was conducted through the ice on lakes. Salmon was the most abundant species, but trout, char, whitefish and others were also harvested. Meat and fish were preserved by drying, smoking and processing into pemmican, stored in caches mounted on posts. These foods were supplemented by the gathering of wild roots and berries. The prevailing diet was high in calories and fat, ideally suited to the harsh climate. It is recorded that amongst the Chipewyan, favourite delicacies were caribou tongue, caribou marrow fat, beaver tail and moose nose.

During autumn and winter, people lived and hunted in small extended family groups of up to 30 people, which often combined into larger hunting bands. It was normally the men's task to hunt, whilst the women made camp. During the summer, separate bands would gather together on the shores of lakes and rivers for communal fishing, socialising, exchanging goods, singing, dancing and games. There was no formal political organisation and the only acknowledged leaders were for group hunting or spiritual activities. The bands, which were often linked by intermarriage, were informal and sometimes temporary associations. Friendly bands sometimes met together in council to make group decisions, with each extended family represented by a male or female spokesperson acting in consultation with elders.

Many Subarctic peoples lived in conical tents called 'wigwams'; others built dome-shaped lodges. Both types of house were covered by hides or sheets of birch bark, depending on local resources. There was usually a central fireplace and the place of honour for guests was opposite the door. Tools made of wood, bone, hide and stone were hung from poles inside, as were moccasins and fish for curing. Clothes made from caribou or moose skins were beautifully decorated with natural paints, porcupine quills, bone buttons, seeds and shells; sometimes designs were painted inside the garment to give the wearer spiritual power. Water travel was conducted by birchbark canoe or raft. Overland journeys were made either by dog-sledge – often driven by women – or on foot, using snowshoes during the winter. Goods were carried on people's backs, by pack-dogs or on toboggans dragged by women.

Subarctic people had a close spiritual relationship with the wild animals upon which they depended for all their material needs. Each creature was believed to be imbued with a spirit. Their preserved bones, teeth and claws were often used as talismans, or for divination by shamans. Dreams were equated with visions, and amongst some peoples, children were sent into the wilderness on vision quests, in which animals bestowed them with supernatural power. The prevailing ethical code was one of individual responsibility.

LIFE IN THE SUBARCTIC
WHEN THESE STORIES WERE COLLECTED

Subarctic peoples' contact with Whites began in the early 17th century. Due to the challenging terrain and climate, Whites did not initially settle in the region in significant numbers, or claim the lands for themselves. Their main interest was in obtaining large quantities of high-quality animal pelts for the burgeoning European fur trade. This was facilitated by introducing the Native Americans to firearms for hunting.

As demand for furs expanded, Subarctic suppliers in the more accessible regions found their time-honoured hunting grounds encroached upon by opportunist White trappers. These were soon followed by other immigrants. Increasing numbers of staff came to man the expanding network of trading posts, dominated by the Hudson's Bay Company (see p. 23). Christian missionaries moved in, bringing teachers to run the schools they established. Government Indian Agents arrived, forcing local people to adopt a White lifestyle, and driving them off the most commercially promising land into less fertile reservations. Railways were built across previously virgin landscapes, making the whole region accessible to outsiders. Several gold rushes, particularly in 1897-98, brought an influx of prospectors and miners. These incomers had no sense of what the Carrier (Dakelh) nation call 'letting the earth heal itself – giving the land a rest so the berries will grow again and the fish and beaver will multiply'; instead, they brought profound and turbulent changes to the Subarctic ecosystem and peoples.

The traders' voracious appetite for furs caused trappers to disregard the accustomed closed season during the fur-bearing animals' breeding periods, and to kill them in unsustainable numbers. The flesh of these animals had previously formed local people's staple diet, so the result was widespread severe food shortages. This was exacerbated by the building of roads and railways, opening up the land for timber extraction and mining. Dams were built, disrupting fishing rivers, and flooding salmon runs and family camping grounds; and local people's fishing activities were officially restricted. As their lands became increasingly exploited for commercial purposes, the Subarctic peoples found themselves forcibly moved from their ancestral hunting grounds onto reserves, which were then repeatedly reduced in size. They became increasingly dependent on the Hudson's Bay Company, both to buy their furs and dried meat, and to supply them with trade goods for their daily needs; many were forced to rely on government 'relief' to avoid starvation. There was virtually universal conversion to Christianity, though at the turn of the 20th century ceremonies from the old religions were also still performed. Fatal European diseases such as smallpox, measles and flu drastically reduced the local population.

STORYTELLING IN THE SUBARCTIC

Amongst some Subarctic peoples, storytelling traditionally took place during the autumn or winter. For others, it was a popular activity at summer gatherings, when different groups could share and thus disseminate their own tales.

A vivid picture of a Cree storytelling session on the shore of James Bay, at the southern end of Hudson's Bay was given by Fred Swindlehurst in 1905:

'Seated around a blazing campfire, a group of Cree Indians, silent and moody, had just finished supper, and were enjoying their evening smoke. The night was cold and dark, and save for the crackling of the fires everything was as still as death. Suddenly one of the Indians began to relate a story. At first his voice was low and pleasing; then as he spoke of fighting, excitement obtained the mastery and his narrative was accompanied with wild but appropriate gestures. The audience occasionally grunted approval. There was not a sign of incredulity... The tales are told only in the fall of the year. Should an Indian relate them during winter or summer, the belief is that misfortune will attend all his endeavours during the year. If told in fitting season, however, the narration will bring good luck.'

Sadly, Swindlehurst found that amongst these Cree at least:

'The young Indians do not take the trouble to learn the stories, and the custom of storytelling in the autumn is kept up by only a few of the older men, who dread the ridicule of the White man and are for the most part silent in his presence.'

Likewise, Alanson Skinner reported in 1911:

'It is now very hard to find anyone able to relate the myths and legends... The younger generation usually remembers only fragments of the stories, and they object strongly to relating them in this form.'

Perhaps because of this, relatively few Subarctic myths were recorded, and then only as sparse outlines and synopses which retained little vitality from the originals.

However, G.T. Emmons, writing in the same year, saw more encouraging signs amongst the Tahltan:

'History and legends were generally known to all, but they were particularly in the keeping of individuals who taught them to the children at night about the fire. A few days after each lesson the children were all questioned and made to recite what they had been told, and the most apt pupils were given a thorough course of instruction. The writer's limited experience in this matter, however, led him to believe that the older women were generally the better informed in questions of history and legend, for in conversation with the men when relating old stories they would often appeal to the older women for aid.'

THE PEOPLES BEHIND THE STORIES

Chipewyan (Denesoline)

Originally spread across Alberta, Manitoba, Northwest Territories, Nunavut and Saskatchewan, they became middlemen between White traders and other Subarctic peoples in remoter regions. Today about half still speak their mother tongue and they are currently reviving traditional hunting and trapping practices.

Cree

Since the 18th century, they have been the largest First Nations group in Canada. Today many are of mixed race. They are spread across Alberta, Manitoba, Northwest Territories, Ontario, Quebec, and Saskatchewan in numerous bands, speaking various dialects. A Cree community in Montana, USA, is descended from a group who moved to the Great Plains in the late 17th century.

Kaska (Kaska Dena)
They were originally divided into five groups. Today they still live in their old homelands of northwestern British Columbia, the southern Northwest Territories and southeastern Yukon.

Koyukon
They are based along the Koyukuk and Yukon rivers in northern Alaska, where many still practise traditional hunting and trapping.

Loucheux (Gwich'in, Kutchin)
They still live in their original homelands in the forests of Alaska, Northwest Territories and Yukons. Today some families maintain outlying summer and winter camps, where hunting, trapping and fishing remain important activities.

Slavey (Dene)
They live in Alberta, British Columbia and Northwest Territories. Their English name possibly comes from previous enslavement by more powerful Subarctic peoples. Although increasingly urbanised, some still practice traditional hunting, trapping and fishing.

Tahltan
Their homelands were in the interior of British Columbia, extending into Yukon. Their laws are based on the matrilineal system of inheritance through the mother. There are two Tahltan clans, the Crow and the Wolf, each split into several family groups.

Research for this section also covered stories from the following Subarctic peoples: Beaver (Dunne-za), Carrier (Dakelh), Naskapi and Yellow Knives (T'atsaot'ine).

THE LONG WINTER

Slavey (Dene)

A long time ago, before People came into the world, there was an everlasting winter. It snowed and snowed, on and on, layer upon layer. The Sun vanished behind thick clouds and it was constantly dark, with no difference between day and night. The Moon and the stars, even the northern lights, all vanished too. This went on for three years.

It was a total catastrophe. The animals, birds, fish and insects were constantly shivering and almost starving.

In the end, the various species put aside their differences and gathered together in a grand council to discuss what to do. Even the fish attended, alongside all the birds and animals... Well, not quite *all* the animals. For as they began their debate, they realised that Bear was missing. This caused a lot of speculation:

'I haven't seen her for ages.'

'Nor me – not since this terrible winter set in.'

'Maybe she's stayed permanently in hibernation.'

Then the discussion turned to the main subject – what had happened to all the world's warmth:

'Maybe someone's stolen it and hidden it somewhere...'

'Under the water? Under the Earth?'

'It can't be down there, because the warmth would seep up and melt the snow.'

'Then it must be up in the Sky.'

'Yes!'

'We'd better go up there, find the warmth and bring it back.'

Everyone agreed, and everyone was eager to help. So a great mass of creatures set out on the quest. However, as no one knew the way to the Sky, they split up into groups, each going in a different direction. Some crawled or slid weakly over the frozen land; others fluttered shakily through the air. At last, after interminable nights of travelling and searching, one small group found an opening through the clouds that led up to the Sky.

Lynx spotted it first. He clambered up a nearby tree trunk, then leaped elegantly from the upper branches and through the hole. He stretched back his paw and screeched at the others, 'This way!'

Fox, Wolf and Wolverine all scrambled up after him, followed by three much smaller ones: Mouse, and two fish, Pike and Burbot. They all stood there quivering, and looked around.

The Sky World was just like the Earth used to be in early summer. The creatures basked in the soft warmth for a while and nibbled morsels of the food that they found scattered all around. Gradually they felt their blood flowing more strongly. So they set out to explore, and soon noticed a lake ahead. On the bank there was a small camp, with smoke curling up from the wigwam. They hurried towards it and saw two cubs gambolling outside: Bear's children.

'What are you doing here?' Wolverine demanded.

'Why shouldn't we be here? It's our home, where we were born,' the cubs replied.

'Where's your mother?'

'Out hunting. She'll be back soon,' they said.

Wolverine continued to question them. Meanwhile, Fox, Lynx and Wolf sneaked into the wigwam and sniffed around it. Then Fox poked his head out, winked at Wolverine and called to the cubs in a gentler voice: 'Little ones, could you tell me what's in this?'

With his front paw, he touched a round bag hanging from a hook. It was stuffed so full that its seams were almost bursting.

'Oh,' said the Bear cubs, 'that's where Mama keeps the rain.'

'And what's in this bag hanging next to it?'

'The wind,' they answered.

'And in this third bag?'

'It's the fog,' said the cubs. 'But don't ask what's in the fourth bag – we're forbidden to tell anyone.'

'Why ever not?'

'Mama says it's a great secret. If we tell anyone, she'll nip us and cuff us and toss us about.'

Fox strode out of the wigwam and sat down by the cubs, fixing them with his shrewd yellow eyes. 'Don't worry, little ones,' he said gently. 'Your mother won't know. Anyway, all animals are friends, and friends don't keep secrets from each other. Tell us, please.'

The cubs whispered for a moment, then said in unison, 'That's Mama's special bag – the one where she keeps all the warmth.'

Fox snickered. He didn't touch the bag, but led the other animals a short way off. They had a quiet consultation and hastily agreed a cunning plan.

Fox went back to the Bear cubs, grinning brightly, and said, 'We've seen a deer on the opposite side of the lake.'

'Oh, we love deer meat,' they said.

'Yes, it's the tastiest meat of all, isn't it,' said Fox. 'Your mother could catch it on her way back. Go and keep a lookout, so you can tell her about it as soon as you see her coming.'

The cubs rushed excitedly down to the shore and stood gazing out across the water.

Meanwhile, Lynx was slinking through the undergrowth around the edge of the lake. As he went, he began to transform. By the time he reached the far side, he had turned into a huge deer, with a magnificent pair of antlers.

At the same time, little Mouse scuttled silently down to the beach and into Bear's canoe. She jumped onto the paddle and gnawed a deep hole halfway along the handle.

The others hid together in the brush behind the wigwam.

Suddenly the stillness was broken by the sound of grass being crunched underfoot. Bear herself was emerging from the trees. On the far side of the lake, the 'deer' that was really Lynx grunted several times. The sound carried loudly across the water.

'Mama, Mama!' the cubs cried. 'Look, there's a delicious deer on the far shore!'

Bear turned, saw it, quickened her pace, hurried to her canoe, climbed in and paddled speedily across the water. The 'deer' ambled along the shoreline, apparently oblivious. Bear's eyes were glued to it as her canoe drew near.

However, as she reached the opposite beach, the 'deer' suddenly doubled back the other way, breaking into a run. Bear roared feverishly, and leaned her weight on the paddle to turn the canoe round and chase it. But the paddle snapped clean in two where Mouse had gnawed it. This unbalanced the whole canoe – which capsized with a loud *splash*, tossing Bear into the water.

As she flailed about, the others emerged from their hiding place. They shoved the squealing cubs out of the way and dived into the wigwam. Wolf grabbed the bag of warmth in his mouth and manoeuvred it off its hook to the floor, then dragged it out and away. The others ran ahead, shouting back encouragement. But it was so heavy that Wolf was soon lagging far behind. So Fox took over from him; and when he too began to tire, Wolverine took a turn. Then Lynx caught it in his sharp teeth and hauled it further. Even little Mouse tried to have a go, though Wolf soon pushed her away and took the burden back himself. And so on. In this way, the animals pulled the bag of warmth all the way back through the Sky World, towards the hole through which they had come.

They had almost reached it, when they heard pounding footsteps. Bear had recovered and was galloping after them!

Fox had the bag of warmth in his mouth; but when he heard the others groan, he glanced behind, saw Bear and dropped the bag in despair. Lynx seized it, but he had no strength left. Then Wolf tried but he just couldn't keep a grip on it, and nor could Wolverine. Mouse's efforts were pathetic. So that just left the two fish. Bravely, Pike caught the bag on his small teeth and slithered away with it. Bear was closing in on them. Then Burbot seized the bag. A bit further, a bit further... Bear was almost upon them... Ah, there at last was the hole that led down to Earth!

In a flash, Pike slid through it, bringing the heavy bag tumbling behind him. Burbot wriggled after him. And then – squeezing through, all tangled together in a single mass – came Fox, Lynx, Mouse, Wolf and Wolverine. They dropped to the ground beside the fish in an untidy, panting heap.

The whole Earth was still frozen solid. Their breath steamed in the bitter air.

'Open it!' gasped the two fish.

Claws scrabbled at the bag and tore it apart. A blaze of warmth came rushing out. It showered up and shot around in all directions, spattering the surrounding countryside. In a flash, all the snow and ice began to melt. The clouds lifted and the air lightened. For the first time in three years, the Sun came out.

Before their dazzled eyes, the Earth turned from white to brown, and then to green. The trees budded and burst open, shoots pushed up and unfurled into leaf and flower. On and on, the warmth spread and thickened. Snowmelt gathered into rivulets and creeks in every direction; it gushed into torrential rivers, which rose and burst their banks.

The land flooded. The animals fled.

Others joined them, racing from all directions, filling the air with terrified shrieks as the water rose: 'Help! We'll drown, we'll drown!'

Every eye turned to one tree in the forest, which towered above all the others. Soon its trunk was lost under a mass of claws, as animals desperately shinned up it. Birds soared overhead and directed other creatures towards the peaks of a nearby mountain, until its slopes were covered by a swarming mass of refugees.

As they reached safety, they all cried: 'Who will help us now? Who will take away this flood?'

A deep voice boomed, 'I will.'

A gigantic fish broke through the surface of the deluge, its mouth opening and shutting as it took huge gulps of flood water. The fish grew and swelled until it was as big as the mountain where some of the animals were hiding.

But they did not need to hide there any more. For, thanks to the gigantic fish, the water subsided to exactly the level it should be. The good dry land was there again, covered with a soft carpet of growing plants.

Since then, there have been no more everlasting winters. And the whole Earth has looked just as it does today.

Bell: *Legends of the Slavey Indians*, 1901
No information is given in the source about the original narrator.

Winter is also explored in a Naskapi story. A hunter, annoyed that a mild, slushy winter makes travelling difficult, complains to a being called the North Man. Shortly afterwards, he meets a 'Snow Man', who promises to help him on this matter in the future. The hunter spends all summer building up a store of firewood and grease ready for the next winter – which, as he anticipates, is uncommonly severe. The Snow Man visits his camp and turns the weather even worse, constantly challenging the hunter to deal with it. The hunter avoids defeat by piling more and more fuel and grease onto his fire. Finally, the Snow Man starts to melt, and has to admit that the hunter's power is superior to his own. Ever since then, the story concludes, winters have been less extreme.

There are a number of other Subarctic myths about the Sky World. One, told by the Kaska, says that entry can be gained by travelling to the edge of the Earth, where the Sky moves up and down; it is possible to cross into it by slowing down this movement.

It is interesting to compare this story with THE THEFT OF FIRE (p. 277) and RAVEN STEALS DAYLIGHT (p. 373).

THE BEAVER WIFE

Cree

There was a man, long ago, who hoped to find the most capable wife in all the world. He didn't care at all what she looked like. He just wanted a really hard worker, someone who would spare no trouble in taking care of him, and keep his house to perfection.

He looked around carefully and considered all the unmarried women who camped in his area. But he was so conceited, that none of them would do. So the man declared that he would search amongst all the different animals and birds, until he found a female who could meet his demands.

He went out, caught a Caribou cow, brought her into his wigwam and ordered her to work. Unfortunately, the Caribou didn't have a clue what he was talking about, so that arrangement quickly came to an end.

'Aha, I know,' thought the man, 'Wolves are smart animals. They're related to Dogs, so they're bound to understand human ways.' Out he went, set up a loud howling and soon lured a she-Wolf to his wigwam. Sure enough, she was very quick-witted. However, she was also ravenously hungry, and before he could stop her, she gobbled up all his food. So the man threw her out.

But he didn't give up. He tried a Moose cow, but she was too lumbering and clumsy. He brought in a female Fisher, but the way she slunk about gave him the creeps. Then he trialled a Lynx. This one was not only clever, but also a diligent housekeeper. The man felt more optimistic and asked her to stay. But the Lynx couldn't stand company and soon walked out. Next he persuaded an Otter to take his test; but she didn't last long either, because her constant squealing and chuckling drove him nearly crazy.

'Maybe a bird would be better,' he thought.

So he tested a whole series of different kinds of Owls. But they were all too greedy, and too uppity to do his chores.

Just as he was starting to despair, a gentle Grey Jay knocked at his door. 'Try me,' she begged, 'I'll do whatever you ask.'

Sure enough the Grey Jay worked hard all day long. She never complained, and kept his lodge sparkling clean, with plenty of water and a blazing fire ready when he came home from hunting. Finally, the man thought he'd found the one he was seeking...

But he made the mistake of ordering the Grey Jay to carry in a very heavy hunting catch. Willingly, she grabbed it in her beak and started to drag it inside to cook. But her spindly legs couldn't cope with the weight. With a loud *cra-a-kk*, they buckled and the poor, puny bird collapsed on the floor.

The man said he was sorry and bound her broken legs with a bow string. But as soon as she recovered, he sent her away.

The man resigned himself to living alone.

However, one day, when he was out hunting, he came upon a she-Beaver. She was scurrying to and fro across his path, dragging heavy branches through the forest to the river, where she quickly and skilfully wove them into a very impressive building.

'Hey there,' called the man admiringly, 'we haven't met before.'

'Sorry, can't stop,' the Beaver answered. 'Can't you see I'm busy? Some of us have work to do, you know.'

The man stepped out and blocked her way. 'I've been searching everywhere for a hard-working female like you,' he said. 'Would you like to move in with me?'

She tried to skirt round him, but he wouldn't let her. So she clasped her hands together and gazed up at him with her black eyes. 'What's in it for me?'

'You won't have to wear yourself out any more with building,' said the man. 'You can move into my cosy lodge instead. I'll keep you safe and bring you the best food to eat.'

'And what's the catch?'

'All you need do is keep house for me.'

'Hmm,' said the Beaver, 'that's easy enough. It sounds quite a good deal. All right, I'll give it a try.'

So she turned her back on the river, and went to live on dry land in the man's wigwam. She was so bored with no building work to do, that she willingly undertook every task he set her. Even better, she was always cheerful. She chirruped, sang and chattered away all day long – but so softly that the man didn't mind at all. She was brilliant at every job she turned her nifty little hands to; surely no one else alive could dress furs as well as her. In fact, she was so useful, that the man soon asked if she would marry him.

The Beaver slapped her tail hard on the ground then said, 'Hmm…before I make any promises, I must warn you that it won't be easy for either of us. I do quite like your home, but I still can't totally get used to living on dry land. I really belong to the water, as well you know – and because of that, once we're husband and wife, you need to be very careful.'

'In what way?'

'Whenever you come to a small creek,' said the Beaver, 'you must always perform some special medicine. And you must do exactly the same whenever you come to a dry valley.'

'Why?' asked the man.

'If you don't, there's a terrible danger of flooding. Only you can prevent it.'

'How?'

'Oh, it's easy enough,' said the Beaver. 'You must simply break off a stick and lay it over the creek, or across the valley bottom. Only after you've done that, may you cross it. You *must* do it, even if you're in a terrible hurry, even if you're exhausted.'

'Whatever for?'

'Because that will stop it turning into a huge river – which would change our lives for ever, in a way that you'd find disturbing. If you promise always to do this, I'll make my own promises to you.'

And so he did, and she did, and they became husband and wife. The Beaver kept house to the highest standard, and the man always filled their stores with excellent meat. Although they never had any children, by all accounts they were happy.

But after a while, like any fond married couple, they couldn't help taking each other for granted. And that made them careless.

One spring day, the man and his Beaver wife were walking through the forest together, looking for a new place to camp. He was leading, way out in front, hauling the sledge with their wigwam on it. She was following a long way behind, singing happily as she dragged along their household goods. The man emerged from the trees to a valley – a very wide, completely dry valley. Of course, he was always mindful of her warning; but surely it didn't apply here?

He looked behind to ask his Beaver wife for advice. But she was dawdling way behind in the spring sunshine.

'I really don't believe I need to lay a stick across this valley,' he said to himself. 'There's no water here at all and not a single cloud in the Sky – how could it possibly flood?'

So he hurried on, crossed the valley, walked into the foothills and found a good place to camp. He parked his sledge there and went off hunting, reckoning that his wife would soon catch up and pitch their wigwam. The hunting was good, and he dragged his kill back eagerly, thinking what a splendid meal they would have together that night. However, when he arrived at the camping place, there was no sign at all of his wife.

'Beaver!' he called. 'Beaver, my love, where are you?'

She made no answer.

What could have happened to her? He hadn't noticed any dangers on the way...oh!...except for that dry valley where, for the first time ever in their marriage, he hadn't laid a medicine stick.

The man panicked. He flung down his meat and ran back. Just as the Beaver wife had warned him, the place had transformed. The valley had vanished under a great, rushing river, a thundering torrent.

He stood on the bank, his heart beating fast. Suddenly, he saw a movement – and recognised the dripping head of his wife, fur plastered to her forehead, skimming smoothly through the water.

'My love,' he shouted, 'come here!'

'Can't stop, I'm busy,' she called back.

'What are you doing?'

She dived, vanished for a few moments, then bobbed up again by a great pile of pebbles and wood.

'Can't you see? I've finished making a new dam, and now I'm building a lodge.'

'But we have our own splendid lodge, my love. It's waiting on the sledge, ready for you to put up like you always do so well.'

The Beaver wife clambered out onto her dam and stood there trembling. 'Husband,' she said, 'you failed to work the medicine today. Our pact is broken! I can't live in the human way any more. If you want our love to last, now *you* must come to *me*.'

'But I can't live under the water!'

'Not *under* the water, but within and upon it,' she said. 'My lodge is almost finished. Inside the air is fresh and it's completely dry, comfortable and warm.'

'But how can I reach it without drowning on the way?'

'Hold your breath, dive in, streak through the water until you find an entrance near the bottom, then rise up inside it.'

'But I'm a man, not a Beaver.'

'As I am a Beaver, not one of the People. I adapted, and so can you. Be bold, my love, just as I was bold in marrying you. Look, there's a safe place to enter the water here; see, I'm swimming out to meet you. That's right, dive in, hold your breath and follow me.'

He dived, swam after her and soon emerged on the first level inside her Beaver lodge. He copied her by shaking himself dry, then followed her up to the higher level. Ah, here indeed was a very cosy space! It was lined with a thick, soft spread of chewed wood fragments, far better, much snugger than any human could imagine. He agreed to stay.

'But how will I go hunting?' he asked.

'You don't need to hunt any more,' she told him. 'We Beavers don't eat meat. You must share my meals of leaves and buds, twigs and bark.'

'But I'll get ill. I'll starve.'

'No you won't. As I learned to eat meat, so you will learn to relish the taste of things that grow from the earth. Go back ashore if you wish; but if you still love me, if you want me to continue keeping house for you, you must learn to live like me.'

What could the man do? After all these years, he'd be lost without his wife, he couldn't manage without her.

So he stayed there with her. He came to relish the taste of plants. He became a strong swimmer. He learned to hold his breath underwater for long periods, to sleep all day and work at night. He discarded his clothes and grew hair all over his body. He became an expert builder with sticks and branches, pebbles and mud. His teeth grew sharper; though never sharp enough to fell a tree. Gradually he settled down into his new life...

But not for ever. For this man had a brother, and as the years went by, the brother missed him. One night he had an incredible dream, about the man transforming into a Beaver. In the dream, the brother saw the Beaver lodge, and he went out to search for it.

The Beaver man had a dream too. He warned his wife, 'I fear our days together are coming to an end.'

It was midwinter when his brother arrived and set up a big trap of stakes and nets. It covered the whole Beaver lodge, and also all the burrows in the surrounding bank where they would sometimes hide. There was no escape. It didn't take long for the brother to catch and slaughter the Beaver wife. Soon after, he caught hold of the man and hauled him out onto the bank.

'You look disgusting,' the brother said. 'This is what comes of marrying a dirty animal. Here, take these clothes, get dressed.'

The man didn't resist. Now that his beloved wife, the rock of his life was dead, what was the point? He dried himself, put on the clothes, then followed his brother home.

'When did you last eat meat?' the brother asked him.

'So long ago, I've forgotten.'

'No wonder you look so scrawny,' said the brother. 'Eat this now and get your strength back.'

'What is it?'

'Beaver flesh, of course.'

'I can't eat that!' cried the man. 'If I do, I'll turn into a Beaver completely and you'll never see me again in human form.'

The brother didn't argue. He fed the man up on the meat of many other creatures, and the man gradually grew strong again.

He lived the rest of his life as a human, until he died.

Skinner: *Notes on the Eastern Cree and Northern Salteaux,* 1911
This story was collected by Skinner in 1908, when he travelled to remote regions by canoe and on foot, and met many Woods Cree bands 'who had come from their far off hunting grounds to barter their winter's catch of furs'. He does not name the narrator of this particular myth.

Beaver meat, which is rich in the fat needed for a healthy outdoor life in a cold climate, formed an important part of the Subarctic diet. Skinner described a sacred custom of the hunters:

'Beaver bones are always thrown back into the water in order that
the dogs may not get them, for this would so offend the spirit of the
Beaver that it would warn those still alive not to be caught.'

After the arrival of Whites, local people increased their Beaver trapping activities to sell surplus pelts into the European fur trade, thus entering the commercial economy.

Beavers are iconic animals with their industrious habits and remarkable ability to change the landscape and waterways by constructing huge dams, canals, and dens. Perhaps because of this, they feature in a number of other Subarctic stories. For example, a lengthy Kaska myth features Beaver as 'a great transformer' who outwits and destroys a series of monstrous animals and other beings.

HUNTER'S LULLABY

Koyukon

Over the mountain
slowly staggers the hunter.
Two bucks' thighs on his shoulders,
bladders of fat between them,
twenty deers' tongues in his belt...

Wake, little sleeper,
and call to your father!
He brings you back fat,
marrow and venison
fresh from the mountain.
Tired and worn,
he has carved a toy of deer's horn
while he sat and waited long
for the deer on the hillside.
Wake and see the crow
hiding from the arrow.
Wake, little one, wake,
for here is your father!

– Unnamed woman, singing as she sewed
and hushed her child to sleep.
(Quoted in Dall: *Alaska and its Resources*, 1870)

483

RAVEN GETS MARRIED

∧∧∧∧∧

Chipewyan (Denesoline)
& Loucheux (Gwich'in)

There was a widow who had just one great wish in life: she wanted to find the perfect husband for her only daughter. But unlike most people, she wasn't simply looking for a steady, decent and reliable hunter. For this widow had once been married to a chief, so she was seeking a man as rich and powerful as her late husband. She also had a son; he shared her concerns for his sister's future, and saw that a wealthy brother-in-law would also bring many advantages for himself.

So the family erected their wigwam near a busy river and whenever he had a spare moment, the girl's brother eagerly kept watch on the passing canoes for a suitable candidate. In this way, he met countless eligible men, both young and old; but for a long time he couldn't find anyone to match the family's aspirations.

However, one day, a very distinguished-looking man came paddling past. His canoe was decorated with marvellous ornaments. His clothes were made of the softest white skins, adorned with shells and beads that sparkled in the sun like brightly coloured fish. His hair was sleekly swept back from his prominent, proud nose, and his eyes were piercing and confident.

As the canoe approached, the brother hastily jumped up and put out a hand to hail it. 'Hello there, friend,' he called. 'Welcome to our camp. Come up to our wigwam and share a meal with us.'

The stranger shook his head and answered in a harsh, rasping voice. 'I can't stop, young man – I have urgent business upstream.'

This impressed the brother even more; the stranger was clearly an important man.

The mother had been spying through the doorway and came hurrying down to make sure that the canoe did not pass by. Her first impression of the stranger was a good one. So she beamed at him encouragingly and forcefully repeated her son's invitation, saying, 'You're bound to handle your dealings better if you share a meal with us first. Come, let us look after you for a while.'

Then she turned to her son, saying: 'A distinguished man like this can't trudge up through the mud. Let's make a dry path for him.'

After they had gone to this effort, the stranger could not refuse their hospitality. He smiled suavely, secured his boat and followed them up to the wigwam. There they placed him in the seat of honour, while the mother prepared a fine meal. Naturally, she set her daughter to serve him first. However, the stranger didn't notice the young woman, for his eyes were fixed on the family dog, which was sniffing and staring back at him with suspicion.

'Good lady,' he spluttered, 'I can't eat with that revolting cur sitting there. Get rid of it.'

The mother swallowed her dismay, for the dog was their faithful friend and of great help to her son's hunting. But her daughter's future had to come first. So she led the dog outside and deep into the forest – where she quickly stabbed it to death.

When she returned, her regret was completely overcome by the sight of the stranger deep in conversation with her daughter. The pair went on talking long into the night, after the rest of the family had gone to bed. The mother lay awake until at last she heard her daughter settle down. After that, she heard the stranger go outside for a short time, then come back and go to bed himself.

The next morning, the stranger asked if he could marry the daughter. The mother readily agreed. She was elated: at last, her long-held wish was granted!

Despite all the excitement, the mother had to do her usual daily chores, and hurried out to fetch firewood. As she walked into the trees, she couldn't help brooding about the innocent dog that she had killed the night before. She felt really upset, and decided to say a last goodbye to the dear old family friend. She soon found its corpse lying just where she had left it. But, to her dismay, some wild creature had already found it – and pecked out its eyes.

'It must have been a bird of prey,' she said to herself. Sure enough, the ground was covered in three-toed footprints.

She couldn't help bursting into tears. And as she wept, her thoughts began to drift: 'Bird of prey, probably a raven...'

Suddenly her heart missed a beat. 'Oh no! Supposing… It can't be! But what if it's *the* Raven? Supposing it's him marrying my daughter!'

Her mind raced back over everything that had happened the previous day. She recalled the stranger's sleek black hair, his beak-like nose, the rasping sharpness of his voice…

'Don't be ridiculous, he's a very rich and successful man,' she scolded herself. 'He'll be absolutely perfect as a son-in-law.'

She busied herself with gathering sticks, and hastily carried them home. When she got there, everyone was excitedly discussing the daughter's future. The mother tried to join in, but every time she glanced up at the stranger now, she felt a terrible chill.

There was only one solution: she must use cunning to discover the truth. So she said, 'My son-in-law, I'd like to make you a specially fine new pair of moccasins as a wedding gift. Could you take off your old ones, please, so I can measure your feet.'

'That's very good of you,' he said casually. 'Just make them the same size as the ones I'm wearing.'

'But I do need to look at your actual feet,' she said, 'to ensure a perfect fit.'

'I never let anyone see my feet,' he said, lowering his voice, 'because I have some…er…problems with them.'

'But I really can't make the moccasins without seeing them.'

'Well, just a very quick glance then. There.'

He whipped off one moccasin – then, quick as a flash, put it back on again. The brief glimpse revealed his feet to be thin, wrinkled and dark. Her heart missed a beat again but she said nothing.

However, her son had seen the same thing. He sidled up to her and whispered in her ear, 'Mama, he's only got three toes…and they look like *claws*.'

'I know,' she whispered back.

'Mama, I don't like this. He's not what he pretends to be.'

'I know. We've made a big mistake! But we have to be careful.'

While they were whispering, the stranger was busy talking to the daughter. He turned to the mother and said, 'Dear lady, obviously my bride must move into my home, which is much finer than yours. I want to take her upriver at once to see it.'

The mother threw her arms round her daughter, crying, 'Oh my darling, I don't want you to go! Don't leave your mother like this!'

'But Mama, I'm going to be a married woman now. I've found the splendid husband that you always wanted for me.'

The mother clung to her and whispered quickly, 'Be careful! Your brother and I are worried that he's not what he seems…'

'Don't be silly,' the girl whispered back. 'It's just because you don't want to lose me.'

'Come, dear wife,' the stranger chided her, 'we must be off.'

He took the daughter's arm, hurried her down to his canoe and got into it. She clambered in excitedly, sitting behind him and enjoying all the wonderful ornaments.

'Goodbye, Mama!'

'Take care, my darling!'

It was a bright sunny day. The stranger pulled away from the bank and paddled fast. The daughter leaned back behind him, daydreaming about her forthcoming life, married to the most magnificent man she had ever met.

After a while, she noticed that clouds were gathering. Soon it began to rain. She shivered and huddled closer to her new husband… But then jumped back with a start.

Drops of rain were pouring off the stranger's hair and down his back. As they rolled under his shirt, his skin seemed to dissolve away. She stared at it. Yes, it really was happening. His smooth skin wasn't real, it was just a cover… A cover for something soot-black… Black feathers!

Her mother's words came echoing back into her head: *He's not what he seems.*

She reached out to touch him. Yes, they were definitely feathers.

'What are you doing?' he asked sharply.

'Nothing, husband. I'm just admiring the beads on your clothes, and thinking I must learn to work something similar for you.'

'Ah,' he said in his rasping voice, 'I'm glad to have found such an industrious wife.'

She sat very still for a while. *Splash, splash* went Raven's paddle. What could she do? How could she escape?

The bottom of his shirt was shaped in a long triangle like a bird's tail. Surreptitiously, she leaned forward and caught hold of it.

'Now what are you doing?'

'My dear husband, I'm examining the fringe of your shirt, and wondering if I could ever make anything so exquisitely neat.'

With nimble fingers, she tied the shirt tail tightly to a cross-bar of the canoe. Then she called out, 'Oh look husband! There's a nest over there by the bank, full of new laid duck eggs. Set me ashore for a moment, and I'll fetch some to cook tonight for your supper.'

Raven's stomach rumbled enthusiastically. He steered to the bank and waited while she got out. 'Don't be long,' he rasped.

'I won't,' she promised. But as soon as she was on dry land, she ran off into the trees.

'Wait!' Raven called. 'Come back!'

The daughter didn't answer; she didn't even hear him. She was already racing down the familiar forest tracks towards her home.

Raven gave an angry squawk and tried to leap up to follow her – but he couldn't because she had securely fastened him to the cross-bar. He writhed about, trying to free himself.

Then, with a final effort, he transformed back into his true shape, the shape of a huge and menacing bird. He let out a raucous laugh, broke free and went wheeling away into the storm.

Russell: *Athabascan Myths*, 1900
Bell: *The Fireside Stories of the Chippwyans*, 1903
Camsell & Barbeau: *Loucheux Myths*, 1915
This retelling combines the various versions, which are all very similar.

Russell obtained the story from a Captain J. W. Mills, who had collected it in turn from an unnamed Loucheux woman. Bell gives no information about his informant, but says that he often heard such old tales told on winter nights around the tipi fires, and paddling along rivers and lakes in summer.

Camsell was working for the Geological Survey of Canada when he heard it (with many other tales) one night in 1905, at Fort McPherson in Northwest Territories. It was told by a Loucheux man called Peter Ross, while he sat making a net in his camp. Camsell had previously heard similar tales as a child from an old Cree woman. He names the central character 'Crow' rather than 'Raven', although the North American crow does not actually live within that area. He quotes Ross as saying:

'From the beginning, the Crow [Raven] has always been the enemy of the Indians, annoying them in every possible way. He plunders their caches and removes the bait from their traps.'

It is interesting to compare this simple trickster tale to the Northwest Coast myths (see pp. 373 and 378), in which Raven combines mischief with important sacred powers. A few of these were also known in the Subarctic, presumably transmitted along trade routes.

The style of shirt Raven wears, with hem fashioned into a long triangle at the bottom, can clearly be seen in a painting dating from 1847, called *Gwich'in Hunters at Fort Yukon* in the journal of Alexander Hunter Murray.

MOULDY SALMON GIRL

Tahltan

In late summer just before the salmon run starts, there's often a shortage of food. That means everyone has to share whatever few scraps are left.

One autumn a long time ago, there was a young girl who wouldn't stop complaining about this. All day long it was 'I'm hungry, I'm starving,' whinge and moan, begging for something to eat. Her mother gave her the only thing she could spare, which was a very old piece of dried-out salmon. The girl took one look at it and turned up her nose in disgust.

'Ugh!' she cried. 'It's going mouldy. This isn't food – it's muck. I'm not eating that!'

She tore the salmon in half and hurled it into the bushes – where, no doubt, some wild creature was very pleased to find it.

A day or two later, the first salmon of the new season appeared, swimming frantically upstream. Soon the whole river was overwhelmed by them. The fishing got underway and with all that rich food, hunger soon gave way to over-indulgence. The girl's silly tantrum was completely forgotten. Once the salmon run was over, everything settled down to normal for the coming winter. But not *quite* to normal...

For as the nights drew in and heavy rain fell, the girl's mother went running round the camp, and along to the next one too, frantically weeping and wailing, shouting into all the lodges: 'Has anyone seen my daughter? I don't know where she is! Oh, oh, what's happened to her?'

No one knew. No one had seen her.

The mother was inconsolable. She reckoned there was only one explanation – somehow, her wayward daughter must have tumbled into the overflowing river and drowned.

She was right about the first thing, but wrong about the second. The girl *had* fallen into the river, but she wasn't dead.

For as she swirled around in the foaming torrent, a salmon found her. It's said that all salmon die after spawning, but this one hadn't. Maybe it had swum upriver before its proper time had come, maybe it was just lucky, or maybe it had a purpose. Anyway, somehow the salmon took control of the floundering girl and led her off to its other country, in the sea.

It was a long journey, for Salmon Country is far away. In some respects, it's similar to our own country, for there's land in it as well as water, and when its people are living there, they take human form. The Salmon People took the girl in and looked after her. They called her Mouldy Salmon Girl, because somehow they all knew about her foolish outburst before they'd come up on the run.

They made her welcome and they weren't unkind to her. However, the food they offered their youngsters didn't agree with Mouldy Salmon Girl at all: it was mostly things like grubs and insects. She didn't dare have another tantrum over this, so she quietly went off by herself along the beach looking for something tastier. She found loads of herring roe, which she quite liked. But unfortunately, some of the Salmon People spotted her stuffing it into her mouth and found the sight really funny. Soon a big crowd had gathered round to mock her: 'What are you eating, Mouldy Salmon Girl? Sea dung?'

She didn't dare answer them back and she couldn't change her tastes. So in future she had to forage for food in secret.

Winter passed, spring came and gave way to summer. As the grasses started to turn brown, the Salmon elders became excited. Naturally, Mouldy Salmon Girl wanted to know why.

'We'll be going upriver and inland soon,' they told her, 'to see our friends.'

'Who are your friends?' she asked.

'Who do you think? They're your own kind – human beings.'

'But my people kill you. How can they be your friends?'

'They don't kill us. When we meet them, we're already close to dying. Your people give us back our lives.'

'Can I come with you?' the girl begged. 'Can I go home?'

The elders said that she could.

The Salmon People had been busy mending their old canoes and building new ones. Now those who were going on the journey upriver got into them. A huge old man, the Salmon Chief, told Mouldy Salmon Girl to travel in his canoe. At a signal from him, they all set off across the sea, heading towards a great river estuary.

When they reached it, they paddled upstream, riding the currents easily, jumping over waterfalls, spinning round rapids and onwards, laughing at the torrent's deafening roar. They saw bears peering out of the forest, otters poking their heads above the surface, eagles soaring overhead, all watching hopefully. Whenever they passed through a difficult stretch, some of the canoes capsized, their inhabitants fell out and turned back into real salmon. At once, the wild creatures came hurrying to the bank to scoop them out and eat them. Mouldy Salmon Girl shuddered, but there was no time to worry, because they were still moving rapidly up the river.

Every so often, a section branched off into a smaller creek. Some of the canoes paddled down it, with the people inside waving goodbye to the others. Those who were left behind looked very sad; indeed, some of them were weeping.

'Where are they going?' Mouldy Salmon Girl asked the chief.

'Back to their spawning grounds, to the place where they were born,' he told her.

'How do they know the way?'

'They just do.'

'Why are people crying?' she asked.

'Because we won't see the others for such a long while,' said the chief. 'They'll lay their own eggs in their birthplace and then they'll die. Just as we will, when we get to where we're going.'

'In that case, none of you will see each other *ever* again.'

'Yes we will,' said the chief. 'To die is to be reborn.'

'I don't understand.'

'That's why we've let you come with us,' he said, 'so we can teach you, and you can teach your people.'

Gradually, the number of canoes sailing up the main river grew smaller. The chief led the way out of a steep canyon, on and on, to an area where the forest sloped gently down to the grassy bank. In the distance, Mouldy Salmon Girl saw a camp... And let out a cry of delight: 'That's my home!'

As she stood up to get a better view, something strange happened. The canoe seemed to melt away into the water, taking her with it. Without noticing how, she found she was swimming easily along with the river flow. Her body was fat and silver. Her arms had become fins; her legs fused into a tail. She turned round to look for the chief, and found that he too had become a fish.

'Can I go and look for my parents?' she asked him.

He made a deep dive to show his approval. In her new shape, Mouldy Salmon Girl swam easily up to the bank and idled along it just under the surface, every so often making a leap out into the fresh air. That's how she caught sight of her mother. She had set up a bench just above the bank, and was standing by it, cutting up the fish that her menfolk had already caught.

Mouldy Salmon Girl jumped out and tried to call her. But of course, now she was a fish, humans couldn't understand her, they couldn't even hear her. All her mother saw was a fat, gleaming salmon.

Being back at the salmon run had brought back the poor woman's aching grief for her lost daughter. As she worked, she kept wiping away her tears. Still, she knew it was vital to prepare as much fish as possible to last them through the coming winter. So she swallowed her sorrow and called to her husband: 'There's a really fine big one down here. Quickly, bring your spear.'

Mouldy Salmon Girl was terrified. She spun round in the water and swam rapidly back to the Salmon Chief.

'My own mother and father want to kill me!' she told him.

'Don't be afraid,' said the chief. 'Let them. You can't die. Your father will hit you on the head, but that won't be the end of you, because straight away, your soul will pass down to your tail. Soon after that, your fish body will die completely – but your soul will live on.'

'What will happen to it?'

'It'll go back to the Salmon Country, and come back next spring as a new hatchling. That's what happens to all my people, that's why every year there are always countless salmon swimming upstream.'

'What about the ones that aren't killed by human beings or eaten by bears, the ones I can see laying their eggs all over the place, and then collapsing, all smelly and rotting?'

'They're not dead either,' said the chief. 'Their souls have already returned to the Salmon Country, and they're preparing to return here in the future, when they're ready.'

Mouldy Salmon Girl tried to make sense of this, but she couldn't. Besides, she was desperate to go back to her parents, so she swam up to them and lingered around the bank.

'There it is!' her mother yelled.

Her father came rushing down, brandishing his spear, and stabbed her. After that, Mouldy Salmon Girl knew nothing more.

'This is a really good catch,' said the father. 'I think we should eat it straight away, while it's still lovely and fresh. We both need feeding up, after all the mourning we've done. Go on, get it ready to cook.'

The poor woman didn't have the strength to argue, so she laid the salmon on her bench and started cutting it up. As she did so, her knife suddenly hit something hard and glanced off.

'Ach, that's tough for a fishbone,' she muttered.

She reached in to try and loosen it – but found that instead of a bone, she was touching a dentalium shell. The fish must have swallowed it. Her first reaction was to burst into fresh tears, because on the day her daughter had vanished, she had been wearing a necklace of such shells.

When her husband came up, she showed him what she had found. He felt inside the fish himself, gave a tug – and sure enough, a whole necklace came slithering out.

The woman gasped. 'It's hers!' she cried. 'I'm sure it is.' And then, as she and her husband gazed at it in wonder, realisation dawned: 'This fish must be *our own girl*. When she fell into the river last year, somehow she must have transformed into a salmon!'

The mother stayed with the body of the salmon. Her husband ran out to consult with the shamans and women elders, then came back with some mysterious advice.

'We're to wrap up the whole salmon in a bundle of feathers,' he said, 'and on top of that we're to wrap it in a clean mat. Then we must keep it here, and eat nothing, keep on fasting, until something happens. It'll take eight days, they reckon.'

And so they resisted all the fresh-caught fish and fasted instead. Every day, they peeped under the wrappings. Gradually, they saw the scales fall away, the skin turn smooth, the body reshape, the fins and tail become legs and arms. On the ninth day, they dared to pull the wrappings right away – and there was their own daughter! She was alive, she was well, she was just the same as on the day they had lost her.

'Oh our dearest, whatever happened to you?' they cried.

'Such strange medicine, I can't possibly describe it,' she answered. 'I've been living with the Salmon People, and I've come back to tell everyone about them. We must always treat them with great respect, never speak evil of them or criticise them. If we break their sacred laws, they'll take revenge. But if we do the right thing by them, they promise everything will go well.'

Teit: *Tahltan Tales*, 1921
This myth was collected in either 1912 or 1915. Teit says he obtained most of his Tahltan stories from a man called:

'Tuu'ts ('Strong Rocks'), also known as Dandy Jim, of the Nahlin clan of the Raven phratry of the Tahltan. He was selected by the tribe as the best-qualified person to give me information on their general ethnology, mythology, and so on.'

Tuu'ts lived near the Stikine River, British Columbia, which even today is regarded as an important salmon run.

Salmon are born and begin to mature in fresh water, but later swim out to sea, where they spend most of their adulthood. Once they are mature, they return upriver to spawn, usually to the very same location where they were born. The migration, which can include leaping up waterfalls and overcoming rapids, is a challenging and exhausting process for the fish; after spawning, all salmon from the Pacific Ocean (the species that migrate into Tahltan territory) die. The run usually occurs each year between September and November. This is the prime time for fishing – not just for people, but also for other species, most notably bears, eagles and otters.

The dentalium shells in the girl's necklace were widely used by Native Americans to make jewellery. They were also used as units of exchange for trading between different peoples within reach of the Pacific coast from where they were harvested. They come from marine molluscs and resemble long, hollow teeth; hence the name.

It may be significant that the central character in this important food myth is a girl, since the Tahltan are matrilineal, tracing inheritance through the female line; today this still forms the basis of their society and local government.

Compare this story to the Northwest Coast myth, A JOURNEY TO SALMON COUNTRY (see p. 384).

THE TWO BROTHERS
AND THE GIANTS

Kaska

Two brothers got lost during a family hunting trip. It didn't matter; they were more than old enough to look after themselves.

'Let's travel about together,' said the elder brother, 'and make camp wherever it suits us. It'll be good to make our own decisions without constantly being told what to do.'

The younger brother agreed.

'As our mother and sisters aren't with us,' said the elder brother, 'one of us will have to keep house. I volunteer to do that, while you do the hunting.'

The younger one agreed to that too.

At first, everything went well. The younger brother caught plenty of game and carried it home to the elder one, who proved adept at cooking it and keeping the hut he'd built neat and clean. However, before long, he got get fed up with domestic life; after all, what lusty young man in his right mind wants to do women's work? But instead of speaking out, he just brooded on his resentment.

One frozen winter's day, when the younger brother brought his kill home, the elder snatched it from him, cooked it – and ate all the meat himself.

'Hey, where's my share?' said the younger one.

'In my belly,' said his brother.

The younger one stared at him. 'So...don't we work together any more?'

'No. I'm sick of hanging around at home all day, and I'm sick of you.'

The younger one shrugged. 'All right, brother, this was all your idea, but suit yourself. You can catch your own meat in future.'

He wasn't particularly bothered. He stomped off and soon caught a fat porcupine, skinned it, made a fire and hung the flesh over the flames to cook. While it was roasting, he quickly built a makeshift shelter, then slipped off his snowshoes to go inside and make it cosy.

While he was doing this, a giant came along. A *cannibal* giant.

The giant sniffed the air: '*Fffff.* Hmm, that stinks of half-cooked porcupine. *Fffff.* And also fresh young human! Lovely!'

He picked up the snowshoes, crammed them into his mouth and crunched them up with his sharp yellow teeth. 'Not bad for a taster,' he grinned. 'But where's the human that wears them?' He strode to the fire and poked it around with the handle of his axe.

The younger brother, hiding in his shelter, watched the giant nervously. As soon as the brute turned his back, the younger brother scuttled out of the hut and shinned up the nearest tree.

But the giant heard him! He spun round, pulled the hot meat from the fire with his bare hands and chucked it away. Then he went over to the tree and shouted up, 'Don't think you can escape me so easily, you little gobbet. My guts are rumbling at the thought of your sweet young flesh. I'm going to chop down this tree, so you'll come tumbling out of it into my arms. Then I'll toss you into your own fire to singe your outsides, and eat the rest of you raw.'

Up in the tree, the younger one was jittering with fear. 'Brother!' he screamed. 'Help, help!'

He didn't expect any response. But the truth was that the elder brother was feeling really guilty about how he'd behaved. As soon as he heard the screams, he dropped what he was doing and raced outside. He soon found the younger one's tracks in the snow, and quickly followed them until he saw the giant, and his little brother clinging for his life to the treetop.

The giant saw the older brother coming and licked his lips: 'Yummy! *Two* tender humans in one go!'

The elder brother swallowed his fear. 'Good morning to you, sir,' he called. 'Would you like some help?'

'Help?' said the giant. 'Why would a little wretch like you want to help a savage man-eater like me?'

'Because of that boy up the tree,' said the elder brother. 'I hate him. He's mean and useless. I'd love to see you eat him.'

'Really?' said the giant.

'Yeah, really. Let me cut down the tree to help you. Here, give me your axe.'

The giant was so surprised that he didn't argue. He put the axe into the elder brother's hand.

'Aw, this is heavy!' said the elder brother. 'I need to practise with it for a while, get the feel of its weight.' He started swinging it backwards and forwards through the air.

'Ow!' the giant yelled. 'You just hit me.' He put his big hand up to his brow, which was bleeding from a very nasty-looking wound.

'Sorry,' said the elder brother. 'You'd better stand back: I don't want to catch you again once I'm actually chopping.'

'Let me do it,' said the giant.

'No, no, I want to help. And I want to take revenge on that awful brother of mine.'

Up in the tree, the younger brother's fear mingled with rage. To think that his own closest kin would betray him like this! But there was nothing he could do.

The elder brother started striking the axe in earnest, hacking at the tree. *Thwack! Thwack!* Now the great trunk had a deep gash in it. With every blow it shook violently. The younger one knew his end was near. He closed his eyes and prepared to meet his fate. Then suddenly, as the elder brother swung the axe, he spun round, ran at the giant – and sliced off the brute's head!

The whole forest fell silent. The younger brother opened his eyes and stared down in disbelief.

'You…you saved me after all,' he cried.

'Of course I did. You're my brother. Come on down, let's celebrate together.'

The younger one slid down the trunk. They stood over the decapitated giant, side by side.

'That head is hideous.'

'Yeah.'

'Wonder what it's like inside.'

'Let's cut it open and see.'

So the elder one picked up the axe again and smashed it down on the giant's skull. It split in two with a loud crack – and at once, a thick cloud of tiny insects burst out of it. *Zzzzzzzzzz.* They flew round and round the youths' heads, buzzing maddeningly – then started to settle on their skin and bite them.

'Ow, that's a sharp nip.'

'Ooof, and on me too… And another one…'

'They're all over me!'

They began to slap their faces, their arms, even the bits of their bodies hidden under their thick clothes.

'I'm all itchy.'

'Me too. Hey, you're coming up in red lumps.'

'Don't mock me, so are you.'

That's how the first mosquitoes came into the world. They're cannibals, like the cannibal giants they came from. And that's why most giants are so stupid: they have mosquitoes instead of brains.

But not all giants are stupid. Haven't you heard of Big Man?

Big Man was in the world right at the beginning. He had no hair on his head and he was so tall that, when he stood erect, his head touched the Sky – which in those days was very close to the Earth. Because of that, everything was permanently frozen, covered in snow and ice; and Big Man had to crawl about. He got so angry about this, that he pushed the Sky up until he could stand at his full height. This made the weather on Earth a lot milder, much as it is now. Big Man was a good giant, and never harmed people.

Anyway, back to the brothers. After that adventure, the elder one finished cooking the porcupine that the younger one had caught, and gave him his fair share.

'I was wrong to treat you like I did before,' he said.

'It's all right,' said the younger one.

'Let's try to get on and work together again.'

The younger brother was more than happy to agree. So the next morning they resumed their travels together, hunting and making new camps every day. Everything went very well for a while.

But eventually, they came to an open region where they couldn't find any game, nothing at all. Before long, they'd eaten all the dried meat they'd been carrying; and then they began to starve. It was still the middle of winter and freezing cold. Eventually, the elder brother became so weak with hunger that he couldn't take another step. 'Let's build a camp here,' he said.

'That's fine by me,' said the younger brother. He did most of the work, knocking up a brushwood shelter and making a blazing fire. They sat on opposite sides of it, holding out their hands gloomily to the warmth.

'Pity there's nothing to cook on it,' said the younger one.

The elder brother didn't answer.

'You all right?' said the younger one.

The elder brother just grunted. The truth was, he was hatching a treacherous plan. He was working out how he could manage to get hold of his sibling and toss him onto the fire – so that he could save his own life by cooking and eating him.

The flames flickering on his face lit it with ugly shadows. The younger brother noticed this and felt uneasy. He got up and edged away towards the trees. He was ready to run if necessary, knowing that the elder one was too weak to follow him.

But just then, the elder brother yelped: 'Hey, did you hear that?'

'What?' said the younger one suspiciously.

'Something sizzling. Like meat roasting.'

'You're imagining it,' said the younger one. 'Hunger's making you have waking dreams.' He didn't move, but stayed where he was, half facing the trees, poised to race away if need be.

The elder brother stumbled to his feet and round the fire. He took a long stick and poked it into the burning logs. From afar, the younger one watched him. The elder brother squatted down and used the stick to scrape away the snow on the edge of the fire. As he did, a delicious smell drifted out. Now even the younger one could hear the sizzling.

'I can smell meat cooking too!' he called.

'Yes, it's real! There's a whole buffalo carcass under here. It must have died fighting and got buried in the snow. You didn't realise it, but you lit the fire in the best possible spot, right on top of it. It's thawed and already half cooked, a ready-made meal for us, a whole animal to eat!'

So that night they both feasted to their hearts' content. The next day they went back to their old habits, with the younger brother hunting and the elder one keeping house. The younger one soon brought back another buffalo carcass that he had killed himself. Since the elder brother was still incapacitated, the younger one did all the butchering and cooking too.

'Here, feed yourself up on this,' he said to the elder one. He gave him a huge helping of ribs and fat, then more and more.

'Stop!' the elder one protested. 'I'll burst if I eat any more.'

'You didn't worry about that when we were sitting round that fire a couple of days ago.'

'How do you mean?' said the elder one nervously.

'I knew what was in your mind. You were planning to eat *me*.'

The elder one couldn't deny it. He sat very still for a long time, hanging his head in shame. At last he said, 'That's twice I've tried to harm you, brother. What can I do, what can I say to make amends? Only that, from the bottom of my heart, I apologise.'

The younger one answered, 'Well... I've only got you, and you've only got me. We were born from the same mother, raised by the same fire. So from the bottom of my own heart, I willingly accept your apology.'

After that, the elder brother put all evil thoughts from his mind for ever, and the pair travelled on together in true harmony. Months went by. The snow melted and the buds opened. They left the buffalo country behind and went back into the forest. There were loads of animals to hunt here, and they lived well. Now the two brothers divided their tasks more equably, hunting together and keeping house together.

One day, they happened upon a big porcupine den, a deep hole dug out between two rocks. They were just getting ready to set up a trap there, when they heard footsteps behind them – thudding so heavily that the ground shook.

Another giant!

This time, the younger brother wasn't taking any chances. He dived straight into the porcupine hole, as far as he could go, and curled up into a ball.

The elder one stood his ground outside it.

Stomp. Stomp. The giant drew closer. He stopped a few paces away, then bent down slowly and looked the elder brother straight in the eye.

'Don't be afraid of me, grandson,' he said.

'I...I'm not,' the elder brother whispered.

'I think you are. But you should know I won't hurt you. I'm not the common type of giant, I'm not a cannibal.'

'You're not? Well, that's a relief. So what kind are you?'

'I'm not any "kind". There's only one of me.' Now the giant stood up very straight and beat his chest proudly. 'I am Big Man.'

'Big Man! I've heard of you! You're the one who once pushed up the Sky, aren't you?'

'That's me.'

'Fancy being lucky enough to meet you, Big Man. I can't wait for my little brother to meet you too. Hold on while I call him.' He went to the den hole, put his hands to his mouth and yelled down it: 'Hey, stop hiding down there and come out! This giant isn't a cannibal, he's Big Man. Come and say hello'.

But the younger brother hadn't forgotten the elder one's previous treachery. 'I can't trust him,' he thought. So he stayed right where he was, and didn't answer.

'Isn't he coming?' said Big Man.

'I'll call him again.'

He did, but the younger one just called back, 'Go away! This is just your original trick all over again, isn't it? I'm not coming out until you get rid of that brute!'

'He's very rude,' said Big Man. He put his own face to the hole and yelled: 'Oi! Stop insulting me.'

Nothing happened.

'Please excuse him,' said the elder brother placatingly.

'No,' said Big Man. 'Since he won't come out now, he'll have to stay down there for ever.'

He snapped his fingers. There was a loud creaking noise, and before the elder brother's eyes, the two rocks that surrounded the hole slowly moved towards each other. The patch of darkness between them grew smaller and smaller... And then it was gone.

The elder brother stood rooted to the spot, trembling with horror and grief. He knew that was the end of his younger brother and that he'd never ever see him again.

Suddenly, Big Man snapped his finger in his face 'What's the matter with you, grandson?' he said, as if nothing significant had happened. 'Don't stand there daydreaming. You and I have important work to do.'

'Um... What kind of work?'

'You've got to help me rescue my wife. She's been stolen by the cannibal giants.'

The elder brother didn't have time to argue. Big Man gave a loud, piercing whistle. The next moment, a grizzly bear and a black bear came racing towards him, both heavily laden with baskets like pack dogs. Big Man fondled them, then tucked the elder brother under his brawny arm, and strode off into the distance.

He walked so fast, that it didn't take long to reach the strange country where he was heading. Everything there was giant-sized, including all the animals. Big Man made a camp by a lake, where he caught some gigantic beavers to cook, and shared the feast with the elder brother. When they had finished, Big Man said, 'Grandson, see that hill over there? Climb it and look out in all directions until you spy a lake with an island bang in the middle of it; then come back and tell me which way to go to reach it.'

The elder brother did as he was told, and soon came hurrying back to say, 'The island in the lake lies over there.'

At this news, Big Man began to rock with laughter. 'Ahah, I thought it would fool you, grandson! What you saw isn't really an island – it's the giant who stole my wife. He's hunched up in the middle of the water, fishing. Come on, let's get ready to fight him.'

Big Man set to work, making a bow, arrows and a spear.

'What shall I do?' said the elder brother.

'Make an axe.'

'What shall I make it out of?'

'A beaver tooth.'

So the elder brother went to the pile of enormous beaver bones left over from their meal, and searched through them for some teeth. They were mostly so big and heavy that he couldn't lift them; but eventually he found a manageable one from a baby beaver, and fixed it to a stick.

Then he went to Big Man, who carried him under his arm again towards the enemy's lake. He put him down some distance from the shore and said, 'Go down there and bark like a dog.'

'Whatever for?' asked the older brother.

'Because that stupid giant's scared to his guts of dogs. As soon as he hears you, he'll run home. But I'll be waiting to ambush him, so he won't get away.'

Everything happened almost as Big Man had planned it. The evil giant was squatting in the middle of the lake, scooping up some grotesque fish that were all covered in hair. As soon as the elder brother crept down to the beach and started barking, the giant stood bolt upright, let out a bloodcurdling screech and went splashing out of the water towards his home. Meanwhile, Big Man had hidden himself along the trail. As the evil one passed him, he fired an arrow... But the giant leaped aside and the arrow missed.

Big Man leaped from his hideout, brandishing his spear and hurled it at the other giant, but missed again. The other giant flung himself onto Big Man and the two began to wrestle. Backwards and forwards they went. First one was almost hurled to the ground, then the other. But they were an exact match in strength, so neither made any serious headway. The fight went on and on, the two great beings groaning and cursing, their feet thundering on the ground, sweat pouring down their bodies.

At last Big Man called out to the elder brother, 'Grandson, help!'

The elder brother picked up his beaver-tooth axe. Whatever could he do against the towering evil giant? And supposing he struck Big Man by mistake? He danced around the battle for a while, then suddenly saw his chance. He stepped forward and slammed the axe against the evil giant's hamstrings, slicing right through them. The giant gave a yelp of pain and fell to the ground. Big Man and the elder brother both leaped on him, and after a few blows of their weapons, easily finished him off.

The elder brother stood there, gasping for breath, but Big Man cried, 'No time to lose! We've got to rescue my poor wife.'

He led the way down the trail to a huge stone lodge at the far end. As they approached, the door opened and an ugly giantess came out. She stood there, arms folded, glaring at them fiercely; then stooped, picked up an armful of rocks as if they were leaves, and started hurling them at Big Man and the elder brother.

'Take that!' she yelled. 'And that! You killed my husband! Don't think you'll get away with it!'

More rocks came hurtling towards them. The elder brother dodged into the trees. Big Man went towards the giantess, ducking and leaping first to one side, then to the other, so that her stones never managed to hit him. She strode to meet him; and when they stood face to face, she pulled off her dress and put her breasts on top of Big Man's shoulders, one on each side. They were as heavy as boulders, and their weight almost made Big Man fall down. But he wriggled free of her and they began to wrestle, just as he'd done with her husband. This went on for another long time. All the while, the elder brother was watching and calculating – and then suddenly hamstrung her too. After she'd collapsed from this, Big Man easily finished her off; then they went into her house and killed all her evil children.

When that was done, they heard a gentle voice calling out, and found Big Man's wife bound with thick ropes in a corner. He quickly freed her and they had a gigantic hug. Seeing their affection, the elder brother felt quite homesick for his parents.

'I couldn't have freed you, my dear, without this little fellow's help,' Big Man said to his wife.

'Then you ought to reward him,' she said.

'I ought to, indeed. What would you like best of all, grandson?'

'I'd really like to go home,' said the elder brother.

'And so you shall,' said Big Man. 'It's a long way off, but to make things easier, you can ride one of my dogs.' By this he meant one of his bears, of course. 'After a while, you'll run out of food. But don't worry, you have my permission to kill the dog and eat it.'

'Are you sure that's all right?' said the elder brother.

'Of course it is. Just always remember the rule: after you've eaten, keep one bare bone from its forelimb and sleep with it close to your head. When you wake up, the bone will be covered in meat again. Do that every night and you'll never run out of food.

'Also, take this special walking stick. When you go to sleep, always stand it upright near your head. When you wake up, it'll point in the direction you're to take that day, so you'll never get lost. But one morning you'll find that, although you've done what you should, the bone's still bare and the stick's fallen flat on the ground. Don't worry, that's a sure sign that you'll arrive home before the end of the day.'

'Thank you, Grandfather,' he replied. 'Even though I still miss my brother, I don't hold it against you for trapping him in the rocks. It's been exciting travelling with you. I'm eager to get home now, but I'll miss you. Will we ever meet again?'

'No,' said Big Man. 'But you'll see me, up in the Sky. There'll be a special sign, by which you'll know that I've passed away.'

'Big Man, surely a great person like you won't die?'

'Don't worry about that now,' said Big Man quickly. 'It's time for you to go home.'

Big Man helped the elder brother mount the grizzly bear, and off they went. However, they'd only gone a few paces, when the grizzly began to growl and buck. The elder brother was afraid it would attack him, so he called back to Big Man, who willingly swapped his mount for the black bear. This gave him a smooth ride, and they travelled a long way together every day, guided by the medicine stick, finding food as they went. After many days, they arrived in the country the two brothers had passed through together long ago, the place where there was no game to kill. So he thanked the bear for his transport then quickly killed him. When he'd finished feasting on the meat, he kept one bone as Big Man had told him, and in this way, he never ran out of food.

Then one day he woke to found that the bone was bare and his direction stick had fallen down. As the Sun came up, he realised he had arrived in the countryside near his home. He continued his journey on foot, and sure enough, just as darkness fell, he found himself going into his parents' lodge. They were overjoyed that at least one of their sons had come home safe and sound!

Shortly after that, something woke him very early. He went outside and was awed to see the entire Sky streaked with red. He remembered Big Man saying that the Sky would show signs that he had passed away, and guessed that gentle giant must have been killed by an enemy, for the red streaks were his blood. And when a heavy rain began to fall, he knew that this was Big Man's tears.

Teit: *Kaska Tales*, 1917
Teit collected the Kaska stories:
    '…at the foot of Dease Lake in 1915, my informants being Tsonake'l,
    also known as Albert Dease, and his wife Nettie Mejade'sse…I
    collected all the tales my informants knew.'
Regarding the use of bears as pack dogs and food, the story concludes:
    'That is why black bears are much better eating than grizzly bears, and
    also why grizzly bears are mean sometimes and want to fight people.
    That is also probably why people say that bears were originally dogs.'
In a different source, Teit says that the Tahltan, who were neighbours of and closely related to the Kaska, believed:
    'There were giants of two kinds. One kind, called *Yatsedu'sa'tz*, were
    very tall, almost, reaching the sky. They did not kill people, but
    sometimes stole them and made pets of them. The other kind were
    much smaller; they were cannibals, and ate people.'
The Tahltan had the same tradition of mosquitoes originating from an evil giant's brains, giving rise to their derogatory expression 'You're like a giant – with mosquito brains'.

Another Kaska story tells of two boys that a giant gives to his wife to fatten. However, she decides to keep them to help with her chores. She kills one, the survivor flees and eventually escapes to a fishing camp, where the people help him to trap and kill the giant and his wife.

A Chipewyan tale tells of a man ensnared in sunbeams by a cannibal giant, who takes him to his camp and hangs him up in a sack. Though he eventually escapes, 'the giant is still chasing him'. In a Naskapi myth, a giant kills a giant beaver, but on the way home is carried off by a giant eagle that strands him on a mountain top. His family 'wish' him back to earth, enabling him to climb inside the eagle's body and float safely down.

505

PEACE SONG

Tahltan

My brother was killed fighting.
When word came to me,
my heart was sad
and I wanted to die.
But now I am a hostage like a deer
and I love peace.
Now I do not want to kill any more.
Now I do not bear hatred
towards the one who killed my brother.

– Sung after the end of a conflict between families or tribes,
to celebrate an exchange of hostages
(Quoted in Emmons: *The Tahltan Indians*, 1911)

THE BOY WHO GAMBLED HIS FAMILY AWAY

∿∿∿∿∿

Tahltan

A wealthy clan chief had a young son who was obsessed with gambling. Nothing interested this boy except the stick game; no one could persuade him to learn the hunting and fishing skills that he needed to become a man. He insisted he didn't need to know such things, because he was such a good gambler. True enough, he won almost every time and thus became very rich in his own right.

Because of this, the chief indulged the boy's passion, and spread news of his talent far and wide. Sometimes other noted gamblers in distant places would invite him to take part in competitions. The chief always encouraged his son to accept the challenges, and it always proved to be well worth his while.

Not surprisingly, all this success made the boy arrogant. He would stride around the village bragging about how invincible he was, and no one ever contradicted him.

One day, a well-dressed stranger came to the village and went straight to the chief's house, asking, 'Is this the place where the famous young gambling champion lives?'

The boy stepped forward eagerly. 'That's me,' he said.

The stranger looked him up and down. 'I hear that you boast no one can beat you,' he said. 'I find that hard to believe; everyone has a weak spot. I challenge you to play against me now.'

'Of course,' said the boy, 'I'll be glad to.'

They went outside together and the boy led the stranger to his favourite gambling spot on the grass behind his father's house. The stranger showed the boy the stakes he had brought: exquisitely made clothing, weapons, tools and necklaces. The boy fetched his own treasures, which were of similar quantity and quality.

The stranger had brought his own set of sticks, which were very long and beautifully painted with fantastical designs and feathers. He showed the boy the trump stick, the one he had to find. 'Take note,' he said, 'it's only very slightly different from the others.'

'That's no problem,' said the boy calmly. 'I like difficult games.'

The stranger shuffled the sticks, and the game began. The boy guessed correctly the first time. So did the stranger. The boy guessed correctly the next time too, but the stranger got it wrong. For the next few rounds, they both played strongly; they were very well matched. A crowd gathered to watch and cheer on the chief's son; he turned round, grinned at them and punched the air.

Then suddenly the boy's luck changed and the stranger started to win every single time. Soon his pile of treasures was overflowing, and the boy had nothing left at all.

'I think I've proved my point,' said the stranger. 'Time to stop, eh? You put up a fine game at first, I was really impressed. But you really didn't have any chance against a mighty fellow like me.'

The boy bit his lip. He stared at the stranger's winnings, then at the bare patch of grass where his own treasures had been piled up earlier on. 'I'm not giving up,' he muttered.

'But you've got nothing left to wager,' said the stranger.

'Yes I have. I'll stake one of my father's slaves.'

'Are you sure? Hadn't you better ask your father first?'

'There's no need for that, he always trusts me.' The boy gave a nervous laugh. 'I only let you win all those rounds to tease you. From now on I'm going to beat you every time.'

The stranger looked round at the crowd, one eyebrow raised questioningly. Someone went to check with the chief, who sent back a message that he had absolute faith in his son's ability.

The game went on. The boy lost again; and thus had to send one of the slaves over to the stranger. He staked the other slaves, one by one – and lost them all.

'Well,' said the stranger. 'You're only a young lad. I really think we ought to stop now.'

'No,' said the boy.

'But you haven't got anything left to offer me.'

'Yes I have. I stake my mother.'

A gasp ran around the watchers, and someone shouted, 'Wicked boy! You can't do that.'

'Who are you to tell me?' the chief's son shouted back. He steadied his voice and went on, 'Don't worry, I won't have to pay her over. And sir,' he added, turning to the stranger, 'as my mother is obviously very, very valuable – how about staking two slaves in your possession against her?'

'If you wish,' said the stranger softly.

They played the next round and the stranger won again. 'Now we really must stop,' he said.

'No, no!' shouted the boy.

So they played on. After handing over his poor mother, gradually the boy gambled away all his other relations: uncles, aunts and cousins. He even gambled away his father, so that by the time the chief arrived, he was no longer his own man. The boy had also gambled away every single person in the whole village. Only then did he agree to stop.

'Well,' said the stranger, 'that was certainly exciting, thank you. I'll gather up my takings and be on my way now.'

The chief was standing grimly in front of the outraged villagers. The boy ran over to him and whispered, 'Father, I'm sorry. But surely you don't have to go with this man?'

'Of course I must,' said the chief. 'It's a question of honour. Also, your opponent is no ordinary person: he is a Water Man. His house stands at the bottom of the ocean, which is where we must all go – except you.'

The boy turned pale.

'Goodbye, my son,' said the chief sadly. 'I have not quite lost faith in your abilities – so I hope that one day we may meet again.'

Then he led his people in a sombre line, following the Water Man on a long, long journey, through the forest and over the mountains to the distant ocean.

The boy was distraught. He wandered in and out of the empty houses, crying and tearing his hair. Since he hadn't bothered to acquire any everyday skills, he had no idea how to look after himself. Luckily there was still a fire burning in his father's house and plenty of food there. He spent the next few days in loneliness and misery, eking out his supplies and wondering what ever he could do.

Eventually, he wandered into the forest. As he stood helplessly in a clearing, he noticed smoke rising from a pile of grass. He squatted down to investigate, using a twig to gently brush away the soil. Underneath, he found a miniature house, no higher than the width of his hand.

As he stared at it, suddenly the door opened, and a black mouse came scuttling out. It turned its pale nose up towards him, fixing him with beady eyes. Then it spoke with the voice of an old woman: 'Grandson, where are you going? Ah, I see in your face that you are in some kind of trouble. Tell me, what's the matter?'

The boy choked back his tears. 'Oh, Grandmother! I've been so foolish, so wicked. I've gambled away everything I ever treasured. I have nothing left in all the world.'

'That's not good. But remember this, child: people are worth far more than material goods.'

'I know. But I've gambled away all the people in my life too!'

For a long moment, Black Mouse Woman just stood there, twitching. Then she said, 'Well, I'll help you as best I can. Come in, come in.'

Somehow, the boy found himself inside her little house. It was such a relief to have company again, with such a kindly old person too. He sat by the fire while she filled a cooking pot with water and put it over the flames to heat. Then she fetched a single fish egg from a basket and split it into two with a wedge. Each half was so small that the boy could scarcely see it. She dropped one half into the pot and waited until it began to steam. Then she scooped it out carefully, placed it on a tiny dish and handed it to the boy, saying, 'Here, grandson, this will make you feel better.'

The boy put the tiny morsel into his mouth and politely chewed it, mumbling his appreciation. To his great surprise, once he swallowed it, his hunger completely vanished.

Black Mouse Woman invited him to stay with her, and made him a very comfortable bed. He slept soundly for the first time since he had gambled everyone away. But it seemed no time at all before she was shaking him awake, whispering, 'Grandson, dawn is breaking and it's time to get up. Don't eat anything but go straight down to the river to wash. Then walk towards the sunrise, to a steep hill with bare slopes. Continue up it until you find a solitary plant. Pull this up, roots and all, then eat it.'

The boy did as he was instructed. After he had bathed, he found the hill and walked up it, crunching over dry shingle, despairing that there was nothing growing there at all. Then, right in the middle of the wilderness, he suddenly spotted a beautiful flower. He tugged it free, and ate it warily. It tasted good. Afterwards, he was overcome by sleepiness. He lay down until the feeling passed, then returned to Black Mouse Woman.

'Well done, grandson,' she said. 'The plant you ate will bring you luck. Now, to ensure everything continues to go well, you mustn't use the fire tonight. Tomorrow, I will wake you at the same time and, just like yesterday, you must fast before you go out. This time go to the beach and look for a creature washed up there. Skin it, throw the body into the water, and keep the hide to use later.'

The boy did as she bade him, going out the next day and returning with a fine sea-otter skin.

Black Mouse Woman nodded in approval. 'Now here is something else to help you.' She went to a dark corner of her house and brought forth a Goldeneye Duck, which she placed gently into his arms. The duck turned his glossy, green-black head and looked at the boy kindly with his yellow eye.

'This is your brother,' said Black Mouse Woman. 'He will accompany you on the next part of your journey, which is to the Water Man's house. When you arrive there, challenge the Water Man to gamble against you again. This time, as you play, listen carefully to your duck brother's advice.'

That night, Black Mouse Woman did not light the fire. She woke the boy at dawn again and told him the way to the distant ocean. So now the boy embarked on a long, long journey of his own, through the forest and over the mountains, accompanied by Goldeneye Duck. At last they reached that awesome place where the edge of the land ends by an expanse of water, stretching as far as it is possible to see.

Goldeneye Duck said, 'Tell the Water Man you have arrived.'

So the boy walked right down to the edge of the land, cupped his hands around his mouth and bellowed: 'Water Man, here I am, your gambling rival who you once bled dry!'

Almost at once, the waters of that great ocean peeled right apart like a door opening. Inside, the boy saw another door, this one part of a great house, twice as big and magnificent as his father's. This door opened too – and the Water Man stepped out.

'Welcome,' he said to the boy. 'So you couldn't keep away from me, you can't live without gambling, eh?'

'I've come to win back everything you tricked me into losing,' the boy answered.

'Have you now?' the Water Man mocked him. 'Well, step inside, see how I have put my recent gains to good use.'

As the Water Man turned his back, the boy picked up Goldeneye Duck and carefully hid him in his shirt. Then he followed the Water Man through the door. Once inside, he gazed around in wonder. Every nook and cranny of the house was piled with marvellous treasures – many of which had once belonged to him. The whole place was bustling with slaves – most of whom were his father's former slaves, alongside all the free people from his village. Amongst them, he was shocked to see his own mother and father, both bowed down with heavy burdens.

'Don't regret what has already happened,' Goldeneye Duck whispered. 'This time, together, we shall beat him.'

The Water Man called the boy to the centre of the house. There his ornate sticks were already set up for a game. 'Well, young friend,' he sneered, 'what would you like if you win the first round?'

'My father,' said the boy at once.

'Oho, you think you can win him, do you? Well, I'm not playing a one-sided game. What will you give me if I win – as I surely will? Or have you got nothing left?'

The boy pulled out the sea-otter skin he had found the previous morning. The Water Man nodded scornfully, saying, 'Huh! Is that all you think your poor father's worth, boy? Well, never mind, let's agree these stakes. Are you ready to begin?'

The boy was trembling with nerves. From inside his shirt, Goldeneye Duck whispered, 'Take a risk on this round. I'll watch carefully and work out how you can win the next one.'

They began to play. The boy tried with all his might to do well – but to his great dismay, he lost.

'Another round?' suggested the Water Man.

The boy was about to shake his head, get up and flee. But inside his shirt, Goldeneye Duck whispered, 'Brother, I've discovered your opponent's deceit. His trump stick is actually a fish! You've pointed at it correctly each time, but it kept slithering aside to make it appear you'd chosen the wrong one.'

The boy turned his back on the Water Man and whispered back, 'How can I overcome it?'

'Keep playing and pointing at the fish, so that it has to keep moving,' said Goldeneye Duck. Soon it will become too tired to react in time. I'll watch and let you know when it reaches that state. Then point directly at the fish really fast, so that the Water Man can't deny you've made the correct choice.'

Sure enough, now the boy began to win. The Water Man had no idea how he had overcome his trick. Like all compulsive gamblers, though he was now losing, he kept trusting his luck would turn.

In this way, the boy won freedom for his chief, mother, aunts and uncles, all the other villagers and his father's slaves. He also won back all his lost treasures.

Once he had achieved this, he bid a courteous farewell to the Water Man, who made no effort to detain him. Then, deferring humbly to his father, he accompanied his people back home.

This is why it is bad for young people to gamble too much.

Teit: *Tahltan Tales,* 1921
For information on the original informant, see p. 494.

Of the gambling game, Teit says:

'In this stick-game, common to many Western tribes, one man has to guess a particular stick out of a number. The sticks are rolled in grass and shuffled. The method of playing varies from tribe to tribe.'

It was described in detail by Culin in *Games of the North American Indians* (1907). The sticks could vary from simple and undecorated to elaborately painted ones; and the number used in a game could range from ten to over 100. They were divided into two bundles, and the object was to guess the location of an odd or particularly marked stick, sometimes using a pointer. The count was kept with the sticks themselves, the game continuing until one player had won them all.

The motif of the Water Man living under the sea may seem strange for an inland people divided from the Pacific Ocean by the peaks of the Rockies. However, Teit describes how trading links ensured that the Tahltan often met with Northwest Coast tribes, particularly the Tlingit, for weeks at a time. On such occasions, a favourite shared activity was storytelling, sometimes in the form of competitions to decide which had the most stories. He says that the Tahltan acknowledged their inferiority to the Tlingit in this matter.

A malicious Water Man also appears in a story of the neighbouring Kaska people, in this instance living in a lake where 'he fooled and ate people'.

The Carrier people had a similar, though more prosaic, story; in this case, after the gambler wins everything back, he recklessly continues playing until he has lost it all again, spending the rest of his life in destitution. Here the game was called 'atlih' and used finely polished 'bone-sticks'. It was said to have once been extremely popular, though by the late 19th century only a few elderly men continued to play it.

Stories about the dangers of gambling were common throughout North America. See the Californian story THE END OF DARKNESS, p. 259.

COPPER MOUNTAIN

Chipewyan

A woman was out hunting with her family when she fell behind and lost the others. She searched everywhere for them without success and finally found herself standing in an unknown place before a vast stretch of water. There she heard the splashing of paddles, and saw a strange sealskin boat approaching. The men who stepped out of it were Eskimos, dressed in thick furs. They spoke to her, but she could not understand a single word they said. In the end, they seized her and dragged her into their boat.

They took her on a long journey, across the water then overland to their village, which lay far away in the north. It was a bleak country. There was no forest there; just open, windswept tundra in all directions. Shortly after they arrived, winter drew in, the days grew dark and the whole land was smothered in snow.

Since the woman could not speak their language, and did not know their ways, none of the men wanted her for a wife. Instead, they used her as a slave. The life was harsh, the work hard and she desperately missed her family.

Years went by.

At last, late one summer, she found the courage to leave. She had no idea where she was or how to get home. Her only guide was the sun, which she knew she must follow southwards through the barren land. For food on her journey, she managed to kill small birds and rabbits as she went along. Eventually, she found herself walking along some kind of animal track, and this led her back to the lonely grey water.

The woman had always been strong; she had never given in to despair during all her years of captivity. However, now she began to weep. For she knew she must cross this water; but how could she, without a boat, and with no trees in this land from which she could make one? She sat down on the shore, rested her head on her knees and sobbed bitterly.

Suddenly she became aware of a presence close by. Her heart turned over. It must be her Eskimo captors, come to haul her back to slavery! She looked up fearfully. But instead of men, she saw…a Wolf.

The rest of the pack was surely nearby! She did not dare move, in case it provoked them to attack. But no other animals appeared.

For a long moment, the lone Wolf stared at her intently. Then it took a step towards her and came up very close. She flinched and braced herself…

But all the Wolf did was push its nose against hers to nuzzle her. Then it put out its tongue and gently licked away her tears. When it had finished, it lay down beside her for a few moments, panting. Then it stood up, walked slowly down the beach to the water's edge and waded out into the waves. As it went, it turned its head every so often, as if willing her to follow.

The woman watched as the Wolf splashed further. The water was very shallow; no matter how far out the Wolf went, the waves never rose above its flanks.

The Wolf paused some way out, as if waiting for her. The woman stood up uncertainly, picked up two driftwood sticks to steady herself, and began to follow. As soon as she did, the Wolf waded out further still.

They went on in this way together for some time, with the Wolf constantly glancing back to make sure she was keeping up. All the while, the water stayed at the same level, no lower than her ankles, no higher than her knees. Day melted into thin summer twilight. Still the Wolf and the woman trudged on. Every so often, she stopped, leaned on her sticks and dozed with exhaustion; each time she did, the Wolf waited patiently. When she awoke and waded forward, the Wolf continued its advance. Thus they travelled for four whole days and nights.

On the fifth morning after they had entered the water, the Wolf led the woman onto dry land. It loitered nearby for a while, as if to be sure that she was safe; then turned and hurried back across the water, the same way that they had come.

The landscape here was very different from the endless tundra that she had fled from. Oh joy – there was the edge of the forest!

She ran into it, and the first thing she saw in the dappled light was a cluster of ripe berries. She picked a load and ate her fill, then felt much better.

Very soon she spied a broad trail dotted with the unmistakable hoof prints of caribou. The woman had often watched her menfolk hunt them, and was eager to have a go herself. She still had the awl that her captors had given her for working their skins; now she tied it onto a stick to form a spear. She hid in the brush, and was soon rewarded by thundering hooves as a huge herd came running past. The woman leaped up and deftly speared as many as she could. When they had gone, she saw with pride that she had killed more than enough to feed herself through the coming winter. She took out her knife and quickly butchered them, then carried the meat to a clearing to dry in the wind.

There she scrabbled in the soft leaves and pine needles of the forest floor and used her bare hands to dig out a sunken house, like the one she had lived in as an Eskimo slave. She smoothed the caribou hides to make floor coverings and folded them into a bed. Thus she made herself a very cosy home. The cold, dark season was already drawing in. But she was snug as a bear below the frozen ground, feasting on caribou steaks that she roasted on firewood collected from the surrounding trees. How good it felt to be back in her own country, how wonderful to be free!

Winter passed. One spring morning, the woman stepped outside into a chorus of birdsong, and saw an extraordinary sight. A hill in the distance had caught the sunlight, which had turned its slopes into a curious, dark red shimmer. It was the wrong season for the trees to be turning red and it was too still to be a forest fire. So the woman set off to investigate.

When she reached the hill, she found it was completely barren, yet formed of neither rocks nor sand. Instead, it was smooth all over, red-brown in colour, burnished as if some mysterious being had rubbed it with soft leather. Under her touch it felt cool.

Copper!

She moved her hands over it in wonder, picked up a sharp stone and chipped away carefully at the mountainside. In this way, she broke off some lustrous shards, slivers and nuggets. She held them in her palm, astonished by their soft sheen, moved by their beauty. She tried bending the pieces and found they were pliable.

Laughing with excitement, she sat down, piled them into her lap and started working them into shapes. She ran her fingernails over the surfaces and found it was easy to carve swirls and lines into them. She forced them into curved strips, which she scratched with beautiful, decorative patterns, thus forming a wondrous set of bracelets.

She pushed the bracelets up her arms, broke off more shards and hung some from her dress as ornamental rattles. She stuffed the rest for safe-keeping into her pack. Then, laden with her hoard, she resumed her journey southward, marking the route she took with piles of stones at every junction, to ensure she could find her way back to the copper mountain.

As she went along, she started singing. Her song was so loud and happy, that it carried far across the forest. Two youths, setting traps some way off, heard it. They wondered who it was and what was the cause of such merriment. They left what they were doing and hurried towards it.

The woman saw them coming along the path towards her; they were dressed like her own people! And as they drew close enough to make out what they were saying, she realised they were indeed speaking her own language, the tongue that she hadn't heard for years. She ran up to them and flung herself into their arms, weeping with relief.

The two youths exchanged glances. What kind of woman was this, with her dress covered in jingling sparkles, and leaping on them so brazenly?

'What's the matter?' they asked.

The woman pawed them in excitement. 'Come with me, I want to show you my treasure!'

The youths winked at each other. Her treasure? Oho, this was a come-on, for sure!

'Lead the way,' they guffawed.

All those years in exile had made the woman completely forget how to behave. She took the hand of one youth and beckoned eagerly to the other, then led them back along her trail of piled-up stones, until they reached the copper mountain. By that time, the youths were totally intoxicated by the woman's own excitement. They glanced only briefly up at the shimmering slopes, then feverishly caught each others' eyes again. The next moment, they both pounced on her, tore off her clothes and brutally tried to ravish her.

517

But this was the woman who had survived abduction and slavery; who had walked through water alongside a wild wolf; who had endured winter in the wilderness alone. She fought back at them with the savagery of a she-bear; and when her strength was almost spent, she kicked them aside and clambered up the gleaming slopes of the copper mountain, right to the top.

As soon as she reached its peak, the mountain split open. Then it swallowed her up, enveloping her into its heart.

The youths went home, full of shame. They never dared tell their families what they had done. Because of that, they could never tell anyone about the copper mountain either. So no one ever found it again.

Since then, copper has only existed in small pieces, scattered in rare places, in hidden corners of the earth.

This happened in the earliest age of the world.

Hearne, Samuel: *Journey from Fort Prince Wales,* 1802
Franklin: *Narrative of a Journey to the Shores of the Polar Sea,* 1823
Goddard: *Chipewyan Texts,* 1912

This retelling calls the woman's captors 'Eskimos' rather than 'Inuit', since that was the name always used in English during the 19th century and earlier.

The story seems to have been very widely known, judging from the number of versions that were independently collected. The oldest, very brief, record was made following Hearne's 1771 expedition to the Coppermine River, which runs through Northwest Territories and Nunavut.

Franklin heard the story at the Fort Chipewyan trading post in 1820, from an elderly Chipewyan man called Rabbit's Head, the stepson of a late chief. It was narrated in the Chipewyan tongue, and translated by a Mr Dease, of the Northwest Company, a European fur trading enterprise that later merged with the Hudson's Bay Company (see p. 23).

Goddard collected his version nearly a hundred years later in 1911 at the Chipewyan Cold Lake Reserve in Alberta. It was narrated by a 35-year old man called Jean Baptiste Ennou, who had received a basic education on the reserve and spoke fluent English. Goddard says his book reproduces it almost exactly as it was told. He does not mention the rape at the end, and claims that the men who the woman led to the copper were French.

Very similar stories were recorded amongst the Beaver and Slavey peoples. Both say that after the men abused her, the woman slowly sank into the copper, until only her head was protruding. The Beaver say she was still seen alive there two years later, whilst the Slavey claim that her living head could still be seen there after ten years. However they agree that in the end she completely vanished.

Both Goddard's Chipewyan version and the Beaver version state that the woman had a child, though they do not say whether he was born in or out of wedlock. According to these, she took him with her when she fled the Eskimos, but abandoned him during the journey because he was too greedy.

Copper occurs naturally as a pure metal and was used by Native Americans for many thousands of years before the European settlement. As well as the deposits found along the Coppermine River mentioned above, the Copper River in southern Alaska is similarly named from the abundant mineral deposits along its upper reaches; and the T'atsaot'ine people of Northwest Territories were called 'Yellowknife' or 'Copper Indians' by Whites because they used and traded tools made from copper deposits.

The account of a wolf helping a human is less unlikely than it may seem. Recent scientific studies of Arctic wolves on Ellesmere Island in the extreme north of Canada have found that wolves with little experience of people have no natural fear of them and are prepared to venture in close proximity.

A Carrier tale, collected in 1893, tells of people congregating on the seashore by a tower-like mountain of copper, and holding a shouting match with the Haida people of the Northwest Coast, to decide which nation should own it. It says that the Haidas' voices were so loud that the tower tottered over to their side; thus they came to dominate the copper trade. Several Northwest Coast stories mention copper as a valuable material, including THE COUNTRY UNDER THE SEA (see p. 392). Another Tsimshian myth features a supernatural 'sky prince' who teaches people the art of smelting.

Le grand conseil des femmes, chez les Wyandot
('The great council of women, among the Wyandot')
Illustration by unnamed artist
from Reclus & Reclus: *L'homme et la Terre,* 1905.

MYTHS OF THE NORTHEAST

PEOPLE OF THE NORTHEAST

Canada:
New Brunswick, Nova Scotia and Prince Edward Island.
Southern parts of Ontario and Quebec, small part of Manitoba.

United States:
Connecticut, Delaware, Illinois, Indiana, Kentucky, Maine,
Maryland, Massachusetts, Michigan, New Hampshire, New Jersey,
New York State, Ohio, Pennsylvania, Rhode Island and Vermont.
Parts of: Iowa, Minnesota, Missouri, North Carolina,
Tennessee, Virginia, West Virginia and Wisconsin.

The Northeast cultural region covers southeastern Canada and the northeastern area of the United States, including the Great Lakes, the St Lawrence River area, the east coast and the islands. The terrain ranges from mountains to low-lying river basins and coastal plains. Summers tend to be warm and winters cold with significant snowfall. Historically, much of the region was covered by both deciduous and conifer forest.

Northeast societies were all hunters and gatherers. Where landscape and climate permitted, they were also farmers, and for those with good access to waterways, fish was an important food. Their political systems were characterised by egalitarianism, negotiation and democratic debate to reach group consensus; and they followed strong ethical codes of moderation and respect. Their religions were based upon belief in inner spiritual powers which resided in people, animals and natural phenomena such as storms. These could be harnessed by prayer and song, and were used for healing, success in hunting and love charms. Shamans and unusually successful hunters were believed to have particularly strong manifestations of these powers.

Within these broad parameters, Northeast peoples fall into two distinct groups. One was characterised by their permanent villages of large, sturdily built, communal longhouses. The other group were seasonal migrants, who moved about to harvest wild foods, using separate homes for summer and winter.

The Iroquois, or Haudenosaunee – 'People of the Longhouse' – was and still is a confederacy of adjacent nations. Its initial five members were the Cayuga, Mohawk, Oneida, Onondaga and Seneca. They were later joined by the Tuscarora, and also absorbed the Huron-Wendat (Wyandot) confederacy, itself an alliance of five nations. All shared a similar language and lifestyle.

The confederacy was founded at an unknown date, long before White settlement. According to tradition, it was inspired by a vision of the prophet Deganawida, 'The Peacemaker' and his disciple Aionwatha (Hiawatha). Also called 'The Great League of Peace', its aims were to stop inter-tribal warfare, to live in harmony, to promote peaceful decision-making, and to provide a united front against outside enemies.

Each member nation had its own council for internal affairs. Their all-male chiefs were chosen by, and answerable to, councils of women. A similarly organised 'grand council' dealt with cross-member affairs. Historical and legal records were kept, and treaties formalised, by the use of 'wampum belts'. These were made from white and purple shell-beads, woven into symbolic patterns on collars and belts. Debating and negotiation were highly valued, and some Haudenosaunee chiefs became famed for their formidable oratory when dealing with the colonial and then the Canadian and US governments.

At a lower level, the longhouse people were organised into clans, each represented by an animal: bear, beaver, deer, eel, hawk, heron, snipe, turtle and wolf. These transcended national boundaries; for example a Mohawk Wolf-clan member and a Seneca Wolf-clan member regarded themselves as kin. Each clan originated from a single female ancestor and was led by a woman.

Women enjoyed high status in longhouse society, which was matrilineal. Ancestry was traced through the female line from the original 'clan mother'. Children belonged to their mother's clan;

the significant men in their lives were not their fathers, but their mothers' brothers. Upon marriage, the husband moved into his wife's family house alongside her sisters and their husbands. Women owned the property, and could end an unhappy marriage by ordering the husband to leave the house, leaving their children behind.

Women had prime responsibility for food production, carrying out all agricultural work, apart from the hard physical task of clearing the land of trees and brush. They worked in groups, often helped by slaves or prisoners of war, while the children helped guard against vermin. It is estimated that longhouse people grew 80 per cent of their food – mainly beans, maize and squash, known as the 'three sisters'. Tobacco was grown for ceremonial smoking, and European crops were later added. Meat was brought in by male hunters, working in groups and often away from their families for extended periods. The most important game was deer but they also caught bears, beavers, frogs, muskrats, owls, rabbits, squirrels and wildfowl. Fishing in lakes, rivers and streams was another important male activity. Both women and men gathered wild fruit, nuts, roots, bark, stems, leaves and fungi. Syrup was extracted from wild maple trees for use as a sweetener.

The longhouse peoples lived year-round in fortified villages, each surrounded by a set of fields. The villages were linked by networks of trails, dotted with travellers' lodges, each set a day's journey apart. Every few decades the intensively farmed fields would stop yielding enough crops; so the people would relocate and clear new tracts of land by slashing-and-burning.

A village comprised a number of communal longhouses owned by female elders, each accommodating a large extended family. The men constructed them using pole frameworks covered by overlapping slabs of bark. They were windowless, with a door at either end. Inside, each nuclear family had its own apartment, with a platform for sitting and sleeping, covered with mats or hides, and storage space above. The central corridor contained a row of fires, each shared by two families whose apartments faced each other.

A major preoccupation of longhouse men was warfare against outside nations. This was highly ritualised, conducted both to demonstrate the warriors' bravery and to settle scores. War would typically begin with a feast, and featured singing and dancing as the warriors travelled to attack their chosen enemy. Some of these would be killed, and their scalps collected as trophies. Others, including women and children, were taken prisoner, destined for slavery or adoption into the victors' nation, though some enemy men were ritually tortured to death.

For spiritual matters, including healing, there were secret rites and societies, with both male and female priests.

The Seasonal Migrants included members of the Wabanaki Confederacy (see p.531) the Algonquins, and other related peoples, spread across a wide area.

During the winter, they lived in small family groups scattered deep in the forest, enabling the men to maximise the hunting and trapping of bear, beaver, caribou, deer, moose, otter, porcupine and rabbit. In some areas, the spring thaw brought the popular activity of collecting sap from maple trees to be processed into syrup. During the summer months, families gathered together en masse in villages near rivers, lakes or the coast. Here they co-operated in fishing and shooting waterfowl; and gathering eggs, shellfish, wild herbs, roots and fruits. Where the terrain and climate were suitable, the women also grew crops similar to the longhouse people. Some peoples harvested wild rice from streams and lakes at the end of the summer, with men paddling the canoes as women gathered the rice with sticks. Summer was also the time for holding group councils to discuss matters of mutual concern.

Birch bark, freely available from the forest trees, was an important resource. It was used to cover rectangular cabins in summer, and dome-shaped or tipi-shaped 'wigwams' in winter, the latter lined with hides for warmth. On inland and coastal waterways, strips of bark were sewn together with spruce roots to make lightweight canoes, waterproofed with spruce resin and bear grease. It was also widely used for containers. The Micmac and Ojibwe made bark scrolls, inscribed with pictographs using bone tools or charcoal, for recording facts, ancestral songs and teachings.

The seasonal migrants were mostly organised into clans, each with its own animal totem. Clans were often split into two moieties, within which marriage was forbidden. Chiefs represented a particular clan, moiety, village, band or district and periodically met together in councils. Other types of leader were respected for their skill in hunting or war, or because of their visionary dreams. Most, though not all, of the seasonal migrant societies were patrilineal, with descent passing through the male line and women moving in with their husbands' families upon marriage. However, women were usually treated as respected equals, and their opinions were valued in decision-making.

LIFE IN THE NORTHEAST
WHEN THESE STORIES WERE COLLECTED

The oldest story in this book is a Northeast one, collected from the Wyandot people in the early 17th century (see THE KEEPER OF THE BRAINS OF THE DEAD, p. 551). At that time, the coast of modern Massachusetts was being settled by the British 'Pilgrim Fathers'. They were initially welcomed and helped by local Native Americans, agreeing a treaty that brought 40 years of peace between them. British, Dutch and French fishermen, whalers, fur traders and missionaries, were also living and working in the area.

Many Native Americans succumbed to the European diseases these incomers brought. Amongst the survivors, some prospered as major suppliers to the European fur trade. However, the White trade goods they obtained in exchange for their furs caused steep cultural changes, which were exacerbated by the French enforcing conversion to Christianity in return for their coveted weapons. As demand for fur increased, the hunting season was extended, and the guns and steel traps introduced by the Whites killed game with unprecedented efficiency. This caused unsustainable drops in the target animal populations, so some hunters reinvented themselves as middlemen, sourcing furs from distant interior peoples, particularly in the Subarctic, and selling them on.

By the time most of the stories in this section were collected, some 250 years later, life for the Northeast peoples had been dramatically transformed. They were forced off their ancestral land by a series of spurious treaties, broken first by European governments on behalf of the colonists, and later by the independent Canadian and US governments. Numerous Native Americans succumbed to disease, the ravages of alcohol introduced by White settlers and the attempted annihilation of their cultures. Some were now living on small reservations; outside these, others had adopted a White lifestyle, enforced by the compulsory education of their children. A number had intermarried with Whites and most had converted to Christianity.

STORYTELLING IN THE NORTHEAST

One of the oldest records of Northeast storytelling dates to 1645, when the Jesuit missionary Paul Ragueneau wrote of the Wyandot:

'The elders of the country were assembled this winter for the election of a very celebrated captain. They are accustomed, on such occasions, to relate the stories which they have learned regarding their ancestors...so that the young people, who are present and hear them, may preserve the memory thereof, and relate them in their turn, when they shall have become old. They do this in order thus to transmit to posterity the history and the annals of the country...

'They offer, to the person from whom they desire to hear something, a little bundle of straws a foot long, which serve them as counters for calculating the numbers, and for aiding the memory of those present, distributing in various lots these same straws, according to the diversity of the things which they relate... The turn having come to a Christian old man, to tell what he knew... When he came to name God...as the Creator of the world, the eldest captain of those present seizes the straws from his hands, imposes silence upon him, and tells him that he does wrong to relate the stories of the French, and not those of the Hurons [Wyandot].'

Despite the march of White culture and Christianity, even by the late 19th century, ethnologists were able to collect many surviving myths and traditional tales. Charles G. Leland wrote:

'When I began, in the summer of 1882, to collect among the Passamaquoddy Indians at Campobello, New Brunswick, their traditions and folklore, I expected to find very little indeed [from] these Indians, few in number, surrounded by White people, and thoroughly converted to Roman Catholicism... What was my amazement, however, at discovering, day by day, that there existed among them, entirely by oral tradition, a far grander mythology...illustrated by an incredible number of tales. I soon ascertained that these were very ancient.'

He added that they:

> '...always distinguish very accurately between their ancient lore and that derived from the Whites.'

Even in their reduced state, Native American storytellers in this region continued to revere and uphold the ancestral styles of narration. In the early 20th century, Skinner & Satterlee found that Menominee storytellers:

> '...were invariably referred to as being able to tell the tales in the old way, as they ought to be told... The Menominee lay great stress on adherence to pattern, especially with regard to the culture hero stories and sacred myths.'

Ancient storytelling customs were carefully preserved, including the widespread rule that it was best kept as an activity for the winter months. The Algonquin said:

> 'It is not proper to tell stories in summer, lest one die; but, if stories are told, they must be told for ten successive evenings in order to prevent evil.'

There was a sense that the old narratives were in danger of dying out. Leland tells of an elderly Algonquin man called Edward Jack with 'an endless store of Indian lore', sitting by the fire, smoking tobacco mixed with willow bark and saying sadly:

> 'All these things there are many and long traditions...the old people know them; the young forget them and the wisdom which is in them.'

Working with the Seneca during the same period, Curtin found:

> 'It was only the old who possessed any knowledge of Seneca Mythology – middle-aged and young men had "thrown it away"... If the collecting of it had been delayed a few years the opportunity to gather it would have been lost for ever.'

Nevertheless, research for this book unearthed some 300 stories from the Northeast – one of the largest canons of any of the cultural areas.

Arthur C. Parker was of partial Seneca descent, and adopted into the nation as an honorary member (see p. 538). Writing of his experiences around the turn of the 20th century, he vividly described a typical storytelling session amongst those people:

> 'As the night grows darker, a shout is heard outside and all the children run to the door. "Dajoh, dajoh!" they exclaim, and rushing out surround a tall man of middle age, one taking his hand and leading him in. We can hear the shout of 'The storyteller has come!' His entrance to the lodge puts the young

people in a state of suppressed excitement. Even the older people are pleasantly disposed towards him, and one matron draws forth a bench which she sets before the central fire. Several corn-husk mats are then placed around on the floor and the company draws into a circle...

'The storyteller has two bags, one containing his pipe and tobacco, and the other filled with mysterious lumps – the trophies that remind him of his stories – bear teeth, shells, bark dolls, strings of wampum, bunches of feathers, bits of bark with hieroglyphs upon them, and the claws of animals. He takes his seat and, after smoking a pipeful of sacred tobacco, throws some of this fragrant herb upon the fire, at the same time saying a ritualistic prayer to the unseen powers, about whom he is soon to discourse. Finally he exclaims, "Hauh, oneh djadaondyus," and all the people respond, "Hauh oneh!" He plunges his hand into his mystery bag and draws forth a bear's tusk. "Ho!" he says. "This is a tale of Bear. All now listen!"... Another trinket comes forth, and again another, as a new tale unfolds.

'When the night has grown old, and the youngsters show signs of weariness by falling asleep, the storyteller closes his bag, carefully ties it and then starts to smoke again. The listeners have been thrilled by his dramatic recitation, they have been moved to uproarious laughter or made to shudder with awe... Everyone files past the storyteller with a small gift – a brooch, a carved nut, a small bag of tobacco or a strand of sinew for thread. No gift is large and most gifts are pinches of native tobacco. The storyteller then finds a comfortable bed.'

THE PEOPLES BEHIND THE STORIES

Algonquin (Omamiwinini, Anishnabek)

Their ancestral homeland was mainly in southern Quebec, where nine bands of the Algonquin nation are still currently based, with a further band in Ontario. Their mother tongue, still spoken today, inspired many modern Canadian place names; for example Quebec is named from the Algonquin word 'kebec', meaning 'place where the river narrows'. Their modern ethical code promotes treating the Earth and one's fellow beings with respect, and working together for the benefit of all.

Iroquois (Haudenosaunee)
For membership and historical details of this confederacy, see p. 523; the modern Haudenosaunee Confederacy still follows its founding principles. They claim to be one of the oldest participatory democracies in the world, and to have inspired the US Constitution with their values of unity, peace and freedom to pursue individual success. Today about half live on their main reserve in southern Ontario, forming the largest population of Canadian First Nations. The rest live in the United States, spread between New York State, Oklahoma and Wisconsin.

Menominee (Mamaceqtaw)
The name 'Menominee' means 'Wild Rice People' in the Ojibwe language, reflecting that both nations harvested wild rice as a staple food. Historically they lived in Wisconsin, which is the location of their modern reservation, and part of Michigan. They have five ancestral clans: Bear, Eagle, Wolf, Moose and Crane.

Micmac (Mi'kmaq)
Today their main communities are in New Brunswick and Nova Scotia – which, alongside Prince Edward Island, were their ancestral homelands. They also have smaller communities in Maine, Massachusetts Newfoundland and Quebec. They had a traditional system of writing with charcoal on birch bark to keep important records. Many still have some knowledge of the mother tongue. They are part of the Wabanaki Confederacy (see below).

Passamaquoddy
Their ancestral and current homelands are Maine and western New Brunswick. Today some still speak the Malecite-Passamaquoddy language which they share with their related neighbours, the Maliseet people. They are part of the Wabanaki Confederacy (see below).

Penobscot
They mainly live in Maine along the Penobscot River, with other groups living across the border in New Brunswick, Nova Scotia and Prince Edward Island. They are currently working to revitalise their ancestral language and to protect their historical treasures. They are part of the Wabanaki Confederacy, see below.

Seneca (O-non-dowa-gah)
They are the largest member of the Iroquois Confederacy (see above), and in the 19th century were said to be the most powerful. They are known as 'Keepers of the Western Door' due to their location in relation to the other confederacy members. Today most live in New York State, with others in Oklahoma and Ontario.

Wabanaki Confederacy
This comprises five Algonquian-speaking peoples: the Abenaki, Maliseet, Micmac, Passamaquoddy and Penobscot. They are spread across New Brunswick, Nova Scotia, Prince Edward Island and southern Quebec; and in the US, in New Hampshire, Maine, Massachusetts and Vermont. Their name means 'Children of the Dawn Country'. Their annual gathering, revived in the 1990s, now welcomes sympathetic outsiders such as environmental activists.

Wyandot
Originally an alliance of five nations in Ontario (the Huron-Wendat confederacy), in the 17th century they were absorbed by the Iroquois (see above), sharing a similar culture and language. Some groups remained separate and today live near Quebec City, with a further small number in Oklahoma. French settlers called them 'Huron', meaning 'boar's head', from the men's hairstyle.

Winnebago (Ho-Chunk)
The Ho-Chunk Nation of Wisconsin is based in their original homeland, with a separate group in Nebraska. They are working to restore use of their mother tongue and other elements of their traditional culture.

Research for this section also covered stories from the following Northeast peoples: Delaware (Lenni Lenape), Maliseet, Ojibwe (Chippewa), Oneida, Onondaga, Sac and Fox (Meskwaki).

THE STORY STONE

◇□◇▷◇□◇

Seneca (O-non-dowa-gah)

This happened long, long ago, way back in the time of our forefathers.

There was a boy called Crow, whose mother and father had both died. No one wanted to adopt him, so he had to take care of himself. Luckily, he was resourceful. He managed to build himself a rough shelter out of branches, and for food he hunted small game: birds and squirrels. But without a mother to scold him to wash, or to mend his clothes and heal his scratches, he was always ragged and smelly, covered in scabs. So everyone in his village mocked him and yelled abuse at him, calling him 'Filthy One' and 'Good for Nothing'.

In the end, he couldn't stand it any more. 'Why should I put up with this?' he thought. 'It's not my fault I'm an orphan, and I've never caused any trouble. I'll go off somewhere else, teach myself to become a great hunter, and never go near these brutes again.'

So Crow secretly packed his bow and arrows, some scraps of food and a little tobacco, all scavenged from the villagers' leavings. Then he set off through the forest. He walked a long way, until he came to a river. Hauled up on the bank there, he saw a small canoe. He pushed it into the water and got in.

However, before he could pick up the paddle, the canoe began to move of its own accord – not through the water, but up into the air! It rose as fast as an arrow flies. Then it spun round to face south, and flew steadily away through the clouds.

On and on it went, until at last it began to sink towards a strange country. It came to rest on another river, this one overshadowed by high cliffs. Crow paddled it to a narrow beach and got out. He looked up and saw plenty of hand- and foot-holds in the rocky cliff-face above him, so he climbed up it and soon reached the top. He walked through the forest until he found himself in a clearing that was open to the sun and stars, but sheltered from the wind. Here he set to work, stripping bark from the trees and using it to build a small but cosy cabin. When he had finished, he looked around for somewhere to sit and eat his scraps.

At once, he noticed a large, round stone, waist high, with a flat, smooth top. He sprang onto it, made himself comfortable and unwrapped his humble meal.

He was just about to take the first bite, when he almost jumped out of his skin. For here, right in the middle of nowhere, a voice suddenly said: 'Have you come to hear a story?'

Crow gazed around nervously. There was definitely no one in the clearing except for him. He jumped down from the stone and ran into the trees in each direction, but couldn't see any sign of anyone or any living thing, and no tracks except his own. He went back to sit on the stone, scratching his head in bewilderment.

At once the voice said again, 'Have you come to hear a story?' It seemed to come directly from the stone itself.

'What...what is a story?' he managed to answer.

'It is a treasure,' said the Stone. 'It is an account of things that happened long, long ago,'

'What kind of things?'

'Marvellous events, mysterious happenings, sacred people. There was a world before this. The things I can tell you about happened in that world.'

'Oh! I would very much like to hear them,' Crow said.

'Very well,' said the Stone, 'but I cannot give away such a treasure for nothing. If you wish to hear one of my stories, in return you must give me a gift.'

'I'm afraid I've nothing to offer you but some half mouldy bird-flesh or some scraps of tobacco,' Crow said sadly.

'Give me the tobacco,' said the Stone, 'and I will begin.'

So Crow tipped all the fragments of tobacco that he had out onto the Stone, and waited. After a short time, the Stone began to speak again: 'Long ago, in the time of your forefathers when the world that existed before this one was young...'

As Crow listened, his eyes grew large and his mouth dropped open. He had never heard such wondrous things before.

All too soon, the Stone said, 'This story is finished. Now night is falling and you must rest.'

'Tomorrow,' begged Crow, 'will you tell me more?'

'I will indeed,' said the Stone. 'But for next time, you must learn and carry out the correct rituals for listening to stories. This evening, as it was your first time, I have been willing to speak simply in return for your gift; but in future you must say and do certain things to show that you appreciate what you are hearing and giving me your full attention.'

'I'll do whatever you wish,' cried Crow.

'This is good,' said the Stone. 'Now listen carefully. In future, when I announce that I am about to tell a story, you must say "Nio"; and as I speak you must say "Hen", so that I know you are listening. You must never fall asleep but continue to listen intently until I say "Da'neho nigaga'is", to show that my story is finished. Then you shall give me gifts and I shall be as satisfied as you.'

'I will,' Crow promised.

He slept well that night, better than he had ever done before. Perhaps it was because he was away from his tormentors in the village. Perhaps it was also because the wonderful story he had just heard sweetened his dreams. The next morning he rose early and went out hunting. By midday he had managed to kill a great many birds. He lit a fire and roasted them, boiling the carcasses into soup. Afterwards, he worked at making their bones into arrow points. When the Sun began to sink, he ran back to the Stone, with a good clutch of birds. He sat down and waited.

Very soon, the Stone began to speak again: 'Shall I tell you another story?'

'Nio!' answered Crow.

'Long ago...' began the Stone.

'Hen,' said Crow, to show he was paying attention.

And so the Stone proceeded to tell him of more extraordinary people, creatures and events. Its voice was rich and deep; it filled the twilight shadows with such magic, such terror and such great deeds that Crow thought his head was scarcely big enough to hold them all.

When at last the Stone said, "Da'neho nigaga'is", to show that he was finished, Crow laid out the birds in the centre of the Stone as his gift for the night.

'Thank you,' said the Stone. 'You have done well with your hunting and your learning today. Tomorrow I shall tell you more.'

And so it went on, evening after evening. Crow felt as if he was bursting with all the wonderful stories he had heard. One day, he spoke about this to the Stone. 'I would like to remember all your stories for ever,' he said, 'but there are so many, and they are all so long, I'm afraid I might forget them.'

'Ah,' said the Stone, 'then it is time for you to travel towards the sunrise.'

'How far must I go and why?' Crow asked.

'Travel until you reach a big village.'

'I don't want to go to a village. In the one where I grew up, the people who lived there were cruel to me.'

'This place will be different,' said the Stone. 'None of these people will know anything of what has gone before.'

'What shall I do there?'

'When you arrive, you will know.'

So the next morning, Crow packed up his bow and arrows and made his way eastwards through the forest. By the end of the day, he came to a village, just as the Stone had told him. He entered it nervously. Some boys were playing in the centre, and called out to him to join them. They were so impressed by his strength and speed, that they didn't notice how ragged he was.

'Our fathers are teaching us to hunt deer,' they said. 'Why don't you join us tomorrow?'

So he did, and the men were impressed by him too, because he had been hunting birds for himself for so long, that he quickly adapted to bringing down larger game. He generously shared his kill with these people who had treated him so kindly, and in return the village families eagerly befriended him. They especially enjoyed hearing the stories he had learned from the Stone, although in truth he could only remember a few of them, and some were incomplete. Nevertheless, just as the Stone had ordained it, they gave him gifts in return. As a result, he soon had a fine new suit of deerskin clothes. Then, one day, an old widow invited him into her house.

'My daughter has a present for you,' she said. 'Come this way, come in.'

Inside her house, a young woman stepped forward. 'I made this for you, storyteller,' she said. And she handed him a pouch, covered with exquisite quillwork embroidery. Crow accepted it happily; so the girl stepped forward and offered him another gift, a loaf of bridal bread. Crow accepted that as well. In this simple way, the pair were married.

Unfortunately, they had only been together for a matter of days, before trouble came to them.

'I'm afraid my elder sister is very jealous that I've married you,' said his wife. 'So jealous, that she wants to kill you. I think we should run away together before she can cause us any harm.'

So they crept out in the middle of the night, and followed the trail back westwards to the forest clearing where Crow had built his bark hut. They arrived just as the Sun was setting, and straight away, Crow took her to sit on the Stone. At once the Stone welcomed them both and began telling them a new story.

When it finally said 'Da'neho nigaga'is' and the stars came out to light the night, the young couple went to his hut.

'Now you know how I learned the stories I shared with your people,' said Crow.

'Oh, I knew that already,' his wife answered. 'The Stone is my grandfather.'

Crow stared at her in amazement.

'And it was my grandfather who told me to make the pouch for you,' she went on. 'It is to keep all his stories safe. From now on, every time you hear one, you must put a small memento inside the pouch. In future, each memento will remind you of the story it is associated with, and so you will never forget any of them.'

They lived in the forest clearing all through the winter. Every day, Crow went out hunting while his wife kept house, preserved the stores of meat and sewed clothes. Every evening the Stone told them more stories, and for each one Crow added to the mementos inside his pouch.

At last, the snow began to melt and it was spring. One evening when Crow and his wife went to sit on the Stone, it was silent for a long while. Finally it said:

'I have finished. I have told you everything. Now, listen carefully to what you must do. Keep these stories as long as the world lasts. Tell them to your children and grandchildren, generation after generation. It is true that some people will remember them better than others, and some will tell them differently. None of this matters, so long as when you visit one another, you tell the stories, and keep them up always.'

The next morning, Crow's wife said she would like him to take her to the village where he was born.

'No,' he said. 'The people there all despise me. None of them will be pleased to see me again.'

'Well,' she said, 'we must go there anyway.' She led him down the cliff to the riverbank where, long before, he had left the flying canoe.

'I expect you have often wondered where this came from,' she said. 'Well, now I can tell you. I sent it to you, following the orders of my grandfather, the Stone. Come on, let's get in. You paddle, and on the way I shall teach you some new things – some songs.'

Once again, the canoe rose into the air. As they soared through the clouds, Crow listened to his wife singing, and by the time they landed he had committed all her songs to memory too. They were back in the very spot where he had originally found the canoe waiting for him. They both got out.

'So,' he said gloomily, 'we'd better go to my old home, since you're so anxious to see it.'

His wife took his hand and led him to a great fallen, moss-covered tree. It had lain there for so long that its core had rotted away, leaving it completely hollow.

'Before we go there,' she said, 'take off your clothes, then crawl through this tree.'

Crow did as she asked him, though he was ashamed to stand naked before her, for the abuse he'd suffered as a boy had left him disfigured by scars. To avoid her gaze, he quickly slipped into the opening and crawled through it. When he re-emerged into the dappled sunlight, he stared down at himself in amazement: all his scars had vanished!

He dressed again quickly and they set off for his village. When they arrived, no one there realised who he was.

'It's me,' he said. 'Remember? You used to call me Filthy One.'

At first, they didn't believe him. But when they looked more closely, they recognised the features of the ragged orphan who they used to abuse. 'Where have you been?' they cried. 'What's happened to you?'

'I'm changed,' he said. 'And I've brought you great treasures. If you want to know what they are, gather round me at nightfall, and make sure you come with gifts.'

Though they were all sceptical, they were curious too, so they did as he said. Crow showed them the embroidered pouch his wife had made him, drew out a memento from it, and began to tell them one of the Stone's stories. All the people were totally astonished and enthralled. Never before had they heard words of such truth, beauty and wisdom. At the end they all clamoured to give him the small gifts they had brought, and promised that if he would only continue with his storytelling, they would give him much, much more.

So despite his unpromising start in life, Crow became a very great man.

It was the Stone that first gave us all knowledge of the world before this one. But it was thanks to Crow that its stories have survived; and also thanks to the many people since him who have taken care to remember them, and keep them alive for the future.

Curtin: *Seneca Indian Myths,* collected 1883, published 1922
Curtin & Hewitt: *Seneca Fiction, Legends and Myths,* collected 1896, published 1918
Parker: *Seneca Myths and Folk Tales,* collected 1903-4, published 1923
This retelling is an amalgam of three versions, sourced from different Seneca informants who all lived on Cattaraugus Reservation in New York State. Some of the wording closely mimics both Curtin's 1883 source, and Parker's own account. The latter has the most complete and detailed storyline, though it is sparsely told. The ritual words used during storytelling are reproduced from his text.

Parker was actually born on Cattaraugus Reservation: his father was descended from the great Seneca teacher, Handsome Lake, though his mother was British. Discussing his childhood on the Reservation in his Foreword he says:

'[I] cannot remember when [I] first began to hear the wonder stories of the ancient days. [My] earliest recollections are of hearing the wise old men relate these tales of the mysterious past. They were called "Ka'kaa" or "Ga'kaa", and when this word was uttered, as a signal that the marvels of old were about to be unfolded, all the children grew silent and listened. In those days, back on the Cattaraugus Reservation, it was a part of a child's initial training...

'Many years later...in 1903 [I] returned to...Cattaraugus [with a colleague]...for the purpose of making an archaeological survey... To our camp came many Indian friends who sought to instruct [us] in the lore of the ancients... I filled my note-books with sketches and outlines of folk fiction, and after our return to New York, I began to transcribe some of the stories. The following winter was spent on the reservation among the non-Christian element in a serious attempt to record folk tales, ceremonial prayers, rituals, songs and customs...

Later I was able to go over my original notes with Edward Cornplanter, the local authority on Seneca religion, rites and folkways, and to write out the material here presented... Though differences will be found between our texts and those of Curtin, it must be remembered that variations are bound to occur. All versions of folk tales recorded by different individuals at different or even identical times will vary in certain particulars.'

Curtin's version, recorded some twenty years earlier, has much less plot: it simply tells of the orphan hunting alone, happening upon the storytelling stone, and keeping it secret. Eventually, his kindly foster mother gets suspicious and sends men to spy on him. With the secret out, the stories are now shared with the whole village. The description of the Stone comes from here, as do its statements about the significance of stories, and the opening sentence.

Curtin, a field worker for the American Bureau of Ethnology, was instructed in the Seneca language by a man called Sim Logan. He followed Logan back to Cattaraugus Reservation in 1883, and stayed there for three months. Initially his efforts to collect myths and legends were hindered by an influential young man called Two Guns, who accused Curtin of intending to steal the Seneca religion and use it as a 'curiosity'. Many others agreed. Fortunately, an old-timer called Solomon O'Beal (also descended from Handsome Lake) understood the value of Curtin's work and successfully overcame this opposition. O'Beal shared all the stories and traditions he himself remembered with the ethnologist, and this was supplemented by other Seneca elders. This particular story came from a man called Henry Jacob, who also provided three other stories in Curtin's collection. By the end of his stay, Curtin was so highly regarded, that he was formally adopted into the people, and given the name of Hiwesas, 'Seeker of Knowledge'.

A briefer account was translated from the indigenous language by Hewitt. He does not say exactly who told it to him, but names his informants as:

'Mr Truman Halftown, Mr John Armstrong, and Chief Priest Henry Stevens, all of the Cattaraugus Reservation, N.Y. These worthy men, who have all passed away, were uniformly patient, kind, and interested. They were men whose faith in the religion of their ancestors ennobled them with goodwill, manliness, and a desire to serve.'

The myth does not appear to have been told by any other peoples. However, the motif of a wretched orphan who eventually becomes a highly respected man is very common right across the continent.

THE GREAT SPIRIT AND THE EARTH

Wabanaki

The Great Spirit is in all things;
he is in the air we breathe.
The Great Spirit is our father.
But the Earth is our mother.
She nourishes us;
that which we put into the ground she returns to us,
and healing plants she gives us likewise.
If we are wounded,
we go to our mother
and seek to lay the wounded part against her,
to be healed.
Animals too, do thus,
they lay their wounds to the Earth.

– Bedagi (Big Thunder)
(Quoted in Curtis: *The Indians' Book*, 1907).

SMALL TURTLE AND THE MOON

◇▣◇▣◇▣◇

Wyandot

In the beginning:

After the Mother of the People fell through a hole from the Sky and landed in the infinite water...

After she was found by Big Turtle Woman, who ordered the other water animals to dive to the bottom...

After they brought back fragments of soil from there and fixed them to Big Turtle's back...

After this soil spread across Big Turtle, to form Turtle Island, which is also called the Earth...

...Even after all this, the Earth was not yet finished. For the only light in it was dim, no brighter than the faint glow given off by snow. So Big Turtle summoned all the other animals to a grand council.

'It's not good enough,' she said. 'We've made this beautiful world for the Mother of the People, but she can hardly see it. When she has descendants, they won't be able to see it either. Who can suggest a remedy?'

All those assembled fell into a deep discussion. Some suggested one thing, some another, and each idea was debated thoroughly; but none seemed a good solution. Finally, a new voice spoke up, the voice of Small Turtle. Everyone turned to peer at her and listen.

'Because I am small and look insignificant,' she said, 'you may think that I have no contribution to make. However, you are wrong, for it happens that I possess great powers. It is possible that I could use these to climb up to the Sky. And if I do that, it is equally possible that I could gather some light up there, and shine it over the Earth.'

'If that's the case,' said Big Turtle, 'I propose that you try.' And all the others nodded in agreement.

So Small Turtle stood up and cried, 'Cloud, arise!'

At once, the air darkened in the distance and an enormous, louring cloud came rolling slowly over the infinite ocean. As it drew near the animal council, they saw that it was formed of great lumps of rock, broken tree trunks and uprooted bushes, all mingled with lakes and running water. Soon it was so close and so low, that Small Turtle was able to leap into one of the streams. Then the cloud rose, slowly and steadily, up and up, spitting out dazzling flashes of lightning, until it had carried Small Turtle into the Sky.

When she arrived, she stepped off and stood back. Fragments of lightning were still spattering from the cloud. Small Turtle gathered them up and nudged them together into a tightly packed ball. She breathed into the ball and gave it a male spirit.

'Welcome!' she said to it. 'You are Sun. I have made you to travel across the Sky every day, to shine down onto the People who will be born in the future to live on Turtle Island.'

'I don't wish to be alone,' Sun answered her. 'Give me a wife.'

So Small Turtle gathered more fragments of lightning and made them into a smaller ball, that shone with a gentler light.

'You are Moon,' she said. 'Welcome! Your task is to follow Sun, for he is your husband.'

After that, Small Turtle travelled back to the world below and reported on what she had done. 'Each day,' she said, 'Sun will travel across the Sky spreading his light. When he reaches the end of his trail, he'll pass under the Earth then rise again at the same starting point. Moon will always follow some way behind him. While Sun is below ground, it will be her turn to light the Sky.'

'This is all very good,' said Big Turtle. 'Now the People who will be born on Earth will be able to see very well. But how will Sun and Moon pass underneath on their daily journeys?'

'I need the other animals' help for that,' said Small Turtle. 'With your permission, they must bore a hole through your shell, Big Turtle, and make an underground passage for Sun and Moon to pass through.'

Big Turtle agreed to this proposal, and the passage was made.

For a while, everything went well and the Earth was brightly lit. Every day, Sun travelled across the Sky then passed through the passage under Turtle Island, ready to rise again. Moon, with her softer light, followed him in exactly the same way.

However, after a while, Sun became lazy. When he entered the underground passage, he took to loitering in it, staying underground there for much longer than he should. Moon tried to fit in with his new routine, and slowed down whenever he did.

However, one day she could not help herself: she went too fast and found herself bumping into Sun under the Earth. Sun was furious. In the darkness below, where no one could see or hear, he rushed at her in a rage. He shouted at Moon, making her cower; he fell on her and beat her brutally, on and on, until she was almost dead. Then Sun pushed savagely past her and resumed his journey.

That day, after he had completed his travels, it grew completely dark. The next day he reappeared, but again after he finished his trail, the darkness returned.

'Where is Moon?' the animals wanted to know. 'What has become of her?'

They sent Small Turtle back to the Sky to find out. She searched everywhere. At last she found Moon, lingering in the underground passage. She was weeping bitterly. A weak, trembling light still flickered from her and by this, Small Turtle saw how badly Sun had abused and broken her. She was almost as cold as winter. There was only a tiny, bent sliver of her left.

Gently, Small Turtle drew Moon out into the open. Tenderly, she healed and mended her. After a while, Moon grew a little stronger and a little bigger. Then she recalled her suffering at her husband's hands and relapsed again, shrinking and trembling. Small Turtle repeated her healing; Moon recovered a little more, then relapsed again, recovered, relapsed and so on. After a long time, under Small Turtle's care, she managed to grow almost as round and big as when she was first created.

'I will go and see Sun,' she said.

'Are you sure?' said Small Turtle. 'Can you really forgive him that terrible beating?'

'Of course I can,' said Moon. 'In fact, it is *me* who should apologise. I will tell him how sorry I am for going too fast.'

Small Turtle shook her head sadly. She watched Moon run hopefully after Sun, heard her timid but eager voice call out. She saw Sun travel steadily on, not even turning his head to acknowledge his gentle wife.

After a while, Moon came creeping back, steps dragging, head hung low. Again, she had turned pale and dim.

'Well?' said Small Turtle.

'He ignored me,' wept Moon. 'He would not listen, he did not even acknowledge I was there.' As she spoke, she continued to fade and tremble, until there was barely anything of her left.

Small Turtle tried her best to help. She punished the Sun for his brutality (though how she did this, has long been forgotten). To help the Moon light the Sky at night, Small Turtle created the stars to be her children. However, she never managed to heal Moon completely. The best she could do was to revive her former radiance for a short time every so often; but then, almost at once, Moon would start to decay again. Each month it was always the same, over and over.

That is why, to this very day, the moon is constantly waxing and waning.

As for Small Turtle, since she went above to fix things and did it so well, she became known as the Keeper of the Sky, and lived up there ever after. However, sometimes the animals would ask her to attend their councils to share her wisdom and power. Then a herald whose voice went a long way would call her, and she would ride her cloud down to join them.

Barbeau: *Huron and Wyandot Mythology*, 1915
An outline of the opening section, about the creation of Earth by Big Turtle, was also recorded by the Jesuits in 1636 (see p. 556), confirming the considerable antiquity of at least part of the story. A similar creation story appears in Onondaga, Seneca and other Iroquois myths. See also the Californian story, COYOTE AND EARTH MAKER, p. 233.

Barbeau gives the story as a segment of a longer myth which contains a number of different episodes. He recorded it in English, at Wyandotte, Oklahoma, in September 1911. His informant was a man called B. N. O. Walker, who had a Wyandot mother and a partly Wyandot father. He was educated, and worked as chief clerk in a US Indian agency. He had heard the myth when he was growing up, from his Canadian aunt, Kitty

Greyeyes. She in turn had learned the myths from Theresa Brown ('Aunt Hunt') and Jim Clarke, who both lived in Ontario.

Barbeau gives another version, published by W. E. Connelley in 1899. It was one of many he collected over 50 years from various Wyandot informants at Kansas City and Wyandotte Reservation Oklahoma. Connelley says that Small Turtle's epithet, 'Keeper of the Sky', was used as a name for women of the Wyandot Little Turtle Clan.

He adds a colourful note on how he first heard this myth:

'The Wyandot believe the comet is the cloud in which the Little Turtle went up to the sky, burnished and brightened by the Little Turtle with rays taken from the midday sun. In this she rides through the heavens to perform her duties. About 1882 there was a large comet, visible in Kansas City... On my way to my office very early one morning, late in the fall, I met Matthias Splitlog. From where we stood we had a splendid view of the comet. "See!" said Mr Splitlog, "there is the chariot of our Grandmother, the Little Turtle." Then he told me why it was so called.'

There are various turtle species in the old Wyandot homeland in Ontario. The smallest is the inconspicuous ten-centimetre (four inches) long stinkpot, or musk turtle, which is dark brown and lives at the bottom of lakes, bogs and marsh pools. One of the largest is the snapping turtle which can grow up to 43-centimetre (seventeen inches) long.

Some modern Native American people refer to North America as 'Turtle Island'.

FIRST MOTHER

◇▢◇▢◇▢◇

Penobscot

Long ago, the great teacher Kloskurbeh lived in the world alone.

One day, when the Sun was high in the Sky, a young man suddenly appeared before him saying, 'Greetings, my mother's brother.'

'Greetings, nephew,' Kloskurbeh replied. 'Where have you come from, and why?'

'I have come from the waters where I was born,' the young man said. 'The wind blew over them until the waves quickened into foam. The Sun shone on that foam and warmed it. The warmth made life – and that life is me. See, I am young and swift. I have come to live with you and help you.'

Kloskurbeh made him welcome. Another day dawned and this time, when the Sun was high, a young woman suddenly appeared. She went and stood before Kloskurbeh and the young man, saying, 'Greetings, my children.'

'Greetings, Mother,' Kloskurbeh replied. 'Where have you come from, and why?'

'I have come from the most beautiful plant in the world, from which I was born,' the young woman said. 'The dew fell on the leaf. The sun warmed the dew. The warmth made life, and that life is me. I have come to live with you – and I have brought love to give you. If you will love me in return and grant my wish, this love will grow all over the world; even the animals will know it. I bring strength too, and comfort. Though I am young, I will spread these gifts all across the Earth.'

Kloskurbeh lifted his hands towards the Sun and praised the Great Spirit. Afterwards, the young man and the young woman were married. Thus, when their children were born, she became the First Mother.

Kloskurbeh spent many years teaching their children everything they needed to know. Finally, his work was finished and he told them he would go away to live in the Northland. 'I will wait there, and you may come to me there if you wish,' he said. 'Or, if you need me here, I will return.'

First Mother's children had many children of their own, who in turn had children, and so on, until the world was full of People. Unfortunately, there was not enough food for them all, and they tasted the bitterness of famine.

First Mother was deeply distressed by this. Every day at noon she took to going out, leaving her husband alone, staying away until the shadows grew long. She did not tell him where she went. The husband too was sad, not just because of the famine, but also because of his wife's sorrow, for he loved her dearly.

One day he followed her to the place where she was accustomed to ford the river, and waited for her return. When she came, she stepped deep into the water and at once began to sing. How happy she seemed as she stood there! – as happy as the day when she first came to live on Earth and took him as her husband. He watched her carefully, trying to understand the cause of this brief moment of joy…and saw that something was trailing behind on her right foot: a long green blade. When at last she emerged from the water, she stooped and cast the blade away. After that, her sorrow at once returned.

She did not speak to him. Silently, the husband followed her home. When they arrived, and the Sun was streaking the horizon with soft colour as it sank, he broke his silence.

'My wife,' he said, 'come out and share the beauty of the Sky with me.'

So they stood side by side, drinking in this ever wondrous sight. But when only a few moments had passed, they heard footsteps approaching. Seven small children came running and stood before them with tears streaming down their cheeks.

'What is the matter?' First Mother asked gently.

'Oh, Mother,' they whispered, 'we are so hungry! The night is coming. Where is our food?'

First Mother began to weep too. 'Hush, my little ones,' she answered. 'Be patient. One day, I promise, you will hunger no more.'

The children hung their heads in silence and crept away. But the husband reached out and wiped away First Mother's tears. 'My wife,' he said, 'what can I do to help overcome this terrible famine? And what can I do to make you happy?'

'Both sorrows have the same cure,' she answered.

'Then tell me, I beg you.'

'Do you love me?' she said. 'Would you do anything I ask to make my happiness return?'

'If it is in my power,' he said, 'I will willingly do it.'

'Then kill me,' said First Mother.

'How can you ask such a thing of me?' the husband cried. 'Surely there is something else I can do – anything at all! – to make you happy?'

'Nothing else,' First Mother answered.

The husband took his leave of her wretchedly and hurried away to the Northland, to seek out Kloskurbeh. The trail there was very, very long. The seasons and years slowly turned. Only after seven long years had passed, did he finally return.

'Did you find Kloskurbeh?' said First Mother.

'Indeed I did,' he answered.

'And what did the wise one tell you?'

'He told me to do the very thing that you asked for. He told me to take your life.'

'He spoke wisely and I am glad,' said First Mother. 'Now, listen carefully. After you have killed me, call two men to help you. They must take hold of my hair, and by that means draw my dead body around the edge of an empty field.'

The husband shuddered; but since he had spoken to Kloskurbeh, he knew he could not argue. Still he asked her, 'Will you at least tell me why they must do such a terrible thing?'

'I will tell you nothing except what must be done,' she answered. 'When the men reach the very centre of the field, they must bury my bones there, then come away. After this, let seven months pass in peace. Then the men must return to the same field and gather everything they find there. They must distribute it fairly amongst all our children. Then everyone shall eat it.'

'What is it that they will find, my wife?'

'My own flesh,' she told him. 'It is my flesh that must be eaten, for that is what I give you all. But listen further. A portion of it must be saved and put in the ground again.'

'And what of your bones that were buried?'

'They are not to eat, but to burn. The smoke will bring peace to you, and to your children.'

The next day, the man rose in great sorrow while the Sun was still low in the Sky. He went to his wife for the last time, then took her life as she had asked him: his last great act of love to her. Afterwards, he called two of the men and ordered them to draw her body all around an open field, until the flesh was worn away. In the centre of the same field, they buried her bones. Then all the people waited, grieving and hoping, for the waxing and waning of seven moons.

After that time, the husband went back to the field. He found it completely filled with beautiful, tall plants, each one heavy with ripe fruits. He tasted the fruit and it was sweet. He called it 'corn'.

Then he pushed through the swaying corn plants to the centre of the field, where First Mother's bones were buried. There a different plant was growing, with broad leaves; he tasted them and found them bitter. He called this plant 'tobacco'.

He ran to tell the People – his children, his children's children and all their countless descendants. When they heard the news, their hearts were filled with joy. They all ran to the field at once, they worked hard and harvested the corn and the tobacco.

However, when it was all gathered in, they did not know how to divide it. So the husband sent messengers to Kloskurbeh, asking him to come and give them counsel. Kloskurbeh came; he too was gladdened by the great harvest. 'First,' he said, 'we must give thanks to the Great Spirit.'

This was done.

Then Kloskurbeh went on, 'The words of First Mother have come to pass. She said she was born of the leaf of the beautiful plant, and that her power should spread across the whole world, and that all People should love her. Now you know that she has gone into this substance. Take care that this corn, the seed of First Mother, is always with you – for it is her flesh. Her bones have also been given for your good: burn them, and the smoke of tobacco will bring freshness to the mind.

'Since these things came from the goodness of a woman's heart, see that you hold her always in your memories. Think of her when you eat. Remember her when the smoke of her bones rises before you. And because you are all brothers and sisters, divide her flesh and bones among you. Let all share alike. For in this way First Mother's love will be fulfilled.'

Curtis: *The Indians' Book,* 1907

A short note to the story says:

> 'Joseph Nicolar, a Penobscot Indian, compiled and wrote the legends of his people, and published them himself in the year 1893, in a small volume entitled *The Red Man.* [This story] is adapted from the book and is here contributed by Nicolar's wife, who is still living at Oldtown, Maine. The same story [was also] told to [Curtis] by Big Thunder. [It] differs somewhat in detail, but is essentially the same.'

The original narrative is beautifully and hauntingly told, so it is reproduced here more or less exactly, with just a little editing.

Kloskurbeh, described in the source as 'the great teacher' seems to be essentially the same as the Algonquin Glooskap (see GLOOSKAP THE MASTER, p. 560).

Corn – the cereal usually known in the UK as maize – was one of the important crops called 'the three sisters' by many Northeast peoples, grown alongside beans and squash. There are numerous different varieties, which range in colour from pale yellow to dark red and blue. It was often ground in a pestle and mortar for bread, or used whole in stews and soups. An Iroquois myth tells of an elderly chief praying on a mountain top to the Great Spirit for better food. He is told to take his family away to the Plains and wait there for three years. By the end of that time, they have fallen asleep and transformed into corn plants. Another tells of a youth sleeping near his sweetheart's lodge to guard her from danger and any rivals. One night he sees her sleepwalking, chases her and manages to seize her; when she wakes, she transforms to the first corn plant. See also THE ORIGIN OF HUNTING AND FARMING, p. 121, and TOBACCO AND CORN, p. 168.

Tobacco was traditionally used over much of North America, not as in the modern world, but for ritual and medicinal purposes. When smoked or burnt as incense, it provided a symbolic link to the spiritual world. It was also chewed, sniffed and mixed in drinks and buried with the dead. A Wyandot myth tells of a couple grieving at the death of their two young daughters. The bereaved father sees a hawk fall to the ground from a screeching flock flying overhead. When he approaches it, the hawk is consumed by fire. Within a coal left behind, he finds his elder daughter, who gives him a 'precious gift' – a handful of seeds. She plants them in the ashes, which become a tobacco field, then teaches the people how to grow, cure and smoke it.

This myth strongly reflects the matrilineal nature of Penobscot society. Alongside the key role played by First Mother, note that in the opening passage, the young man shows his respect to Kloskurbeh by addressing him as 'my mother's brother' rather than 'father'.

THE KEEPER OF THE BRAINS OF THE DEAD

◇□◇□◇□◇

Wyandot

There was a man whose sister died before her time. She had always been his favourite, so when he lost her he was inconsolable.

But a man can only weep for so long. After a while, he pulled himself together and resolved to deal with his grief in a more practical way. 'I'll try and get her back,' he thought. He didn't mean her poor, wasted body – which had long been laid to the winds on a scaffold – but her *real* self: her soul. 'I'll go and seek her out in the Village of Souls. I'll persuade the people in charge there to let her come back to me.'

He felt a little better now he had made this decision. He was confident his quest would not fail; he had a talent for arguing a case. There was no reason to postpone his start, nothing to pack; carrying food on the journey would only be a hindrance. So he set off without delay, heading for the place where the Sun sets, which is where the Village of Souls lies.

He walked non-stop, never pausing to hunt or forage or eat. On and on he went, always following the long trail towards the sinking Sun. Four days passed, ten days, twelve days. By then his unfed body was no more than bones and skin; but he had really got into his stride. He felt as if he could keep going for ever.

Suddenly, in the fading twilight, he saw a woman standing before him. He stared at her in disbelief for a few moments, then cried out, 'Yes, it's really you – my poor, dear, beloved sister!'

She was as vague as the dusk shadows that surrounded her. She did not answer him, not a word, not even a sigh. Her translucent hands were holding a bowl filled with porridge. She thrust it at him. Trembling, he took it, then reached out to touch her... And at once she vanished.

But the bowl was still there in his hands, real and solid. He ate the porridge ravenously, smiling fondly at the familiar flavour, just like she used to cook it while she was still alive. When he had finished it, he strode on with renewed zest and hope.

The next evening, the ghost of his sister appeared again with another bowl of food. Everything happened just as before. After that, she brought him food day after day, in exactly the same way. In-between her visitations, he trudged on stoically, journeying westwards for three more months.

At last, he found his way was blocked by a wide, rushing river. Its dark waters surged past him with the force of a waterfall. On the opposite bank, he saw a broad swathe of land that had been cleared to plant crops; and beyond this, right on the forest edge, there was a small cabin. Apart from his wife's ghost, this was the first sign of people that he had seen since he set out. His heart leaped: this must be the outskirts of the place he was seeking.

But how could he cross such a torrential river? There was not anywhere shallow enough to wade through; and if he tried to swim it, he would be swept away at once.

He put his hands to his mouth and shouted with all his might towards the cabin: 'Hoi! Is anyone there? Is this the way to the Village of Souls?'

At once, the cabin door opened. A figure briefly appeared in its frame...then hastily withdrew, slamming the door behind it with a bang that carried loudly across the water.

The man shouted again and again, to no avail. 'I've got to get across,' he thought. He looked urgently up and down the banks. He saw now that, upstream, several great trees had fallen across the river, forming a rough, rickety bridge. He ran to them, climbed onto the trunks and stumbled across to the far side. There he leaped down onto the grass and headed straight for the cabin. When he reached it, he pushed the door, then shoved it with his shoulder, but it was shut fast. So he started beating on it with his fists, over and over. 'Open up!' he yelled. 'I know you're in there, so either let me in, or else come outside and speak with me!'

At last, a voice from within called back to him: 'Wait. If you wish to enter, first you must pass in your arm and let me examine it.'

The door was pulled open a crack. The man pushed his hand through it, then his whole arm. He felt the person inside catch hold of it and squeeze it firmly.

The voice cried, 'You are a living person! How can this be? How did you manage to cross the river? This country is forbidden to all except the souls of the dead.'

The man was ecstatic: he had definitely reached the right place! 'I know,' he called back. 'That's exactly why I've come. I'm looking for the soul of my beloved sister, who recently died.'

The door swung right open and the figure beckoned him into the cool darkness within, saying, 'You've done well to find your way here, very well indeed. Few before you have ever succeeded.'

The man bowed his head. 'I'm very glad to have arrived. May I ask what is your name, Grandfather?'

'You may ask, but the only answer I shall give to satisfy your curiosity is this: I am the Keeper of the Brains of the Dead.'

'I understand,' said the man. 'I'm glad to meet you. Can you tell me if it's possible to find my sister's soul, and carry it back with me?'

'It is certainly possible,' the Keeper said. 'You must go out from here and walk a little further still until you come to a group of houses. That is the Village of Souls.'

'The very place! And what shall I do when I get there?'

The Keeper said, 'Follow the sound of music to a house where all the souls are gathered for a dance.'

'What are they dancing for, Grandfather?'

'This house is where Aataensic lives,' said the Keeper. 'She is sick, so they are dancing there to heal her.'

'Do you really speak of Aataensic herself?' cried the man. 'She who is the mother of the People? Aataensic who fell to Earth from the Sky at the beginning of all things?'

'It is her house indeed. Do not be afraid to enter. You will find your sister's soul there.'

'And what shall I do when I find her? How can I take her back with me?'

The Keeper turned to a dark corner and drew out a pumpkin. He took a knife, cut a complete circle round the top, scooped out the flesh and returned the top to its place like a lid. 'You must put her in here. Do not ask any further questions: when the time comes, you will know how.'

The man took the pumpkin carefully. 'Thank you for trusting me, Grandfather, and for all your advice. Shall I see you again?'

'Yes indeed. Once you have your sister's soul safely shut inside the pumpkin, bring it here before you return home, so I can give you something else that you will need.'

The man thanked him again, and set out in the direction that the Keeper pointed out to him, carrying the hollow pumpkin. He soon reached the Village of Souls, and heard the sound of drums and singing. He followed this to a large house, the house of Aataensic. Its door was open. He peered inside and saw a mass of ghostly people gathered there, dancing. He walked boldly in.

At once, the music gave way to a soft hiss like an intake of breath. As one, the dancers turned to look at him and fell still. He stared at them intently, desperately seeking his sister... But even as he searched, the dancers began to float softly upwards; then they faded like mist in morning sunshine, until they had completely vanished.

He sat down in the centre of the house, by the fire, and placed the pumpkin beside him. The flames died down to glowing embers. He waited there alone in the silence. For a long time, there was neither sound nor sight of the vanished dancers. Through the open door, he watched the day melt into the blue glow of twilight.

Eventually, he sensed a presence. Then he glimpsed a movement, and heard the muted tread of feet and drumming. The dancers were returning. He stayed very still, not even shifting his head, scarcely even blinking. Soon the house was filled again with the souls, they surrounded him completely, swaying and stepping in their former solemn dance.

He watched them in silence, not moving, but letting his eyes dart about. And so it was that he saw his sister.

He jumped up, stretching out his hands to seize her. But before he could even touch her, she had slithered away and vanished. He groaned in frustration, then crept outside, forcing himself to hold back.

His patience paid off. The dancers returned. Slowly and gravely they circled past him. Motionless, he waited. Several times he saw his sister, moving close then passing him. He resisted the temptation to make another false move. She drew near again... And this time he jumped up and managed to catch hold of her.

How soft and pliant she felt, how insubstantial! Yet even as she struggled and shook and writhed, he clung to her with one hand, while in the other he gripped the pumpkin. Gradually, he grappled his sister towards the door. As they moved, she seemed to shrivel and shrink. They stumbled outside, she still fighting, he still clinging on with all his might. In the grey dawn he saw that she had dwindled to almost nothing. He picked her up easily, thrust her into the hollow pumpkin and secured her inside it with the lid. This ended the struggle; his sister's soul was completely drained of strength.

The man carried the pumpkin triumphantly back to the Keeper's house. The Keeper was expecting him. He welcomed the man inside and gave him a second pumpkin almost identical to the first.

'What is this for?' the man asked.

'It contains your sister's brains,' said the Keeper.

The man thanked him again and asked what he should do next.

'Go home,' said the Keeper. 'Then go to the cemetery where your sister's body lies. Take its remains from the scaffold, carry it to your house, and place it alongside the two pumpkins. Then invite all your kin and neighbours to a great feast. Once they are all assembled at your house, order them to be still, to lower their eyes and to keep them lowered. In this way, they must wait quietly until you tell them that the ordeal is over. It is absolutely vital that everyone is there, and equally vital that no one should see you carry out the following ceremony. Place your sister's body over your shoulders, lift the pumpkins, one in each hand, and walk the length of your house, thus carrying all the parts of your sister. If everything is done absolutely correctly, your sister will become whole once more and return to life.'

Then the Keeper of the Brains of the Dead sent the man away. He retraced the steps of his long journey eagerly, hardly able to contain his excitement. All the way, he took great care of the two pumpkins, one containing his sister's soul, the other with her brains.

At last he reached his village. He placed the pumpkins in a safe place inside his house, then went to the cemetery. There he found his sister's corpse, turned dry and stiff by long months of exposure to the wind. He carried it carefully home, then sent out messengers inviting everyone to a feast. His family and neighbours and friends were all very glad to see him back safely, especially as he seemed to be over the worst of his grief. They gathered eagerly at his house to celebrate.

The man told them about his long journey and his extraordinary experiences at the end of it. He revealed that he was about to bring his beloved sister back to life and explained the ritual he must conduct in their presence to achieve this.

'You all have a part in this ceremony,' he said. 'The Keeper of the Brains of the Dead emphasised that it is vital. While I carry my sister's parts through the house, you must all stay here, but avert your eyes and keep them averted. I earnestly beg you to do this.'

'Of course we will,' the guests answered as one. They all bent their heads, and either lowered their eyes or closed them tightly.

The man laid his sister's body across his shoulders, took the two pumpkins in the palms of his upraised hands, and began to walk ceremoniously down the centre of his house. Step by slow step he made his way, glancing from one side to the other, to be sure that all the guests were doing as he had asked them. Every head he saw was bent, every eye was either fixed upon the floor or shut. Step by step, the body balanced on his shoulders grew heavier. Step by step, it grew warmer. He fancied he could feel a gentle motion in it, as of soft breathing. His heart began to pound. Now he was only three steps away from the end of his walk, now only two...

But at that moment, one of the guests far back along the line was overcome by an insuperable pang of curiosity. Was it a man or a woman? Who knows, who cares? For whoever it was, that person lifted their head only very slightly, and peeped out furtively through the cover of their eyelashes.

It was impossible that anyone else could have noticed. Yet it was enough. It put an end to everything.

The pumpkin in which the sister's soul was interred suddenly burst open. The soul flew out of it and away. It is not told what happened to her brains. But her body, which just an instant before had been stirring back to life, grew cold and stiff once more.

After that, the distraught man had no choice. He had to carry it back to the cemetery. And he had to accept that his beloved sister was truly lost for ever.

Thwaites: *The Jesuit Relations*, story collected in 1636
The Jesuits' reports, over 70 in number, are said to be the oldest written records of Native American life. The text gives no indication of the manner in which this story was originally narrated, and it is peppered

with extremely disparaging remarks about the Wyandot people and their mythology. Nevertheless, it seems to give an accurate account of the story, and is introduced by some interesting background information about Wyandot beliefs:

'As to what is the state of the soul after death, they hold that it separates in such a way from the body that it does not abandon it immediately. When they bear it to the grave, it walks in front, and remains in the cemetery until the Feast of the Dead; by night, it walks through the villages and enters the Cabins, where it takes its part in the feasts, and eats what is left at evening in the kettle...

'At the Feast of the Dead, which takes place about every twelve years, the souls quit the cemeteries, and in the opinion of some are changed into turtle doves, which they pursue later in the woods, with bow and arrow, to broil and eat; nevertheless the most common belief is that after this ceremony...they go away in company, covered...with robes and collars which have been put into the grave for them, to a great village, which is toward the setting Sun – except, however, the old people and the little children who have not as strong limbs as the others to make this voyage; these remain in the country, where they have their own particular villages...The souls of those who died in war form a band by themselves; the others fear them, and do not permit their entry into their Village, any more than to the souls of those who have killed themselves.'

Wyandot funeral customs were also described by the Jesuits:

'The corpse placed in a crouching posture in the midst of the circle of friends and relatives; the long, measured wail of the mourners; the speeches in praise of the dead, and consolation to the living; the funeral feast; the gifts at the place of burial; the funeral games, where the young men of the village contended for prizes; and the long period of mourning to those next of kin. The body was usually laid on a scaffold, or, more rarely, in the earth. This, however, was not its final resting-place. At intervals of ten or twelve years, each of the four nations which composed the Huron [Wyandot] Confederacy gathered together its dead, and conveyed them all to a common place of sepulture. Here was celebrated the great Feast of the Dead...their most solemn and important ceremonial.'

The source gives no details about how the sister's body was disposed of in the myth, though it mentions a 'tomb' at the end; so the retelling follows the above information and assumes it was laid on a scaffold. Placing the deceased's body on a scaffold or tree was a widespread Native American funeral practice, protecting the corpse from being dug up by wolves, bears or other wild animals.

Aataentsic, at whose house the healing dance of the Souls of the Dead is held, is described in the same source as the 'head of the nation'. She originally lives in a parallel world above the sky. One version of her myth says she falls through a hole to Earth after her dog, which in turn is pursuing a bear. An alternative version says that she has a tree cut down to obtain healing fruit from it for her ailing husband. The felled tree leaves a hole which she jumps through. Her fall is observed by Turtle Woman, who calls all the other sea creatures to a council to discuss what to do with her. Beaver leads them all to dive to the water bottom and bring up soil, which is placed on Turtle's back. Aataentsic lands gently there and gives birth to a daughter, who in turn quickly gives birth to two sons. They fight and one is killed. The surviving son, Iouskeha, becomes the Sun, whilst Aataentsic herself becomes the Moon; they live together at the ends of the earth near the sea. It says that both are believed to be somehow 'present' at village feasts and dances, which perhaps explains why Aataentsic appears in this apparently unrelated story. See SMALL TURTLE AND THE MOON, p. 541.

The Jesuits took a poor view of Wyandot religion and were dedicated to converting them to Christianity. However, the limited effect of this policy, even after over 150 years of missionary work, was demonstrated in 1798 by the Reverend James B. Finley, who recorded the following acerbic Wyandot tale:

'Once, in the days of our grandfathers, many years ago, this white man's God came himself to this country and claimed us. But our God met him somewhere near the great mountains, and they disputed about the right to this country. At last they agreed to settle this question by trying their power to remove a mountain. The white man's God got down on his knees, opened a big Book, and began to pray and talk, but the mountain stood fast. Then the red man's God took his magic wand, and began to pow-wow, and beat the turtle-shell, and the mountain trembled, shook, and stood by him. The white man's God got frightened, and ran off, and we have not heard of him since, unless he has sent these men to see what they can do.'

The early date when this myth was first collected, long before the Wyandot were overwhelmed by European culture, demonstrates that the motif was entirely indigenous, even though it bears similarities to the Ancient Greek story of Orpheus and Eurydice.

There are many related Native American 'land of the dead' myths; see THE YOUTH AND HIS EAGLE, p. 195; THE WAR TWINS AND THE UNBORN, p. 219; THE DRESSES, THE SPIRIT HOUSE AND THE BONES, p. 353; and GHOST COUNTRY, p. 458.

WIZARD'S CHANT

Passamaquoddy

I sit and beat the wizard's magic drum,
and by its mystic sound I call the beasts.
From mountain lair and forest nook they throng;
Even mighty storms obey the dreadful sound.

I sit and beat the wizard's magic drum;
The storm and thunder answer when it calls.
Aplasemwesit, the mighty whirlwind, stops
To hear the mystic sound I make…

The lightning, thunder, storm and forest sprite,
whirlwind, night ghost, spirit of the deep
all come together reverently
to hear the mystic sound I make.

– Ancient oral poem supplied by Louis Mitchell,
Passamaquoddy scholar and politician
(Quoted in Leland & Dyneley: *Kuloskap the Master,* 1902)

GLOOSKAP THE MASTER

◇▣◇▢◇▢◇

Micmac (Mi'kmaq) & Passamaquoddy

Wonderful traditions come down to us from olden times, very old indeed!

Many are the tales of the birth of the world. At that time, darkness was everywhere and the only living things were the wild spirits of forest and rock. Then Glooskap arrived. He was the Master, the greatest being who ever came to our land. He brought the first light. He shot arrows into the trees, from which the first human beings emerged, our ancestors, the People of the Early Dawn. He made the animals too, and when they threatened to kill the People, Glooskap shrank them, weakened them and banished the worst ones to the ice wilderness. Then he blessed the People by teaching them how to hunt, how to build houses and canoes, how to use plants for medicine and food. He showed them the stars up in the Sky, revealing their names and wonderful stories about them.

Glooskap built his home on an island in the forest. His companions there were an old Bear woman who he called Grandmother, and his faithful boy-servant, Marten. They both had power from fasting in the wilderness with prayers and visions – but not nearly as much power as Glooskap.

The seasons turned and the years turned. Gradually, evil beings entered the world: giants, witches and monstrous birds. They hated Glooskap and often tried to harm him, but he always overcame them.

One of these evil ones was a monster who mimicked human form. He was enormous, fat and bloated, really hideous to behold. His great, round, yellow eyes stuck out from his head like knots in a pine branch. His stringy lips stretched from ear to ear. His feet were broad and flat, with unnaturally long toes. His voice was a hoarse, blood-chilling croak.

The monster's dwelling was on top of a mountain where a mighty river rose. One day, he built an impenetrable dam around this river, completely blocking its flow. In this way, he kept all the water, every last drop of it, for himself. So the good People who lived in the village at the mountain bottom found themselves with no water to drink unless it rained. They began to waste away from thirst.

Glooskap took pity on them. He appeared before the monster and asked him courteously to share the water.

'What do I care if they die?' the monster snarled. 'If they want water, let them go somewhere else.'

Glooskap reported back to the villagers to see what they would do. He watched as they all offered their last few drops of water to their bravest warrior, to give him strength to attack the monster. Glooskap was so impressed by their fortitude, that he told them he would undertake this task himself.

He stretched himself until he stood ten feet tall. He dressed his scalp lock with a plume of 100 black and scarlet feathers. He painted his face as if with blood, and daubed green rings around his eyes. He hung a huge clam shell from each ear. Then Glooskap marched up the mountain, followed by a fearsome eagle that flapped its wings at every step. He strode into the monster's village and called out to a boy he saw there, 'Good boy, fetch me a drink.'

The boy recognised him and trembled. But he said, 'I'm sorry, Master, I can't, it's forbidden. Only the chief can distribute drinks.'

'Then tell the chief that Glooskap orders him to bring one.'

The boy sidled off. Glooskap waited. Finally, the boy came back carrying a tiny cup, less than half-full of foul, discoloured liquid.

Glooskap cast it away, pushed the cowering boy aside and strode around the village. Before long, he found where the monster was lurking and went to confront him. 'Bring me a drink of pure water,' he roared. 'And bring it at once!'

'I'm not bringing you anything,' the monster croaked back at him. 'Begone! Get out of my land, Glooskap, go back to the valley. If you want a drink, you can scavenge for it down there.'

Glooskap shot him a single glance, then seized his spear and thrust it deep into the monster's body. A mighty river gushed out from the wound. For the monster had crammed all the dammed up water into his belly, to keep it from the People.

Glooskap seized the monster and crumpled him up in his hands. He transformed him into a Bullfrog and hurled him into the river. 'Stay there for ever!' he cursed him. 'The wrinkles in your back shall always remind everyone of how I squeezed the evil from you!'

Meanwhile, back in the village at the bottom of the mountain, the thirsty People were growing weaker and weaker. To distract themselves, they discussed what they would do if they ever managed to find a mass of water again:

'I'd live in the soft smooth mud and always be wet and cool,' said one. 'How wish I could!'

'I'd plunge from the rocks into the deep, cold stream, drinking as I dived,' said another. 'How wish I could!'

'I'd ride up and down with the rippling waves between land and water,' said a third. 'How wish I could!'

'I'd swim in the water all the time for ever,' said a fourth. 'How wish I could!'

And so it came to be. As the water came pouring down the mountainside, the first became a leech. The second was transformed into a spotted frog. The third changed into a crab, carried up and down with the tide. The fourth became a fish. Until then, none of those creatures had existed.

The river rushed and roared down. It swept them all headlong down into the endless ocean, carrying them to many lands all over the world, where they have lived in their new shapes ever since.

An even worse evildoer was the Sorcerer who struck at the heart of Glooskap's household.

One day, when Glooskap was hunting in the far north, this sorcerer led a war party to the Master's island. There he brutally abducted Grandmother and Marten. He carried them away over several stormy oceans to his lair, where he forced them to be his slaves.

When Glooskap returned home and found his loved ones gone, he wailed with sorrow. Desperately, he searched the woods for them. Wretchedly, he combed through the corners and crannies of his wigwam, seeking some sign of their fate. In this way, he found Marten's magic dish, which the boy-servant had hastily concealed as the sorcerer's cronies seized him. As soon as Glooskap glanced at the dish, he knew everything that had happened.

He did not attempt to rescue them at once. Instead, he went out to the wilderness to fast and pray. After seven long years of this, he grew so powerful that nothing on Earth could ever defeat or resist him.

He went to the shore and sang a magic song. A whale heard it and at once swam to him, saying, 'Master, what can I do for you?'

'Sadly, nothing, my friend, for you are too small,' said Glooskap gently.

The little whale turned back, disappointed. Glooskap sang again. This time, the great Whale Chieftainess herself answered his call.

'Master,' she said, 'I am sturdy. If you wish, I will gladly carry you across the great water.'

'How far?' said he.

'As far as you wish to go. Come, step onto my back.'

So Glooskap stepped onto the Whale Chieftainess, standing upright and noble on her body. She swam with him speedily across the waves. When at last she stopped, a strange land loomed ahead.

'Master,' she said, 'do not ask me to go any further, I beg you. For I can see shells on the seabed below, and that means we have reached the shallows. Unless I turn back now, I shall beach!'

But Glooskap said, 'My friend, you must trust me and swim on.'

The Whale Chieftainess trembled, but even one as mighty as she must obey the Master's command. As she glided slowly and fearfully on through the shallows, she began to hear strange voices rising from the seabed like bubbles.

It was the song of the Clams, who were great enemies of the Master. But the Whale Chieftainess did not know this, nor could she understand their language. That was fortunate, for this is the treacherous song they chanted:

'Save yourself,
Chieftainess,
Hurry, hurry!
Toss him off
And drown him!'

'Master,' the Whale Chieftainess called, 'what are they saying?'

Glooskap's own voice rang out loud above those evil words, urging her: 'Don't worry, dear friend. Just swim on!'

She knew she must obey him. But by now the water was so shallow, she was barely still afloat.

'Master,' she wept, 'you're riding me to my death. I'll be stranded here for ever!' Sure enough, the next moment, she came to a juddering halt on solid land.

Glooskap leaped from her back, thrust his bow against her and used it to give her a push. The Whale Chieftainess wobbled... Then she began to slide back and back, through the shallows, until she was totally submerged in deep water again.

'Ah, Master,' she cried, 'I trusted you as you urged me, and truly you did not let me down! You are like a dear, beloved grandson to me. I am so happy to have helped you on your journey.'

'As I am so grateful for your help,' said Glooskap. 'Here, let me reward you.'

He drew out his pipe, filled it with tobacco from his pouch, lit it and passed it to the Whale Chieftainess. She accepted it and at once began to smoke merrily. As she sailed away, it looked like a long cloud trailing behind her − just as whales still blow today.

Glooskap watched her go, then strode on boldly northwards. He passed through wild lands peopled by loathsome spirits and witches, easily fending them off. He crossed the country now called Newfoundland. From its furthest shore, he rode on the back of another whale to a distant, lonely beach.

There he found a solitary wigwam. Inside the wigwam sat his beloved Grandmother and Marten. Grandmother had wept so long and so bitterly that she had become a mere shadow of her former self. Marten had almost wasted away and died.

The evil sorcerer was lurking nearby, ready to resume tormenting them. Glooskap revealed himself and provoked the sorcerer to anger.

Then the two faced each other. Each began to stretch, taller and taller.

However, anger is the falsest of all passions, and it caused all the sorcerer's strength to drain away. He became so feeble, that he could only manage to make his head rise above the forest. Glooskap's head, on the other hand, went so high that it actually touched the clouds.

Glooskap gave a laugh that rumbled across the land like thunder. Then he took his bow and shot the sorcerer dead.

Time went on and time went by. Glooskap suppressed numberless evil beings until safety and peace ruled the world again.

Yet did this make the People happy? No. Instead, they themselves turned to evil. They became obsessed with pride, violence and deceit.

The Master grew angry. His love for them thinned and trickled away, like oil in the sea.

He sent messengers out, inviting everyone to a grand feast on the silver water's edge. All the People and all the animals of the forest hurried to it in great excitement, eager to make merry. However, when Glooskap greeted them, he did not share their happiness.

He stood before them, solemn and grim. 'At the end of this feast,' he announced, 'I am leaving you for ever. I do not need to tell you why.'

He said nothing else. All too soon, the dreaded time came. Glooskap began to sing his songs of enchantment. He entered his great stone canoe and paddled away over the shining waves. The People watched in stunned silence until they could see him no more. His voice grew faint, then faded right away.

After that, everything changed.

Before Glooskap departed, all the animals had spoken one common language. Now they found themselves talking in different tongues; they could no longer understand each other. They scattered and fled, some to the sea, others to the forest. Since that day, the animals have never again met together in council.

Of all the creatures who mourned Glooskap's departure, none grieved more than the great white Snowy Owl. In despair, he flew far to the north, constantly calling to the night, *'Kukuxkmw!'* – 'I am sorry, oh so sorry!' The Loons were equally devastated, for they had been Glooskap's hunters and messengers. The most faithful ones followed him, leaving the others to flee on an endless journey over mountain, valley and lake, wailing hopelessly for his return…

But listen. It is told that Glooskap is living still, in solitude, in a wigwam far away in some unknown lonely land. Some say it is beyond the peaks, others claim it to be above the Sky. No one knows exactly where. He spends his time there constantly making arrows.

It is said that he is waiting for any of the People who are strong and steadfast enough to seek him out in his hiding place. If they can endure the seven-year journey; if they can climb up and down a sheer, smooth mountain; if they can dodge the tongues of venomous snakes, and evade the crushing Wall of Death beyond them – then they may surely reach Glooskap's lonely lodge. Such heroes will be made most welcome and receive a fine reward.

For Glooskap grants a single wish to each successful traveller. However, such visitors should be wary, for the results are not always as they might seem.

There were three brothers who once managed to complete the journey to Glooskap. One wished to be taller; the second wished simply to stay and admire the view; the third wished to live for ever. The Master granted their wishes by turning them all into trees. Another man who reached him wished for the love of countless women. Glooskap granted this in the form of a bag filled with amorous spirits; but their passion quickly smothered him to death.

Meanwhile, Glooskap continues to work his arrows. One day, there will finally be enough to fill his lonely wigwam from end to end. Then he will stride forth to make his final battle. The sea will rise and boil away into mist; and the world will end in a storm of flames.

Is this is true? Who can tell for sure? For such things are beyond all knowing…

Leland: *The Algonquin Legends*, 1884
Leland: *Kuloskap the Master and other Algonkin Poems*, 1902
This story is distilled from a selection of separate narratives from both sources. Some were in prose, some in verse and some appeared in both forms. The retelling here reproduces much of the flavour, narrative style and imagery of the originals. The opening sentence is directly lifted from the first poem in *Kuloskap the Master*.
Leland started collecting the prose narratives in 1882, from Passamaquoddy people living at Campobello in New Brunswick, Canada. He supplemented this with further material from the Micmac, also of New Brunswick, and the Penobscot of Maine, USA. These three nations are part of the Wabanaki Confederacy (see p. 531). The name Wabanaki,

meaning 'Children of the Dawn Country', is clearly linked to the Glooskap origin myth. Leland says that all his informants were certain of the stories' antiquity. For information on the *Algonkin Poems* source, see p. 591.

Looking at the sources in more detail, Glooskap's myth actually begins before his birth, inside his mother's womb, alongside his malevolent twin brother, Wolf. The pair discuss how they should be born. Glooskap is happy to come into the world in the conventional way, but Wolf insists on bursting out through their mother's side, thus killing her. After the twins grow up, Wolf persuades Glooskap that each should reveal to the other the unique secret method that could kill him. Glooskap, mistrusting his brother, first pretends that he can only die by being stroked by an owl's feather, then later changes the specific weapon to a pine root. Wolf tries, and fails, to slay Glooskap with each of these. Later, one of Wolf's cronies, Beaver, overhears Glooskap whispering to himself that he could really be killed by a flowering rush. Beaver hurries to tell this to Wolf and claims, as a reward, a pair of wings to enable him to fly. Wolf mocks him and refuses. At this, Beaver rushes to confess to Glooskap, who seeks out his brother and kills him to save his own life. Lamenting for his lost twin, he turns Wolf into a mountain.

Other narratives describe Glooskap living with his younger brother or boy-servant, Marten, who can change at will from a young baby to a powerful youth, and whose magic dish can foretell their fate. Martens are slender forest animals related to minks, weasels and wolverines. Their lodge is kept by an old woman who he calls 'My Grandmother'. Instead of a dog, he keeps either Squirrel – who can grow larger to kill enemies, when required – or two Wolves who pull his travois.

Leland says that the name Glooskap means 'liar' – either because he has never kept his promise to return to Earth; or because of the episode in which he lies to stop his twin brother killing him.

There are many further stories about people visiting Glooskap to request the granting of wishes – usually cautionary tales. The Menominee and Ojibwe had similar narratives about about their trickster, Manabus (see p. 568) or Nanabozho.

Glooskap continues to inspire the modern Mi'kmaq people as a cultural icon. His name is given to a tourism trail and a heritage centre in Nova Scotia, where a giant statue representing him was erected in 2005.

MANABUS AND LITTLE BROTHER

◇☐◇☐◇☐◇

Menominee

Up in the Above World, the Creator held a council to consult with his attendants. They all agreed he should make an island and put it down below. So he did. This was the Earth.

When it was finished, the attendants asked, 'Who should walk upon the Earth?'

The Creator said, 'To start with, I'll make two women. One shall be the daughter of the other.' He did this, and breathed life into them both.

It was early spring. The two women talked about what they needed to do to live comfortably, and soon got to work. First, they built themselves a shelter to live in, then they started digging roots to eat. By the time they were settled, it was midsummer.

Up in the Above World, another council was in progress.

The Creator said, 'We need someone to watch over the Earth, to be its guardian and teach the future People how to live.'

'This is a very good idea,' said his attendants. 'But where will this person come from?'

The Creator said, 'I'll make the daughter pregnant, so she can give birth to him.'

While the two women were digging roots, they suddenly heard a great wind roaring. It billowed around the daughter, making her dress fly up; and in that way, the Creator put a new life into her body. Straight away, she began to feel strange. The older woman took her home and later that very same night, she helped her daughter give birth to a beautiful baby boy.

The older woman called the baby Manabus, then put him in his cradle to sleep. But her daughter hadn't finished giving birth yet. The next moment, a Buffalo emerged from her womb, all wet and new. After this came a Moose, an Elk and many, many others – all the different types of animal that live on Earth today. She was the mother of them all.

As soon as each animal was born, it rose to its feet. The older woman led them all outside, and let them walk away.

When she went back in, she found that her daughter had died. She wept bitterly. But then she said to herself, 'The Creator chose for this to happen, so it must be good. And I am very fortunate to be given the care of Manabus.'

Manabus was no ordinary child. Within three days, he had grown from a baby into a boy who could walk and talk. Within the passing of a month, he had become a man. He made himself a bow and arrow and set off to explore.

He stayed away all day; but that night he returned to the old woman, his Grandmother. He did the same thing the next day and the next, and so on.

'Where do you go each day?' Grandmother asked him. 'What do you do there?'

'I walk all over the world, Grandmother,' Manabus said, 'for it is my duty to take care of it. As I travel, I often meet up with my younger brothers – the animals that were born after me. I give them advice: I tell them what kind of food is good to eat, and where is best for each kind to live.'

'Ah,' said Grandmother, 'you were the first person born on Earth, Manabus. That's why you are the leader and guardian of us all.'

'Yes,' he said, 'but, unfortunately, there are also certain creatures who don't respect me. They are the Lower Spirits, monstrous snakes who live in the Underneath World. They wish to bring trouble to the Earth. So whenever I meet them, I make a point of reminding them that my power is greater than theirs, to keep them under control.'

'Grandson,' said the old woman, 'you have important work to do. It's right that you should go out and do it. I am here if you ever need me, but don't feel any obligation to keep coming home.'

Manabus thanked his Grandmother. He continued to go out day after day, visiting his numerous younger animal brothers.

Despite this, he spent most of his time travelling by himself, and he often felt lonely. He thought, 'If only I had a *proper* brother, a companion to talk to and share things with. It's bad luck that I was the only human that my mother gave birth to; but that shouldn't stop me choosing one of the others to be my special friend. But which one? I need someone brave and strong, someone knowing... Ah yes, the Wolves have that kind of power. And if I had a Wolf to walk beside, he could hunt for me and ensure we always had plenty of meat. So that's decided. I wish I could meet up with a pack of Wolves very soon.'

The next moment, he saw a pack of Wolves approaching. They walked towards him in single file, the younger Wolves in front, with the patriarch bringing up the rear.

Manabus greeted them warmly: 'Well, here I am, my brothers, walking in solitude day after day – and I've had enough of it. May I follow you and enjoy your company? May I share your kill?'

The patriarch answered, 'You are very welcome, Manabus, come this way.'

So Manabus accompanied the Wolves all day. He had to run really fast to keep up with them. When night fell, they made a rough camp out of fallen branches, then the younger Wolves went out hunting. One by one they returned, stood before Manabus and vomited up part of their kill. That was how they shared it with him, that was what he had to eat.

The next morning, the patriarch said to Manabus, 'Older brother, you have seen for yourself that our habits are very different from yours. Also, we travel at a speed which is difficult for you to match. The truth is, you are not suited to live as one of us. But I am eager to help you, so I shall give you the best of my sons, White Wolf. He will willingly keep you company and take care of you on your own terms.'

So White Wolf left his pack and became Manabus's special companion. They spent the next day together, talking very amiably, then lay down to sleep side by side. In the middle of the night, Manabus changed White Wolf into a human being.

When his companion woke in the morning, he looked at himself in wonder. 'What's happened to me?' he cried. 'I promised to bring you meat every day, but now I am no longer a Wolf, how can I?'

'I changed you into a form to match mine, to make it easier for us to walk side by side for always,' Manabus told him. 'From now on, you have a new name in honour of our special relationship:

you are called Little Brother. But don't worry, you haven't lost your Wolf power, you'll still be able to do all the things you could do before.'

They settled into their new life together and it went well for both of them. Each day, Little Brother caught a deer, which they cooked and ate together. Time went by. The weather grew colder and colder. One morning, they awoke to find that everything was frozen.

Now they spent more time sitting inside their wigwam and talking. Little Brother listened eagerly as Manabus told him many things he had not known before.

'You must always take care,' Manabus said. 'Never stay out after sunset. Never try to cross the great water. That way, the evil Lower Spirits, the monstrous snakes of the Underneath World, will never be able to get you.'

Little Brother listened and nodded.

Manabus went on, 'Although we must be wary of the Lower Spirits, always remember that you and I are the most powerful beings on Earth. No one else on this island can rival our power. No one can get the better of us.'

He often repeated this last statement. He would say it in the morning, and again in the evening. It never occurred to him that the Underneath World beings could hear him. He had no idea that his constant boasting was provoking them, and making them really angry. After a while, the Lower Spirits had had enough of his arrogance and called a council to discuss how to deal with it. They resolved to show Manabus how limited his power really was, by doing something that would hurt him sorely. They plotted to snatch away Little Brother.

They summoned White Deer to carry out their cruel plan. 'Run across the Earth, straight past Little Brother,' they ordered him. 'Entice Little Brother onto the frozen lake, so we can trap him.'

White Deer quickly found the place where Manabus and Little Brother were camping. As they slept, White Deer made clear tracks in the snow beside his camp. As soon as Little Brother awoke, he found the tracks and followed them, using his Wolf skills. However, he never quite caught up with White Deer, who was always tantalisingly ahead. On and on, Little Brother tracked him, as the Sun moved across the Sky. It grew later and later; the Sun sank and gave way to twilight. Suddenly, Little Brother skidded to a halt.

'Oh no!' he thought, 'Manabus warned me always to be home before sunset. I'd better return at once.'

He looked around to get his bearings. He was standing on the shore of the lake – and on the far bank, directly opposite, he could see the cheerful sight of their wigwam.

He thought, 'The quickest way home is straight across the ice. I know Manabus warned me never to cross the great water, but as it's frozen, maybe that doesn't apply. Surely it will be safer than going all the way round the edge, and not getting back until long after dark.'

He put a cautious foot onto the ice by the shore. It was so thick, it held him firmly. He picked up a branch and smashed it onto the surface. It didn't make any impact. He decided to risk it.

He ran out onto the ice, sliding across it with all his Wolf speed. However, when he was right in the centre, he suddenly heard a rumbling noise. The ice was beginning to crack! All around him, channels of dark water appeared, seething and frothing as if it were on the boil.

Little Brother didn't panic, but leaped nimbly from one floe to another. The gaps between them grew larger and larger. He leaped desperately again – and missed his footing.

'Manabus, help!' he screamed.

But it was too late. With a great splash, he sank down, down down, right into the depths.

Meanwhile, Manabus sat in their wigwam, watching the Sun move across the Sky. As it got lower, he began to feel anxious for Little Brother to come home. Then he heard his brother's voice in the distance and thought, 'He must be shouting to say he's on the way.'

But Little Brother did not appear. In the end, Manabus fell asleep – and dreamed about what the Lower Spirits had done. He woke up in great distress. 'It can't be true!' he cried. 'He's just got lost. I'll go and look for him – I'll seek him all over the Earth if need be.'

He went out as soon as it was light. He walked and walked, he searched and searched. He couldn't find Little Brother anywhere on the island, so now he concentrated on the rocky cavities that led to the Underneath World. He called down each one he came to: 'Does anyone know what happened to my Little Brother?' But the answers he received were always the same. No one had seen Little Brother, no one knew anything of his fate.

Manabus was bereft. He realised that the Lower Sprits were the culprits. He had been so happy with his brother, and now he felt lonelier than ever before. He sat in darkness, talking to himself. He wept so bitterly that the Earth itself shook, sending the lake waters heaving up in great waves.

'Maybe if I wait four days,' he thought, 'the evil ones who snatched Little Brother away will send him back to me. Then I'll be so happy, I'll forgive the suffering they've caused.' But then a new worry occurred to him. 'Supposing they've done something to him, supposing even if he returns, he's not the same as before? If he's changed, I can't accept him back, I'll have to send him away.'

After the four days had passed, Little Brother did indeed return. But just as Manabus had feared, he was not his old self at all. He had become a shadow.

'Stop!' Manabus cried when he saw him. 'Don't come any closer! I can't take you back like this, not as a shadow. I don't want you! Go away, as far as possible – to the country where the Sun sets. I order you to make your home and your fire there.'

Little Brother listened as he had always listened. He stopped obediently, as he had always been obedient. But he spoke what was in his thoughts.

'My older brother,' he said sadly, 'it's a great pity that you have spoken to me in this way. By doing so, you have changed the future for all the People who will come to live on Earth. It had been intended that when they were lost to their loved ones, they would return to life four days later. But your action has made this impossible. Because of you, the dead must always remain as shadows, in the place where I am banished.'

At this, Manabus's anguish grew worse than ever.

The Creator looked down from the Above World and saw this. He called another council and said, 'Manabus is so distressed, there's a real danger he'll start causing trouble on Earth. The Lower Spirits are to blame for this. Summon them here to discuss how they can make amends.'

This was arranged. All the Lower Spirits, the monstrous snakes, came up from Underneath, to join the Creator and his attendants at the medicine lodge in the Above World. They sat along its north side, while the Creator and his attendants sat along the south. Soon they were joined by leaders from every bird species in the world. They agreed that one of the birds, a small yet very powerful one called Mesinikake, should visit Manabus and invite him to the council, so that they could resolve his grievance.

Mesinikake flew down to Earth and went to Manabus in the wigwam where he sat alone with his grief.

Manabus did not receive him well. He said, 'It wasn't *your* fault that I lost my beloved Little Brother, Mesinikake. So your invitation is worthless. I refuse to accept it.'

Mesinikake carried this message back to the Above World. When the Creator heard it, he was angry – not with Manabus, but with the Lower Spirits who had offended him so badly. He was also angry with his attendants for failing to find a solution. The entire council brooded in silence for a while.

Meanwhile, down on the Earth, Otter was sitting high on a rock, eavesdropping on the Above World council. 'I wonder why they didn't ask me to help,' he thought. 'After all, I'm the greatest of my kind and have often used my power to help others out of trouble. Well, I won't wait any longer for them to call me. I'll go straight up there and offer my services.'

He leaped down from his rock and gathered specks of coloured dust from the ground around his lodge – some the colour of the Sky, others the colours of growing things: green, yellow and red. He used this to paint himself, then hastened to the medicine lodge in the Above World. There he stood at the door and addressed both sides who were assembled there:

'My cousins,' he said, 'I've come to help you achieve your mission. I'm not sure why you overlooked me; but I won't hold that against you. You all know that I have as much power as the best of you. Even better, I always get on with everyone, be they good or bad. I can entertain even the most aggrieved people, and make them laugh. No need to discuss this any further: I'll go to Manabus at once, and bring him up here in no time.'

So Otter went off to Manabus's wigwam, squeaking and chirping gently. Manabus heard him coming but he didn't get off his bed. He didn't even stir when Otter let himself in.

'Get up, my friend,' said Otter. 'Come with me. Your great-grandfather wants you to join the other powerful spirits in their council.'

Manabus said, 'It wasn't *your* fault that I lost my beloved Little Brother, Otter. So your invitation is worthless. I refuse to accept it.'

'Ah, but I am on good terms with the Lower Spirits,' said Otter. 'I often dive down to their world and they make me welcome there.' He narrowed his eyes at Manabus, then grinned at him. 'So think of me as one of them, let me share their blame.'

Manabus considered this. Then he nodded, rose from his bed and followed Otter to the Above World.

When he arrived, the Lower Spirits were waiting to welcome him. They said, 'Manabus, we have invited you here so we can apologise for the distress we caused you. We are all your grandfathers, and we all recognise that we made a grave mistake in leading your beloved Little Brother to his death. We wish to make amends for this error by giving you gifts.'

Each stood up and held out a medicine bag to him.

After all their past treachery, Manabus found it hard to trust them. 'What's in these bags?' he said. 'What are you offering me?'

'Roots, medicines,' they answered.

'What are they for? How can they be used? How can I tell if they are good – or another trick? Show me, tell me, before I accept your gifts.'

The Lower Spirits let him take time to examine them carefully. They explained each bag's purpose and how it should be used. When they had finished, Manabus said, 'Yes, I can see that these will be useful for the People who will come to live on the Earth after me.'

He stayed in the medicine lodge in the Above World for four days. He learned how to stop grieving for Little Brother. He was accepted into the medicine society and learned all the important rituals and medicines which People in future should use to heal themselves whenever anyone died.

When he had learned everything, he thanked all his grandfathers for teaching him these things. But he also said this:

'You have taught me well. But I fear that an evil spirit will come into this world to meddle with your gifts; it may conceal bad roots amongst them to injure the future People. So I only accept your good medicines, the ones that heal. Likewise, of the rituals which you have taught me, I will only use the good ones. The Creator must agree to these terms.'

Michelson says this myth was narrated over several sittings by Judge Peroute, a priest of the Grand Medicine Society, and translated by John Satterlee, a mixed-race man who was the official interpreter at the Menominee Reservation at Keshena, Wisconsin. The end of the original story goes into considerable detail about the medicine society rituals. This is not included in the retelling, but the rest is similar to Satterlee's translation, including the narrative style and the rather abrupt ending.

The original translation uses the word 'God' at the beginning of the text, though later the same character is called the Creator. It also uses the word 'servants', which this retelling replaces with 'attendants', for a footnote says that the Menominee word translating as 'servants of the Greater Creator...is not menial in sense. The greatest of these servants is Big Eagle.'

The translation calls the Lower Spirits 'the gods underneath', with more information given in another footnote:

"'Monster snakes" is a stricter rendering. These are located in tiers. Those on the fourth and lowest tier are the most powerful.'

According to Michelson, this was the most sacred myth of the Menominee, forming the basis of their Medicine Society. When telling stories about Manabus, or even mentioning his name, it was customary to throw a handful of tobacco on the fire.

Other ethnologists collected different versions of it during the same period, but these seem to have been corrupted and downgraded so that the religious dimension is partly or entirely absent. In some variants, it seems to have become jumbled up with elements of plot from the *Glooskap* stories (see p. 560). The most common Manabus stories from around the turn of the 20th century are light-hearted folk tales that characterise him as a mere trickster; as happened with sacred characters from other regions such as Coyote, Old Man and Raven.

An unusual one tells of the Upper Beings challenging the Lower Beings to a game of lacrosse on Lake Michigan, with goals at Chicago and Detroit, but failing to invite Manabus. In revenge, he causes huge waves on the lake that threaten one of the goals. The players chase him up a mountain, and he escapes on a 'growing tree' as a flood rises.

One interesting early 20th century tale does explicitly recognise Manabus's spiritual status in a very pertinent way. Here, the Supreme God creates the world by putting islands in the water, then moulds soil to form two men: Manabus and Jesus. They live on separate islands, each protecting his own people, and maintaining a peaceful friendship – until Columbus reaches the Americas, and causes conflict between them.

Amongst the Ojibwe, the same character is known as Nanabozho. There are a number of trickster tales about him, but also variants of the myth retold here.

FLYING WITH THE THUNDERS

◇☐◇☐◇☐◇

Wyandot

There was a youth who went out raiding with two companions. On the way home, right out in the wilderness, he fell and broke his leg. It was damaged so badly that he couldn't walk at all.

The other two made a rough litter out of branches and carried him on it. But the youth was heavy and the ground was rough. By the time they'd trudged up a steep trail to a mountain ridge with him, the other two had grown weary of their burden. As the injured youth dozed fitfully, they put the litter down and drew aside to discuss their situation.

'What shall we do?' said one. 'Dragging him along means that instead of getting home in a few days, we might not make it before the first snow comes.'

'You're right,' said the other. 'So… What do you suggest?'

The first one hedged around a bit. 'He's in a really bad way, you can see that. The wound must be infected: he's burning with fever and he's hardly even raised his head since we started carrying him.'

The other said, 'You think we should put him out of his misery?'

'We could throw him down that cliff,' whispered the first one. He pointed across the ridge to a deep ravine. 'He'll hit the bottom so hard, he'll die instantly. And we won't have to worry about anyone finding his body down there.'

'It would be a kindness. He won't even have time to suffer,' the other agreed.

They went back to the litter. The injured youth was in a swoon and didn't even realise they were lifting him again. It only took a few moments to carry him to the cliff edge and toss him over.

They listened for the distant thud as he hit the bottom, then paid their respects to his spirit. Afterwards, they continued their journey as fast as they could. When they reached home, they went to see his mother and told her that the youth had died honourably in battle.

'He put up a brilliant fight, totally fearless, but the enemy outnumbered him,' they lied. 'You should be really proud of him.'

Of course, that was not much comfort to the mother, who was a widow, with no other children. She was distraught with grief.

But in truth, the youth was not dead. He lay stunned, and injured even more badly than before, at the bottom of the cliff, deep in the twilight shadows of the ravine. There he gradually drifted back into consciousness.

The first thing he saw was a stranger, a wrinkled old man with grey, spiky hair, crouching close beside him.

'Ah, good! You've managed to wake up, my son,' said the old one. 'Your companions have betrayed you, yet you've ended up lucky; for I can heal your wounds and get you on your feet again. And I am lucky too –' he rubbed his hands together and licked his lips '– because I've been living on nothing but leaves until now; but once you recover, you shall stay and hunt for me, supply me with meat.'

'Who are you?' the youth croaked. 'Where am I? How did I get here? Where are my friends?'

The old man did not reply, but scuttled off. He soon returned, bringing herbal pastes and brews, and bundles of leaves for bandages. He used these to doctor the youth, then helped him stagger to his own shelter under some rocks within the ravine. There he nursed the youth back to health.

Days and months passed. Finally, the youth was completely recovered and all his energy returned. Then his saviour sent him out hunting, far into the wilderness that lay beyond the end of the ravine. It was winter. The youth travelled easily over the firm snow and found plenty of game. He diligently brought home everything he killed.

The old one greedily devoured a large share of this food. Every day, he made a point of praising the youth: 'See how strong I've grown, thanks to the meat you bring me. There'll be no stopping me now.'

The youth wondered what he meant. The old one did not explain, but just encouraged him to hunt even harder: 'Keep on like this. And don't let the fact that you must hunt alone hold you back; if ever you kill an animal that's too big to haul back by yourself, come and fetch me to help with it.'

The winter snows melted. Warm winds and rain showers heralded the coming of spring. One day, the youth had to travel further than usual to find any game, right to the edge of a forest. There he came upon a bear, newly emerged from its den after the winter sleep. It was still drowsy and stumbling around, easy prey. He shot it dead with a single arrow, then ran across to examine his catch. He stooped over it, trying to guess its weight: it was huge. Maybe it was time to take up his master's offer of help.

As he considered this, suddenly he was startled by the sound of voices murmuring behind him. Whoever could it be? In this deserted country, he had never met anyone apart from his strange master. He leaped up and spun round. A short way off, he saw three big men watching him intently.

They were unlike anyone he had ever seen before. Their skin was damp with dew. Their robes were vague, drifting and vaporous, as if sewn from clouds.

The youth hastily fitted another arrow to his bow and held it up threateningly. But the strangers only laughed.

'Put your weapon down, friend,' said one.

'Who are you?' the youth cried. 'What do you want?'

'We are the Thunders,' said another.

'Thunders?' he cried in astonishment.

'We soar from Sky to Earth, from Earth to Sky,' said the third. 'We watch here, there, everything, everywhere. We bring rain, we nurture life, we punish evil.'

'But…why have you come here?' said the youth.

'To root out and destroy a monster.'

They were all staring at him intently. The youth felt they could see right into his heart. He said nervously, 'I think you've come to the wrong place. There are no monsters here.'

'Don't be so sure,' they said. 'Things are not always as they seem. A monster has been very close to you ever since you came to this wilderness.'

'I don't understand,' said the youth.

'The old man who cured your wounds, the one you now work for, is not what he seems. He is filled with gluttony and vice. He

579

chews trees to death, eats through houses. You must lure him to us so he can be destroyed.'

The youth was trembling so much, he could scarcely answer them. 'I…I don't know. He…he saved my life. You're asking me to betray him. Surely…surely that's totally wrong…?'

'It would do the world a great service.'

How could he break faith with his saviour? Without that old one, he would certainly have died. And yet…even more than that, how could he dare argue against the Thunders, who were the Earth's protectors? He hesitated a few moments more, while their gaze burned into him. Then he hurried back to find the old one.

As usual, he was lurking inside the shelter. He had grown so massive from his new, meat-rich diet that he seemed to fill it entirely. 'Where have you been all this time, my son?' he grumbled. 'I've been growing anxious for your return.'

'I was delayed because I killed a huge bear,' said the youth. 'It's oozing with fat, enough to last for months, but it's too big for me to drag home by myself. I remember you saying I should ask your help in such a matter if ever I need to. Now that time has come.'

'Very well then, I'll help you,' the old one said. 'But wait, my son! First tell me – for my own eyes are poor – is there any sign of rain, even a speck of dark cloud? If there is, the bear meat must wait, for such weather puts me in great danger.'

'But if we delay, wild animals will steal the meat.'

'Never mind. Go outside and check for me.'

The youth went out to look, then returned and said truthfully, 'The weather's dry and the Sky's completely clear.'

'All right, I'll risk it. But we must hurry and get this over with as fast as we can. It's dangerous for me to be out in the open. Keep a sharp eye out as we go, and if the weather changes in any way, tell me at once: we might have to retreat.'

The old one rose, came outside and sniffed suspiciously. The air was unnaturally still, as before a storm, yet the Sky was indeed cloudless. So he followed the youth along the trail. All the way he kept muttering to himself: 'Why can I smell death? Is it the bear, or is it my fate? Should I go back? No, I can't refuse such a hoard of meat; my power will increase so much when I've devoured it. I'll have to risk it.' Then aloud he cried, 'Hurry, hurry!'

At last, they reached the dead bear. When the old one saw it, he smacked his lips, drew out his knife and signalled the youth to do the same. Working side by side, they quickly skinned the bear and cut it up. The old one hastily began to shove all the joints into a sack. Then suddenly he froze, hissing: 'Listen! What is that?'

A soft rumbling had started up in the distance. It grew louder and the Sky darkened. The clouds burst and the rain that the old one had dreaded came bucketing down.

The old one shrieked. He jerked. He started to spin – round and round, faster and faster, until his body was little more than a blur...

The rain parted. The Thunders were revealed. Lightning flashed from their fingers.

The old one was gone. He had not vanished, but transformed into his true shape: a gigantic porcupine, three times the size of a man! His spines gleamed with poison. He ran into the bushes, his great teeth slicing through the tangle of saplings and overhanging branches. Quills loosened from his back, flying towards the youth and the Thunders like arrows.

The youth dodged to one side as the Thunders smashed their way through the brush after their foe. They roared and clapped: bolt after bolt of lightning shot through the air – until at last, the evil giant porcupine lay dead.

The storm quietened as suddenly as it had begun. The youth sank to the ground, exhausted and confused.

After a while, the Thunders came to him. 'Get up,' they said. 'Be proud to have helped us rid the world of a malicious destroyer. As a reward, we shall send you straight back to bring joy to your mother – hastened by our own gift of flying.'

The youth watched in awe as the Thunders broke off fragments from their cloud robes and draped them over his own shoulders. They weighed nothing and filled him with light and air.

'Move your arms inside them,' the Thunders told him.

The youth did as he was told, and found himself rising from the ground like a bird. When his arms stilled, he sank again.

'These robes will carry you back to your mother's house,' they said. 'When you arrive, hide them somewhere safe and live well. After a full year has turned, we will fetch you to fly again – this time with us. Then you will see more of the work that we do each year for the High One, to keep the Earth safe from those whose greed would otherwise ruin it.'

The youth did as they told him and flew home. His mother cried with happiness to see him. He buried his cloud robes in the forest, kept the secret of his adventure close to his heart, and waited.

The year turned, summer to autumn, to cold winter. Spring peeled open again and the first rains fell in torrents. Most people huddled indoors, but every day the youth went out and stood under the dark clouds alone. In that way, he was ready when at last the Thunders came again to fetch him.

'Fly with us!' they roared. 'Hunt with us, from Sky to Earth, from Earth to Sky, until we have struck down every shoot of this year's evil!'

They swept him up and away. All through the spring rains he flew in the clouds with them, helping them seek out many evil creatures, helping to destroy them. In each country they did this, the air cleared and new growth pushed vigorously through.

One day, as they flew over the mountains, the youth was overcome by thirst. Looking down, he saw a pool and swooped to Earth to drink from it. It tasted unusual, but he thought nothing of it. However, when he returned to the Sky, the Thunders stared at him for a long moment, then circled close, sniffing.

'Where have you been?' they demanded.

'I was thirsty.' The youth pointed beneath him. 'I went down and drank from that pool.'

'Your lips are smeared with foul oil from its waters. We know that smell: it is the poisonous spittle of the Chief of all Maggots, an evil one we have been hunting down for years. Every spring he devours the corn and beans that the women in the country below try to grow in their gardens. If you had not been flying with us, we might never have found him. What luck you have brought to us – and also to the women who have suffered years of despair from his gluttony!'

The three Thunders gathered together, hovering directly over the pool. They pointed at it and released a mighty thunderbolt. From its flames came a spiralling pillar of steam, sucking up all the water, dispersing it into the grey blanket of rain that veiled the Sky.

'Look down, friend,' they cried. 'There is one of the great shapes of evil!'

The youth looked. Moments ago, the waters of the pond had been rippling there. Now there was only a hollow of arid, cracked dirt. Sprawled hideously in the middle of it, big as a longhouse, lay a dead maggot.

'Thus we are finished for this spring,' said the Thunders. 'But within the coming months, new evils will grow, so next year we will return to resume our work. Meanwhile, go back to your village and tell your people what you have seen, and what we promise: If they dig the ground each spring with pure hearts, the Thunders will kill the creatures that spoil the forest and steal their crops, and bring rain to make them grow.'

For the last time, the youth flew with the Thunders. This time, they led him home. There the cloud robes fell from his shoulders and dissolved right away like morning mist.

He called his people around him and told them everything that had happened and what he had witnessed. They were amazed.

Ever since then, no one fears the Thunders. The people honour them instead.

Hale: *Huron Folk-Lore,* 1891

Hale recorded this story in 1874, from his 'esteemed Wyandot friend and instructor, Chief Joseph White (Mandarong)'. It was 'carefully translated and explained by Mrs White.' He comments:

'The narrative, in its present shape, must be regarded as a comparatively modern composition, or at least recension, due to some native mythologist of much imaginative genius, who lived within the last two centuries, or since the removal of the Hurons [Wyandot] from their ancient seat... But the myths comprised in the narrative certainly embody...the most ancient and widespread beliefs of the tribes of the great Huron-Iroquois family.'

He includes some interesting notes at the end of the story:

'Thence originated the honour in which the Thunder is held among the Indians. The Wyandots were accustomed to call [Thunder] their grandfather...

'The chief added that the young man learned from his divine friends the secret of rain-making, which he communicated to two persons in each tribe. They were bound to strict secrecy, and possessed, the chief affirmed, the undoubted art of making rain. He had often known them to accomplish this feat. He himself had become partly possessed of this secret, and had been able in former days to bring rain. Of late years, in obedience to the injunctions of the Church, he had forborne to exert this power. I asked him if he had any objection to disclose the secret. His wife urged him to tell; but on consideration he said that he would rather not. He had received it in confidence; the Church had forbidden the practice of the art; and he thought it best that the knowledge of it should perish. It was evident that he entertained the most entire faith in the power of this charm.'

It seems that Thunder could be a single deity or appear in multiple forms. Hale says:

'When thunder is heard to roll from many parts of the heavens, it is because there are many of the Thunders at work. They…[may] be regarded as one god or many…'

The Delaware have a related story with some interesting beliefs attached. An old man and a young boy set out together to explore the world. Sleeping on an island in a great lake, they are awakened by a strange man, elaborately decorated with paint and feathers. He takes them to meet the Thunder people who bring rain to make crops grow. The Thunders explain how they take a fair reward from the people's fields, causing familiar scenes of crop damage:

'We take a little from a great many fields. When you see a small or withered squash, or bad kernels of corn on an ear, or dried-up beans in a pod, you may know that we have taken our part from them. We have taken the spirit and left the shell. If you see a whole field of withered corn, you may know that we have taken the spirit from it, but we seldom destroy a whole field; we take only a little.'

The old man and boy are asked to use their powers to kill some gigantic enemies: a porcupine, a fish and a flying monster. The boy manages to shoot them all dead, and his reward is to live and work with the Thunders permanently:

'…and to this day the little boy goes with them everywhere. After the great Thunders roar we hear the little fellow with his alto voice, and we say, "That is Wishakon," and we burn tobacco saying, "This is all we have to give," and we thank him for rain.'

Thunder personified as a benevolent, evil-destroying force is important in a number of other Northeast myths associated with the spring rains. Many such stories also feature malevolent snakes. In a Passamaquoddy tale, a woman impregnated by an evil snake is saved by Lightning Woman and her brother Thunder. She marries the latter, and their son is given wings to make thunder. As in the story retold here, the woman visits her own people and tells them never to fear storms. The Menominee said the Thunders took the form of birds of prey, with an invisible Golden Eagle as their chief. They tell of an orphan girl adopted by ten Thunderbird 'uncles', then changed into a tiny, creeping toad, who sings to make the rain.

See the Great Plains story, THE THUNDERBIRDS, p. 91.

Hale concludes with an interesting comment on the mythology of the Wyandot and Iroquois peoples:

'Not only [their] principal deities…but almost all their minor divinities – spirits of the winds, of the plants, etc. – are of a benign nature. If the character of a people, as is commonly assumed, can be inferred from the character and attributes of the objects of their worship, the tribes of this race must be deemed a naturally kindly and peace-loving people.'

A FABLE

Winnebago (Ho-Chunk)

Once there were some mice under a crooked log
and they believed they were the only people in the whole world.
One of them, standing up and stretching his little arms,
could just touch the underside of the log.
He thought that he was very tall
and that he touched the Sky.
So he danced and sang this song:

'Throughout the world
Who is there like little me?
Who is like me!
I can touch the Sky,
I touch the Sky indeed!'

– Narrated and sung by Chash-chunk-a (Peter Sampson).
(Quoted in Curtis: *The Indians'* Book, 1907)

SUMMER AND HER GRANDMOTHER RAIN

◇□◇□◇□◇

Passamaquoddy

In ancient days,
in a land near the Sun,
lived a pretty young woman
in her wigwam of flowers.
Green were her garments,
all of fresh leaves.
Summer was her name.

Her grandmother, Rain,
lived far away
but oft came to visit
her beloved Summer.
'Grandchild,' said Rain,
'never go wandering
to the far distant Northland!
For there dwells Winter,
our deadliest foe.
If you went to his country,
he'd steal all your beauty,
wither you and weaken you
and cause you to die.

But Summer was callow
and Summer was wilful.
She paid no heed
to her grandmother's warnings.

One sunny morning
she sat by her wigwam
looking afar to the land in the north.
She saw shimmering lakes,
bright rushing rivers,
exquisite blue mountains,
aglow with beauty.
She heard a voice calling her,
beguiling, enchanting:
'Come, sweet Summer,
come dance in the Northland!'
How could she resist?

So she rose and set out
on the perilous journey,
though her grandmother's voice
chased her on the wind:
'Stop, dearest child!
Turn back from the Northland!
Ignore evil Winter
who's luring you there!'
But Summer was deaf
to wise Rain's warning.
Summoned by the mountains
bewitched by the rivers,
drawn to the gleaming land,
she journeyed resolutely
with fever in her soul.

Days passed, months passed.
The trail seemed endless,
while still Rain called her:
'Stop, my dear grandchild!

Turn back to safety!'
But Summer was scornful,
tossed back her hair
and went eagerly on,
northward and northward,
further and further…

Until an uncanny feeling
seeped into her bones.
It was chilling and horrible,
heavy and wearying –
the deadly power
of freezing cold.
Her smooth skin wrinkled.
Her glossy black hair
turned white and brittle.
Her dress of green leaves
faded and wilted.

'What's happened to the Sun?'
Summer cried weakly.
It dimmed then vanished.
'Where are the rivers?'
They'd all turned to ice.
'The lakes and the mountains?'
All smothered by snow.

Now foolish Summer
saw the trap she'd entered.
Regret overwhelmed her.
Heartbroken, weakened,
she swooned to the ground,
frozen to the centre,
knowing she must die.

Far away, her grandmother
called up her warriors,

strong yet invisible:
'Warming Breeze the valiant,
South Wind and East Wind!
Fly fast, I order you,
to the far Northland!
Fight there, my heroes!
Rescue fair Summer
from the death-clasp of Winter!'

They raced out eagerly,
reached the distant Northlands
in the blink of an eye.
Winter saw them coming,
summoned his own warriors:
North Wind the terrible,
wild Northwester, chill Northeaster,
Frost spirit, Sleet spirit,
murderous Snow.
'Hurry!' he roared.
'Our foes from the south
have come to attack us –
Prepare for war!'

Thus battle broke out
between fair winds and foul winds,
warm gales and hurricanes,
thunder, lightning,
and mild summer rain –
beating and heating,
freezing and melting...

Until warm winds thawed cold ones.
Evil Winter's ice cheeks
softened into sweat beads,
indestructible strength
beginning to fail.
No longer roaring,
his voice barely squeaking,

as he groaned to his men:
'We'll all perish
unless we free Summer.
The one I enchanted
and tried to vanquish
is destroying *me* instead.
We must set Summer free!'

        At that very instant
        the winds all fell silent,
        the snow and rain stopped.
        Summer's eyes opened.
        Slowly, she rose from
        the ground where she lay frozen.
        Weakly, she turned back
        for the long trudge home.
        She was old and half-broken,
        her hair thin as snow wisps,
        weary and tottering,
        stiffened by frost.

Many moons she travelled.
The Sun grew warmer,
days and shadows longer,
the air much softer,
the mountains green.
Ice cracked up
in the lakes and rivers.
Petals unfolded,
rich with perfume,
warmed by the breeze.
Butterflies saw her,
fluttered around her.
Summer's heart grew lighter,
her skin more radiant,
her beauty restored.

On the way home
she called at old Rain's wigwam,
wet with showers and
swathed in clouds.
She found her grandmother
lying sick in darkness.

'Dear child,' said Rain,
'your foolish disobedience,
and the fear of losing you
struck me harder
than you can know.
Without my struggle
against cruel Winter,
all life would have perished
in the ice and snow.
So never again
let temptation entrap you
if you care at all
for our beautiful world!'

Leland: *Kuloskap the Master and Other Algonkin Poems,* 1902
Leyland explains the provenance of the verse narratives in his book as
follows:

'There has perished, or is rapidly perishing, among the…Indians of
North America, far more poetry than was ever written by all the
White inhabitants; and…this native verse is often of a very high order.
…I was made aware by Louis Mitchell, a Passamaquoddy Indian, who
had been in the Legislature of Maine…that there were in existence
certain narratives and poems quite different in kind from anything
which I possessed… Three of the poems Mitchell wrote out for me
in exact, though often quite ungrammatical language, which was so
close to the original that the metres betrayed themselves
throughout… I, with great care, put the Mitchell Anglo-Algonkin into
English metre, having been impressed, while at the work, with the
exquisitely naive and fresh character of the original, which…in many
passages had strictly a life and beauty of its own.'

Leland asked J. Dyneley Prince, a scholar of the Algonquian languages, to
compare his metrical version against Mitchell's original text, and also to
revise and correct it. Of the metre, Leland explains:

'When an Indian…would spin off some long romantic yarn, he… frequently begins to intone or chant the tale in a manner which is something between plain-song and…singing…by one who has no vocal gift. Then the voice falls into one or the other of two measures which I believe I have accurately followed in the present work. This… rhythm is quite irregular, following only a general cadence rather than observing any fixed number of beats in each line. I have endeavoured to represent this peculiarity in the English version by not adhering too strictly to an unvarying measure.'

This retelling is closely based on the imagery, style and metre of the original text in Leland's book.

The Iroquois have a very similar story. They also tell a myth in which the Great Spirit punishes some powerful chiefs who insult him, by sending storms and snow that cause extreme cold and starvation. Eventually mild weather returns, but in remembrance of their insults, the Great Spirit brings back winter each year, and turns the corpses of those frozen to death into poisonous plants.

In a Menominee myth, a hunter mocks the snow for fleeing the springtime sun. An invisible voice responds by challenging him to a trial of strength the following winter. The man prepares by laying in massive stores of oily firewood and fat He then sends his family to a safe place and makes his camp alone. During a bout of extremely cold weather, he peers through a chink in the wall and sees the Snowman approaching. As it turns colder and colder, he piles up his fire for four days – until the Snowman begins to melt and is forced to retreat, vowing his power will continue in the far north. The Subarctic Naskapi people told exactly the same story.

An Ojibwa story says summer is in the power of certain birds; when a man holds these captive, it causes permanent winter in the north, until they are freed. The Seneca tell of old man Winter building an impenetrable ice house, then banning entry to everyone except for his friend North Wind. Together they plot to make the weather even worse. Then the youth, Spring, enters with his own friend, South Wind. They prove their greater strength by making all the snow melt until Winter shrinks to nothing.

There are also other Northeast myths about battles of the winds. In an Iroquois story, a young boy visits the West, North and East Winds in turn, using trickery to overcome their aggression. Finally he meets the South Wind in a place of flowers and birds, and obtains from him the first crop seeds. A Passamaquoddy Glooskap story (see p. 560) describes a great bird called Wind Blower, who lives at the northern end of the sky. Flapping his wings, he makes such a violent wind that Glooskap binds them together and throws the bird into a chasm. The air now becomes so still, that all the water stagnates. So one of his wings is freed and since then the winds have been moderate.

WHY ANIMALS
DO NOT TALK

◇□◇□◇□◇

Iroquois (Haudenosaunee)

Long ago, so long that books cannot tell of the time, all the animals in the forest could talk.

At that time, the animals were also the sole guardians of all wisdom and knowledge. The People envied them for this and longed to know everything too. The animals considered the matter and agreed that, in the name of fairness, they should share their knowledge. So they invited the People to sit around their council fire. There, each species appointed the best of their kind to share with the People everything that they knew.

Beaver taught the women where to snare pike and salmon, and how to build houses to keep out rain and frost.

Bear and Wolf joined forces to teach their special skills of tracking and following trails through the forest and the plains.

Dog demonstrated his patience and endurance, showing the People how to keep watch for many days without growing weary.

Raccoon gave lessons in climbing the highest trees.

Horse demonstrated the secrets of swift running.

Mountain Lion showed the warriors how to hide in a thicket, on the branches of an overhanging tree, or behind a rocky ledge – then to burst out on an enemy like an unexpected whirlwind.

Thus from every animal the People took lessons in the crafts of the woods and plains, until they believed they had learned all there was to know. But at that point, Fox had one last lesson for them, the greatest lesson of all. He led them into the deepest part of the forest and there, hidden from all outsiders, he taught them cunning.

Now at last, the People were fully equipped for everything, and thus they were content.

However, the animals did not share their happiness. For as time went by, the People used their new skills to dominate the animals and become their masters. Because of this, whenever there were no People around to eavesdrop, the animals constantly complained to each other.

'It's not fair,' Beaver grumbled. 'Wouldn't you think that the women would be content with the excellent fishing places I pointed out to them? Oh no, those aren't good enough for *them*! They've been wandering around all over the place looking for even better ones – and they've found the secret streams which I was keeping for myself. Even worse, I've often caught them staring me up and down with very malicious gleams in their eyes. I'm terrified they're planning to tear the warm fur off my back and use it to cover themselves. And have you seen the new houses those People are building? They're far better than my own. And their boats: it was me who felled the trees for them, and how do they thank me? With mockery! They shape their paddles to look exactly like my own tail, then use them to dart across the water much faster than I can. I wish I'd never taught them anything, they've done nothing but abuse their new skills.' Beaver gave a deep sigh of utter misery

Whenever Bear and Wolf went wandering in the woods, they now often noticed People following their trail. But the People disguised their own tracks so cunningly that the animals could not keep up with them at all. Also, the People used the skills that Bear had given them to find the trees where the bees stored their honey – and thus robbed him of his favourite food.

One day, Wolf actually heard a warrior promise a young woman that, if she moved into his wigwam, she would rest on a couch made of Wolf skins, and be covered with Bear fur! With a great howl, he ran to find Bear and share this dreadful news with him. Both animals hurried their children away and hid them in lonely caves, as far as possible from the homes of People.

Mountain Lion was furious too. He always took every precaution to conceal himself. But now he kept seeing branches parting silently, as if swayed by a summer breeze, to reveal a man laughing at Mountain Lion's pathetic attempts to hide.

As for Raccoon, human boys kept following him around with shouts of mockery, hanging from the ends of the swaying branches so recklessly, that old Raccoon felt dizzy. He couldn't stand any more of it, so he went away to the hills to be by himself.

Fox was furious to discover that the People could not only match his cunning, but had become even craftier than him. He tried so carefully to conceal his trail: walking in the beds of streams, circling round and round the mountains until he almost lost his way – yet the People always found him. When he tried to lead them astray by subtle wiles, they quickly uncovered his ploys with roars of laughter, causing him to shrivel with humiliation before his friends and neighbours.

Dog and Horse, however, accepted the changes.

True enough, Dog found that he was no longer the best at keeping watch; but that didn't make him angry with his human brothers and sisters. Instead, he willingly spent long nights on guard out in the wilderness, side by side with the People. Dog really enjoyed the challenge of seeing who was most vigilant, and the fun afterwards, when they discussed the results of their friendly contest.

Horse was pleased to see that the People had thoroughly mastered the running skills he had taught them. He admired their diligent practice to improve their stamina and speed. Although they no longer needed him for their races, he still liked watching them. And afterwards, when the People returned to their village, he took pleasure in following them. For the young women would take turns to mount his back and ride him to the council fire, which made him very proud.

Despite Dog's and Horse's happiness, all the other animals were outraged that the People now surpassed them in everything.

To discuss this terrible calamity, a council was summoned in great secret. For the first time ever, the People were not invited. News of the council was spread in hurried whispers. The fire was not lit in its usual place; instead, its flames were concealed in a remote spot under the darkest trees, well away from any trails. The animals gathered round it in the dead of night, at a time when they knew all the People were fast asleep.

It was Wolf who opened the discussion. 'My brothers and sisters,' he declared, 'we are all too aware of our terrible situation. Personally, I can see only one way forward. We must rush in upon their villages at once and kill all the People as they sleep, including their children!'

Bear spoke next, and he took a nobler stance. 'It's true,' he said, 'that we animals cannot tolerate this dangerous situation any longer. We are are all living in fear. However, I have to say that my brother Wolf's proposition of attack by stealth is despicable. Instead, we should do the honourable thing and challenge the People to open war.'

Beaver had a more original suggestion. 'Let's wait until the chill winds of winter arrive,' he argued. 'Then, in the middle of the night, we'll tear away the People's houses, to expose them and their children to the freezing cold. Right now they believe they're more powerful than us – but a taste of winter storms will soon reveal their weakness! They'll come grovelling to us, desperate to reach an agreement – which, of course, we shall make in our own favour.'

Each of these proposals brought strong murmurs of support. However, when it was Horse's turn to speak, he strongly opposed the three who had gone before him.

'No, no, no!' he cried. 'It would be wrong to carry out any of these vile suggestions. In my experience, the People aren't really bad neighbours; it's just that they've become too arrogant. My ancestors and the People have been on the best of terms for many years, and not even a tiny ripple of trouble ever disturbed our relationship before. I refuse to support any plan which involves loss of their lives or causes them pain.'

He tossed his mane and went on: 'Now then, listen, for I have a much better solution. I've heard that way beyond the mountains, there's another fine country – not quite as pleasant and fertile as this one here, but still a good place to live. I therefore propose that we invite the People to go there on a great harvest expedition. Once they're safely on the far side of the mountains, we animals can sneak away in the night and reclaim the forest for ourselves.'

'That's totally ridiculous!' scoffed Mountain Lion. 'And in my opinion, even Beaver's idea is much too lenient. These People are downright wicked and dangerous. Only total extermination of the human race can save us from further trouble. Tell me, Horse, what good would it really do to lure the People over the mountains, then run away from them? They're not helpless nurselings or invalids. They'd never just lie down across there and give up their beloved streams, lakes and forests here. They'd come rushing back – and the ground would turn red with our own blood when they attacked us in revenge. If we animals are to retain any freedom and independence, we must follow the simple advice of Wolf. I second an immediate attack upon the People's villages – and we should do it now. No one can persuade me otherwise.'

When he had finished, Raccoon stood up. All eyes turned hopefully towards him, for he was from a very ancient family, and was held in high respect by all the inhabitants of the forest.

'I can't agree with Wolf and Mountain Lion,' he said. 'To be honest, the People have never done me any great harm. Nevertheless, they have become far too clever for us, and I too am convinced that we'd be better off without them. Too much power in the hands of one group always makes trouble for the others. So I favour Beaver's plan. If we carry it out carefully, we can surely bring about a treaty to keep the People under control.'

'I have a better idea than any of you,' Fox interrupted. 'First, I'll teach you all to become expert cheats and tricksters...'

At these words, the others all roared and howled in disgust.

'Be quiet and let me finish,' Fox went on. 'Once you've learned my little lesson, we'll all cosy up to the People and pretend we're their undying friends. It will be a deceit, of course, because having won their trust to go on their land, we'll sneak off and strip their fields of corn. Then we'll loosen their boats and fishing nets from their moorings, and float them downstream to be lost in the rapids. That will get the People at our mercy! Then we can force through a treaty on the lines proposed by Beaver. Unlike Wolf and Mountain Lion's nasty plan, it won't cause the People any serious harm. I assure you, that's the best way forward.'

While everyone at the council was considering all these speeches, Dog asked for a turn to be heard, and this was granted.

Dog stepped forward and gazed bleakly around the council fire, his voice grim. 'Never before,' he said, 'no, *never,* have I ever realised what it means to be a lowly "beast". Today, however, I have learned that most of the animals here are beasts. I am ashamed of you all! I also feel bitterly ashamed of my own weakness in attending this council, which excludes my human brothers and sisters. That goes against one of our most ancient and sacred customs – a custom that has existed since the Great Spirit first sent us to live in this beautiful country. I expect we will all be punished for such treachery. Indeed, we *deserve* to be punished.

'Listen. The People have always treated us all with kindness and respect. Have you forgotten all those winters, when the snow lay deep and no food could be found? Do you not remember how the People fed you all, and sheltered even the biggest amongst you in their own homes? In hard times, they have always helped us animals, and often saved us from starvation.'

Dog gazed around the circle of listeners. No one denied what he had said.

'No human being,' he went on, 'has ever refused aid to a needy, sick or suffering animal. What does it matter that they have acquired knowledge that previously was ours alone? This has not impoverished us, we have lost nothing by it. Why should we be jealous and find fault with them for it? Would it not be far wiser to follow the People's example, and take trouble to learn each others' different skills? Surely that is better than letting jealous, vengeful passion break the longstanding peace? I cannot, and will not, be party to any of the other plans proposed.'

No one spoke against him, but the air was tense.

Dog continued, 'If the rest of you persist with your treacherous, schemes, consider it your moral duty to leave the council now. Go on: go to the village and warn the sleeping People – our sisters and brothers, and their innocent children – of their imminent danger!'

Nobody moved.

'I have one more thing to say,' said Dog. 'If war comes, I will not fight with you; I will fight on the side of the People. I will help them defend their lives and homes from any attack the rest of you bring against them.'

By the time Dog had finished speaking and sat down, Wolf and Mountain Lion were both incandescent with rage.

'You coward!' howled Wolf.

'You faithless bribe taker!' screeched Mountain Lion. 'We all know what this is about, Dog: you've been bought for a meagre crust of maize-cake that's too hard for the People's own teeth to crush. Think of your forefathers, the long line of noble Dogs who lived before *you* were born to disgrace them. Does their memory not stir you? No? Then you have betrayed the honour of the Dog race. You deserter, you traitor!'

'That's too flattering for him,' snarled Wolf. 'You're too weak even to be a traitor, Dog. You're a pathetic fool, a mindless baby. You've been turned by the simpering praise and soft caresses lavished on you by human girls. I saw you the other day, lying at the feet of the chief's daughter. You only had to raise your eyes at her, and she was taking you in her arms, laying her cheek against you, stroking your back and singing to you. What a level you've sunk to, selling yourself to the People, while the rest of us are exploited and enslaved!'

'Yah, go play with the human newborns!' mocked Mountain Lion. 'Go snore in the sun with the old men!'

'Be warned, Dog,' said Wolf. 'If you dare expose this council's secrets to the People – we shall set upon you and kill you!'

This hot-tempered language caused a huge sensation, with all the animals talking at once. However, Dog remained calm and dignified. He showed no outward sign that he had even heard the abuse from Mountain Lion and Wolf.

The next moment, Horse again spoke up, springing into the open place before the fire. From there he hurled his most powerful eloquence at the two accusers.

'I speak as a champion of Dog,' he cried. 'You have insulted and maligned him in a manner that should be condemned by all honourable animals. Despite our differences, and even though I am his superior in size, I look up to Dog as a wise brother. I love him, for he is gentle, affectionate, trustworthy, noble and brave.

'You, Mountain Lion, and you, Wolf, are keen to brag about your own so-called bravery. Yet which of you ever dared rush into the burning forests as Dog did, to lead the blind and helpless Deer to safety? Which of you ever plunged into the river when it was dangerously swollen and foaming with snowmelt, to rescue a weak and drowning friend who'd stumbled over the bank? Only Dog does such great deeds.

'I used to love you all, but from now on I am ashamed even to acknowledge Wolf and Mountain Lion as distant kin. They seem to think that bravery consists of savage attacks with glistening teeth. Nonsense! True bravery is only found in noble deeds. I vow to follow Dog to the homes of the People, and together we will defend them from your wickedness.'

As Horse ceased speaking, a stunned silence suddenly fell over the assembly. However, this was not due to Horse's words, remarkable as they were; it was because a most unexpected visitor had appeared at the council fire –

The Great Spirit himself!

Jaws dropped open. Eyes stared in brief amazement then were quickly averted. Heads bowed in humility.

'What is going on?' said the Great Spirit. He spoke quietly but ominously. 'My messengers reported voices at the council fire raised loud in inexcusable dispute, so I myself came to listen. I heard everything. You have broken the ancient pact between the People and the animals. My children, you have brought me unfathomable sorrow.'

They all listened, trembling, overcome with shame.

'I shall punish you all,' the Great Spirit said. 'I shall change the language of my human children, the People, so that you animals will never again be able to speak with them. But that is not all; I have more specific punishments for each of you.

'Wolf and Mountain Lion: from now on and for all time, you shall be hunted and killed by the People. They will regard you as their most despicable foes.

'Bear: you at least expressed more honour in your aggression. So though I will allow the People to attack you if you provoke them, I shall not permit them to molest you without reason.

'Beaver and Raccoon: because of your callous plans for the vanquishing your human kin, I give the People the right to hunt you. You will sacrifice your thick furs to keep their children warm.

'Fox: you longed to be a thief, to steal the People's food and make them hungry. Well, you shall have a chance to try and fulfill your desire... But beware, for the People will constantly outwit you with traps and snares. And when they catch you, they will use your fur just like Beaver's and Raccoon's.

'Horse and Dog: Your noble words brought me some comfort. So I will permit you both to keep the ability to understand the speech of the People. However, even you two are guilty of breaking an ancient treaty, by attending a council from which a key group was excluded. So you must also be punished, though more mildly than the others. I will deprive you of the ability to talk back to the People.

'Nevertheless, for your loyalty to them, they shall always be your champions and friends. You shall live in the People's homes, be present at their great feasts and festivals, share the products of their hunt, be loved and petted by the women and children, and share both their victories or defeats.

'On these terms, you, Dog, and you, Horse, shall be the companions and brothers of the People for ever.'

Canfield: *Legends of the Iroquois, told by The Cornplanter, 1902*
(Collected 1816-1836)

This story collection claims to have roots extending back hundreds of years. Canfield describes its origins as follows:

'A few years after the close of the war of the Revolution [1775–1783] one of the pioneers of western New York...made the acquaintance and won the friendship of the Seneca chief, The Cornplanter (Gyantwahchi or Garyanwahga). The friendship continued as long as the two men lived and was marked by its cordiality...They were thrown together many winters, and The Cornplanter was led to talk freely of his people, their past, their present condition, and their future, and it was during these confidences that the Indian told his White friend many of the Iroquois legends. To the recollections of the Cornplanter was added the knowledge possessed upon the subject by... Governor Blacksnake, who resided upon the same reservation and in the immediate vicinity, and that of "other old men and leaders of these Indians". The legends were preserved in outline notes upon the blank pages of some diaries and civil engineer field-books...and these outlines, with full oral explanations, came finally into the possession of the present writer.

'About 25 years ago, the work of their further verification by means of enquiries made of some...Indians in New York State was commenced. Many of those consulted had only imperfect knowledge of the legends, others knew one or more of the stories, and, by aid of the outlines referred to above, were able to assist in the work of their restoration. Among those who gave most valuable assistance was Simon Blackchief and his mother. The latter spoke only in the Indian tongue, and her version of such of the stories as she had heard in her girlhood was translated by her son...

'The author [later made] a number of visits to several of the reservations. Through these helps, and by a study pursued [during] residence in close proximity to the Allegany Reservation, the present writer believes that he has succeeded in bringing these legends to a point approximating their original beauty. In their elaboration care has been taken not to depart from the simplicity and directness of statement characteristic of the Indian, and only such additions that seemed to be warranted have been made.'

Nevertheless, Canfield's presentation of The Cornplanter's narrative is strongly flavoured with a 19th century literary style. The retelling here restores its oral feel, and replaces terms now considered derogatory; but otherwise closely follows Canfield's structure, imagery and oratory.

The Cornplanter was of mixed race, the son of an 'Indian Princess of the Turtle Clan' and a White man called John Abeel or O'Bail, who traded with the Indians. He was probably born in 1732 in Conewangus on the Genesee River and died in 1836 at the age of 104. Canfield says:

601

'He was more thoroughly acquainted with the traditions of his people than any contemporary chief in the nations comprising the Iroquois... From his earliest recollection, The Cornplanter had a pronounced hatred of the Whites, caused, no doubt, by...the cruel treatment to which his mother was subjected by his father, who seems to have taken an Indian wife in order that he might gain the friendship of the Indians, and thus secure good bargains in trade... [The Cornplanter] spent his early years at the council fires, and became one of the most celebrated orators in the Confederation of the Six Nations.'

The animals' passionate speeches in this story reflect the Iroquois' own eloquent debating techniques, which they employed both during their own council meetings, and later in their ill-fated attempts to negotiate with the White authorities.

Canfield continues:

'[The Cornplanter] travelled from village to village and sought wisdom from the sages of the Iroquois. It was during this portion of his life that he listened to the traditions that had descended from chief to chief over a period of three centuries. When he had acquired a reputation for bravery and woodcraft second to none of his race, he was unanimously chosen Chief of the Senecas, and came at once into prominence as the leader of the war-parties of that nation in alliance with the French against the English...

'It was during the last twenty years of the Cornplanter's life that the legends herein contained were recalled and told. He did not speak of them generally, for he held them sacred, but reserved them for the ears of those in full sympathy with the people of which he was one of the last true representatives. He told them with an intensity of feeling that was pitiful, for it was plain he realised that the greatness of his people had disappeared... The Cornplanter died a strong believer in the religion of the Indians, and looked forward with an eye of faith towards the Happy Hunting Grounds, for which countless generations of his people had been taught to hope.'

The 'Happy Hunting Grounds' were supposedly the Iroquois land of the dead; however, modern scholars dispute the authenticity of this term.

Although this is clearly a myth of great antiquity, the role of the Horse in the story must have been a fairly modern addition, since horses did not arrive in the region until the early 18th century.

THE MASTER OF NIGHT

Menominee

There is a little man three or four feet high
who has a body like a human being, yet is invisible.
He exists on this island, however, and is a shadow
of something that has power, or perhaps he himself is a spirit.
Anyway, he does only one kind of work.
He is the Master of Night and drives sleep into every human being.

When dusk approaches, he is already about his business.
His magic is unavailing with some, why we do not know, but a
great many are easily overcome by his sleep. He stares at the
person he has selected and wills that he or she shall fall asleep. He
motions or waves with his hand a few times and the person is
stunned or numbed with slumber, his head nods, his eyes are heavy.
He goes to some who have sought their beds a second time, and
knocks them on their heads with something very soft like a pillow.
Some know it, hear it, feel it, but others do not even sense it,
and some flinch or jerk away at the blow.
Babies and children he visits first and so on up to the old people.
It is said that those who surmise they are struck
by the Master of Night live to a very old age.

– Unnamed informant
(Quoted in Skinner & Satterlee: *Folklore of the Menomini Indians*, 1915)

603

LITTLE LEAF
AND LITTLE FIRE

⬧◻⬧◻⬧◻

Passamaquoddy

It was long ago, the dawn of the world:
no mouldering trees yet in the valleys,
no fish yet swam the cold, deep rivers,
The forest trails as yet untravelled
by curious woodchuck and bear.

In that early time, on the great Mountain,
Little Leaf watched the year unfolding.
When spring was coming and sunlight shining,
he climbed a tree and there, all summer,
dressed in green, the branches rocked him.
He listened all day to the birds and breezes,
and slept by night to the song of the owl.
When autumn came and the days grew shorter,
Little Leaf dressed up in scarlet.
Then, as the nights grew cold and longer,
he donned a coat of brown and yellow,
let go his hold and fell to the ground.
And there he slept beneath a snowdrift,
curled up like a bear all through winter –
until in spring the bluebird called him.
Then little Leaf, gladly waking,
dressed in green and climbed in the sunshine,
up through the tree and upon its branches,
lived as he did the summer before.

This tale begins on a bright spring morning.
Little Leaf, stretched out in the sunshine,
heard from afar some wondrous music, like
a rippling flute and a woman singing.
He looked up and saw a beautiful bird,
vividly dressed, head to tail, in scarlet.
'Who are you, fair bird?' he shyly asked her.
'They call me Little Fire,' she answered,
'for when I fly from forest to sunshine
I seem like a flame that leaps in darkness.'
'And why do you sing exquisite music?'
'My grandfather, mighty Mountain, sent me
to win the heart of one called Little Leaf,
who, I believe, now stands before me.
Mountain wishes that you and I should wed!'

Little Leaf listened in wary silence.
Always cautious, he did not trust her.
For often had his grandmother warned him:
'Dear child, beware all living creatures!
The smallest insect may eat your life out.
The worm that slips through a needle's eye,
may cut your stem or blight your beauty.
Anything moving may bring you death!'
Though Little Leaf was charmed by her beauty,
as she spoke, he was deeply suspicious.
Was she a friend or a false-hearted foe?

Little Fire of his doubts knew nothing,
so warbled again her lovely song.
So sweetly the tune spread through the forest!
Every leaf on the tree was listening,
branches waving. The ants stopped running,
butterflies alighted on flowers to hear it.
Like liquid, the music soared then fell
to a final long note, sweet as honey.
Little Leaf's doubts faded, his heart melted.
'Little Fire,' he cried to her, 'be mine!'

So the red bird and leaf now lived together.
When other singers came to visit,
to serenade the happy couple
and hold singing contests with Little Fire,
the sweetest voice was always hers.

One day, the couple went off to visit
their grandfather, the mighty Mountain, who'd
brought them together; they wished to thank him.
Inside his cave, he greeted them warmly;
but then his voice grew sober and solemn.
'Grandchildren,' he said, 'heed well what I tell you.
Never leave this Mountain! For if you do,
you'll both face terrible deadly dangers.
Little Fire: beware the boy with arrows
who shoots forest birds and takes them home
where his grandfather roasts and eats them.
Little Leaf, your danger lies with Whirlwind.
He blows leaves off branches, drives them headlong
in flocks towards the brutal Storm, who
tramples them to total oblivion.'

Little Fire took Little Leaf in her beak,
carried him back to their tree in the forest.
Safely secluded, concealed on the Mountain,
secure in their wigwam on the top branch,
safe from all dangers, always so happy!

But some folk too easily get disgruntled;
even when all's well, they don't believe it.
One morning, Little Leaf glimpsed in the distance
a beautiful land, in the sunshine gleaming.
'How fine,' he thought, 'seem those lakes and valleys,
much lovelier than this place we live in!'
He felt in his heart a desperate longing.
So he called Little Fire and spoke these words:
'Look, beloved, at that beautiful country!
In that far land we'd be much happier.'

The gentle red bird did not wish to argue.
So she took her beloved in her beak,
flew fast and far, over rock and river,
all the way to the land that he longed for.
Perched on a tree, they built a new wigwam.

Unfortunately, it was not long
before the boy that Mountain had warned of
heard Little Fire's exquisite singing.
Amazed, he stood for a while and listened,
then beheld her wondrous feathers.
He bent his bow and let fly an arrow.
Down fell the red bird, sorely wounded.
The boy snatched her up, ran proudly homeward.

Soon after that, the Whirlwind rushed in,
saw Little Leaf, seized him in triumph,
took him to his grandfather, mighty Storm.
'This,' said the chief, 'is no common captive
but the Leaf of all leaves – priceless riches!'

That night, bad dreams came to the Mountain,
showing Little Leaf taken prisoner.
Waking in anger he called for his son.
'Go to chief Storm,' he said, 'and tell him
To return the leaf.' His son departed
and when he came to the mighty Whirlwind
said, 'Free Little Leaf – or before the evening
my grandfather's people will be on the warpath!'
Quickly the Whirlwind gave up his captive
and the son of the Mountain carried him home.

So the leaf was safe, back in his wigwam
on the great tree. But he lived in sorrow,
and whenever the notes of a bird came ringing
out of the forest, his grief was greater.
For his life with Little Fire was finished.

But what had become of Little Fire?
The boy was showing her to his father,
who examined the red bird carefully.
'You've caught a marvellous creature,' he said,
'a treasure! It's well you didn't kill it.
We'll hide it safely inside our wigwam.
Take care, my son – don't let it escape.'

So Little Fire was now their prisoner.
But day by day, her wounds were healing,
and soon her colour grew bright as ever.
Then, one fine morning when least expected,
her voice burst out like a stream in sunshine.
These were her words: 'If the Wind could hear me
I would no longer be held captive,
for he would carry the news to Mountain.
Then Mountain would quickly send his warriors,
to fight and give me back my freedom
then take me to Little Leaf again!'

When the old chief heard Little Fire singing,
her words made his heart grow weak with fear.
'Truly,' he thought, 'it was a foolish deed
to shoot this bird, and to keep her captive.
If the Mountain learns what we have done,
we're bound to meet a terrible ending!

While he thought it over, his grandson came home
bringing some birds he'd killed in the forest.
When they were cooked, and the chief had eaten,
Down by the fire he lay on a bearskin.
The door was shut fast; there was not a crack
through which the red bird could creep to freedom.
Soon the old chief's head drooped on his shoulder,
and the sleep spirits soothed him to slumber.
At once, Little Fire saw the opening
through which the smoke from the fire ascended;
so softly, the red bird rose and taking

a bucket of birch, she filled it with water.
Dipping her wing in, she sprayed the fire
till the bright, hot flame died in the ashes.
Out of the smoke hole, in careful silence ,
flew the red bird, away from her captor.

In the fresh air of soft, warm autumn,
she heard other songbirds far beneath her.
Joyful, she flew across the forest,
leaving death behind, with love before her,
never had she been half so happy!
Imagine her joy when she reached the Mountain
and saw from afar on the great tree rising
a bright red leaf which shone in the sunset.
She flew to him straight and swift as an arrow.
Little Leaf who slept, half dead with grieving,
woke in joy to find her wings wrapped round him!
Thus in a moment, without any warning,
Little Leaf's grief turned into gladness.
Together they wept such tears of rapture.

Ever since then, Little Fire and Little Leaf
have lived all summer upon the Mountain,
singing in shadows, shining in sunlight.
And so it will be while the Mountain endures.

Leland: *Kuloskap the Master and other Algonkin Poems*, 1902
For information on the provenance of the ancient Algonquin verse
narratives, see p. 591. This is an edited version of Leland's translation,
following the original imagery and metre.
  The source names the red bird as a scarlet tanager. This is a medium-
sized songbird which is common in deciduous forests in eastern North
America. The male birds are vivid red; however, the old storytellers
employed some poetic licence in describing Little Fire, for the females are
actually an olive colour with yellowish underparts.

THE BOY WHO WAS RAISED BY A BEAR

◇▯◇▯◇▯◇

Wyandot

A man once married a woman who already had a child, a little boy. From the very first, this man did not like his stepson and was constantly haunted by the idea of getting rid of him.

When the summer was over, the family went out far into the woods for the hunting season, and built a house for the winter in a lonely spot. The man started hunting right away. While he was out in the woods, he came upon a large, rocky cave. He explored it carefully and noticed that there were a lot of big boulders lying around nearby. By the time he got home that night, he had hatched a vicious plan.

'Wife,' he said, 'it's time that boy of yours learned to hunt. I want to take him out with me tomorrow.'

The woman knew his feelings for her son, and tried hard to refuse him. But the hunter insisted, and she feared he might do something rash unless she gave in.

So the next day, the lad followed his stepfather out into the woods, and before long they reached the rocky cave. The man told his stepson to enter the cave and look around. The boy started sobbing, for he was afraid. But the man scolded him and ordered him to go in at once, and not come out again until he had explored it thoroughly. The boy had no choice but to submit.

As soon as the boy was inside, the stepfather hastily set to work, piling many great boulders in the opening. He was a strong man, the stones he used were very heavy; and he wedged them together tightly. Thus, within moments, the boy's worst fears came true – he was shut up in the cave.

As soon as the man had finished, he went away, so he could not hear the boy crying. And cry he certainly did, yelling and screaming, 'Wah, wah, wah!' on and on and on, for he was far too young to know what to do.

Suddenly, above his sobs, he heard someone calling him: 'Grandson, come this way!' The voice seemed to be coming from a long way off, right at the back of the cave.

The boy was so shocked, he fell silent and listened. The voice called again: 'Grandson, come this way!' The boy dried his eyes, swallowed his fear and walked towards it, into the dark. All the time the voice kept calling and encouraging him. Finally, it became so loud that he realised he was very close to it.

Now the voice said, 'Stop there, in front of me, grandson! Don't come round me or behind me.'

The boy obeyed and peered through the darkness. He made out a large figure that appeared to be lying down. 'Grandson,' the unknown person said kindly, 'don't cry. I'll try and do something to help you.'

'Thank you,' whispered the boy. 'I'm very hungry.'

At this, the figure got up. In the gloom, the boy got another surprise. For it was not an old man as he had thought – but a big Porcupine! That was why he had not wanted the boy to come behind him, for fear that his quills might hurt him. The Porcupine reached into a bag, pulled out a small cake and offered it to the boy.

'I don't know whether you can eat this kind of thing,' he said, 'for it's some of my own food – slippery elm bark. Try it and see what you think.'

The child took it, tasted some, and found that it was good. So he ate until he was satisfied and no longer hungry. Then the Porcupine said, 'Grandson, let's go to the entrance of the cave together: I'll try to open it, so you can get out.'

When they reached the boulders blocking up the cave, the Porcupine tried his best to shift them, but they were much too heavy. The boy began to cry again, but the Porcupine said, 'Hush, don't worry, for I know another way.'

Although the stones were packed together tightly, there were several gaps between them. The Porcupine stuck his nose through one of these and shouted at the top of his voice: 'All you animals, come round here!'

Before long, many animals of all kinds had gathered at the cave entrance. Among them were the Deer, the Fox, the Raccoon, the Turtle, the Wolf, the Turkey and other birds of all shapes and sizes.

The Porcupine told them, 'A boy has been forced into this cave where I was sleeping, and barricaded inside. Neither of us can get out. I'm hoping one of you can manage to open it.'

So the animals took turns to try. First, the Raccoon reached his hand round a large stone and tried to move it; but he achieved nothing at all. The birds and many other animals all tried without success. The Fox and the Wolf came up together to scratch and bite the stones, but this was of no use, and they both ended up with blood streaming from their mouths. The Deer, a large buck, stuck one of his long horns between the stones and tried to lever them out, but he only succeeded in breaking his horn; then he tried with the other horn, with the same result, so he ended up with no horns at all. In this way, one after another, all the animals tried but failed.

Just at that moment, a Bear came along. The Porcupine explained the situation, and the Bear said that he would willingly try. He stretched his arms around one of the largest boulders, took a firm grip on it – and heaved it right out of the way.

The Porcupine and the boy ran straight outside and took deep breaths of fresh air. Then the Porcupine said to the other animals, 'There is something I need to tell you. This child, who I regard as my grandson, has been shut up in here for some time. I've looked after him as well as I could, but I haven't got the proper kind of food for him, and I don't know how to bring up a human child. I'm hoping that one of you will bring some suitable food to make him grow strong, and thus prove yourself qualified to take care of him.'

When they heard this, all the animals scattered and went in search of something for the boy to eat. Some small birds came back first with various seeds and offered them to the child. But they were very small and very hard; he could not eat them. The Turkey brought some different kinds of seeds, but they were no better. The Raccoon came next with some crawfish in his mouth. The boy thought they looked tasty and was on the point of taking them. But the Porcupine said, 'Wait, keep on waiting! Perhaps you will get something more worth your while.'

So he did. The Fox offered some meat to the boy. He hesitated, wondering if this was the right food for him; but the Porcupine said, 'No, hold on, you may find something still better.' The Wolf brought back a large bone with an even bigger portion of meat hanging from it. The boy looked at the Porcupine eagerly; but the Porcupine repeated, 'Not yet, grandson; I know that you badly wish to eat this; but you must not take it.' A large number of other animals came forward with different foods; they too were all dismissed.

Last of all came a Bear Mother. 'Well,' she said, 'I've been watching what's going on, and I think I know what's best for this boy – the kind of food that *my* children eat.' She handed the boy a flat, dark cake.

The Porcupine nodded at the boy. The boy seized the cake and gobbled it down. Oh, it was so good!

The Porcupine saw how much he had enjoyed it. 'So,' he declared to the other animals, 'You have all seen that this Bear Mother is the only one of you who is equipped to look after the child, only she knows how to make him healthy and happy.'

So the Bear Mother took the boy along to her den, and introduced him to her three cubs. They were delighted that a human child had come to live with them. Straight away, they started to jump around and play with their new companion. The Bear Mother was still suckling them, for they were very young. From now on she nursed the boy alongside them. She thus had four little ones to take care of. They lived very comfortably indeed. Every once in a while, she would give the boy some dried blackberry flat-cake – the same kind she had originally offered him.

When spring came, the boy and the cubs went roaming about contentedly in the woods. By now, they were all big enough to eat anything. So the Bear Mother stopped suckling them, and provided them with nuts, grapes and other fruits. All this time, the little boy lived exactly like them.

In this way, nearly a whole year passed happily. One afternoon in late summer, when the blackberries were ripening, a runner came to the Bears' den. When the boy first saw him, he thought he was a man and his heart gave a leap of joy mingled with fear; but then he looked more closely, and saw that it was really another Bear. The runner spoke to the Bear Mother as head of the family. 'I have come to invite you all to the annual gathering at the blackberry patch,' he announced.

The following day, the Bear Mother took her cubs and the boy to the appointed place. A large crowd of other Bears had already assembled there. As with the runner, when the boy looked at them all milling around, at first he thought they were People; but on closer examination, he realised they were definitely Bears.

The chief of all these Bears called for silence. 'Go to work and pick the berries,' he told them.

Soon a great quantity of blackberries had been gathered. The Bears spread them out neatly in the sunshine to dry.

All this time, the Bear Mother had been keeping her little ones and the child close beside her. However, she was so busy working on the blackberries, that one of the cubs – the most mischievous one – called the boy aside. 'Let's go far away from the crowd,' he whispered.

The boy followed him out into the bush.

'Now,' said the cub, 'chase me back towards all the others, like the men chase bears when they're hunting. When the others see us, they'll be afraid and run away. So there'll be no one left to guard all those blackberries drying in the Sun – and we'll be able to eat the lot!'

The boy thought this would be great fun, so he chased the cub, whooping loudly, with all his might, as they rushed back to the crowd. Just as the cub had predicted, the Bears were terrified to see what they believed to be a human hunting party. They all fled into the bush, abandoning the fruit. As soon as they had gone, the two young friends began to gobble down as many berries as they could.

However, soon the Bear Mother retraced her steps, for she was very anxious to ensure that her two missing family members were safe. When she saw them picking up armfuls of dried blackberries, she guessed straight away who the culprit was. She pulled the boy aside and asked him. He didn't want to betray his friend, but he was so respectful of the Bear Mother that he had to confess the truth. The Bear Mother at once reached for a stick, caught her wayward cub and beat him soundly.

While she was doing this, the other bears cautiously returned to the berry patch. The Bear Mother told them what had happened. Then she said, 'These children of mine have piled up far more than our share of berries over here. Come round and help yourselves.'

So they did. By the end of the day, everyone had a fair portion and all the blackberries had been dried. At this point, all the Bears sat down and started smearing some of the dried berries across the soles of their feet. Then they walked around, so that the fruits stuck firmly to their paws. For it is a fact that the berries adhere to the

Bears' feet until the winter is over; and whenever they wake briefly from their long sleep inside a hollow tree, a hole or a cave, they lick some of this preserved food from their paws. This, in truth, enables them to survive without ever having to go out and forage in the cold.

When they had finished this task, the Bears shaped and pressed the rest of the dried berries into cakes, each exactly as flat and and broad as a Bear's paw. They were the same delicious flat-cakes which the boy had grown used to eating with his adopted family. They shared a feast of these. When it was over, they all scattered in different directions – just as People do when they prepare for the cold season's hunting.

The weather by now was growing bitterly cold. The Bear Mother said to her young ones, 'Stay here while I search for a place to spend the winter.' She went off and, after a long while, came back and led her family to a large tree. It was completely hollow, with an opening at the top of the trunk. She climbed it and shouted, 'Come up! Here's our winter home.'

The boy followed the cubs as they climbed up the tree after her, then crawled down to the bottom of the hollow. It was very warm inside, and as cosy as a human house. The Bear Mother gave the boy a small parcel of dried blackberry, telling him to nibble some whenever he felt hungry. But she and her cubs did not need this, for they had the berry juice on their paws to lick when they needed to.

During the winter, on fine nights the cubs would often wake up, climb up the hollow and crawl down the the tree trunk to play in the snow in the moonlight. As they did this, they scratched off strips of bark from the tree, until it looked almost red. The Bear Mother always lived in fear of human hunters at this time of year – particularly as the cubs' marks on the tree was clear evidence that this was their den. In fact, several hunters had already happened to come near. However, so far the Bears had not been discovered, because the Bear Mother had a very clever trick to keep the hunters away. She would grasp a special forked stick in her paw and point it towards the men as they approached. Somehow this seemed to cause them terrible neck pains; they would stop in alarm, then turn round and make a hasty retreat. In that way, for a long time, she kept her family safe.

Even so, she knew her luck could not last for ever, so she instructed the boy on what he should do in case the hollow tree was ever cut down.

One day, her worst fears were realised. The Bear Mother saw a man approaching. He walked up directly to the tree. She seized her forked stick and held it up towards him; but too late, she noticed that the fork was split, and thus no longer of any use.

The man came right up to the tree and cut a prominent mark on it. That was the old custom, to stop any other hunter claiming the same tree. This done, he went home to fetch some friends to help him kill the Bears.

While he was gone, the Bear Mother quickly called the boy to her. 'Remember what I told you before,' she said. 'Very soon the man will come back, with his hunting party, to kill me and the cubs. When that happens, I will be the first to go out. I will let them kill me quickly.'

The boy began to cry, but the Bear Mother scolded him and ordered him to pay attention.

'This has to happen, this is the way of the world. As soon as they have finished with me, tell the two boy cubs to go out next. Then, afterwards, it is your turn to go out. Sit just outside the opening, and call out to the hunters. Say to them, "Look at me! I'm not a Bear but a human being. My sister is still inside the tree. Please don't kill her!"'

The boy had no time to ask for any more advice, for at that moment, the hunters crowded round the tree and started banging on it to frighten out the animals. As she had said, the Bear Mother went out first. She didn't even have time to reach the ground before the hunters shot her dead. Next, the two male cubs went outside. The first one was killed straight away. However, the second one – he who had persuaded the boy to steal the blackberries – was still full of tricks and mischief. He put on a bold show and managed to slip down the tree and run away before the hunters could shoot him. He would have escaped easily, if only their dog hadn't given chase and brought him to grief.

Now the boy was left alone inside the tree with the female cub, his foster-sister. He peeped out of the hole. He was terrified of going out, but he knew he had to honour his dead Bear Mother by carrying out her instructions exactly. So he climbed up and sat at the top of the opening. The hunters were astonished to see a boy appearing from the Bears' den!

While they were wondering what to do, the boy called out to them: 'Don't you remember me? I'm the boy that mysteriously vanished last year. You must have heard about me. Well, here I am.'

'*You!*' the hunters cried. 'Of course, we remember well. But we were told you'd had an accident and met a terrible death. How ever did you get here?'

The boy didn't answer this but said, 'There's still another one left inside the hollow here, a little female cub. She is my sister. I beg you not to kill her. Please, please let her run away!'

The hunters said, 'But why didn't you come out before to warn us? We wouldn't have killed these Bears if you'd shown yourself first; we would have spared them all.'

'I don't know,' said the boy. 'I did exactly as my Mother Bear said I should. Maybe it could not be helped.'

One of the hunters again knocked at the tree to make a noise. Now the female cub came out, trembling with fear. The boy, still sitting up there, cried out, 'Here she is! Please let her run away!'

The men grabbed their dog and held it fast. The cub jumped down onto a nearby log, crawled along it and dropped out of sight at the far end.

Last of all, the boy came down from the treetop. The hunters kept saying how truly sorry they were for having killed these Bears – his foster family. They all hugged him, for they were really glad to have found him safe and well.

Then they skinned the dead Bears, cut them up, packed the pieces of meat into pelts, strapped them to their backs and set off to carry them home. The boy followed.

It so happened that many families had set up camp together that winter. The hunters called everyone out and said, 'Look! We've found that boy who vanished last year!'

They all gathered around and made him very welcome. His own mother and stepfather weren't there, and no one knew where they had gone. The boy wasn't at all sorry to have missed them.

Time went by, various families looked after the boy, and he settled down to normal life. Eventually, he grew up and found a wife. In the autumn, the couple moved camp into the woods for the hunting season, and built a small bark house to live in, just as his mother and stepfather had once done. He went out hunting and succeeded in killing plenty of game: Deer, Raccoons – and Bears.

So they had a good supply of meat and his wife was pleased with his success. But she couldn't help complaining that almost all the Bears that he killed were old, tough ones. Very occasionally, he might bring home a male cub; but he never, ever killed any female cubs. She began to long for some younger, more tender Bear meat. In the end, she complained to him, saying, 'Why do you so rarely kill young Bears? These old ones you keep bringing me really aren't fit to eat.'

She already knew about his boyhood adventure, and he reminded her that he could not kill female cubs. This was because the Bear Mother had warned him, before they parted, 'You must never kill any young she-Bears – for this surely would bring about your death.'

However, his wife was not satisfied. She became ill-tempered, and started nagging him about it. He kept repeating that he would die if he broke this rule; but she refused to believe him.

Unfortunately, after a while he too grew tired of eating the tough, stringy flesh of the old Bears. He kept trying not to think about it, but in the end he decided to listen to his wife's pleading. So the next time he went out Bear hunting, he killed a female cub and brought it back home.

'At last!' his wife cried, 'some good, tender meat!' She dressed it eagerly and made a fine roast of it at once.

However, when she served it, the young man found that he did not feel like eating any of it, even though it was deliciously cooked. Instead, he stretched himself on a deerskin away from the marital bed, and went to sleep all alone. When his wife went to bed later on, she also had to sleep by herself, on the other side of the fire.

The next morning, the woman woke up and was surprised to see that he hadn't risen early, as he usually did.

'What's up with you?' she called. 'Why don't you get up?'

There was no reply. Again she called out; again she got no answer. Now her irritation turned to fear. She walked up to him, and found him motionless, rolled up in the deerskin, cold and dead.

That is all.

Barbeau says that, in collecting the stories, his 'chief aim has been accuracy'. They were recorded directly under dictation in French, English or the Wyandot language; the latter were:

'...subsequently translated with the help of linguistic informants... In every case the author has been careful not to alter the character of the material and, as far as possible, to retain the informant's style and expressions.'

This particular story was recorded in English, in October 1911, from a man called Star (Hiram) Young, who belonged to the Wolf clan and was at least 65 years old. His Wyandot name was Harg'nu (Sky in the Water), and he also had the nickname Tic'g (Morning Star). He lived on the Seneca Reservation in Oklahoma. He stated that he had heard this myth 'a score of times' from the man who had raised him, his late uncle, John Solomon (Ta'harg'nut' – Sticking Out of the Sky) of the Deer clan. It was well told, so here it is presented as an edited version of the original.

The story concludes with a note from Barbeau, in which he says that the taboo on killing female bear cubs seems to indicate that it was for the purpose of conserving and increasing a species which was commonly hunted for food.

The benevolence of the porcupine is in contrast to FLYING WITH THE THUNDERS (p. 577), where the same animal is depicted as an evil villain.

Barbeau recorded three other versions of the same myth, indicating its importance to the Wyandot people. Two came from one of his principal informants, Catherine Johnson, a 60-year-old woman who spoke only Wyandot; they are very brief and the only significant difference is that the young man dies as a result of killing a mother bear rather than a female cub. The other came from 83-year-old Smith Nichols, also exclusively a Wyandot speaker. His extensive knowledge of ancient lore came from his grandmother who, he claimed, had lived to be 125, thus considerably extending the antiquity of the story. According to him, it is the boy's stepmother who hates him and shuts him up in a cave. He is found by a wolf and eventually adopted by a bear, with a similar ending to the others, except that his father kills the stepmother for her abuse of his son. The same story was also told by the Seneca. An Onondaga version has the boy shut up inside a hollow log by some bullies of his own age, and ends with him transforming into a bear.

Another Wyandot myth underlines the esteem in which bears were held. A married couple are abducted by bears and forced to live with them. Though they are treated well, the husband twice tries to escape. On the first occasion, the bears quickly recapture him and break his bones; the second time, they scratch him all over with their claws. They then teach the wife the art of medicinal healing with herbs, so that he completely recovers. Eventually the bears take the couple home, thus disseminating knowledge of healing to the people.

WOOD SPIRITS

Micmac (Mi'kmaq)
& Passamaquoddy

It is a thing well known to all
who keep the ancient faith of the good olden time
that there are wondrous spirits deep in the silent woods…
who are called in Micmac 'Wiguladfimfichiik'
and in Passamaquoddy 'W'nag'meswuk'.
They can work strange deeds
and sing such songs of magic power
that charm the wildest beasts,
tame wolf and bear, and soothe the wolverine.
From them, and them alone, are brought the magic flutes,
which sometimes pass to sorcerers or great warriors.
When these are played upon,
women who hear the tone are all bewitched with love;
the moose and caribou
follow the winning sound even to their death.
And when the forest spirits are pleased with anyone
they transform him to a spirit like themselves.

– Louis Mitchell,
Passamaquoddy scholar and politician
(Quoted in Leland & Dyneley: *Kuloskap the Master*, 1902)

THE SINGER IN THE DUSK

◇□◇□◇□◇

Algonquin

In ancient days, deep in the boundless forest, there stood a birch tree. And on this birch there lived a big, benevolent, very old Tree Fungus.

This Tree Fungus was greatly loved by the smallest forest creatures; the birds, insects and even the creeping ones all regarded him as their kin. They were always crawling up and down the tree trunk to visit him, or hovering above him to talk.

Their favourite time to draw near him was at sunset. For every day as dusk fell, he would chant this special song:

'Fair Tree Fungus,
Fair Tree Fungus
Sits with mouth open!'

This was a signal that the time had come for sleep. As soon as they heard it, the insects folded their wings and fell into sweet slumber as the twilight thickened. None would stir through the long, cold, damp night – until their guardian broke into song again, to announce the coming dawn:

'Fair Tree Fungus,
Fair Tree Fungus
Sits with mouth open!'

As soon as they heard this, all the small creatures called back their own greeting:

'Daylight is breaking:
Beautiful morning!
Let us arise!'

Beyond the spot where Tree Fungus lived, surrounded by his small friends, the forest teemed with other, much bigger creatures. One of these was Flying Squirrel.

One bright morning, Flying Squirrel came gliding through the trees, looking for a place to build a new nest. Soon he found the perfect spot: a fine hole in the trunk of a tall birch tree.

However, just above this hole was the very branch where the venerable Tree Fungus lived. Flying Squirrel was horrified when he saw him. 'Ugh, what an ugly old growth!' he thought. 'I can't have that hanging over my nice new nest.'

So he perched on a nearby branch and called out coarsely, 'You, mouldy one! What are you doing here?'

Tree Fungus answered him calmly: 'Greetings, grandchild, and welcome. I am here because I live here.'

'Oh, do you? Since when?'

'Ah, Flying Squirrel,' said Tree Fungus, 'long before your great-great-grandfather was born on that cedar that you came from this morning, I began to grow on this birch.'

'That's certainly a long time,' said Flying Squirrel. 'How much longer do you plan to hang around?'

Tree Fungus said, 'So long as this birch tree sends out its leaves, so long as its pale trunk stands upright in the forest, it will always be my home.'

'No it won't!' Flying Squirrel retorted. 'You've been here far too long already, Fungus. I want to make my own nest in this birch – and you're in the way. I order you to move out. Go on, leave!'

Tree Fungus said quietly, 'Grandchild, I forgive your discourtesy, for I realise you are ignorant. Because you are free to go anywhere, you are blind to the fact that others may not be able to do likewise. I am permanently fixed to this tree, and have depended on its nourishment since I first began to grow. Besides, I have longstanding and important obligations. My numerous small friends in the surrounding forest need me here. Without my song at dusk and dawn, they could not find the peace of sleep, or wake at sunrise. So I cannot comply with your request. Since you are completely mobile, Flying Squirrel, and since no one here relies on your presence, it is *you* who should move. You have skills to make your home in any part of the forest.'

Such honest words, spoken by a distinguished forest sage! But Flying Squirrel was not humbled by them; instead, he flew into a violent temper. He sank his teeth into the branch where he was crouching and started gnawing at it furiously.

Unbeknown to him, just below this branch, a great band of Wasps had built their wigwam. Flying Squirrel's champing made the branch wobble alarmingly. Within moments, over 100 Wasp warriors came flying out, wielding their sharpened stings. They fell upon Flying Squirrel and clung to his back; they stung him furiously all over. Flying Squirrel shrieked in pain. He lost his foothold. He tried to launch into a glide, but failed. He tumbled to the ground, screaming for help.

In the trees nearby, there were many other kinds of Squirrels – red ones, grey ones and striped ones. They heard Flying Squirrel's screams, raced to the rescue and gathered round him for an urgent council. They quickly resolved to remove Tree Fungus for ever from his birch tree and, if necessary, to kill him.

They formed a war band and rushed at the birch, brandishing weapons. Then they began to climb its trunk en masse.

Meanwhile, the Wasps had gone seething out through the forest to seek support. Many other insect warriors now came winging in: gallant Bees, Black-flies, Hornets, Horseflies, Midges, Mosquitoes and more Wasps. Each carried a deadly spear. Crowds of Worms lined up to wave them on.

By now, the leading Squirrel warrior was halfway up the birch. The swarming insect army set upon him fiercely. He lost his grip and pitched over onto the ground. Each Squirrel coming up behind suffered the same fate. Soon the forest floor under the tree was littered with badly wounded Squirrels. Wretchedly, those who could, staggered up and limped back to their council.

All this time, Tree Fungus had watched the battle impassively. Now the Sun began to set. As if nothing were amiss, he chanted his customary song:

'Fair Tree Fungus,
Fair Tree Fungus
Sits with mouth open!'

At once, the insect warriors laid down their weapons. They settled on leaves and logs, folding their wings. The song also overwhelmed the exhausted Squirrels; their furious council debate quickly gave way to the oblivion of sleep.

Early next morning, Tree Fungus's song awakened both armies.

The Squirrel council paid eager attention when Flying Squirrel stood up to speak. 'Listen!' he said. 'Last night I had a dream, and this was revealed to me: we have but a single chance of victory. To conquer Tree Fungus and destroy him, *one of us must touch him –* even for an instant, even very lightly – before he next sings his song at dusk. To do this is to win. To fail means defeat for ever. Come, my friends, to battle!'

The Squirrels massed together, rushed again to the birch tree and eagerly started climbing its trunk. Every eye was fixed upon the great, ancient Tree Fungus looming above; every paw stretched up, desperate to touch and thus overcome it.

Meanwhile, in the leaves and branches all around, the insects were dipping their spears in poison.

Mmmmm! Thousands of the small, winged ones swarmed out around the Squirrels. None cared any longer for their own lives: no Mosquito squealed in protest as he was swatted, no Horsefly lamented that he would lose his wife and children, no Hornet regretted that he would never again warm himself by his wigwam fire; the Bees proudly hummed their own death songs.

Under the insects' spiked spears, one by one, the Squirrels fell. Each was quickly replaced by another equally ruthless warrior. But they were no match for the numberless insects who also constantly renewed their defences. The casualties on both sides quickly mounted up. The battle raged on, fiercer and fiercer...

Meanwhile, another day was drawing to its end. The Sun slowly dipped behind the trees. Soft, blue shadows overwhelmed the forest.

High up on the birch, Tree Fungus still hung safely, stolid as always. He had continued to watched the carnage in silence. Now, as the evening softly gathered, he chanted his age-old summons:

'Fair Tree Fungus,
Fair Tree Fungus,
Sits with mouth open!'

Countless warriors were dead. But not a single Squirrel had achieved the goal of climbing high and close enough to touch Tree Fungus, not even with the tip of a paw. Because of this, as Flying Squirrel's dream had foretold, the Squirrels were defeated.

As Tree Fungus sang, all the survivors on both sides dropped their weapons and sank to the ground. Sleep overwhelmed them.

Everything was over. Peace returned to the forest.

High in the birch tree, Tree Fungus kept watch, safe from all enemies, a friend to all who cared for him.

Leland: *Kuloskap the Master and Other Algonkin Poems,* 1902
This is adapted from one of the ancient Algonquin verse narratives (see p. 591). The original translation is rather rambling, but careful study reveals this unique and mysterious story.

There are two possible identities for Tree Fungus. One is *Piptoporus betulinus* (birch polypore, birch bracket or razor strop), which grows almost exclusively on birch trees. It produces distinctive fruiting brackets which look like mushroom tops growing out from the bark, each lasting for over a year. It is edible and is said to have medicinal properties. It provides a home for many different insect species, which both eat it and breed within it. Another possible candidate is *Inonotus obliquus* (chaga mushroom, clinker polypore, sterile conk trunk rot). This grows slowly on birch and other trees as an irregular dark mass which has been compared to the appearance of burnt charcoal. This too is claimed to be effective in healing.

Flying squirrels are nocturnal, and live in coniferous and mixed forests. They do not actually fly, but use folds of skin between body and legs to glide through the air, adjusting the tautness to steer, and using their tails to brake before landing. Fungus is one of their main foods, alongside insects, carrion, eggs and nestlings; and their feeding helps to spread fungus spores. They are just one of several different North American squirrel species.

Birch tree bark played an important part in traditional everyday Algonquin life (see p. 525).

The Walas'axa (potlatch ceremony, see p. 366)
Painted at Tsaxis, British Columbia (Northwest)
by Wilhelm Kuhnert, 1894.

SOURCES AND BACKGROUND READING

STORY SOURCES

Primary Sources

Collected 'in the field', mainly by ethnologists; with a few less formal collections. Most of these sources can be viewed and downloaded online, via websites such as archive.org, gutenberg.org and sacred-texts.com

Barbeau, Marius: *Huron and Wyandot Mythology, with an appendix containing earlier published records* (Ottawa: Government Printing Bureau, 1915)

Barrett, S.A.: *A Composite Myth of the Pomo Indians* (Journal of American Folklore, 1906)

Bayliss, Clara Kern: *A Tewa Sun Myth* (Journal of American Folklore, 1909)

Beauchamp, W. M.: *Onondaga Tales* (Journal of American Folklore, 1888)

Beauchamp, W. M.: *Onondaga Tales II* (Journal of American Folklore, 1888)

Beauchamp, W. M.: *Onondaga Tales* (Journal of American Folklore, 1893)

Bell, James Mackintosh: *The Fireside Stories of the Chippwyans* (Journal of American Folklore, 1903)

Bell, Robert: *Legends of the Slavey Indians of the Mackenzie River* (Journal of American Folklore, 1901)

Boas, Franz: *The Central Eskimo* (Bureau of American Ethnology, 1888)

Boas, F. & Rink, H.: *Eskimo Tales and Songs* (Journal of American Folklore, 1889)

Boas, Franz: *Eskimo Tales and Songs* (Journal of American Folklore, 1894)

Boas, Franz: *Eskimo Tales and Songs* (Journal of American Folklore, 1897)

Boas, Franz: *The Mythology of the Bella Coola Indians* (New York: American Museum of Natural History, 1898)

Boas, Franz: *Traditions of the Tillamook Indians* (Journal of American Folklore, 1898)

Boas, Franz: *Tsimshian Texts* (Bureau of American Ethnology, 1902)

Boas, Franz: *The Folk-Lore of the Eskimo* (Journal of American Folklore, 1904)

Boas, Franz: *Kwakiutl Tales* (New York: Columbia University Press, 1910)

Boas, Franz: *Tsimshian Mythology* (Bureau of American Ethnology, 1916)

Boas, Franz (Ed): *Folk-Tales of Salishan and Sahaptin Tribes* (New York: American Folklore Society, 1917)

Bushnell, David I.: *The Choctaw of Bayou Lacomb* (Bureau of American Ethnology, 1909)

Bushnell, David I.: *Myths of the Louisiana Choctaw* (American Anthropologist, 1910)

Camsell, Charles & Barbeau, C. M.: *Loucheux Myths*, collected in 1905 (Journal of American Folklore, 1915)

Canfield, William Walker: *The Legends of the Iroquois, told by 'The Cornplanter'* (New York: A Wessels Co., 1902)

Carmichael, Alfred: *Indian Legends of Vancouver Island* (Toronto: The Musson Book Company Ltd, 1922)

Connelley, William Elsey: *Wyandot Folk-Lore* (Topeka, Kansas, Crane & Company, 1899)

Costello, J. A.: *The Siwash, Their Life, Legends and Tales; Puget Sound and Pacific Northwest* (Seattle: Calvert, 1895)

Curtin, Jeremiah: *Creation Myths of Primitive America* (Boston: Little Brown, 1898)

Curtin, Jeremiah: *Myths of the Modocs* (Boston: Little, Brown, 1912)

Curtin, Jeremiah & Hewitt, J. N. B.: *Seneca Fiction, Legends and Myths* (Bureau of American Ethnology, 1918)

Curtin, Jeremiah: *Seneca Indian Myths* (New York: E.P. Dutton & Company, 1922)

Curtis, Edward S.: *The North American Indian, Vol. 1* (publisher unknown, 1907)

Curtis, Natalie: *The Indians' Book* (New York and London: Harper and Brothers Publishers, 1907)

Cushing, Frank: *Creation and the Origin of Corn* (from Zuni Breadstuff, Millstone 9, No. 1, 1884)

Cushing, Frank Hamilton & Hodge, Frederick Webb: *Outlines of Zuni Creation Myths* (Bureau of American Ethnology, 1896)

Cushing, Frank Hamilton: *Zuni Folk Tales* (New York: G.P. Putman's Sons, 1901)

Dawson, George M.: *Geological Survey of Canada – Report on the Queen Charlotte Islands, 1878* (Montreal: Dawson Brothers, 1880)

Deans, James: *The Story of the Bear and His Indian Wife: A Legend of the Haidas of Queen Charlotte Islands BC* (Journal of American Folklore, 1889)

Deans, James: *A Daughter of the Sun. A Legend of the Tsimshians of British Columbia* (Journal of American Folklore, 1891)

Deans, James & Triggs, Oscar Lovell: *Tales from the Totems of the Hidery* (Chicago: Archives of the International Folk-Lore Association, 1899)

Dixon, Roland B.: *Some Coyote Stories from the Maidu Indians of California* (Journal of American Folklore, 1900)

Dixon, Roland B.: *Achomawi and Atsugewi Tales* (Journal of American Folklore, 1908 and 1909)

Dixon, Roland B.: *Shasta Myths* (Journal of American Folklore, 1910)

Dixon, Roland B.: *Maidu Texts* (Publications of the American Ethnological Society, 1912)

Dorsey, George A.: *Wichita Tales, 1, 2 and 3* (Journal of American Folklore, 1902, 1903 and 1904)

Dorsey, George Amos: *Traditions of the Caddo* (Washington: Carnegie Institution, 1905)

Dorsey, George: *The Pawnee Mythology Part I* (Washington: Carnegie Institute, 1906)

Dorsey, George A. & Kroeber, Alfred L.: *Traditions of the Arapaho* (Chicago: Field Columbian Museum, 1903)

Dorsey, Rev. J. Owen: *A Teton Dakota Ghost Story; Ponka Stories; Abstracts of Ponka and Omaha Myths* (Journal of American Folklore, Vol. I, 1888)

Dorsey, James Owen: *The Cehiga Language* (Washington: Contributions to North American Ethnology, Government Printing Office, 1890)

Dorsey, James Owen & Swanton, John R.: *A Dictionary of the Biloxi and Ofo languages accompanied with thirty-one Biloxi texts and numerous Biloxi Phrases* (Bureau of American Ethnology, 1912)

Du Bois, Constance Goddard: *The Mythology of the Diegueños* (Journal of American Folklore, 1901)

Du Bois, Constance Goddard: *Mythology of the Mission Indians* (Journal of American Folklore Society, 1904 and 1906)

Eastman, Charles A. & Eastman, Elaine Goodale: *Wigwam Evenings – Sioux Folk Tales Retold* (Boston: Little Brown, 1909)

Emmons, G. T.: *The Tahltan Indians* (Philadelphia: The University Museum, 1911)

Farrand, Livingston: *Traditions of the Chilcotin Indians* (New York: American Museum of Natural History, 1900)

Farrand, Livingston, with Kahnweiler, W. S.: *Traditions of the Quinault Indians* (New York: American Museum of Natural History, 1902)

Farrand, Livingston & Mayer, Theresa: *Quileute Tales* (Journal of American Folklore, 1919)

Fewkes, Jesse Walter: *Casa Grande, Arizona* (Bureau of American Ethnology, 1912)

Frachtenberg, Leo J.: *Coos Texts* (New York: Columbia University Press, 1913)

Frachtenberg, Leo J.: *Alsea Texts and Myths* (Bureau of American Ethnology, 1920)

Franklin, Sir John: *Narrative to the Shores of the Polar Sea, in the Years 1819, 20, 21 and 22* (London: John Murray, 1823)

Gatschet, Albert S.: *Some Mythic Stories of the Yuchi Indians* (American Anthropologist, 1893)

Gifford, Edward Winslow: *Miwok Myths* (University of California Publications, 1917)

Goddard, Pliny Earle: *Hupa Texts* (University of California Publications, 1904)

Goddard, Pliny Earle: *Jicarilla Apache Texts* (New York: American Museum of Natural History, 1911)

Goddard, Pliny Earle: *Chippewyan Texts* (New York: American Museum of Natural History, 1912)

Goddard, Pliny Earle: *The Beaver Indians* (New York: American Museum of Natural History, 1916)

Goddard, Pliny Earle: *Myths and Tales from the White Mountain Apache* (New York: American Museum of Natural History, 1919)

Golder, F.A.: *Tales from Kodiak Island* (Journal of American Folklore, 1903)

Golder, F.A.: *Eskimo and Aleut Stories from Alaska* (Journal of American Folklore, 1909)

Grinnell, George Bird: *Pawnee Hero Stories and Folk-Tales* (New York: Forest and Stream Publishing Company, 1889)

Grinnell, George Bird: *Blackfoot Lodge Tales – The Story of a Prairie People* (New York: Charles Scribner's Sons, 1892)

Grinnell, George Bird: *A Blackfoot Sun and Moon Myth* (Journal of American Folklore, 1892)

Grinnell, George Bird: *Pawnee Mythology* (Journal of American Folklore, 1893)

Grinnell, George Bird: *A Pawnee Star Myth* (Journal of American Folklore, 1894)

Grinnell, George Bird: *The Story of the Indian* (New York: D. Appleton and Company, 1898)

Grinnell, George Bird: *Some Early Cheyenne Tales* (Journal of American Folklore, 1907)

Grinnell, George Bird: *Some Early Cheyenne Tales II* (Journal of American Folklore, 1908)

Grinnell, George Bird: *A Cheyenne Obstacle Myth* (American Anthropologist, 1920)

Grinnell, George Bird: *Falling Star* (Journal of American Folklore, 1921)

Gunn, John Malcolm: *Schat-Chen: History, Traditions and Narratives of the Queres Indians of Laguna and Acoma* (Albuquerque, New Mexico: Albright & Anderson, 1917)

Hale, Horatio: *Huron Folk-Lore III: The Legend of the Thunderers* (Journal of American Folklore, 1891)

Harrington, John Peabody: *A Yuma Account of Origins* (Journal of American Folklore, 1908)

Hearne, Samuel: *Journey from Fort Prince Wales, in Hudson's Bay, to the Northern Ocean: for the discovery of copper mines and a north west passage, performed between the years 1769 and 1772* (Philadelphia: Joseph & James Crukshank, 1802)

Hewitt, J. N. B.: *Iroquoian Cosmology* (Bureau of American Ethnology, 1903)

Hoffman, W. J.: *Mythology of the Menomoni Indians* (American Anthropologist, 1890)

James, George Wharton: *Indian Blankets and their Makers* (New York: Tudor Publishing Co., 1914, 1937)

Judson, Katharine Berry: *Myths and Legends of the Pacific Northwest: Especially of Washington and Oregon* (Chicago: A.C. McClurg & Co., 1910)

Judson, Katharine Berry: *Myths and Legends of California and the Old Southwest* (Chicago: A. C. McClurg & Co., 1912)

Kohl, J. G.: *Kitchi-Gami: Wanderings Round Lake Superior* (London: Chapman and Hall, 1860)

Kroeber, A. L.: *Animal Tales of the Eskimo* (Journal of American Folklore, 1899)

Kroeber, A. L.: *Tales of the Smith Sound Eskimo* (Journal of American Folklore, 1899)

Kroeber, A. L.: *Cheyenne Tales I* (Journal of American Folklore, 1900)

Kroeber, A. L.: *Ute Tales* (Journal of American Folklore, 1901)

Kroeber, A. L.: *Gros Ventre Myths and Tales* (New York: American Museum of Natural History, 1907)

Kroeber, A. L.: *Origin Tradition of the Chemehuevi Indians* (Journal of American Folklore, 1907)

Kroeber, A. L.: *Indian Myths of South Central California* (University of California, 1907)

Kroeber, A. L.: *Sinkyone Tales* (Journal of American Folklore, 1919)

Kroeber, A. L.: *Handbook of the Indians of California* (Bureau of American Ethnology, 1919, 1925)

Kroeber, A. L. & Marsden, W. L.: *Notes on Northern Paiute Ethnography* (originally published in 1923; reprinted University of California, 1972)

Kroeber, Henriette Rothschild: *Wappo Myths* (Journal of American Folklore, 1908)

Kroeber, Henriette Rothschild: *Pima Tales* (American Anthropologist, 1908)

Kroeber, Henriette Rothschild: *Papago Coyote Tales* (Journal of American Folklore 1909)

Kroeber, Henriette Rothschild: *Traditions of the Papago Indians* (Journal of American Folklore, 1912)

Lasley, Mary: *Sac and Fox Tales* (Journal of American Folklore, 1902)

Leland, Charles G.: *The Algonquin Legends of New England* (Boston: Houghton, Mifflin & Co., 1884)

Leland, Charles Godfrey & Prince, John Dyneley: *Kulóskap the Master, and other Algonkin Poems* (New York: Funk & Wagnalls Company, 1902)

Lloyd, J. William: *Aw-aw-tam Indian Nights, Being the Myths and Legends of the Pimas of Arizona* (Westfield, N.J: The Lloyd Group, 1911)

Lofthouse, Right Rev. Bishop: *Chipewyan Stories* (Transactions of the Canadian Institute, 1913-1915)

Lowie, Robert H.: *The Northern Shoshone* (American Museum of Natural History, 1909)

Lowie, Robert H.: *Chipewyan Tales* (American Museum of Natural History, 1912)

Lowie, Robert H.: *Myths and Traditions of the Crow Indians* (American Museum of Natural History, 1918)

Lummis, Charles Fletcher: *The Man who Married the Moon, and other Pueblo Indian Stories* (New York: Century Co., 1894)

Lummis, Charles Fletcher: *Pueblo Indian Folk-Stories* (New York: Century Co., 1910)

Lyman, William Denison: *History of the Yakima Valley, Washington; comprising Yakima, Kittitas and Benton Counties* (Chicago: S. J. Clarke, 1919)

Mackenzie, Sir Alexander: *Voyages from Montreal: through the continent of North America to the frozen and Pacific oceans in 1789 and 1793 with an account of the rise and state of the fur trade* (Toronto: The Courier Press Ltd., 1911)

Maclean, John: *Blackfoot Mythology* (Journal of American Folklore, 1893)

Mason, J. Alden: *Myths of the Uintah Utes* (Journal of American Folklore, 1910)

Mason, J. Alden: *The Papago Migration Legend* (Journal of American Folklore, 1921)

Matthews, Washington: *The Gambler: A Navajo Myth* (Journal of American Folklore, 1889)

Matthews, Washington: *Navaho Legends* (Boston and New York: Houghton, Mifflin & Co., 1897)

Matthews, Washington: *Navaho Myths, Prayers and Songs with Texts and Translations* (Berkley University Press, 1907)

McDermott, Louisa: *Folklore of the Flathead Indians of Idaho: Adventures of Coyote* (Journal of American Folklore 1901)

McLaughlin, Marie L.: *Myths and Legends of the Sioux* (publisher unknown, 1916)

Merriam, C. Hart: *The Dawn of the World: Myths and Weird Tales Told by the Mewan (Miwok) Indians of California* (Cleveland: Arthur H. Clarke Co., 1910)

Michelson, Truman: *Piegan Tales* (Journal of American Folklore, 1911)

Michelson, Truman: *Menominee Tales* (American Anthropologist, 1911)

Michelson, Truman: *Ojibwa Tales* (American Anthropologist, 1911)

Mooney, James: *Myths of the Cherokees* (Journal of American Folklore, 1888)

Mooney, James: *Calendar History of the Kiowa Indians* (Bureau of American Ethnology, 1898)

Mooney, James: *The Jicarilla Genesis* (American Anthropologist, 1898)

Mooney, James: *Myths of the Cherokee* (Bureau of American Ethnology, 1902)

Morice, A.G.: *Notes, archaeological, industrial and sociological on the Western Dénés: with an ethnographic sketch of the same* (publisher unknown, 1893)

Morice, A. G.: *Three Carrier Myths* (Transactions of the Canadian Institute, 1895)

Morison. O.: *Tsimshian Proverbs* (Journal of American Folklore, 1889)

Neff, Mary L.: *Pima and Papago Legends* (Journal of American Folklore, 1912)

Nelson, Edward William: *The Eskimo About Bering Strait* (Bureau of American Ethnology, 1899)

Parker, Arthur C.: *Iroquois Sun Myths* (Journal of American Folklore, 1910)

Parker, Arthur Caswell: *Seneca Myths and Folk Tales* (Buffalo NY: Buffalo Historical Society, 1923)

Powers, Stephen: *Tribes of California* (Washington: Contributions to North American Ethnology, 1877)

Pradt, George H.: *Shakok and Miochin: Origin of Summer and Winter* (Journal of American Folklore, 1902)

Radin, Paul: *Winnebago Tales* (Journal of American Folklore, 1909)

Radin, Paul: *The Winnebago Tribe* (Bureau of American Ethnology, 1923)

Rasmussen, Knud & Herring, G.: *The People of the Polar North: a Record* (London: Kegan Paul, Trench, Trübner & Co., 1908)

Rasmussen, Knud & Worster, W.: *Eskimo Folk-Tales* (London: Gyldendal, 1921)

Rigs, Stephen Return and James Owen Dorsey (ed.): *Dakota Grammar, Texts and Ethnography* (Washington: Government Printing Office, 1893)

Rink, Henry: *Tales and Traditions of the Eskimo* (Edinburgh and London: W. Blackwood and Sons, 1875)

Russell: *Myths of the Jicarilla Apaches* (Journal of American Folklore, 1898)

Russell, Frank: *Athabascan Myths I* (Journal of American Folklore, 1900)

Sapir, Edward & Curtin, Jeremiah: *Wishram Texts, Together with Wasco Tales and Myths* (Publications of the American Ethnological Society, 1909)

Sapir, Edward: *Two Paiute Myths* (University of Pennsylvania Museum of Archaeology and Anthropology, 1910)

Sapir, Edward & Dixon, Roland B.: *Yana Texts together with Yana Myths* (University of California Publications, 1910)

Sapir, E.: *A Flood Legend of the Nootka Indians of Vancouver Island* (Journal of American Folklore, 1919)

Schoolcraft, Henry R.: *The Myth of Hiawatha, and other Oral Legends, Mythologic and Allegoric, of the North American Indians* (Philadelphia: J. B. Lippincott & Co. / London: Trubner & Co., 1856)

Skinner, Alanson: *Notes on the Eastern Cree and Northern Salteaux* (New York: American Museum of Natural History, 1911)

Skinner, Alanson: *Plains Cree Tales* (Journal of American Folklore, 1916)

Skinner, Alanson & Satterlee, John V.: *Folklore of the Menomini Indians* (New York: American Museum of Natural History, 1915)

Smith Erminnie A.: *Myths of the Iroquois* (Bureau of American Ethnology, 1883)

Speck, Frank G.: *Some Mohegan-Pequot Legends* (Journal of American Folklore, 1904)

Speck, Frank Gouldsmith: *Myths and Folk-Lore of the Timiskaming Algonquin and Timagami Ojibwa* (Ottawa: Government Printing Bureau, 1915)

Speck, Frank G.: *Some Naskapi Myths from Little Whale River* (Journal of American Folklore, 1915)

Speck, F. G.: *Some Micmac Tales from Cape Breton Island* (Journal of American Folklore, 1915)

Speck, F. G.: *Penobscot Tales* (Journal of American Folklore, 1915)

Spinden, Herbert J.: *Myths of the Nez Perce* Indians (Journal of American Folklore, 1908)

Stevenson, Matilda Coxe: *The Sia* (Bureau of American Ethnology, 1894)

Stevenson, Matilda Coxe: *The Zuni Indians:Their Mythology, Esoteric Fraternities and Ceremonies* (Bureau of American Ethnology, 1904)

St. Clair, H. H. & Lowie, R. H.: *Shoshone and Comanche Tales* (Journal of American Folklore, 1909)

Swanton, John R.: *Haida Texts and Myths* (Bureau of American Ethnology, 1905)

Swanton, John R.: *Tlingit Myths and Texts* (Bureau of American Ethnology, 1909)

Swanton, John R.: *Animal Stories from the Indians of the Muskhogean Stock* (Journal of American Folklore, 1913)

Swanton, John R.: *Some Chitimacha Myths and Beliefs* (Journal of American Folklore, 1917)

Swanton, John R.: *Myths and Tales of the Southeastern Indians* (Bureau of American Ethnology, 1929)

Swindlehurst, Fred: *Folk-Lore of the Cree Indians* (Journal of American Folklore, 1905)

Teit, James: *Traditions of the Thompson River Indians of British Columbia* (Boston and NewYork: Houghton, Mifflin & Co. / London: David Nutt 1898)

Teit, James: *Traditions of the Lillooet Indians of British Columbia* (Journal of American Folklore, 1912)

Teit, James A.: *Kaska Tales* (Journal of American Folklore, 1917)

Teit, James A.: *Tahltan Tales 1 and 2* (Journal of American Folklore, 1921)

Thompson, Lucy (Che-na-wah Weitch-ah-wah): *To the American Indian* (California: Eureka, 1916)

Thompson, Stith: *Folk Tales of the North American Indians* (Indiana University Press 1929)

Thwaites, Reuben Gold (ed.): *The Jesuit Relations and Allied Documents, Travels and Explorations of the Jesuit Missionaries in New France 1610 - 1791. Hurons, Vol. X, 1636 and Vol. XII, Quebec 1637* (Cleveland: the Burrows Brothers Company, 1898)

Turner, Lucien M.: *Ethnology of the Ungava District, Hudson Bay Territory* (American Bureau of Ethnology, 1894)

Voth, H. R.: *The Traditions of the Hopi* (Field Columbian Museum Publication, 1905)

Voth, H. R.: *Arapaho Tales* (Journal of American Folklore, 1912)

Wissler, Clark: *Some Dakota Myths 1 and II* (Journal of American Folklore, 1907)

Wissler, Clark & Duvall, D.: *Mythology of the Blackfoot Indians* (New York: American Museum of Natural History, 1908)

Secondary Sources

Appleton, Le Roy H.: *American Indian Design & Decoration* (New York: Dover Publications, 1950, 1971)

Edmonds, Margot & Clark, Ella E.: *Voices of the Winds – Native American Legends* (New York: Facts on File, 1989)

Erdoes, Richard and Ortiz, Alfonso: *American Indian Myths and Legends* (New York: Pantheon Books, 1984)

Ghandl of the Qayahl Llaanas: *Nine Visits to the Mythworld,* translated by Robert Bringhurst (Vancouver: Douglas & Mcintyre, 2000)

Marriott, Alice & Rachlin, Carol K.: *American Indian Mythology* (New York and Scarborough, Ontario: Mentor, New American Library, 1968)

McNeese, Tim (ed.): *Myths of Native America* (New York: Four Walls Eight Windows 1998, 1999)

CULTURAL AND HISTORICAL BACKGROUND

Books

Bancroft-Hunt, Norman: *People of the Totem, The Indians of the Pacific Northwest,* with photographs by Werner Foreman (London: Orbis Publishing, 1979)

Bancroft-Hunt, Norman: *The Indians of the Great Plains,* with photographs by Werner Forman (London: Orbis Publishing, 1982)

Barrett, S. A.: *Ceremonies of the Pomo Indians* (University of California Press, 1917)

Brown, Dee: *Bury My Heart at Wounded Knee – An Indian History of the American West* (London: Picador 1975)

Catlin, George: *North American Indians,* edited by Peter Matthiessen, based on 'The Manners, Customs and Condition of the North American Indian' published in 1841 (New York: Penguin Books USA, 1989)

Culin, Stewart: *Games of the North American Indians* (Bureau of American Ethnology, 1907)

Dall, William H.: *Alaska and its Resources* (Boston: Lee and Shepard, 1870)

Denig, Edwin Thompson: *Five Indian Tribes of the Upper Missouri,* based on papers written by Denig during his career as a fur trader on the Upper Missouri 1833–56 (University of Oklahoma Press, 1961)

Densmore, Frances: *Teton Sioux Music* (Bureau of American Ethnology, 1918)

Dickason, Olive Patricia with David T. McNab: *Canada's First Nations - A History of the Founding Peoples from Earliest Times* (Don Mills, Ontario: Oxford University Press, Fourth Edition, 2009)

Emmons, George Thornton: *The Tahltan Indians* (Philadelphia: The University Museum, 1911)

Gatschet, Albert S.: *Songs of the Modoc Indians* (American Anthropologist, 1894)

Johnson, Michael: *The Native Tribes of North America, A Concise Encyclopedia* (London: Windrow & Greene Ltd., 1993)

Joseph, Alvin M. Jr: *500 Nations - An illustrated History of North American Indians* (New York: Alfred A. Knopf Inc., 1994)

McLuhan, T. C. (ed.): *Touch the Earth – A Self-Portrait of Indian Existence* (London: Abacus, Sphere Books, 1973)

Mooney, James: *The Sacred Formulas of the Cherokees* (Bureau of American Ethnology 1891)

Radin, Paul: *Literary Aspects of North American Mythology* (Ottawa: Government Printing Bureau, 1915)

Taylor, Colin F.: *The Native Americans – The Indigenous People of North America* (London: Tiger Books International, 1991, 1995)

Waldman, Carl: *Atlas of the North American Indian* (New York: Facts on File, 2000).

Wilson, James: *The Earth Shall Weep – A History of Native America* (London: Picador, 1998)

Zimmerman, Larry J.: *Native North America* (London: Macmillan, 1996)

Native American Peoples' Websites

Wherever possible these have been used for the most reliable cultural and historical information. All web addresses were correct at the time of research. Numerous other websites were also visited to check specific points of query, too many to list here.

ARCTIC CULTURES
Aleuts – aleutians.org
Canadian Inuit – www.itk.ca
Greenlanders – greenland.com

CALIFORNIA CULTURES
Achomawi – pitrivertribe.org
Luiseno – pechanga-nsn.gov, rincontribe.org, paumatribe.com
Maidu – maidu.org, bigchicocreek.org
Serrano and other southern California tribes – dorothyramon.org
Shasta – shastaindiannation.org

Tolowa – tolowa-nsn.gov
Yokuts – tachi-yokut-nsn.gov
Yuki (Round Valley Indian Tribes) – rvit.org
California storytellers – cistory.org

GREAT BASIN CULTURES
Chemehuevi – chemehuevi.net
Pauite – utahpaiutes.org,   historytogo.utah.gov,
Shoshone and Bannock – sbtribes.com
Ute – southernute-nsn.gov, utetribe.com utahindians.org

NORTHEAST CULTURES
Algonquin – algonquinnation.ca, algonquinsofpikwakanagan.com
Iroquois – haudenosauneeconfederacy.com, sixnations.ca
Menominee – menominee-nsn.gov, mpm.edu
Micmac – benoitfirstnation.ca, muiniskw.org
Passamaquoddy – passamaquoddy.com
Penobscot – penobscotnation.org, penobscotculture.com
Seneca – sni.org
Wabanaki – wabanaki.com
Winnebago – ho-chunknation.com
Wyandotte – wyandotte-nation.org

NORTHWEST CULTURES
Coos – ctclusi.org
Cowichan – cowichantribes.com
Haida and Tlingit – ccthita.org
Nuxalk (Bella Coola) – nuxalknation.ca, nuxalk.net
Quileute – quileutenation.org
Quinault – quinaultindiannation.com
Tillamook – ctsi.nsn.us
Tlingit – thetlingitpeople.weebly.com
Tsimshian – tfntreaty.ca

PLAINS CULTURES
Arapaho – colorado.edu/csilw/newarapproj2.htm
Blackfoot – bloodtribe.org, siksikanation.com
Cheyenne and Arapaho – c-a-tribes.org
Comanche – tshaonline.org
Crow – crow-nsn.gov
Gros Ventre – ftbelknap.org
Montana Tribal Nations – tribalnations.mt.gov
Omaha – omaha-nsn.gov

Pawnee – pawneenation.org
Ponca – poncatribe-ne.org
Sioux – aktalakota.stjo.org, shakopeedakota.org

PLATEAU CULTURES
Coeur D'alene – cdatribe-nsn.gov
Klamath, Modoc and Yahooskin – klamathtribes.org
Klickitat (Yakama) – yakamanation-nsn.gov
Lillooet – lilwat.ca, statimc.ca, statimc.net
Modoc – modoctribe.com
Nez Perce – nezperce.org
Okanagan (Silyx) – syilx.org
Pend d'Oreilles (Kalispel) – flatheadwatershed.org, kalispeltribe.com
Salish and Kootenai (Flathead) – cskt.org
Sanpoil, Okanagan, Nez Perce and others – colvilletribes.com
Stolo (Fraser River People) – stolotribalcouncil.ca
Thompson River People – lnib.net

SOUTHEAST CULTURES
Alabama – alabama-coushatta.com, alabama-quassarte.org
Caddo – caddonation-nsn.gov
Cherokee – cherokee.org, visitcherokeenc.com

SOUTHWEST CULTURES
Acoma Pueblo – acomaskycity.org, puebloofacoma.org
Apache – wmat.nsn.us
Hopi Pueblo – hopi-nsn.gov
Isleta Pueblo – isletapueblo.com, isleta.com
Laguan Pueblo – lagunapueblo-nsn.gov
Navajo – navajoindian.net, navajo-nsn.gov, navajopeople.org
Papago – tonation-nsn.gov
Pima – gilariver.org
Pueblos (general) – indianpueblo.org
Zuni – ashiwi.org

SUBARCTIC CULTURES
Carrier (Dakelh) – carriersekani.ca
Cree – creeculture.ca
Dene Nations – denenation.ca
Gwich'in – gwichin.ca
Naskapi – naskapi.ca
Tahltan – tahltan.org

OTHER BOOKS BY ROSALIND KERVEN

Medieval Legends of Love & Lust

Viking Myths & Sagas

Faeries, Elves & Goblins: The Old Stories

Arthurian Legends

English Fairy Tales and Legends

*'The stories are short and lively…
There is a strong focus on character and dialogue.'*
– TLS

*'Rosalind Kerven's selection and retelling is very good…
Her copious notes draw the reader into a world of other stories,
and whets the appetite to read and listen further.'*
– Folklore

'Authentically and accessibly retold'
– The Bookseller

workingwithmythsandfairytales.blogspot.co.uk